ON RECORD

Routledge
Taylor & Francis Group
OCM 5497628
LONDON AND NEW YORK

ON RECORD

ROCK, POP, AND THE WRITTEN WORD

○ ▲ ○ ▲ ○ ▲ ○ ▲ ○ ▲ ○ ▲ ○ ▲

Simon Frith and Andrew Goodwin,
Editors

First published in Great Britain in 1990
by Routledge
2 Park Square, Milton Park, Abingdon, Oxon, OX14 4RN

Simultaneously published in the USA and Canada
by Routledge
270 Madison Ave, New York, NY 10016

Reprinted 1994, 1996, 1998, 2000, 2003, 2004, 2006

Routledge is an imprint of the Taylor & Francis Group

Printed in Great Britain by T J International Ltd, Padstow, Cornwall

British Library Cataloguing in Publication Data

On record: rock, pop and written word.
1. Pop music
1. Frith, Simon II. Goodwin, Andrew
782.42164

ISBN 0–415–05305–6 (hbk)
ISBN 0–415–05306–4 (pbk)

*Due to limitations of space, acknowledgements for previously published
essays may be found on pages 491–92.*

BOOK DESIGN BY ANNE SCATTO

Contents

Preface　　　　　　　　　　　　　　　　　　　　　　　*ix*

PART ONE · GROUNDWORKS　　　　　　　　　　　1

David Riesman　　Listening to Popular Music　　　　5
Donald Horton　　The Dialogue of Courtship in Popular Song　　14
Stuart Hall and Paddy Whannel　　The Young Audience　　27

**PART TWO · FROM SUBCULTURAL TO
CULTURAL STUDIES**　　　　　　　　　　　　　39

Paul Willis　　The Golden Age　　　　　　　43
Dick Hebdige　　Style as Homology and Signifying Practice　　56
Angela McRobbie　　Settling Accounts with Subcultures:
A Feminist Critique　　　　　　　　　　　66
Gary Clarke　　Defending Ski-Jumpers: A Critique of Theories
of Youth Subcultures　　　　　　　　　　81
Will Straw　　Characterizing Rock Music Culture: The Case
of Heavy Metal　　　　　　　　　　　97
Lawrence Grossberg　　Is There Rock After Punk?　　111

PART THREE · THE ORGANIZATION OF THE MUSIC BUSINESS   125

Paul M. Hirsch   Processing Fads and Fashions: An Organization-Set Analysis of Cultural Industry Systems   127

Richard A. Peterson and David G. Berger   Cycles in Symbol Production: The Case of Popular Music   140

Roger Wallis and Krister Malm   Patterns of Change   160

PART FOUR · THE CREATIVE PROCESS   181

Antoine Hennion   The Production of Success: An Antimusicology of the Pop Song   185

Edward R. Kealy   From Craft to Art: The Case of Sound Mixers and Popular Music   207

H. Stith Bennett   The Realities of Practice   221

Mavis Bayton   How Women Become Musicians   238

Andrew Goodwin   Sample and Hold: Pop Music in the Digital Age of Reproduction   258

PART FIVE · MUSICOLOGY AND SEMIOTICS   275

Susan McClary and Robert Walser   Start Making Sense! Musicology Wrestles with Rock   277

Roland Barthes   The Grain of the Voice   293

Theodor W. Adorno   On Popular Music   301

Andrew Chester   Second Thoughts on a Rock Aesthetic: The Band   315

Mark W. Booth   Jingle: Pepsi-Cola Hits the Spot   320

Dave Laing   Listen to Me   326

Barbara Bradby   Do-Talk and Don't-Talk: The Division of the Subject in Girl-Group Music   341

PART SIX · MUSIC AND SEXUALITY   369

Simon Frith and Angela McRobbie   Rock and Sexuality   371

Sue Wise   Sexing Elvis   390

Sheryl Garratt   Teenage Dreams   399

Richard Dyer   In Defense of Disco   410

Simon Frith   Afterthoughts   419

PART SEVEN · READING THE STARS 425

David Buxton Rock Music, the Star System, and the
Rise of Consumerism 427

Tom Carson Rocket to Russia 441

Holly Kruse In Praise of Kate Bush 450

Simon Reynolds New Pop and Its Aftermath 466

Greil Marcus Corrupting the Absolute 472

PART EIGHT · LAST WORDS: THE FANS SPEAK 479

Fred Vermorel and Judy Vermorel Starlust 481

Acknowledgments 491

Preface

False assumptions about the way pop music progresses sometimes mirror shaky notions about the manner in which popular cultural theory develops. In theories of progress by attrition, each musical "revolution" is held to wipe out the last. Rock 'n' roll supersedes rhythm and blues. Progressive rock defeats pop. And punk kills them all—until "postmodern" hip-hop incorporates even *that* attempt to up the stakes of pop teleology.

What such histories deny is the continuing existence and development of nearly every major post–rock 'n' roll form. And so it is in the academy, where generations successively attempt to establish new paradigms that either incorporate or obliterate previous methodologies, which are then consigned to the bargain bins of cultural theory.

It should be obvious from this caricature of musical and theoretical common sense that this book is organized around different assumptions. We assume that each of the disciplines that have contributed to the study of pop music still have something to teach us, and that the study of popular music (like popular culture in general) must remain interdisciplinary.

The unifying theme among the pieces collected here is a determination to take pop music seriously (even while, in some cases, the authors are having fun with it). The aim of this collection is, simply, to promote popular music theory. It offers a representative selection of ways of studying rock and pop, and charts the shifts in method that researchers have used through more than thirty years of analytical work. In mapping out the agenda of rock and pop studies during this period, the book also implies an argument; for while we certainly cannot assent to every position taken in this book (many are, of course, contradictory), we do see merit in each of the different methods used to understand the pleasures and politics of pop.

The problem for teachers, researchers, and students at present is that most of the best arguments about pop and rock are hidden in specialist or out-of-print publications. To this end our book gathers together many of the most significant studies of pop music ever published—most of which are available only in relatively obscure journals or within the pages of books about *other* things. (And we are sorry that we don't have room for Jean-Paul Sartre's thoughts about the hit parade, hidden in his philosophical tome *The Critique of Dialectical Reason*.) The field of pop music studies has only one international academic journal (*Popular Music*—first published in 1981), but journals of sociology and cultural studies have been open on occasion to studies of pop, and many of these articles deserve a wider readership.

In gathering together the most significant theoretical writings on rock and pop we have stressed analytical approaches, rather than pop history or rock criticism. There are numerous histories and critical anthologies available at present. But there is no book which collects the writings that have set the terms and agenda of popular music studies. We emphasize, then, that we are concerned with *arguments* about music and its meaning, rather than factual or descriptive material, or judgments of personal taste. This collection does not, therefore, cover the history of rock, nor does it pretend to include all the best rock writers (and so there are no pieces from Charlie Gillett or Peter Guralnick, on the one hand, or from Nik Cohn, Robert Christgau, or Lester Bangs, on the other). Furthermore, there is no attempt to cover a representative selection of pop genres, since the pieces were gathered for their analytical content, not for the range of music discussed. It is for readers and teachers to use the concepts and frameworks established here in order to fill the gaps in history and genre, for it is just that kind of work that this collection is intended to provoke.

If *On Record* does not function as a history of the music itself, it will, we hope, serve as a guide to theoretical developments in the study of pop. We have organized the readings thematically so that the book may function as a guide to theory, offering key examples of the kinds of work that go on in a wide variety of disciplines. This has sometimes meant sacrificing pieces whose musical pertinence or insight appealed to us as pop fans, in favor of a piece which better illustrated the methodology. The accounts gathered together in the first four sections of the book cover the early "groundworks" that helped to establish the study of pop in the academy, the subsequent development of ever more sophisticated versions of cultural studies and subcultural theory, the analysis of the music industry itself, and studies of the process of pop production. These areas form the core of sociological approaches to pop, and it is our view that each of them has made a contribution to the field that remains useful today—albeit to varying degrees, given the relative simplicity of methods used in some of the earlier studies.

In the second half of this book we turn to the interpretation of pop and rock, in a series of extremely diverse kinds of text analysis. We group musicology and semiotics together, since both attempt a similar project, despite the very different language used in the two fields. Now that semioticians from cultural studies have begun talking to the musicologists (in organizations such as the International Association for the Study of Popular Music), some synthesis of these approaches cannot be far away. The hermeneutic tradition of pop studies is then pursued further, through the relation between pop and sexuality, and the related issue of stardom and its meaning. One purpose of *On Record* is to show that popular music studies require an interdisciplinary approach—in the end, sociological, political, and semiotic arguments cannot be disentangled from one another. Once we approach pop with a sufficiently complex method it also becomes clear that generalization across all the various forms of popular music is highly dubious.

The "last words" from pop music fans that form the final sequence of this reader serve warning to all the theory (including our own) that comes before: in the last instance, pop meanings are forged in the hearts and minds of pop fans, not pop theorists or rock critics. We make this final statement with a proviso, however, since that knowledge is not so much an excuse to evacuate theory as a challenge to students of pop to analyze the process of consumption with *all* the conceptual tools at their disposal.

Simon Frith and
Andrew Goodwin

ON RECORD

PART ONE

Groundworks

○ ▲ ○ ▲ ○ ▲ ○ ▲ ○ ▲ ○ ▲ ○

The academic study of pop and rock music is rooted in sociology, not musicology (for which, even now, popular music is at best of marginal interest), and the sociology of pop and rock is, in turn, rooted in two nonmusical concerns: the meaning of "mass culture" and the empirical study of youth (and delinquency). These were individual topics of academic interest in the 1930s, but they merged with the rise of rock 'n' roll in the mid-1950s. Rock 'n' roll was the first unavoidable mass cultural commodity explicitly aimed at teenagers, and it therefore stood symbolically for the more general fifties phenomenon of a commercial teen culture (which soon had its own complement of teen-market researchers, a phenomenon sardonically observed at the time by Dwight MacDonald).[1]

The basic attitude of the educated establishment to rock 'n' roll—in universities and the media alike—was a sometimes anxious, sometimes amused disdain. The educated taste for popular music might extend to the "authentic" sound of blues and jazz, on the one hand, or to the "sophisticated" sound of Broadway, on the other, but not to rock 'n' roll, which was clearly a low-grade gimmick. The only real question, again echoed in both scholarly and mass market magazines, was whether or not it was actually a corrupting influence.

This is the context in which the three pioneering articles in this section need to be read. They each attempt, from different theoretical positions, to rescue young people's music from the contempt of the academy. And they each follow the same strategy, one which was to be immensely influential on subsequent rock sociology: they take for granted the commercial production of pop and rock (the standardization, market manipulation, etc., described by the mass culture critics) but suggest that young people's consumption of the music is much more active, more creative, more complicated than mass culture theory implied.

David Riesman's piece, written in 1950, was prescient in a number of ways. It reflected his general concern to read American popular culture not in terms of market exploitation but as expressive of certain deeply held social-psychological values.[2] Although he was writing before the recognition of rock 'n' roll as a market genre, he did pick up on the postwar emergence of specific youth music culture—his division of the youth audience into a casual mainstream and a hip elite remains commonplace today (not least in its gender assumptions about "passive" female pop fans and "active" male rock fans). His paper, in short, asked what became the basic sociological rock question: What is the relation between commerce and youth? Riesman gave what became the recurring answer: it depends on the music, it depends on the youth.

Donald Horton's 1957 article is an example of what was until the mid-sixties the most common form of academic pop writing: content analysis of lyrics. This appealed to empirical sociologists because it employed an apparently scientific method. It was used both to expose the shallow fantasies of commercial pop and to measure changes in Americans' underlying value system. The problem of such studies was their assumption that one can read the "meaning" of song words without reference to either their musical or performance context. But Horton's article is important because he did, at least, ask the question, "How do people *use* pop songs?" He is more interested, that is, in the active place of songs in people's lives than in how lyrics passively reflect audience values. He suggests that love songs (which then, as now, dominated the charts) work in dramaturgical terms: what is at issue is a *rhetoric* of romance. His approach, in short, remains interesting not just as a sign of its own times but also for its suggestiveness as a kind of discourse analysis.

Stuart Hall and Paddy Whannel's 1964 book, *The Popular Arts*, was written in the context of British anxiety about the effects of mass culture. Their work was informed not so much by either Marxist or elitist contempt for commercial taste in toto as by arguments developed in the 1930s by literary critic F. R. Leavis and his followers.[3] Two aspects of Leavis's work are important here: First, because it emerged from literary rather than sociological theory, it involved critical readings of mass cultural *texts* (rather than content analysis); second, it was an educational project—the task was to protect young people from mass culture by teaching them to "discriminate."

These concerns for texts and teaching are apparent in Hall and Whannel's work too, but like Riesman, they also describe the positive role young people can play in their own culture (while, unlike Riesman, raising questions about popular culture and class). We have edited their discussion of popular music to bring out the way it captures a moment of transition in both pop music itself (they were writing in 1964, the year of the Beatles) and in academic attitudes to it (one of the Beatles' most profound achievements was to make music that academics liked!). And so, as the general sociological (and media) category was shifting from "teen" culture to "youth" culture, here we find the first hints of both the subcultural theory that was to develop under Stuart Hall's direction at the Centre for Contemporary Cultural Studies in the 1970s, and of the "serious" criticism of pop music that was to characterize the ideology of rock.

NOTES

[1] Dwight MacDonald, "A Caste, a Culture, a Market," *The New Yorker*, 22 and 29 November 1958, p. 24.
[2] See also David Riesman, *The Lonely Crowd* (New Haven: Yale University Press, 1950/1961).
[3] For a further discussion of this see Simon Frith, *Sound Effects* (New York: Pantheon, 1981).

David Riesman

LISTENING TO POPULAR MUSIC

1 9 5 0

○ ▲ ○ ▲ ○ ▲ ○

The study of popular culture—radio, movies, comics, popular music, and fiction—is a relatively new field in American social science. Much of the pioneering in this field has been done by or on behalf of the communications industry to prove to advertisers that it can influence buying habits, and to pretest its more expensive productions, such as potential bestsellers and movies. At a more theoretical level, a good deal of current interest in popular culture springs from the motives, seldom negligible in scientific investigation, of dismay and dislike. Gifted Europeans, horrified at the alleged vulgarization of taste brought about by industrialization, or left-wing critics in the traditions of Marx or Veblen who see popular culture as an antirevolutionary narcotic, highbrows who fear poaching on their preserves by middlebrow "culture diffusionists"—all these have contributed approaches, and sometimes methods as well, to the present state of research in this field.

In using Harold Lasswell's formula—"who says what to whom with what effect"—the question of effects has proved most intractable to study, being at the same time in my opinion the most important and rewarding area. By its very nature, popular culture impinges on people unceasingly; it is part of their environment, part of the background noise, color, and verbal imagery of their lives from the age at which they can first listen to the radio, watch television, or "read" comics. The researcher has two courses open to him. He can either question listeners and readers to see what uses they make of popular culture materials, or he can study the materials themselves and make guesses about the uses made of them. He is usually pushed by the difficulties of interviewing toward the latter procedure, that is, toward some form of content analysis. This is especially the case where he wants to discover the effects of nonverbal materials such as music and paintings. For he will find that, on the whole, people can talk more readily about their responses to words than about their responses, say, to a tune. Yet this very readiness to talk, this availability of a critical vocabulary, may hinder as well as help the researcher; words about words may screen rather than reveal underlying meanings. The current preference for the Rorschach test or the Thematic Apperception test ("inkblot" or pictorial stimuli) as a way of getting at underlying character is evidence that verbal responses to verbal cues are likely to be stereotyped and conventionalized.

I do not mean to deprecate content analysis where this is used to suggest possible audience effects. We must be on guard against a tendency to sniff at library or armchair research as against fieldwork; certainly the quickest shortcut to understanding what popular culture does for people—and hence to understanding a great deal about American culture as a whole—is to make oneself the relevant audience and to look imaginatively at one's own reactions. But the danger exists then of assuming that the *other* audience, the audience one does not converse with, is more passive, more manipulated, more vulgar in taste, than may be the case. One can easily forget that things that strike the sophisticated person as trash may open new vistas for the unsophisticated; moreover, the very judgment of what is trash may be biased by one's own unsuspected limitations, for instance, by one's class position or academic vested interest.

While fieldwork may not cure this attitude, it may chasten and modify it, provided that we can find the vocabulary to talk to people about experiences which are not particularly self-conscious ones. My judgment is that the same or virtually the same popular culture materials are used by audiences in radically different ways and for radically different purposes; for example, a movie theater may be used to get warm, to sleep, to neck, to learn new styles, to expand one's imaginative understanding of people and places—these merely begin an indefinitely expansible list. What these various ways and purposes are, we can scarcely imagine all by ourselves; we must go out and talk to various sorts of people in various moods to get at them. It may then appear that it is the audience which manipulates the product (and hence the producer), no less than the other way around.

This is a particularly important consideration in the field of popular music, where the music industry, with its song pluggers, its jukebox outlets, its radio grip, seems to be able to mold popular taste and to eliminate free choice by consumers. The industry itself may like to think it can control matters, even at the price of feeling a good deal of guilt over trashy output or dubious monopolistic practices. Nevertheless, there seems to me no way of explaining by reference to the industry controllers the great swings of musical taste, say, from jazz to sweet in the last decade; actually the industry ignores these swings in consumer taste only at its peril. Even in the field of popular music, there is always a minority channel over which less popular tastes get a hearing, eventually perhaps to become majority tastes.

These, then, are some of the very general assumptions which guided me in setting down the following hypotheses about a majority and a minority audience for popular music among teenage groups. These hypotheses were directed to the Committee on Communication of the University of Chicago as a tentative basis for research, and in the period since their drafting several students have been working in this area. They have, as was to be anticipated, come up against the great methodological obstacles already indicated: how to isolate music from the influences of other media; how to understand the relations between musical conventions and the conventions of the peer groups (the groups of age mates); how, in the case of popular tunes, to separate the mélange of words and music, performer and piece, song and setting.

It has proved easy enough, through *Billboard, Variety,* and other trade sources, to establish popularity ratings for hits; through a study of jukebox preferences in particular neighborhoods to get an indication of class and ethnic, sex, and age differences; through an analysis of chord progressions or arrangements to get clues to what musical patterns and conventions might be common to a group of hit tunes. But to move from there to the more basic problems of the use of music for purposes of social adjustment and social protest, or the role of music in socializing the young, teasing the adolescent, and quieting the old—such things as these loom on the far horizon as unsolved problems.

Bearing the difficulty of these problems in mind, I venture to suggest, nevertheless, that one role of popular music in socializing the young may be to create, in combination with other mass media, a picture of childhood and adolescence in America as a happy-go-lucky time of haphazard clothes and haphazard behavior, jitterbug parlance, coke-bar sprees, and "blues" that are not really blue. Thus the very problems of being young are evaded— the mass media also furnish comparable stereotypes for other deprived groups, such as Negroes, women, GIs, and "the lower classes." I do not mean to suggest that in thus presenting the young with a picture of Youth drawn by adults there is conspiratorial intent—rather there is a complex interplay of forces between the adults, who are the producers, and the young, who are the consumers.

Most teenagers, though much more "knowing" than the picture gives them credit for being, do not think about this situation at all. Among those who do, some are aware that their group standards are set by outside forces. But their loss of innocence has made them cynical, not rebellious; and they are seldom even interested in the techniques of their exploitation or its extent.

A small minority is, however, not only aware in some fashion of the adult, manipulative pressure but is also resentful of it, in many cases perhaps because its members are unable to fit themselves by any stretch of the imagination into the required images. Such a "youth movement" differs from the youth movements of other countries in having no awareness of itself, as such, no direct political consciousness, and, on the whole, no specialized media of communication. If we study, for instance, the hot rodders, we see a group of young (and pseudo-young) people who, in refusing to accept the Detroit image of the automobile consumer, create a new self-image—though one in turn liable to manipulation. Likewise, the lovers of hot jazz, while not explicitly exploring the possibilities of how youth might take a hand in formulating its own self-images, do in fact resist certain conventional stereotypes. But they do so by making a differential selection from what the adult media already provide.

Thus, we may distinguish two polar attitudes toward popular music, a *majority* one, which accepts the adult picture of youth somewhat uncritically, and a *minority* one, in which certain socially rebellious themes are encapsulated. For the purposes of this analysis, I shall disregard the many shadings in between, and also neglect the audiences of hillbilly and "classical" music.

Most of the teenagers in the majority category have an undiscriminating taste in popular music; they seldom express articulate preferences. They form the audience for the larger radio stations, the "name" bands, the star singers, the hit parade, and so forth. The functions of music for this group are *social*—the music gives them something to talk or kid about with friends; an opportunity for competitiveness in judging which tunes will become hits, coupled with a lack of concern about how hits are actually made; an opportunity for identification with star singers or band leaders as "personalities," with little interest in or understanding of the technologies of performance or of the radio medium itself.

It is not easy at this stage to state the precise way in which these indiscriminate listening habits serve to help the individual conform to the culturally provided image of himself. To discover this is one of the tasks of research. And to this end some further lines of inquiry suggest themselves.

First, it has often been remarked that modern urban industrial society atomizes experiences, isolating each experience from other experiences. Does this same pattern operate, as T. W. Adorno suggests, in the auditory experience of popular music? Such music is presented disconnectedly, especially over the radio—where it is framed by verbal ballyhoo and atomized into individual "hits"—like the disparate items on a quiz program. Can it be established that this mode of presentation reinforces the disconnectedness often associated with modern urban life?

Second, by giving millions of young people the opportunity to share in admiration for hits, hit performers, and the hit-making process, are identifications subtly built up which serve to lessen the effects of social conflicts and to sustain an ideology of social equality?

Third, does the music tell these people, almost without their awareness, how to feel about their problems in much the same way that the daytime serials package their social lessons?

Fourth, since this music is often dance music, does it help to create and confirm postural and behavioral attitudes toward the other sex? Does the facial expression assume the "look" the music is interpreted as dictating? Is the music felt as inculcating the socially right combination of "smoothness" with stylized "spontaneity," of pseudosexuality with reserve? Do these psychic and gestural manifestations then carry over from the dancing situation to other spheres of life? We should not be surprised to find that such molding of the body image and body responses affects girls more powerfully than boys; as the subordinate group, with fewer other outlets, girls can less afford even a conventionalized resistance.

It is not unlikely that we will discover that the majority role represents in many of its aspects a pattern of "restriction by partial incorporation." That is, the majority is continuously engaged in the process of adapting elements of the minority's musical outlook, while overtly ignoring or denigrating minority patterns. Jazz itself, many of the dance steps, and lyrical images are almost entirely minority products to begin with. But they undergo significant changes in being incorporated into the majority style, just as radical intellectual and ideological developments are modified by academic acceptance.

The minority group is small. It comprises the more active listeners, who are less interested in melody or tune than in arrangement or technical virtuosity. It has developed elaborate, even overelaborate, standards of music listening; hence its music listening is combined with much animated discussion of technical points and perhaps occasional reference to trade journals such as *Metronome* and *Downbeat*. The group tends to dislike name bands, most vocalists (except Negro blues singers), and radio commercials.

The rebelliousness of this minority group might be indicated in some of the following attitudes toward popular music: an insistence on rigorous standards of judgment and taste in a relativist culture; a preference for the uncommercialized, unadvertised small bands rather than name bands; the development of a private language and then a flight from it when the private language (the same is true of other aspects of private style) is taken over by the majority group; a profound resentment of the commercialization of radio and musicians. Dissident attitudes toward competition and cooperation in our culture might be represented in feelings about improvisation and small "combos"; an appreciation for idiosyncrasy of performance goes together with a dislike of "star" performers and an insistence that the improvisation be a group-generated phenomenon.

There are still other ways in which the minority may use popular music to polarize itself from the majority group, and thereby from American popular culture generally: a sympathetic attitude or even preference for Negro musicians; an equalitarian attitude toward the roles, in love and work, of the two sexes; a more international outlook, with or without awareness, for example, French interest in American jazz; an identification with disadvantaged groups (not only Negroes, from which jazz springs), with or without a romantic cult of proletarianism; a dislike of romantic pseudosexuality in music, even without any articulate awareness of being exploited; similarly a reaction against the stylized body image and limitations of physical self-expression, which "sweet" music and its lyrics are felt as conveying; a feeling that music is too important to serve as a backdrop for dancing, small talk, studying, and the like; a diffuse resentment of the image of the teenager provided by the mass media.

To carry matters beyond this descriptive suggestion of majority and minority patterns requires an analysis of the social structure in which the teenager finds himself. When he listens to music, even if no one else is around, he listens in a context of imaginary "others"—his listening is indeed often an effort to establish connection with them. In general what he perceives in the mass media is framed by his perception of the peer groups to which he belongs. These groups not only rate the tunes but select for their members in more subtle ways what is to be "heard" in each tune. It is the pressure of conformity with the group that invites and compels the individual to have recourse to the media both in order to learn from them what the group expects and to identify with the group by sharing a common focus for attention and talk.

Moreover, many factors, including the youth orientation of the culture generally, lower the age at which children venture into the "personality markets" to be judged by their success in terms of popularity. As high schools adopt the social customs and listening habits previously postponed until college, so the grammar school tends to ape the high school in dating patterns, proms, and so on. At the same time, the personalities of the popular music industry have every reason to cultivate the child market and are quite willing to "rob the cradle." This convergence of forces means that children are compelled to learn how to respond to music, in a fashion their peer group will find acceptable, at increasingly earlier ages. Under these pressures, music can hardly help becoming associated with both the excitements and the anxieties of interpersonal relationships.

So far, I have obtained some fifteen long interviews with young people about popular music. Since these interviews were in the nature of a limited pretest, simply part of the long process of developing a questionnaire which could then be used on a selected sample, I made no effort to obtain a sample but engaged in random house and street interviewing in white (and Nisei) South Side Chicago, seeking to vary only sex, age, and economic standing in a very rough way. The respondents ranged from fourteen to twenty-two and from probably upper-lower to middle-middle class. In addition, I sought data on the higher social strata from the always available "sample" of traditional social psychology—namely, my students—and data on the Negro community from a few discussions with Negro students and musicians.

One advantage in interviewing teenagers about their music listening habits is that—as compared, for instance, with interviewing on politics—one meets little resistance (save for an occasional overprotective mother), since all do listen and like to talk about their tastes; if the interviewer had cards with hits listed on them, they would doubtless enjoy ranking the cards and then explaining their rankings. However, the group as a whole—as compared with housewives—tended to be inarticulate, even if not shy; a good deal of direction was needed in some portions of the interview, and this ran the obvious risk of tilting the responses. After introductory questions concerning the respondent's age, schooling, family data (for example, siblings, father's occupation, residential mobility, and, where possible, socioeconomic status and mobility strivings), I turned to general questions about radio listening habits: length of time, place (that is, where, and with whom, listening occurs), favorite types of programs, and the like. Then came the questions about music. (Depending on the rapport, the order was sometimes reversed.) The schedule was long and open-ended, pointing toward the problems indicated in the analysis above.

One question which sometimes led to illuminating answers was this: "How do you and they (your friends) decide what is a good or bad piece?" One seventeen-year-old girl, the daughter of a railroad telegrapher, said, "If it's popular we go for it, if it's played on the Hit Parade." Her answer to whether her social life would be affected if she hated music was, "That's all there is to do for kids our age." Yet the time she craved music most was when she was alone; the somewhat sultry love ballads that were her favorites were perhaps vicarious company. Like virtually all the other respondents, she vigorously denied attending broadcasts or having any desire to meet her favorite performers. "I don't swoon over anybody," she said.

I also discovered that respondents generally felt much safer in stating their musical dislikes than their musical likes; the former were volunteered readily, while the latter came out only if approval for the preference seemed in the offing. That is, many would quickly reject a whole area: "I hate hillbilly," or "I can't stand fast music," or "Negroes are too jumpy." More rarely something specific was rejected: "I dislike Tommy Dorsey; he has no rhythm, just blasting of horns." Or, " 'Bubble Gum' is the craziest song." Many said they disliked commercials and several that they would not buy anything that was advertised. As in highbrow circles, so in middlebrow and lowbrow ones, enthusiasm would seem to be a greater social danger than negativism: the fear is to be caught liking what the others have decided not to like.

Among these young people, music seemed to be one of the principal areas for peer-group training in the appropriate expression of consumer preferences; by learning to talk about music, one also learned to talk about other things. Yet the vocabulary used to discuss music, as it turned up in the interviews, was in the majority of cases not a very differentiated one, but rather the "swell," "lousy," "I go for that," and so on which signify preferences for other cultural commodities, tangible and intangible. Indeed, one differentiation, as already indicated, between my hypothetical majority and minority wings lies in the latter's development of strict and often highly articulate standards for judging jazz.

This leads us to a final paradox. The hot jazz lovers are protesters. They are individualists who reject contemporary majority conformities. In the very process, however, do they not in many, perhaps most, cases simply move into another peer group, which holds them fast, and adopt a new conformity under the banner of nonconformity? While my handful of interviews in white South Side Chicago brought to light only a single hot jazz fan, there have been a number of such fans among the students at the University of Chicago. Sometimes these are young men—strikingly enough there are very few hot jazz girls, save in an occasional "symbiotic" relation to a hot jazz boy—who grew up as somewhat rebellious individuals in a small high school group where they stood almost alone in their musical orientation. Then, when they came to the university, they found many other such people and for the first time experienced the security and also the threat of peers who shared their outlook.

What happens then, when this discovery is made, is something we are far from understanding; obviously, the problem touches on the whole congeries of issues connected with social and intellectual mobility, the American *rites de passage*, the role of big cities and intellectual centers. We may perhaps assume that the hot jazz fan can employ his *musical* deviations (from the standpoint of the great majority) to conceal from himself other surrenders he makes to his peer group. Or, he may find within the field of jazz further possibilities of protest by taking a still more esoteric stance, for example in favor of "pure" Dixieland or of some similar now-frozen cult. But what if his peer group, conceivably as the result of his own initiative, moves with him there also? Does popular music itself offer him enough variety to permit him to use it alternatingly to establish prestigeful social distance from others and needed ties to them? And how does it compare in this respect with other cultural products, such as books, movies, art, and modern furniture?

Difficult as these questions are, it seems to be easier to understand the uses of music in this sociological sense than it is to understand the variations in what people of different psychological types actually hear when they listen to music. Is it foreground noise for them or background noise? What is it, precisely, that they "perceive?" Ernest Schachtel has made a brilliant beginning on the question of what meaning physical forms have for people, through seeing what they make of Rorschach inkblots. Experts in auditory perception have not succeeded, so far as I know, in finding an auditory stimulus as useful as the Rorschach test in circumventing cultural stereotypes. Our problem is to reach the people for whom music or plastic art or the movies are appealing in part just because they are more comfortable with sounds and images than with print and words. We are brought back to our problem of how to communicate with them.

While the interview guide I developed on the basis of these research suggestions covered movies, magazines, and favorite radio programs as well as music, it did not explore the whole range of popular culture activities (and inactivities, such as just sitting), or pay sufficient attention—though it did pay some attention—to hobbies, pets, dating, and other leisure pursuits. I am convinced that we cannot understand the role of any communication medium in isolation from the other media and from other leisure activities, any more than we can understand individual manipulation of the materials in the media without understanding the group which the individual belongs to, wants to belong to, or wants to be set apart from.

This truism led me to the further conclusion that one cannot hope to understand the influence of any one medium, say music, without an understanding of the total character structure of a person. In turn, an understanding of his musical tastes, and his use of them for purposes of social conformity, advance, or rebellion, provides revealing clues to his character, to be confirmed and modified by a knowledge of his behavior and outlook in many other spheres of life. Plainly, we cannot simply ask "who listens to what?" before we find out who "who" is and what "what" is by means of a psychological and content analysis which will give us a better appreciation of the manifold uses, the plasticity of music for its variegated audiences.

Donald Horton

THE DIALOGUE OF COURTSHIP IN POPULAR SONG

1957

○ ▲ ○ ▲ ○ ▲ ○

American popular songs are frequently written in the mode of direct address, of intimate conversation, in which the speaker and the person spoken to are identified as "I" and "you." In some the "I" is identified as masculine or feminine, while in others no clues to the sex of the speaker are given, and the same verses could be used by either sex in addressing the other. The relationships described or implied in the lyrics are those of dating and courtship. Some merely express an attitude or sentiment of the speaker toward the one addressed. More often the content is an appeal, request, demand, complaint, or reproach, soliciting response, as though the songs were fragments of dialogue. Musical comedies, motion pictures, and television programs such as *Your Hit Parade* regularly dramatize them as intimate conversations between lovers.

We might surmise, then, that the popular song provides a conventional conversational language for use in dating and courtship, one whose highly stylized and repetitious rhetorical forms and symbols are confined to the expression and manipulation of a narrow range of values. The questions asked here are: What can be said in this language? To what situations is it appropriate? What relationships between speaker and others are recognized in it? With what problems of social interaction can it deal?

The important role of language in motivating and directing social interaction has been discussed by numerous social psychologists whose empirical studies have, however, been few in number. The present paper is intended as a discussion of the social-psychological functions of language as found in popular song lyrics but also as a contribution to the analysis of other forms of art, both popular and sophisticated. The data are verses published in the June 1955 issues of four periodicals devoted to song lyrics: *Hit Parader, Song Hits Magazine, Country Song Roundup*, and *Rhythm and Blues*. The four magazines contained 290 lyrics, but with some duplication; a net total of 235 different lyrics constituted the material for analysis. Of these, 196 (83.4 percent) are conversational songs about love. The various phases or stages of the love relationship represented in them may be arranged as "scenes" in a drama of courtship.

THE DRAMA OF COURTSHIP

Prologue: Wishing and Dreaming

A few songs belong to what might be called a prologue to the drama; they voice the anticipations of youngsters who have not yet begun to take part in love affairs. "Someone to Watch over Me" is a girl's prayer for a lover ("I hope that he'll turn out to be someone to watch over me"); in a complementary song, "A Girl to Love," the boy may sing, "Here I wait with open arms for a girl to love." Two of the lyrics seem to represent lines to be said by a more experienced actor to a reluctant neophyte. A girl may quote from "Dance with Me Henry" (subtitled "The Wallflower"), "Hey baby, what do I have to do to make a hit with you?" and advise the timid boy to "get the lead out of your feet," for, "If you don't start trying, / You're gonna end up crying." In the other the boy who knows from experience tells the one who does not: "If you ain't lovin' then you ain't livin'." To the prologue belong also some general recommendations of the state of love: "When You Are in Love" ("When you are in love / You will discover a wonderland") and "Cherry Pink and Apple Blossom White" ("It's cherry pink and apple blossom white / When your true lover comes your way").

Act I: Courtship

We might expect a boy and girl on first meeting to go through a period of friendship preceding love; but such a stage is not provided for in our songs, or at least there is no characteristic dialogue for it. The more aggressive of the two prospective lovers is provided with gambits for winning the reluctant other which might be called the "direct," the "sweet," and the "desperate" approaches. No doubt one might be used successfully without the others, but in the hypothetical drama they are successive scenes.

In Scene 1 the direct approach is provided with words like "Oh, what I'd give for a moment or two, / Under the bridges of Paris with you" ("Under the Bridges of Paris") or "I'd love to gain complete control of you, and handle even the heart and soul of you" ("All of You"). For the brash and boisterous there is "Here Comes All My Love," in which the lover can say: "You been teasin' long enough—now I'm gonna call your bluff," or "Main Event," which says: "Now that we've done a little fancy dancin', / Sparred with each other to our heart's content, / If you intend to do some real romancin' (Boing), / Let's get to the main event."

We may doubt that this kind of attack is often successful. At any rate, the current crop of songs provides the sweet dialogue of Scene 2, in which the lover makes some show of devotion and offers simple declarations of love in a variety of dialects: "I love you, / For sentimental reasons" ("I Love You"); "I love you more than Jambalaya Creole shrimp and crawfish pie" ("I Love You More and More"); and "Honey Bunch, I go for you" ("Honey Bunch"). The lover's demands may be excessively modest: "A little love that slowly grows and grows / . . . That's all I want from you" ("That's All I Want from You"). He asks for a return of love ("Do, do, do what your heart says, / Love me as I love you" ["Do, Do, Do"]) but may accept a policy of gradualism ("Little by little our dreams will come true" ["Do, Do, Do"]) and patience ("Someday you may love me the way I love you" ["It's Your Life"]).

When neither simple appeal nor gentle persuasion wins, the heroic and desperate songs of Scene 3 are available. In the language provided here the lover may plead, "How can I make you love me, / What can I say or do?" ("How Can I"), or "Your love is all I'm needing, / Why can't you hear my pleading?" ("Your Love"). If these supplications fail, he may make heroic promises: "For you my love I'd do most anything" ("For You My Love"); "I would laugh, I would cry, / For your love I'd gladly die" ("Sweet Brown-eyed Baby"). He may humble himself with "I'm just a fool, / A fool in love with you" ("Earth Angel"); "I confess pretty baby 'cause I'm just a fool for you" ("I Confess").[1] Reaching the depths of self-pity and self-humiliation, he may cry, "Bring me tears, bring me pain, / Fill my days with never-ending rain, / But bring me your love" ("Bring Me Your Love"); or "Treat me like a fool, / Treat me mean and cruel, / But love me" ("Love Me").

Before the beloved yields to these entreaties, he (or more probably she) may ask, in Scene 4, for further reassurances and commitments. The developing love relationship may seem dangerous and overwhelming: "First you think it's fun to try to kiss and run, / But each time you do, then love comes running after you . . . / That's why I tried to run away, / Fly with panic in my heart" ("Boomerang"). Are the lover's avowals genuine? Can he be entrusted with love? Will the new relationship be founded on mutual respect and mutual obligations? "Are you in love with me honestly, honestly? . . . / Is this dream a perfect dream that we can share? / Is it love or is it just a love affair?" ("Honestly"); "If I give to you my kisses, / I've got to know that you know how to handle it. . . . / Whatever we arrange, / Let's make it a fair exchange" ("Fair Exchange"); "Darling, say that you'll be true, / Let each kiss express, / Just how much I mean to you" ("Fill My Heart with Happiness"); "Handle me with gentleness and say you'll leave me never" ("Softly, Softly"). The lover who cannot give these assurances is resisted: "Please stay away from my heart, / And please don't let me love you, / 'Cause I know you'll be untrue" ("Please Don't Let Me Love You"). Marriage or the promise of marriage may be added as a condition to these questions and pleadings, although only two songs in the present collection go so far: "You gotta walk me, walk me, walk me down that well-known aisle" ("D'ja Hear What I Say"); and "If I'm only dreaming, you'll make those dreams come true, / On the day I'm hearing wedding bells, / Walking down the aisle with you" ("Wedding Bells").

The ritual responses to these demands are provided in songs like "Pledging My Love" ("Forever my darling, / My love will be true") and "I'm Sincere" ("I'm sincere when I cry that I'll love you 'til I die"). Fidelity is sworn in such words as "Never will my lips be for any one but you" ("You're the Heart That Loves Me"), and considerateness is promised in "I'd never forgive myself / If I ever made you cry" ("I'd Never Forgive Myself"). In the song "Are You Mine?" a section of dialogue has alternate lines for the boy and the girl: "[Boy] Are you mine? [Girl] Yes, I am. [Boy] All the time? [Girl] Yes, I am. [Boy] Mine alone? [Girl] Yes, sirree. [Boy] All my own? [Girl] Yes, sirree." Only one song provides a specific answer on the marriage question: "So, baby, if you'll just tell me you want me to, / I'll book a weddin' for me and you" ("I've Been Thinking").

It is quite possible, of course, that the actors may go through this drama more than once. The same lyrics, read with different overtones and connotations, may serve at different (should we say "higher" or "lower"?) levels of experience. The metaphors of "heart," "love's wonderland," "make your dreams come true," "make you mine," and so on are serviceably ambiguous to confound the censors. In the songs themselves, however, references to prior loves or conflicts between a new love and an old are scarce. It is perhaps in Scene 4, the scene of appeals, promises, reassurances, and final commitments, that we should note the songs in which a struggle of loyalties is expressed. In "Make Believe" the lover sings: "You belong to another . . . / I belong to someone too, / But they can't seem to see / That our love has to be. / We'll make believe 'til / We can make it come true." In "Conscience" the conflict is more agonizing: "Conscience, keeper of my heart . . . / Let me live and let me love . . . / Please don't treat a love like ours /

As just an evil thing. . . . / Will I choose the one I love / Or the one I'm tied to?" If this conflict is resolved, then the songs of pledge and counter-pledge quoted above may be invoked.

In Scene 5 one of the lovers is becoming impatient. Mere acknowledgments, mere kisses, are not enough. "How long must I wait for you, / To do what I ask you to, / Baby, how long?" ("How Long Must I Wait"); and "Let's stay home tonight . . . / There's a message in your eyes and if I'm right, / Let's stay home tonight" ("Let's Stay Home Tonight"). To these urgencies the other may respond with some anxiety: "Your love's like quicksand, I'm sinking deeper by the hour. / I'm up to my heart, I'm helpless in your power" ("Quicksand"); or can warm himself (herself) with "Look out, little fool, you're not wise, not wise to love so completely, / Or fall for the look in her [his] eyes" ("Danger, Heartbreak Ahead"). The other may reply: "Come a little closer, don't have no fear. . . . I heard what you told me, / Heard what you said. / Don't worry, my pretty, won't lose my head." The timid, yielding, might whisper: "Take my all, darling, do, / But don't unless you love me too, / There's no right way to do me wrong" ("There's No Right Way to Do Me Wrong"); while the bold, putting all fears behind, might say: "Starting with the 'A, B, C' of it, / Right down to the 'X, Y, Z' of it, / Help me solve the mystery of it, / Teach me tonight" ("Teach Me Tonight").

Act II: The Honeymoon

"The first thing I want in the morning, and the last thing I want at night, / Is Yoo-hoo, baby" ("My Heart's Delight"), sings the intoxicated lover in Scene 1 of Act II; "You sweet as honey that comes from a bee, / You precious as an apple that comes from a tree" ("Nothing Sweet as You"). This is the honeymoon period whose songs describe the exhilaration of mutual (and perhaps fulfilled) love: "Tweedle tweedle tweedle dee, I'm as happy as can be" ("Tweedle Dee"); "Baby when you hold me in your arms I feel better all over" ("Feel Better All Over"). The lover is by turns boastful ("I got a sweetie way over town, / He's so good to me . . . / I feel so proud walkin' by his side, / Couldn't get a better man, / No matter how hard I tried" ["I Got a Sweetie"]), or humble ("I will pray to every star above; / And give them thanks for you / And drink a toast to love" ["A Toast to Lovers"]), or astonished ("I found out since we've been kissin', / All the things I've been missin', / The wilder your heart beats, / The sweeter you love" ["The Wilder Your Heart Beats"]). Here is the appropriate place for the old favorite, "Carolina in the Morning":[2] "No-one could be sweeter / Than my sweetie when I meet her in the morning. . . . / Nothing could be finer / Than to be in Carolina in the morning."

If this happiness is troubled, it is only by a doubt that anything so wonderful could be real—"If you are but a dream, I hope I never waken" ("If You Are But a Dream")—and by the pain of parting at night, for these lovers are not yet legally married: "Please don't say goodnight to me so soon, / Hold me close some more, / That's what arms are for" ("Please Don't Go So Soon"). Even in this euphoric stage only one song refers to marriage: "I'm so happy, so happy, / This is my wedding day" ("My Wedding Day").[3]

Act III: The Downward Course of Love

The first uncertainties may occur in the new relationship if the lovers are temporarily separated, an event not unlikely among youngsters who do not yet control their own lives. Scene 1 provides for simple loneliness: "There's a hope in my heart that you'll soon be with me" ("The Sand and the Sea"); but loneliness may be touched with anxiety: "I've hungered for your touch a long lonely time . . . / And time can do so much. / Are you still mine?" ("Unchained Melody"); "Don't forget how much I love you . . . / And tho' other eyes may shine, / Tie a string around your heart, / Ev'ry moment we're apart" ("Don't Forget"); "I can't stay away like this, / I'm afraid that you'll get careless, and someone will steal a kiss" ("I Can't Stand It Any Longer").

In Scene 2 forces hostile to love's happiness appear. Parents may intervene: "My mother, she is scoldin' me / Because I love you so" ("Oh, Mother Dear"). Jealousy, even jealousy of past loves, may arise: "How important can it be / That I've tasted other lips?" ("How Important Can It Be?"). Malicious talk is a danger: "Don't listen to gossip whatever you do, / It's usually lies that you'll hear, / What they say about me they say about you, / So kiss me and dry up your tears" ("Gossip"). The lover may be unfaithful or simply unkind: "Give me your love instead of all those heartaches . . . why must you make me cry?" ("Give Me Your Love"); "Mama he treats me badly" ("He Treats Your Daughter Mean"); and, as one of the partners begins to "cool" (for whatever reasons), the other instantly detects it: "A heart may be fickle, / And words may deceive . . . / But kisses don't lie / . . . I know you are changing, that I'm losing you . . . / You don't want to hurt me, / But kisses don't lie" ("Kisses Don't Lie").

The answer to infidelities and unkindness is the threat of leaving (Scene 3) and the offending lover's remorse, "Maybe when I've said my last goodbye, / Your anxious heart will cry and cry" ("Anxious Heart"); "If you can't be true, I'm gonna fall out of love with you" ("I'm Gonna Fall Out of Love with You"); "If you can't give me half the love / That I've been giving you, / You'd better hold me tighter dear / 'Cause I'll go slipping through" ("Butterfingers"); and, finally, "Nobody loves me, / Nobody seems to care. / I'm going to pack my suitcase, / Movin' on down the line" ("Everyday I Have the Blues"). In reply to such threats, one may plead inexperience, as in "Give a Fool a Chance" ("If I make you cry at times, / If I tell a lie at times, / It's my first romance, / Give a fool a chance"),[4] or simply, as in "One Mistake," beg for pity ("Oh, oh baby, why don't you forgive and forget, / Or will I have to spend the rest of my life / Paying for my one mistake?"). Now the final parting occurs, Scene 5 furnishing the melancholy dialogue: "One more kiss before I leave you . . . / You have caused a lot of trouble. / Darling, you have broke my heart" ("Don't This Road Look Rough and Rocky"); "I thought our love was here to stay / And now you tell me / That you don't love me, / And you must go, / And you must go" ("Is It True— Is It True"). The deserted lover may plead, "Why don't you reconsider, baby" ("Reconsider, Baby"), and the other may reply, "Let me go, let me go" ("Let Me Go, Lover"). The braver course is to say: "I'll step aside . . . / Your happiness means everything to me. / I'll step aside just for your sake, / Altho my heart will surely break" ("I'll Step Aside"); or "I'm losing you and it's grieving me, / But I'll say 'Goodbye' with a smile" ("No Tears, No Regrets").

Act IV: All Alone

"Time goes by and I still love you" ("Time Goes By") is the new motif. "Ever since my baby's been gone, I sure have a hard time living alone" ("Ever Since My Baby's Been Gone"). The forsaken lover still loves and dreams of persuading the other to come back. He may appeal to her pity for his miserable state: "Can't eat no more and my clothes don't fit right . . . / Since you left me baby / Can't sleep no more at night" ("Carry On"); "Since you've gone from me dear / And we've lost the flame, / Tears fall like rain on my window pane. / Please come back, all my dreams are in tatters." ("Parade of Broken Hearts"). To appeals for pity he may add apologies: "I made a horrible mistake / To ever try a new romance, / And now my heart will surely break / Unless you give me one more chance" ("Change of Heart"); "Thoughtlessly I know I hurt you" ("In the Year You've Been Gone"); "I guess I took that gal of mine / For granted too darn long" ("I Gotta Go Get My Baby"). Or, while blaming the other, he may forgive: "I gave you my heart / And carelessly, you broke it so carelessly . . . [yet] / If you'd call again, I'd give my all again" ("Foolishly"); "It may sound silly, / For me to say this, / After the way you broke my heart, / But I still love you . . . / It may sound silly, / But if you 'phoned me and asked forgiveness for doing me wrong . . . / I'd be waiting with open arms" ("It May Sound Silly"). But love, broken, is not easily mended. There are few lyrics for answering these appeals, unless, perhaps, some of the business of

Act I may be repeated, with demands for new reassurances and new pledges. There is one song, however, giving an answer in the negative: "Don't ask me while we dance / To start a new romance, / I just can't take the chance, / No, not again" ("No, Not Again").

Scene 2 opens a prospect of hopeless love. The abandoned one no longer thinks of winning back the other: "There goes my heart, / There goes the one I love, / There goes the girl I wasn't worthy of . . . / There goes somebody else in place of me" ("There Goes My Heart"); "I'll keep remembering forever and ever, I'll love you dear / As long as I live" ("As Long as I Live"). The symbol of unrequited love appears to be the faded rose petal: "Now our love is a mem'ry / Where it's gone nobody knows, / But I'll hold so dear as a souvenir / Just a petal from a faded rose" ("A Petal from a Faded Rose").

Some actors in Scene 2 are less stoical and more given to tears: "Tomorrow I'll be twice as blue, / Because I'm still in love with you" ("Tomorrow's Just Another Day to Cry"); "When a romance sours, / Smiles are just a lie. / Play me hearts and flowers, / And let me cry" ("Play Me Hearts and Flowers"); or, still more forlornly, "Where does a broken heart go when it dies of pain? / Is there a heaven for broken hearts? / Will it live again?" ("Where Does a Broken Heart Go?").

A bitter dialogue is available as an alternative conclusion of Scene 2 in phrases such as "I trusted you, believed your lies" ("Unsuspecting Heart"). The other is cruel, unfeeling, selfish: "To each new love a lot of pain is all you'll ever bring, / Because to you one broken heart just doesn't mean a thing" ("One Broken Heart Don't Mean a Thing"). In "Why Should I Cry over You?" the forsaken one says, "All my love was a waste of time" and ends, with a touch of malice, "Someday your heart will be broken like mine, / So why should I cry over you?" In "I Hope" this uncharitable wish is expressed: "If another fool is blinded by a lie, I hope this time it's you."

In Scene 3, the lover, having thrown off the old love, may face the future with "My baby don't love me no more," but ending with the lines, "Somehow I'll find me a baby new, / And maybe I'll pick on you, / You'll hear me knocking at your door, / 'Cause my baby don't love me no more" ("No More"); or "You done messed around until I've found myself somebody new" ("All Gone"); or, finally, celebrate a new freedom by singing, "Let me be among the crowd, / I like the way I'm living now, / Untied, untied, untied" ("Untied").

These categories of the content are derived from 196 (83.4 percent) of the total of 235 songs and include all the songs about love written in the mode of direct address. Among the remainder are 9 narrative and descriptive ballads on love (3.8 percent), bringing the total of songs about love to 205 (86.8 percent). In addition, there are 6 religious songs, 8 ballads on other themes, 4 comic songs, 6 "dance songs," 3 "tune" songs, and 3 "miscellaneous" songs.[5] In Table I the "acts" and "scenes" are entered as categories, and the frequencies and percentages for the four magazines, taken together, are shown.

Table 2 shows the distribution of songs according to content in the four magazines. Here the subcategories—"scenes" of the drama and subdivisions of the "other" category—are not shown separately because of the small numbers resulting from dividing the cases among four magazines.

The judgment that the four magazines belong to a common universe of discourse is supported by Table 2. The major categories are represented in similar proportions in all four. The subcategories are not represented, because of the smallness of the sample, but it can be reported that, with very few exceptions, songs for each of these are found in each of the magazines. The only statistically significant difference in the percentages in Table 2 occurs in the "All Alone" category between *Country Song Roundup* (22.1) and *Hit Parader* (10.9) and *Song Hits* (8.8), confirming the common impression that the hillbilly songs largely concentrate upon the doleful condition of hopeless love. Near-significant differences are found in the emphasis on the "Downward Course" in *Rhythm and Blues* (30.5) as compared with *Hit Parader* (20.5), and the converse emphasis in the latter on songs of "Courtship" (31.5 as against 24.6 in *Rhythm and Blues*)—perhaps reflecting a tendency of the public of *Rhythm and Blues* to spend less time on preliminaries and more on the troubles they subsequently get into.

In general, identical situations and dialogues occur in the four magazines. The country songs include a few more concerned with marriage or married people and often favor a manly, semiliterate style suitable for "cowboy" and "ranch-hand" singers; but their conceptions are the same—merely expressed on occasion in a folksy patois filled with standard symbols of rural and western life. The songs in *Rhythm and Blues*, too, have their characteristic dialect, the most substantial difference being that a few songs suggest sexual feelings and relations in a less ambiguous language than the usual "hearts" and "kisses" (e.g., "How long must I wait for you / To do what I ask you to?" and "I need love so bad, / It's driving me mad"); and a few verses imply that the lovers are or have been living together. But it cannot be said that these are typical. We are not commenting here, of course, on the distinctive character of much of the Negro music.

FUNCTIONS OF THE SONG LANGUAGE

The Dialectic of Courtship

It is striking that in so large a number of instances the dialogue reflects discordances in the relative positions of the lovers in the "career" of love

TABLE 1
DISTRIBUTION OF SONG LYRICS BY CONTENT

CONTENT	NO.		PERCENTAGE
Prologue: Wishing and Dreaming		9	3.8
Act I: Courtship		76	32.3
Scene 1 (direct approach)	6		2.6
Scene 2 (sentimental appeal)	13		5.5
Scene 3 (desperation)	21		8.9
Scene 4 (questions and promises)	23		9.8
Scene 5 (impatience and surrender)	13		5.5
Act II: The Honeymoon		19	8.1
Act III: The Downward Course of Love		34	14.5
Scene 1 (temporary separation)	5		2.2
Scene 2 (hostile forces)	11		4.7
Scene 3 (threat of leaving)	9		3.8
Scene 4 (final parting)	9		3.8
Act IV. All Alone		58	24.7
Scene 1 (pleading)	25		10.6
Scene 2 (hopeless love)	29		12.4
Scene 3 (new beginnings)	4		1.7
TOTAL LOVE SONGS IN CONVERSATIONAL MODE		196	83.4
Narrative and descriptive ballads on love themes	9		3.8
Religious songs	6		2.6
Other ballads	8		3.4
Comic songs	4		1.7
Dance songs	6		2.5
Tune songs	3		1.3
Miscellaneous	3		1.3
TOTAL OTHER SONGS		39	16.6
TOTAL ALL TYPES		235	100.0

TABLE 2*

SONG LYRICS IN FOUR SONG MAGAZINES, BY MAJOR CATEGORIES

CONTENT	HIT PARADER		SONG HITS		COUNTRY SONG ROUNDUP		RHYTHM AND BLUES	
	NO.	PER-CENT	NO.	PER-CENT	NO.	PER-CENT	NO.	PER-CENT
Prologue	4	5.5	3	3.8	2	2.9	1	1.5
Courtship	23	31.5	22	27.5	17	25.0	17	24.6
Honeymoon	11	15.1	14	17.5	7	10.3	9	13.0
Downward Course	15	20.5	21	26.3	18	26.5	21	30.5
All Alone	8	10.9	7	8.8	15	22.1†	9	13.0
Others	12	16.5	13	16.1	9	13.2	12	17.4
TOTAL	73	100.0	80	100.0	68	100.0	69	100.0

*The base for this table consists of all the songs (290) published in the four magazines, including duplications.
†Differences between 22.1 percent and 8.8 percent *(Song Hits)* and 10.9 *(Hit Parader)* are significant at the 5 percent level. No other differences in the table are significant at the 5 percent level.

and provides appeals by the one to bring the other "into step." In the earlier scenes of the drama, one lover is characteristically "ahead" in moving toward increasing intimacy and commitment while the other lags behind. Both parties to this changing and tense relationship are provided with an appropriate rhetoric—the one with devices of persuasion and reassurance, the other with ways of saying, "Go slow. I'm not ready. I'm not sure." In the later scenes, one is typically moving away from the relationship, while the other tries to restore it. There is a lexicon of appeals, promises, self-defenses, and self-accusations for the one; a lexicon of reproaches, refusals, and forgiveness for the other. Only in the "Honeymoon" period of Act II is untroubled mutual acceptance expressed. The drama reflects the dialectical progression of a complex and difficult relationship, and this is undoubtedly the character of romantic love generally and of adolescent love in particular. Not only are those involved developing at different rates and often making conflicting demands upon each other, but their mutual adjustment is also subject to environmental difficulties and pressures. However stereotyped and sometimes ludicrous the song may be, it is functionally adapted to this phase of adolescent experience.

Vicarious Discourse

One would not suppose that young people carry on extensive colloquies in verse, although casual observation confirms the fact that they do murmur the lyrics of the songs to which they are dancing and repeat lines or phrases of songs in teasing and joking at social gatherings. In a culture in which skill in the verbal expression of profound feelings is not a general trait and in which people become embarrassed and inarticulate when speaking of their love for each other, a conventional, public impersonal love poetry may be a useful—indeed, a necessary—alternative. It is not essential that such a language be used in direct discourse, for, if two people listen together to the words sung by someone else, they may understand them as a vicarious conversation. By the merest gestures it can be made clear that one is identified with the speaker, and the other with the one addressed. This is undoubtedly one of the chief functions of the professional singer, whose audience of lovers finds in him their mutual messenger.

For the young adolescent, the neophyte in the drama of courtship, everything lies in the future; and in the popular songs of the day he or she finds a conventionalized panorama of future possibilities. These include standard situations and contingencies, and the dialogue expressing appropriate standard attitudes and sentiments, for both one's own sex and the opposite sex as well. They offer the opportunity to experiment in imagination with the roles one will have to play in the future and the reciprocal roles that will, or should be, played by the as-yet-unknown others of the drama. Again, it may be the function of the popular singer, in dramatizing these songs, to show the appropriate gestures, tone of voice, emotional expression—in short, the stage directions—for transforming mere verse into personal expression. The singer is at the same time available as an object of vicarious identification or as a fancied partner with whom in imagination the relationships and emotions of the future may be anticipated.

The Self as Lover

As the youngster progresses in age and experience, he moves through the successive stages of the drama, finding that in each new situation the dialogue once practiced in play now can be said in earnest. At the same time, the songs appropriate to the stages already passed will have acquired the private meanings of personal history. When the cycle has been completed, the whole of this symbolic universe will have been reinterpreted, its meaning "reduced" from an abstract, conventional possibility to a concrete, completed personal experience. In the course of this continuous translation of cultural patterns of rhetoric into personal expression, the songs, like other formulas of personal communication, may promote a sense of identity.

The adolescent, especially, is preoccupied with the ceaseless construction and reconstruction of conceptions of who and what he is. He must not only learn the specifications of numerous interacting and reciprocal roles but come to identify some roles as his own. The working-out of a socially valid and personally satisfactory conception of himself and his role in relation to the opposite sex is one of his most urgent and difficult tasks, at least in contemporary America, where so much of the responsibility for this phase of development is left to the young people themselves, aided by their cynical and somewhat predatory allies of the mass media. If television, motion pictures, and popular literature demonstrate and name the roles he may properly assume, the popular songs provide a language appropriate to such an identity.

NOTES

[1] In the lexicon of songwriting "fool" does not mean silly or stupid but rather not responsible for one's condition—a helpless, though willing, victim.

[2] Originally copyrighted in 1922 but reprinted in *Hit Parader*.

[3] One song ("Where Will the Dimple Be?") is appropriate to the married state—but only for the pregnant wife: "Now I wake up ev'ry night, / With such an appetite, / Eat a chocolate pie topped off with sauerkraut. . . ."

[4] Here "fool" does imply stupidity.

[5] "Dance songs" are those whose subject matter is the dance, perhaps suggesting the mood of the dance, describing the steps and movements, or providing a chant to accentuate the rhythm. "Mambo Rock" does all three· "There's an island in the Caribbean Sea, / Where the natives dance and rock with glee . . . / You can grab your chick right by the hand, / Then you clap your hand and stomp your feet . . . / Hey mambo, mambo rock. / Hey mambo, mambo rock." Conversely, in "tune songs" the lyrics concern the music, either describing it, interpreting it, or providing nonsense syllables to accompany it: "Keep it moderato / Like that Crazy Otto / Not too hot, oh" ("The Crazy Otto Rag"); or "Tinkle, tinkle tay listen to him play / Tinkle tinkle tee happy melody" ("The Water Tumbler Tune").

THE YOUNG AUDIENCE

1 9 6 4

○ ▲ ○ ▲ ○ ▲ ○

For many young people, Britain in the fifties and sixties has been a society in transition, a society throwing out a number of confusing signals. Teenage culture is, in part, an authentic response to this situation, an area of common symbols and meanings, shared in part or in whole by a generation, in which they can work out or work through not only the natural tensions of adolescence, but the special tensions of being an adolescent in our kind of society. Sometimes this response can be seen in direct terms—kinds of radical political energy with certain clear-cut symbolic targets (the threat of nuclear weapons, political apathy, the bureaucratic quality of political life, all that is summed up in the term "the Establishment"). Sometimes, the response takes the form of a radical shift in social habits—for example, the slow but certain revolution in sexual morality among young people. In these and other ways the younger generation have acted as a creative minority, pioneering ahead of the puritan restraints so deeply built into English bourgeois morality, toward a code of behavior in our view more humane and civilized. Much of the active participation of the younger generation in their own subculture has this flavor about it—a spontaneous and generative response to a frequently bewildering and confused social situation. In these conditions the problems of the young seem important largely because they are symptomatic of the society as a whole. The shift in sexual attitudes, for example, draws attention to itself not only because it contrasts sharply with the code of behavior subscribed to by adult society (though rarely lived up to), but also because it illuminates in a striking way the confusion about these questions among people of all ages and all backgrounds. There is no common consensus any longer among adults about sexual attitudes or about the role of authority in society, or even about our expectations of how young people should behave. The young sense the absence of this consensus. And this stimulates the trend toward independence, self-reliance, and spontaneity, and exposes them as well to powerfully suggestive alternative models such as the media put forward.

Of course, there is always a gap between the generations, and it is difficult to judge whether the gap is now wider than it has been in the past. The conflict between generations is really one form of the maturing process in adolescence, and should trouble us only when it is so wide that the maturing process itself is disrupted. But it does seem likely that when we have, on the one hand, parents occupied with making the adjustment to a new tempo of life and, on the other, a young generation which is itself the product of those changes to which adults are adjusting, the gap in social experience and feeling between the generations can become dangerously wide. Parents are always one generation behind their children: today they seem to be two generations behind. Naturally, there are many young people who don't experience these tensions at all, and one must be constantly aware of how varied the pattern is. But there is something like a majority feeling, even if the trends are really set by a small minority, and in the age of the mass media these tensions communicate themselves much more rapidly from place to place, group to group. One of the special features of this is the role of the media in speeding up the fashion cycle among the young.

This helps to isolate teenagers as a distinct grouping from the rest of society. Paul Goodman suggests that youth is the only subculture which behaves as if it were a class. And this isolation is often stressed and validated by the media themselves. Some teenagers are genuinely "misunderstood": Dr. Winnicott has suggested that at this stage of adolescence they don't really want to be understood. But many more learn to feel misunderstood because they are told so often that they are. One could cite a host of articles, features, and reports which, without trying to probe to the heart of the problem, loosely glamorize this feeling of group isolation.

The isolation of the subculture also becomes a major emphasis in the songs, lyrics, interviews with pop stars, teenage films, comics, and stories. The culture provided by the commercial entertainment market therefore plays a crucial role. It mirrors attitudes and sentiments which are already there, and at the same time provides an expressive field and a set of symbols through which these attitudes can be projected. But it also gives those attitudes a certain stress and shape, particularizing a background of feelings by the choice of a certain style of dress, a particular "look," by the way a typical emotion is rendered in a song or depicted in a drawing or photograph.

Teenage entertainments, therefore, play a cultural and educative role which commercial providers seem little aware of. Their symbols and fantasies have a strong hold upon the emotional commitment of the young at this stage in their development, and operate more powerfully in a situation where young people are tending to learn less from established institutions—such as the family, the school, the church, and the immediate adult community—and more from one another. They rely more on themselves and their own culture, and they are picking up signals all the time, especially from the generation just ahead.

Teenage culture is a contradictory mixture of the authentic and the manufactured: it is an area of self-expression for the young and a lush grazing pasture for the commercial providers. One might use the cult figure of the pop singer as an illustration. He is usually a teenager, springing from the familiar adolescent world and sharing a whole set of common feelings with his audience. But once he is successful, he is transformed into a commercial entertainer by the pop music business. Yet in style, presentation, and the material he performs, he must maintain his close involvement with the teenage world, or he will lose his popularity. The record companies see him as a means of marketing their products—he is a living, animated, commercial image. The audience will buy his records if they like his performances, and thus satisfy the provider's need to keep sales high; but they will also regard the pop singer as a kind of model, an idealized image of success, a glamorized version of themselves.

The economic base for this revolution in cultural tastes is the increased spending power of unmarried young people. This has been much exaggerated—it is part of the current myth that teenagers all over the country have money to burn. In fact, consistently high earnings are limited to a minority of jobs and to certain parts of the country. There is now some evidence that the contribution made to home and upkeep has been underestimated. Thousands of young people are in badly paid dead-end jobs, and the employment situation has noticeably worsened in recent years. Their prospects are not good. However, Mark Abrams estimated in his early study, *The Teenage Consumer* (since supported by further studies), a growth in the real earnings of unmarried teenagers of 50 percent as compared with 1938. This is double the rate for adult earnings in the same period. In 1958 he estimated that Britain's five million unmarried teenagers were grossing about £1.48 billion annually. More significant was the proportion of uncommitted or "discretionary" spending money they had available—about £900 million. This is a rise in discretionary spending of 100 percent as compared with 1938. The significant point is the high concentration of spending in certain limited fields. Nearly a quarter of that sum went for clothing and footwear (£210 million); another 14 percent on drink and tobacco (£125 million); 12 percent on sweets, soft drinks, and snacks (£105 million); £40 million on records, record players, papers, and magazines; £25 million on bicycles and motorcycles. These sums are decisive in the chosen fields of purchase: 25 percent of all consumer spending on bicycles and motorbikes, records and record players, cinema and other entertainments; and between 15 percent and 25 percent of all expenditure on sweets, soft drinks, footwear, women's clothing and cosmetics. On the other hand, in the main consumer range (household purchases and fuel, furniture and consumer durables, insurance) their contribution is negligible—less than 3 percent of the total.

These large sums reflect the rise in living standards generally as well as the trend toward personal consumption in Britain in recent years. But the teenage contribution is most significant because it is concentrated in the whole range of goods and services which reflect cultural tastes, social life, gregariousness of the group or gang or clique, leisure and entertainment, and the consumption of provided teenage culture. It is in these fields that the most noticeable increases are to be found.

Commercial providers have been quick to cash in on this volatile market—one which is easily stimulated because turnover is high and the market is highly fashion conscious. The providers know that fashion and style play a key role in governing the flow of teenage purchase. As Mark Abrams remarked, "Teenagers more than any other section of the community are looking for goods and services which are highly charged emotionally." In a contribution to a BBC symposium on *The Young Affluents* a social worker described the teenage propensity to consume in this way: the woman who wants a sweater primarily to keep warm will buy a single one; but the teenager who wants a pink sweater in order to feel bright and gay and extrovert on one day, and a purple sweater to feel dark and intense and introspective the next will feel she needs two, and perhaps many more, if she can afford them. We are all subject to the play of fashion, but teenagers seem to be particularly so. The search for a "style" among young people is really part of a deeper search for a meaning and identifiable pattern in life.

When commercial providers become involved in creating new fashions and setting styles, they are inevitably caught up in the psychological processes of adolescence, in the crisis of identity which many experience at this age. They provide one set of answers to the search for more meaningful and satisfying adult roles. And the danger is that they will short-circuit this difficult process by offering too limited a range of social models for young people to conform to, a kind of consumer identity, which could be dangerous even when ultimately rejected by them. There seems to be a clear conflict between commercial and cultural considerations here, for which commercial providers take no responsibility.

The commercial images sometimes work in this way because they invoke such powerful elements in the teenage culture. They play upon the self-enclosed, introspective intensity of the teenage world. One aspect of this tribalism which the media exaggerate can be seen lying behind the remarks of a young girl interviewed in a series on adolescents on BBC Schools Television. "You see a woman who is well dressed," she said, "in the latest fashion, made-up and all that . . . Well, you wouldn't say she's 'modern'— she's 'smart,' but 'modern' is more for young people." This innocent comment catches a feeling which is stressed again and again in advertising for the teenage market. In a different mode, the song "Teenage Dream," sung by Terry Dene, carried precisely the same message:

> Mum says we're too young to love
> And Dad agrees it's so,
> But the joy and bliss I find in your kiss
> Is a thrill they'll never know.

This inward-turning, self-pitying quality of many of the slower teenage ballads, the community-of-lost-souls feeling invoked in words and rhythms, is both an authentic rendering of an adolescent mood and a stylized exaggeration of it.

This apparent self-sufficiency in teenage culture is not simply a matter of keeping adult experience at arm's length; it is also a by-product of the limited subject matter and emotions dealt with in commercial entertainments. A study of the lyrics of teenage songs and the situations dramatized in them shows the recurrence of certain set patterns. These all deal with romantic love and sexual feeling. The emotion is intensely depicted, but the setups recur with monotonous regularity and the rendered style stereotypes the emotion. They deal exclusively with falling in love, falling out of love, longing for the fulfillment of love, the magic of love fulfilled. Of course, this has been the typical subject matter of popular song throughout the ages. But one has then to compare the actual quality of the statement in pop music with, say, the folk song or the blues or even the pointed Johnny Mercer lyric of the twenties to appreciate the particular flavor, the generalized loneliness and yearning—a yearning of "no-body in particular for anyone-at-all," as Philip Oakes once wrote.

> Johnny An-gel
> He doesn't even know I exist
> . . . I pray someday he'll love me
> And together we will see
> How lovely Heaven will be.

These songs, and the romantic stories with which they have so much in common, portray what Francis Newton calls "the condition, the anxieties, the bragging and uncertainty of school-age love and increasingly school-age sex." They reflect adolescent difficulties in dealing with a tangle of emotional and sexual problems. They invoke the need to experience life directly and intensely. They express the drive for security in an uncertain and changeable emotional world. The fact that they are produced for a commercial market means that the songs and settings lack a certain authenticity. Yet they also dramatize authentic feelings. They express vividly the adolescent emotional dilemma. And since they are often written on behalf of the adult providers of the entertainment world by teenage stars and songwriters, who share the cultural ethos of their audiences, there is a good deal of interaction and feedback going on all the time.

These emotions, symbols, and situations drawn off from the provided teenage culture contain elements both of emotional realism and of fantasy fulfillment. There is a strong impulse at this age to identify with these collective representations and to use them as guiding fictions. Such symbolic fictions are the folklore by means of which teenagers, in part, shape and compose their mental picture of the world. It is in this identification that we find an explanation for the behavior of the teenage "fan" and the contrived absurdities of the fan club, with its sacred relics, ritual strippings of the "hero," and personally autographed images. Fan club behavior has now extended to younger teenagers, as can be seen on any public occasion, such as the personal appearance of pop groups like the Beatles. At the same time the teenage magazines have to some extent institutionalized fan club behavior in their pages. Roy Shaw remarked that the tone of some of these magazines for young girls is so intimate that "the readers feel, and are intended to feel, that they are members of a vast teenage club, where no do-good youth leader obtrudes his presence." The same contrived intimacy is characteristic of teenage films—the Cliff Richard films, *The Young Ones* and *Summer Holiday*, are good examples of the deliberate manufacturing of this mood.

Because of its high emotional content, teenage culture is essentially nonverbal. It is more naturally expressed in music, in dancing, in dress, in certain habits of walking and standing, in certain facial expressions and "looks," or in idiomatic slang. Though there is much to be learned from the lyrics of pop songs, there is more in the *beat* (loud, simple, insistent), the *backing* (strong, guitar-dominated), the *presentation* (larger than life, mechanically etherealized), the *inflections* of voice (sometimes the self-pitying, plaintive cry, and later the yeah-saying, affirmative shouting), or the *intonations* (at one stage mid-Atlantic in speech and pronunciation, but more recently rebelliously northern and provincial). One can trace a whole line of development in popular music by listening to intonations—Louis Armstrong's gravelly rasp on the last word in "I Can't Give You Anything but Love, Baby" becomes Elvis Presley's breathy, sensual invocation, "Bab-eh," is then anglicized into Adam Faith's "Boi-by," with a marked Cockney twist (in "What Do You Want if You Don't Want Money?"), and provincialized by groups like the Beatles.

Certain attitudes seem not only to recur with emphasis in the provided culture, but to have found some specially appropriate physical image or presence among teenagers themselves. This teenage "look" can be partly attributed to the designers of mass-produced fashions and off-the-peg clothes and to the cosmetic advice syndicated in girls' and women's magazines. But these styles have a deeper social basis. The very preoccupation with the image of the self is important—pleasing, though often taken to extremes. Dress has become, for the teenager, a kind of minor popular art, and is used to express certain contemporary attitudes. There is, for example, a strong current of social nonconformity and rebelliousness among teenagers. At an early stage these antisocial feelings were quite active—the rejection of authority in all its forms, and a hostility toward adult institutions and conventional moral and social customs. During this period, adult commentators often misread this generalized nonconformism as a type of juvenile delinquency, though it had little to do with organized crime and violence. The "teddy boy" style, fashionable some years ago, with its tumbling waterfall hair style, fetishistic clothes, long jackets, velvet collars, thick-soled shoes, and the accoutrements which went along with them— string ties with silver medallions, lengthy key chains, studded ornamental belts—was a perfect physical expression of this spirit. Contrary to expectations, this style did not disappear, but persisted in the dress of motorcycle addicts and "ton-up" kids, and reappeared with the "rockers." A variant of this nonconformity could be found among "ravers" or beatniks, with the trend to long hair, heavy sweaters, drain-piped jeans and boots, or black stockings and high heels. The teddy boy look, a historical throwback, with its recall of Edwardian times, matched exactly the primitivism of the attitudes it expressed.

Sometimes this attitude is more inward and internalized, relating to real failures in the relationships between children and parents, and the sense of being misunderstood. For two teenage generations at least, James Dean did much to embody and project this image and to give it a style—his films *Rebel Without a Cause* and *East of Eden* are classics which, despite their exaggerations (e.g., the chicken-run scene in *Rebel*) and emotional falsity (the relationship between Dean and his parents in the same film), have a compulsive and hidden quality, due largely to Dean's true dramatic gifts. *Rebel Without a Cause*, directed with disturbing indulgence by Nicholas Ray, who seemed incapable of placing any distance between his dramatization of the teenage world and his own point of view, is really a cult film, and its most impressive moments are ritualized scenes from the teenage fantasy viewed from within the culture itself. In all his films, James Dean portrayed the ideal of blue jean innocence, tough and vulnerable in the same moment, a scowl of disbelief struggling with frankness for mastery in his face and eyes, continual changes of mood and expression on his features, still, as Edgar Morin describes him, "hesitating between childhood's melancholy and the mask of the adult," and with a studied inarticulateness in his gestures and walk. The Dean films have never left the circuit, playing continuously since his death to teenage audiences at the local cinema.

Related to the same set of attitudes, but more recent in origin, is that style of "cool" indifference—a kind of bland knowingness about the ways of the world, even, at times, a disenchantment, an assumed world-weariness. This detachment can be either cynical or sad. It is best described by that evocative word "beat"—but *not* beatnik. It lies behind the masklike, pasty-faced, heavily mascara'd look which became fashionable among teenage girls—originally a copy of a Paris style, but when assumed by teenagers suggestive of so much else. There is something of it, too, in the variations of the "continental" or "Italian" style which became required wear for teenage boys when dressed up (elsewhere, jeans are ubiquitous), with its modern, lazy elegance; its smooth, tapered lines; light materials; pointed shoes or boots; and the flat, rather dead "college" haircut which often accompanies it. A model of innovation in this field was the drained face and the whole casual ensemble of Adam Faith. This style, with certain bizarre innovations, is that of the "mods."

The Adam Faith look contrasts sharply with the more moody, insolently sensual appeal of, say, the early Elvis Presley or his transatlantic mirror image, Cliff Richard (both Faith and Presley became the prototype for illustrations in the girls' romantic comics) or the "poppett" appeal of the Beatles.

Against the somewhat limited range offered in the provided culture, we have to set the real access of independence and the genuine charm—the naivete as well as the assuredness—which allow teenagers to play, mold, or conjure with their experiences and derive pleasure from them. This life and spontaneity is never far from the surface, however powerful is the pull of fashion toward conformity. A light-footed, freewheeling quality comes through, both in the elegance of casual dress and the grace of movement in dancing, walking, or animated conversation—a real growth of sophistication which has taken place since the "teenage thing" first began. The sullen teddy boy style was a copy of an already exaggerated upper-class fashion; now the balance has shifted, and the fashion trends move the other way—the wool shirt and the slim Italian line penetrated to the West End and Chelsea from the outer working-class suburbs.

The Melody Maker (August 1959) reported that when jazz critic Bob Dawbarn asked Larry Parnes, the pop music impresario, whether he thought teenage tastes had changed much over the past couple of years, Parnes replied, "They have not so much changed as had their tastes changed for them." One of the main controls which the record and promotion companies exercise over the teenage taste in the pops is the pop singer himself, around whom in recent years there has developed something of a youthful religion of the celebrity. But the intensity of rapport between audience and singer cannot be explained wholly in terms of the contrived engineering which makes the singer an idol. As Edgar Morin said in relation to cinema idols, "In the last analysis it is neither talent nor lack of talent, neither the cinematic industry nor its advertising, but the need for her which creates the star."

Something in this primitive force depends upon the representative character of the idol's biography. These singers are not remote stars, like Garbo, but tangible idealizations of the life of the average teenager—boys next door, of humble beginnings, almost certainly of working-class family, who have like the Greek gods done their "labors" as van boy, messenger, truck driver, filmcutter, or clerk in a routine occupation (that is, if they have not come straight from the "labors" of the classroom). What makes the difference between himself and his fellows is that he has been touched by success—picked out by a talent scout from Denmark Street or given a break in some provincial beat club or created a stir in the columns of a provincial paper. He is marked out, not so much by his musical talents (which more than once recording manager has said can be a distinct handicap in the business) as by his personality. He's got "something," and luck has come his way.

In the pop music business, "personality" as well as names is manufactured and marketed. What the audience sees (or saw: stars now seem more real and audiences less naive) as a magical process is very Big Business in the pop world. A whole industry has gone into the "production" of the star.

In the production of the pop-singing idol the manager comes first. He takes the risks on which there is no certain return, backing unknown singers whom he believes to have "star quality"—though most managers today hedge their bets by running a whole stable of singers so that losses on the swings can be made up on the roundabouts. Bunny Lewis, one of the successful managers, says that he looks first of all for the boy who is physically attractive, vocally individual, easily recognizable. Then, he advises, the embryo star has to be groomed—"style their hair, fix their teeth, dress them properly, coach them vocally. Instill a little sanity into them—they are going from a few pounds a week to a lot of money, and they must remain sound about it all." The manager not only grooms the star but often chooses the appropriate look for his personality, for this is the point of real connection with the audience.

The next important link in the promotion chain is the Artists and Repertoire (A&R) man, who is either employed by a record company or freelance. He is really the record producer, who puts the singer and his manager in touch with the media through the disc company. He selects the artist and the song, decides the style, length, and accompanying group as well as the place for recording. His role is vital, for he exercises a real power of choice over what material gets recorded. He is also closely in touch with composers of teenage ballads—very often themselves teenagers.

The recording engineers will be almost as responsible as the singer, in many cases, for the final quality of the record. A song can be recorded many times until it sounds just right to the A&R man's ear, and, if necessary, a good first chorus can be spliced with a good second chorus from a different take to make the perfect record. Depth, resonance, volume, and pitch can all be created in the modern recording studio. The voice can be made to resound from the heavens by the skillful use of an echo chamber. A heavy hand on the guitar can be softened, or a beat of the bass accentuated, by the turn of switches.

But making records is only one aspect of the pop singer's career. There is the whole business of keeping the star fixed in the teenage firmament. This is partly a matter of sheer hard grind on the part of the star and the agent or manager—one-night stands in different towns, the summer season in a seaside town, a good deal of traveling and rehearsals. It is also a matter of highly organized and sustained publicity—radio and television appearances and interviews, feature articles, gossip news, original or ghosted columns in the teenage papers. For example, as well as the photographs of the stars which are found in the illustrated love comics for teenage girls, each one of these papers has a pop singer or two as resident columnist, plus large color photo insets, details about the singers' tastes and love life, letters requesting information about them from fans, their horoscopes, and so on.

In what terms is it possible to establish even rough standards of judgment about this kind of music? There are many forces at work which inhibit any judgment whatsoever: pop music is regarded as the exclusive property of the teenager, admission to outsiders reserved. In these terms, disqualification is by age limit. But, of course, this is nonsense. Like any other popular commercial music, teenage pop is light entertainment music, intended for dancing, singing, leisure, and enjoyment. It differs in character, but not in *kind*, from other sorts of popular music which have provided a base for commercial entertainment since the advent of jazz, and before. If we are unable to comment on its quality and to make meaningful distinctions, it is largely because we lack a vocabulary of criticism for dealing with the lighter and more transient qualities which are part of a culture of leisure. We need that vocabulary very much indeed now, since this is the area in which the new media are at play.

On the other hand, there are counterforces at work which dismiss *all* pop music simply because of its teenage connections and its cult qualities. This reaction is just as dangerous since it is based upon prejudice. It springs in part from the inability of adults to establish their own points of reference in relation to popular culture—even though, lying behind the rejection of Elvis Presley, there is often a secret addiction to Gracie Fields or Vera Lynn or the Charleston or Al Jolson or Nelson Eddy. There must also remain the suspicion that pop music provides a sitting target for those who have, for some unaccountable reason, to work off social envy or aggression against the younger generation. From this point of view, contemporary pops could not be better designed, since they are basically loud, raucous, always played at full volume, an obvious affront to good taste. They are frankly sensual in appeal, with persistent themes of youth, love, and sex. These themes are given a physical image in the pop singer himself, whose behavior on and off stage is a challenge to British modesty and reserve. Worst of all, the music itself is an affirmation of a spirit of adolescent rebelliousness and independence, and therefore, it is supposed, symbolizes some sort of deep undermining of adult authority and tastes.

Pop music may well be all of these things, but that does not help us much at the end of the day. For it is more difficult to judge, keeping one's respect both for the lively qualities embodied and the standards of light entertainment generally, the quality of a music which is so entwined with the cult of its own presentation, so mixed in with the mystic rites of the pop singer and his mythology, and so shot through with commercialism. It might be said, then, that the pops cannot be judged at all—but have rather to be seen as part of a whole subculture, and handled as one would the chants and ceremonies of a primitive tribe. Are the only standards anthropological?

This method, too, has its pitfalls. It invites a slack relativism, whereby pop music of any kind is excused because it plays a functional role in the teenage world. Functional it is—but the relationship between what is authentically part of teenage culture and what is provided for that culture by an adult and organized industry is not a simple one. If we add the evidence of the first part of this chapter, which deals with authentic features of the culture, to the second part, which describes the organization of the industry, we see how necessary it is to view this phenomenon both from within and without teenage culture itself. And this consideration brings us back to one of the basic problems in popular culture—does the audience get what it likes (in which case, are those likes enough?) and needs (in which case, are the needs healthy ones?), or is it getting to like what it is given (in which case, perhaps tastes can be extended)? Nowhere in this whole field is it so true that the real answer lies in an understanding of how these two factors interact in contemporary popular culture.

PART TWO

From Subcultural to Cultural Studies

○ ▲ ○ ▲ ○ ▲ ○ ▲ ○ ▲ ○ ▲ ○

Pop music studies undertook its most sophisticated engagement with cultural theory (and its first break with traditional sociology) not through a study of the sounds, but through an analysis of style—dress style, hair style, life-style. The roots of this work were at first sociological and arose from research in the 1970s undertaken by British sociologists in the National Deviancy Conference. In their studies of the meaning of social "deviance" these researchers inevitably looked at the emergence of youth subcultures in Britain—the teds, the rockers, and the mods (the latter were to be celebrated in the Who's album/film *Quadrophenia*). The key book was Stan Cohen's *Folk Devils and Moral Panics*, an analysis of the social function of deviancy that beat a path for numerous later studies of political deviance, crime, homosexuality, hooliganism, drugs, . . . and pop.[1]

Soon this work was taken up by researchers at the University of Birmingham's Centre for Contemporary Cultural Studies (now the Department of Cultural Studies). They began a Marxist strain of subcultural analysis whose impact is revealed in the fact that all but one of the contributors to this section was associated at one time with the Centre. The Centre's *Working Papers in Cultural Studies* carried a number of important contributions to this debate, including Phil Cohen's important attempt to relocate the relations between subcultural identity and the larger class cultures.[2] (In the popular publishing marketplace jazz singer and writer George Melly wrote *Revolt into Style*—a bestselling account of subcultures and music.)[3]

By the mid-1970s the Centre was involved in a heady fusion of Marxist and feminist approaches, using "textual" analyses of cultural meaning based on linguistic and semiotic models. Its efforts to understand youth subcultures culminated in the seminal text of subcultural theory: a collection titled *Resistance Through Rituals*.[4] This book, along with Dick Hebdige's *Subculture: The Meaning of Style*,[5] established the key facets of subcultural analysis—subcultural identity as a response to the breakup of a traditional "parent" culture, the analysis of style as *bricolage*, the notion that subcultures present imaginary solutions to real problems, and the use of signs and icons as what Hebdige calls "semiotic guerilla warfare." This work drew on Levi-Strauss, Althusser, Barthes, and Kristeva, among others, to produce the most heavily theorized analysis of pop of its time.

While subcultural analysis has not always said a great deal about the music of subcultural groups, this kind of analysis remains a key element in understanding pop and rock for two reasons. It is important first because it represents the first attempt to offer analysis of the *meanings* embodied in pop music consumption. Subcultural analysis provides an alternative to quantitative methods of audience research and stresses the active role of youth in constructing its own meanings from the field of pop. Secondly this work remains important because pop is a visual medium every bit as much as it is an aural one; and the subcultural analysis of style is therefore central to any engagement with pop and its iconography.

Despite the apparent neglect of the music in some subcultural work, each of the writers in this section shows a keen awareness of the history and function of pop itself, and of its interaction with style. The extract from Paul Willis is an early attempt to understand the role of music in the lives of a subcultural group—and in his analysis of the music of the motorcycle boys Willis offers some suggestive (if rudimentary) stabs at musical analysis in his attempt to demonstrate a homology between the concept of time held by the boys and the rock 'n' roll music they listen to.

Similarly, Hebdige hints at the role of punk rock as noise and its correspondence with ideals of anarchy and chaos. He goes on to draw a parallel between the punk subculture and a certain avant-garde aesthetics which typifies the more heavily theoretical wing of cultural analysis. Hebdige's point, which is very close to the arguments made in cultural studies about film and television, is that subcultural style is not merely a matter of content (different signs), but one of form (different signifying practices).

The zenith of subcultural theory's influence was surely the late 1970s, when (as McRobbie points out) a dense theoretical treatise by Hebdige could be reviewed favorably in the British pop newsweekly *New Musical Express*. By the 1980s a number of disparate critiques of the approach were beginning to crystalize into a significant "rethinking" of the field. Willis and Hebdige are typical of subcultural theory in their focus on male sounds and styles to the near exclusion of girls and young women. Angela McRobbie's essay is thus a moment of transition in the debate and acts to frame their work (from a feminist perspective) and redirect it so that the politics of class (and, in Hebdige's case, ethnicity) are supplemented with an analysis of gender. Gary Clarke's critique of subcultural theory is more radical still. His original paper makes a number of points about gender which overlap with McRobbie—here we reproduce the arguments he mobilizes on behalf of "ordinary" youth and the important comments on music which butress his critique of the selectivity of subcultural accounts. Clarke's analysis serves as a prescient comment on the problems of analyzing music and style in an era that seems to refuse notions of counterculture.

What is obvious now is that the academic study of pop and rock that began in sociology departments in the 1950s and continued in the development of subcultural theory in the 1970s, has come to rest—in the 1980s—in the discipline of "cultural studies." In the U.S.A. this has emerged from departments of communications by way of British subcultural theory, but in practice what it involves is a combination of sociological approaches to the institutions and audiences of popular culture (if, alas, without sociology's empirical grounding) with interpretative theories drawn from semiotics, psychoanalysis, and literary criticism. The problem of the latter is that they were developed first with respect to written texts and then with reference to images—photographs, films, television, advertisements, etc. It remains less clear how they relate to sounds, and the next stage in the development of cultural studies will undoubtably be its appropriation of musicology.

Will Straw's pioneering piece on heavy metal is thus still emphatically sociological in tone. Heavy metal has been a genre mostly despised by critics and neglected by subcultural theorists (it doesn't have the glamor of mod or punk) but it is probably the essential (male) rock form, and though Straw's article (written in 1983) is dated in places, it remains an excellent example of what comprehensive cultural analysis of a pop phenomenon can accomplish.

Lawrence Grossberg tries to define rock 'n' roll itself in addressing its supposed death. Grossberg is the most ambitious of American cultural studies scholars, and his purpose here is to use rock analysis as the basis of a general theory of cultural empowerment. But what's most interesting about this 1986 essay is how clearly it echoes David Riesman's 1950s arguments: the stress is still on youth and music, on the use of records as a means of social *differentiation*. If these points are now placed in a much more densely theorized set of arguments than they used to be, this tells us as much about the changes over the last forty years in the academy as about the changes either in youth culture or the music business itself.

NOTES

[1] Stan Cohen, *Folk Devils and Moral Panics* (London: MacGibbon & Kee, 1972).
[2] Phil Cohen, "Sub-cultural Conflict and the Working-class Community," *Working Papers in Cultural Studies*, No. 2 (University of Birmingham: Centre for Contemporary Studies, 1972).
[3] George Melly, *Revolt into Style* (London: Penguin, 1972).
[4] Stuart Hall and Tony Jefferson (eds.), *Resistance Through Rituals* (London: Hutchinson, 1976).
[5] Dick Hebdige, *Subculture: The Meaning of Style* (London: Methuen, 1979).

THE GOLDEN AGE

1 9 7 8

○ ▲ ○ ▲ ○ ▲ ○

"You know this type of music, all this loud stuff, you know, it sort of goes with leather-jacketed kids, you know. . . . You might not have heard a record before, and you come down here and hear it, and like it, but—it's still in you that type of music, because if you've got a likings, it's there isn't it?"

MICK

Pop music was a manifest and ever-present part of the environment of the motorbike boys: it pervaded their whole culture. In simple quantitative terms, there was a massive interaction with pop music. It is clear, however, that the significance of this relationship went very much further than an arbitrary or random juxtaposition.

The motorbike boys had very specific tastes that were not part of the current pop music scene and were not catered for in the ongoing mass media sources. They liked the music of the early rock 'n' roll period between 1955 and 1960. By current standards in the commercial market and the pop music provided by mass media channels their tastes were at least ten years out of date. By deliberate choice, then, and not by the accident of a passive reception, they chose this music. This alerts us to the dialectical capacity which early rock 'n' roll had to reflect, resonate, and return something of real value to the motorbike boys.

Their preferred music, especially that of Buddy Holly and Elvis Presley, was part of the first really authentic and integrated period of rock 'n' roll. It marked the first distinctive break between the record as an artifact and the sheet music it was based on. Because these singers brought together a number of elements first made available by the initial pop opening explosion, unified them in a unique way, and combined this with a distinctive personal style, it was virtually impossible that another artist could repeat the performance simply from the sheet music. For the first time the single record really came into its own, and the stylistic integrity of the singer made *hearing* the record more important than seeing the musical score. Buddy Holly's distinctive style lay mainly in the restless, exclamatory, alert quality of his voice. There was no mournful submission to fate but an active confrontation with life and an awareness of the possibility of change: "You say you're gonna leave . . . but that'll be the day when I die." Elvis Presley's distinctive treatment of the songs relied on the easy riding of the urgency in the rhythm from the bass and the guitar. His voice was close, personal, and confiding, though always ready to take a defiant stand on his own cultural identity: "Get off my blue suede shoes." This historic period of rock 'n' roll came to an end with the death of Buddy Holly in an air crash in February 1959: an event which sealed the authenticity of the genre: early rock 'n' roll.

The bike boys' musical preferences, therefore, were *objectively* based on the identification of fundamental elements of the musical style. The music did have a distinctiveness, a unity of construction, a special and consistent use of techniques, a freshness and conviction of personal delivery, a sense of the "golden," "once and for all" age, which could parallel, hold, and develop the security, authenticity, and masculinity of the bike culture.

The social nature of this general consonance of structure was apparent in the bike boys' comments about music. A need for security and authenticity, the lack of relativity and concreteness in their life-style, was almost literally *seen* in the qualities of their preferred music. Early Elvis Presley and Buddy Holly were changeless and secure; 78s were preferred to singles; original versions of songs were preferred to repeat versions. The masters of the golden age were absolutely unchallengeable:

> JOE: Yes, after all this time, people are still recording him. Mick Berry tries to take him off, and Bobby Vee and Tommy Roe, they've all had a bash at taking him off, so it must be good . . . there's more in his fan club now than there ever was. . . . I do though he's got more fans than he's ever had now . . . and they're still releasing tracks of his LPs, and that's still after ten years. . . .
>
> FRED: Any rock 'n' roll singer that's worth his weight in song, like, has always recorded some of Buddy Holly's . . . you go all through the top groups, they've all recorded one or two . . . always, every group, so there he must be liked by even modern singers, mustn't he? . . . "True Love Ways" by Peter and Gordon.

To dignify this sense of "the tradition" with a platonic parallel would be foreign to the boys' own expression, but it may help in illuminating the essential status of the valued originals. One could regard these originals as ideal creations: holding the ultimate in musical value in their ontological genuineness. Records that were repeats, or similar in form and style, were just shadows cast on later years. Records owing nothing to the originals were meaningless and were ignored. They did not even have the reflection of authenticity played across them. They were without identity. Thus, even though a repeat record may be preferred in its immediate impact, it could never replace or seriously challenge the original. Records in altogether different styles were not responded to for their own qualities—they were dismissed at a deeper level. The originals had a value which was beyond demonstrable qualities, and could therefore never be challenged by demonstrable qualities.

The motorbike boys' preference for 78s over 45s can be understood in this light. Although their technical quality was demonstrably inferior to the more recent 45s, they had a bulk, a brittleness, a distinctive tactile presence that all spoke of genuine origins in the golden age. The scratchiness of the reproduction, far from detracting from this total effect—as it would for a neutral observer—enhanced the "soul" of the song for them simply because it was overriding evidence of the music's authentic origins.

With a grounding of their life-style in ontological security, the motorbike boys expected their music to have a similar integrity. There was not a field for the free play of choice in music, as there was not a field for a free play of feeling about reality. The music, in one sense, had to be the only possible music, and secure within its own distinctive style. Veneration for the golden era implied a location of personality and group identity, in just the way that the physical world did—the same demands of genuineness could be made upon it.

It is in the light of the "golden age" and its cultural resonance for the motorbike boys that we can understand their attitudes to later artists. The Beatles' albums *Revolver* and *Rubber Soul* and *Sergeant Pepper* were immensely successful records, but they had clearly deserted the spirit of early rock 'n' roll. With their melodic asymmetry and complexity of rhythm, they had an authenticity of their own, but it was not the authenticity of the "big beat," rock 'n' roll era. These records did not have the intrinsic capacity to return anything of significance to the motorbike boys. They were in fact disliked, they were considered daft. However, for a brief period after *Sergeant Pepper*, on singles at any rate, the Beatles returned to a simpler, more intense vocal style, based on the work of much earlier singers. "Lady Madonna" was reminiscent of Fats Domino's styling, and "Get Back" of Chuck Berry's. For the motorbike boys these were the last flowerings of the Beatles' genuine rock 'n' roll personality. They were greatly appreciated, but everything after (except for some of the records from the Plastic Ono Band, who deliberately returned to earlier styles) was despised.

The Rolling Stones, too, whom the boys consistently rated highly, can be seen as giving a rebirth in the 1960s to the rock 'n' roll of the mid-1950s. The Stones' music began with strong simple rhythms and conventional chord patterns and meter taken fairly directly from Chicago rhythm and blues. The vocal style was that of black singers such as Chuck Berry, Muddy Waters, Bo Diddley, and Howlin Wolf. The only influence from a white singer was, in fact, from Buddy Holly. There was experimentation, often accidentally, but it was always—apart from a brief digression in *Her Satanic Majesty Requests*—from a hard rock base. The Rolling Stones were most successful with numbers of their own composition, such as "Satisfaction," "Get Off My Cloud," and "19th Nervous Breakdown," because these more accurately reflected the English cultural situation, but musically they remained consistent with the atmosphere and spirit of the original rhythm and blues sources. Although Mick Jagger's copying of Negro speech rhythms sometimes seemed inauthentic, his consistent alignment with early rhythm and blues, and the successful adaptation of rhythm and blues to the English setting without loss of its essential spirit, completely outweighed this factor for the motorbike boys. Basically Mick Jagger was, if not an original, at least an inheritor of hard rock. He held the internal codes. In this he answered their need for authenticity, security in identity, and straightforward belief in a fixed-center universe.

Early rock 'n' roll bore authentic potential meaning for the motorbike boys in another important way—the powerful *social* meaning with which it was historically invested. Early rock 'n' roll was seized upon by the young in the mid-1950s in America and England as their very own music. It was mainly theirs because it so clearly was not their parents'. Early rock 'n' roll films were associated with rioting, fighting, and seat slashing in the movie theaters. The new dancing was violently active compared to any of its predecessors, and the live performance of the stars (particularly Elvis Presley) was openly sexual in a way that only American Negroes had been held to be capable of before. Parents and established society could not condone such open subversion of traditional values. The dissociation of one group is the association of another. A large-scale distinctive musical genre became, perhaps for the first time, truly available to the young. This was the beginning, the first distinctive awakening, of what we refer to generically as youth culture. It was crucial for the motorbike boys that this takeover, this social furnacing of an expressive form, was characterized—aided and abetted by lurid media treatment of particular incidents—by violence, aggression, and antisocial feeling. Rock 'n' roll, then, came to the motorbike boys rich in absorbed, highly appropriate social meanings. This "double fit" of the music—its *prior* social imbuement and its particular *objective* structure—explains much of the motorbike boys' attachment to the music.

* * *

Not only was the motorbike culture about security of consciousness and authenticity, it was also about the linked expression of these things in movement, in style, in physicality, in "handling yourself."

One of the most noticeable things about the music they liked was the prominence of its beat. It is music for dancing to, for moving to, and clearly has the ability to reflect, resonate, and develop in a particular way a lifestyle based on confidence and movement. Elvis Presley was consistently best in his fast-moving beat songs. With his gyrating hips, outflung arms, and coy angling of the head, he altogether did away with the image of the stationary singer. Almost every early record cover shows him moving and, of course, his stage name will always be Elvis the Pelvis. Buddy Holly's style, too, relied on a strident beat, and the alert quality of his voice was enhanced and projected by the clear beat. For the period and for his color (white) he was very strongly influenced by black rhythm and blues music: this is one of the reasons why he was the only white singer seriously to influence Mick Jagger. The driving, dancing rhythm of more traditional rhythm and blues comes through in his records time and again. Sometimes, as in "Not Fade Away," the music is virtually taken over by beat and rhythm, with the melody totally subjugated to a transfixing rhythm pattern. The Beatles, as we have seen, in their early days played a kind of updated rock 'n' roll, which again relied on a fundamental "big beat."

The progress of the Beatles could be described simply in terms of the loss of this big beat. They became more sophisticated, using melodic asymmetry and complex rhythm patterns. The later music became very much harder to dance to, especially in the concrete, direct, bopping-to-the-rhythm dance patterns of the early rock era—a style of dancing which had none of the freaky free-form movements that later styles developed to match the asymmetry of progressive music. The motorbike boys ranked the early Beatles very highly. They became progressively cooler about the later Beatles. They despised some of their late "really stupid stuff." To simplify, the process of the bike boys' disillusionment was commensurate with the disappearance of the big beat from the Beatles. The Rolling Stones, much more consistently than the Beatles, kept to the strong, simple beat of rhythm and blues. Of all post–early rock music, the Stones have kept closest to the elemental function of pop—providing music to dance to. Mick Jagger, in performance, with his outlandish talent for movement, mime, and gesture, personified in action the movement potential of his music.

Their preferred music, therefore, was clearly answerable to the restless movement of the bike boys' lives. Musical discrimination was based essentially on the displaced category of social and physical movement. The musical quality they universally disliked was slowness and dreariness. The quality they prized was fastness and clarity of beat. This is from a discussion of Ray Charles:

PW: Say a bit more.

JOE: Just what I said when I heard it before, it's too slow and dreary, isn't it . . . eh? I like music that makes you get up and do something, like.

TIM: You put the Beatles against them and you know straightaway, don't you, or the Stones, you get the Stones or the Beatles with them, they're outclassed, ain't they? You can't understand a word he says . . . and the beat, well, there ain't one, is there?

The antidote to boredom was always movement and the bike boys' preferred music not only reflected this, but provided a concrete, formative outlet. A good strong beat was the prerequisite for dancing. As Joe said: "That's all you need." The importance of being able to dance to music was stressed time and again—and as an internally coded aspect of the music unaffected by particular contexts such as the immediate desire to dance:

JOE: Oh, I do like [Connie Francis], one of the best girl singers out . . . she warn't as good as Buddy Holly, but she was one of the best girl singers out.

PW: Was there anything else about that particular record ["Lipstick on Your Collar"]?

JOE: Oh, yes, you can bop to it, any record I can bop to, I like, that's it.

To praise a record for its relevance to dance was not, therefore, to say that it was actually always danced to, or that it could be appreciated only when dancing. It was meant as a description of a general quality of the music that was quite as evident whether actually dancing or not. Again, a section from the discussion of Ray Charles:

MICK: If people go to a dance, you know to enjoy themselves . . . they don't want to listen to stuff like that . . . you can't get up and dance . . . you'd just sit there moping all night . . . I'd walk out, I would.

The literal meaning of the song lyrics was not often considered. At one level they were taken for granted so that appropriate words and meanings could always be read in: the possible range of meaning was very limited so that the bike boys always knew, and took for granted, the kind of things that were said. Lyrics became important only negatively, when they obtruded, broke expectations, or were not understandable.

In relation to the importance of style and movement in the culture and of the selection and generation of representations of these things, we can understand a further dimension of the bike boys' exclusive preference for singles. Singles were specifically responsive to the active, moving listener. They lasted for only 2½ minutes. If a particular record was disliked, at least it lasted for only a short time. It could also be rejected from the turntable more quickly without the difficulty of having to pick the needle up to miss tracks. Exact selection could also be made so that the order of records was totally determined by individual choice. To play an LP was to be committed—unless you were prepared to go to a great deal of trouble—to someone else's ordering of the music. By and large, LPs are more popular with an audience which is prepared to sit and listen for a considerable period, and with a certain extension of trust so that unknown material can be appreciated and evaluated. LPs are a cheap way (as opposed to singles) of building up a large collection of songs within particular traditions. Often there will be tracks on an LP which have never been very popular, but which are of interest to the expert or the devotee or the technician. LPs tend to serve the interest more of the "serious" listener, who is concerned to appreciate all the aspects of a particular field, and not simply those to which he is already attracted. Of late, LPs have also been produced which have been conceived as a unit, parallel in a way to the opera or extended musical piece. Dating approximately from *Sergeant Pepper* by the Beatles, the so-called progressive groups particularly have been concerned to produce LPs which are imaginatively conceived as a whole in this way and which are meant to be taken as a whole at one sitting. All this implies an audience which is stationary, sitting, not engaged in other activities, and prepared to devote a substantial length of time to the appreciation of the music alone. Of course, there are many exceptions to all this. An LP, *Elvis's Golden Hits*, for instance, is specially produced as a cheap collection of Elvis's singles. The attraction is specifically that of a cheap package of popular singles. However, generally, and especially in contrast to singles, it holds true that the LP audience is stationary and mono-channeled toward the music.

This kind of situation is clearly completely inappropriate to the motorbike boys. The connotations of the LP form were quite contrary to the fundamental elements of their life-style. They are usually moving, engaged in other activities, responsive to music only when it is not boring, and most interested where music responds to their particular mood. Their preference for singles was so overwhelming, indeed, that, quite apart from inherent musical qualities, the absence of a single version of a song was held as *prima facie* evidence of its inferiority, and even well-liked songs were passed over if the LP version only was available. This might be taken as clottish, obstinate inflexibility until it is realized that, in fact, the experience of listening to the same track on an LP (as on a single) would not have been so enjoyable for the motorbike boys: it would not have been the same experience precisely because they would have felt a lack of control, an implied seriousness, an unresponsiveness, which would have inhibited the free flow of response. Their preference for singles was simply an honest, logical projection of a coherent set of attitudes on to an appropriate object—not the random obstinacy of the unimaginative.

The assertive masculinity of the motorbike boys also found an answering structure in their preferred music. Elvis Presley's records were full of aggression. Though the focus was often unspecified and enigmatic, the charge of feeling was strong. In the atmosphere of the music, in the words, in the articulation of the words, in his personal image, was a deep implication that here was a man not to be pushed around. His whole presence demanded that he should be given respect; though, by conventional standards, the grounds for that respect were disreputable and antisocial. Buddy Holly's music was not so aggressive, but it was utterly secure in its own style: it insisted that its range and interests were important and deserving of recognition. The Rolling Stones' music and image has remained entirely "unrespectable" in its opposition to the adult world, and its espousal of hooliganism and permissiveness. Their 1960s music especially was harsh and angry—striking cruel or sardonic poses. The violence of the vocal delivery invested the lyrics with meaning far beyond the power of the cold words. There was also, in the Stones' music, an assumed superiority over women, and a denial to them of personal authenticity, which was very close to the attitudes of the boys themselves. The Beatles were not aggressive in such an outright fashion, and did not symbolize hooliganism in the same way, but there was a vigorous release of feeling, and an utter confidence in their style of playing, which gave the music considerable power and muscular control. In some ways the Beatles' early songs were a celebration of youth: they expressed a naive male ethic of control in an alienated world. All this made the music particularly responsive to the special confidence and rumbunctious, masculine movement basic to the bike boys' cultural style.

The motorbike boys preferred music, then, that clearly resonated and developed the particular interests and qualities of the boys' life-style. The music had an integrity of form and atmosphere as well as an immediate, informal, concrete confidence. It belonged to the golden age of pop and yet maintained an immediate responsiveness to living concerns. This dual capacity to answer to the basic ontology, as well as to the surface style, of the bike culture explains the centrality of the music to the culture.

This centrality of rock 'n' roll music is surprising in one sense. In view of the limited power of the motorbike boys to change the internal form of their music, it might be expected that the dialectical power of the music in the culture was limited. They *selected* as between types of music, of course, and the fantastic precision and distinctive type of their taste attest to the degree to which *selection* from what exists can be an important ingredient of cultural development. In the reverse moment, of course, the music itself had exerted an immense influence on the culture and its material practices, which in their turn further modified the culture and forms, ultimately, of appropriating the music—all within a complex unity.

We have looked at the obvious connection between rock music and dancing. There also seemed to be a direct connection between rock music and fast bike riding. Fast riding was incited by the feel of the rhythm in the head. And in reverse all the qualities of fast dangerous riding, movement, and masculinity seemed to be summed up in—were part of—similar qualities in the music. As we have seen, stylistic, assertive masculinity was a generalized quality of the culture as a whole. It owed much to the articulation of feeling between the bike and pop music. There were several half-explained, sometimes obscure statements concerning what seemed to be an experiential synthesis between rock music and riding the motorbike:

TIM: It helps, like, the sound of the engine . . . try and get a beat in my head, and get the beat in my blood, and get on my bike and go.

FRED: If I heard a record, a real good record, I just fucking wack it open, you know, I just want to wack it open.

TIM: You can hear the beat in your head, don't you . . . you go with the beat, don't you.

TIM: I usually find myself doing this all of a sudden (moving up and down) with my feet, tapping on the gear or something stupid like that.

TIM: Once you get the beat in your head, you really go, you start going.

FRED: Yes, the beat of the motorbike, the beat in your head, you want to beat the traffic . . . The more the engine roars, the more I have to give it, and I think, "You bastards."

JOE: Once I've heard a record, I can't get it off my mind, walking or on the bus, humming it, or singing it, you know. I think that's in your head . . . you know . . . if you were on a motorbike, it'd drive you mad that would, it's all in my head, you're bombing down the road.

Interestingly, where dancing as an immediate corollary and physical expression of the music was stretched to the full, or unavailable, then riding took over as an extension of the same mood and feeling. In an important sense that mood or feeling would have remained basically suppressed or undeveloped were it not for the cycle of music–dancing–riding–music:

JOE: If you hear a fast record you've got to get up and do something, I think. If you can't dance any more, or if the dance is over, you've just got to go for a burn-up.

In a more violent way fighting can be seen as an extension of emotion along the same dimension. In a telling comment Joe said to Fred, "He can't dance, you see, I get up and dance, he gets up and hits." Fighting for Fred had an integral relationship with pop in the sense that it was a playing out of emotion embodied by the music—it would not have happened without the music. Though we must condemn this and mark it as one of the final limits of the culture, recognizing here the reproduction of a traditional regressive, self-entrapping, working-class trait, we must also recognize the distorted and displaced fashion in which it marks a distinctive sense of bursting through a block: of communicating *something* deeply. Remember that aggression, "handling yourself," movement, masculine bravado, and courage were important values in the bike culture. Fighting, fired, and furnaced by a primitive rhythm, was a powerful expression of those qualities in the moment that it marked their tragic, self-destructive limits:

JOE: If the dance is over, you've just got to go for a burn-up.

FRED: That's like me, we were at the Alhambra dance and whenever a good record came on with a big beat I had to get up and hit some fucker, or do sommat. It did, it sent me fucking wild . . . it just sends me mad. I'll tell you one thing that used to send me fucking mad, that was "Revolution," "Revolution," any rock anyone with a big beat in it, the fucking sound, I go fucking wild, I do. Me and Pete, you know, we got banned from a dance, and the police came practically every week because we used to fight every week, couldn't help it, it used to send us wild. There'd be a perfect stranger and Pete would go and punch his head in, he wouldn't get back up, only 'cause the records, certain records, they'd send us fucking mad, they would, they're old beat records. . . . If I hear a good record it . . . fucking, you know, I go in a temper, it just puts me in a temper if I'm just there, so I have to thrash out, it sends me wild, that fucking "Revolution" used to get me mad.

FRED: I dunno, but it sends me fucking mad, but . . . all the big fast ones do. I have to bang my feet or do something, I can't help it. Have you ever been in a dance and you get that tensed up over the record, you feel like fucking lashing out on everything and everybody there?

PW: Well, I just have a pint and keep it in.

FRED: No, I don't drink, you do it the easy way, you can do it the other way, you can go and get pissed down the road and come back there to it, and then listen to the record.

PW: How about the bike?

JOE: Yes, give it holy stick down the road . . . fucked up, I get like that, sometimes I fucking shiver with a record like that. . . . You get that tensed up, you know, you just let it . . . get it all out, you know, then your bike, or fighting somebody, takes the heat off you, doesn't it.

Drinking alcohol would be an "easy way out"; it would not recognize the link between emotion and music. A *full* response spilled over into action and real-life movement. There was an integral connection which it was as dishonest to break as it was reprehensible to keep.

The capacity of the music to influence the culture of the bike boys, on the one hand, and the exact and searching selection of music made by the boys, on the other, allowed a real, though limited, dialectic of experience with its own form of material practice to function in their culture. It brought about very clear basic homologies between the social group and its music. We should respect and learn from this creative, cultural achievement in an area normally thought of as "culture-less," deprived, and manipulated.

A POSTSCRIPT

A really adequate account of the internal parameters of the bike boys' preferred music and its specific ability to hold and retain particular social meanings must be more technically rigorous than this chapter has been. Musicology is the discipline which has the formal resources for this task. It is possible to outline a framework for such an analysis.

Fundamentally, rock 'n' roll has opened up "new" possibilities because it has avoided being trapped by the received conventions concerning rhythm, tonality, and melody.

Most importantly, rock 'n' roll escaped from the determinations of the classic bar structure simply by giving equal emphasis to all the beats of the bar. This subverts the bar form, and actually replaces it with a continuous pulse or basic primitive, standardized rhythm. This regular beat, rather than melody or harmony, is the basic organizing structure of the music. Its constancy and continuity mean that the music is, so to speak, a steady stream, rather than a varied structure. The structure of classical music, with its hierarchy of beats in the bar, meant that it existed clearly in a time sequence—some things had to come before others. In subverting the discontinuities of the bar, rock 'n' roll also subverted the sense of order and of ordered time—if all the elements of a piece are the same, it does not matter in which order they appear. Rock 'n' roll music can be stopped or started at any time; it can be turned back or forward; it can be suspended here and carried on over there; it can be interrupted; it does not need an emotional decrescendo with which to finish. One of the most characteristic features of Buddy Holly's singing style is his "hiccup," an interruption and confusion of tone that would never be tolerated in classical music. Elvis Presley's "Jail House Rock" comes to an abrupt stop and then starts again. One of the commonest end-piece forms is the fade, the diminution of a constant beat into nothing—an impossible concept for any previous musical forms and, incidentally, one that relies completely on modern technical methods.

The tonal aspects of rock 'n' roll are also interesting and innovatory. The music was not caught up in the end of the possibilities of harmony in the way that classical romantic music was—resulting finally in atonality and polytonality because it never seriously took them up. Rhythm replaces harmony as the basic organizing principle of the music. The normal rules of progression, and forms of cadence, are replaced in rock'n' roll by a kind of anarchy and the creative exploration of the possibilities of new electronic equipment: electronic "spacing" techniques which anyway eclipse harmony; exploitation of fluidity of the recorded as against the formalism of written music; echo chambers.

By avoiding conventional tonality, the music can also avoid the great emotional structures of crescendo and decrescendo which are the essential characteristics of classical romantic music. In conjunction with the bar, chord progressions fix conventional music in a time sequence—at the very least the decrescendo has to come after the crescendo. The disregard for tonality in rock 'n' roll further enables it to experiment with repetition and "timelessness"—in a sense to experiment with the "space," the here and now, instead of the ordered time dimension of music.

The melodic element in rock 'n' roll is generally unimportant. There is little conventional chord progression and very limited development of linear expression in the form of a tune. Where they exist, melodic pieces are short, repeated several times over, and frequently totally obscured by rhythm. The suppression, breakup, or nonexistence of the melody means that each part of the music can be understood by itself. For its appreciation the music does not need to be taken as a whole, as in the classic bourgeois aesthetic principle. It also means that from the melodic, as well as rhythmic, point of view, the music can be suspended or broken off at any point, or faded at any point. The tonal and melodic features of the music, therefore, add to the pulse effect created by the constant rhythm beat.

If the main lines of this argument are valid, what is the relationship of this internal structure to the culture and style of the motorbike boys? Most crucially this music allows the return of the body in music, and encourages the development of a culture based on movement and confidence in movement. The classical European tradition has steadily forced the body and dancing out of music, and made it progressively unavailable to the masses, and progressively harder to dance to. The absolute ascendancy of the beat in rock 'n' roll firmly establishes the ascendancy of the body over the mind—it reflects the motorbike boys' culture very closely. The eclipse of tonality and melody in the music is also the eclipse of abstraction in the bike culture.

Second, and in a related way, the suppression of structured time in the music, its ability to stop, start, and be faded, matches the motorbike boys' restless concrete life-style. As we have seen, it is no accident that the boys preferred singles, nor is it an accident that the rock 'n' roll form is the most suited to singles and its modern technology (fading, etc.). Both the music and its singles form are supremely relevant to the style of the bike culture. For the boys, music has to accompany, not determine; it has to respond in the realm of their immediate activity, not in a separate realm with its own timing and logic which require acts of entering into.

In one way, and concentrating on its oppositional aspects, the whole motorbike culture was an attempt to stop or subvert bourgeois, industrial, capitalist notions of time—the basic, experiential discipline its members faced in the work they still took so seriously. The culture did not attempt to impute causalities or logical progression to things. It was about living and experiencing in a concrete, essentially timeless world—certainly time-less in the sense of refusing to accept ordered, rational sequences. Hearing the steady strum of the motorbike exhaust (reminiscent of the pulse of their music) riding nowhere in particular is a steady state of being, not a purposive, time-bound action toward a functional end. In a curious way, death on the motorbike stopped time altogether: it fixed and secured this symbolic state forever. In sum, the boys were exploring a state, a space, rather than a linear logic. The streamlike quality of rock 'n' roll matched, reflected, and fitted in with this concern. It could be stopped, or broken off, or easily changed (as with the single) and did not intrude, with its own discipline, into concrete and spontaneous activity. As the music suppressed the discontinuities of the bar structure, it also suppressed ordered, rational time. The stream pulse quality of the music could be taken and used as timelessness—or certainly as an escape from bourgeois time. In this sense, there was a profound inner connection with a life-style that was so utterly concerned with concrete action in the present and the immediate secure experiencing of the world.

STYLE AS HOMOLOGY AND SIGNIFYING PRACTICE

1 9 7 9

○ ▲ ○ ▲ ○ ▲ ○

STYLE AS HOMOLOGY

The punk subculture signified chaos at every level, but this was possible only because the style itself was so thoroughly ordered. The chaos cohered as a meaningful whole. We can now attempt to solve this paradox by referring to another concept originally employed by Levi-Strauss: homology.

Paul Willis first applied the term "homology" to subculture in his study of hippies and motorbike boys, using it to describe the symbolic fit between the values and life-styles of a group, its subjective experience and the musical forms it uses to express or reinforce its focal concerns. In *Profane Culture*,[1] Willis shows how, contrary to the popular myth which presents subcultures as lawless forms, the internal structure of any particular subculture is characterized by an extreme orderliness: each part is organically related to other parts, and it is through the fit between them that the subcultural member makes sense of the world. For instance, it was the homology between an alternative value system ("Tune in, turn on, drop out"), hallucinogenic drugs, and acid rock which made the hippy culture cohere as a "whole way of life" for individual hippies. In *Resistance Through Rituals*,[2] Stuart Hall et al. crossed the concepts of homology and *bricolage* to provide a systematic explanation of why a particular subcultural style should appeal to a particular group of people. The authors asked the question: "What specifically does a subcultural style signify to the members of the subculture themselves?"

The answer was that the appropriated objects reassembled in the distinctive subcultural ensembles were "made to reflect, express and resonate . . . aspects of group life." The objects chosen were, either intrinsically or in their adapted forms, homologous with the focal concerns, activities, group structure, and collective self-image of the subculture. They were "objects in which (the subcultural members) could see their central values held and reflected."[3]

The skinheads were cited to exemplify this principle. The boots, braces, and cropped hair were considered appropriate and hence meaningful only because they communicated the desired qualities: "hardness, masculinity and working-classness." In this way "the symbolic objects—dress, appearance, language, ritual occasions, styles of interaction, music—were made to form a *unity* with the group's relations, situation, experience."[4]

The punks would certainly seem to bear out this thesis. The subculture was nothing if not consistent. There was a homological relation between the trashy cut-up clothes and spiky hair, the pogo and amphetamines, the spitting, the vomiting, the format of the fanzines, the insurrectionary poses, and the "soul-less," frantically driven music. The punks wore clothes which were the sartorial equivalent of swear words, and they swore as they dressed—with calculated effect, lacing obscenities into record notes and publicity releases, interviews, and love songs. Clothed in chaos, they produced Noise in the calmly orchestrated Crisis of everyday life in the late 1970s—a noise which made (no) sense in exactly the same way and to exactly the same extent as a piece of avant-garde music. If we were to write an epitaph for the punk subculture, we could do no better than repeat Poly Styrene's famous dictum: "Oh Bondage, Up Yours!" or somewhat more concisely: the forbidden is permitted, but by the same token, nothing, not even these forbidden signifers (bondage, safety pins, chains, hair dye, etc.) is sacred and fixed.

This absence of permanently sacred signifiers (icons) creates problems for the semiotician. How can we discern any positive values reflected in objects which were chosen only to be discarded? For instance, we can say that the early punk ensembles gestured toward the signified's "modernity" and "working-classness." The safety pins and bin liners signified a relative material poverty which was either directly experienced and exaggerated or sympathetically assumed, and which in turn was made to stand for the spiritual paucity of everyday life. In other words, the safety pins and other objects "enacted" that transition from real to symbolic scarcity which Paul Piccone has described as the movement from "empty stomachs" to "empty spirits"—and therefore an empty life notwithstanding [the] chrome and the plastic . . . of the life style of bourgeois society."[5]

We could go further and say that even if the poverty was being parodied, the wit was undeniably barbed; that beneath the clownish makeup there lurked the unaccepted and disfigured face of capitalism; that beyond the horror-circus antics a divided and unequal society was being eloquently condemned. However, if we were to go further still and describe punk music as the "sound of the Westway," or the pogo as the "high-rise leap," or to talk of bondage as reflecting the narrow options of working-class youth, we would be treading on less certain ground. Such readings are both too literal and too conjectural. They are extrapolations from the subculture's own prodigious rhetoric, and rhetoric is not self-explanatory: it may say what it means but it does not necessarily "mean" what it "says." In other words, it is opaque: its categories are part of its publicity. As J. Mepham writes, "The true text is reconstructed not by a process of piecemeal decoding, but by the identification of the generative sets of ideological categories and its replacement by a different set."[6]

To reconstruct the true text of the punk subculture, to trace the source of its subversive practices, we must first isolate the "generative set" responsible for the subculture's exotic displays. Certain semiotic facts are undeniable. The punk subculture, like every other youth culture, was constituted in a series of spectacular transformations of a whole range of commodities, values, commonsense attitudes, etc. It was through these adapted forms that certain sections of predominantly working-class youth were able to restate their opposition to dominant values and institutions. However, when we attempt to close in on specific items, we immediately encounter problems. What, for instance, was the swastika being used to signify?

We can see how the symbol was made available to the punks (via David Bowie and Lou Reed's "Berlin" phase). Moreover, it clearly reflected the punks' interest in a decadent and evil Germany—a Germany which had no future. It evoked a period redolent with a powerful mythology. Conventionally, as far as the British were concerned, the swastika signified enemy. Nonetheless, in punk usage, the symbol lost its "natural" meaning—fascism. The punks were not generally sympathetic to the parties of the extreme right. On the contrary, the conflict with the resurrected teddy boys and the widespread support for the antifascist movement (e.g., the Rock Against Racism campaign) seem to indicate that the punk subculture grew up partly as an antithetical response to the reemergence of racism in the mid-seventies. We must resort, then, to the most obvious of explanations—that the swastika was worn because it was guaranteed to shock. (A punk asked by *Time Out* why she wore a swastika replied: "Punks just like to be hated.")[7] This represented more than a simple inversion or inflection of the ordinary meanings attached to an object. The signifier (swastika) had been willfully detached from the concept (nazism) it conventionally signified, and although it had been repositioned (as "Berlin") within an alternative subcultural context, its primary value and appeal derived precisely from its lack of meaning:

from its potential for deceit. It was exploited as an empty effect. We are forced to the conclusion that the central value held and reflected in the swastika was the communicated absence of any such identifiable values. Ultimately, the symbol was as "dumb" as the rage it provoked. The key to punk style remains elusive. Instead of arriving at the point where we can begin to make sense of the style, we have reached the very place where meaning itself evaporates.

STYLE AS SIGNIFYING PRACTICE

We are surrounded by emptiness but it is an emptiness filled with signs.[8]

It would seem that those approaches to subculture based upon a traditional semiotics (a semiotics which begins with some notion of the "message"— of a combination of elements referring unanimously to a fixed number of signifieds) fail to provide us with a "way in" to the difficult and contradictory text of punk style. Any attempt at extracting a final set of meanings from the seemingly endless, often apparently random, play of signifiers in evidence here seems doomed to failure.

And yet, over the years, a branch of semiotics has emerged which deals precisely with this problem. Here the simple notion of reading as the revelation of a fixed number of concealed meanings is discarded in favor of the idea of *polysemy*, whereby each text is seen to generate a potentially infinite range of meanings. Attention is consequently directed toward that point—or more precisely, that level—in any given text where the principle of meaning itself seems most in doubt. Such an approach lays less stress on the primacy of structure and system in language (*langue*), and more upon the *position* of the speaking subject in discourse (*parole*). It is concerned with the *process* of meaning construction rather than with the final product.

Much of this work, principally associated with the Tel Quel group in France, has grown out of an engagement with literary and filmic texts. It involves an attempt to go beyond conventional theories of art (as mimesis, as representation, as a transparent reflection of reality, etc.) and to introduce instead "the notion of art as 'work,' as 'practice,' as a particular *transformation* of reality, a version of reality, an account of reality."[9]

One of the effects of this redefinition of interests has been to draw critical attention to the relationship between the means of representation and the object represented, between what in traditional aesthetics have been called respectively the form and content of a work of art. According to this approach, there can no longer be any absolute distinction between these two terms, and the primary recognition that the *ways* in which things are said—

the narrative structures employed—imposes quite rigid limitations on *what* can be said is of course crucial. In particular, the notion that a detachable content can be inserted into a more or less neutral form—the assumption which seems to underpin the aesthetic of realism—is deemed illusory because such an aesthetic "denies its own status as articulation. . . . [in this case] the real is not articulated, *it is*."[10]

Drawing on an alternative theory of aesthetics, rooted in modernism and the avant-garde and taking as its model Brecht's idea of an "epic theater," the Tel Quel group sets out to counter the prevailing notion of a transparent relation between sign and referent, signification and reality, through the concept of *signifying practice*. This phrase reflects exactly the group's central concerns with the ideological implications of form, with the idea of a positive construction and deconstruction of meaning, and with what has come to be called the productivity of language. This approach sees language as an active, transitive force which shapes and positions the "subject" (as speaker, writer, reader) while always itself remaining "in process" capable of infinite adaptation. This emphasis on signifying practice is accompanied by a polemical insistence that art represents the triumph of process over fixity, disruption over unity, "collision" over "linkage"—the triumph, that is, of the signifier over the signified. It should be seen as part of the group's attempt to substitute the values of fissure and contradiction for the preoccupation with wholeness, which is said to characterize classic literary criticism.

Although much of this work is still at a tentative stage, it does offer a radically different perspective on style in subculture—one which assigns a central place to the problems of reading which we have encountered in our analysis of punk. Julia Kristeva's work on signification seems particularly useful. In *La Révolution du language poétique* she explores the subversive possibilities within language through a study of French symbolist poetry, and points to "poetic language" as the "place where the social code is destroyed and renewed."[11] She counts as radical those signifying practices which negate and disturb syntax—"the condition of coherence and rationality"[12]—and which therefore serve to erode the concept of "actantial position" upon which the whole "Symbolic Order," is seen to rest.[13]

Two of Kristeva's interests seem to coincide with my own: the creation of subordinate groups through *positioning in language* (Kristeva is specifically interested in women) and the disruption of the process through which such positioning is habitually achieved. In addition, the general idea of signifying practice (which she defines as "the setting in place and cutting through or traversing of a system of signs") can help us to rethink in a more subtle and complex way the relations not only between marginal and mainstream cultural formations but between the various subcultural styles themselves. For instance, we have seen how all subcultural style is based on a practice which has much in common with the "radical" collage aesthetic of surrealism, and we shall be seeing how different styles represent different signifying practices. Beyond this I shall be arguing that the signifying practices embodied in punk were "radical" in Kristeva's sense: that they gestured toward a "nowhere" and actively *sought* to remain silent, illegible.

We can now look more closely at the relationship between experience, expression, and signification in subculture; at the whole question of style and our reading of style. To return to our example, we have seen how the punk style fit together homologically precisely through its lack of fit (hole: T-shirt::spitting:applause::bin liner:garment::anarchy:order)—by its refusal to cohere around a readily identifiable set of central values. It cohered, instead, *elliptically* through a chain of conspicuous absences. It was characterized by its unlocatedness—its blankness—and in this can be contrasted with the skinhead style.

Whereas the skinheads theorized and fetishized their class position in order to effect a "magical" return to an imagined past, the punks dislocated themselves from the parent culture and were positioned instead on the outside: beyond the comprehension of the average (wo)man in the street in a science fiction future. They played up their Otherness, "happening" on the world as aliens, inscrutables. Though punk rituals, accents, and objects were deliberately used to signify working-classness, the exact origins of individual punks were disguised or symbolically disfigured by the makeup, masks, and aliases which seem to have been used, like Breton's art, as ploys "to escape the principle of identity."[14]

This working-classness therefore tended to retain, *even in practice, even in its concretized forms*, the dimensions of an idea. It was abstract, disembodied, decontextualized. Bereft of the necessary details—a name, a home, a history—it refused to make sense, to be grounded, "read back" to its origins. It stood in violent contradiction to that other great punk signifier—sexual "kinkiness." The two forms of deviance—social and sexual—were juxtaposed to give an impression of multiple warping which was guaranteed to disconcert the most liberal of observers, to challenge the glib assertions of sociologists no matter how radical. In this way, although the punks referred continually to the realities of school, work, family, and class, these references made sense only at one remove: they were passed through the fractured circuitry of punk style and re-presented as "noise," disturbance, entropy.

In other words, although the punks self-consciously mirrored what Paul Piccone calls the "pre-categorical realities" of bourgeois society—inequality, powerlessness, alienation—this was only possible because punk style had made a decisive break not only with the parent culture but with its own *location in experience*.[15] This break was both inscribed and reenacted in the signifying practices embodied in punk style. The punk ensembles, for instance, did not so much magically resolve experienced contradictions as *represent* the experience of contradiction itself in the form of visual puns (bondage, the ripped T-shirt, etc.). Thus while it is true that the symbolic objects in punk style (the safety pins, the pogo, the ECT hair styles) were "made to form a *'unity'* with the group's relations, situations, experience," this unity was at once "ruptural" and "expressive," or more precisely, it expressed itself through rupture.[16]

This is not to say, of course, that all punks were equally aware of the disjunction between experience and signification upon which the whole style was ultimately based. The style no doubt made sense for the first wave of self-conscious innovators at a level which remained inaccessible to those who became punks after the subculture had surfaced and been publicized. Punk is not unique in this: the distinction between originals and hangers-on is always a significant one in subculture. Indeed, it is frequently verbalized (plastic punks or safety-pin people, burrhead Rastas or Rasta bandwagon, weekend hippies, etc., versus the "authentic" people). For instance, the mods had an intricate system of classification whereby the "faces" and "stylists" who made up the original coterie were defined against the unimaginative majority—the pedestrian "kids" and "scooter boys" who were accused of trivializing and coarsening the precious mod style. What is more, different youths bring different degrees of commitment to a subculture. It can represent a major dimension in people's lives—an axis erected in the face of the family around which a secret and immaculate identity can be made to cohere—or it can be a slight distraction, a bit of light relief from the monotonous but nonetheless paramount realities of school, home, and work. It can be used as a means of escape, of total detachment from the surrounding terrain, or as a way of fitting back in to it and settling down after a weekend or evening spent letting off steam. In most cases it is used, as Phil Cohen suggests, magically to achieve both ends.[17] However, despite these individual differences, the members of a subculture must share a common language. And if a style is really to catch on, if it is to become genuinely popular, it must say the right things in the right way at the right time. It must anticipate or encapsulate a mood, a moment. It must embody a sensibility, and the sensibility which punk style embodied was essentially dislocated, ironic, and self-aware.

Just as individual members of the same subculture can be more or less conscious of what they are saying in style and in what ways they are saying it, so different subcultural styles exhibit different degrees of rupture. The conspicuously scruffy, "unwholesome" punks obtruded from the familiar landscape of normalized forms in a more startling fashion than the mods, tellingly described in a newspaper of the time as "pin-neat, lively and clean," although the two groups had nonetheless engaged in the same signifying practice (i.e., self-consciously subversive *bricolage*).

This partly explains or at least underpins internal subcultural hostilities. For example, the antagonism between the teddy boy revivalists and the punk rockers went beyond any simple incompatability at the level of content—different music, dress, and so on—beyond even the different political and racial affiliations of the two groups, the different relationships with the parent community, and was inscribed in the very way in which the two styles were constructed: the way in which they communicated (or refused to communicate) meaning. Teddy boys interviewed in the press regularly objected to the punks' symbolic "plundering" of the precious fifties wardrobe (the drains, the winklepickers, quiffs, etc.) and to the ironic and impious uses to which these "sacred" artifacts were put when "cut up" and reworked into punk style, where presumably they were contaminated by association (placed next to "bovver boots" and latex bondage-wear!). Behind punk's favored "cut ups" lay hints of disorder, of breakdown and category confusion: a desire not only to erode racial and gender boundaries but also to confuse chronological sequence by mixing up details from different periods.

As such, punk style was perhaps interpreted by the teddy boys as an affront to the traditional working-class values of forthrightness, plain speech, and sexual puritanism which they had endorsed and revived. Like the reaction of the rockers to the mods and the skinheads to the hippies, the teddy boy revival seems to have represented an "authentic" working-class backlash to the proletarian posturings of the new wave. *The way in which it signified*, via a magical return to the past, to the narrow confines of the community and the parent culture, to the familiar and the legible, was perfectly in tune with its inherent conservatism. Not only did the teds react aggressively to punk objects and "meanings," they also reacted to the way in which those objects were presented, those meanings constructed and dismantled. They did so by resorting to an altogether more primitive language: by turning back, in George Melly's words, to a " 'then' which was superior to 'now' " which, as Melly goes on to say, is "a very anti-pop concept."[18]

We can express the difference between the two practices in the following formula: one (i.e., the punks') is kinetic, transitive, and concentrates attention on *the act of transformation* performed upon the object; the other (i.e., the teds') is static, expressive, and concentrates attention on the *objects-in-themselves*. We can perhaps grasp the nature of this distinction more clearly if we resort to another of Kristeva's categories—*significance*. She has introduced this term to describe the work of the signifier in the text in contrast to signification, which refers to the work of the signified. Roland Barthes defines the different between the two operations thus:

> Significance is a *process* in the course of which the "subject" of the text, escaping (conventional logic) and engaging in other logics (of the signifier, of contradiction) struggles with meaning and is deconstructed ("lost"); signifiance—and this is what immediately distinguishes it from signification—is thus precisely a work; not the work by which the (intact and exterior) subject might try to master the language . . . but that radical work (leaving nothing intact) through which the subject

explores—entering not observing—how the language works and undoes him or her. . . . Contrary to signification, significance cannot be reduced therefore, to communication, representation, expression: it places the subject (of writer, reader) in the text not as a projection . . . but as a "loss," a "disappearance."[19]

Elsewhere, in an attempt to specify the various kinds of meaning present in film, Barthes refers to the "moving play" of signifiers as the "third" (obtuse) meaning" (the other two meanings being the "informational" and the "symbolic" which, as they are "closed" and "obvious," are normally the only ones which concern the semiotician). The third meaning works against ("exceeds") the other two by "blunting" them—rounding off the "obvious signified" and thus causing "the reading to slip." Barthes uses as an example a still from Eisenstein's film *Battleship Potemkin* which shows an old woman, a headscarf pulled low over her forehead, caught in a classical, grief-stricken posture. At one level, the level of the obvious meaning, she seems to typify noble grief but, as Barthes observes, her strange headdress and rather "stupid" fishlike eyes cut across this typification in such a way that "there is no guarantee of intentionality."[20] This, the third meaning, flows upstream as it were, against the supposed current of the text, preventing the text from reaching its destination: a full and final closure. Barthes thus describes the third meaning as "a gash rased [sic] of meaning (of the desire for meaning) . . . it outplays meaning—subverts not the content but the whole practice of meaning."

The ideas of "significance" and "obtuse meaning" suggest the presence in the text of an intrinsically subversive component. Our recognition of the operations performed within the text at the level of the signifier can help us to understand the way in which certain subcultural styles seem to work against the reader and to resist any authorative interpretation. If we consider for a moment, it becomes clear that not all subcultural styles "play" with language to the same extent: some are more straightforward than others and place a higher priority on the construction and projection of a firm and coherent identity. For instance, if we return to our earlier example, we could say that whereas the teddy boy style says its piece in a relatively direct and obvious way, and remains resolutely committed to a "finished" meaning, to the signified, to what Kristeva calls "signification," punk style is in a constant state of assemblage, of flux. It introduces a heterogeneous set of signifiers which are liable to be superseded at any moment by others no less productive. It invites the reader to "slip into significance" to lose the sense of direction, the direction of sense. Cut adrift from meaning, the punk style thus comes to approximate the state which Barthes has described as "a *floating* (the very form of the signifier); a floating which would not destroy anything but would be content simply to disorientate the Law."[21]

The two styles, then, represent different signifying practices which confront the reader with quite different problems. We can gauge the extent of this difference (which is basically a difference in the degree of *closure*) by means of an analogy. In *The Thief's Journal*, Jean Genet contrasts his relationship to the elusive Armand with his infatuation with the more transparent Stilittano in terms which underline the distinction between the two practices: "I compare Armand to the expanding universe. . . . Instead of being defined and reduced to observable limits, Armand constantly changes as I pursue him. On the other hand, Stilittano is already encircled."

The relationship between experience, expression, and signification is therefore not a constant in subculture. It can form a unity which is either more or less organic, striving toward some ideal coherence, or more or less ruptural, reflecting the experience of breaks and contradictions. Moreover, individual subcultures can be more or less "conservative" or "progressive," integrated *into* the community, continuous with the values of that community, or extrapolated *from* it, defining themselves *against* the parent culture. Finally, these differences are reflected not only in the objects of subcultural style, but in the signifying practices which represent those objects and render them meaningful.

NOTES

[1] Paul Willis, *Profane Culture* (London: Routledge & Kegan Paul, 1978).
[2] Stuart Hall and Tony Jefferson (eds.), *Resistance Through Rituals* (London: Hutchinson, 1976).
[3] Ibid.
[4] Ibid.
[5] Paul Piccone, "From Youth Culture to Political Praxis," *Radical America 3* (15 November 1969).
[6] John Mepham, "The Theory of Ideology in *Capital*," *Working Papers in Cultural Studies*, No. 6 (University of Birmingham: Centre for Contemporary Cultural Studies, 1972).
[7] *Time Out*, 17–23 December 1977.
[8] Henri Lefebvre, *Everyday Life in the Modern World* (London: Allen Lane, 1971).
[9] Sylvia Harvey, *May 68 and Film Culture* (British Film Institute, 1978).
[10] Colin MacCabe, "Notes on Realism," *Screen 15*, No. 2 (1974).
[11] Julia Kristeva, *La révolution du langage poétique* (Paris: Seuil, 1974).
[12] Allon White, "L'éclatement du sujet: The Theoretical Work of Julia Kristeva," University of Birmingham (1977), photocopy.
[13] Kristeva's "Symbolic Order" is used in a sense derived specifically from Lacanian psychoanalysis. I use the term merely to designate the apparent unity of the dominant ideological discourses in play at any one time.
[14] "Who knows if we are not somehow preparing ourselves to escape the principle of identity?" A. Breton, Preface to the 1920 Exhibition of Max Ernst.
[15] Piccone, "Youth Culture."
[16] Hall and Jefferson, *Resistance Through Rituals*.
[17] Phil Cohen, "Sub-cultural Conflict and the Working-class Community," *Working Papers in Cultural Studies*, No. 2 (University of Birmingham: Centre for Contemporary Cultural Studies, 1972).
[18] George Melly, *Revolt into Style* (London: Penguin, 1972).
[19] Roland Barthes, "The Third Meaning," in Stephen Heath (ed.), *Image–Music–Text* (London: Fontana, 1977).
[20] Ibid.
[21] Roland Barthes, "Writers, Intellectuals, Teachers," in Heath (ed.), *Image–Music–Text*.

Angela McRobbie

SETTLING ACCOUNTS
WITH SUBCULTURES

A Feminist Critique
1 9 8 0

○ ▲ ○ ▲ ○ ▲ ○

Although "youth culture and the "sociology of youth"—and particularly critical and Marxist perspectives on them—have been central strands in the development of Cultural Studies over the past fifteen years, the emphasis from the earliest work of the National Deviancy Conference onward has remained consistently on *male* youth cultural forms. There have been studies of the relation of male youth to class and class culture, to the machinery of the state, and to the school, community, and workplace. Football has been analyzed as a male sport, drinking as a male form of leisure, the law and the police as patriarchal structures concerned with young male (potential) offenders. I don't know of a study that considers, never mind prioritizes, youth and the family; women and the whole question of sexual division have been marginalized. This failure by subcultural theorists to dislodge the male connotations of "youth" inevitably poses problems for feminists teaching about these questions. As they cannot use the existing text straight, what other options do they have?

One is to dismiss the existing literature as irrevocably male-biased and to shift attention toward the alternative terrain of girls' culture, to the construction of ideologies about girlhood as articulated in and through various institutions and cultural forms—in schools, in the family, in law, and in the popular media. The danger of this course is that the opportunity may be missed of grappling with questions which, examined from a feminist perspective, can increase our understanding of masculinity, male culture, and sexuality, and their place within class culture. This then is the other option: to combine a clear commitment to the analysis of girls' culture with a direct engagement with youth culture as it is constructed in sociological and cultural studies. Rather than simply being dismissed, the subcultural "classics" should be reread critically so that questions hitherto ignored or waved aside in embarrassment become central. An examination of their weaknesses and shortcomings can raise questions of immediate political relevance for feminists. What, for example, is the nature of women's and girls' leisure? What role do hedonism, fantasy escapes, and imaginary solutions play in their lives? What access to these spheres and symbols do women have anyway?

In this article I am going to explore some questions about youth culture and subcultures by attempting this sort of feminist rereading of two recent books, Paul Willis's *Learning to Labour* and Dick Hebdige's *Subculture*.[1] The point, therefore, is not to condemn them—they represent the most sophisticated accounts to date of youth culture and style—but to read "across" them to see what they say (or fail to say) about working-class male sexuality, bravado, and the sexual ambiguity of style. Willis investigates the relation for a group of "lads" between working-class youth cultural "gestures" and the places to which they are allocated in production. The expressions of resistance and opposition which characterize this relation are fraught with contradiction. Willis suggests that the vocabulary articulating their distance from structures of authority in school and workplace simultaneously binds the lads to the basically rigid positions they occupy in these spheres; their rowdy shouts of disaffiliation quickly become cries of frustration and incorporation. A particular mode of class culture is thus seen in a complex way to serve two masters: capital *and* labor. The emphasis of Hebdige's *Subculture* is quite different. He focuses elliptically on subcultural style as *signifier* rather than as a series of distinct cultural expressions. Style, he claims, takes place several steps away from the material conditions of its followers' existence and continually resists precise historical analysis. One of its objectives, then, is to be forever out of joint with mainstream dominant culture: it evaporates just as it crystallizes.

Willis and Hebdige both show how male adolescents take already coded materials from their everyday landscapes (and, though this is not spelled out, from their fantasies) and mold them into desirable shapes, into social practices and stylish postures. Both accounts draw on the notion that control and creativity are exercised from within subordinate class positions and that, as a result of this subordination, cultural gestures often appear in partial, contradictory, and even amputated forms. These insights can be taken further by focusing on the language of adolescent male sexuality embedded in these texts. Questions around sexism and working-class youth and around sexual violence make it possible to see how class and patriarchal relations work together, sometimes with an astonishing brutality and at other times in the teeth-gritting harmony of romance, love, and marriage. One of Willis's lads says of his girlfriend:

> "She loves doing fucking housework. Trousers I brought up yesterday, I took 'em up last night and her turned 'em up for me. She's as good as gold and I wanna get married as soon as I can."[2]

Until we come to grips with such expressions as they appear across the subcultural field, our portrayal of girls' culture will remain one-sided and youth culture will continue to "mean" in uncritically masculine terms. Questions about girls, sexual relations, and femininity in youth will continue to be defused or marginalzed in the ghetto of Women's Studies.

SILENCES

One of the central tenets of the women's movement has been that the personal is political. Similarly, feminists recognize the close links between personal experience and the areas we choose for study—our autobiographies invade and inform what we write. Even if the personal voice of the author is not apparent throughout the text, she will at least announce her interest in, and commitment to, her subject in an introduction or foreword. Although few radical (male) sociologists would deny the importance of the personal in precipitating social and political awareness, to admit how their own experience has influenced their choice of subject matter (the politics of selection) seems more or less taboo. This silence is particularly grating in the literature on the hippie and drug countercultures, where is seems to have been stage-managed only through a suspiciouly exaggerated amount of "methodological" justification.

It is not my intention here to read between the lines of writing about subcultures and unravel the half-written references, the elliptical allusions, and the sixties rock lyrics. The point is that this absence of self (this is quite different from the authorial "I" or "we") and the invalidating of personal experience in the name of the more objective social sciences goes hand in hand with the silencing of other areas, which are for feminists of the greatest importance. It's no coincidence, for example, that while the sociologies of deviance and youth were blooming in the early seventies, the sociology of the family—still steeped in the structural-functionalism of Talcott Parsons— was everybody's least favorite option. If we look for the structured absences in this youth literature, it is the sphere of family and domestic life that is missing. No commentary on the hippies dealt with the countercultural sexual division of labor, let alone the hypocrisies of "free love"; few writers seemed interested in what happened when a mod went home after a weekend on speed. Only what happened out there on the streets mattered.

Perhaps these absences should be understood historically. The sociology of crime/deviance/youth culture was one of the first areas from which the hegemony of Parsonianism was challenged. Many of the radical young sociologists in the vanguard of this attack were recruited from the New Left, from the student movement of the late sixties, and even from the hippie counterculture. At this time, before the emergence of the women's movement in the early seventies, the notions of escaping from the family, the bourgeois commitments of children, and the whole sphere of family consumption formed a distinct strand in left politics. Sheila Rowbotham has described how women were seen in some left circles as a temptation provided by capital to divert workers and militants alike from the real business of revolution, and she has also shown how hypocritical these antifamily, antiwomen platitudes were.[3] Clearly things have changed since then but, although the work of feminists has enabled studies of the family to transcend functionalism, the literature on subcultures and youth culture has scarcely begun to deal with the contradictions that patterns of cultural resistance pose in relation to women. The writers, having defined themselves as against the family and the trap of romance as well as against the boredom of meaningless labor, seem to be drawn to look at other, largely working-class, groups who appear to be doing the same thing.

In documenting the temporary flights of the teds, mods, or rockers, however, they fail to show that is it monstrously more difficult for women to escape (even temporarily) and that these symbolic flights have often been at the expense of women (especially mothers) and girls. The lads may get by with—and get off on—each other alone on the streets, but they did not eat, sleep, or make love there. Their peer-group consciousness and pleasure frequently seem to hinge on a collective disregard for women and the sexual exploitation of girls. And in the literary sensibility of urban romanticism that resonates across most youth cultural discourses, girls are allowed little more than the back seat on a drafty motorbike.

> Just wrap your legs around these velvet rims
> And strap your hands across my engines
> We'll run till we drop baby we'll never go back
> I'm just a scared and lonely rider
> But I gotta know how it feels.[4]

Writing about subcultures isn't the same thing as being in one. Nonetheless, it's easy to see how it would be possible in sharing some of the same symbols—the liberating release of rock music; the thrill of speed, of alcohol, or even of football—to be blinded to some of their more oppressive features.

I have oversimplified in this account, of course—there is a whole range of complicating factors. In the first place, feminists also oppose the same oppressive structures as the radical sociologists and have visions of alternative modes of organizing domestic life—although ones which are *primarily* less oppressive of women, because historically women have always suffered the greatest exploitation, the greatest isolation in the home. Second, to make sense of the literature on subculture *purely* in terms of male left identification with male working-class youth groups would mean devaluing the real political commitment behind the work and ignoring its many theoretical achievements. The attempts to explain the ways in which class fears on the part of the dominant class have been inflected during the postwar period onto sectors of working-class youth—and dealt with at this level— remains of vital significance; also important has been the ascription of a sense of dignity and purpose, an integrity and a rationale, to that section of youth commonly labeled "animals" in the popular media. Third, there have been political and theoretical developments. The NDC (National Deviancy Conference) of the late sixties grew out of a libertarianism which rejected both reformist and old left politics in favor of grassroots politics (especially cultural and "alternative" politics) and which emphasized the importance of community work and action research. Many of these ideas have since been refined in an engagement with the work of Althusser and of Gramsci.

Yet the question of sexual division still remains more or less unexplored. In *Learning to Labour*, Paul Willis convincingly argues that the culture which the lads bring to the school and workplace and its consequent relation to the position they occupy in the labor hierarchy provides the key to many of the more contradictory aspects of male working-class culture. But what do these expressions mean for girls and female working-class culture? One striking feature of Willis's study is how unambiguously degrading to women is the language of aggressive masculinity through which the lads kick against the oppressive structures they inhabit—the text is littered with references of the utmost brutality. One teacher's authority is undermined by her being labeled a "cunt." Boredom in the classroom is alleviated by the mimed masturbating of a giant penis and by replacing the teacher's official language with a litany of sexual "obscenities." The lads demonstrate their disgust for and fear of menstruation by substituting "jam rag" for towel at every opportunity. What Willis fails to confront, I think, is the violence underpinning such imagery and evident in one lad's description of sexual intercourse as having "a good maul on her." He does not comment on the extreme cruelty of the lads' sexual double standard or tease out in sufficient detail how images of sexual power and domination are used as a kind of last defensive resort. It is in these terms that the book's closing lines can be understood. When Paul Willis gently probes Joey about his future, he replies, "I don't know, the only thing I'm interested in is fucking as many women as I can if you really want to know."

Although Willis shows how male manual work has come to depend on the elaboration of certain values—the cultural reproduction of machismo from father to son, the male pride in physical labor and contempt for "pen pushing"—he does not integrate these observations on masculinity and patriarchal culture into the context of the working-class family. The family is the obverse face of hard, working-class culture, the softer sphere in which fathers, sons, and boyfriends expect to be, and are, emotionally serviced. It is this link between the lads' hard outer image and their private experiences—relations with parents, siblings, and girlfriends—that still needs to be explored. Willis's emphasis on the cohesion of the tight-knit groups tends to blind us to the ways that the lads' immersion in and expression of working-class culture also takes place outside the public sphere. It happens as much around the breakfast table and in the bedroom as in the school and the workplace.

Shopfloor culture may have developed a toughness and resilience to deal with the brutality of capitalist productive relations, but these same "values" can be used internally. They are evident, for example, in the cruel rituals to which the older manual workers subject school leavers newly entering production. They can also be used, and often are, against women and girls in the form of both wife and girlfriend battering. A full *sexed* notion of working-class culture would have to consider such features more centrally.

DISCOURSES OF DISRESPECT

Because it consistently avoids reduction to one essential meaning and because its theses are almost entirely decentered, it's not easy to contain Dick Hebdige's *Subculture* within the normal confines of a critical review. Ostensibly his argument is that it is on the concrete and symbolic meeting ground of black and white (implicity male) youth that we have to understand the emergence and form of subcultural style, its syncopations and cadences. From an account of the "black experience," he works outward to the ways in which this culture has been taken up and paid homage to by white male intellectuals and by sections of working-class youth. At the heart of this process he places rock music—black soul and reggae, white rock (especially the music and style of David Bowie), and, of course, the "mess" of punk. Acknowledging—and fleetingly pleading guilty to—the tendency to romanticism in such subcultural tributes, Hebdige stresses the danger that such hagiography can overlook the unmitigated ferocity of the oppression and exploitation which have created black culture as it is. He does not try to prove his case with a barrage of empirical facts, but presents his reading of style as one which the reader can take or leave. Yet the sheer partiality of extrapolating race as signifier *par excellence* makes that which he chooses *not* to deal with all the more shocking. Despite his emphasis on the neglect of race and racism in youth and subcultural work, he seems oblivious to the equal neglect of sexuality and sexism.

His book twists and winds its way around a variety of themes. At some moments it goes off into flights of densely referenced semi-sociological stream of consciousness. At others it addresses itself with foreceful clarity to mainstream theoretical debates on youth culture: two of his arguments here are worth dwelling on in that a feminist critique would demand they be pushed further than he is willing to do. From the start Hebdige acknowledges his debt to the theoretical overview in *Resistance Through Rituals*,[5] in particular its application of Gramsci's concept of hegemony to the question of youth in postwar Britain, and places his own work broadly within the parameters defined by John Clarke's essay on style in that collection. The problem is that Hebdige's assumptions actually run counter to those of *Resistance Through Rituals*. Briefly, he posits that the youth subculture is the sum of those attempts to define it, explain it away, vilify it, romanticize it, and penalize it. The moral panic and smear campaign construct what the subculture "becomes" just as much as the kids on the street. Linked to this is his important recognition that there is no necessary relation between the peculiarities of subcultural style and the area of (presumably) working-class life from which it is drawn, that "one should not expect the subcultural response . . . to be even necessarily in touch, in any immediate sense, with its material position in the capitalist system." Working-class self-images are just as constricted by the limitations and historical specificities of available codes as youth cultures. Their "raw materials" may be material, but they are never completely "uncooked."

In one of the most perceptive and exciting parts of the book, Hebdige uses punk to illustrate this. It is here, in spelling out his argument that punk was a response to already articulated "noises" (especially in the popular press) of panic and crisis, that he contradicts the logic of the *Resistance Through Rituals* position, which argued for the *deconstruction* of the ideological debris and clutter about youth and for the reconstruction from these ruins of a more adequately theorized account. The important point is that, precisely because it used a phenomenal forms / real relations model, *Resistance Through Rituals* was unable to engage directly with the sort of concepts at play in Hebdige's account. The significance of "Outsider Mythology," for example, or of representations of youth in film, literature, or music, would have been consigned to the sphere of ideology or (worse) "idealism," given the same logical, if not political, status as the "moral panic" and therefore also in need of "deconstruction."

Hebdige, in contrast, argues that ultimately the radical/Marxist account is logically no more true than any other: it is valuable to the extent that it engages critically not only with the phenomenon in question but also with the inadequacies of the different existing accounts. Although its "politics" cannot be read off—it may have little to say about youth politics in the activist sense—it nevertheless has a material political force in that it disrupts commonsense wisdoms about youth and their more respectable academic revisions. Whereas in *Resistance Through Rituals* it is class that provides the key to unlocking subcultural meanings (though not, the authors stress, in a reductionist way),[6] in *Subculture* style and race are selected as the organizing principles for prying them open. Although neither book takes us very far in understanding youth and gender, Hebdige's account at least makes it possible to explore the theme *without* continual recourse to class and so may disrupt (in a positive sense) some of our own commonsense wisdoms about class and class culture. But although his method draws on the work of feminists like Kristeva and is one widely used by feminists working in Media Studies, Hebdige by and large reproduces yet another "silence." The pity is that he thereby misses the opportunity to come to grips with subculture's best-kept secret, its claiming of style as a male but never unambiguously masculine prerogative. This is not to say that women are denied style, rather that the style of a subculture is primarily that of its men. Linked to this are the collective celebrations of itself through its rituals of stylish public self-display and of its (at least temporary) sexual self-sufficiency. As a well-known ex-mod put it:

> "You didn't need to get too heavily into sex or pulling chicks, or sorts as they were called . . . Women were just the people who were dancing over in the corner by the speakers."[7]

If only he had pushed his analysis of style further, Hebdige might well have unraveled the question of sexuality, masculinity, and the apparent redundancy of women in most subcultures.

What is clear, though, is that Hebdige revels in style. For him it is a desirable mode of narcissistic differentiation—"You're still doing things I gave up years ago," as Lou Reed put it. There's nothing inherently wrong with that; the problem is that as a signifier of desire, as the starting point for innumerable fantasies or simply as a way of sorting friends from enemies, Hebdige's usage of "style" structurally excludes women. This is ironic, for in "straight" terms it is accepted as primarily a female or feminine interest. What's more, women are so obviously inscribed (marginalized, abused) within subcultures as static objects (girlfriends, whores, or "faghags") that access to its thrills—to hard, fast rock music, to drugs, alcohol, and "style"— would hardly be compensation even for the most adventurous teenage girl. The signs and codes subverted and reassembled in the "semiotic guerilla warfare" conducted through style don't really speak to women at all. The attractions of a subculture—its fluidity, the shifts in the minutiae of its styles, the details of its combative *bricolage*—are offset by an unchanging and exploitative view of women.

HOMAGES TO MASCULINITY

Rather than just cataloguing the "absences" in *Subculture*, I want to deal with three questions raised by a feminist reading: the extent to which subcultural *bricoleurs* draw on patriarchal meanings, the implications of ambiguous sexuality for youth cultures, and the question of gender and the moral panic.

Dick Hebdige claims that style breaks rules and that its "refusals" are complex amalgams taken from a range of existing signs and meanings. Their "menace" lies in the extent to which they threaten these meanings by demonstrating their fraility and the ease with which they can be thrown into disorder. But just as the agents who carry on this sartorial terrorism are inscribed as subjects within patriarchal as well as class structures, so too are the meanings to which they have recourse. These historical, cultural configurations cannot be free of features oppressive to women. Machismo suffuses the rebel archetypes in Jamaican culture which, Hebdige claims, young British blacks plunder for suitable images. The teds turned to the style of Edwardian "gents." The mods, locating themselves within the "modernism" of the new white-collar working class, looted its wardrobe as well as that of smart young blacks around town. The skins, similarly, turned simultaneously to both black style and that of their "fathers" and "grandfathers." More tangentially, punks appropriated the "illicit iconography of pornography," the male-defined discourse *par excellence*. Of course, it would be ludicrous to expect anything different. The point I'm stressing is how highly differentiated according to gender style (mainstream or subcultural) it is—it's punk girls who wear the suspenders, after all.

If, following Eco's dictum,[8] we speak through our clothes, then we still do so in the accents of our sex. Although Hebdige does fleetingly mention sexual ambiguity in relation to style (and especially to the various personas of David Bowie), he doesn't consider it as a central feature right across the subcultural spectrum—for him subcultural style *is* Sta-prest trousers, Ben Sherman shirts, or pork pie hats. I'm not suggesting that all subcultures value transvestism—far from it—but that subcultural formations and the inflections of their various "movements" raise questions about sexual identity which Hebdige continuously avoids. Does subcultural elevation of style threaten the official masculinity of straight society, which regards such fussiness as sissy? Does the skinheads' pathological hatred of "queers" betray an uneasiness about their own fiercely defended male culture and style? Are subcultures providing relatively safe frameworks within which boys and young men can escape the pressures of heterosexuality?

For feminists the main political problem is to assess the significance of this for women. If subculture offers a (temporary?) escape from the demands of traditional sex roles, then the absence of predominantly girl subcultures—

their denial of access to such "solutions"—is evidence of their deeper oppression and of the monolithic heterosexual norms which surround them and find expression in the ideology of romantic love. Whereas men who "play around" with femininity are nowadays credited with some degree of power to choose, gender experimentation, sexual ambiguity, and homosexuality among girls are viewed differently. Nobody explains David Bowie's excursions into female personas (see the video accompanying his "gay" single "Boys Keep Swinging") in terms of his inability to attract women. But any indication of such ambiguity in girls is still a sure sign that they couldn't make it in a man's world. Failure replaces choice; escape from heterosexual norms is still synonymous with rejection. (Even the fashionable bisexuality among the women of the Andy Warhol set is less willingly dealt with in the popular press as hot gossip.) My point, then, is not to label subcultures as potentially gay, but to show that the possibility of escaping oppressive aspects of adolescent heterosexuality within a youth culture or a gang with a clearly signaled identity remains more or less unavailable to girls. For working-class girls especially, the road to "straight" sexuality still permits few deviations.

Finally I want to comment on the way in which Hebdige deals with the processes of reaction and incorporation accompanying the subcultural leap into the limelight of the popular press and media. He exposes with great clarity the inadequacies of the old "moral panic" argument and suggests that the Barthesian notion of trivialization/exoticization/domestication[9] offers a better account of how youth cultures are "handled." But again, because his model is not gendered, he fails to recognize that these are gender-specific processes. Ultimately the shock of subcultures can be partially defused because they can be seen as, among other things, boys having fun. That is, reference can be made *back* to the idea that boys should "sow their wild oats"—a privilege rarely accorded to young women. This does not mean that the "menace" altogether disappears, but at least there are no surprises as far as gender is concerned. Even male sexual ambiguity can be dealt with to some extent in this way. But if the Sex Pistols had been an all-female band spitting and swearing their way into the limelight, the response would have been more heated, the condemnation less tempered by indulgence. Such an event would have been greeted in the popular press as evidence of a major moral breakdown and not just as a fairly common, if "shocking," occurrence.

WALKING ON THE WILD SIDE— IT'S DIFFERENT FOR GIRLS

Rather than dealing with more mainstream sociological criticisms of *Subculture* (its London-centeredness, for example) or making my rather oversimplified comments on youth culture more specific (historically and in relation to such institutions as school, family, and workplace), I now want to look briefly at some of the meanings ensconced within some of the objects and practices constituting the subcultural artillery.

Rock music has been so much a part of postwar youth cultures that its presence has often just been noted by writers; the meanings signified by its various forms have not received the attention they deserve. Dick Hebdige does something to redress this, but again without developing a perspective sensitive to gender and sexual division. My points here are tentative and simple. Such a perspective would have to realize that rock does not signify alone, as pure sound. The music has to be placed within the discourses through which it is mediated to its audience and within which its meanings are articulated. Just as reviews construct the sense of a particular film in different ways, so an album or concert review lays down the terms and the myths by which we come to recognize the music. One myth energetically sustained by the press is the overwhelming maleness of the rock scene. Writers and editors seem unable to imagine that girls could make up a sizable section of their readership: although at a grassroots level virulent sexism has been undermined by punk, Rock Against Racism, and Rock Against Sexism, journalistic treatment remains much the same. As "the exception," women musicians are now treated with a modicum of respect in the *New Musical Express* or *Melody Maker*, but women are dealt with more comfortably in the gossip column on the back page, as the wives or girlfriends of the more flamboyant rock figures.

The range of drug scenes characterizing subcultures reveals a similar pattern. The inventory is familiar—alcohol for teds, rockers, and skins; speed and other pills for mods, punks, and rudies; hallucinogenics for hippies; cocaine and to a lesser extent heroin for other groups closer to the rock scene. So intransigently male are the mythologies and rituals attached to regular drug taking that few women feel the slightest interest in their literary, cinematic, or cultural expressions—from William Burroughs's catalogues of destructive self-abuse and Jack Kerouac's stream-of-consciousness drinking sprees to Paul Willis's lads and their alcoholic bravado. It would be foolish to imagine that women don't take drugs—isolated young housewives are among the heaviest drug users, and girls in their late teens are one of the largest groups among attempted suicides by drug overdose. Instead I'm suggesting that for a complex of reasons the imaginary solutions which drugs may offer boys do not have the same attraction for girls. One reason is probably commonsense wisdom deeply inscribed in most women's consciousnesses—that boys don't like girls who drink, take speed, and so on; that losing control spells sexual danger; and that drinking and taking drugs harm physical appearance. A more extreme example would be the way that the wasted male junkie can in popular mythology, in novels and films, retain a helpless sexual attraction which places women in the role of potential nurse or social worker. Raddled, prematurely aged women on junk rarely prompt a reciprocal willingness.

The meanings that have sedimented around other objects, like motorbikes or electronic musical equipment, have made them equally unavailable to women and girls. And although girls are more visible (both in numbers and popular representation) in punk than earlier subcultures, I have yet to come across the sight of a girl "gobbing." Underpinning this continual marginalization is the central question of street visibility. It has always been on the street that most subcultural activity takes place (save perhaps for the more middle-class oriented hippies): it both proclaims the publicization of the group and at the same time ensures its male dominance. For the street remains in some ways taboo for women (think of the unambiguous connotations of the term "streetwalker"): "morally dubious" women are the natural partners of street heroes in movies like Walter Hill's *The Warriors* and in rock songs from the Rolling Stones to Thin Lizzy or Bruce Springsteen. Few working-class girls can afford flats and so for them going out means either a date—an escort and a place to go—or else a disco, dance hall, or pub. Younger girls tend to stay indoors or to congregate in youth clubs; those with literally nowhere else to go but the street frequently become pregnant within a year and disappear back into the home to be absorbed by childcare and domestic labor.

There are of course problems in such large-scale generalizations. Conceptually it is important to separate public images and stereotypes from lived experience, the range of ideological representations we come across daily from empirical observation and sociological data. But in practice the two sides feed off each other. Everyday life becomes at least partly comprehensible within the very terms and images offered by the media, popular culture, education, and the "arts," just as material life creates the preconditions for ideological and cultural representation. This complexity need not paralyze our critical faculties altogether, however. It is clear from my recent research, for example, that girls are reluctant to drink precisely because of the sexual dangers of drunkenness. This doesn't mean that girls don't occasionally "get pissed"; my data suggest that they will drink with more confidence and less tension only when they have a reliable steady boyfriend willing to protect them from more predatory, less scrupulous males. It's difficult to deal so schematically with drug usage, and particularly involvement in hard drug subcultures. Particularly interesting, however, are the warnings to girls against hard drugs in the West German media (the addiction rate there is much higher than in Britain). These are couched entirely in terms of the damage heroin can do to your looks, your body, and your sexuality. They reinforce and spell out just how "it's different for girls": a girl's self-evaluation is assumed to depend on the degree to which her body and sexuality are publicly assessed as valuable.

THE POLITICS OF STYLE—
TWO STEPS BEYOND

I noted earlier that a "politics of youth" cannot simply be read off from Dick Hebdige's book. Although this hesitancy is preferable to the sloganizing with which much writing on youth culture ends, it still barely disguises the pessimism deeply rooted in all structuralisms, the idea that codes may change but the scaffolding remains the same, apparently immutable. Hebdige's conclusion seems to point to a convergence between gloomy existentialism and critical Marxism as the gap between the "mythologist" and the working class appears to expand. The sadness pervading the closing pages of *Subculture* hinges on this failure to communicate which, Hebdige claims, characterizes the relation between intellectuals and the class whose life they write about. But just because *Subculture* won't appear alongside the *Guinness Book of Records* on the bestseller lists or the shelves of Smith's is no real cause for such pessimism. Instead we should develop a clearer idea of the sectors of "youth" potentially responsive to Dick Hebdige's intervention (male ex-mods, hippies, skins, and punks at art colleges, apprentices on day-release courses in tech colleges, rock fans and young socialists . . . ?) and also a broader vision of our spheres of political competence.

Radical and feminist teachers could well, despite the usual resistance they encounter, popularize many of Hebdige's arguments (as well as some points of feminist critique). It's also conceivable that some young people may read the book unprompted by youth "professionals" (teachers or community workers). After all, the *New Musical Express*, which sells over 200,000 copies, recently reviewed it in glowing terms, and Hebdige's ideas have clearly influenced several of the paper's feature writers. So there's no doubt that, apart from being one of the most important books to date on the question of youth culture, it is also likely to reach, if often indirectly, an unprecedentedly wide audience. That's why its lack of attention to gender matters: it could have opened up questions of style *and* sexual politics. Also, had he addressed himself more directly to this potential audience, Hebdige might have made clearer the implications of the "escape" from the working class into the subcultural bohemia of an art college or rock band, or simply into the independence of a rented flat. As it is, *Subculture* should become a landmark within the politics of culture inside the notoriously traditional art colleges because of its emphasis on style and image as *collective* rather than *individual* expression and its investigation of the *social* meaning of style. The problem is just that Hebdige implies you have to choose either style *or* politics and that the two cannot really be reconciled.

My own guess is that to understand these questions about youth culture and politics more fully, it will be necessary to supplement the established conceptual triad of class, sex, and race with three more concepts—*populism*, *leisure*, and *pleasure*. It's not possible to develop a full-blown theoretical justification for that project here, however. And as I opened this article by condemning the self-effacement of male writers, it would perhaps be appropriate to end on a personal note about the ambivalence of my own responses to subcultures (I too lace my texts with rock lyrics) and the possible links between youth subcultures and feminist culture.

For as long as I can remember, collective expressions of disaffiliation from authority and the hegemony of the dominant classes (by either sex) have sent shivers of excitement down my spine. Despite their often exaggerated romanticism and their bankrupt (frequently sexist) politics, the "spectacle" of these symbolic gestures has got a hold on my consciousness which I cannot completely exorcise. Sitting on a train in West Germany, surrounded by carefully coiffured businessmen and well-manicured businesswomen, the sight of two Felliniesque punks (male) in the next compartment cannot fail to make me smile, just as it cannot fail to make some convoluted political statement.

In a similar way, punk is central to an understanding of the resurgence of "youth politics" in Britain over recent years. It's not a *deus ex machina* which will banish the unpopularity of left politics but, as a set of loosely linked gestures and forms, it has proved a mobilizing and energizing force which has helped to consolidate developments like Rock Against Racism. There have also been overlaps between the nuances of punk style and feminist style which are more than just coincidental. Although the stiletto heels, miniskirts, and suspenders will, despite their debunking connotations, remain unpalatable to most feminists (with the exception of Nina Hagen), both punk girls and feminists want to overturn accepted ideas about what constitutes femininity. And they often end up using similar stylish devices to upset notions of "public propriety."

What this indicates is a mysterious symbiosis between aspects of subcultural life and style in postwar Britain and aspects of a "new" left and even feminist culture. However precious or trivial the question of style may seem in contrast to concrete forms of oppression and exploitation (unemployment, for example, or the strengthening of the state apparatus), it cannot be hived off into the realm of personal hedonism. The sort of style Dick Hebdige describes is central to the contradictory nature of working-class male culture, and it plays a visible role in the resistance by youth in Britian today. The style of West Indian boys *and* girls is as much an assault on authority as outright confrontation. In our daily lives, feminists wage a similar semiotic warfare. Knitting in pubs, breastfeeding in Harrods, the refusal to respond to expressions of street sexism, the way we wear our clothes—all the signs and meanings embodied in the way we handle our public visibility play a part in the culture which, like the various youth cultures, bears the imprint of our collective, historical creativity. They are living evidence that although inscribed within structures, we are not wholly prescribed by them. For many of us too, escaping from the family and its pressures to act like a real girl remains the first political experience. For us the objective is to make this flight possible for all girls, and on a long-term basis.

I'm not arguing that if girls were doing the same as some boys (and subcultures are always minorities) all would be well. The "freedom" to consume alcohol and chemicals, to sniff glue and hang about the street staking out only symbolic territories is scarcely less oppressive than the pressures keeping girls in the home. Yet the classic subculture does provide its members with a sense of oppositional sociality, an unambiguous pleasure in style, a disruptive public identity, and a set of collective fantasies. As a prefigurative form and set of social relations, I can't help but think it could have a positive meaning for girls who are pushed from early adolescence into achieving their feminine status through acquiring a "steady." The working-class girl is encouraged to dress with stylish conventionality (see the fashion pages of *Jackie*); she is taught to consider boyfriends more important than girlfriends and to abandon the youth club or disco for the honor of spending her evenings watching television in her boyfriend's house, so saving money for an engagement ring. Most significantly, she is forced to relinquish youth for the premature middle age induced by child-birth and housework. It's not so much that girls do too much too young: rather, they have the opportunity of doing too little too late. To the extent that all-girl subcultures, where the commitment to the gang comes first, might forestall these processes and provide their members with a collective confidence which could transcend the need for "boys," they could well signal an important progression in the politics of youth culture.

NOTES

[1] Paul Willis, *Learning to Labour* (London: Saxon House, 1977); Dick Hebdige, *Subculture: The Meaning of Style* (London: Methuen, 1979).
[2] Willis, *Labour*.
[3] Sheila Rowbotham, *Women's Consciousness, Man's World* (Harmondsworth: Penguin, 1973), p. 19.
[4] "Born to Run," © Bruce Springsteen 1975.
[5] Stuart Hall and Tony Jefferson (eds.), *Resistance through Rituals* (London: Hutchinson, 1976).
[6] For a different interpretation, see Ros Coward's angry attack in " 'Culture' and the Social Formation," *Screen 18*, No. 1 (Spring 1977).
[7] From an interview with the now deceased Pete Meaden in *New Musical Express 17* (November 1979).
[8] See Umberto Eco, "Social Life as a Sign System," in D. Robey, ed., *Structuralism* (London: Jonathan Cape, 1973).
[9] From Roland Barthes, *Mythologies*, quoted in Hebdige, *Subculture*, pp. 97–99.

DEFENDING SKI-JUMPERS

A Critique of Theories
of Youth Subcultures*

1 9 8 1

○ ▲ ○ ▲ ○ ▲ ○

THE SEARCH FOR RESISTANCE

Since its publication, the "new subcultural theory" contained in the Centre for Contemporary Cultural Studies' collection *Resistance Through Rituals*[1] has become the new orthodoxy on youth; the collection and its spinoffs are firmly established on course reading lists at a time when youth has become a major focal concern of the state and parties across the political spectrum. To a large extent, the acceptance of the literature and its acclaim are justified: the authors realistically outlined the lived experience of postwar working-class youth subcultures in a sympathetic manner which was hitherto unknown. However, the approach has not been without its critics.

The major emphasis of the Centre for Contemporary Cultural Studies has been to explain the emergence of particular youth styles in terms of their capacity for problem solving. Phil Cohen's "Sub-cultural Conflict and the Working Class Community"[2] set the pace, and most of the Centre's analyses are based on an amplification of the ideas, and consequently the problems, in Cohen's paper.

---

* Ski-jumpers are cheap, imported, acrylic sweaters depicting a row of three skiers as a band across the chest. The origin of the style or the cult is impossible to trace, yet they are worn by a large majority of working-class youth, regardless of race or gender.

Cohen's complex analysis takes into account the full interplay of economic, ideological, and "cultural" factors which give rise to subcultures. Subcultures are seen as

> a common solution between two contradictory needs: the need to create and express autonomy and difference from parents . . . and the need to maintain parental identifications.[3]

Cohen explains the development of subcultures on the basis of the redevelopment and reconstruction of the East End of London, which resulted in the fragmentation and disruption of the working-class family, economy, and community-based culture. Cohen suggests that the subcultures among working-class youth emerged as an attempt to resolve these experiences. Subcultures are seen as collective solutions to collectively experienced problems. Mods are seen to correspond to, and subsequently construct a parody of, the upwardly mobile solution, while skinheads are read as an attempt to recover magically the chauvinisms of the "traditional" working-class community.[4]

However, Cohen (and adherents) are imprecise on the necessary extent of the connection between actual structural location and the problem-solving option. Is it possible, say, to have an upwardly mobile skinhead? Also, we are given little explanation as to how and why the class experiences of youth crystallize into a distinct subculture. The possible constituency of a new style is outlined, but where do the styles come from? Who designed the first fluorescent pink or leopardskin drape suit, for example, and how do we analytically leap from the desire for a solution to the adoption of a particular style? This is a significant problem when it seems that *both* skins and teds seek to revive and defend the "traditional" working-class community, but through different styles. Furthermore, since any discussion of life chances is regarded as a "Weberian deviation," we are given no clues as to how we can explain the different degrees of commitment to a subculture other than through some neopositivist reference to the extent of the problems which stimulate the emergence of subcultures. The subcultures as discussed in *Resistance Through Rituals* are essentialist and non-contradictory. As Chris Waters has argued,[5] the subcultures are treated as static and rigid anthropological entities when in fact such reified and pure subcultures exist only at the Centre's level of abstraction which seeks to explain subcultures in terms of their genesis. Hence there is an uncomfortable absence in the literature of any discussion as to how and with what consequences the pure subcultures are sustained, transformed, appropriated, disfigured, or destroyed. It is extremely difficult to consider the individual life trajectories of youth within the model laid down by Cohen. If each subculture is a specific problem-solving option, how are we to understand how individuals move in and out of different subcultures? Cohen, for example, classifies Crombies and Parkas as distinct subcultures, but surely the only "problem" which distinguished them from skins and mods respectively was the need to keep warm.

The fundamental problem with Cohenite subcultural analysis is that it takes the card-carrying members of spectacular subcultures as its starting point and then teleologically works backward to uncover the class situation and detect the specific set of contradictions which produced corresponding styles. This could lead to the dangerous assumption that all those in a specific class location are members of the corresponding subculture and that all members of a subculture are in the same class location. A basic problem is that the elements of youth culture (music, dancing, clothes, etc.) which are discussed are not enjoyed *only* by the fully paid-up members of subcultures. If we reverse the methodological procedure adopted by the Centre and start with an analysis beginning with the social relations based around class, gender, and race (and age), rather than their stylistic products, we have to examine the whole range of options, modes of negotiation, or "magical resolution" (and the limitations of access and opportunity that exist) that are open to, and used by, working-class youth. Such an approach would require a break from the Centre's paradigm of examining the "authentic" subcultures in a synthetic moment of frozen historical time which results in an essentialist and noncontradictory picture. Any empirical analysis would reveal that subcultures are diffuse, diluted, and mongrelized in form. For example, certain skins may assert values of "smartness" which are considered by the authors to be restricted to the mods. The anthropological analysis of unique subcultures means that descriptions of the processes by which they are sustained, transformed, and interwoven are absent. Similarly, the elitist nature of the analysis (that is, the focus on "originals") means that we are given no sense of how and why the styles became popular (and how and why they eventually cease to be in vogue) other than through a simplistic discussion of the corruption and incorporation of the original style.

By focusing on subcultures at their innovatory moment, the authors are able to make elaborate and generalized readings of the symbols from a few scant observations of styles and artifacts. Youth subcultures are seen not simply as "imaginary solutions" but also as symbolic resistance, counterhegemonic struggle, a defense of cultural space on a "relatively autonomous" ideological level. For example, Hebdige considers the mods to have won a magical "victory":

> The style they created therefore, constituted a parody of the consumer society in which they were situated. The mod delivered his blows by inverting and distorting the images (of neatness, of short hair) so cherished by his employers and parents which while being overtly close to the straight world was nonetheless incomprehensible to it.[6]

Similarly, the teds' "reworking" of Edwardian dress is seen as a reassertion of traditional working-class values in the face of affluence, and the model-worker image of the skins is interpreted as part of a symbolic return to the "traditional" working-class community.

The paradigm developed in *Resistance Through Rituals* has more recently been taken to extremes in *Subculture: The Meaning of Style*, in which Dick Hebdige presents a detailed analysis of postwar subcultures.[7] Hebdige is the theorist of style and subculture *par excellence*: wheeling in the entire left-of-field gurus of art, literature, linguistics, and semiotics "to tease out the meanings embedded in the various post-war youth styles." Springing from the art-school tradition himself, Hebdige prioritizes the creativity of subcultures, their "art," "aesthetics," the "signs of forbidden identity" contained in the styles. This lies in the *bricolage* of subcultures, in their ability to create meaning and transform "everyday objects" as if they were a walking Andy Warhol exhibition. Since Hebdige's problem is to witness and understand the transformative moment in which new meanings are created (in the same way that the *Resistance . . .* project was set up to understand the emergence of deviant values), the resultant "semiotic guerilla warfare" is restricted to a flashpoint of rebellion. This is necessary by definition in Hebdige, since it seems that the symbolic potency of a style rests entirely upon the innovatory and unique nature of a subculture's "appearance." Hence, for all the discussions of "the subversive implications of style . . . the idea of style as a form of refusal . . . a gesture of defiance or contempt," when it all boils down, the power of subcultures is a temporary "power to disfigure." The politics of youth is not only restricted to a consideration of the symbolic power of style, but this is also confined to the moment of innovation since, as we shall see, stylistic configurations soon lose their shock potential in Hebdige's analysis.

But what is the symbolic power of style in Hebdige's analysis? Quite simply it is a case of "shocking the straights": the power of subcultures is their capacity to symbolize Otherness among an undifferentiated, untheorized, and contemptible "general public." Subcultures "warn the straight world in advance of a similar presence—the presence of differences—and draw upon themselves vague suspicions, uneasy laughter, white and dumb rages."

This dichotomy between subcultures and an undifferentiated "general public" lies at the heart of subcultural theory. The readings of subcultural style are based on a necessary consideration of subcultures at a level of abstraction which fails to consider subcultural flux and the dynamic nature of styles; second, and as a result, the theory rests upon the consideration of the rest of society as being straight, incorporated in a consensus, and willing to scream undividedly loud in any moral panic. Finally, the analysis of subculture is posited upon the elevation of the vague concept of style to the status of an objective category. In *Subculture* the degree of blackness of a subculture provides the yardstick, but generally, the act of basic consideration (like the old song) is that "you either have or you haven't got style."

Such a dichotomy between the public, or straights, and the subcultures (even if it is not always explicit) is extremely surprising, particularly in light of the Centre's appropriation of Gramsci. However, I wish to argue that in Hebdige's case, the straight/subculture divide is premised upon a misreading of the concept of "common sense." Even though he quite categorically argues that ideology is not the same as false consciousness, both in the use of the term "common sense" and the treatment of the working-class "straight" culture, Hebdige constantly counterposes the stylists as possessing an (albeit inarticulate) creative and radical consciousness while "the public" are drowning in "mythologies" and suffocated by the *Daily Mirror*. Despite the inclusion of the theoretical equivalents of 12-inch import disco mixes to supplement the analysis, Hebdige fails to comprehend the nature of working-class culture (which is rooted in a highly contradictory "common sense") other than as a form of imposed false consciousness. Hence we find references such as this: "representations . . . are shrouded in a 'common sense' which simultaneously validates and mystifies them." Consequently references to "straight" working-class culture conflate "normalcy" and common sense; the working class are presumably locked in a subordinate acceptance of capitalist social relations as natural and possess a bland culture of normalcy and naturalness. For Hebdige this is reflected in the very absence of style in their attire; the clothes of these undifferentiated normals "masquerade as nature." Furthermore:

> Each ensemble has its place in an internal system of difference—the conventional modes of sartorial discourse—which fit a corresponding set of socially prescribed roles and options . . . Ultimately, if nothing else they are expressive of normalcy as opposed to deviance (i.e. they are distinguished by their relative invisibility, their appropriateness, their "naturalness").

This counterposition of normal and subcultural styles is clearly rooted in the failure to examine the ways in which styles are dynamic and diffuse. However, holding this dichotomy is a necessary part of Hebdige's analysis if he is to suggest that subcultures are to signify the Other and subvert naturalness through *bricolage*. The uncreative, bland, and incorporated nature of working-class commonsense culture is consequently necessarily (and wrongly) overstated.

Commonsense culture is not simply a form a mystification or ideological snow which falls from above. The crucial concept is that of "good sense" which requires closer attention—particularly if the current trend toward derogatory uses of common sense (or its conflation with false consciousness) is to be halted.

THE PUNKY REGGAE PARTY

The most intriguing part of Hebdige's *Subculture* lies in his break from an exclusive emphasis on class to assert the centrality of race in youth subcultures. After a convincing and sympathetic outline of black cultural forms, Hebdige suggests that youth subcultures provide a "phantom history of race relations since the war." I shall return to this, but I wish to begin by examining punk, since it is central in the thesis.

Hebdige's analysis of punk is unique since it breaks from the theoretical tradition laid down by Phil Cohen. Rather than being seen as an attempt to retrieve elements of the parent culture in light of the restructuring of the working-class community, "the punks seem to be parodying the alienation and emptiness which have caused sociologists so much concern." This is achieved by "celebrating in mock heroic terms the death of the community and the collapse of traditional forms of meaning."

Thus, the cartoon characteristics of punk—the bondage trousers, ripped and zipped shirts, the safety pins, the leathers, the S&M clothing so vividly described by Hebdige—are seen as a parody of the poverty and the crisis which had been represented in the media: "punk reproduced the entire sartorial history of post-war working-class youth cultures in its 'cut up' form, combining elements which had originally belonged to completely different epochs."

This reading of the "anarchy in the U.K." aspect of punk is fairly accurate and well documented, but I would like to raise some objections. First, Hebdige concerns himself only with the innovative punks, the original "authentic" and "genuine" punks concentrated in the London area. This is characteristic of most of the Centre's subcultural theory—it explains why certain youths develop a particular style say, in the East End, but youth subcultures elsewhere are usually dismissed as part of the incorporation and containment of the subversive implications of that style. We are never given reasons why youths "in the sticks" are inclined to adopt a particular style. Hebdige's analysis of punk begins with a heat wave in Oxford Street and ends in a Kings Road boutique.

This metropolitan centeredness contradicts Hebdige's emphasis on working-class creativity, since most of the punk creations that are discussed were developed among the art-school avant-garde, rather than emanating "from the dance halls and housing estates." Hebdige's vision of punk is extremely elitist; despite punk's proletarian stance (constantly emphasized), his concern is typically for the "art" of the innovators:

This is not to say of course that all punks were equally aware of the disjunction between experience and signification upon which the whole style was ultimately based. The style no doubt made sense for the first wave of self-conscious innovators at a level which remained inaccessible to those who became punks after the subculture had surfaced and been publicized. Punk is not unique in this: the distinction between originals and hangers-on is always a significant one in subculture.

For whom is this distinction significant? Certainly most punks would like to have been one of the few regulars at the Roxy or the 100 Club in the early days, but Hebdige's distinction between "the faces" (the term for the elite mods) and what he terms "the unimaginative majority" in each subculture is highly problematic. I cannot accept style as an objective category to be measured, and the original/hangers-on distinction is particularly problematic when there is no discussion of the restrictions on access and opportunity to become an "authentic" subcultural member. Such questions are of great relevance in considering the relationship of girls to subcultures and the possible effects the recession may have on youth styles.

But what of the readings or decoding of these authentic subcultures? Hebdige pathetically admits that "it is highly unlikely that the members of any of the subcultures described in this book would recognize themselves reflected here."

I would suggest that this is largely due to the failure to examine how subcultures make sense to the members themselves—a project which Hebdige sets up but never achieves. Indeed this would require Hebdige to enter a different terrain. By defining subcultures in terms of their style and symbolic power, by extension, Hebdige and company elevate themselves to the privileged position of expert semioticians, as those able to read the signs, to "decipher the graffiti, to tease out the meanings." This eliminates any question of intent, any consideration that the members of a subculture are knowing subjects. Rather than taking the meaning which style has for youths as the starting point, the self-images of youth are explicitly denied, for example:

> If we were to go further still and describe punk music as the "sound of the Westway" or the pogo as the "high-rise leap" or to talk of bondage as reflecting the narrow options of working-class youth, we would be treading on less certain ground. Such meanings are both *too literal* and too conjectural. They are *extrapolations from the subculture's own prodigious rhetoric* and *rhetoric is not self-explanatory: it may say what it means but it does not necessarily "mean" what it "says"*: In other words, it is opaque: its categories are part of its publicity. (my italics)

Thus subcultures are allowed to speak only through their clothes. Earlier and more crudely, Phil Cohen drew on linguistics to make a similar point:

> Delinquency can be seen as a form of communication about a situation of contradiction in which the delinquent is trapped, but whose complexity is excom-

municated from his perceptions by virtue of the restricted linguistic code which
working class culture makes available to him.[8]

To return to punk, although Hebdige correctly chastises Taylor and Wall[9]
and produces an interesting analysis of the Bowie-ites, he makes the fatal
faux pas in (expertly) judging punk as a reaction to glam rock, which "tended
to alienate the majority of working-class youth." For Hebdige, glam consisted of either contemptible teenybop or the music and styles of Bowie,
Lou Reed, and Roxy Music, "whose extreme foppishness, incipient elitism,
and morbid pretensions to art and intellect effectively precluded the growth
of a larger mass audience."

This is simply wrong; glam rock *did* achieve a popular mass audience.
Furthermore, punk was not simply proletarian in style; it drew heavily on
the glam rock forms—particularly its use of makeup. Several punk bands
produced cover versions of glam hits, Bowie remained popular with the
punks, and Marc Bolan and Lou Reed competed for the title "Godfather
of Punk." Rather than being "an attempt to expose glam rock's implicit
contradictions . . . an addendum designed to puncture glam rock's extrav-
agantly ornate style," punk emerged via "pub rock" as a response to the
excesses of "technobores," "pomp rock," and the "progressive scene," a
gesture against the Pink Floyd, Led Zeppelin, Yes, Genesis, and Emerson,
Lake and Palmers of the world and not a reaction to Alvin Stardust, Mud,
Roxy Music, and company.

Let us now turn to the question of race. Hebdige argues that youth
subcultural styles represent a coded recording of race relations, since each
subculture can be interpreted as a symbolic adoption or rejection of the
presence of black culture. Hence the hipsters, beats, mods, early skins, and
punks can be seen as emulations of black style, while the later skins, glam
rock, and the ted revival are seen as a retraction into a purely white culture,
either out of "chauvinism" or in response to an increasingly black consciousness reflected in the politicization of reggae music.

Hebdige claims that the reader can either take or leave the "phantom
history" thesis. I would accept that stylistic links are generally evident (white
rock and pop music in all its forms has constantly drawn on black musical
forms), but as the thesis stands it has major problems. I would have preferred
an analysis of the impact of black culture on white working-class youth
culture as a whole rather than the use of black style connections with a few
elite members of a white subculture as evidence; in addition, there is no
discussion of racism among the subcultures.

Hebdige's site of "phantom history," that of subcultural styles, thus has
several notable absences; blackness is expressed through early soul music
and reggae while other elements of youth culture—particularly the long
hippie period—are ignored. More significantly, his approach forbids any

analysis of the connection between black culture and the straights. To read Hebdige, soul music ended after the mods (though, for example, Tamla Motown has dominated turntables for over twenty years), and funk and disco music are something to be sneered at. Consequently, he fails to fulfill the potential of his analysis since he examines only selected areas of articulation as opposed to the mass appropriations of black music. Hence Hebdige (wrongly) suggests that black and white links were absent during the early seventies and that "left to his own devices, pop tended to atrophy into *vacuous disco-bounce and sugary ballads*" (my emphasis).

The problem is that Hebdige tends to equate black culture with a Jamaican culture (Asians are noted by their absence)[10] which is unproblematically imported. Although he presents an excellent and sympathetic account of Rastafarianism, we are given no account as to how it might have been transformed as it became a youth subculture. Furthermore, he tends to equate reggae with the "armagidion" sound of the roots rockers; there is no mention of the lighter "lover's rock" which also fosters black solidarity and is particularly popular among black girls. Forms of non-Rasta black culture equally require examination.

Generally, then, Hebdige's accounts of the black/white nexus are too tenuous and brittle and, of course, restricted to the level of style: "For example, one of the characteristic punk hair-styles consisting of a petrified mane held in a state of vertical tension by means of vaseline, lacquer or soap, approximated to the black 'natty' or dreadlock styles." Of course, black and white musical fusions cannot be denied, but it should be noted that black culture is *transformed* when it is adopted by whites—the reggae of white bands like the Clash or the Police is not the same as that of, say, Black Uhuru. Since punk there have been conscious attempts to adopt black styles, as evident in the explicitly antiracist music of "two-tone" bands such as the Specials, and in the pop success of UB40, who unleashed the possibility of reggae and dub for white audiences.

But soul, disco, funk, Latin, and salsa are also areas where rock and pop have appropriated black styles, and it would be a mistake to see punky reggae as the only viable form of contemporary youth culture.

SUBCULTURES AND WORKING-CLASS CULTURE

Any future analysis of youth must transcend an exclusive focus on style. The Centre's subculturalists are correct to break away from a crude conception of class as an abstract relationship to the forces of production. However, subcultures are conceived as a leisure-based career, and the "culture" within "youth subculture" is defined in terms of the possession of particular artifacts and styles rather than as a whole "way of life" structured by the social relations based on class, gender, race, and age. Consequently we are given little sense of what subcultures actually *do*, and we do not know whether their commitment is fulltime or just, say, a weekend phenomenon. We are given no sense of the age range, income (or source of income), and occupations of the members of a subculture, no explanation as to why some working-class youths do not join. Individual subcultural stylists are, ironically, reduced to the status of dumb, anonymous mannequins, incapable of producing their own meanings and awaiting the arrival of the code breaker.

Even if we accept that it is possible to read youth styles as a form of resistance, the Centre's claims that subcultures "operate exclusively in the leisure sphere" mean that the institutional sites of hegemony (those of school, work, and home) are ignored. Surely these are the sites in which any resistance is located, and they need to be considered in order to examine the relationship between working-class youth and working-class culture in general. Paul Willis's *Learning to Labour* presents such an analysis, examining boys' resistance at school to explain the reproduction of a shopfloor culture of masculinity.[11] Unfortunately, Willis's categories of the "lads" and the "earoles" reproduce the dichotomy between deviant and "normal" working-class youth which underlies the rest of the literature. The "lads" are the focus of attention in the study, while the modes of negotiation (probably based on instrumentalism) adopted by the "earoles" are ignored since they are presumed to be unproblematically incorporated into state schooling.

I would argue generally that the subcultural literature's focus on the stylistic deviance of a few contains (albeit implicitly) a similar treatment of the rest of the working class as unproblematically incorporated. This is evident, for example, in the distaste felt for youth deemed as outside subcultural activity—even though most "straight" working-class youths enjoy the same music, styles, and activities as the subcultures—and in the disdain for such cults as glam, disco, and the ted revival, which lack "authenticity." Indeed, there seems to be an underlying contempt for "mass culture" (which stimulates the interest in those who deviate from it) which stems from the work of the Marxism of the Frankfurt School and, within the English tradition, to the fear of mass culture expressed in *The Uses of Literacy*.[12]

Hebdige has more recently argued that a form of cultural conservatism tends to pervade the working class as a whole—as evident in the rituals of the Labour movement.[13] I would argue that we need to examine the forms of "popular memory" which pervade society as a whole. The desire to return to a mythical past as a "magical solution" is not restricted to the skinhead subculture. The "swing" and "Gatsby" revivals, for example, popular among many working-class youths in the early seventies, involved a magical return which has been hitherto ignored by academic analysts. More importantly, the hippie movement (which has been dismissed as simply contributing toward a new post–Protestant ethic hegemony) constructed its own influential forms of nostalgia. This conflated a return to a whole-food, preindustrial age (see the work of bands like Jethro Tull, Family, Stackridge, and folk rockers such as Steeleye Span and Fairport Convention) and a return to a mythical Garden of Eden in a long Edwardian summer, an assemblage of Victorian antiquaria, *Sergeant Pepper*, Lord Kitchener posters, and other elements of a middle-class, quintessential colonial Englishness. Since the hippies are absent in Hebdige's "phantom history," it would be interesting and rewarding to examine how this nostalgia combined with Eastern mysticism to produce a reaction to a black presence which would fit neatly into his theory.

THE "INCORPORATION" OF YOUTH CULTURES

The death knell of a style in youth culture is its appropriation by younger age groups, "bubble gum" groups, or its mass production by chain stores. THIS POPULARISATION MEANS THAT THE STYLE HAS BEEN ROBBED OF ITS MESSAGE. *Another complication is separating the part-time and full-time adherents, separating the* RIGHTEOUS *from the* POSEURS. *In a subculture with* LITERARY *and* ARTISTIC *affiliations, these are core members at the centre of the culture, often* CREATIVE ARTISTS, *but followers and peripheral members who may adopt the lifestyle or appearance and who may or may not be perceived as "real members."*[14] *(my emphasis)*

Each subculture moves through a cycle of resistance and defusion . . . subcultural deviance is simultaneously rendered "explicable" and meaningless in the classroom, courts and the media at the same time as the "secret" objects of subcultural style are put on display in every high street, record shop and chain store boutique. STRIPPED OF ITS UNWHOLESOME CONNOTATIONS, THE STYLE BECOMES FIT FOR PUBLIC CONSUMPTION.[15] *(my emphasis)*

Subcultural theory concerns itself with the original authentic members of a subculture and *their* creativity rather than how the styles dissipate and become used among working-class youth more generally. The two quotes above reveal the consequent logic of the approach: the conflation of the escalation and castration of these "secret" coded styles. Hence, we are to presume that the subcultures are brought back into line, rendered meaningless, "incorporated" within the consensus, as their creativity is adopted by the ranks of the "artless" working class.

It is true that subcultures do lose their potency, but the discussions of the "incorporation" of styles are inadequate for various reasons. First, the "creativity" of the initial members of a subculture is overstated and the "relative autonomy" of youth from the market is inadequately theorized. Within these accounts, the "moment" of creative assemblage is *before* the styles become available. However, such innovations usually have a firm stake in the commodity market themselves. For example, the partnership of Malcolm McLaren and Vivienne Westwood was central in the manufacturing and selling of both punk ("cash from chaos") and the "warrior chic" of the eighties. If we are to speak of the creativity of working-class youth in their appropriations from the market, the journey from stylistic assemblage to mass selling must be reversed. In light of Hebdige's admission that, "in the case of the punks, the media's sighting of punk style virtually coincided with the invention of punk deviance,"[16] I can see little point in any analysis which worships the innovators yet condemns those youth who appropriate that style when it becomes a marketed product and splashed across the *Sun*'s center page. Surely, if we are to focus on the symbolic refusal contained in items of clothing such as bondage trousers, we ought to focus on the moment when the style becomes available—either as a commodity or as an idea to be copied (for example by attaching zips and straps to a pair of old school trousers); any future analysis of youth should take the breakthrough of a style as its starting point. It is true that most youths do not enter into the subcultures in the elite form described in the literature, but large numbers do draw on particular elements of subcultural style and create their own meanings and uses of them. The concept of *bricolage* does not apply simply to an exclusive few—most working-class youths (and adults) combine elements of clothing to create new meanings. If anything, what makes subcultures outstanding is *not* their obvious *bricolage* (as Hebdige argues), but the lack of any fashion confusion as a style becomes a "uniform." An examination of male working-class youth quietly reveals that "normal" dressing means using elements drawn from government surplus stores, sportswear (such as training shoes, track suits, rugby shirts, "Fred Perry" tops, hunting jackets, rally jackets, flying suits, etc.), subcultural clothing appropriated from different historical eras via the secondhand clothing markets, and, finally, mass market fashion, which itself contains forms of recontextualized meaning, be it ski jumpers or work overalls. Girls are less free to experiment, but a closer examination is required here, since women's fashion cannot be simply conflated with an unchanging cult of femininity. In particular, it may be possible for our semioticians to make detailed readings of the *bricolage* which passes off as "accessories" on the fashion pages.

If we are to consider the "symbolic refusals" contained in items of clothing, we should not be content to read the styles of subcultural mannequins during their leisure time while dismissing other styles as if they were merely bland. Instead we should focus on the diluted "semiotic guerilla warfare" in certain sites: in particular, those of school, home, and the workplace. This is evident for example in the stylistic disruptions of school uniform, the nonregulation jumper; earrings (on boys and girls); hair that is too long or too short; the trousers that are too wide, too straight, or that should be a skirt; the shirt or blouse of an unacceptable color or with a collar that is too short or long; the wearing of sneakers in class, and so forth. Similarly, a youth does not have to adopt the complete uniform of a subculture to be sent home from work or a training course, to annoy parents, to be labeled "unmasculine" or "unfeminine," to be refused service in a bar or café, to be moved on by the police, and so forth. Clearly, the diffusion of styles cannot be classed as a simple defusing of the signifying practice of an elite few.

BEYOND A PARODY OF THE CRISIS

I would like to conclude by examining the significance of what has been taken to be "youth culture" in the period of crisis. Since working-class youth are not denied the sources of income which financed the spectacular subcultures of the sixties and seventies, a deemphasis on style could be expected—the relative cheapness of the attire could explain the current popularity of skins. However, the removal of the restrictions imposed by wage labor mean that youths are also more free to experiment with dyed mohican haircuts or long, one-sided fringes. On the whole, the absolute distinction between subcultures and "straights" is increasingly difficult to maintain: the current diversity of styles makes a mockery of subcultural analysis as it stands.

Punk and two-tone had two very important consequences. First, in disinterring the entire wardrobe of postwar styles, they both decoded these styles and greatly expanded the field of stylistic options for an increasingly self-reflexive and stylistically mobile youth culture. After punk, virtually any combination of styles became possible. To name but a few examples: the revival of skins, mods, and teds; rude boys; suedeheads; a psychedelic revival; rockers—both the traditional type and the younger, denim-clad heavy metalists; Rastafarians; soulheads (short-haired blacks); disco; Antpeople; Northern soul; jazz-funkateers; Bowie freaks; punk (subdivided into Oi, "hardcore," or "real" punk, plus the avant-garde wing); futurists; new romantics; glam revivalists; beats, zoots, and so on.

Second, the "new wave" eroded the distinction between "teenyboppers" and youth, which was largely based on the distinction between progressive LPs and pop singles of the early seventies. Punk made singles and singles artists acceptable. Much to the industry's delight, the current stars—Madness, Adam and the Ants, and the new romantic bands—"cross over" conventional market categories. The possible effects of this, such as the potential nurturing of some degree of solidarity among youths of different backgrounds, have yet to be considered or realized; but this may be important if class-based politics becomes increasingly meaningless to the unemployed.

Another interesting development has been the increasing amount of semiotic readings conducted by cult leaders themselves. For example, the unification of black and white colors in the design of the "two-tone" movement was consciously intended to be part of the antiracist struggle. More recently, Adam Ant's theatrical images of pirate/Indian/highwayman have been consciously used to symbolize a defense of the oppressed, while Malcolm McLaren's piracy/"go for gold" image for Bow Wow Wow has been explicitly theorized as an attempt to irritate monetarist belt tighteners.[17] Even the latest trend in zoot suits has been understood as being one in the eye for austerity.[18]

Such analyses reveal that subcultural theory has had an impact—although the stylist's own readings seem more down to earth than, say, Hebdige's flights of fantasy. I would argue that the politics of youth cultural styles is not contained within the semiotic value of particular artifacts. Rather, the very existence of a youth culture, the quest for "good times" and "good clothes," contains an element of resistance as part of a struggle over the quality of life. State monetarism involves an attempt to lower working-class expectations, to "tighten our belts"; youth culture represents an anchor for refusal, for resistance to a return to austerity. Young people now expect a certain standard of living based on good clothes, records, nights out, or whatever. Such relatively high expectations explain the growing feelings of frustration and anger among youth. Note, for example, that articles looted during the 1980 and 1981 British inner-city riots tended to be those associated with commercial youth culture—clothes, records, radios, tape decks, and the like.

The decadence and the glamor of the new romantics may be important in this—particularly as the style has become widely accepted by "straights" since its diffusion from the elite London clubs. Furthermore (following the popularity of the Human League), girls have become increasingly dominant within the cult and may become more selective in their choice of partner, rejecting "drab" patriarchs—although, of course, a great deal of empirical work is required to verify this.

The current crisis in capitalist social relations also demands an analysis of the culture of unemployed youth—the means by which unemployment is negotiated, survived, and transformed into leisure and how this relates to conventional "youth culture." Forms of negotiation such as the home taping of records and radio programs, jobs in the "black economy," second-hand clothes, daytime TV, lie-ins, and reduction in cinema charges for the unemployed require closer examination. Obviously "doing nothing" reaches a new importance.

I would like to end by focusing on a local example in Birmingham. The recent introduction of a two-pence flat bus fare for those under 16 years of age (and anyone who dares to pass themselves off as under 16—and many do) has resulted in a moral panic concerning the way in which youths kill time by riding around on buses—particularly the circular routes. Usually clad in the semiotically innocent ski-jumper, youths have appropriated the upper decks as an area of cultural and physical space. Alternatively, the cheap fare provides the opportunity to "do nothing" in the town center:

> When is the West Midlands County Council going to appreciate the misery it is causing shoppers and shopkeepers. . . . They have nothing better to do than cause havoc among shoppers and shopkeepers. We are having to pay pounds more to finance the 2p policy that helps them play their game. (Mailbox letter in *Birmingham Evening Mail*, November 4, 1981)

The autumn letters to the editor of the *Birmingham Mail* were bursting with a moral panic over the buses, orchestrated in relation to a campaign against rate increases in the area. However, the main focus has been on youths. Assorted letters complained about noise, truancy from school, youths occupying seats, unemployed youths wasting time and not looking for jobs, overcrowding in the town center—with the possibility of theft or "trouble"—youths smoking, drinking, or sniffing glue on buses, and so forth, as Birmingham youths have created new meaning from the conventional activities of shopping and public transport.

What is required is an analysis of the activities of all youths to locate continuities and discontinuities in culture and social relations and to discover the meaning these activities have for the youths themselves. This paper has shown that youth culture is far from being the overworked topic it initially seems to be.

NOTES

[1] Stuart Hall and Tony Jefferson (eds.), *Resistance Through Rituals* (London: Hutchinson, 1976).
[2] Phil Cohen, "Sub-cultural Conflict and the Working-class Community," *Working Papers in Cultural Studies*, No. 2 (University of Birmingham: Centre for Contemporary Cultural Studies, 1972).
[3] Ibid.
[4] Dick Hebdige, "The Meaning of Mod," and John Clarke, "The Skinheads and the Magical Recovery of Community," in Hall and Jefferson (eds.), *Resistance*.
[5] Chris Waters, "Badges of Half-formed, Inarticulate Radicalism: A Critique of Recent Trends in the Study of Working Class Youth Culture," *International Labour and Working Class History*, No. 19 (Spring 1981), pp.23–37.
[6] Hebdige, "The Meaning of Mod."

[7] Dick Hebdige, *Subculture: The Meaning of Style* (London: Methuen, 1979). The following references and quotes are from this book.

[8] Cohen, "Sub-cultural Conflict."

[9] I. Taylor and D. Wall, "Beyond the Skinheads," in G. Mungham and G. Pearson (eds.), *Working Class Youth Cultures* (London: Routledge & Kegan Paul, 1978), writing in defense of the "progressive rock" of the seventies, suggested that glam rock (particularly Bowie) was part of a manufactured conspiracy to destroy the skin subculture.

[10] I would tentatively suggest that Asian boys have built up a youth culture (literally) of self defense based on training in the martial arts and the numerous kung fu–derived films.

[11] Paul Willis, *Learning to Labour* (London: Saxon House, 1977). Despite the richness of the analysis, Willis's explanation of "how working class kids get working class jobs" is ultimately based on the unproblematic socialization of sons into the values of their fathers.

[12] Richard Hoggart, *The Uses of Literacy* (Harmondsworth: Penguin, 1958).

[13] Dick Hebdige, "Skinheads and the Search for White Working Class Identity," *New Socialist*, No. 1 (September/October 1981).

[14] Mike Brake, *The Sociology of Youth Culture and Youth Subcultures* (London: Routledge & Kegan Paul, 1980).

[15] Hebdige, *Subculture*.

[16] Ibid.

[17] See the interview with McLaren and subsequent debates in the *New Musical Express* (August/September 1980).

[18] C. Sullivan, "The Zoot Suit: A Historical Perspective," *The Face* (September 1981).

CHARACTERIZING ROCK MUSIC CULTURE

The Case of Heavy Metal

1 9 8 3

○ ▲ ○ ▲ ○ ▲ ○

The decomposition of psychedelic music, in the late 1960s, followed three principal directions. The first of these, in the United States, involved a return to traditional, largely rural musical styles, with the emergence of country rock, of which the stylistic changes in the careers of the Byrds (in 1968) and the Grateful Dead (in 1970) offer examples. In Britain, a second tendency took the form of a very eclectic reinscription of traditional and symphonic musical forms within an electric or electronic rock context, with groups such as King Crimson, Jethro Tull, Genesis, Yes, and Emerson, Lake and Palmer. The third trend, which may be found in both American and British rock music of this period, was toward the heavy metal sound, frequently based in the chord structures of boogie blues, but retaining from psychedelia an emphasis on technological effect and instrumental virtuosity. In groups on the periphery of psychedelia—such as Blue Cheer, the Yardbirds, Iron Butterfly—many of the stylistic traits that would become dominant within heavy metal were already in evidence: the cult of the lead guitarist, the "power trio" and other indices of the emphasis on virtuosity, the "supergroup" phenomena, and the importance in performance of extended solo playing and a disregard for the temporal limits of the pop song. Their coherence into a genre was reinforced, through the 1970s, by the sedimentation of other stylistic attributes (those associated with stage shows, album-cover design, and audience dress and life-style) and by the relatively stable sites of institutional support (radio formats, touring circuits, record industry structures).

INSTITUTIONS AND INDUSTRIES IN THE EARLY 1970S

Heavy metal music came to prominence at a time when institutions associated with the psychedelic period were either disappearing or being assimilated within larger structures as part of widespread changes within the music-related industries. The overriding tendency in these changes was the diminishing role of local entrepreneurs in the processes by which music was developed and disseminated. The end of the sixties meant the end of free-form radio, a large number of independent record labels, the ballroom performance circuit, and the underground press, all of which had contributed, at least initially, to the high degree of regionalization within psychedelia and associated rock movements.

For many record company analysts, the number of hit-making independent record labels is an index of the degree of "turbulence" within the industry. The modern history of the American recording industry has thus been divided into three epochs: one running from 1940 to 1958, marked by concentration and integration within and between the electronics, recording, and publishing industries; the 1959 to 1969 period, characterized by the "turbulence" associated with the introduction on a large scale of rock music; and, finally, the period that began in 1970, and that saw the return of oligopoly to the extent that, in 1979, the six largest corporations accounted for 86 percent of *Billboard*'s total "chart action."[1] Two other statistics are worth noting: by the late 1960s, the album had displaced the single as the dominant format in record sales, and during the 1970s, in large part as a result of the overhead costs associated with oligopoly, the break-even point for album sales went from 20,000 to nearly 100,000 copies.

While the oligopolization of the American record industry in the 1970s is undeniable, it is less certain that one can assume the usual production effect, the sequence oligopoly–bureaucracy–conservatism–standardization. Writers such as Paul Hirsch have argued that the "centralization" of decision making in the industries producing cultural "texts" is rarely like that found in other businesses and that entertainment industries more closely resemble the house construction industry, with its organization of production along craft lines. Within the record industry, horizontal integration has frequently meant assimilating smaller, specialized labels within conglomerates (through purchases or licensing-distribution agreements), such that those involved in the selection and production of music stay in place. The record industry in the 1970s thus relied far more on outside, contracted producers or production companies than it did in the old days of the salaried artist and repertoire director.

The defining characteristic of much rock music production in the early 1970s was, further, its domination by rock elites, by people already established in creative capacities within the industry. The supergroup phenomena of this period is symptomatic of this, as is the fact that most of the leading heavy metal bands (such as Humble Pie) were formed by remnants of groups popular in the 1960s. And many of the country-rock groups and singer-songwriters who achieved high market penetration in the early 1970s had in one capacity or another long been record company employees (for instance Leon Russell, Carole King, and the members of the Eagles).

The implications of this for the American record industry during these years are not obvious. The reliance on industry elites is indicative of industry conservatism insofar as it displaced "street-level" talent-hunting and might be seen as a resistance to innovation. However it meant neglect too of the process whereby musicians with local followings and local entrepreneurial support established themselves regionally and proved their financial viability by recording first for minor labels. The majors were now signing acts without this form of market testing (a contributing factor in the increasingly high ratio of unprofitable to profitable records), and the selection and development of talent, the initiation of new styles, was increasingly the responsibility of the established creative personnel. Recording contracts in this period of growth gave artists unprecedented control over the choice of producers and material.

"Centralization" in this context meant, therefore, a *loosening* of divisions of labor. It is clear, for example, that many of those formerly involved in support capacities (songwriters, session musicians, etc.) achieved star status because of the ease with which they could move between divisions or combine the production, composing, and performing functions (just as members of groups now took it for granted that they could record solo albums).[2] Loose role definitions, and the continuing prosperity of performers and the industry as a whole, also encouraged international record production, with, as one of its effects, the free movement of session personnel (and their musical concerns) between Great Britain and North America (Joe Cocker's *Mad Dogs and Englishmen* album and film remains a useful document of this). While the bases for comparison are limited, the American record industry in the 1970s was not unlike the American film industry following the antitrust decisions of the 1940s, which divorced the production and distribution companies from those involved in exhibition: in both cases, one finds a high reliance on licensing agreements between major companies and smaller production outfits; in both cases, there is a fluidity of movement between roles and a tendency (for financial—often tax-related-—reasons) for stars to build corporate entities around themselves and work in a variety of international locales. Much of the rock literature of the mid- to late 1970s, describing industry growth in terms of the co-optation and destruction of the energies unleashed in the 1960s, regards this as exemplifying a process inevitable within mass culture,[3] but it can be argued that the changes are better understood as the triumph of craft-production structures. In this regard, the punk critique of early 1970s rock—which focused on its excesses and its eclecticism, on its "empty" virtuosity and self-indulgence rather than on an assumed standardization—was a necessary counterweight to the recuperation argument.

The changes that occurred in the programming policies of FM radio stations in the United States and Canada between the late 1960s and mid-1970s are well documented elsewhere, as is the decline of the local underground press.[4] In both cases, rising overhead costs and an increased reliance on large advertising accounts (with record companies the prominent spenders) grew out of and furthered the desire—or need—for market expansion. Either way, both radio stations and magazines paid less attention to marginal or regional musical phenomena. The rise of overhead costs and group performance fees were, similarly, the major factor in the replacement of the mid-sized performance circuit by the large arena or stadium, a process that continued throughout the 1970s, until the emergence of punk and new wave reestablished the viability of certain types of small venues.

These developments certainly did lead to standardization on FM radio and in the rock press. Radio playlist consultants, automated stations, and satellite-based networks all became significant elements in the evolution of FM radio throughout the 1970s, and the development of the rock press from local, subculturally based publications to national magazines is evident in the history of *Rolling Stone*, one of the few rock papers to survive. It would be wrong, though, to see these developments as local examples of the general "standardizing" trend. Radio playlist consultants became important because of the eclecticism and sheer bulk of record company product—individual station directors simply didn't have the time or skill to listen to and choose from all this product. At the same time the increasing rigidity of formats was an effect of demographic research into the expansion of the rock audience beyond its traditional youth boundaries—the recession of the 1970s called for a more accurate targeting of listening groups.[5] It was because such targeting remained a minor aspect of record company strategy (except in the most general sense) that it became crucial in shaping the formats of radio stations and magazines, media commercially dependent on the delivery of audiences to advertisers.

HEAVY METAL AUDIENCES AND
THE INSTITUTIONS OF ROCK

On one level, Led Zeppelin represents the final flowering of the sixties' psychedelic ethic, which casts rock as passive sensory involvement.

JIM MILLER[6]

In discussing heavy metal music, and its relationship to rock culture in a wider sense, I am assuming a relative stability of musical style and of institutional structures from 1969–70 until 1974–76. (Near the end of this period, dance-oriented music began to achieve popularity with segments of the white audiences, with a variety of effects on the sites within which music was disseminated, while the gradual acceptance, in the United States and Canada, of British symphonic or progressive rock resulted in a generic cross-fertilization that eroded the stylistic coherence of heavy metal.)

The processes described earlier as leading to the renewed importance of the *national* rock audience also worked to constitute it as a "mass" audience—the media disseminating music or information about it (radio and the press) now relied on national formats rather than on their ties to local communities (or on the popularity of local personalities). These developments made more important an audience segment that had been somewhat disenfranchised by movements within rock in the late 1960s— suburban youth. In the 1970s, it was they who were the principal heavy metal constituency.

In stressing the geographical situation of heavy metal audiences rather than their regional, ethnic, racial, or class basis, I am conscious that the latter have had wider currency in theoretical studies of rock, and it is obvious that race and class are, for example, highly determinant in the audience profile for soul or opera. Nevertheless, for reasons that should become evident, habitation patterns are crucial for the relationship between music, the institutions disseminating it, and life-styles in a more general sense. The hostility of heavy metal audiences to disco in the late 1970s is indicative in this respect; the demographics of disco showed it to be dominated by blacks, Hispanics, gays, and young professionals, who shared little beyond living in inner urban areas.[7] The high degree of interaction between punk/ new-wave currents and artistic subcultures in America (when compared with Great Britain) may also be traced in large part to the basis of both in inner urban areas such as New York's Soho; those living elsewhere would have little or no opportunity to experience or become involved in either of these cultures.

Suburban life is incompatible for a number of reasons with regular attendance at clubs where one may hear records or live performers; its main sources of music are radio, retail chain record stores (usually in shopping centers), and occasional large concerts (most frequently in the nearest municipal stadium). These institutions together make up the network by which major-label albums are promoted and sold—and from which music not available on such labels is for the most part excluded.

My argument is not that this institutional network gave major labels a free hand in shaping tastes but that, in conjunction with suburban life-styles, it defined a form of involvement in rock culture, discouraging subcultural activity of the degree associated with disco or punk, for example. Heavy metal culture may be characterized in part by the absence of a strong middle stratum between the listener and the fully professional group. Only in rare cases in the early 1970s could there be found an echelon of local heavy metal bands performing their own material in local venues. What I have referred to as the dominance of music in general by elites, in conjunction with the overall decline in small-scale live performance activity in the early 1970s, worked to block the channels of career advancement characteristic of other musical currents or other periods within rock history. It might also be suggested that the economy of North American suburbs in most cases discourages the sorts of marginality that develop in large inner urban areas and foster musical subcultures. High rents and the absence of enterprises not affiliated with corporate chains mean that venues for dancing or listening to live music are uncommon. If, for the purposes of this discussion, a music-based subculture may be defined as a group whose interaction centers to a high degree on sites of musical consumption, and within which there are complex gradations of professional or semiprofessional involvement in music together with relatively loose barriers between roles (such that all members will be involved, in varying degrees, in collecting, assessing, presenting, and performing music), then heavy metal audiences do not constitute a musical subculture.

The lack of intermediary strata between heavy metal audiences and groups was further determined by another characteristic of the music. Most of the groups that were predominant—Led Zeppelin, Black Sabbath, Uriah Heep, Humble Pie, Deep Purple, and so on—were British. They were instrumental in establishing a major characteristic of North American rock culture in the 1970s: regular, large-scale touring. The dependence of certain British bands on the North American market has become a structural feature of the rock industry, and is quite different in its significance from the periodic "British invasions" of the charts.

The American rock-critical establishment had a negative response to heavy metal, or at least to the form British musicians gave it. This had two effects on the place of heavy metal within rock culture and its discourse. On the one hand, critical dismissal encouraged heavy metal musicians to employ a populist argument, whose main tenet was that critics had lost touch with the tastes of broad sections of the rock audience. On the other hand, this placed critics in the dilemma of how to respond negatively to the music without employing the terms traditionally used to condemn rock overall (sameness, loudness, musical incompetence, etc.)—the critical terms with greater acceptability within rock culture (commercialism, conservatism) were, at least initially, inappropriate. The explicitly sociological or ethnographic bent of critical writing on heavy metal, its attention to the social/political implications of the music, were symptomatic of the cleavages heavy metal had effected within rock discourse.

In the early and mid-1970s, and particularly in *Rolling Stone*, rock criticism adopted more and more of the terms of journalistic film criticism, valorizing generic economy and a performer's links with the archives of American popular music. (The consistent high regard for singers such as Bruce Springsteen, Emmylou Harris, and Tom Waits, for performers like Lou Reed who played self-consciously with rock and roll imagery, stands out in a rereading of *Rolling Stone* from this period.) The emphasis on the individual career or the genre as the context within which records were meaningful accompanied the rise of the "serious" record review. This not only diminished the interest of heavy metal for its own sake, but also made the audience a relatively minor focus of rock criticism, as the latter moved away from the pop-journalistic or countercultural concerns of a few years earlier.

A major characteristic of heavy metal was its consistent noninvocation of rock history or mythology in any self-conscious or genealogical sense. The iconography of heavy metal performances and album covers, and the specific reworking of boogie blues underlying the music, did not suggest the sorts of modalization (that is, ironic relationships to their design principles or retrospective evocation of origins) that country rock, glitter rock, and even disco (with its frequent play upon older motifs of urban nightlife) possessed. As well, there was nothing to indicate that heavy metal listeners were interested in tracing the roots of any musical traits back to periods preceding the emergence of heavy metal. While the terms "rock" and "rock and roll" recur within song lyrics and album titles, this is always in reference to the present of the performance and the energies to be unleashed now, rather than to history or to myth. Any "rebel" or nonconformist imagery in heavy metal may be seen as a function of its masculine, "hard" stances, rather than as a conscious participation in rock's growing self-reflexivity. That the recent neo-punk movements in Anglo-American rock have found much of their constituency within heavy metal audiences is partly due, I suspect, to the redefinition of punk's minimalism as the expression of raw energy.

Equally striking is the almost total lack of hobbyist activity surrounding heavy metal music. Observation suggests that heavy metal listeners rarely become record collectors to a significant extent, that they are not characterized by what might be called "secondary involvement" in music: the hunting down of rare tracks, the reading of music-oriented magazines, the high recognition of record labels or producers. To the extent that a heavy metal "archive" exists, it consists of albums from the 1970s on major labels, kept in print constantly and easily available in chain record stores. There is thus little basis for the presence in heavy metal audiences of complex hierarchies based on knowledge of the music or possession of obscure records, on relationships to opinion leaders as the determinants of tastes and purchases. An infrastructure of importers, specialty stores, and fanzines was almost nonexistent in heavy metal culture during the early 1970s and emerged only in the 1980s, with the recent wave of newer heavy metal groups.

In its distance from both Top 40 pop culture and the mainstream of rock-critical discourse, heavy metal in the early 1970s was the rock genre least characterized by the culture's usual practices of contextualization. It is rarely the case, for example, that heavy metal pieces are presented on the radio for their nostalgic or "oldie" value. Rather, they are presented as existing contemporaneously with recent material, with none of the transitory aspects of Top 40 or setting down in individual careers or generic histories which the rock press and radio bring to bear upon other forms. The specificity of the heavy metal audience, then, lies in: (1) its nonparticipation in the two dominant components of rock culture, the Top 40 succession of hits and hobbyist tendencies associated with record and information collecting; and (2) its difference, nevertheless, from the casual, eclectic audience for transgeneric music (such as that of Carole King or, more recently, Vangelis). It is this coexistence of relatively coherent taste, consumption, and, to a certain extent, life-style with low secondary involvement in rock culture that in the 1970s most strongly distinguished audiences for heavy metal from those for other sorts of rock music.

HEAVY METAL CULTURE: MASCULINITY AND ICONOGRAPHY

On the whole, youth cultures and subcultures tend to be some form of exploration of masculinity.

MIKE BRAKE

That the audience for heavy metal music is heavily male-dominated is generally acknowledged and easily observable, though statistical confirmation of this is based largely on the audiences for album-oriented rock

(AOR).[9] Clearly heavy metal performers are almost exclusively male (recent exceptions such as Girlschool being accorded attention most often for their singularity). Is it sufficient, then, to interpret heavy metal's gender significance simply in terms of its "cock rock" iconography?

One problem here is how to reconcile the hypothesis that heavy involvement in rock music—as critic, record collector, reader of the rock press, or performer—is primarily a male pursuit[10] with the observation that these activities are for the most part absent from the most "masculine" of rock audiences, that for heavy metal. The point is that involvement in rock music is simply one among many examples of critieria by which status is assigned within youth peer groups, albeit one that involves a high degree of eroticization of certain stances and attributes.

Within male youth culture (particularly in secondary school or workplaces), a strong investment in archivist or obscurantist forms of knowledge is usually devalued, marginalized as a component of what (in North America, at least) is called "nerd" culture. I would emphasize that this marginalization is not simply directed at intellectual or knowledgeable males; rather, it involves specific relationships between knowledge and the presentation of the physical body. In recent American youth films (such as *The Last American Virgin*), the nerd is stereotyped as unstylishly dressed and successful at school: it is precisely the preoccupation with knowledge that is seen as rendering the boy oblivious to dress, grooming, posture, and social interaction (particularly as related to sexuality).

If, within a typology of male identity patterns, heavy metal listeners are usually in a relationship of polar opposition to "nerds," it is primarily because the former do not regard certain forms of knowledge (particularly those derived from print media) as significant components of masculinity—if the "nerd" is distinguished by his inability to translate knowledge into socially acceptable forms of competence, heavy metal peer groups value competencies demonstrable in social situations exclusively. Interestingly, within rock culture, neither of these groups is seen to partake of what the dominant discourse surrounding rock in the 1970s has regarded as "cool."

"Cool" may be said to involve the eroticization and stylization of knowledge through its assimilation to an imagery of competence. There developed in the 1970s a recognizable genre of rock performance (Lou Reed, Patti Smith, Iggy Pop, even, to a lesser extent, Rod Stewart) based on the integration of street wisdom, a certain ironic distance from rock mythology, and, in some cases, sexual ambiguity (whose dominant significance was as an index of experience) within relatively coherent musical styles and physical stances. The recurrence of black leather and "rebel" postures in the iconography surrounding such music never resulted in its full assimilation in the more masculine tendencies of rock culture, since these motifs overlapped considerably with those of gay culture or involved a significant degree of intellectualization; but in North America, much of the original constituency for punk and new wave included people whose archivist involvement in rock centered on a tradition dominated by the Velvet Underground and East Coast urban rock in general. Many of those in this current (such as Lenny Kaye and Lester Bangs) became important figures within American rock criticism, and it remains the purest example of secondary involvement in rock music becoming a component of a highly stylized subculture. Since the mid-1970s, performers on its fringes have contributed an alternative constellation of male images to those found in heavy metal, one that participates in what rock culture defines as "cool," but that lacks the androgynous aspects of the bohemian underground. Bruce Springsteen, Bob Seger, and John Cougar Mellencamp are American rock performers who have all achieved mainstream AOR success while presenting, as important components of their styles, an archivist relationship to rock music and a tendency to play self-consciously with the mythologics that surround it.

Another rock culture that may be fruitfully compared with heavy metal emerged around British progressive rock (or what is now derisively called "pomp rock"): symphonic groups such as Yes, Genesis, and Emerson, Lake and Palmer. While certain of these groups—for example, King Crimson and ELP—achieved North American success in the early 1970s, others, such as Genesis and Gentle Giant, did not become popular until the middle of the decade. The audiences for this music, like those for heavy metal, were predominantly male; but to a much greater extent than with heavy metal, one can trace complex gradations of involvement in this music, at least until 1975 or so.

Progressive rock fostered secondary involvement among North American listeners for a number of reasons. Both the earlier albums of many of these groups, and records by minor groups within the same genre, were often available only as imports, and the subculture that sprang up thus both spawned, and centered on, import-oriented record stores, fanzines, and the British musical press (the pattern was repeated by latter new wave fans—large numbers of record stores currently marketing postpunk music began by selling progressive rock imports). Interest in British progresive rock was also closely correlated with the frequent reading of, and subcultural involvement in, science fiction (another component of "nerd" culture).[11] These interests overlapped as well with those of audiences for European electronic music and American minimalism, though the more recent alignment of this music and its audiences with trends within postpunk music has obscured these links. Like heavy metal, progressive rock received little critical favor in the American rock press, which tended to regard jazz-rock fusion as the most important of the avant-garde tendencies during this period.

The distinction between heavy metal and progressive rock audiences began to weaken in the middle and late 1970s. American groups that combined features of these two forms emerged and achieved considerable success (Boston, Kansas, Styx, etc.), and this hybrid sound came to be characteristic of album-oriented rock radio. One effect of this was the growing mainstream acceptance of progressive rock in general and decline in the subcultural activity surrounding it.

The convergence of heavy metal and progressive rock audiences is in several respects paradoxical, as is the later penetration of adult contemporary radio formats by heavy metal bands such as Journey. It is tempting to suggest that, despite progressive rock's consistent nonemployment of erotic motifs and heavy metal's aggressive staging of masculine sexuality—and despite the former's aspirations to status as "serious" music and the latter's populist promise of rock in its purest form—both displayed similar forms of opposition to the constraints and concerns of the Top 40 single. While heavy metal is commonly and justifiably perceived as an expression of violent sexuality, many of its most popular manifestations are explorations of nonromantic and nonerotic themes, whose fantastic and "philosophical" components are evidence of heavy metal's links to a continuing drug-based culture and to many of the same remnants of psychedelia that recurred in progressive rock. (Led Zeppelin's song "Stairway to Heaven" is the best-known example of this.)

The major stylistic components of heavy metal iconography may be inventoried as follows: long hair for both performers and audiences; denim jackets and jeans among audience members; smoke bombs as an element of stage performances; marijuana smoking and the taking of depressant drugs (Quaaludes and alcohol, etc.). On album covers: eclecticism at the beginning, but the gradual cohering of an iconography combining satanic imagery and motifs from heroic fantasy illustration, which could be found increasingly too on the backs of jean jackets, automobiles and vans, T-shirts, pinball machines (and, with the later influence of punk, on buttons). The remarkable aspect of traits such as long hair and denim jackets is their persistence and longevity within heavy metal culture long after they had ceased to be fashionable across the wider spectrum of North American youth culture. This itself reflected a decade-long shift whereby the heavy metal look came to acquire connotations of low socioeconomic position. While this might seem incompatible with my characterization of heavy metal audiences as largely suburban—and therefore, presumably, middle class—it would seem that the heavy metal audience, by the early 1980s, consisted to a significant extent of suburban males who did not acquire postsecondary education and who increasingly found that their socioeconomic prospects were not as great as those of their parents.

The iconography prevalent in heavy metal culture may be seen as the development of (1) certain tendencies emergent within psychedelia, which were in part responsible for the popularization of (2) types of fantasy and science fiction literature and illustration, which, in heavy metal iconography, saw their (3) heroic or masculine features emphasized. It is well known, for example, that, within the hippie counterculture, fantasy literature such as Tolkien's *The Lord of the Rings* was widely read and provided motifs for a wide range of poster art, songs, album covers, and so on. In progressive rock of the early 1970s, related themes dominated, and the commercialization (in poster and book form) of the album covers by artists such as Roger Dean testified to the market for this style. In many cases (Jethro Tull, Genesis) fantastic motifs accompanied the musical invocation of early British history or mythology.

However, the most successfully popularized of these styles was the "heroic fantasy" associated with Conan and spinoff fictional characters. From the late 1960s through the 1970s, this form of fiction passed from paperback novel to high-priced illustrated magazine to conventional comic book format to, ultimately, the cinema: each step was evidence of the genre's broadening appeal and entry into mainstream youth culture. By the mid-1970s, the artwork of Frank Frazetta and others associated with the genre was widely merchandised in poster and calender form, and on the covers of heavy metal albums by such groups as Molly Hatchett. Highly masculine (dominated by an imagery of carnage) and mildly pornographic, this illustrative style has cohered around heavy metal music and its paraphernalia.

The satanic imagery associated with heavy metal iconography almost from its inception (by Black Sabbath) grew out of stylistic traits present within psychedelia (such as those found on early Grateful Dead albums), and its convergence with elements of heroic fantasy illustraion came near the middle of the decade. However, it is arguable whether the readership of fantasy literature overlaps significantly with the audience for heavy metal music (though the audience for heroic fantasy films likely does). The readership of *Heavy Metal* magazine, for example, despite its title, includes more fans of progressive rock than of heavy metal, which is to be expected in that both the magazine and these types of music are the centers of subcultural activity. Studies have demonstrated the low involvement of heavy metal audiences in print media and their high movie attendance.[12]

What heavy metal iconography did do was contribute to the development of a 1970s kitsch, to the proliferation of fantasy and satanic imagery as vehicle and pinball arcade decor, as poster art and T-shirt illustration. For the most part, this has meant inscribing a masculine-heroic element within the fantastic or mystical motifs that surrounded psychedelic and, later, progressive rock. These motifs increasingly stood out against the geometrical-minimalist and retro design principles that became widespread within rock music following the emergence of punk and new wave.

CONCLUSION

Heavy metal is at once the most consistently successful of forms within rock music and the most marginalized within the discourse of institution-alized rock culture. That literary criticism is not regularly unsettled by the popularity of Harlequin romances while American rock culture regards heavy metal as a "problem" is symptomatic of the tension in the 1970s between the ascension of critical discourse on rock music to respectability and the importance to it of a rock populist reading.

Heavy metal in North America provides one of the purest examples of involvement in rock music as an activity subordinate to, rather than deter-minant of, peer group formation. While involvement in disco or punk may determine people's choices of types and sites of love and friendship (and even the selection of places to live and work), heavy metal—perhaps because of the inaccessibility of the institutions that produce and disseminate it—does not.

For young men, at least, involvement in rock music is perhaps the most useful index of the relationship between knowledge/competence and physical/sexual presence. Despite my concentration on heavy metal, the most male-dominated of rock's forms, and the most blatant in its associations of masculinity with physical violence and power, I regard the 1970s as significant precisely for the ways in which certain types of rock (glitter, punk) accomplished important interventions in sexual politics. That these interventions and their effects were major, while heavy metal remained the most popular form of rock during this decade, is evidence of the complexity and breadth of rock culture.

NOTES

[1] B. Anderson, P. Hesbacher, K. P. Etzkorn, and R. S. Denisoff, "Hit Record Trends, 1940–77," *Journal of Communications* 30, No. 2 (Spring 1980), p. 41; R. Peterson and D. Berger, "Entrepreneurship in Organizations: evidence from the popular music industry," *Administrative Science Quarterly* 16 (1971), pp. 97–107; P. Titus, "The Rise and Fall of the First Album," *New York Rocker* (September 1980), pp. 24–25.

[2] It is true that this fluidity of roles was a characteristic as well of early 1960s pop-rock, wherein songwriters such as Goffin and King might write a song and record it under a concocted group name. The crucial difference is that creative activity in the early 1970s was not based on small-scale enterprise and the anonymity of certain roles. Rather, the high level of freelance activity and the critical discourse within the early 1970s resulted in producers and groups being seen as highly personalized artists, whose work with others was regarded as creative collaboration.

[3] See for example S. Chapple and R. Garofalo, *Rock 'n' Roll Is Here to Pay* (Chicago: Nelson-Hall, 1980).

[4] Ibid.

[5] See H. Mooney, "Twilight of the Age of Aquarius? Popular music in the 1970s," *Popular Music and Society* 7 (1980), p. 185.

[6] Jim Miller, "Led Zeppelin," in J. Miller (ed.), *The Rolling Stone Illustrated History of Rock and Roll* (New York: Rolling Stone Press/Random House, 1976), p. 306.

[7] See P. Fornatele and J. Mills, *Radio in the Television Age* (Woodstock, N.Y.: Overlook Press, 1980), p. 77.

[8] M. Brake, *The Sociology of Youth Culture and Youth Subcultures* (London: Routledge & Kegan Paul, 1980), p. vii.

[9] See Fornatele and Mills, *Radio*, p. 74.

[10] Simon Frith and Angela McRobbie, "Rock and Sexuality," *Screen Education*, No. 29 (Winter 1978/1979), p. 8. (Their article is reprinted in Part 6 of this volume.)

[11] The source of the demographic information on science fiction reading and muscial preferences is a personal interview with Len Mogel, publisher of *Heavy Metal* magaizine, in July 1981. The link between subcultural involvement and science fiction and "nerdishness" is no more absolute than are the definitions of these attributes, but is based on my reading of several hundred science fiction fanzines from this period. The "nerd" quality of a high percentage of those involved in science fiction fandom is often readily acknowledged by those active therein, and their marginality within youth peer groups has been confirmed in sociological examinations of this subculture, such as Fredric Wertham's extremely flawed *The World of Fanzines*.

[12] See G. C. Bruner, "The Association Between Record Purchase Volume and Other Music-related Characteristics," *Popular Music and Society* 3 (1979), p. 237.

IS THERE ROCK AFTER PUNK?

1 9 8 6

○ ▲ ○ ▲ ○ ▲ ○

I want to talk—sympathetically—about the current situation of rock and roll in the United States. To understand its specificity and possibilities, we must first ask how rock and roll works for its fans for, as I will argue, to call something "rock and roll"—and more than music is encompassed by that term—is to say that it works for its fans. Hence, I define "rock and roll" as a mode of functioning. I do not intend to speak either as a fan (although I am one) or as a critic (although I have been one) for, from either of these positions, one can only make judgments about the quality of the music or the appropriateness of the audience's response.

The uniqueness of the present situation is visible, subjectively, as a "crisis" for many fans and, objectively, in the changing place of rock and roll within both the larger category of popular music and the economic practices that surround the rock and roll culture. As evidence of the former, I might point to the increasingly common rhetoric of the "death of rock and roll" and to the changing tastes at both the upper and lower chronological boundaries of the potential rock and roll audience. Although these have occurred before, they are so widespread within the culture today that it seems reasonable to take them as indicating significant shifts. As evidence of the objective crisis, I can point to the decreasing sales of records (despite the industry's claim that the recession is over, the number of gold and platinum albums has significantly declined) and the decreasing attendance at live venues.

Furthermore, the industry increasingly segregates rock and roll from popular music, which contrasts sharply with the tendency of the past twenty-five years to collapse these categories. For example, the major format distinction in radio today sets "contemporary hits," with its flavor of fifties AM radio but with a wider range of musical sounds and styles, against "album-oriented rock," which plays predominantly heavy metal and new wave. The former is described as "horizontal" because it appeals to diverse audiences (including teenage girls and parts of the "adult-contemporary audience"), while the latter defines the narrower, "vertical" appeal of rock and roll (teenage boys and college-age youth). Finally, we may point to the increasing ease and rapidity with which various styles of rock and roll have been incorporated into, and exploited by, commercial interest (e.g., network television has discovered the virtues of rock, not only in sports but in dramatic programming; and is there any product that has not tried to use breakdancing?) and reduced to harmless stereotypes.

These "facts" are neither merely symptoms of some hidden causal determination nor the causes of the changing articulations of rock and roll. What I will offer, then, is not an exhaustive causal explanation of this situation but a description that places these "facts" in a context of mutual determination. The contemporary effects of rock and roll are inseparable from its conditions of existence, from the contradictory structure of the rock and roll culture itself, from the lines of force—the "political" tendencies and contradictions—that have displaced and redefined its effects. In particular, I will point to two intersecting vectors that have deconstructed (and perhaps reconstructed) the possibility and power of rock and roll. First, punk not only opened up new musical and sociological possibilities, it also restructured the music's relation to itself and its audience. Second, the very notion of youth culture, so crucial to rock and roll, is being dismantled and undermined, partly by rock and roll itself, but also by other social and cultural discourses.

ROCK AND ROLL AS
AFFECTIVE EMPOWERMENT

Rock and roll is a cultural event that emerged at a particular moment into a particular context. Part of its power is, in fact, that it has constructed its own history through which it has maintained a unity for itself within its differences. That is, despite the changing musical, stylistic, and political parameters of rock and roll and its fans, the category itself is constantly reiterated, created, albeit not quite anew, with both a changing past and a confident future ("Rock and roll will never die"). My concern is to identify what it is that constitutes this unity and opens a space within which differences function positively: What does it mean to say that rock and roll works?

Three features of rock and roll mitigate against treating it primarily within the terms of communication theory. First, and it should come as no surprise to communications researchers, whether one looks for meanings (interpretations) or uses (gratifications), one finds heterogeneity. Different people not only interpret the music differently but use it differently as well. A 13-year-old girl, a college student, and a blue-collar worker may all be fans of the Police or Prince or Van Halen, but all for very different reasons. Even further, there is no necessary correspondence between the meaning someone gives a genre or text and the ways they use it. The issue is not one of individual taste because one can identify audiences, but the crucial correlations remain unexamined.

Second, in many cases, the music appears "hollow." The significance of the music is not in the music, nor in the fan. For example, the meaning may be found outside the text, in the way it marks our history. Or the meaning may be irrelevant, subservient, or simply absent. As many a rock and roll fan has commented, the power of the music lies not in what it says but in what it does, in how it makes one move and feel. To find how rock functions, it is necessary to explore effects that are not necessarily signifying, that do not necessarily involve the transmission, production, structuration, or even deconstruction of meaning. Rock and roll is corporeal and "invasive." For example, without the mediation of meaning, the sheer volume and repetitive rhythms of rock and roll produce a real material pleasure for its fans (at many live concerts, the vibration actually might be compared to the use of a vibrator, often focused on the genital organs) and restructure familial relations (by producing immediate outrage and rejection from its nonfans, e.g., parents). If we assume, further, that rock and roll fans are not "cultural dopes," then we must examine the contradictions and struggles that are enacted around, and in, rock and roll in various contexts. Thus, while it is often true that the "ideology" of rock and roll appears conservative and that its consumption merely reinforces the capitalist hegemony, there is always a remainder of nonsignifying effects in such calculations. The fact that we think of it as "pleasure" is often used to justify our dismissing it as the sugar coating that makes the ideological pill go down. I will argue that it is much more.

The third feature of the way rock and roll exists within youth cultures is that, oddly enough, the genre cannot be defined solely in musical terms. Different audiences not only define the boundaries of rock and roll differently but are differentially capable of listening to, and finding "pleasure" in, different forms of rock and roll.

These three features suggest that one cannot approach rock and roll by using anyone's experience of it, or even any collective definition of that experience. Yet one cannot deny its popularity, not merely in quantitative and economic terms, but also in terms of its importance in the lives of its fans and its role in the "youth cultures" of the United States. Further, they suggest that one cannot read the political effects of rock and roll off the text (although this does not deny the relevance of the musical/lyrical text). Understanding rock and roll requires asking what it gives its fans, how it empowers them and how they empower it. What possibilities does it enable them to appropriate in their everyday lives? Treating functions/effects in terms of empowerment avoids the textual and social-psychological reductionism of communication theory. It may help to give some rather simple examples of "empowerment": a record is a commodity to be purchased, consumed, and disposed of. But within the larger networks I want to investigate, such an accommodation to capitalism may also empower its fans in ways that contradict the consumer economy's attempt to regulate the structures and rhythms of daily life. For the disposability of the commodity also places the record at the disposal of its fans: they can control its uses, use it in new and unintended ways, restructure and recontextualize its messages, and so forth. Second, a song may, in both its ideological messages and the patterns of its gendered consumption, reproduce the social definitions of sexuality and social roles. And yet, in its restructuring of the body as the site of pleasure, in the ways it makes a space for and inserts the female body and voice into its physical and social environment, it may challenge hegemonic constraints on sexuality, desire, and even gender construction. And finally, to combine these two examples, although early rock and roll (especially rockabilly) was marketed as if it were male produced and consumed, women were not only fans of the music, but also sang and even recorded it. The politics of the economic decision not to market such efforts is not the same as the politics of the functioning of the music within the everyday lives of its fans.

Furthermore, looking at the networks of empowerment within which rock and roll functions also points to its potentially oppositional role in American culture. Rock and roll has, repeatedly and continuously, been attacked, banned, ridiculed, and relegated to an insignificant cultural status. The fact that so much effort has been brought to bear in the attempt to silence it makes it reasonable to assume that some struggle is going on, some opposition is being voiced. And despite the changing social sites and discourses of the attack, it is consistently as a way of behaving that rock and roll is seen as dangerous. For example, it is not that the music sounds like black music but that it makes its fans act like "animals" (in the rhetoric of the fifties, blacks).

This suggests that we look at the ways of behaving—the practices—that define the rock and roll culture, including the fact that particular texts exist and are popular, which is not the same as being commercially successful. That is, rock and roll is not defined by the *Billboard* charts. Even the briefest study of the rock and roll culture points to the existence of a boundary between popular music and rock and roll, but again, this distinction cannot be made in solely musical terms. Not all popular music is rock and roll, and not all of the fans of popular music are rock and roll fans. Both the music itself (in its self-references, in the fact that performers—from the slick commercialism of Culture Club to the avant-gardism of Fred Frith— struggle to assert that they make "rock and roll," in the use of cover versions of songs, etc.) and the fans compulsively encapsulate rock and roll. The power of rock and roll depends upon that part of the population which makes a particular investment in it, which empowers it within their lives, which differentiates both the music and themselves. Rock and roll fans (used now in this narrower sense) enact an elitism (an inverse canonization) in their relation to music. Rock and roll does not belong to everyone, and not everything is rock and roll. This is visible in the judgments they make: rock and roll fans distinguish not only between good and bad rock and roll, but also between rock and roll and music that cannot be heard within the genre (they have a variety of names for it: co-opted, sold-out, boring, straight music). While a rock and roll fan may enjoy other forms of popular music, the boundary is always drawn. If there must always be something that is not rock and roll (and that the fan can recognize because he or she knows what is really rock and roll), how does this boundary work?

I will make three general claims about this encapsulation. *First*, it works on the audience as well as the music; it marks them as different without necessarily defining any positive (visible, readable) identity: you are not what you don't listen to, which cannot be simply reduced to you are what you listen to. One cannot predict individual tastes; one can only invoke, in Bourdieu's words, a "social cartography" of taste. Encapsulation creates what I would call "nomination groups" (rather than taste cultures) which function, by naming rock and roll, to create not subcultures but what are only nominal groups. *Second*, the music always functions in a larger context, a rock and roll apparatus. That is, the way in which particular music is inserted into the everyday lives of its fans depends upon the overdetermined relations between the music and a variety of other social, cultural, economic, sexual, and discursive practices. Rock and roll is always located within a seemingly random collection of events that interpenetrate and even constitute the specific rock and roll culture, including styles of dance, dress, and inter-action; images of the band and its fans; and so on. *Third*, rock and roll's importance in the experience of its fans depends upon its functioning af-fectively within their everyday lives. A rock and roll apparatus (there are always many competing ones) locates what sorts of "pleasures" or energizing possibilities are available to its fans; it restructures social life by rearranging the sites at which pleasure can be found and energy derived, at which desire and power are invested and operative. For example, the rock and roll culture transforms many of the structures of contemporary boredom (repetition and noise) into the structures and pleasures of its musical and listening practices.

The work of encapsulation might be clarified by comparing it with the common argument that the car has become an extension of the house. Inversely, rock and roll might be seen as an invasion of the house; it creates a kind of "bubble," a mobile environment surrounding its fans, sometimes weak and transparent, sometimes strong and opaque. It radically reshapes the real, not merely symbolically, by placing the rock and roll apparatus in a (limited) struggle within and against the structures of everyday life.

Thus, I want to locate the effects of rock and roll at the level of an (at least potentially) oppositional politics that produces a rupture between the rock and roll audience (in their everyday lives) and the larger hegemonic context within which it necessarily exists. But how is this politics constructed? There are two analytic moments to this work. The first I have already implicitly described: rock and roll selects and uses pieces of its material environment as the raw material with which to articulate a youth culture or, more accurately, a series of different and allied youth cultures embodied within the various rock and roll apparatuses. In fact, rock and roll at all levels of its existence constantly steals from other sources, creating its own encapsulation by transgressing any sense of boundary and identity. This is the stage of *bricolage*. The second moment actively structures this material context into an organization of "pleasure" and power, of the social energy that defines the possibilities for both domination and resistance within everyday life. The rock and roll apparatus is a kind of machine which, like a cookie cutter constantly changing its shape, produces or imprints a structure on the fans' desires and relations by organizing the material pieces of their lives, within the apparatus, along certain axes. The rock and roll apparatus works by inscribing a geography of desire on its youth culture, on the space within which the audience exists.

I now want to describe briefly the circuits of empowerment. Most obviously, the energy of the rock and roll apparatus is constructed around the categories of youth and the body. Rock and roll celebrates youth, not merely as a chronological measure but as a difference defined by the rejection of the boredom of the "straight" world. The politics of youth celebrate change, risk, and instability; the very structures of boredom become the sites of new forms of empowerment. The powerlessness of youth is rearticulated into an apparatus in which it becomes the site of "pleasure" and power. The "pleasure" of empowerment / empowerment of "pleasure" is, furthermore, articulated around the material pleasures of the body. It is its emphasis on rhythm and dance, and its affirmation of sexual desire which may, occasionally, challenge the dominant gender categories. Rock and roll seeks pleasure in the different ways the body can be inserted into its social environment.

However, it is the third axis of "attitude" that locates the radical specificity of rock and roll as a response to the specific structures of contemporary everyday life. This response is manifested in rock and roll's celebration of surfaces, styles, and artifice. In Baudrillard's terms, "reality" has disappeared, leaving only its image; without origins, everything becomes a rerun, another style. Given the rapid rate of continuous change, the increasing knowledge of risk and danger, the sense that the rules for survival no longer guarantee a good life, the commodification of all value, life is increasingly lived in "a controlled panic." The rock and roll apparatus, in short, not only energizes new possibilities within everyday life, it places that energy at the center of a life without meaning: the postmodern situation.

This postmodern context makes one historical appearance of the generation gap into a permanent difference, and the practice of "excorporation" defines a response by which the rock and roll apparatus constantly reinscribes a boundary between "us" and "them." It steals and transforms the practices, fragments, and signs of other cultures and cultural moments, both those marginalized and repressed by the hegemonic culture and those located in the heart of the hegemony; it relocates them within its own reduction to surfaces—all a matter of attitude (or in its more visible forms, style).

I want to use this framework to suggest two of the elements—one specific and one general—that have contributed to the current uncertainty marking the rock and roll culture. The first, only briefly discussed here, concerns the appearance and effects of punk rock. Punk was, after all, a watershed of some sort, at least in the sense that everything that has come after it— and there has been a real explosion of musics and styles—must be read as "postpunk." The second concerns the growing historical contradictions within the social meanings and material existences of youth itself. The very possibilities of resistance that helped construct a youth culture around rock and roll have become an agent, along with other social changes, in the deconstruction of youth.

Punk emerged at, and responded to, a particular moment in the history of rock and roll. It is, after all, not coincidental that in 1976 the first of the baby boomers were turning thirty. Punk attacked rock and roll for having grown old and fat, for having lost that which puts it in touch with its audience and outside of the hegemonic reality. It attacked rock and roll in the guise of megagroups and arena rock, hippies and baby boomers who had clearly become part of what was supposed to be outside of rock and roll. If the rock and roll apparatus works when it draws a line between "them" and "us," encapsulating its fans in a mobile environment of their own, punk did so more clearly and outrageously than at any point in the seventies, precisely by articulating a particular structure of the apparatus. While it denied that rock and roll represented the emotional life or real social experiences of its fans, it reconnected the music and the fan. When it looked inside itself, it did not find nothing; it found the emptiness of the "blank generation," postmodern youth. Even as it seemed to celebrate anarchy and the pure negativity of its deconstruction (the insanity, dissonance, its threatening difference), even as it projected a potentially expansive pluralism of apparatuses and styles (a pluralism that could arise only after punk celebrated its own death), it reencapsulated rock and roll within a surprisingly circumscribed range of sounds, styles, and attitudes. It celebrated rock and roll as the music of manic fun and risk even as it called that attitude into question.

By foregrounding rock and roll's attitude, by making obvious the artificality of any attitude, punk not only problematized the investment in any particular attitude, but also in the body and pleasure as well. But this attack on rock and roll's central investments, offered in the form of deconstruction as an attitude (pose), was articulated to, and limited by, the axis of youth. Youth remained the site of rock and roll's investment and empowerment, even if it was a youth with neither a past nor a future. By reinvesting the axis of youth at the center of the apparatus and displacing the question of style, punk was able to reaffirm its existence as rock and roll. But this was obviously a strategy/structure that was condemned to failure. In fact, punk reproduced, almost perfectly, the contradictions—the impossible situation—in which youth and youth culture increasingly found itself.

THE DECONSTRUCTION OF YOUTH

The place of youth in the rock and roll culture has been unsettled by the conjunction of the history of rock and roll and a series of other social events. In the eighties, the contradictions of "youth" are becoming increasingly explicit. We might begin trying to make this visible by returning to the contemporary discussions of the death of rock and roll. For the real power of this discourse lies not in its connection with that part of the audience struggling to rediscover or reinvest its faith in rock and roll, but rather in its pointing to a part of the audience for whom rock and roll is neither possible nor desirable.

The typical description of the crisis of the rock and roll audience goes something like this. There is, apparently, a new generation of youths who have confronted a number of events: (1) Style and culture have been increasingly commodified and incorporated into hegemonic discourses through advertising, fashion, and the media. (2) They have been raised under the threat of continuous economic recession. While rock and roll has survived earlier recessions, its fans had previously believed that there was something after the recession and that fun was a sufficient strategy (on the surface) for getting through it. Rock and roll offered an economy of transitions, of magical transformations. (3) Images of youth which so dominated postwar baby boom America, have been replaced increasingly with images of the baby boomers' attempts to deal with growing old and having responsibility. (4) Rock and roll has become nostalgic. It is not only the music of parents but of advertising as well. How can it possibly mark a difference and constitute some kind of resistance? Its claims to have provided some form of transcendence or revolution have been dissolved in the gray morning of the 1980s. (5) A new generation of conservative youth has appeared—variously characterized as the "me generation" and the "mean generation." (6) New technologies, and in some cases, older cultural forms, have replaced rock and roll as the dominant leisure activities of youth. The result is that, for many young people, rock and roll has become just another moment of hegemonic leisure, background music to which they relate in ways more reminiscent of an earlier generation's relation to Tin Pan Alley's music.

There is, obviously, a good deal of truth in all of these observations. And young people do seem to have turned to other forms of culture to seek their own strategies of "pleasure" and survival within a context of "controlled panic." But in all the contemporary discussions of youth, we are caught in the uncertainty of generations. Youth is caught already in the contradiction between those who experience the powerlessness of their age and the generations of the baby boomers who have tried to redefine youth as an attitude. If the former is increasingly uncertain, it is partly because the status of the latter has also become problematic. As more and more people point to the increasingly troubled and adultlike qualities of young people, they are also observing the failure of the baby boomers to accept and arrive at traditional notions of adulthood. But we must not assume that we already understand these relations. If we too quickly reduce the context to simple questions—Is youth disappearing? Are youth and adulthood merging?—we are in danger of ignoring the real struggles and frustrations that still characterize the different groups and their relations to each other and other social groups.

The parameters marking the social identities and spaces of youth are shifting on a number of levels. In both public policy and familial commitment, the economic and moral "DMZ" that has surrounded youth for the past decades is being eroded. As these walls, which have disciplined (imprisoned, nurtured, and constructed) youth crumble, the place of youth in the social networks of knowledge has changed. Events have made punk cynicism hip (and accurate!), but without the anger and frustration. Beginning with the artificiality of all styles and commitments, young people are increasingly obsessed with their own survival and the transition into adulthood.

There is also a change in the ways that youths are represented. In the late seventies, movies and television offered few, if any, positive images of or heroes for youth. The models that were offered were so simplistic that they could be taken only ironically. Increasingly, youths are often represented only in their absence. This absence may function not only as a real lack, but also by placing youths in a position in which it makes no difference that they are, in fact, young. In a large number of popular horror movies of this period, youths are represented either as pure victim or as pure evil. In fact, it makes no difference that they are young unless it is as the victims of some unnamed social rage; it only deconstructs the very difference being obliterated. Tom Carson has recently described the new "sour view of children" on prime time television in which either "negative characteristics usually associated with adulthood" are displaced onto children—"children are treated as mercenary and calculating while parents are seen as passive, endearingly hapless"—or they are seen as "alien, inherently Other."

The enormous popularity of Spielberg's films (*Close Encounters, ET, Poltergeist, Gremlins*) is the most recent manifestation of this shifting representational code. These films are all structured around the disappearance of children and their eventual return. The movies offer themselves as a new "fountain of youth"; they project adult fantasies of youth and their surfaces resemble advertising. The category of youth has been appropriated by others who not only define but essentialize it. They speak as if from a position of youth, for youth, but they speak as adults, for adults. Thus it is increasingly common to find the baby-boomer heroes and heroines of prime time television confronting their ambiguous relations to both youth and adulthood, appropriating the former category and dissolving it into their reluctance to enter the latter category. Perhaps all this encodes a new resentment of youth by a generation that was never taught to be adults or even to value that identity, and whose identity is still imbricated in their investment in youth. This incorporation of youth into adulthood has taken on a new form in the past few years: the increasing sexualization of youth (and more recently, even childhood, perhaps partly in response to an increasing ambivalence about out willingness to make the necessary personal and economic sacrifices that have constructed the category). This sexualization is also taking place within the rock and roll / youth culture itself. One need only look at the way in which dancers present themselves, not to each other but to the camera, on programs such as *American Bandstand* to realize that the sexualization of youth has taken on new inflections.

In fact, it was perhaps almost inevitable that rock and roll would define and, even more, help bring about its own death, that the rock and roll apparatuses would dismantle their own possibility of empowering alliances. Consider where rock and roll constructed its own culture, the physical spaces that it appropriated and created as its own: the street, the jukebox, the party, and the "hop/dance." The significance of these spaces is that, to some extent, they all attempt to exist outside of the family and the school. In fact, it is these two institutions which rock and roll has most consistently attacked. Frith and McRobbie have argued that the antidomesticity of rock and roll is an expression of its basic male orientation and its antifemale ideology. I disagree: the antidomesticity of the rock and roll apparatus is an attack on the place in which its own youth is constructed. It is a resistance to the very discipline that is, paradoxically, constitutive of its "youth." Such resistance is a crucial aspect of the rock and roll apparatus. But what if rock and roll begins to succeed in challenging the control of the hegemony over the category of youth? For example, if youth is defined in part by its ambiguous and risky relation to sexual practice (especially intercourse), what happens to it when that relationship is fundamentally changed?

The antidomesticity of rock and roll (as well as its antischool stance) is increasingly supported by other hegemonic discourses, and such alliances surely make rock and roll's status problematic. The family as an adequate site for the protection of the child is increasingly under attack. For example, although issues of childbeating and incest have been raised by feminists since the nineteenth century, they have never been taken up in widespread public debate until the present moment. And the demand for more flexible social and sexual arrangements similarly challenges the stability and adequacy of the traditional nuclear family. One might add that, similarly, the other institutions that have direct responsibility for the discipline, control, and construction of youth—schools, medicine, juvenile courts—are coming under broad attack.

Finally, these changes can be related to one other reconstruction of youth and its relationship to the body in the contemporary world. This makes pleasure something to work for (not merely a political struggle, it is a physical and economic one). Youth is something to be held on to by physical effort. That is, youth has become a state of the body, presumably one that offers its own pleasurable rewards. This emergent cultural formation is most clearly embodied in the current transformation of sports/health into a form of leisure with its own styles, and to the remarkable appearance of the "yuppies" on the public scene. It is interesting to note that this emergent culture not only has grown out of the rock and roll audience, but often continues to use at least some of the music within its own structures of empowerment (*Flashdance* and Michael Jackson's *Thriller*, two of the most successful albums of 1983, are widely used for various styles of exercise).

The result is that while rock and roll has been crucial in constructing a youth culture, it has also been crucial in eroding the conditions for the particular construction of "youth" upon which it is built, not merely because of its own practices but in conjunction with a whole series of events that have intersected and interacted with it. But if the institutions and disciplines that construct youth are deconstructed, how can rock and roll define itself by its resistance to them? How can the rock and roll apparatus invest itself in an unstable axis of youth? The relationship between rock and roll and youth has become contradictory: rock and roll exists not within the rise of youth but rather at the cusp between the rise and the decline of a particular construction of youth, one that so privileges its transitional status as to reify and celebrate transitions. The rock and roll apparatus attacks the very conditions of its existence.

I have attempted to do three things in this article: (1) to lay out a conceptual vocabulary with which we can investigate the politics of rock and roll in more subtle and complex ways, a framework within which rock and roll is a set of strategies for struggle, the nature and effects of which are never predetermined; (2) to argue that at least two significant vectors of change have to be taken into account as we consider the present political position of rock and roll. This is not to deny other vectors of determination, merely to acknowledge that the complex array of changes that have taken place over the last twenty-five years have changed the relations between rock and roll, youth and society; (3) to suggest a different approach to the empirical question of rock's "death." Let me, in conclusion, make an explicit comment about this last concern.

We will not arrive at an adequate practical understanding—"pessimism of the intellect, optimism of the will"—of the current situation in rock and roll by focusing on either the phenomenology of its fans or the message of its texts, even if we locate both within the context of a conservative hegemony. The crucial contradiction, the point at which rock and roll is inserted, is that between everyday life and the ideological struggles of contemporary politics. For those ideologies—both of the left and the right—continue to mystify that which rock and roll empowers: the changing structures of our affective existence. Thus, the limits that I place on rock and roll are defined by the lines of what Goldstein calls its "mattering maps," by the axes along which it organizes the affective investments of its fans. These maps empower sites of struggle and resistance; "rock and roll" cannot mean *anything* (although anything can be rock and roll, i.e., located within a rock and roll apparatus). Similarly, although any song outside of any context (apparatus) can mean anything, as rock and roll the song never exists outside of some apparatus within which its meaning is constructed or articulated according to the particular affective organization of the apparatus. "Rock and roll," then, is a floating signifier of a historically changing and multiple affective machinery, a machine articulated into particular relations within larger social and cultural formations.

The parameters of this affective organization are constituted by the contradictions between three lines of effects: youth, the body (pleasure), and attitude (postmodernity). Rock and roll's empowerment is a function of the historically articulated relations between these unstable and discontinuous vectors.

If punk, in conjunction with other historical events, has made rock and roll problematic, it has not "argued itself out of a future." I have not argued that rock and roll is dead nor that its affective empowerment is no longer possible. I have tried to make sense of some of the contemporary forms and practices that form the heart of various rock and roll apparatuses. Obviously, there is still rock and roll music, and obviously, it still has an important affective place in its fans' lives. But the affective machinery and organization of the contemporary rock and roll apparatuses have undergone significant transformation as a result of the increasingly visible contradiction between postmodernity and the forms of rock and roll's empowerment (the punk effect) and the increasingly contested nature of youth formations in contemporary society. I am not proclaiming rock and roll's death. On the contrary, my best guess is that rock and roll will find new forms of empowerment and investment (e.g., through its visualization) which, while remaining within the basic affective organization I have described, will offer new strategies around the common expressions of our postmodern condition. The question is whether we, as cultural critics, will be able to find ways of articulating it into an oppositional politics rather than dismissing it as conservative, selfish, merely entertainment, or consumerist.

PART THREE

The Organization of the Music Business

○ ▲ ○ ▲ ○ ▲ ○ ▲ ○ ▲ ○ ▲ ○

The organization of the popular music industry is a topic that has been much written about but rarely theorized. There are numerous histories of rock and pop, and dozens of books about the economics of the business; but few of these offer much beyond an unacknowledged auteur theory and simplistic accounts of the "commercialization" of a form that is (wrongly) assumed to be more authentic in its (nonexistent) precapitalist form.

The essays in this section provide a more vigourous engagement with the organization of the music business than is usual. The writers employ three models, each derived from sociology. Paul Hirsch's seminal essay on fads and fashions has been excerpted so as to focus attention on his discussion of popular music (in its original form the piece also considers publishing and cinema at greater length). Hirsch uses concepts from organization theory to study the interrelation between music production and the promotion of pop via the mass media—a concern that has proved to be of increasingly empirical importance in understanding contemporary pop music.

Peterson and Berger's highly influential study argues that pop production is a cyclical process governed by organizational determinants which derive from the competition between the major record companies and their smaller rivals. Their study is interesting for its attempt to link organizational and textual issues, since they conclude that musical diversity is related to the breadth of marketplace competition—and vice versa. This view has been challenged by some critics, and the debate is taken up elsewhere in this collection, by Barbara Bradby.

Wallis and Malm explore the international perspective through the concept of "cultural imperialism." The debate about this approach is a key one in modern pop studies,[1] and Wallis and Malm's study contributes to this in being both empirically founded (upon the "Music Industry in Small Countries" research project) and open-minded in its judgment on the possible effects of the internationalization of pop. Their concluding comments anticipate the burgeoning world music (or world beat) movement that has surfaced throughout the West in recent years. Once again, even in international perspective, the centrality of the mass media is stressed as a factor in understanding the workings of today's music industry.

NOTES

1 Dave Laing, "The Music Industry and the 'Cultural Imperialism Thesis,'" *Media, Culture & Society 8*, No. 3 (July 1986).

Paul M. Hirsch

PROCESSING FADS AND FASHIONS

An Organization-Set Analysis of Cultural Industry Systems

1 9 7 2

○ ▲ ○ ▲ ○ ▲ ○

DEFINITIONS AND CONCEPTUAL FRAMEWORK

Cultural products may be defined tentatively as "nonmaterial" goods directed at a public of consumers, for whom they generally serve an aesthetic or expressive, rather than a clearly utilitarian, function. Insofar as one of its goals is to create and satisfy consumer demand for new fads and fashions, every consumer industry is engaged to some extent in the production of cultural goods, and any consumer good can thus be placed along the implied continuum between cultural and utilitarian products. The two poles, however, should be intuitively distinct. Movies, plays, books, art prints, phonograph records, and pro football games are predominantly cultural products; each is nonmaterial in the sense that it embodies a live, one-of-a-kind performance and/or contains a unique set of ideas. Foods and detergents, on the other hand, serve more obvious utilitarian needs. The term "cultural organization" refers here only to *profit-seeking firms producing cultural products for national distribution.* Noncommercial or strictly local organizations, such as university presses and athletic teams, respectively, are thus excluded from consideration. A fundamental difference between entrepreneurial organizations and nonprofit agencies is summarized by Toffler:

> In the non-profit sector the end-product is most frequently a live performance— a concert, a recital, a play. If for purposes of economic analysis we consider a

live performance to be a commodity, we are immediately struck by the fact that, unlike most commodities offered for sale in our society, this commodity is not standardized. It is not machine made. It is a handicrafted item. . . . Contrast the output of the non-profit performing arts with that of the record manufacturer. He, too, sells what appears to be a performance. But it is not. It is a replica of a performance, a mass-produced embodiment of a performance. . . . The book publisher, in effect, does the same. The original manuscript of the poem or novel represents the author's work of art, the individual, the prototype. The book in which it is subsequently embodied is a [manufactured] replica of the original. Its form of production is fully in keeping with the level of technology in the surrounding society.[1]

Our frame of reference is the cultural industry system, comprised of all organizations engaged in the process of filtering new products and ideas as they flow from "creative" personnel in the technical subsystem to the managerial, institutional, and societal levels of organization.[2] Each industry system is seen as a single, concrete, and stable network of identifiable and interacting components. The concept of organization levels, proposed initially to analyze transactions within the boundaries of a single, large-scale organization, is easily applied to the analysis of interorganizational systems. Artist and mass audience are linked by an ordered sequence of events: before it can elicit any audience response, an art object first must succeed in (a) competition against others for selection and promotion by an entrepreneurial organization, and then in (b) receiving mass media coverage in such forms as book reviews, radio station airplay, and film criticism. It must be ordered by retail outlets for display or exhibition to consumers and, ideally, its author or performer will appear on television talk shows and be written up as an interesting news story. Drawing on a functionalist model of organizational control and facilitation of innovations proposed by Boskoff, we view the mass media in their gatekeeping role as a primary "institutional regulator of innovation."[3]

A number of concepts and assumptions implicit in this paper are taken from the developing field of interorganizational relations and elaborated on more fully by Thompson.[4] Studies in this emerging tradition typically view all phenomena from the standpoint of the organization under analysis. They seldom inquire into the functions performed by the organization for the social system but ask rather, as temporary partisans, how the goals of the organization may be constrained by society. The organization is assumed to act under norms of rationality, and the subject of analysis becomes its forms of adaptation to constraints imposed by its technology and "task environment." The term "organization-set" has been proposed by Evan[5] as analogous to the role-set concept developed by Merton[6] for analyzing role relationships:

Instead of taking a particular status as the unit of analysis, as Merton does in his role-set analysis, I take . . . an organization, or a class of organizations, and trace its interactions with the network of organizations in its environment, i.e., with elements of its organization-set. As a partial social system, a focal organization depends on input organizations for various types of resources: personnel, matériel, capital, legality, and legitimacy. . . . The focal organization in turn produces a product or a service for a market, an audience, a client system, etc.[7]

After examining transactions between the focal organization and elements of its task environment, I will describe three adaptive strategies developed by cultural organizations to minimize uncertainty. Finally, variations within each industry will be reviewed.

INPUT AND OUTPUT ORGANIZATION-SETS

The publishing house, movie studio, and record company each invests entrepreneurial capital in the creations and services of affiliated organizations and individuals at its input (product selection) and output (marketing) boundaries. Each affects volume sales by linking individual creators and producer organizations with receptive consumers and mass media gatekeepers. New material is sought constantly because of the rapid turnover of books, films, and recordings.

Cultural organizations constitute the managerial subsystems of the industry systems in which they must operate. From a universe of innovations proposed by "artists" in the "creative" (technical) subsystem, they select ("discover") a sample of cultural products for organizational sponsorship and promotion. A distinctive feature of cultural industry systems at the present time is the organizational segregation of functional units and subsystems. In the production sector, the technical and managerial levels of organization are linked by boundary-spanning talent scouts—for example, acquisitions editors, record "producers," and film directors—located on the input boundary of the focal organization.

To this point, cultural industries resemble the construction industry and other organization systems characterized by what Stinchcombe calls "craft administration of production." The location of professionals in the technical subsystem, and administrators in the managerial one, indicates that production may be organized along craft rather than bureaucratic lines.[8] In the cultural industry system, lower-level personnel (artists and talent scouts) are accorded professional status and seldom are associated with any one focal organization for long time periods. Although company executives may tamper with the final product of their collaborations, contracted artists and talent scouts are *delegated* the responsibility of producing marketable creations, with little or no interference from the front office beyond the setting of budgetary limits.[9] Due to widespread uncertainty over the precise ingredients of a bestseller formula, administrators are forced to trust the professional judgment of their employees. Close supervision in the production sector is impeded by ignorance of relations between cause and effect.[10] A highly placed spokesman for the recording industry has stated the problem as follows:

> We have made records that appeared to have all the necessary ingredients— artist, song, arrangements, promotion, etc.—to guarantee they wind up as best sellers. . . . Yet they fell flat on their faces. On the other hand we have produced records for which only a modest success was anticipated that became runaway best sellers. . . . There are a large number of companies in our industry employing a large number of talented performers and creative producers who combine their talents, their ingenuity and their creativity to produce a record that each is sure will captivate the American public. The fact that only a small proportion of the output achieves hit status is not only true of our industry. . . . There are no formulas for producing a hit record . . . just as there are no pat answers for producing hit plays, or sell-out movies or best-selling books.[11]

Stinchcombe's association of craft administration with a minimization of fixed overhead costs is supported in the case of cultural organizations.[12] Here we find, for example, artists (i.e., authors, singers, actors) contracted on a *royalty* basis and offered no tenure beyond the expiration of the contract. Remuneration (less advance payment on royalties) is contingent on the number of books, records, or theater tickets sold *after* the artist's product is released into the marketplace. In addition, movie-production companies minimize overhead by hiring on a per-picture basis and renting sets and costumes as needed,[13] and publishers and record companies frequently subcontract out standardized printing and record-pressing jobs.

The organization of cultural industries' technical subsystems along craft lines is a function of (a) demand uncertainty and (b) a "cheap" technology. Demand uncertainty is caused by shifts in consumer taste preferences and patronage; legal and normative constraints on vertical integration; and widespread variability in the criteria employed by mass media gatekeepers in selecting cultural items to be awarded coverage.[14] A cheap technology enables numerous cultural organizations to compete in producing a surplus of books, records, and low-budget films on relatively small capital investments. Mass media exposure and volume sales of a single item generally cover earlier losses and yield additional returns. Sponsoring organizations tend to judge the success of each new book or record on the basis of its performance in the marketplace during the first six weeks of its release. Movies require a far more substantial investment but follow a similar pattern.

These sources of variance best account for the craft administration of production at the input boundary of the cultural organization. It is interesting to note that in an earlier, more stable environment, that is, less heterogeneous markets and fewer constraints on vertical integration, the production of both films and popular records was administered more bureaucratically: lower-level personnel were delegated less responsibility, overhead costs were less often minimized, and the status of artists resembled more closely the salaried employee's than the freelance professional's.[15]

At their output boundaries, cultural organizations confront high levels of uncertainty concerning the commercial prospects of goods shipped out to national networks of promoters and distributors. Stratification within each industry is based partly on each firm's ability to control the distribution of marginally differentiated products. Competitive advantage lies with firms best able to link available input to reliable and established distribution channels.

The mass distribution of cultural items requires more *bureaucratic* organizational arrangements than the administration of production—for example, a higher proportion of salaried clerks to process information, greater continuity of personnel and ease of supervision, less delegation of responsibility, and higher fixed overhead.[16] Whereas the building contractor produces custom goods to meet the specifications of a clearly defined client-set, cultural organizations release a wide variety of items that must be publicized and made attractive to thousands of consumers in order to succeed. Larger organizations generally maintain their own sales forces, which may contract with smaller firms to distribute their output as well as the parent company's.

The more highly bureaucratized distribution sector of cultural industries is characterized by more economic concentration than the craft-administered production sector, where lower costs pose fewer barriers to entry. Although heavy expenditures required for product promotion and marketing may be reduced by contracting with independent sales organizations on a commission basis, this practice is engaged in primarily by smaller, weaker, and poorly capitalized firms.

Contracting with autonomous sales organizations places the entrepreneurial firm in a position of dependence on outsiders, with the attendant risk of having cultural products that are regarded highly by the sponsoring organization assigned a low priority by its distributor. In the absence of media coverage and/or advertising by the sponsoring organization, retail outlets generally fail to stock new books or records.

A functional equivalent of direct advertising for cultural organizations is provided by the selective coverage afforded new styles and titles in books, recordings, and movies by the mass media. Cultural products provide "copy" and "programming" for newspapers, magazines, radio stations, and television programs; in exchange, they receive "free" publicity. The presence or absence of coverage, rather than its favorable or unfavorable interpretation, is the important variable here. Public awareness of the existence and availability of a new cultural product often is contingent on feature stories in newspapers and national magazines, review columns, and broadcast talk shows, and, for recordings, radio station airplay. While the total number of products to be awarded media coverage may be predicted in the aggregate, the estimation of *which ones* will be selected from the potential universe is problematic.

The organizational segregation of the producers of cultural items from their disseminators places definite restrictions on the forms of power that cultural organizations may exercise over mass media gatekeepers to effect the selection of particular items for coverage. Widely shared social norms mandate the independence of book review editors, radio station personnel, film critics, and other arbiters of coverage from the special needs and commercial interests of cultural organizations.[17] Thus, autonomous gatekeepers present the producer organization with the "control" problem of favorably influencing the probability that a given new release will be selected for exposure to consumers.

For publishing houses and record firms, especially, it would be uneconomical to engage in direct, large-scale advertising campaigns to bring more than a few releases to public attention.

> Record companies are dependent on radio . . . to introduce new artists as well as to introduce new records of all artists and to get them exposed to the public. . . . [We] cannot expose their performances because it's just on grooves and the public will not know what they sound like. (Q.) "Would it be fair to say that radio accounts for 75, or 90 percent of the promotion of new releases?" (A.) I think your figures are probably accurate, yes.[18]

For book publishers, record companies, and, to a lesser extent, movie studios, then, the crucial target audience for promotional campaigns consists of autonomous gatekeepers, or "surrogate consumers" such as disc jockeys, film critics, and book reviewers, employed by mass media organizations to serve as fashion experts and opinion leaders for their respective constituencies.

The mass media constitute the institutional subsystem of the cultural industry system. *The diffusion of particular fads and fashions is either blocked or facilitated at this strategic checkpoint.* Cultural innovations are seen as originating in the technical subsystem. A sample selected for sponsorship by cultural organizations in the managerial subsystem is introduced into the marketplace. This output is filtered by mass media gatekeepers serving as "institutional regulators of innovation." Organizations in the managerial subsystem are highly responsive to feedback from institutional regulators: styles afforded coverage are imitated and reproduced on a large scale until the fad has "run its course."[19]

We see the consumer's role in this process as essentially one of rank-ordering cultural styles and items "preselected" for consideration by role occupants in the managerial and institutional subsystems. Feedback from consumers, in the form of sales figures and box office receipts, cues producers and disseminators of cultural innovations as to which experiments may be imitated profitably and which should probably be dropped. This process is analogous to the preselection of electoral candidates by political parties, followed by voter feedback at the ballot box. The orderly sequence of events and the possibility of only two outcomes at each checkpoint resemble a Markov process.

This model assumes a surplus of available "raw material" at the outset (e.g., writers, singers, politicians) and pinpoints a number of strategic checkpoints at which the oversupply is filtered out. It is "value added" in the sense that no product can enter the societal subsystem (e.g., retail outlets) until it has been processed favorably through each of the preceding levels of organization, respectively.

ORGANIZATIONAL RESPONSE TO TASK-ENVIRONMENT UNCERTAINTIES

My analysis suggests that organizations at the managerial level of cultural industry systems are confronted by (1) constraints on output distribution imposed by mass media gatekeepers and (2) contingencies in recruiting creative "raw materials" for organizational sponsorship. To minimize dependence on these elements of their task environments, publishing houses, record companies, and movie studios have developed three proactive strategies: (1) the allocation of numerous personnel to boundary-spanning roles; (2) overproduction and differential promotion of new items; and (3) cooptation of mass media gatekeepers.

Proliferation of Contact Men

Entrepreneurial organizations in cultural industries require competent intelligence agents and representatives to actively monitor developments at their input and output boundaries. Inability to locate and successfully market new cultural items leads to organizational failure: new manuscripts must be located, new singers recorded, and new movies produced. Boundary-spanning units have therefore been established, and a large proportion of personnel allocated to serve as "contact men,"[20] with titles such as talent scout, promoter, press coordinator, and vice-president in charge of public relations. The centrality of information on boundary developments to managers and executives in cultural organizations is suggested in these industries' trade papers: coverage of artist relations and selections by mass media gatekeepers far exceeds that of matters managed more easily in a standardized manner, such as inflation in warehousing, shipping, and physical production costs.

Contact men linking the cultural organization to the artist community contract for creative raw material on behalf of the organization and supervise its production. Much of their work is performed in the field.

Professional agents on the input boundary must be allowed a great deal of discretion in their activities on behalf of the cultural organization. Successful editors, record "producers," and film directors and producers thus pose control problems for the focal organization. In fields characterized by uncertainty over cause-and-effect relations, their talent has been "validated" by the successful marketplace performance of "their discoveries"—providing high visibility and opportunities for mobility outside a single firm. Their value to the cultural organization as recruiters and intelligence agents is indicated by high salaries, commissions, and prestige within the industry system.

Cultural organizations deploy additional contact men at their output boundaries, linking the organization to (1) retail outlets and (2) surrogate consumers in mass media organizations. The tasks of promoting and distributing new cultural items are analytically distinct, although boundary units combining both functions may be established. Transactions between retailers and boundary personnel at the wholesale level are easily programmed and supervised. In terms of Thompson's typology of output transactions, the retailer's "degree of nonmember discretion" is limited to a small number of fixed options concerning such matters as discount schedules and return privileges.[21] In contrast, where organizations are dependent on "surrogate consumers" for coverage of new products, the latter enjoy a high degree of discretion: tactics employed by contact men at this boundary entail more "personal influence"; close supervision by the organization is more difficult and may be politically inexpedient. Further development of Thompson's typology would facilitate tracing the flow of innovations through organization systems by extending the analysis of transactions "at the end of the line"—that is, between salespeople and consumers or bureaucrats and clients—to encompass boundary transactions at all levels of organization through which new products are processed.

A high ratio of promotional personnel to surrogate consumers appears to be a structural feature of any industry system in which (a) goods are marginally differentiated; (b) producers' access to consumer markets is regulated by independent gatekeepers; and (c) large-scale, *direct* advertising campaigns are uneconomical or prohibited by law. Cultural products are advertised *indirectly* to independent gatekeepers within the industry system in order to reduce demand uncertainty over which products will be selected for exposure to consumers. Where independent gatekeepers neither filter information nor mediate between producer and consumer, the importance of contact men at the organization's output boundary is correspondingly diminished. In industry systems where products are advertised more directly to consumers, the contact man is superseded by full-page advertisements and sponsored commercials, purchased outright by the producer organization and directed at the lay consumer.

Overproduction and Differential Promotion of Cultural Items

Differential promotion of new items, in conjunction with overproduction, is a second proactive strategy employed by cultural organizations to overcome dependence on mass media gatekeepers. Overproduction is a rational organizational response in an environment of low capital investments and demand uncertainty.

Under these conditions it is apparently more efficient to produce many "failures" for each success than to sponsor fewer items and pretest each on a massive scale to increase media coverage and consumer sales. The number of books, records, and low-budget films released annually far exceeds coverage capacity and consumer demand for these products. Fewer than 20 percent of over 6,000 (45 rpm) "singles" appear in retail record outlets.[22] Movie theaters exhibit a larger proportion of approximately 400 feature films released annually, fewer than half of which, however, are believed to recoup the initial investment. The production of a surplus is facilitated further by contracts negotiated with artists on a royalty basis and other cost-minimizing features of the craft administration of production.

Cultural organizations ideally maximize profits by mobilizing promotional resources in support of volume sales for a small number of items. These resources are not divided equally among each firm's new releases. Only a small proportion of all new books and records "sponsored" by cultural organizations are selected by company policymakers for large-scale promotion within the industry system. In the record industry:

> The strategy of massive promotion is employed by policymakers in an attempt to influence the coverage of their product by media over which they exert little control. They must rely on independently owned trade papers to bring new records to the attention of radio programmers and disk jockeys, and upon radio airplay and journalists to reach the consumer market. For this reason, selected artists are sent to visit key radio stations, and parties are arranged in cities throughout the country to bring together the artist and this advanced audience. It seems likely that if . . . . policymakers could better predict exposure for particular releases, then fewer would be recorded. . . . Records are released (1) with no advance publicity, (2) with minimal fanfare, or (3) only after a large-scale advance promotional campaign. The extent of a record's promotion informs

the policymakers' immediate audience of regional promoters and Top 40 pro-grammers of their expectations for, and evaluation of, their product. In this way the company rank orders its own material. The differential promotion of records serves to sensitize Top 40 programmers to the names of certain songs and artists. Heavily promoted records are publicized long before their release through full-page advertisements in the trade press, special mailings, and personal appearances by the recording's artists. The program director is made familiar with the record long before he receives it. It is "expected" to be a hit. In this way, though radio stations receive records gratis, anticipation and "demand" for selected releases are created. . . . The best indicator of a record's potential for becoming a hit at this stage is the amount of promotion it is allocated.[23]

Most cultural items are allocated minimal amounts for promotion and are "expected" to fail. Such long shots constitute a pool of "understudies," from which substitutes may be drawn in the event that either mass media gate-keepers or consumers reject more heavily plugged items. I see the strategy of differential promotion as an attempt by cultural organizations to "buffer" their technical core from demand uncertainties by smoothing out output transactions.[24]

Co-optation of "Institutional Regulators"

Mass media gatekeepers report a wide variety of mechanisms developed by cultural organizations to influence and manipulate their coverage deci-sions. These range from "indications" by the sponsoring organization of high expectations for particular new "discoveries" (e.g., full-page adver-tisements in the trade press, parties arranged to introduce the artist to recognized opinion leaders) to personal requests and continuous barrages of indirect advertising, encouraging and cajoling the gatekeeper to "cover," endorse, and otherwise contribute toward the fulfillment of the organiza-tion's prophecy of great success for its new product.

The goals of cultural and mass media organizations come into conflict over two issues. First, public opinion, professional ethics, and, to a lesser extent, job security all require that institutional gatekeepers maintain in-dependent standards of judgment and quality rather than endorse only those items which cultural organizations elect to promote. Second, the primary goal of commercial mass media organizations is to maximize revenue by "delivering" audiences for sponsored messages rather than to serve as pro-motional vehicles for particular cultural items. Hit records, for example, are featured by commercial radio stations primarily to sell advertising:

Q: Do you play this music because it is the most popular?
A: Exactly for that reason. . . . We use the entertainment part of our programming, which is music, essentially, to attract the largest possible audience, so that what

else we have to say . . . in terms of advertising message . . . [is] exposed to the largest number of people possible—and the way to get the largest number to tune in is to play the kind of music they like . . . so that you have a mass audience at the other end.

Q: If, let's say that by some freak of nature, a year from now the most popular music was chamber music, would you be playing that?

A: Absolutely . . . , and the year after that, if it's Chinese madrigals, we'll be playing them.[25]

Goal conflict and value dissensus are reflected in frequent disputes among cultural organizations, mass media gatekeepers, and public representatives concerning the legitimacy (or legality) of promoters' attempts to acquire power over the decision autonomy of surrogate consumers.

Cultural organizations strive to control gatekeepers' decision autonomy to the extent that coverage for new items is (a) crucial for building consumer demand and (b) problematic. Promotional campaigns aimed at co-opting institutional gatekeepers are most likely to require proportionately large budgets and illegitimate tactics when consumers' awareness of the product hinges almost exclusively on coverage by these personnel. As noted earlier, cultural organizations are less likely to deploy boundary agents or sanction high-pressure tactics for items whose sale is less contingent on gatekeepers' actions.

VARIABILITY WITHIN CULTURAL INDUSTRIES

Up to this point, I have tended to minimize variability among cultural organizations, cultural products, and the markets at which they are directed. My generalizations apply mainly to the most *speculative* and entrepreneurial segments of the publishing, recording, and motion picture industries: that is, adult trade books, popular records, and low-budget movies. Within each of these categories, organizations subscribe, in varying degrees, to normative as well as to the more economic goals I have assumed thus far. Certain publishing houses, record companies, and movie producers command high prestige within each industry system for financing cultural products of high quality but of doubtful commercial value. To the extent they do *not* conform to economic norms of rationality, these organizations should be considered separately from the more dominant pattern of operations described earlier.

Coverage in the form of radio station airplay is far more crucial in building consumer demand for recordings of popular music than for classical selections. Control over the selection of new "pop" releases by radio station programmers and disc jockeys is highly problematic. Record companies are dependent on radio airplay as the *only* effective vehicle of exposure for new pop records. In this setting—where access to consumers hinges almost exclusively on coverage decisions by autonomous gatekeepers—institution-alized side payments ("payola") emerged as a central tactic in the overall strategy of co-optation employed by producer organizations to assure desired coverage.

Radio airplay for classical records is less crucial for building consumer demand; the probability of obtaining coverage for classical releases is also easier to estimate. Whereas producers and consumers of pop records are often unsure about a song's likely sales appeal or musical worth, criteria of both musical merit and consumer demand are comparatively clear in the classical field. Record companies, therefore, allocate proportionately fewer promotional resources to assure coverage of classical releases by mass media gatekeepers, and record company agents promoting classical releases employ more legitimate tactics to influence coverage decisions than promoters of pop records employ to co-opt the decision autonomy of institutional regulators.

Thompson has proposed that "when support capacity is concentrated but demand dispersed, the weaker organization will attempt to handle its dependence through coopting."[26] In my analysis, cultural organizations represent a class of weaker organizations, dependent on support capacity concentrated in mass media organizations; demand is dispersed among retail outlets and consumers. While all cultural organizations attempt to co-opt autonomous consumer surrogates, the intensity of the tactics employed tends to vary with degree of dependence. Thus, cultural organizations most dependent on mass media gatekeepers (i.e., companies producing pop records) resorted to the most costly and illegitimate tactics; the institution of payola may be seen as an indication of their weaker power position.

NOTES

[1] Alvin Toffler, *The Culture Consumers* (Baltimore: Penguin, 1965).

[2] Talcott Parsons, *Structure and Process in Modern Societies* (Glencoe, Ill.: Free Press, 1960).

[3] Alvin Boskoff, "Functional Analysis as a Source of a Theoretical Repertory and Research Tasks in the Study of Social Change," in George K. Zollschan and Walter Hirsch (eds.), *Explorations in Social Change* (Boston: Houghton Mifflin, 1964).

[4] James D. Thompson, *Organizations in Action* (New York: McGraw-Hill, 1967).

[5] William M. Evan, "Toward a Theory of Inter-organizational Relations," *Management Science 11* (1963), pp. B217–30; reprinted in James D. Thompson (ed.), *Approaches to Organizational Design* (Pittsburgh: University of Pittsburgh Press, 1966).

[6] Robert K. Merton, *Social Theory and Social Structure*, rev. ed. (Glencoe, Ill.: Free Press, 1957).

[7] Evan, "Inter-organizational Relations," pp. 177–79.

[8] Arthur L. Stinchcombe, "Bureaucratic and Craft Administration of Production: A Comparative Study," *Administrative Science Quarterly 4* (September 1959), pp. 168–87.

[9] Richard Peterson and David Berger, "Entrepreneurship in Organizations: Evidence from the Popular Music Industry," *Administrative Science Quarterly 16* (March 1971), pp. 97–107.

[10] "Production" here refers to the performances or manuscripts created by artists and talent

scouts for later replication in the form of books, film-negative prints, and phonograph records. The physical manufacture of these goods is sufficiently amenable to control as to be nearly irrelevant to this discussion.

[11] Henry Brief, *Radio and Records: A Presentation by the Record Industry Association of America at the 1964 Regional Meetings of the National Association of Broadcasters* (New York: Record Industry Association of America, 1964).

[12] Stinchcombe, "Bureaucratic and Craft Administration"; and *Constructing Social Theories* (New York: Harcourt, Brace & World, 1968).

[13] Stinchcombe, *Constructing Social Theories*.

[14] Paul M. Hirsch, *The Structure of the Popular Music Industry* (Ann Arbor: Survey Research Center, University of Michigan, 1969).

[15] Roger L. Brown, "The Creative Process in the Popular Arts," *International Social Science Journal 20*, No. 4 (1968), pp. 613–24; Peterson and Berger, "Entrepreneurship."

[16] Stinchcombe, "Bureaucratic and Craft Administration."

[17] Public reaction to the "payola" scandals in the late 1950s demonstrated a widespread belief that the disseminators of mass culture should be independent of its producers. Disc jockeys, book reviewers, and film critics are expected to remain free from the influence or manipulations of record companies, book publishers, and movie studios, respectively. This feeling is shared generally by members of each industry system and is embodied as well in our legal system.

[18] Clive Davis, "The Truth about Radio: A WNEW Inquiry," mimeograph (New York: WNEW, 1967), p. 5. This is a transcript of an interview with the general manager of CBS Records.

[19] Boskoff, "Functional Analysis"; Rolf Meyersohn and Elihu Katz, "Notes on a Natural History of Fads," *American Journal of Sociology 62* (May 1957), pp. 594–601.

[20] Harold Wilensky, *Intellectuals in Labor Unions* (Glencoe, Ill.: Free Press, 1956).

[21] James D. Thompson, "Organizations and Output Transactions," *American Journal of Sociology 68* (November 1962), pp. 309–24. Sponsoring organizations that lack access to established channels of distribution, however, experience great difficulty in obtaining orders for their products from retail outlets and consumers. Thompson's typology of interaction between organization members and nonmembers consists of two dimensions: degree of nonmember discretion, and specificity of organizational control over members in output roles. Output roles are defined as those that arrange for the distribution of an organization's ultimate product (or service) to other agents in society.

[22] Sidney Schemel and M. William Krasilovsky, *This Business of Music* (New York: Billboard) 1964.

[23] Hirsch, *Popular Music Industry*, pp. 34, 36.

[24] Thompson, *Organizations in Action*.

[25] Peter R. Strauss, "The Truth about Radio: A WNEW Inquiry," mimeograph (New York: WNEW, 1966).

[26] Thompson, *Organizations in Action*, p. 36.

● Richard A. Peterson and David G. Berger ●

CYCLES IN SYMBOL PRODUCTION

The Case of Popular Music

1 9 7 5

○ ▲ ○ ▲ ○ ▲ ○

This study examines two related questions: (1) the relationship between market concentration and homogeneity of the cultural product and (2) the form of the changes in these variables over time. Focusing on one symbol-producing domain, popular music, it will be possible to identify a number of the specific mechanisms that condition the associations that are observed. The popular music industry is a strategic research site for a number of reasons. There are more systematic data available over time than in the case of any of the "fine arts" where creations are not mass produced. More systematic data are available than for television, movies, or popular magazines, because the record output of the music industry is the input for the radio and jukebox industries. Thus, trade magazines publish weekly performance figures for currently popular records and periodically aggregate these data. Finally, the record industry is convenient because it has received more scholarly attention than any other popular arts industry. There have been periodic analyses of the ideological content of lyrics, and studies of the complex structure of the industry and its changes over time.

This study examines the 26-year period from 1948 to 1973. Nineteen forty-eight was chosen as the initial year for three reasons: by that year the materials shortages caused by the war and pent-up consumer demand had been eliminated; the protracted and stormy labor negotiations with the American Federation of Musicians' President Petrillo, had been successfully completed, making possible the uninterrupted production of records; and finally, the 45 and 33⅓ rpm record formats had been established.[1]

To facilitate discussion, the 26-year period under investigation has been divided into five eras of unequal duration. The cutting points have been determined by inspecting the four- and eight-firm concentration ratios (Table 1, columns 4 and 5). For each era, three questions will be addressed. What is the level of market concentration? What are the mechanisms that make for the observed level of concentration? And finally, what is the corresponding level of innovation and diversity in the music produced? Specific segments of Tables 1 and 2 will be cited throughout the paper as appropriate.

CORPORATE CONCENTRATION: 1948—1955

In the eight-year period from 1948 to 1955, the record music industry was dominated by four firms: RCA Victor, Columbia, Decca, and Capitol.[2] They controlled the Broadway musical, country, and classical music record market to which all of our data refer unless otherwise indicated.

Few firms had hits on more than one of the labels that they owned in the 1948–55 era, as can be seen by comparing columns 1 and 2 of Table 1. The weekly Top 10 charts were completely filled by as few as eight and no more than fourteen firms, and in 1955 when fourteen reached the Top 10, half of these had but one hit during the year. The annual proportion of all hits owned by the four leading companies, what economists call the "four-firm concentration ratio,"[3] was declining slowly over the period but remained above 70 percent. That these data for the hit singles market are representative of the total industry as well is suggested by a *Fortune* survey (May 1961) which estimates that in 1948 the four major companies controlled over 75 percent of the total record market. As column 5 of Table 1 shows, the top eight firms accounted for virtually all of the hit singles during the period.

Such concentration ratios are high as compared with other manufacturing industries. While some, including autos, electrical lamps, and chewing gum, have four-firm concentration ratios above 90, a United States government survey of 416 manufacturing industries found that only 6.5 percent have concentration ratios greater than 80, and an additional 11.3 percent have concentration ratios above 60.[4] The market concentration ratio in the record industry is surprisingly high, especially when one considers that the final product, a 45 rpm record, is nothing more than a song stamped in plastic. It could be created for as little as two or three hundred dollars, and could be manufactured and marketed for a few thousand more, thus affording no barrier to companies desiring to enter the market. Patent law and copyright

TABLE 1
NUMBER OF FIRMS AND MARKET SHARES IN THE WEEKLY TOP 10 OF
THE POPULAR MUSIC SINGLE RECORD MARKET, BY YEAR

COLUMN	1	2	3	4	5
				CONCENTRATION RATIO	
YEAR	LABELS	FIRMS	FIRMS WITH ONLY ONE HIT	4-FIRM	8-FIRM
1948	11	11	5	81	95
1949	9	8	3	89	100
1950	11	10	3	76	97
1951	10	8	2	82	100
1952	12	11	5	77	95
1953	12	11	3	71	94
1954	13	12	4	73	93
1955	16	14	7	74	91
1956	22	20	10	66	76
1957	28	23	8	40	65
1958	35	31	19	36	60
1959	46	42	29	34	58
1960	45	39	20	28	52
1961	48	39	16	27	48
1962	52	41	21	25	46
1963	52	36	15	26	55
1964	53	37	17	34	51
1965	50	35	16	37	61
1966	49	31	13	38	61
1967	51	35	15	40	60
1968	46	30	17	42	61
1969	48	31	14	42	64
1970	41	23	5	51	71
1971	46	21	7	45	67
1972	49	20	5	48	68
1973	42	19	4	57	81

regulations afforded no protection of oligopoly during this period.[5] What then, were the barriers to effective competition in the 1948–55 era?

VERTICAL INTEGRATION

Based on much evidence, we will argue that the four large firms did not maintain their dominance over the market by continually offering the product that consumers most wanted to purchase. Rather, oligopolistic concentration of the record industry was maintained by control of the total production flow from raw materials to wholesale sales. This is a strategy that economists call "vertical integration."[6] The effectiveness of vertical integration can be seen by examining how it helped to reduce competition at three key points in the production process: the artistic factor, merchandising, and distribution.

The major firms tried to monopolize artistic factors, including songwriting, publishing, and performing talent.[7] In and of itself, this strategy would not have been successful because substitutes for these artistic factors could always be found. Over the years, new independent firms have secured a market position based initially on the talents of a single artist or group. Examples include Decca in 1934 with Bing Crosby, A&M in 1961 with Herb Alpert and his Tiajuana Brass, and Capricorn in 1972 with the Allman Brothers Band.

While absolute control of the artistic sector was impossible, the high market concentration during the 1948–55 era was guaranteed by the control of two key areas "downstream" in the production process. The four leading companies controlled the media of merchandising music and the channels for distributing records. In 1948 new songs were merchandised by inclusion in musical movies, Broadway productions, live network radio variety programs (such as that hosted by Jack Benny), and recorded music programs (such as Martin Block's WNEW "Makebelieve Ballroom").

The big four record companies used each of these media to great advantage, and they were able to do so because of their corporate links with radio and movie firms. RCA Victor was linked with the NBC network and a number of radio stations. In addition, it was corporately affiliated with the RKO Film company.[8] Columbia also had its own network, CBS. Decca was affiliated with the Music Corporation of America, a powerful Hollywood movie and radio talent agency, and eventually it came to own Universal movie studios as well. Capitol Records was linked to Paramount Pictures until 1950. Two other entrants into the record market in this era, MGM Records and ABC-Paramount, were branches of movie firms (the latter originally formed as a combine with the American Broadcasting Company.) In this era the major companies offered disc jockeys various sorts of inducements to feature their releases, a practice that was stigmatized as "payola" and was made explicitly illegal only much later in the 1950s, when many new independent record companies imitated the practices of the majors.[9]

The second means that the majors used to maintain their market position was monopolization of the channels of record distribution. Each of the majors maintained a system of wholesale dealerships, warehouses, and record jobbers. While they did not own many retail record outlets, they could discourage individual retailers from handling the records of independent companies by threatening to delay shipments of their own most fast-moving records. Mercury Records, a Chicago-based company formed in 1947, was the only independent firm to garner a significant share of the market in this era. It is reputed to have used the channels of organized crime to market its product and force its records on jukebox operators.[10]

Another standard tactic used by the major companies was quickly to record and market a version of a fast-selling song recorded by another oligopolist or independent company. These are called "cover" records. Column 2 of Table 2 shows the frequency with which multiple recordings of the same tune reached the Top 10 in this early era. With their more systematic channels of distribution, the major companies were often able to co-opt the hit of an independent and drive it out of the market. Analyzing data from the entire *Billboard* popular singles chart, Anderson and Hesbacher find that as many as seven versions of a song were charted, and fully 70 percent of the songs had more than one version reach the chart during the years 1946–50.[11] Beginning in 1952, black rhythm and blues performers were most often the victims of the cover tactic, but it was a longstanding practice.[12] The 1947 hit songs "Near You" and "Open the Door, Richard" are good cases in point. Both were first released by independent companies. Both were covered by the four major companies, and both had five versions in the Top 10 record charts in a period of several weeks.[13] These cases not only illustrate a tactic the majors used to maintain market control, but it also suggests one of the consequences of their dominance, a homogeneity of cultural products.

HOMOGENEITY OF PRODUCT

Did the oligopolistic concentration of the industry during the 1948–55 era correlate with homogeneity in cultural output, as predicted? Uncontestable evidence is difficult to generate. One judge's homogeneity may be another's diversity. Two types of evidence will be examined to confront this question. The first involves the sheer number of records and performers reaching the Top 10 weekly charts. The second concerns the lyrical content of hit records.

Table 2 presents the data on records and performers. It shows that during the era, between 48 and 66 records made the weekly Top 10 hit list per year and that the number nearly doubled in subsequent years. The table also shows that cover records were a significant part of the charts during the era, but disappeared entirely by 1958. Column 3 shows the number of records to become "Number 1" during the year. For the early period, the average was ten. Thus, records retained the top chart position for an average of over five weeks. By contrast in three recent years, hits have averaged less than two weeks in the Number 1 chart position.

Columns 4, 5, and 6 of Table 2 deal with the artists who performed on the Top 10 records already discussed. In a period of oligopolistic control, one would expect the introduction of few new "products," in this case new performers. Column 4 shows that for the first five years of the era, between 22.9 and 38.8 percent of all Top 10 performers had their first hit that year. However, in the next two years the percentage of new performers exceeded 40 percent, and in 1955 it reached 57.4 percent. The data on "established performers"—those having Top 10 hits in at least three of the preceding four years—show the opposite trend. For 1948–49 over half of all performers were established hitmakers, but the figure dropped over the next five years and fell drastically in 1955 to 17 percent of the total. What this means is that a generation of hitmakers including Bing Crosby, the Mills Brothers, the Andrews Sisters, Vaughn Monroe, Les Brown, Dinah Shore, Jo Stafford, Mitch Miller, Doris Day, Tommy Dorsey, Tony Bennett, and many more were swept out of the popular music charts by 1955.

Evaluation of the content of any cultural product is hazardous. But a number of different sources agree on the homogeneity of popular music during the 1948–55 era. It was written by formula, and expressed a quite restricted range of sentiments in conventionalized ways.[14] Several systematic content analyses of lyrics of the music of this era substantiate the view of homogeneity. Donald Horton and David Berger both found that over 80 percent of all songs fit into a conventionalized love cycle where sexual references are allegorical and social problems are unknown.[15]

UNSATED DEMAND

The argument to this point is that market concentration creates a homogeneity of product. As long as the market-controlling mechanisms just described continue to operate unchanged, the trend to greater homogeneity continues because each of the oligopolists focuses on winning the greatest share of the mass market. As a result, the total market may be static or

TABLE 2
NUMBER OF RECORDS AND EXPERIENCE OF PERFORMERS IN THE
WEEKLY TOP 10 OF THE POPULAR MUSIC SINGLES RECORD MARKET
AND CHANGE IN AGGREGATE SALES, BY YEAR

COLUMN	1	2	3	4	5	6	7
				% OF PERFORMERS			% CHANGE IN
YEAR	RECORDS	COVER RECORDS	NUMBER 1 RECORDS	NEW	ESTABLISHED	FADING STAR	RECORD SALES IN CONSTANT DOLLARS
1948	57	14	9	29.3	48.8	30.0	− 20.4
1949	63	20	9	22.9	60.0	33.3	− 10.4
1950	66	21	12	38.8	40.8	30.0	+ 7.6
1951	51	6	8	29.4	44.1	53.3	− 2.3
1952	56	6	13	28.2	43.6	29.4	+ 4.8
1953	48	3	7	46.9	40.6	30.8	+ 1.5
1954	56	9	11	43.6	46.2	44.4	− 3.0
1955	62	11	9	57.4	17.0	50.0	+ 23.2
1956	59	4	11	55.3	19.1	77.8	+ 25.5
1957	70	3	16	70.0	10.0	40.0	+ 15.2
1958	77		15	61.0	10.2	66.7	+ 7.5
1959	92		15	73.1	11.9	25.0	+ 14.5
1960	95		18	60.3	14.7	40.0	− 2.1
1961	105		18	66.2	16.2	8.3	+ 5.3
1962	107		19	60.0	20.0	43.8	+ 5.8
1963	110		19	67.0	14.8	69.2	+ 0.4
1964	104		23	68.6	7.1	80.0	+ 6.7
1965	111		27	65.3	9.3	57.1	+ 10.5
1966	120		27	55.1	10.3	25.0	+ 16.3
1967	108		19	48.1	18.5	60.0	+ 9.2
1968	90		16	57.5	19.2	28.6	+ 17.9
1969	101		17	44.6	20.3	26.7	+ 2.1
1970	97		21	55.8	14.3	54.5	− 1.4
1971	94		19	61.3	14.7	63.6	+ 0.4
1972	101		22	57.1	11.9		+ 5.0
1973	98		28				− 4.5

even shrink because potential consumers, whose tastes are not met by the homogenized product, withdraw from the market. Thus under conditions of oligopoly, there is hypothesized to be a growing *unsated* demand. It is impossible to know exactly what music consumers would have bought during the 1948–55 era if they could have, but two quite different lines of inferential evidence suggest that the unsated demand was tremendous. The first has to do with the aggregate consumer expenditures for records, and the second involves the growth of alternative marketing mechanisms for providing music.

Music industry officials proudly point to the growth of aggregate record sales from $189 million in 1948 to almost $2 billion in 1973. When one adjusts these figures for changes in the cost of living and then computes the annual growth rate, the picture is not always quite so rosy (see column 7 of Table 2). While the great sales loss of 1948 may have been due to consumer confusion over the introduction of the 45 and LP format records, their great advantage over 78 rpm in audio fidelity, durability, and convenience should have made for great market advances in the succeeding years of general economic growth. Rather than increase, however, the adjusted aggregate sales for 1954 were slightly less than those of 1948! That there had been a great reservoir of unsated demands is suggested by the explosive five years of growth from 1955 to 1959, when industry sales increased by 261 percent.

Another indicator of unsated demand in the early 1950s is the proliferation of diverse kinds of what Peterson and Berger call "communal music—that is, music not merchandised through the mass media but disseminated primarily through live performance."[16] Jazz, rhythm and blues, country and western, gospel, trade union songs, and the urban folk revival are cited as examples. Following World War II, independent record companies catering to each of these kinds of music developed and flourished. By 1948 the popular music industry trade press began to take cognizance of both the country and western (country) and the rhythm and blues (soul) markets. As late as 1953, however, it did not see that the increasing interest in these styles might be an index of the audiences' growing disenchantment with the available popular music records,[17] an observation David Riesman had made as early as 1948.[18]

COMPETITION: 1956—1959

In 1955 rock 'n' roll, a guitar-based meld of soul and country music, burst onto the national popular music scene threatening to displace the brass and reed-based dance band music. In 1956 Elvis Presley, its most visible exponent, became a national media sensation. With the exception of Buddy Holly and Billy Haley, all of the new generation of "boppers" first recorded for independent recording companies founded in 1948 or thereafter.

Table 1 graphically shows the growth of competition from 1955 to 1959. The number of firms producing hits tripled, while the number of firms with just one hit quadrupled. At the same time, the four-firm concentration ratio was more than cut in half, dropping from 74 to 34, and the eight-firm concentration ratio dropped from 91 to 58.

To find the cause of this rapid shift to competition between 1955 and 1959, we must return to examine the two guarantors of oligopoly, control of record merchandising and distribution. In 1948 the U.S. Supreme Court finally decreed in a decade-long antitrust case that movie production companies had to divest themselves of their theater chains. In a single stroke, this blow to exclusive distribution ended the dominance of the eight major Hollywood film companies over the American movie industry. Moreover, by 1951 television was beginning to reduce movie attendance severely. These events had two distinct effects on the record industry. First, the movie companies curtailed the production of musicals that showcased new songs. Second, MGM, United Artists, Paramount, Warner Brothers, 20th Century Fox, and Columbia Pictures entered the recorded music industry.

While these record-making movie companies have become a significant element in the industry in recent years, only MGM was significant in the market during the 1956–59 period. The new competition did not come from the movie industry transfers but rather from a spate of underfinanced independent companies including Atlantic, Chess, Dot, Imperial, Monument, and Sun Records.[19]

MERCHANDISING VIA RADIO

The independents were able to establish a substantial market position primarily because the big four lost control of merchandising new records via radio airplay. The reasons for this are complex and relate to the advent of television. By 1952 there were nearly 20 million TV sets in use. As a result, major national sponsors transferred their advertising budgets to the new medium, and from 1948 to 1952 radio station income from broadcasting dropped by an alarming 38 percent. In the light of these events, many strategically located people predicted the dissolution of network programming and the death of radio. Their predictions appeared to be confirmed when the network shows were terminated or, like the single great mass audience, transferred to television. Yet the medium did not die. Between 1955 and 1960 the number of radio sets in use, sparked primarily by the introduction of truly portable, cheap transistor radios, increased by

30 percent. The number of AM radio stations increased by 27 percent. Total broadcasting income increased by 4 percent despite a three million dollar loss by the radio networks.

This turn-around was based on a profound transformation in radio programming. Although the new idea was simple, it took a decade to perfect. Instead of defining the audience as a unitary conglomeration, it was redefined as a number of discrete taste groups. As a result stations aimed their programming at one or another of these segments. Thus, by 1960, rather than four networks duplicating each other's programming hour by hour, but changing the fare over the course of the day, each of the local stations in a city had evolved a distinct format, which it broadcast with little change throughout the day.[20] Because it was inexpensive, most of these new single-format stations relied on recorded music. As a consequence, diverse sorts of music styles from pop tunes to soul, country, gospel, Latin, classical, and jazz received unprecedented merchandising over the air.[21] Because of a methodological artifact of the way radio audience surveys were conducted in that era, records aimed at teenagers received an inordinate amount of airplay. Thus, teen-oriented records profited most by the change in radio programming.

In this period, disc jockeys became celebrities. They vied with each other for the honor of introducing new records and discovering new performers. Repeated airplay meant greater aggregate exposure for a style of music. It also increased the speed with which particular tunes rose and fell in popularity. Both factors increased the demand for a new product. Columns 1, 2, and 3 of Table 2 reflect this increased circulation of hits. Between 1955 and 1959, cover renditions dropped from the Top 10, while the number of records increased by half and Number 1 records increased by two-thirds.

The new demand for records not only affected merchandising but also induced record distributors to stock the product of the independent companies. As a result, the feasibility of vertical integration at this vital stage in the production process was substantially reduced.

DIVERSITY AND SATED DEMAND

In line with the earlier theoretical discussion, increased competition among music producers should make for a greater diversity of product and a more nearly sated demand. As already noted, the first three columns of Table 2 show a marked increase in the number of records reaching the Top 10 during the 1956–59 period. Columns 4, 5, and 6 of the table show the effects of the changes on performers. Beginning in 1955, there was a marked increase in the number of successful new artists and a corresponding decrease in the predominance of established performers. In addition, each of the years from 1955 to 1958 recorded an unusually high proportion of "fading stars," established performers who enjoyed their last Top 10 record.

Column 7 of Table 2 shows the explosive growth of the record industry from 1955 to 1959. That this growth was caused by satisfying what had been unsated consumer demand is suggested by the comments of those who were involved in the communal music traditions of country, soul, and jazz. They worried that these forms were being incorporated into the popular music mainstream and might wither away as distinct cultural traditions. Numerous commentators noted the influx of rock 'n' roll. The lyrics and associated dance styles were attacked as suggestive and lewd. Frank Sinatra, once a teen idol himself, called rock 'n' roll "phony and false, and sung, written and played for the most part by cretinous goons."[22] Rather than play them, some of the older generation of disc jockeys ostentatiously smashed rock 'n' roll records while they were on the air. Several "riots" at rock concerts got wide publicity, and a growing immorality was attributed to the musical "craze." This reaction paralleled in many ways the moralistic reaction against jazz during the 1920s. Whatever else it signified, the controversy about rock 'n' roll during the late 1950s shows that the music was viewed as important and significantly different from the music that had preceded it.

The studies that focused on the early development of rock 'n' roll show that the standard love themes were dealt with in more candid and personal terms. Moreover, numerous songs cited the conflict of youth with their parents at home, in school, at work, and over love. Peterson and Berger's content analysis of hit tunes from each year through this period shows that the content and diversity of themes changed slowly during the 1956–59 shift from corporate concentration to competition.[23] They argue that rock 'n' roll was filling a previously unsated demand, and also that the new music, together with its associated youth culture, was creating a demand for ever more diverse and polemical lyrics.

SECONDARY CONSOLIDATION: 1959–1963

Table 1 shows the change in market shares during the 1960–63 period. The number of firms in the market stabilized at about forty, the four-firm concentration ratio dropped to one-quarter of the total, and the eight-firm concentration stabilized at about half the market. What is more, the market shares of the individual firms changed rapidly from one year to the next. In 1954 the old "big four" of the recording industry held the first four places among corporations in the popular singles record market for the last time. Only RCA remained among the top four sellers each year through 1963, and after 1955 it held its position only because of the spectacular success of Elvis Presley. While the big four were losing their hegemony in the singles market, they did not necessarily lose revenues, because the total industry was expanding explosively from 1955. (See column 7 of Table 2.) While the oligopolists were losing their preeminence, several new corporate entries, including MGM and Warner Brothers, together with a number of independent companies, Dot, Parkway, and Imperial, were establishing a strong market position. Their rise stabilized the eight-firm concentration ratio.

As Gillett has shown, the majors made no concerted effort to buy the contracts of successful "rockers" or develop their own.[24] They thought that rock 'n' roll was a fad that would soon pass, and they were convinced that the industry would soon return to pre-1955 "normalcy." They believed that the interest in rock 'n' roll had been artificially stimulated by bribing radio disc jockeys and television teen show hosts. In consequence, they supported the 1959–60 federal government investigation of "payola." The new Federal Communications Commission regulations resulting from these investigations eliminated only the grossest forms of payola. They did not return the major companies to their favored position in merchandising records. As Peterson and Berger conclude, quite the opposite occurred. The product of *all* independents was opened to wider mass media exposure.[25]

By 1960, rock 'n' roll did seem to be a passing fad. Most of the early rock stars were dead, in forced retirement due to personal legal problems, or like Elvis Presley, in the army and singing more like a prerock crooner.[26] Their replacements were ever less inventive imitations who created little genuine excitement. The sluggish state of the market is reflected in the figures in column 7 of Table 2. From 1959 to 1963, total industry sales rose less than 10 percent, compared to greater gains in four of the five previous years.

Apparently, near the end of this period, RCA, Capitol, Decca, and Columbia decided that they could never recover the singles market on the strength of their prerock artists. In 1962 and 1963 they bought the contracts of numerous established young white artists such as Paul Anka, Dion and the Belmonts, Bobby Darin, Duane Eddy, Eydie Gorme, and Ricky Nelson. In the same period Capitol and Columbia scored their first successes in picking distinctive new talent, the Beach Boys and Bob Dylan, respectively. While the concentration ratios were still at their low ebb, the strategy of buying into the newer rock music was beginning to bear fruit. In 1963, for the first time in almost a decade, three of the old big four held the first three positions in the number of Top 10 singles charts.

RENEWED GROWTH: 1964—1969

The six-year period 1964 through 1969 brought innovation and transition on all fronts. Fueled by "Beatlemania" in 1964, and recharged by California psychedelic sounds in 1967, a second generation of rock innovators reached the market. Diversity in lyrics peaked and sales soared. At the same time, however, a trend toward reconcentration began.

While the number of firms competing in the pop music market remained high, comparing 1963 to 1969, the eight-firm concentration ratio increased 14 percent, and the four-firm ratio increased by 61 percent. (See Table 1.) During the period, total record sales doubled, reaching $1.6 billion. For the first time record sales surpassed the gross revenues of all other forms of entertainment.

Both Decca and RCA were out of the top eight sellers until 1969. Columbia remained among the top three with a diversity of artists, while Capitol retained a high rank primarily on the strength of Beatle hits. Like the Beatles, the spate of English groups which followed in their wake were released by corporate firms rather than independents, because the English groups had been contracted to one or another of the four firms dominating the English market before their records were released in the United States.[27] Three movie companies, Warner Brothers, United Artists, and Paramount, bought strong market positions by acquiring Reprise, Liberty, and Dot Records, respectively. Several independent powers like Cameo-Parkway did not survive the payola scandals, but two others, Atlantic and Motown (the latter black-owned and -managed), reached positions among the top four firms.

The turnover of performers remained considerable but was greatly reduced by 1969 (see Table 2). The number of new Top 10 artists was decreasing while the proportion of established artists was increasing from an all-time low of 7.1 in 1964. None of the established performers the major companies had acquired in the 1962–63 period survived the British invasion of 1964, and another wave of established performers was driven from the Top 10 by the shift to psychedelic sounds in 1967.

The number of hits reached an unprecedented peak in 1966. Songs were on the Top 10 for an average of four weeks, and the Number 1 song held that position for an average of only two weeks. By way of comparison, the comparable figures for 1963 were ten and seven weeks, respectively. As the content analysis of lyrics of the period show, love themes still predominated, but these were often put in the context of broader social issues.[28] In addition there were many hit songs dealing with subjects never mentioned prior to 1955. These included songs of sexual freedom, bourgeois hypocrisy, racial integration, black pride, drugs, politics, and war. While the themes were usually liberal, they were by no means all of one kind. For example, in 1966 RCA sold over a million copies of Barry Sadler's jingoistic Number 1 single "Ballad of the Green Berets." Numerous commentators tried to diciper the underlying implications of this second generation of rock. What they found ranged from the dawn of a new consciousness to a Communist plot, capitalistic avarice, sexual decadence, drug mania, white theft of black creativity, and male chauvinism.

According to the theory that diversity of cultural products is a function of competition, one would predict that the greatest diversity of lyrical themes would have occurred during the 1960–63 period when industry concentration was at its lowest, rather than four years later. Three possible explanations will be offered for this lag of diversity behind competition. First, during the early 1960s a gap may have developed between the potential diversity made possible by competition and that which people in the industry provided. The timidity of industry personnel in the early 1960s is suggested by writers who argue that only the success of the Beatles and Bob Dylan in the mid-1960s encouraged wide-ranging musical and lyrical experimentation.[29]

Second, while corporate concentration reached a low ebb in 1962, it was not until the mid-1960s that the search for new talent became so intense that performers could demand unprecedented artistic freedom in selecting what they could record. Finally, the peaking of lyrical diversity during the 1964–69 period may have been a function of the increasing range of public controversy over civil rights and the Vietnam War in society at large. But social turmoil is not inevitably mirrored in popular music. In the earlier period of great turmoil, the Depression years of the 1930s, the music industry was controlled by three companies, and popular music took no cognizance of the calamitous events of the time.[30]

RECONCENTRATION: 1970–1973

The cycle theory outlined initially leads to the prediction of slowly increasing concentration. The figures in Table 1 show a trend that is far from slow. From 1969 to 1973 the four- and eight-firm concentration ratios increased by 36 percent and 27 percent respectively. At the same time the total number of firms having hits dropped by 61 percent, and the number with only one hit dropped dramatically from 14 to 4. Thus, there was not only an increase in the market shares of the leading firms, but far fewer firms were able to successfully compete in the popular music market at all.

Each year since 1969 *Billboard* has computed the market shares held by the ten leading firms on the total "Hot 100" singles chart by weighting records according to their chart rank. Four- and eight-firm concentration ratios computed from these data are consistently lower than, but roughly parallel to, those in Table 1.[31] These data also show a marked increase in concentration during 1973, suggesting that a new period of significantly higher concentration may be beginning.

The strategies that have made for reconcentration can be seen by examining the structure of the leading firms of 1973. The same four firms, Columbia, Warner Brothers, Capitol, and Motown, have leading market shares in *Billboard's* singles market data and our own. The diversified conglomerates, Warner Communications and CBS, lead with a 15 percent share of the market each. Warner led the way and Columbia followed in successfully employing the dual strategies of acquiring the contracts of established artists and buying once independent companies.[32] Almost half of the records that give Capitol, now a division of the English conglomerate EMI, a third-place ranking come from ex-members of the Beatles group. Motown is the one independent that has established and maintained a position in the top four without being acquired by one of the conglomerates. A&M Records is the only other independent that survives in the top eight firms. Both had been firmly established a decade earlier in the period of much greater competition. The other firms in the top eight include the conglomerates ABC, Philips Lamp, and Columbia Pictures.[33] Decca and RCA hold the ninth and tenth positions, respectively. This review of the top ten companies in the 1973 popular singles market supplements the quantitative data on reconcentration. It shows that, with two important exceptions, all of the leading firms are diversified corporations with major holdings in industries other than recorded music.

CONGLOMERATE COMPETITION

While the stage performance of groups like Alice Cooper and the various bisexuals seemed to become ever more bizarre, audiences and commentators of the 1970s were less shocked than their counterparts had been with the less extreme behavior of earlier rock 'n' roll groups. Everyone seemed to understand these as staged performances. As Melly asserts, what began as a revolt against bourgeois society had degenerated into a self-conscious posed style.[34] The faltering growth in industry sales during these years may reflect growing boredom with the sorts of popular music provided (see Table 2). Unfortunately, no systematic content analysis of the popular singles covering the entire 1970–73 period has yet been published. Peterson and Berger interpret their 1969–70 sample songs as showing a trend toward greater conventionality.[35] A brief inspection of the hit song lyrics from 1973, however, does not suggest a return to pre-1955 homogeneity. There were songs about sexual intercourse, homosexuality, interracial dating, drugs, filicide, abortion, and the folly of being a war hero. Certainly the data in Table 2 show that the number of songs reaching the Top 10 and the Number 1 position had not declined. While the rapid turnover of records does not necessarily mean diversity, slow change was correlated with homogeneity in the 1948–54 period.

If the 1970–73 period *does* prove to exhibit a continuing diversity, as suggested by Hesbacher and Keesing, it contradicts the theory that concentration leads to homogeneity.[36] The behavior of the major firms fits the economics theory of product differentiation under conditions of high market concentration.[37] Whereas the majors had been caught off-guard by the rock explosion in the mid-fifties, they now had discovered a means of capitalizing on each new fad. Since they have a wide range of artists under contract with one or another of their various subsidiary labels, they can take advantage of every changing nuance of consumer taste. Arthur Taylor, president of the Columbia Broadcasting System, neatly articulated the strategy in a talk to a group of New York stock market securities analysts in November 1973:

> We think Columbia Records is particularly well suited to maintain its leadership of the recorded music industry. Because of the versatility of our catalog— which covers literally every point of the music spectrum—we can and do capitalize on the rapidly changing public tastes. As I speak, black music and country music appear to be two primary growth areas in the coming year. If that perspective changes by the time you leave this room, I can still assure you Columbia Records will have a major entry into whatever new area is broached by the vagaries of public tastes.

As Stan Cornyn, vice-president of Warner Brothers Records, candidly admitted at a record merchandisers' convention, "We don't cover hit records any more, we cover hit philosophies."[38]

THE FRAILTY OF DIVERSITY

Diversity was maintained in the 1970–73 era because the largest firms in the industry allowed their various divisions to compete with one another. While this may be viewed as desirable from a number of perspectives and may have been necessary to maintain market preeminence, accountants in the major firms undoubtedly viewed in-firm competition as wasteful, inefficient, and unnecessary.

One would expect the large firms to try to economize by regaining control over the three key areas of production identified earlier: artistic creation, merchandising, and distribution. There is ample evidence in the industry trade press that the major companies are asserting increasing central control over the creative process. The most spectacular instance was the 1973 ouster of Columbia Records' divisional president Clive Davis, who had engineered the company's diversification policy, which had returned it to the top position in the singles maket. Davis was fired amid charges of misuse of company funds, including the wholesale use of drugs for payola.

As noted previously, the key to market control in the earlier era of high concentration was merchandising. While the Clive Davis case suggests that the majors have tried to control radio airplay by drug payola, in the 1970s the independents were prevented from successfully competing in the market because the total cost of promotion, legal as well as illegal, was prohibitively high. Economists have noted that economies of scale give large firms a competitive advantage in advertising competition. It has been estimated that promotion expenses account for 44 percent of the cost of marketing an LP record.[39] As one record company executive explained in 1973, he would not launch an independent record company in the popular record market without a promotional budget of one million dollars.[40] RCA has spent half that amount in promoting one performer, David Bowie. The majors have also moved to regain a controlling position in record distribution by buying chains of retail record stores. Industry structure seems to be approaching the conditions of 1948.[41]

CONCLUSION

Data on the music industry have been examined to bring into sharp focus the common observation that cultural forms tend to go through cycles. The first hypothesis, that the degree of diversity in musical forms is inversely related to the degree of market concentration, has been supported. The observation that changes in concentration lead rather than follow changes in diversity contradicts the conventional idea that in a market consumers necessarily get what they want. What is more, the counterassertion that repetitive presentation can induce consumers to buy whatever they hear is also brought into question, for as we have found, consumers may simply withdraw from the market.

The second hypothesis, that the cycle consists of a relatively long period of gradually increasing concentration and homogeneity followed by a brief burst of competition and creativity, has been supported. Such bursts of creative innovation have been noted in diverse art forms, and in science and religion as well. While the degree of market concentration is by no means as complete in 1973 as it was in 1948, the data for these 26 years fit the hypothesized model quite well. By the time scale of the jazz revolution, the reconcentration phase of the cycle is not yet complete, for it was 35 years from the time that jazz exploded on the highly concentrated

Tin Pan Alley music industry in 1919 until rock 'n' roll again broke through the barriers of music industry concentration.

Beyond providing evidence for these two hypotheses, much of the text has been devoted to detailing the mechanisms that condition the cyclical development of popular music. While these have been presented in concrete terms, the singular importance of the factors in the immediate task environment of the music industry lends weight to the assertions of Crane and Peterson that the sociology of culture would be greatly facilitated by the comparative analysis of the various networks in which symbols (be they in the arts, science, politics, or religion) are created, manufactured, marketed, and consumed.[42]

NOTES

[1] On the production of records see R. D. Leiter, *The Musicians and Petrillo* (New York: Bookman, 1953). On establishing record formats see Olvier Read and Walter L. Welch, *From Tin Foil to Stereo* (Indianapolis: Bobbs-Merrill, 1959).

[2] Catherine S. Corry, *The Phonograph Record Industry: An Economic Study* (Washington, D.C.: Library of Congress, Legislative Reference Service, 1965). Throughout the discussion, the most familiar names for records companies will be used rather than their official corporate titles. For example, the American Decca Company has been absorbed into the Music Corporation of America, and no records are now released in the United States on the Decca label. Capitol is a division of the English firm EMI; Columbia is a division of CBS industries; and London is the American label of British Decca Records, Co. Ltd.

[3] F. M. Scherer, *Industrial Market Structure and Economic Performance* (Chicago: Rand-McNally, 1970).

[4] U.S. Senate, "Concentration Ratios in Manufacturing Industry: 1963," Committee on the Judiciary, Subcommittee on Antitrust and Monopoly, Washington, D.C., 1966.

[5] Read and Welch, *Tin Foil to Stereo*; Paul M. Hirsch, "The Organization of Consumption," Ph.D. dissertation, University of Michigan, 1973.

[6] Joe Bain, *Industrial Organization* (New York: Wiley, 1959), pp. 155–59; Scherer, *Industrial Market Structure*, pp. 69–71.

[7] Katharine Hamill, "The Record Business, It's Murder," *Fortune* (May 1961), pp. 149–50; Corry, *Phonograph Record Industry*; Paul M. Hirsch, "The Structure of the Popular Music Industry," Survey Research Center, University of Michigan, 1969; Richard A. Peterson and David G. Berger, "Three Eras in the Manufacture of Popular Music Lyrics," in R. Serge Denisoff and Richard A. Peterson (eds.), *The Sounds of Social Change* (Chicago: Rand-McNally, 1972).

[8] Read and Welch, *Tin Foil to Stereo*, pp. 287–89.

[9] Arnold Passman, *The Deejays* (New York: Macmillan, 1971), pp. 69–82; Erik Barnouw, *The Golden Web: A History of Broadcasting in the United States*, Vol. 2, *1933 to 1953* (New York: Oxford University Press, 1968), pp. 216–18; Barnouw, *The Image Empire: A History of Broadcasting in the United States*. Vol. 3, *From 1953* (New York: Oxford University Press), pp. 125–66.

[10] For understandable reasons, the three individuals who independently supplied this information have asked not to be cited by name.

[11] Bruce W. Anderson and Peter Hesbacher, "Popular American Music: Changes in the Consumption of Sound Recordings, 1940–1955," unpublished manuscript, Unversity of Pennsylvania, Philadelphia, 1974.

[12] Charlie Gillett, *The Sound of the City* (New York: Outerbridge & Dienstfrey, 1973), pp. 46–48; R. Serge Denisoff, *Solid Gold* (New Brunswick, N.J.: Transaction Books, 1975), pp. 116–19.

[13] Joel Whitburn, *Top Pop Records: 1940–1955* (Menomonee Falls, Wisc.: Record Research, 1973), pp. 65–66.

[14] Arthur Korb, *How to Write Songs That Sell* (New York: Greenberg, 1949); David Ewen, *The Rise and Fall of Tin Pan Alley* (New York: Funk & Wagnalls, 1964); S. I. Hayakawa, "Popular Songs vs. the Facts of Life," *A General Review of Semantics 12* (Winter 1955), pp. 83–95; Hughston F. Mooney, "Songs, Singers, and Society," *American Quarterly 6* (Fall 1954), pp. 221–32; David Riesman, "Listening to Popular Music," *American Quarterly 2* (Fall 1950), pp. 359–71.

[15] Donald Horton, "The Dialogue of Courtship in Popular Songs," *American Journal of Sociology 63* (May 1957), pp. 569–78; David Berger, "The Unchanging Popular Tune Lyric, 1910–1955," unpublished manuscript, Columbia University, New York, 1966.

[16] Peterson and Berger, "Three Eras," p. 287.

[17] Gillett, *Sound of the City*, p. 18.

[18] Riesman, "Popular Music."

[19] Sceptor Records provides a good illustration of the almost casual way in which record companies entered the music field during that period. The company was founded in 1959 by Florence Greenberg of Passaic, New Jersey, to record a four-girl singing group who were her daughter's classmates. This group, the Shirelles, sold well in the soul market for eight years. They had six Top 10 popular music hits between 1959 and 1963, securely establishing the company in the popular music market.

[20] William H. Honan, "The New Sound of Radio," *New York Times Magazine* (3 December 1979), pp. 56–76; R. Serge Denisoff, "The Evolution of Pop Music Broadcasting: 1920–1972," *Popular Music and Society 2* (Spring 1973), pp. 202–26.

[21] Paul M. Hirsch, . . .

[22] Jerry Hopkins, *The Rock Story* (New York: New American Library, 1970), p. 247.

[23] Peterson and Berger, "Three Eras."

[24] Gillett, *Sound of the City*.

[25] Peterson and Berger, "Three Eras," p. 296.

[26] Hopkins, *Rock Story*, pp. 201–37.

[27] Gillett, *Sound of the City*, pp. 171–73.

[28] James T. Carey, "Changing Courtship Patterns in the Popular Song," *American Journal of Sociology 74* (1969), pp. 720–31; Carey, "The Ideology of Autonomy in Popular Lyrics: A Content Analysis," *Psychiatry 32* (1969), pp. 150–64, Peterson and Berger, "Three Eras."

[29] George Melly, *Revolt into Style* (New York: Doubleday, 1971); Gillett, *Sound of the City*; Anthony Scaduto, *Bob Dylan* (New York: Grossett & Dunlap, 1971).

[30] Ewen, *Tin Pan Alley*; Berger, "Popular Tune Lyric."

[31] The lower concentration ratios may be due to a difference in the basis of computation. The ratios reported in Table 1 weight all Top 10 songs equally, whereas the *Billboard* figures weight all records by their chart positions in the entire Top 100. Alternatively, the difference in ratios may mean that smaller companies still have a larger share of the market below the Top 10.

[32] Beside Warner Brothers, the Warner Communications labels include Reprise, Electra, Nonesuch, Bearsville, Atlantic, Atco, Asylum, and Rolling Stone. CBS labels include, among others, Columbia, Monument, Philadelphia International, Stax, Mums, T-Neck, and Enterprise Records.

[33] ABC is affiliated with Dunhill and has acquired Famous Music, Dot Records, and Paramount from Gulf & Western. Philips Lamp is a Dutch conglomerate that now owns Polydor, Mercury, Smash, MGM Records, James Brown Productions, Verve, Deutsche Grammophon, and Chappell Music. Columbia Pictures' record division has used several labels over the years including Colpix, Colgems, Bell, and Arista Records.

[34] Melly, *Revolt into Style*.

[35] Peterson and Berger, "Three Eras."

[36] Peter Hesbacher, "Contemporary Popular Music: Directions for Further Research," *Popular Music and Society 2* (Summer 1973), pp. 297–310; Hugo A. Keesing, "The Pop Message: A Trend Analysis of the Psychological Content of Two Decades of Music," paper presented at the Eastern Psychological Society meeting, Philadelphia, 18–20 April 1974.

[37] Scherer, *Industrial Market Structure*, pp. 324–45; John M. Vernon, *Market Structure and Industrial Performance* (Boston: Allyn & Bacon, 1972), pp. 67–77.

[38] Stan Cornyn, "The Rock Morality," address to the National Association of Record Merchandisers, Los Angeles, 27 February 1971.

[39] John Bream, "Record Prices," *Minnesota Daily* (15 October 1971), p. 9.

[40] Personal interview with Jim Foglesong, president of the Dot Records division of ABC Records, 28 August 1973.

[41] The *Billboard* figures for corporate shares of the 1974 "Hot 100" released January 12, 1975, show continuing "reenoligopolization." The four- and eight-firm concentration ratios are 47.9 and 74.2, a gain of one and seven percentage points, respectively.

[42] Diana Crane, *Invisible Colleges* (Chicago: University of Chicago Press, 1972); Richard A. Peterson, "The Production of Culture," paper presented at the American Sociological Association meeting, Montreal, 1974.

PATTERNS OF CHANGE

1 9 8 4

○ ▲ ○ ▲ ○ ▲ ○

My fear is that in another 10 or 15 years' time, what with all the cassettes that find their way into the remotest village, and with none of their own music available, people will get conditioned to this cheap kind of music. Then they will lose their own culture. . . . I'm not being sentimental. If this disappears, then the whole world culture will lose one little aspect. However small a nation we are, we still have our own way of singing, accompanying, intonating, making movements and so on. We can make a small but distinctive contribution to world culture. But we could lose it due to lack of organization and finance. The government is all out for nationalism, but when it's a question of development, culture doesn't count for much. Filling our stomachs comes first . . . when they've paid for agriculture, roads, factories, they search in their pockets for their last coin to give it to culture. It's the same in most countries.

W. B. MAKULLOLUWA, SRI LANKA, 1982

When the disco sound originated in Munich, a new star was born, the Producer. Regarding the future, I would predict that the predominance of the producer and the role of the sound, will remain. Recorded music will tend to become more international. The land of origin will become less discernible.

WOLFGANG ARMING, POLYGRAM AUSTRIA, 1979

These two statements spotlight some of the major global effects of the growth of the music industry over the last decade, and some of the dilemma it has caused.

Music industry technology has found its way, in a very short time, into every corner of the earth. Both software and hardware can be found in even the remotest village in every country, irrespective of social or economic system. No other technology has penetrated society so quickly—what is more, the rate of penetration appears to be accelerating. At the same time governments seem to be aware that their traditional cultural heritage could be threatened, but are not sure what to do, or cannot act because of other priorities. Also, international producers of audio and visual products, partly through losses resulting from their own inventions, are forced to try to sell similar products in as many different countries as possible. A transnational form of nationless culture develops. Through a process of integration and concentration different sectors of the music, electronic, and communications industries have been amalgamated into giant conglomerates, so complex in their organizational structure that even individual employees do not know who owns what. At the same time, the amount of music in our environment has increased to such a level that, even if a saturation point has not been reached, it is already getting harder to experience silence! And the problems of identifying usage of music, for the purpose of correctly remunerating creators and performers, is nigh on becoming an insoluble problem.

This scenario, however bleak it might appear at a superficial glance, is not entirely negative. The sound cassette has given thousands of people the opportunity to hear more music. To a certain extent users can decide what music they want to hear on their cassettes. The cassettes can even be used for recording the sound of the small peoples themselves. The very accessibility of music industry technology has brought about another common pattern of change, particularly noticeable in smaller cultures. It has provided the prerequisite for a counterreaction against the transnationalization of music—even if no local music cultures have been totally unaffected by international music products. (We will try to explain this process later by introducing the concept of "transculturation.") The transformation of the business side of the music industry into a number of giant concerns has not stopped small enterprises, often run by enthusiasts, from cropping up everywhere. As regards copyright questions, musicians and composers are becoming more active than ever before in the protection of their rights and in actions aimed at compensating losses.

We will embark on our summary of changes by referring back to the developments prior to the seventies in connection with our minicomparison of four sample countries (Tanzania, Tunisia, Trinidad, and Sweden). We noted similarities regarding changes in mode of performance, style and structure, organization, use and function of music. A continuation of the same patterns of change can be noted throughout our sample. Traditional music forms become subjected to the demands of stage shows. Quality is judged through official competitions or, in the case of commercially reproduced music, through its apparent performance in the marketplace. Such changes affect the music that is played and the musicians who play it. Different styles become streamlined. Virtuosity becomes a measure of individual prowess. This applies equally well to dancers and musicians in Sri Lanka, Tunisia, or Kenya who perform traditional art (out of a traditional context) for tourists as it does to, say, steelpan bands who concentrate all their efforts on performing one piece of music at the annual Trinidad panorama competitions at the expense of the rest of their repertoire. When the stage is an international competition, this process goes one step further (as in, for instance, the Eurovision Song Contest), producing a streamlining effect over national borders. This latter effect is accentuated further by the media industry's need to present a lowest common denominator in terms of cultural products that can be sold in as many countries as possible. There is an interesting interplay here between the value system applied in judging competitions and the choices made by those who enter them. ABBA from Sweden made their name initially by winning the Eurovision Song Contest—this gave them access to a world market. But they won because they prepared the right sort of stage performance for the values applied in judging the Eurovision Song Contest. Their success prompted many other ABBA-type groups to do the same in subsequent years. Selection procedures such as competitions comprise, in other words, a pattern of change.

The significance of the value system in this context is illustrated by the calypso monarch competitions in Trinidad. The 1983 winner, Tobago Crusoe, sang two songs at the finals. One was about black cricketers accepting money to play in South Africa; the other was a critical analysis of the Trinidadian economy. One can hardly imagine a European artist singing anything like that in the Eurovision Song Contest. The common denominator in Eurovision is a total absence of anything that could be interpreted as social, or even worse, political. How do the Trinidadians do it? Obviously the calypso's long tradition of social involvement plays a role. The other factor is the value system applied by the judges. Points are awarded both for subject and lyrics. (Imagine if only the same system could be tried out just once with the Eurovision Song Contest.)

Other patterns in our sample are those concerning:

► the style and structure of music (adaptation to concert hall conditions, decrease in stylistic variations of traditional forms)

► organizational changes (government involvement, integration into the economic system)

► the use and function of music (cementing group identity, use as a time filler, use for political or commercial information).

There is considerable overlap between these areas of change. The actual direction and speed of change are determined by a number of technological, economical, and organizational factors which can affect musical activity on a local, national, and international level.

The most spectacular factor, as we have already indicated, is the development and spread of music industry technology. This can be subdivided into two areas: music instrument and amplification technology, and record and mass media technology.

The effects of technology on music making and music reception also depend on economic and organizational factors. Significant developments here are the development of government policies on a cultural and economic plane, the relationship between different types of music and different sources of finance, the cost and service requirement aspects of new technology, and international agreements and money flows in the area of music, to name but a few.

We will now consider the spread of music industry technology—first regarding instruments and amplification, and second, recording technology.

AMPLIFIED, ELECTRIFIED, AND ELECTRONIC

One of the most significant developments throughout the past two decades has been the spread of amplified, electrified, and electronic instruments. Instruments with microphones present the immediate advantage that, as long as electric current and amplifiers are available, performers can make their presence felt more easily in terms of decibels than with traditional instruments. It is often much easier to play a loud chord on a guitar with a microphone and an amplifier than it is to develop the technique of performing on, say, a traditional instrument that is intended to be heard over large distances. This has had a negative effect on traditional arts of producing volume acoustically rather than resorting to electricity.

Amplification has not been restricted to guitars—virtually every traditional instrument can now be heard in an amplified version. This applies both to violins, cellos and flutes when introduced into jazz or pop in the West, as well as to traditional instruments such as the hand piano (*mbira*) in Africa.

Adding a microphone and connecting it to an amplifier is the simplest form of adapting an instrument to electronic technology. The next stage could be termed the production of electric instruments, where notes are produced in conventional ways, but where the instrument can be used only together with an amplifier. These instruments become totally worthless if there is no electric current. By the early seventies, mass-produced electric guitars had spread to every country in our sample, having a profound effect on the music that was being played (both Western and adaptations of traditional tunes), but also on factors such as stage requirements—an orchestra playing on a lorry would have to have a portable generator, for instance.

Another product of music industry technology in the field of instruments is the development of electronic producers of sounds, where tones are created via electronic circuits. Electronic organs such as the Hammond did have some mechanically rotating parts for tremolo effects, but the generations of synthesizers that emerged through the seventies are entirely solid-state (with the obvious exception of the keyboard). A common goal in the design and use of these instruments is to reproduce synthetically sounds that are as similar as possible to those produced by natural instruments. This has been developed to the stage where certain drum synthesizers even have small departures from regular tempo in their programs to make the results sound more human. Another use of synthesizers is the production of new sounds that traditional instruments have not produced—such electronic effects have often provided the gimmicks that are added to make disco music more attractive. The development of electronic circuit techniques has also enabled these mass-produced instruments to be adapted to different cultures. Some organs imported into Tunisia have microtones so that they can perform Arabic music.

By the early eighties, synthesizers could be found in all the MISC countries.[1] In Tunisia we came across a synthesizer that was being programmed to produce a sound similar to that of the local bagpipes. The resulting sound was mixed with the natural sound on a cassette recording of popular folk music, thus producing different tonal qualities on the recorded version of this music than would be heard under normal conditions—say, at a wedding reception.

Musicians everywhere are now aware of the progression through amplified and electric to electronic instruments and gadgets. There is no critical debate in the popular sector regarding positive or negative effects of always incorporating the latest "black box" into one's music. The desire to have access to the latest means of producing new sounds encourages musicians to try to keep abreast of the state of the art everywhere. Information about new "black boxes" is gleaned from listening to recordings, reading specialist magazines, or through traveling and travelers.

We should stress that the spread of electric instruments has not led to musicians departing entirely from traditional music forms (even if some have developed completely new repertoires for the purpose of, say, entertaining tourists from other countries). It is quite usual to find musicians in any country who turn to their own traditional music for rhythmical or melodic inspiration, popularizing it through their own treatment with electronic instruments and amplification. But the electrified versions of established music forms developed in this way seem to survive at the expense of traditional versions.

* * *

The first case in the spread of instrument technology was the amplification of a very special instrument, the human voice. Common to all our sample countries is the spread of public address systems, involving both the use and abuse of the microphone. This has accompanied and encouraged the development of music performances from being part of traditional events and rituals, often with amateur participants, to be stage performances by professional entertainers. With the advent of the microphone, the art of projecting one's voice over large distances or filling a large auditorium (e.g., an opera house) is fast dying out. We have found this phenomenon everywhere. Prayer callers in the Moslem mosques no longer climb up the tower to call their flock to the fold. A loudspeaker does the job—the prayer caller will be relaxing in a chair somewhere at the bottom of the turret with a microphone. Or he might even be replaced by a recording of some master prayer caller. *An art has been made redundant by technology.* The same applies to many traditional groups who prefer to bathe in a sea of microphones; the tonal impression of their performance becomes the responsibility of the engineer who mixes the sound.

Another common phenomenon we have noted, particularly in countries that have most recently assimilated PA system technology, is the tendency to push the tolerances of the system to its utmost. Sound levels are set on the verge of feedback or distortion. This is not just a phenomenon of youth; even older audiences do not seem to complain or even suffer. The result, of course, is that many of the nuances of the performances disappear in the amplification.

ECONOMIC EFFECTS ON LOCAL MUSIC MAKING

The spread of electric instruments and amplifiers has not necessarily meant that fewer people actually create or perform music. There are probably far more young people playing guitars in Scandinavia and Wales than used to take piano lessons two decades ago. When Sweden had its first pop boom (inspired by the Beatles) in the mid-sixties, there were said to be over five thousand groups singing variants on "All You Need Is Love" in that country of only eight million. The motivating force for many had been the status attached to pop band membership, or even wild hopes of emulating the Beatles. When most of them discovered this was not possible, many stopped playing, and a lot of second-hand equipment came on the market (around 1967–68). When the Swedish music movement emerged around 1970, this equipment proved to be a practical resource.

Guitars, organs, PA systems, and amplifiers place considerable financial strains on the owners. The fact that so many young people got bands going in Scandinavia during the mid-sixties was probably an indication of the buoyant state of the economy. Even if many instruments were bought on hire-purchase agreements, the purchaser would need a steady job or generous parents. In other countries with a larger spread of income it is no coincidence that rock groups are often formed by the children of upper-middle-class families. This is particularly noticeable in a country like Chile, where imported instruments can easily be acquired on hire-purchase. The same applies to the small number of groups playing Western rock music in Colombo, Sri Lanka.

The converse was true of the punk ideology, which embodied such things as second-hand clothing and cheap ways of living. Instruments and amplifiers could well have been salvaged from a garbage dump—the music did not require sophisticated gadgets and gear. By then, Sweden and other countries were experiencing high youth unemployment, so it was natural that punk ideology made a forceful entrance, affecting the music scene in the late seventies.

The costs of acquiring and servicing the equipment of an electric group led not only to new forms of economic dependence, but also to professionalization. Groups often have to rely on some form of sponsorship or grants. In Western Europe cultural grants are normally given purely to art music. Pop and rock, though not pure electronic music, are regarded as commercial phenomenons which should pay their way in the marketplace. (Sweden is an exception here and does give grants, mainly for equipment, to electric rhythm groups.) When the commercial market does not provide enough to cover the costs incurred, some type of sponsorship has to be sought. Thus all the jazz bands in Tanzania are sponsored by organizations, official bodies (e.g., the army), companies, or commercial promoters. The Mlimani Park Orchestra is run by a transport company—all the members are on its payroll. Many groups and artists in Kenya have to turn to commercial entities for sponsorship. Most of the session musicians in Trinidad find regular employment in the Police Band. Electric groups in Tunisia rely on the tourist hotels, as do many of their colleagues in Sri Lanka. The Volvo car company pays the salaries of some of the members of the Gothenburg symphony orchestra.

As regards equipment costs for touring artists, the sky is the limit. This is partly why a group like ABBA performs so seldom in public. An ABBA tour is a gigantic undertaking, involving tons of equipment for sound and lighting as well as a staff of about fifty assistants. The requirements are so high because (a) ABBA must be able to reproduce exactly the sound of their records on stage and (b) the visual effect must correspond to what they regard as their global image.

Even for lesser-known artists on tour, the temptation to have a few extra loudspeakers and synthesizers is too much to withstand. A large percentage of the fee for the show gets eaten up by costs for ancilliaries. An example from the summer of 1983 shows how little can stay in the pockets of the performers: Every year throughout the short, hectic Swedish summer, artists tour the *folkparker* (open air entertainment centers), often putting on a 45-minute show at two or even three different parks in an evening. A new artist on the park scene was one Carola Häggkvist, a 16-year-old girl who entered the Eurovision Song Contest for Sweden. Her show cost 31,000 Swedish kronor (app. £3,000)—park managers complained it was far too expensive. A breakdown of costs shows that over a third of the 31,000 would be eaten up by equipment costs (PA and lights). Another 10,000 kronor would be divided between her backing musicians and the rest of the staff. Traveling expenses, insurance, and manager's commission would consume the remainder, leaving a fee of 3,000 kronor for the artist, Carola. In other words one can assume that of the 31,000 a local promoter pays out for the show, less than a third goes to the artist and her musicians.

To sum up, the spread of attractive music industry instrument technology has increased the costs of the tools for many musicians and with this their demands on regular employment. Access to service facilities becomes essential. Musicians can either rely on the commercial market or seek grants and some form of sponsorship (which increases their dependence on the sponsor). Reliance on the commercial sales of their musicianship can lead to the risk of pricing themselves out of the market, for example, by being replaced by a discotheque.

At the same time many musicians playing popular music find themselves once again in a Scylla and Charybdis situation. Irrespective of whether they live in rich Sweden or poorer Kenya, they still feel the pressure to perform with equipment as good (*read:* expensive or powerful) as that of their colleagues. This inevitably puts them in a position of being highly dependent on others, usually financiers who rent equipment.

RECORDING TECHNOLOGY

By 1983, the resources for making phonograph records (from recording studios through to stamping out discs) were available in all the MISC countries with the exception of Tanzania, where a plant was still under construction. These resources expanded rapidly throughout the seventies. The only general setbacks concerned the supply of vinyl plastic during the first oil crisis (1973), when there was a global shortage while some new plants were put on line. Individual countries have also experienced raw material and spare parts problems arising from currency shortages.

During the seventies, multitrack studio resources became available throughout our sample (except Tanzania, where a multichannel studio has only a 2-track recorder). Jamaica, partly thanks to its international success with reggae, can now boast of up to seven or eight ultramodern 32-track studios.

None of our sample, on the other hand, had the resources for producing more recent recording/video industry inventions, such as the compact disc (Sony/Philips) or Selectavision discs (RCA).

In the latter half of the seventies, cassette technology had spread worldwide, and with it the software of the global record industry. *Grease*, ABBA, Boney M could be heard everywhere. This also led to the infusion everywhere of the same technical norms regarding what recorded popular music should sound like. In other words, the electronic industry's norm regarding the "sound" produced by the average recording studio, as reproduced through the average cassette recorder, provides global standards for recorded music. Anything that departs too far from this norm will be regarded as sounding weird. An illustration of the dependency on recording technique is that groups of musicians rehearsing will often sing and play into a cassette recorder to check that the sound is satisfactory (the significance of acoustic features becomes reproduced by electronic aspects).

The accessibility of recording technology has provided musicians in small countries with the means of reproducing their own music. The spread of the international record industry's products has also affected music making on both professional and amateur levels, even posing a threat at times. In the disco boom of the seventies, recordings such as those in the film *Grease* reached every continent. Disco records provided a cheap alternative to live music in the entertainment sector. These discos functioned merely as entertainment, not primarily as advertisements for the live performances of the artists concerned. A result of this was that musicians who played for tourists in hotels along the Tunisian coast found themselves out of a job. Clubs in Sweden who used to give two or three rock bands a chance to earn enough to pay for the weekly installments on their equipment went over to disco.

"MEDIAIZATION": ADAPTING THE MUSIC TO THE MEDIA

The introduction of music industry technology inevitably affects the way music is performed and the people who perform it. This applies to the prayer caller in a mosque as much as to a vocalist in a traditional folk orchestra who has to learn where to stand without running the risk of feedback. This generalization also covers the process whereby music is fed through a recording studio with all the opportunities for adding extra sound effects.

On an international level, and sometimes even on a national level, a result of this dependency is the emergence of a professional elite who rely ultimately on the media rather than live performances to communicate with their audiences. ABBA, as we have seen, is one such example. The recording introduces an extra level between the performer and the audience. A general effect of this is to separate the world of the successful recording artist from that of the average consumer of these recordings. This in its turn influences the subject matter of their material. Personal problems or general philosophical observations tend to dominate. Artists serving a world market would rarely choose to sing about, say, why the eight o'clock bus is always ten minutes late, or some other subject of local relevance.

Recording technology can affect music on several levels. Adding a synthesizer to the sound of the bagpipes on the cassette of the singer Zoubaier in Tunisia results in the bagpipe accompaniment not sounding the same as it does in a live situation. The listener will get a different impression of the bagpipe sound. The performer will have the dilemma of deciding whether or not to adapt the performance to the sound on the recording, either by playing in a different fashion or by incorporating some electronic gadget.

Sometimes this development can go so far that music becomes almost entirely a studio product. Jamaican reggae is an example. It is only in the sophisticated recording studios of Kingston that the reggae sound the world has learned to recognize is created. Live performances of reggae are extremely rare since the demands on equipment are so great and the finances of all but the top reggae artists are so poor. Reggae can be heard live in Jamaica only at major events, such as the Sunsplash Festival or the newly instigated *Rockers Magazine* awards show. On the other hand, giant discotheques dominate where the spontaneous performance would be by disc jockeys who often improvise lyrics ("toasting" or "rapping") over reggae rhythm tracks ("dubs").

The opposite situation used to exist in Trinidad in the days when calypso singers would produce new songs daily, based on the happenings of the previous twenty-four hours. It was an improvised, spontaneous culture that even encompassed what the calypsonians referred to as "calypso wars." One calypso master would challenge another one to come on stage and engage in a verbal battle where the sword was the tongue and points were awarded for advanced rhymes, usually spiced with an element of insult directed at one's opponent. The calypsonians became walking dictionaries of rhymes and quaint grammatical constructions.

Things are different now. The same pattern can be observed as in Jamaica. Calypso is adapting to the terms of the music industry environment. With the introduction of large sound systems, calypsonians have had to structure their performances more strictly. Advanced arrangements are written for ten- to fifteen-piece backing bands, and the repertoire is restricted. Instead of churning out new songs in a steady stream (albeit often with very similar melodies), the calypsonians will sing only two or three songs for the whole of the carnival/calypso season. Because of the time involved in the recording and manufacturing process (often abroad), the topics cannot be merely of current interest, referring to the events of the night or even the week before. At the start of the three-month run-up period to the carnival, a calypsonian will release a recording and proceed to market the product. Since part of the artist's income arises from sales of discs and cassettes, an effort is made to make the live performance in the calypso tent sound as similar as possible to the recorded version (thus decreasing the value accorded to the art of improvisation and increasing the demands on the sound of the backing group). The disc will also, it is hoped, be played on Trinidad's two radio stations; this will have both a marketing effect, by boosting sales, and a publicity effect for a calypsonian entering the carnival competition for the annual "Calypso Monarch." The calypso has thus become adapted to the available media and music industry technology. Calypso has not gone so far as reggae yet in becoming purely a studio product, but the pattern of change is the same. Live bands used to be very much in existence on the streets of Port of Spain on carnival days. Now many of them have been replaced by disc jockeys, turntables (or cassettes), and giant loudspeaker systems. They are more reliable, functional, and cheaper.

Another live music form in Trinidad has also been affected in much the same way as the calypsos. The steel bands have undergone a process of specialization whereby the National Panorama Championships have become the major goal for each year's carnival activities. A band of up to one hundred members will spend weeks preparing one single piece of music for the competitions. This leaves them with no general repertoire and thus diminishes their social role as entertainers—it is not much fun going out in the streets at carnival knowing only one or two tunes. What is more, the tunes they play are often melodies sung by calypsonians—that is, the hit songs of the year. And when a company decides to record a steel band, all their members might not even be expected to take part. The best players will take a selection of pans into a studio and create the whole effect by using multichannel techniques. What started as a social phenomenon in the ghettoes is fast becoming adapted to the music industry environment, to the demands of recording technology and the media.

This process whereby music becomes affected by the technology through which it is disseminated is a common facet of change everywhere. With all due respect to etymologists as well as our publisher, who reacted, quite rightly, against a surplus of consecutive vowels, we have opted to refer to this process as *mediaization*. This refers to the adaptation of music forms to the constraints of entertainment media, recording technology, recording markets, and so on. The example of the steel bands is particularly relevant in this context. Watching a traditional steel band performing a rousing, rhythmical number live is a very impressive visual and aural experience. On the other hand, it is extremely hard to reproduce the same type of experience through normal recording techniques (a band of one hundred players, for instance, covers a large area). If this problem is solved by using multichannel techniques, then a mediaized version could develop with a different sound. The bands may well then try to emulate this in a live situation, producing a different type of steel band music.

A general conclusion is that a major problem for small countries is not primarily that their own particular types of music are ignored by the local media and establishment (even if this does happen) but that this adaptation process can conflict with their social function. Steel bands concentrate on a competition number—their repertoire suffers. *Baila* in Sri Lanka often functioned as music with social or satirical content that was sung at parties. Its adaptation to the demands of cassette technology has produced two mediaized versions: one with fairly smutty lyrics and another more respectable form performed by artists who would like to be accepted by the official media.

Tanzanian jazz bands still perform an important social function—they play live at clubs. Their simple mono recordings on Radio Tanzania serve merely to advertise the live function. Should they achieve world acclaim, or should Tanzania acquire the same type of technical resources as Jamaica, then an inevitable process of mediaization will take place. The result could be a fascinating "new" sound. It could also be a devastating loss of spontaneity and live music culture.

ACTIVE PARTICIPATION OR PASSIVE LISTENING?

The spread of music industry technology has also changed the listener's role in music making. In former times, music was very much a question of two-way communication. The performer was physically very close to the audience and relied on establishing some sort of rapport. This still happens everywhere in rural areas where traditional music is still part of local rituals. But the incidence is rapidly on the decrease, simply because never before have people had such easy access to so much recorded music. In the first half of the seventies the amount of time the Swedes devoted to listening to recordings increased fourfold. By 1976 young Swedes in the 9–24 age group spent on average one hour a day listening to their own recordings and an extra hour listening to recordings on the radio. Much of this is *secondary listening*; in other words, music provides merely a background to other activities.

This is a global trend. Transistor radios and cassette recorders are every-where. The same goes for television—even in Tanzania where television is virtually absent and video imports are forbidden, there are plenty of VHS machines. In two of the less rich countries in our sample (Sir Lanka and Jamaica) parabolic dishes have been used to pick up television satellite signals and redistribute over local transmitters. New dishes are cropping up every day in Jamaica. Scandinavia will soon find itself in the footprints of a number of European satellites. No one knows how to solve all the legal problems of copyright that these developments entail. But what is clear is that

- ▶ The international distribution of music that has access to modern media is increasing at an extraordinary rate and
- ▶ smaller countries are finding it harder and harder for their own music to compete with international repertoire.

Even rich Sweden finds production of a high percentage of local television programs an impossible financial burden. Since Jamaican Television found it could pick up nearly thirty channels on its dish, local musicians have virtually disappeared from the screen (in a country which is one of the net exporters of music!).

One of the biggest growth rates in the music industry can be found in the area of background music. The same unobtrusive instrumental versions of standard evergreens can be heard when an Air Jamaica plane lands in Montego Bay (no reggae!), in the lobby of any international hotel, or in most supermarkets the whole world over.

Organizations such as Muzak have devoted considerable resources to investigating the positive effects (positive with relation to increased pro-ductivity or purchasing activity) of musical wallpaper. Less has been done to study its negative effects. Little is known about the possible saturation effects of living in a constant environment of recorded music. This study shows that it is not a phenomenon exclusive to large or rich countries, or even the industrialized world. Within less than three years of liberalization of import restrictions, the sound cassette had become a major disseminator of recorded music, both local and foreign, in Sri Lanka. Two years later the videocassette was firmly established in urban areas, and a national television service was inaugurated.

This statement by music researcher W. B. Makulloluwa of Sri Lanka, made in 1982, illustrates the feeling of despair felt by those who see their own heritage being crushed by the onslaught of relatively cheap interna-tional culture:

We are not prepared for television. Cameras and tape recorders don't make television programmes. You have to have trained people to do that. What are we getting now? The pop music of Germany, ABBA, Star Parade and so on. People see these things over and over again. But we don't have the money, experience or capacity to put on shows like that. Even if we do put on something national, it can't compete with all the glittering lights and costumes of the foreign products. People begin to believe that you have to have that sort of thing. This development could destroy everything that has come down through the ages, everything that we can proudly call national culture.

The picture our research presents might seem fairly bleak; there are, however, some bright lights at the end of the tunnel. In every MISC country we have witnessed how people use available technology for their own cultural purposes, not merely for swallowing something that is served up on a plate.

CULTURAL EXCHANGE, CULTURAL DOMINANCE, CULTURAL IMPERIALISM, OR TRANSCULTURATION

The mass communications development during the past decade [i.e., the seventies] has led to a completely new situation regarding the interaction between music cultures and subcultures. Interaction between different local types of music has been a fact since time immemorial. It became more intense throughout the nineteenth century in the industrialized countries as communications developed. This process has continued throughout this century, gradually encompassing more and more areas of the world, before exploding during the seventies.

The kinds of interaction can be classfied roughly in four categories, each one representing a new stage in the pattern of change. The first pattern, which is the simplest form of interaction, can be called *cultural exchange*. Here two or more cultures or subcultures interact and exchange features under fairly loose forms and more or less on equal terms.

CULTURE 1   **CULTURE 2**

This very often takes place on a person-to-person level. For instance, traveling musicians in Europe have picked up ways of making music by playing with musicians in foreign countries ever since the Middle Ages. When groups of Turkish musicians came to Sweden as immigrants around 1970, some of them started to play individually with Swedish jazz and folk musicians. Within a very short time Turkish folk music, Swedish folk music, and jazz were merged into a new kind of music played in Sweden by groups bearing such names as Sevda ("love" in Turkish), Oriental Express, and Oriental Wind.

But cultural exchange is not always a matter of person-to-person interaction. An illuminating example is the case of the musical "round trip" involving Africa and the Caribbean. First the Africans were brought as slaves to the Americas. There they developed Afro-American music forms. During the forties and fifties, records with Caribbean music found their way back to Africa, not as the crow flies, but via Europe. Black intellectuals from the Caribbean and Africa met at universities in England and France and an exchange of music tool place. Colonialists (especially the Belgians) developed a taste for records with Latin American rhythms at their parties. Through such routes, Afro-Caribbean music on disc found its way to African countries and was played in people's homes or on the radio. The music caught on, and African urban areas started to copy rumbas and calypso music. During the fifties Afro-Caribbean and African music were mixed to produce new music forms, especially in Congo/Zaïre, which were to provide the basis for most modern East African popular music. Musicians from Zaïre migrated to East Africa, where a new cultural exchange process took, place when the Tanzanians infused elements of local music into the Zaïrean sounds, producing Swahili jazz. This in its turn was adopted by many Zaïrean musicians during the late seventies. In the late sixties records started appearing mainly in Zaïre and Kenya of Zaïrean and some Tanzanian pop music. Some of these records found their way to the Caribbean (presumably via London and Paris). They were eagerly devoured by young musicians who, in the wake of the black power movement, were seeking their African roots. This led to a new merger of music types in the early seventies when these young West Indians developed Afro-Jazz in Martinique and Guadeloupe and Afro–Dadian music in Trinidad. In the later stages of this musical round trip, recordings were the instrumental medium of cultural exchange.

The second pattern is *cultural dominance*. This is the case when a culture, usually that of a powerful society or group in a society, is imposed on another in a more or less formally organized fashion.

CULTURE 1

CULTURE 2

For example in the development of Afro-American music, the culture of the white slave-master was dominant. Cultural exchange on equal terms was not possible. However, the imposition of white culture on the black slaves was very loosely organized in some parts of the Americas, and more formally in others. This difference led to many variants in the pattern of change, with results varying from almost pure African music with a sprinking of European features to the complete eradication of the African cultural heritage of the black people.

For another example of cultural dominance we can turn to Africa, where missionaries working in Kenya and Tanzania supported by a colonial administration exerted pressure on local culture. Schools were established at mission stations where native pupils were taught a mixture of European and Christian values and music. The dominance even included, and still does at some missions, the banning of traditional African instruments. The form of music tuition practiced by the missions has been incorporated to a large extent into the present-day school curriculum of Kenya, thereby continuing a process of change by cultural dominance. The general school system in all our sample countries teaches music according to a system of norms that reflect what is considered "good" by a ruling or dominant class. In Swedish schools, for instance, the singing style of Western art music is predominant. This singing style differs from that of traditional Swedish folk music, but many Swedes now perform traditional songs in a style modeled on the ideas of Western art music. Traditional songs are also performed in multipart arrangements for choirs, a style introduced through the school system.

Radio and other mass media can also be instrumental in exerting cultural dominance. One example is the domination of North Indian art music in the programming of Sri Lanka Broadcasting Corporation. However, most cases in which mass media function as part of a pattern of change belong to our last two categories.

The third pattern is *cultural imperialism*. Here the cultural dominance is augmented by the transfer of money and/or resources from dominated to dominating culture group.

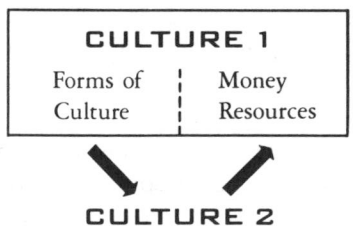

Examples of the money transferred are profits made by subsidiaries of record companies belonging to the dominating culture, or copyright money. The resources can be gifted musicians, pieces of music, or unique traditional musical instruments which are removed to museums in a dominating culture area.

Activities during the past fifty years in the field of culture emanating mainly from the United States but also from some European countries are largely a process of cultural imperialism that has been described by many researchers.[2] For example, there have been cases where pieces of music have been taken from small countries and copyrighted in the United States. To enjoy the financial advantages, many gifted artists have moved from Latin America and the Caribbean to the United States. Some, like Bob Marley, have transferred the right to collect copyright money for their creative work to a U.S. copyright organization.

The financial and other gains involved in cultural imperialism contribute to placing a dominated culture under heavier pressure than from pure cultural dominance. Cultural imperialism speeds up the pace of change, but it also can lead to counteractions, such as the setting up of a local Musicians' Performing Rights Society in Kenya or the establishment by local musicians of small independent "noncommercial" record companies in the Nordic countries.

Most forms of cultural imperialism in the music sector require that music be packaged and made into a product that can be exchanged for money in the form of a recording or a concert in the closed hall where an entrance fee can be charged. This commercial aspect of cultural imperialism has contributed to the spread of the concept of packaging and selling of music to more and more music cultures and subcultures. For instance, during the seventies some Swedish folk fiddlers started to issue and sell recordings of their own music. This was a completely new development in Swedish folk music culture, and of course the technique was learned from the regular recording companies. Learning the art can contribute to effective counteractions!

The three patterns enumerated so far—cultural exchange, cultural dominance, and cultural imperialism—were joined by a fourth and new pattern around 1970: *transculturation*. This pattern of change is the result of the worldwide establishment of the transnational corporations in the field of culture, the corresponding spread of technology, and the development of worldwide marketing networks for what can be termed transnationalized culture, or *transculture*.

Transnational music culture is the result of a combination of features from several kinds of music. This combination is the result of a socioeconomic process whereby the lowest musical common denominator for the biggest possible market is identified by building on the changes caused by the three previously described patterns of change. The production of transcultural music, like any other commodity, can involve pilot tests, industrial processing, and marketing/dissemination through mass media. Disco music, for instance, is a transcultural music. The music of *Grease* or the group Boney M are typical examples. It is a product that has not originated within any special ethnic group. Disco music was marketed during 1975–78 in a massive worldwide campaign involving films, TV shows, recordings, and so-called merchandising—John Travolta T-shirts, Boney M buttons, ABBA posters, and so on. Not only synthetically created music but also styles that have originated in a special ethnic group can be turned into transcultural music. Usually the music in this case is stripped of its most original features. Reggae performed in country and western style or Chopin melodies accompanied by a drum machine are examples. The spread of miniature organs with the *same* limited selection of synthetic rhythms to every market where they are sold is another example. Regardless of their own cultures, all performers have to relate to these predetermined rhythms.

In the previously described patterns of change, the interaction has been bilateral, between two music cultures or, in the case of cultural dominance and imperialism, between a powerful, dominating culture and a number of other less powerful cultures. Through the transculturation process, music from the international music industry can interact with virtually all other music cultures and subcultures in the world due to the worldwide penetration attained by music mass media during the past decade.

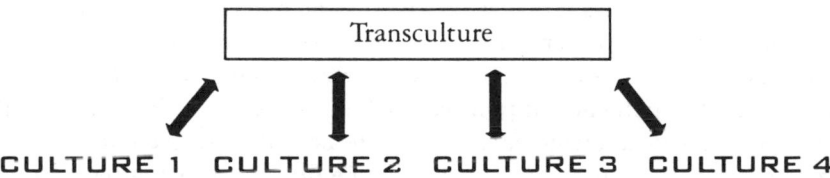

As we have noted, small countries function as marginal markets for international music as well as sources of internationally exploitable culture. What happens in practice is that individual music cultures pick up elements from transcultural music, but an increasing number of national and local music cultures also contribute features to transcultural music. The resulting process is a two-way flow which we have termed *transculturation*. As the music and electronic industries spread their hardware and software to different countries, this process starts.

Before we proceed to a more detailed description of the first stages in the transculturation of music in our sample countries it is important to point out that all the four categories of patterns of change described here still exist today. They overlap, stengthen, or weaken each other in a complex system of relationships. For instance, there can be clear conflicts between cultural imperialism and transculturation. The process of the transculturation of music can be spread by a network of local agents for transnational companies who do not have to transfer money to any other country, or even by local entities whose official ideology is strictly opposed to that of transnational enterprises. This network is often augmented by recording pirates, whose activities can hardly be said to contribute positively to the riches of any "imperialists" (apart from those who sell duplicating equipment and blank tapes).

There are clear similarities in the pattern of change in our sample countries as well as other countries. The speed of change has increased, but not equally fast everywhere. Similar changes have taken place at different points in time and with different intervals between them. A change so profound as the emergence of popular music took place in the Nordic countries during the last decades of the nineteenth century; in Chile during the first decades of this century; in Tunisia, Sri Lanka, and Trinidad during the thirties, in Jamaica during the forties, and in Kenya and Tanzania during the fifties and sixties. Developments in music that have been spread out over more than fifty years in the Nordic countries have occurred within twenty years in Kenya. In the seventies these developments reached a state where the music cultures of most countries had many features in common, maybe much more so than in other fields such as agriculture, industrial development, or economic systems. This situation is a prerequisite for the type of interaction that can lead to a general process of transculturation. In other words, translating this into practical terms, we have here the basis of an explanation for the almost simultaneous emergence of what could be termed "national pop and rock music" in all our sample countries. Access to music industry technology, the influence of transnational music, access to local music culture, and the will to create something different all converged at the same time. The results could be referred to as the first stage of transculturation in these countries.

NATIONAL POP-ROCK OR ONE GLOBAL MUSIC?

The common development that has involved more local music making than anything else in the MISC sample has been the emergence of national styles of pop and rock music during the seventies. These activities have invariably used the recording for distribution. One of the prerequisites, as we have noted, was access to technology by which local music could be documented and spread (first the open-reel tape recorder, then the record and cassette). The world had been flooded with Anglo-American music in the fifties and sixties. This influenced, but did not prevent, local musicians developing their own styles, which were adapted to their own cultures. This seems to have happened about the same time everywhere, in the late sixties and early seventies. Throughout this period, the transnational record companies might have increased or maintained their dominance in terms of sales and market percentages, but were doing less in terms of recordings released (and were probably quite happy to have it this way, since smaller independent entities where taking the risks in the market).

When the Swedish music movement exploded around 1970, thousands of groups suddenly started singing in their own language. The same type of process took place in Wales. (While Swedish groups were emerging from the cellars, singing in their own languages, young people in Wales were appearing at summer youth camps singing in Welsh.) The first pop record sung in Sinhala was released in Sri Lanka in 1969. Through the seventies Jamaica experienced the transition from rock steady to reggae. Kenya was producing the first Lou pop records. Other local tribal variants followed throughout the decade. The Tanzanian jazz bands were developing their own Swahili version of East African popular music. After almost ten years of copying the Beatles, Elvis, or Chubby Checker, musicians in the small nations started trying to develop their own national forms of popular music. Singing in one's own language or dialect was a significant change, since it introduced a new communicative element between performer and listener.

Where recording and manufacturing and organizational resources were available, numerous small music businesses, such as companies and clubs, emerged. The enthisiasts found an outlet for their energy. These changes heralded a very creative period in the cultural history of small countries.

The creative results, however, were not always accepted by the establishment in those small countries. Radio stations sometimes refused to play local popular music. Local politicians were slow to realize the value and importance of this development, particularly for young people. During the following ten years these local forms of pop and rock were to become accepted, first by a youth audience, and then gradually by government authorities and national mass media.

We have defined transculturation as a process whereby elements of music and music technology spread by the transnational industry are incorporated into local music. Much of the music of the Swedish and Welsh music movements was rock with local-language lyrics. Some musicians did include elements of their own culture's melodic traditions. The flow of influences was not merely one-way. Reggae began to influence global popular music, or, to use our terminology, the transculture assimilated elements of reggae. This is a relatively new process, very different from the cultural exchange of previous times. Beethoven's Fifth has always been Beethoven's Fifth; Western art music has stayed more or less intact throughout the process of distribution around the world. Classical composers in Wales might have gone through periods during which they incorporated local Welsh folk melodies into their works, but they have not all started writing variations on Hungarian folk songs in the way that international pop music might include elements of Jamaican pop. We can assume that the transculturation process will continue and accelerate, encouraged by the fact that musicians in smaller cultures will continue to dream about success in the world market (thus contributing to the feedback aspects of transculturation).

It is hard to say what is at the end of the tunnel. In its early stages transculturation has had positive effects on cultural activity. Musicians have made a lot of music but have also looked to their own roots for extra inspiration on top of that supplied by international music. But what are the long-term perspectives? In theory at least, the result could be one single global type of popular music culture which incorporates elements of every subculture the international music industry has penetrated. However, this is a long way into the future and much can happen in the meantime.

NOTES

[1] The Music Industry in Small Countries project, administered by the University of Gothenburg, forms the basis of this study.
[2] See A. Mattelart, *Multinational Corporations and the Control of Culture* (New Jersey, 1979).

PART FOUR

The Creative Process

○ ▲ ○ ▲ ○ ▲ ○ ▲ ○ ▲ ○ ▲ ○

The recording industry, described in the previous section, is the setting in which music (and money) is made, but songs and stars are not just cans of beans. The continuing need for "new" product, the irrationality of aesthetic tastes, and the central place of romanticism (its language of art and genius) in rock ideology mean that the creative process itself—the set of social relations, rules, and practices within which the pop musical product is made—is exceedingly complex.[1] Academic researchers have, on the whole, neglected the microsociology of the music business, have failed to look in detail at how musical decisions are made, why sounds or images emerge the way they do. It remains easier to assume that records are the result of creative routine or individual inspiration; the best single study of the music industry is still Geoffrey Stokes's 1976 journalistic report of the making of a

Commander Cody LP.[2] What we have to understand, as he makes clear, is that commercial routine and individual inspiration feed off each other, and the essays in this section, though written from very different perspectives, all contribute to such an understanding.

Antoine Hennion is France's leading sociologist of music. His work combines detailed empirical observation with subtle readings of what is going on. The article here is an edited extract from Hennion's study of life in a Paris recording studio. After months of listening to producers, musicians, engineers, and A&R men discussing the finest nuances of sound and packaging, Hennion concluded that the one pop interest group not present at some time in the studio—the public—in fact dominated the proceedings. It was with reference to "the public" (and to different studio actors' authority to speak for it) that each musical decision was justified.

Edward Kealy looks at the studio from a narrower perspective, that of the sound mixers and studio engineers themselves, and his particular interest is how their work and work status were changed by the rise of rock. He raises interesting questions about the relationship between "music" and "sound," "art" and "craft" in the recording process, and if his 1979 arguments are now in some ways dated, they remain obviously relevant to the era of digital recording, sound sampling, the continuous remix, and the rise of sound mixer as auteur.

H. Stith Bennett and Mavis Bayton provide complementary accounts of the creative process from musicians' perspective. Bennett's 1980 study, *On Becoming a Rock Musician*, was modeled on Howard Becker's pioneering 1950s work with jazz musicians[3] in which he attempted to get "inside" the musicians' world through participant observation of their everyday language and social interaction. We have extracted Bennett's description of the practice session, which shows how rock musicians learn to play together, not simply by developing their instrumental techniques but, just as importantly, by agreeing on the terms of value judgments and aesthetic decisions—that is, a musical discourse must be learned as well as a musical skill.

Bennett's work is interesting and important, but flawed by its specificities of time and place and, in particular, by its unquestioned assumption that rock musicians are men. Mavis Bayton, former member of the British feminist punk band the Mistakes, takes up Bennett's analytic approach in order to answer the questions he ignores: How do women become rock musicians? What obstacles do they face? How do they overcome them? She raises specific issues about the sexual division of rock, to which we will return in Part 6, but her general point is that the single most obvious (and most neglected) aspect of its "creative process" is its domination by men.

All of these studies employ the same methodology: participant observation and interview material are used to reconstruct the *participants'* understanding of the musical world in which they work, and this remains one of the most fruitful sociological approaches to popular music (much better grounded empirically than subcultural theory, for example). Theoretically, though, such work always runs the risk of celebrating participants' "common sense" rather than criticizing it, and in a world so dependent on myths of creativity this is a decided drawback. In the last essay here, then, on how recent technological change affects the very idea of creativity, author Andrew Goodwin steps back from musicians' and engineers' own accounts of their work to place them in a wider framework of arguments about artistic "aura" and mechanical reproduction, about "authenticity" and postmodernism.

NOTES

[1] For specific discussion of the myths of rock creativity see Simon Frith and Howard Horne, *Art into Pop* (London: Methuen, 1987).

[2] Geoffrey Stokes, *Star-Making Machinery* (Indianapolis: Bobbs-Merrill, 1976).

[3] See Howard S. Becker, *Outsiders* (New York: Free Press, 1963).

Antoine Hennion

THE PRODUCTION OF SUCCESS

An Antimusicology of
the Pop Song

1 9 8 3

○ ▲ ○ ▲ ○ ▲ ○

A t the heart of the frenetic activity of the record industry and of all the conflicting opinion to which this activity gives rise lies a common goal: popular success. This also provides the key to the paradoxes one encounters when one studies the economic aspects of the record industry in France. What does the achievement of success involve in actual fact? Economic, sociological, and musicological analyses tend to evade this issue rather than explain it. Can the ability to achieve success be attributed to a more or less innate sixth sense? Does it reside in the superiority of the smaller producers over the larger ones? Is success achieved through bribery, through massive "plugging," through a dulling of the senses, or through conformism, as the ritual claims of the press would have it? Is it a by-product of profit, of standardization, of alienation, or of the prevailing ideology, as Marxists argue? The sociology of mass media and culture explains it in an equally wide variety of ways.

When one studies the professional milieu on the spot (as I did for three years, from 1977 to 1980), one learns that its fundamental task resides in *the permanent and organized quest for what holds meaning for the public.* Not an arbitrary or a coded meaning, nor a meaning imposed from above, any more than a meaning collected by statistical surveys or market research— these last can reveal only "objective," that is, sociopolitical, categories enabling the powers that be to label their "subjects": age, sex, socioprofessional group, preferences. The meaning in question is to be found "down below," in those areas that carry the public's imagination, its secret desires and hidden passions—one could almost define such categories as *sociosentimental*. They include key phrases, sounds, images, attitudes, gestures, and signs, infralinguistic categories which are all the more difficult to pin down insofar as they escape definition by the official language, and are not autonomous but inseparable from the social context within which a given group attributes a special significance to them. At the same time these infralinguistic categories are ephemeral; as soon as language intervenes, they give up that terrain and re-form elsewhere. Slang, a form of dress, a hair style, a motorcycle, and above all music, that music which "means" nothing, are all the expressions of that which cannot be put into rational discourse—which is always the discourse of other people.

These meanings cannot be manufactured, cannot even be decoded. The professionals of the record industry have to feel them empathetically, to make them resonate, in order to be able to return them to the public. The distribution of roles and the organization of work among producers, authors, musicians, and technicians, as I have observed it, aims chiefly at preserving and developing artistic methods that act as veritable mediators of public taste, while accomplishing a production job that must also be technical, financial, and commercial. Pop music has been able to systematize the very principle of its own diversity within an original mode of production. The *creative collective*, a team of professionals who simultaneously take over all aspects of a popular song's production, has replaced the individual creator who composed songs that others would then play, disseminate, defend, or criticize. This team shares out the various roles that the single creator once conjoined: artistic personality, musical know-how, knowledge of the public and of the market, technical production, and musical execution have become complementary specialisms and skills performed by different individuals. Thus the final product, consisting of highly disparate elements that can be considered individually and as a mixture, is the fruit of a continuous exchange of views between the various members of the team; and the result is a fusion between musical objects and the needs of the public.

In accordance with the way my own research evolved, this article roughly progresses from the musical to the social; first, I sketch out a "formal" analysis of the pop song in which it can be seen that a song's expressive value does not lie in its form and that a musicological assessment cannot explain why certain songs are successful and why most others fail. I then try to trace the song back to its origins and analyze the role played by the producer[1] and his relationship with the singer; for it is the producer who has the task of introducing into the recording studio the ear of the public, whose verdict has little to do with technical considerations; it is he who must assess what effect the song will have on audiences at large. It is also he who must try to "draw out" of the singer what the public wants and conversely to pave the way for the special emotional ties that bind the singer to his public, by himself embodying for the singer an audience that is as yet only potential. It is for him that the singer will try to fashion the right persona. This work of the professionals, which makes possible the operation of a transfer mechanism between singers and their audiences, goes against the grain of musicological analysis: there is here no such thing as the "structure" of a song. None of the elements that go into its creation, none of the dichotomies that the outside observer can detect, are above the process of negotiation. Their meaning varies, wears out, or vanishes. Each song modifies by degrees the basic model, which does not exist as an absolute. The gimmick of yesterday soon becomes the boring tactic of today, as far as public taste is concerned.

If one wishes to analyze pop music, one is always led back to real audiences, in the form of consumers; a pop song, which owes its ephemeral existence to the public in the first place, is sustained only by that which gave it its substance from the start. But this self-consumption of the public by the public is not without certain effects; what is stated does not take the form of self-contained, indefinite repetition, but is inscribed in the blank spaces within everyday life; it expresses what cannot be said any other way. Through the history of pop music, one can glimpse the history of those who have no words, just as feelings that cannot be expressed otherwise find their way into the music. This additional layer of meaning should, in fact, lead us to invert our approach: we ought not to attempt to explain the success of the music through sociology and social relations, but should instead look to the music for revelations about unknown aspects of society.

THE RAW MATERIALS

The Music

A tune, lyrics, and a singer: from the musical point of view, a vocal melody with an accompaniment. These elements make up a very limiting configuration as far as the genre is concerned. They exclude the effects of vocal polyphony, as well as pure instrumental composition and its virtuosic possibilities. The music is subordinated in the song to a single main part: a sung melody of a simple type, which must have an accompaniment.

The tunes are tonal, rarely modal. The principal harmonies are familiar; the form depends on the juxtaposition between an insistent chorus and verses that provide progression. But the simplicity of these traditional musical variables is misleading. The song is nothing before the "arrangement," and its creation occurs not really at the moment of its composition but far more at the moment of orchestration, recording, and sound mixing. The elements, with their somewhat classical musical grammar, are looked upon chiefly as raw materials to be assembled along with the voice, the sound, the "colors," and the effects of volume and density. The real music of the song hides behind the melody and gives it its meaning. The audience notices only the melody and thinks it is the tune itself that it likes.

The Lyrics

The pop song tells a story and comments on it in order to provoke in listeners the feelings appropriate to that song. At first glance, one can see that it is a genre which borrows from a wide variety of other genres; from poetry it borrows the importance and autonomy of certain key words, as well as the use of meter, verse, and repetition; from the lyric theater it borrows the singer's direct appeal to the audience to share feelings expressed in the first person; but perhaps it owes most to the novelette in the way that it almost invariably tells a story, set out in a few words, concerning the relationship between two or three individuals. As one producer put it concisely, the pop song is "a little three-minute novel," in which daydream and reality merge in a sort of fairy tale of love or of anonymous ambitions.[2]

A basic idea is set out, elaborated, and concluded. It often reflects the eternal opposition between rich and poor, between strong and weak, between those who are lucky in love and those who are unlucky, etc. The story is conventional; in other words it is familiar to the casual listener and solidly anchored in popular mythology through the intrigues and situations which that mythology holds dear. The vocabulary takes on a particular significance: it is the words that must give the text its originality while remaining simple and easy to memorize.

The Character

The pop singer is not an instrumentalist who happens to have a vocal technique, an interpreter-musician at the service of a given work. He himself is part and parcel of the song he sings, in the form of the "character" he impersonates. The construction and publicizing of this character are not solely a promotion job, separate from artistic creation; on the contrary, this work is central to the song, which is inconceivable outside the association between the lyrics, the music, and the singer.

The song can, from this point of view, be compared to the cinema; like the star in a popular movie, the singer must *be* the character who speaks in the first person in the song and not just *act* the part. Instead of creating a role like the stage actor, who will play it far better if he is not taken in by that role, the singer has to become a character in whom are confused the singer's own life history and those life stories of which he sings. The producer is there to remind him of this; he makes sure that there is a link between the singer and his songs: the singer's stage personality emerges to the extent that the songs which suit him best, and in which he is best able to please, become clearly established.

The Mixture

These three elements (music, lyrics, character) are conceived of as empirical mixtures based on know-how, as ephemeral alloys that cannot be codified. The song is the result of their articulation and is just as empirical and fugitive. As with a do-it-yourself kit, there are tricks of the trade in the creation of a a song. But far from mechanizing production, these retain the subjective relationship between the three elements: each appears to relegate the other two to the rank of effects destined to underline the third; but in actual fact, none of the three could stand on its own. The success of the song depends on its mobility: the limitations of the music (too repetitious), of the lyrics (too trite), of the character (too artificial) are each in turn displaced by the illusion that the other two elements are taking over when the third grows too thin. When the mixture is right, the ingredients enhance one another in a song that will go down well with audiences, though the observer and at first even the producer would be hard put to analyze what is so successful about each element. But beyond a certain threshold of credibility, the public, hell-bent on obtaining pleasure, is ready to forgive the banalities of a song that succeeds in providing it.

THE TECHNIQUES OF THE SONG

Musical Form

Music is the fundamental ingredient in a song, giving it its form. In pop songs, the choice of tune usually precedes that of the lyrics, which will often be altered completely in the process of adapting the two elements to one another.

The construction of songs has become somewhat formalized. The various elements have technical names to which producers refer.

The Introduction. In a few bars, this serves both as a signal to the listener, enabling him to recognize the song immediately, and as a foreaste, making him want to listen to the rest. The intro reveals enough to suggest the mood; sound, rhythm, type, etc. It conceals enough to stimulate the appetite without blunting it. The object is to use fragments that characterize the rest of the song: a few bars of the tune, a chord, a mixture of timbres, a rhythmic pattern. In the words of an experienced producer:

> "The introduction is merely an aural signal which says: 'Watch it, fellows! Here comes such and such a tune!' As a matter of fact, a song is almost made by the introduction, which has *nothing* to do with the tune. It all depends on how smart the orchestration is: one must admit that, very often, it is the accompaniment which turns the song into a hit. I'm thinking of the song by Caradec, for example, 'La petite fille.' Jean Musy's clever orchestration, very light and very effective, played a big part."

Or as one head of a large international firm put it:

> "They really understood the trick back in the heyday of English pop music in the sixties: 'The House of the Rising Sun,' 'Satisfaction,' 'A Whiter Shade of Pale,' perhaps the biggest hits apart from those of the Beatles, all three made it on the strength of their introduction. You remember the guitar arpeggios of the Animals, the bass in 'Satisfaction,' the Hammond organ in 'Whiter Shade of Pale' . . .

The Alternation Between Verses and Chorus. In the verses, which are in a fluid, recitative-like style, the music subordinates itself to the lyrics, so that the story can unfold. The chorus, on the other hand, is more musical and etches the tune in the memory, a tune whose regular repetition right through the song is expected and gives all the more pleasure because it is eagerly awaited during the somewhat dull verses. The arrangement underlines this opposition by enriching the chorus in a number of ways: the addition of instruments absent during the verses, denser harmonic progressions, the pointing up of a climax whose resolution makes one ready for the calm of the following verse.

As far as musical construction is concerned, a song typically opposes a harmonic *sequence* in the verse (with short, constant rhythmic values in the melody) and a marked harmonic *cadence* in the chorus (with contrasted rhythmic values in the melody: held notes, quaver patterns, etc.). But the opposition can also be achieved through a variety of other means.

To find the right balance between the chorus and the verses is vital for the equilibrium (and the right perception) of a song:

> "I remember the number 'De toi' by Lenorman, one of his first songs to do well. The song was completed and I asked people to listen to it. It was a disaster! I was really surprised because I was almost sure that it was a good song. I went over the sound mixing ten times, but each time the result was the same. I couldn't

understand it. And then, at one stage, I changed the construction of the song: it was the same song, but differently constructed; the chorus, which came after a minute and a half of the song, we put right at the beginning. I played the song again to people I knew and everyone loved it! It was the same song, but they wouldn't even admit the fact! It's the little details which count! The success of a song depends on the accumulation of minor details. Sometimes the song is good, but it hasn't been thought out properly. Or else there's just one thing which doesn't work, and if you can find out what that one thing is, it changes everything."

Verse Progression. Musically speaking, a song consists of alternating verses and chorus: the music of each verse being identical, it is up to the lyrics to build up progression through actions that interconnect. The words are "in opposition," "out of phase" with the music, insofar as musically the listener is eager to hear the chorus, during which the music "explodes," while the lyrics induce a desire to hear subsequent verses, since they, not the chorus, tell the listener what happens next. But a good arrangement can also, in the background, build up different verses upon their identical tune, stressing musically the scenic progression that takes place. By varying the orchestration and the texture, the same tune will alternate from cheerfulness to sadness, from serenity to tension. In the same fashion, the chorus will be stressed to varying degrees as the song proceeds.

The Conclusion. The last verse, which puts an end to the tension by proclaiming the conclusion of the action, leads up to the final chorus, whose ultimate function quite naturally issues from its repetitive character. Pop songs often end, anyway, by fading out the sound on a repeated "loop": one cannot end a dream, "full-stop," just like that. This moment is often underlined by means of a rise in key of a semitone without any harmonic transition.

Creating the Music

The Melody. Though listeners often believe that they pay explicit attention only to the melody and the words, the former does little to give musical ideas any form, preferring rather a kind of neutrality—except in cases where the melody itself is meant to evoke a particular style. Balance, malleability, simplicity, everything happens as though the visible surface element, the melody, and the underlying groundwork that gives it its affective dimension were complementary. In fact the melody is merely a neutral support which the listeners can memorize and reproduce easily, but which is not in itself of significance. A chance idea or two that catch the imagination suffice. From this fragile motif, the arrangement has to provide the musical value of the song, all the while remaining in the background. The final product revealed during the performance will superimpose both elements; the familiar form of the melody will be brightened up a thousandfold. The listener perceives the support and its illumination simultaneously. Later on, when he whistles the melody by itself, thinking it is that which gives him pleasure, little does he realize that it is in fact the accompaniment which, even though forgotten as such, gives intensity to the recollection of the melody. And this is all the more true because the process takes place unknown to the whistler, and because his imagination has a clear field in which to animate as it pleases the musical values submerged in his unconscious.

The Rhythm Section ("La Base"). As in jazz, the rhythm section groups together all the nonsustaining instruments in order to lay down the tempo and the chord changes: bass, drums, keyboards, and rhythm guitars. This kind of instrumental texture, based on the opposition between a rhythmic–harmonic pulsation and fairly autonomous melodic voices, comes directly from the influence of jazz. But more generally speaking the same principle is found in most popular musical styles, both those that still function as dances (tangos, waltzes, etc.) and older ones that do not (minuet, branle, bourrée, gigue). This manner of appealing directly to body movement, separating the beat and the melody in order to have them knock against each other—which swing music carried to an extreme—clearly sets these musical styles in opposition to the continuous and increasing integration of elements typical of classical music.

> "It is often said that the French were the kings of the bourrée; it is not true, because the bourrée has quite a complex rhythm of Greek origins that comes from ancient Occitania. In fact, for us it is simply the branle! The French react to the tum, tum, tum . . . like that. Truly Breughel! You know, disco has become a success in France much quicker than in the USA. Cerrone, Village People, all that is by French producers." [An independent producer]

Without accepting this anthropomorphic interpretation at face value, one should nevertheless note that when speaking of this rhythmic–harmonic *"base,"* professionals insist on its animal, physical, primitive aspect. Its elements are described in physiological rather than musical terms. They are essentially concerned with finding a beat and a "sound" that can evoke a visceral reaction, a blend that finds in the listener a fundamental, irresistible body resonance.

> "There is a *morphological* difference between the Anglo-Saxon and Latin inner ears. This can easily be felt, for example, in the way the Americans and the French mix the same song; in France we put in much more voice than in an

American record. The inner ear has been conditioned by the music people have been hearing for generations. Between town and country it is much the same, the people are not sensitive to the same sounds. The ear reflects an entire social group, an entire country." [A young producer specializing in highly commercial songs, a former singer himself]

Orchestral "Backing" ("Habillage"). This groups together the sustaining instruments, brass, and strings, whose function is to draw counterpoints between the melody and the rhythm sections in order to tone down their opposition, which otherwise would be too sharp. Here, pop music diverges from the spirit of jazz, where this tension is developed to an extreme. "Backing" does not exist at all in small jazz combos and is limited in full orchestras by the absence of strings and by a very rhythmic kind of writing for the brass sections. The fact that pop music is orchestrated does not bring the style any closer to that of classical music. True to the spirit of pop, the orchestration disguises the underlying construction of songs behind familiar appearances and brings together superimposed elements which underneath retain their separate functions, instead of stimulating their integration. It draws the ear toward decorative elements superfluous to the development of the song. It is as if the song were not meant to be consciously perceived, so that it might get through to the listener unawares.

While the *base* should be in a strict, consistent style so as not to detract from the rhythmic tread of the harmonies and the pungency of the timbres, the "backing" is, on the contrary, the favored field for borrowing from other styles (especially from classical music), for tricks of arranging, for varied effects and combinations, through which the talented arranger constantly directs the attention here and there, only to slip away and attract it elsewhere. One of these effects in particular is so systematized it has been given a special name: the *gimmick*, a little dash of spice without any relation to the melody, a "trick" that decorates the song and accentuates its individuality. It may be a rhythm, or a little instumental solo, that keeps coming back, unnoticed as such, but that sticks in people's minds, bringing a smile whenever it crops up, and as a result making the whole song memorable.

"It's the little thing; if you take all of Sheila's records you will see that it is used systematically. I've seen how Carrère did it: first, he took a very, very simple rhythm, and from the start he gave it a particular sound; then he added two effects in the middle of the song—what we call the gimmick in our jargon— which are just nice surprises, like a pretty ribbon around a package. These have nothing to do with the melody, they are two little effects that cross each other, meet each other, and which we are glad to hear each time. That's very important for a song. We find the song pretty, but it is pretty only because of this little effect. It is like sugar. . . . But most of the time it is completely unconscious." [An experienced producer]

These "fills," as they are also called, are not only decorative: they in fact fill in the *acoustic space*, making it more or less dense, clear, spacious. It is this which underlines the construction of the song; it is more important than the notes themselves or the passing harmonies, which are chosen from a very limited vocabulary. When the arranger tries to realize the wishes of the producer, he has to translate ideas of progression, of question, tension, mystery, opening, into musical techniques; choice of instruments and registers, range of tessitura, density of texture, doublings, sound clarity, articulations of the form by means of vocal harmonies in the background, or alternatively by having a solo line emerging in the foreground. This work on the volume and the grain of the acoustic space corresponds neither to composition itself nor to orchestration as these exist in classical music. It lies rather in between the two and is what carries the real "musical ideas."

Creating the Lyrics

The "Story." The best way of characterizing the "idea" of a song (bearing in mind that here, more than anywhere, diversity and constant change are the rule) would probably be to say that it must bridge the gap between current events and timeless myths. This is how one must interpret comments like "It's always the same song, but with new clothing each time." The story itself often tends to be timeless and mythic, especially as regards love, and it is the choice of words that brings in a temporary perspective.

An encounter, then a separation, and so on ad infinitum. The stage is set, the action builds up until the shedding of a little tear "which the public loves," things are in the end resolved by a small victory, a return to the status quo, or by the hero recovering himself. It is not the intention of this article to go into the structural analysis of lyrics, as Propp has done for the folktale, nor to extract hypothetical "audiemes" analogous to Barthes's "gustemes" for cooking. Nevertheless a quick analysis of a few typical situations brings out a major part of the "ideas" in pop music. The underlying mythic themes are ambivalent, lending themselves equally well to submission or revolt, desire or hostility, according to the identifications and projections of the listener. One thus finds romantic longings side by side with a complacent acceptance of love's deceptions.

Alongside ambitions for money, power, success, one finds echoed the tranquility of the hobo, pity for the "down-and-outs," sympathy for the loser. Respect for the law and hatred for the police also get along very well together. This ambivalent attitude explains how different songs so easily change the position of the "I" from positive to negative, varying the dominant emotion. But it is always on the dreams, the desire for revenge, the hatred and the resignation of the unwanted, the dominated (or, as Léo Ferré says, *"les pauvres gens"*) that this centers.

This kind of content analysis leaves out the most important thing, namely, what is done with the content, both during the production and during the performance itself—and it is this which makes the difference. Suffice it to say that the story told is doubly familiar to the listening public: through the basic situation presented and through the contemporaneity of the people who play the roles. The story is to the lyrics what the melody is to the arrangement: it is to the story that listeners direct their attention, in order to put themselves in the place of the protagonist, the "I," without noticing all the work it took to make that identification desirable and plausible for the listener—that is, the care given to the choice of words, to their relationship with the music and the characters, and to the contemporary detail. Conventional simplicity and ancient wisdom: that is the formula for the story.

The Words. More than the story itself, which is quite simple, its only constraint being its plausibility vis-à-vis the singer, it is the wording that is the real problem for the composer and the producer. All their attention will be directed toward finding the right style and especially the right choice of words by successive (and often numerous) rewritings. The problem is that here again one must disguise one's intentions beneath familiar everyday language and construct the song as much outside the text as through it.

The words must be simple and direct, but not clichés. They must apply to current problems, to today's ambiance, to what people are talking about, without being worn out by use. One must somehow conform but in a hip way so that the power to stimulate people's imaginations has not been exhausted. Since the concern is less with developing a theme than with making allusions to it through particular expressions, the vocabulary soon becomes outdated, like current events in the daily papers.

The moment when a record comes out is very important. In 1968, for example, there was a period when it was absolutely ridiculous to put out a record; everything became irrelevant, outdated. Writing lyrics reminds one of a patchwork quilt, made up of quotations cut out individually, often quite out of context, from partially remembered memories whose immediate relevance to the text can be quite tenuous. When Eric Charden sings "L'été s'ra chaud, l'été s'ra chaud, dans les tee-shirts, dans les maillots; l'été s'ra chaud, l'été s'ra chaud, d'la Côte d'Azur à Saint Malo!" (The summer will be hot, in teeshirts, in bathing suits; the summer will be hot, from the Côte d'Azur to St. Malo), the effect seems even to come from the very absence of any link between the song's contents and the slogan it evokes (a slogan of May 1968, when students demonstrated, singing "Hot, hot, hot, the springtime will be hot!").

The word quote is sometimes only an acknowledgment of current fashionable slang; it can make a direct allusion to a topic of current interest. But most often it is used to relay or echo certain social themes in a more general way. Thus, feminism gave new life to the word "woman," which suddenly started appearing in the song titles of several female singers.

The meaning of words depends less on their organization in the text than on the social context they evoke in absentia. "There are no 'trends' in pop music; it just *follows* the evolution of society," according to a producer who is involved with singers of quite different styles. But pop also *expresses* this evolution of society, and in doing so is not so passive after all. Nevertheless, the idea of an absence of voluntarism, of claims to autonomy, in favor of listening to what society as it is has to say is fundamental to pop music. "You must never follow fashions! To be 'in fashion' is a great error. When you follow a fashion, you're already behind it" (Gilbert Bécaud). Or, for a young producer of highly commercial songs:

> "You have to imagine what the public will like three or four months from now, when the record comes out. Not to forget the other records that could come out with something new, musically or otherwise, and in doing so outdate your record! You often see three or four records come out practically at the same time which are trying to get at the same thing, exploiting the same idea, something that was in the air. Generally, of course, only one makes it and the others flop!"

Such success hinges on the lightness of the implicit. One must avoid words with too obvious a connotation, or with a single meaning, or with over-strong effects which tend to replace the allusion by the issue itself. One has to write in an "open" style.

This obligation to be simple does not guarantee a lyric will be good: it might have the necessary familiarity, be related to everyday events, and yet be lacking in appeal. Once again, it is through the selection of words that the appeal must be made; certain key words, in contrast with the obviousness of the other words, which are like tiny reservoirs briefly holding the social significations of the moment, function as pure signifiers: mysteriously, they have an autonomy of their own within the meaning of the text and are selected for the way they ring, for the expressive power which gives them their opacity; they have to engage the imagination of the listener and at the same time effect a sort of disengagement from the everyday words of the text, so that the role of dream can be given full play. These unexpected metaphorical turns of phrase interrupt the unfolding of the text, giving one a shiver of pleasure, in a way very similar to the effect of the musical "gimmick."

This opposition between *word quotes*, which enrich the context, and *key-words*, which serve as metaphors, is obviously not clear-cut in the case of the work of "artistic" singer-songwriters (*chansons "à texte"*), where, for reasons of poetic ambition, there is more integration of formulas and images. But the principle of putting "punch" in songs by means of striking images and evocative phrases remains the rule in lyrics which must be sung and therefore have to be very short and interspersed with choruses.

The Style. The style adapts itself to the vocabulary that is used and to the singer, rather than existing for its own sake. It has only certain limited means of its own with which it can underline a song's construction, which are quite independent of it: repetitions (to point up contrasts between verses and chorus); rhymes (to help in the punctuation of the musical periods), etc. Its role is more important in the context of the storyline, to place the characters and even more the imaginary nature of the drama. The frequent use of the direct style where, for example, the "I" addresses itself to the "you," even though it is obvious from the lyrics that the "you" in question is far away, instantly gives the song the form of a fantasy, of a daydream in which a character speaks aloud to someone who is not there. The direct style not only enables the listener to identify with the hero of the song and allows for the direct expression of feelings, it also invites the audience to put itself in the situation of the dreamer; the song is dreamlike in nature not only because of its content, which describes a situation and proposes an imaginary revenge against a cruel beloved; it is first and foremost, and more discreetly, the style that invites the listener to hear the song as "natural," as though it represented his own fantasies.

The Versification. In this way the style makes the lyrics embrace the action of the song. But the style must also fit the music and the main character. In the world of pop music, it is pretty meaningless to say of a lyric that it is good: it is only one piece of the jigsaw puzzle and must be judged not on its own merits but on the way it fits in with the other pieces, both distinct from them and at the same time completely dependent on them. Producers often assert in a somewhat emphatic fashion: "There is only one text for a tune, and only one tune to which a text can be sung." Or, as the singer might put it: "It's a mistake to think that a song is a poem. A songwriter is not a poet. This means that when I'm given some lyrics for a song without the music, I'm just not interested. I can't judge the words without the music" (Dave). An experienced producer goes into greater detail: "Unlike certain other forms of expression, songs are a composite genre: a song is made up of words and music, certain words for a certain music and none other . . . It's like cooking or like magic: if it doesn't work, there's nothing you can do about it."

The important words must coincide with the musical high points, the density of the text with that of the music, etc. But even more than in these technical ways, the association between lyrics and tune must rest on a succession of converging associations that are able to link the one to the other through analogous images or "colors." The text must express in some way what the music says already. If it is the other way around, the listener will reject it. He will recall only the tune of a song if the right words have not been "found," whereas he will memorize both words and music if the lyrics are "good." This relationship calls for many alterations, for progressive, empirical adaptations according to the results. "For 'La Primavera' with Gigliola Cinquetti, I had nine different lyrics. I had already recorded one text out of the six which I had selected at the beginning. I didn't like it. I took the tape back to Italy, and re-recorded over there . . . I think it's the only way to go about it."

Songwriters, composers, and producers need the "public's ear" for this task. It may be true, as they often claim, that there are no written rules, no infallible tricks to guarantee the success of the equation, that you need intuition, quickness of judgment, and feeling rather than any theories out of a book. But this does not mean that such a talent is a gift from heaven or that it defies analysis. It does require a certain form of sensitivity, a knack for grasping that what words and music say depends less on their internal properties than on the way they call up social meanings. This type of awareness as to which words and musical phrases are pregnant with meaning at any given time stems more from personal experience than from any formal learning. It relates to what a person *is* rather than to what he knows. The good professional is someone who in his own life has felt the meanings held in common by his audience and whose experience enables him to seize upon them before their manipulation blunts their significance.

This intuitive knowledge of public meanings (*valeurs-pour-le-public*) is even more necessary when it comes to the creation of a singer's "persona" and its relationship to the music and the lyrics which, in a sense, it "caps." It is at this level that, through his relationship with the singer, the part played by the producer is decisive.

Creating the Persona

A Voice. When looking for new singers, producers do not judge a candidate by his repertoire—they will build it up from scratch anyway—nor, initially, by his technical skills—these can be tinkered with. What they do try to recognize first and foremost, and to single out wherever possible, is a "voice."

That voice, as they conceive of it, is from the start an element with a double meaning, physiological and psychological. It will be the basis for the relationship that must be established between the singer's persona and his songs. Having a "voice" in pop music terms does not mean possessing a vocal technique or systematically mastering one's vocal capacities. Instead, a voice is an indication of one's personality. "Personally, I prefer a singer who is marvelously himself in front of a mike even if possibly he sings . . . I won't say exactly out of tune, but not absolutely in tune either . . . rather than a singer whose pitch is perfect but who stays cold, like a choral singer, and who doesn't project anything" (an independent producer who specializes in the teenybopper market). When singers practice a lot and take singing lessons, they do so mainly in order to develop their stamina for going on stage and to learn how to sing without straining their voice. Working on their sound might well make them lose their originality even if they did gain in proficiency.

What counts is having an interesting sound that attracts attention: inflections, accents, and a way of expression that is immediately recognizable. One producer's criterion is that "something has to happen even on a 'la-la-la.' " In other words, it is not the voice for its own sake that matters but its expressive power. The producer listens for what the infinite nuances of a particular voice have to say, in order gradually to find coherent translations on other levels: music, lyrics, record sleeve, and so forth.

It is at this first moment of contact more than at any other that the producer assesses the singer for what he is, quite apart from any self-awareness or any technique he might have and regardless of what he can do already. To speak of the singer's inner self, as contained in his voice, does not imply any reductive psychologism nor any unilateral stress on the individual; on the contrary, the details of his personal history, which has made him what he is, will mean nothing to the public unless they refer to a certain social condition, at a conscious or an unconscious level. "Each star is a completely stereotyped product which corresponds to a persona . . . Take Le Forestier: he's exactly what young people are today, nice rebels in clean blue jeans" (a promotions assistant).

An Image. On the visual level, the singer's appearance, the way he moves and stands, the way he dresses, all have a function of expression analogous to that of his voice. He must intrigue us, compel our attention, make us want to get to know him just on the strength of his appearance.

A star's "magnetism" must exist, if only in embryonic form, before success comes and before he learns those techniques which will aid his development. This first impression is the foundation of the image that the singer will construct for his public. But perhaps the comparison between image and voice stops here: in a song, as in real life, the voice is less deceptive than the physical appearance, more revealing of the true personality; it cannot be manipulated at will as easily as can the external appearance. It is the voice first and foremost that conveys a singer's authenticity, sometimes through a raw and bitter quality over which he has no control (having a harsh, cracked, or rasping voice has never stopped anyone from becoming a singer). His image, on the other hand, which is easier to "polish," has the opposite function: it serves as a pleasing, seductive, or amusing facade which conceals under a familiar and neutral aspect the unacknowledged source of the pop star's appeal.

One can make analogies here with the complementary roles played by melody and arrangement in a song. Much more than with the voice, certain rules prevail and are standard practice when it comes to constructing the singer's physical image: tricks of dress, makeup, hairdo, lighting. Around the singer's gaze, which remains more authentic, an image is organized, quite superficial and contrived, which reassures fans that their idol corresponds to the usual canons of physical beauty. Singers who do not have "the face that fits the job" have just as hard a time selling as those who sing "out of character."

> "When Claude-Michel Schönberg sang 'Le premier pas' (The First Step), which was a super song, he didn't appear on TV until about three months later. He had already sold a lot of records. On the very day he appeared on TV, his sales dropped, as he had expected. People were disappointed; they had imagined what he'd look like from his voice, from the song. The day they saw him, the face didn't fit at all!" [His producer]

A "History". The singer's real life story is the source of the meaningfulness of his voice and his image. But, just like them, it is reconstructed according to the way it is projected visually, verbally, and musically in his songs. In the early stages, it tends to comprise the succession of unspoken difficulties that led the candidate to become a singer in the first place, that have forged his special personality and that have made him turn for help to the producer, in obtaining for him the ear of a public. This mediation, by the singer-producer relationship, between the singer's real life story and his public is not just a matter of theory: those involved themselves value it intensely, sensing as they do that success depends on the result of this transfer mechanism.

As far as the singer's life story is concerned, even more than the other elements of song production, one cannot speak of technique, of a musicology of pop music, even in the most general sense. Everything gets mixed up during the discovery/production of the singer's performing personality. He must be able to express himself on stage in a role which, while obeying a precise set of show-business rules, is genuinely "true to life." It is that "truth" which will be heard by the public, which will enable his audience to identify with him, and which will bring him success. It is by reformulating his personal problems, but within the social framework of pop music, as recognized by the public, that the singer becomes human in the eyes of an audience who knows exactly how to decipher the language of stars. "It isn't the song which must give the singer personality but the singer who must give personality to the song." The use of artifice allows him to rediscover his natural self; the tinsel of his romanticized biography gives him a base for talking about his life.

The mediation (or rather the *mass mediation*) that pop music introduces between the social truth of a singer and the public's desire to identify is probably the chief task of the producer. And it is precisely this vital mechanism that most eludes technical description—in terms of conscious methods of manufacture and autonomous know-how, artistic elaboration, or tricks of the trade. On the contrary, it is a gradual process which has to let itself be invaded by outside social forces of every sort; it is these forces that dictate in effect the language of pop music: the combination of words, sounds, and images through which the public loves its idols. The singer's persona is—right down, often, to almost the finest nuances, without which something sounds false—the collective projection of the singer's reality and that of the public on the screen of pop music. A cliché, perhaps, but a social cliché full of meaning, full of actuality, which alone provokes public recognition and through that the lasting success of the singer.

The producer is not a calculator. His knowledge of the pop music scene and his experience of the public are of value only when he has integrated them within an "immediate" sensitivity: only then do they mutely guarantee the genuineness of his taste, which can exercise itself spontaneously and in a subjective, noncerebral fashion. He can forget the criteria that he has interiorized and allow himself to give in to his feelings, to react to what he perceives as purely physical sensations produced by such and such effects: "I select the takes according to what gives me a thrill when I listen. It's completely idiotic, but that's the way it is. I can't even explain why; it's purely physical, I wait until it makes my skin tingle" (a semi-independent producer who specializes mainly in quality songs). It is in terms of this emotional response, this sympathy in the strictest sense of the word, that the decisive moment occurs, that moment when a producer decides to take on a new singer because he feels it is going to "work" between them.

> "We have to have the first 'shock,' the 'love-at-first-sight' feeling, before the public can. We're the middle-men. If we liked it, maybe others will too . . . Different people have different talents but then I meet one I take a violent fancy to, the sound of his voice . . . how can I put it . . . it's got a kind of vibration which does something to me; it strikes a chord and makes me feel good . . ." [One of the pop music producers of an American-owned company]

The heart has its reasons . . . The producer does not so much refuse to listen to logical arguments as consider them of lesser importance; he situates them on another level. Good arguments are useful, but secondary. They are only convenient to back up a case, to rationalize something that has already happened. Reason provides justifications that serve to convince those whose job is not, like the producer's, to feel the "vibes": the money men, the directors, the commercial and radio men. And it helps to encourage those on the "artistic" side, in the studios and at the music publishers, who have not yet caught these "vibes," to stick to the project. But reflection can do no more than back up the producer's initial conviction, and it is this which allows him to hold out when success takes a long time to come and the doors remain shut:

> "I'm incapable of working with certain singers, because I don't have the *conviction* they're any good. I can't tell you why I have this conviction! When I started Maxime Le Forestier off, for example, I was absolutely positive that he had a lot to offer. I wrote to one big company to tell them so and they answered 'no, his voice is too thin.' I cut his first record at Festival and it didn't work, the label wasn't good. Maxime went to Polydor and it took several more years. But in the end, with Jacques Bedos, he became the star I had always thought he could become."

This method of work, subjective and "primitive," must be taken seriously; it is a method whereby a lasting conviction is founded on the immediate pleasure responsible for the producer's initial image, visual and aural, of the singer. It is the same method by which the public will subsequently recognize its idols.

AN ART OF PLEASING

Beyond the specific role played by the producer, it is in the end the overall working relationship between the various members of the pop music professional team that enables them to anticipate the public's reactions; each member of the team constantly switches from producing the song to listening to how it sounds, from techniques to image. The real inventiveness of the professional "hit" producers probably lies in the methods of work they have devised for managing these two aspects of the song—for presenting an *imaginary object*. The characteristics of the mode of production they have created, from the function of the producer to the recording session, all have one aim: the problematic fusion between the universe of techniques, by which objects are made, and that of images, in which an audience wants to invest. Work in the studio consists of eliminating the professional's complacency with regard to his style, watching out for any signs of incipient complicity between those who know what they are up to, bringing back into the "firing line" of "primitive" criticism the finds of each member of the team: all this in order to subordinate the meaning a song may have for its creator to the pleasure it can procure for the listener.

The aim of the entire organization of production is *to introduce the public into the studio* through various means:

- ► through techniques of *cutting* and *mixing*, which introduce elements of everyday reality into the song

- ► through the presence of *witnesses* (such as the young singer himself, who is first and foremost a specimen of his public) and of *representatives* of the public (this is the producer's role both in relation to his singer and in relation to the technicians)

- ► through the working relationships, constituted by *mutual criticism* (each member of the team being an audience for the others), by *subjective listening* (it being pleasure that produces meaning), and by *collective anticipation* (the dynamics of the group constitute a first production–consumption process which one hopes will repeat itself first through the media and later among the public).

The dictatorship of the public (which is obvious everywhere in a genre so often described as manipulation) remains extremely ambiguous. If the public is an ignorant despot with the power to decide once and for all whether a song is a hit or not, it is for this very reason an impotent despot who never has control over the terms of his dictates and whom a clever courtesan can always seduce if she knows better than the despot himself what pleases him. Everything is done for the public, but everything is done on its behalf as well. The real public is not present in the studios. What connection is there between this public and the one that is constantly invoked by the various collaborators in the production of a song? Or rather, what can one do to make the real public sanction the many choices one has made in its name by massively buying the records that have been produced?

The only guarantee of success that producers can hope for—and it is a precarious guarantee at best—lies in the introduction into the studio of a relationship between song and listener analogous to that which will later bind the song to its real public. A song-object is not produced first and consumed later; rather a *simultaneous production-consumption* process takes place first inside the studio, and the impact on those present must be repeated later on outside the studio. Success is a *gamble* by the producer on his identification with the public. This gamble is often a losing one and is always unpredictable, but it pays handsome dividends when he wins. In the studio, the producer could only grope his way to success; this holds true also of his search for public approval.

The notion of a gamble is a fundamental one. First of all, it is relevant to the way pop music is produced. It is the basis for the relationship between the large companies and the small producers, who reap the benefits of being in closer touch with the public. The gamble in question has nothing to do with luck; it accounts for the "hit" form of the record business, the all-or-nothing nature of success that suddenly crystallizes around one number, leaving a dozen other almost identical songs unsold. But beyond that, the notion of a gamble is central to the very nature of the song. If, as has already been stated, the only unifying principle of a song lies in the pleasure it offers to its listeners, it is impossible for the producer to go by a set of hard and fast rules. All he can do is gamble on a given song, which is nothing until the public gives it meaning by appropriating it. There is no such thing as art for art's sake in pop music. A song has no objective reality or value in itself. If it is a flop, there is no posterity to rehabilitate it. It exists only to be accepted by its own times as a sign of those times.

The Images of the Public

At last we come to the public, which gives the song its meaning and its substance. The final consumption of a song is the only measure of its potential, which was purely hypothetical until that moment. If it is successful, the spark that consumes it reveals the reality of its expressive charge, while at the same time annulling it. Pop songs do not create their public, they discover it. The opposition that the sociology of culture operates between statutory consumption by elites, on the one hand, and the industrial production of mass culture, on the other, stresses in both cases the arbitrary imposition of meanings by producers and sellers. The public is looked upon as passive, ready to absorb whatever it is presented with so long as the label fits the social category.

This vision overlooks the active use to which people put pop music, the imaginary existence they lead through it, which is not reducible to the official social hierarchies. To speak of the transmission of codes that map out the stratification of society is to speak of a theory that solves too quickly the problem of social domination within cultural production, by applying to it the political model of a power pyramid. This is to place cultural production within the ordinary causality of the social order: the sociopolitical scene that is characterized by real power relationships, realistic compromises, and objective social categories that construct and impose real experience. But when this reality is projected on the screen of pop music, the picture one gets is reversed, as though one were seeing a negative on which were printed the hidden side of current social life. In a rather unreal way, we catch a glimpse of all that official history, always written in terms of the power structure, leaves unsaid: hopes that are disappointed almost before they are formulated, a bitterness that nobody cares about, useless emotions. Producers are the representatives of a kind of imaginary democracy established by pop music; they do not manipulate the public so much as feel its pulse. They offer up their songs to the public in the hope that it will recognize itself in them, just as one suggests various phrases to a dumb person until he nods in agreement. Producers do not control the public's desires but rather fulfill them. Their power lies not in imposing a particular view on the public, but in proposing one to them. In this imaginary world, social domination gives way to complicity: the complicity of the public which knows it must beg for the idols that the companies offer; the complicity of the singer who knows he must endorse the persona the producer suggests to him. The producer's art lies in trial and error: in guessing, espousing, and fanning the flames of passion for which words are lacking, and in desperation, whose only outlet lies in the periodic infiltration of a new style, which comes, in the nick of time, to speak for the underdogs of society.

Thus the producer's role is so subjective, so bound up with identification and projection, that it becomes even more of a social role; rather than genuinely express the passions that it reflects, pop music organizes youthful, mobile social groups still in the process of forming. It draws together potential groups still ignored by the politicians, whose members share the same unspoken frustrations. It gives a self-image to latent communities whose members have in common the feeling of not belonging to an established social category (whether that of the dominators or of the dominated: thus, "the rocker" may represent the young worker plus the violence that has been stifled through "politicization" by the workers' movements; "the disco fan," the young typist with no future plus the pleasure of being no more than a body abandoning itself to a collective rhythm; "the punk," the "kid" without the likeable constructive enthusiasm that he is blamed for not possessing).

Imaginary identities, sentimental adventures, a taste of what reality represses: pop songs open the doors to dream, lend a voice to what is left unmentioned by ordinary discourse. But pop is not *only* a dream machine: perhaps, like witchcraft in another age, it is the unofficial chronicle of its times, a history of desires existing in the margins of official history, which, except at rare moments of rupture, do not speak but act. In setting out a history of today, popular culture etches the contours of a history of tomorrow in that it "feels" a social atmosphere in its earliest, unformulated stages; pop music senses the current and projects a first image of it, long before the politicians have grasped its real nature or had the time to quell it, before words have been found to express it or to betray it. Pop songs hold up a mirror to their age in the truest sense of the word, for they provide it with a blank screen on which its desires are reflected. It is paradoxical that reflection theories of art, which fail to explain art because they deny its role as a mediation, finally become relevant when the word "art" loses its meaning; in pop music—except that this reflection requires a lot of work, from many professionals—"immediacy" costs a lot.

[*translated by Marianne Sinclair and Mark Smith*]

NOTES

[1] *Directeur artistique*, here and throughout the article, is translated as "producer"; even though in France the *directeur artistique*'s functions overlap those of the A&R man as well as those of the producer (as those roles are understood in Britain and the United States); "producer" seems the nearest equivalent.—Ed.

[2] Most of the quotations in this article come from interviews with producers or other professionals in the record industry. More precise details of their sources are mentioned only when relevant.

Edward R. Kealy

FROM CRAFT TO ART

The Case of Sound Mixers
and Popular Music

1 9 7 9

○ ▲ ○ ▲ ○ ▲ ○

T his essay proceeds from the occupational perspective of a particular popular music collaborator—the one credited on record album jackets as the "recording engineer" or "sound mixer." The sound mixer
is a popular art technician, a type of collaborator also common to theatrical,
radio, television, and film productions, but whose role in shaping the aesthetics of popular art is little understood. In addition to illuminating the
role of the popular art technician, studying the recent history of the sound
mixer's relationships with his collaborators provides the sociology of art
with examples of how a craft becomes art and how craftsmen attempt to
become artists. For, in the late 1960s, recording artists began annexing the
craft of sound mixing to their art, while some sound mixers attempted to
slough off their designation as "technicians" and to establish a new collab-
orative role as "artist-mixers." These reciprocal transformations created
problems for popular music collaborators and led to the emergence of new
institutions for production in this art world.

H. S. Becker has noted that such a transformation is a sequence typical
of art history and has affected in recent years such diverse crafts as weaving,
pottery, glass blowing, furniture making, and clothing design.[1] He posits
that such a transformation occurs when artists become interested in the
craft materials as a new medium for artistic expression and make attempts
to take it over. The results of such a transformation show up primarily in
two ways: (1) a change in the aesthetic conventions for judging the crafted

objects from utilitarian to expressive and (2) a change in the status of the work—and the workers—from technical to artistic. The following study specifies how this process took place in popular music collaborations and transformed sound mixing from a craft to an art.

THE SOUND MIXER

As a cultural artifact, popular music has three major components: the music, the commercial system for promoting and distributing it to a mass audience, and the technology for recording and reproducing it. The division of labor among popular music collaborators reflects these components. Usually present at studio recording sessions are music makers (musicians, composers, arrangers), music marketers (record company artists-and-repertoire men or record producers), and recording technicians (sound mixers).

The sound mixer's work represents the point where music and modern technology meet. A sound mixer must know the characteristics of hundreds of microphones and a variety of acoustic environments, and how to employ them to best record a musical instrument; the capabilities and applications of a large array of sound-processing devices, such as echo chambers; the physical capacities of recording media (such as tapes and discs) for accepting and reproducing sounds; the operation of various recording machines; and, finally, how to balance or "mix" at a recording console the electronic impulses coming into a studio "control room" from a variety of live and prerecorded studio sound sources so as to produce a tape that contains a recognizable and effective musical experience. During the decade 1965–75, the process of mixing and refining tapes after the recording of the original studio performance of the musicians has become almost as complex as the editing process that regularly occurs in filmmaking after the original filming of the actors.

Sound mixers commonly hold an occupational self-image that includes such elements of craftsmanship as technical mastery and artistry. A leading Nashville sound mixer describes his work in this way:

> "A mixer is an engineer who takes all the instruments and voices from the recording studios and blends them into that perfect—or near perfect—sound. It is a little like baking a cake. Not too much flour; not too much sugar; just the right ingredients to come out with a tasteful product."[2]

Another mixer has explained why he thinks recording is artful:

RESEARCHER: In what way is recording an art?

MIXER: The answer to that is that the exact way you cause an instrument to sound or blend them together to create a final sound is the art that's involved. . . . In part how much volume he gives to each instrument at a particular time increases or decreases the dynamics of it—creates an interpretation of it that wasn't in the original performance. How he emphasizes the tones that a guitar makes in addition to the basic note, because after all . . . each note on the scale has a tone and the harmonics will determine whether it's a saxophone or a violin. And enhancing these qualities is the art of the engineer.[3]

Both mixers make it clear that, while their skills are considered technical, the practice of such technical skills also involves aesthetic decision making in order to develop a standard for what sounds good.

Recently, sound-mixer trade journals have adopted editorial policies that encourage the mixer to be more self-conscious of his aesthetic contributions. One such editorial states:

As musical ideas and recording techniques have been refined, the demands upon engineers and producers have grown comparably, to the point where their craft is an art form in and of itself. Today their expertise with a fearsome array of concepts and hardware can easily make or break a record.[4]

As this commentator notes, the degree to which sound mixers have taken part in aesthetic decision making has increased during the history of popular recordings, with resulting changes in the aesthetics of music.

The analysis that follows adds the interactional dimension of collaboration and discusses how the changes in the power relationships among collaborators have variously restricted and facilitated the participation of sound mixers in aesthetic decision making.

MODES OF COLLABORATION IN RECORD PRODUCTION

As an occupation, recording has undergone processes of change and development, such as industrialization and rationalization, that are common to much of modern work. In addition, it has undergone a change that is less common: a decentralization induced by new technology. From this history have emerged three currently observable modes of collaborating on popular music productions: the craft-union mode, the entrepreneurial mode, and the art mode.

Each mode can be characterized in terms of the available technology of recording, the intended recording aesthetic, the social organization of studio collaboration, the job responsibilities of the mixer, and the associated occupational ideology of sound mixing.

Craft-Union Mode

The craft-union mode crystallized during the post–World War II era. During the war the technical needs of the combatants had generated improved capabilities for recording sound information on discs and tapes. However, while this improved the range of frequencies that could be recorded, commercial recording processes remained relatively unchanged. The sound mixer's skill lay in using to advantage the acoustic design of the studio, deciding upon the placement of a handful of microphones, and mixing or balancing microphone outputs as the musical performance was recorded. Very little editing was possible, since the performance was recorded directly on a disc or single-track tape. The primary aesthetic question was utilitarian: How well does a recording capture the sounds of a performance? The technology at this time did not offer the sound mixer a wide range of discretionary choices during the recording.

However, the possibility of improved fidelity prompted record corporations to compete seriously with other media in presenting music such as live radio broadcasts and concerts. The companies encouraged their engineers and mixers to develop their craft skills and strive for a recording aesthetic of "concert hall realism" and "high fidelity." This required the construction of large studios and the development of microphone and mixing techniques in order to record whole symphony orchestras and dance bands in a way that simulated the psychoacoustics of a live performance. During this period, the major record companies promoted the recording aesthetic strongly through their corporate interconnections with the major radio networks and film companies, and thus were able to reach a mass audience.

The major media corporations' investment in research and development not only improved fidelity and standardized production processes, but also had a significant impact on the studio workers employed in corporation-owned studios—studios that recorded primarily for mass distribution. The work force was differentiated through a process of professionalization and unionization. Engineers with extensive technical backgrounds specialized in problems of equipment and studio design. In 1948 the Audio Engineering Society held its first meeting at RCA Victor Studios to "establish audio engineering as a separate profession." Those who performed the day-to-day work of recording worked under a chief engineer and were relegated to the status of engineering technician and given the title of sound mixer. Unionization therefore became an attractive alternative for the large corporation sound mixers.[5] Not only did it enable them to negotiate better wages, but it also gave them increased control over their craft. Soon they controlled access to the technology of recording by forbidding collaborators, such as musicians, composers, and record company personnel, to even touch the studio equipment at recording sessions. And they controlled access to the skills of mixing by establishing union apprenticeship and seniority systems. At the same time, they required that all of a company's contracted recording artists use company studios exclusively.

Since studio musicians had also unionized, a salient characteristic of recording sessions in large corporation studios about 1950 was craft union regulation. In addition, the dictates of the corporations' accounting and marketing departments further structured the relationships among collaborators and decided the pace of their work. The company designated an administrative supervisor to recording sessions, the artists-and-repertoire man or "record producer," whose duties included expediting compliance with the contractual provisions of the collaborators, coordinating their work, keeping the studio sessions within budget and on schedule, and selecting and arranging music to suit the company's intended audience. Thus, increasing rationalization in the studio accompanied the large corporations' investment in sophisticated production facilities.

The relationship among collaborators at such recording sessions tended to be formal and impersonal. The mixer recorded whomever the company brought before his microphones without regard for whether he appreciated the musical style or talents of the artists. Usually, the mixer had no musical training or experience; but, like any good craftsman, his interest was in improving the technical performance of his equipment rather than the musical performance of the artists or the market performance of the recording. His pay was the same whether the recording was a success or failure in the marketplace. Yet, a sound mixer's work was the means by which his collaborators realized their aesthetic and commercial ends.

The basic standard used to judge a sound mixer's work was whether the sound was "in the grooves." The good mixer-craftsman would make sure that unwanted sounds were not recorded or were at least minimized, that the desired sounds were recorded without distortion, and that the sounds were in balance. The recording technology itself, and thus the sound mixer's work, was to be unobtrusive so as not to destroy the listener's illusion that he was sitting in Philharmonic Hall rather than in his living room. The *art of recording* was not to compete for the public's aesthetic attention to *the art that was being recorded.*

Thus, the craft-union mode of production was a by-product of rationalization in the recording industry. Unionization gave sound mixers a defense against further encroachments by the professional audio engineer and further work demands by the record producers. However, it also gave them a defensive occupational ideology that locked them into a narrow, technical, instrumental role among their collaborators, who had limited expectations of them and allowed them limited responsibilities for the final product.

Entrepreneurial Mode

However, in 1949 two technological innovations began undermining the predominance of the craft-union mode of studio collaboration: television and tape recording. The rise of television to mass popularity occurred at the expense of national network radio programming. The radio industry turned to local- and minority-taste programming, which previously had proved uneconomical. Such programming decentralized the creation of popular musical taste and made it more difficult for the major music corporations to shape it.

At the same time, studio technology suddenly became much simpler, cheaper, and more flexible with the replacement of direct-to-disc recording by tape recording. Since only a modest investment could now outfit a new recording studio, the ability to make recordings also became decentralized. Within five years of tape's introduction, the number of companies issuing record albums increased from 11 to nearly 200.[6] During the 1950s the coincidence of the diffusion of these two innovations provided the basis for the growth of another mode for organizing studio collaborations: the entrepreneurial mode.

Small entrepreneurs could profitably record new or previously ignored artists and find an audience for them through radio airplay aimed at local- or minority-taste audiences. They could also, in the management of their companies, avoid the high union wages, strict work rules, and expensive technical standards that had developed at the large corporation studios. Some of these entrepreneurs owned and operated studios themselves; others simply rented facilities when necessary. Much of the rhythm and blues and rock and roll music that came to prominence in American popular culture in the 1950s and early 1960s was produced by entrepreneurial collaborations outside the major corporation studios.

The emergence of the entrepreneurial mode of collaborating brought with it a new recording aesthetic. The entrepreneurs, independent studio owners, and mixers who worked for them did not have the resources in terms of studio facilities, musicians, and music to compete with the recording aesthetic of concert hall realism and high fidelity. However, their intended audience—lower-class whites, blacks, and teenagers—was neither expecting nor familiar with such an aesthetic. The music familiar to this audience was played in improvised acoustic environments: the music of roadside dance halls, small clubs, and high school gyms. Only an ethnomusicologist would be able to appreciate reproduction of this music with "high fidelity."

The solution to the problem provided an opportunity for the entrepreneurial collaborators to create, with the technology and the music available to them, a new recording aesthetic that would develop in this audience an appreciation of studio recording as aesthetically desirable in itself rather than as an attempted simulation of a live performance—all of which encouraged innovation in using the limited studio and artistic resources: the use of echo and reverberation devices instead of cavernous studios, recording at loud volume levels, the use of novel microphone placements, electronically altering the acoustic sound's waveform, and various forms of tape editing in addition to the arrangements for music and new lyrics aimed at the life-style of its audience. The aesthetic and commercial goal was to get a "hit sound" from the studio.

Accomplishing this often required that the collaborators work in new ways together. One of the most successful entrepreneurs of rock music, Phil Spector, described the nature of his collaboration with a sound mixer at an independent studio in the early 1960s:

> "You really needed somebody good alongside of you, and Larry was really helpful . . . for what I was doing, he was invaluable. Everything was an experiment. We were breaking every rule there was to break like 'don't go over the red line with the needle' and 'watch this' and 'it's gonna skip' and who cares? . . . Just make the record."[7]

In contrast to the craft-union mode, with its emphasis on technical correctness, concert hall realism, and strict division of labor, the entrepreneurial mode is a more fluid and open collaboration which allows an interchange of skills and ideas among the musicians, technicans, and music market entrepreneurs. Laing thus describes the mid-1950s collaboration of entrepreneur Norman Petty and rock musicians Buddy Holly and the Crickets in terms of an integration of functions:

> They combined within themselves . . . the role of song writer, musicians, lead and backing vocalists, and record producer. The recording was even done at Petty's own studio in Clovis, New Mexico. . . . Consequent upon this integration of functions was an integration of the musical elements within each song.[8]

However, this integration of functions also had important consequences for the sound mixer. In exchange for the opportunity to contribute to shaping the musical aesthetic, he also had to share his control over, and knowledge of, the studio technology with his collaborators. The craft-union rules, which restricted nonmixer access to the technology, did not apply in most of the small independent studios used by the entrepreneurs. One mixer summed up the consequences of this change by stating: "Then [in the heyday of the craft-union mode] the musician was fitted to the mike. Now the mike must fit the musician." In such collaborations the sound mixer acts more like a service worker who must please his clients without benefit of appeal to a set of craft standards enforceable through his union. Skill at selling studio features and techniques to collaborators became as important as skill at achieving good sound quality. Thus, the occupational ideology of these sound mixers expanded beyond that of narrow, instrumental, craft-union technicians to include a client-oriented, entrepreneurial outlook reflecting the new roles of salesman and producer of hit recordings.

Art Mode

Another important consequence of the integration of functions in the entrepreneurial mode was the integration of the sound of the studio technology with the musical aesthetic of popular music, for among the audiences for this new music was the next generation of rock musicians, and the studio sound of the music set up expectations of what rock music making should be. H. S. Bennett has shown that beginning rock musicians usually learn their musical values by listening to popular recordings reproduced by electromechanical media.[9] The instruments they learn to play and perform with (particularly electric guitars and keyboards, and public address systems) are also electromechanical devices. As they practice with these instruments, they attempt to incorporate the sounds and arrangements of recorded popular music in their playing, developing what Bennett calls a "recording consciousness" before actually entering a studio. The result, as I. I. Horowitz has noted, has been that the modern generation of rock musicians realizes that "the gap between the engineering of sound and the creation of music has narrowed to a remarkable degree."[10] Thus, the accomplished rock musician develops a natural interest in the craft of sound mixing as a means of artistic expression.

In the 1960s, further developments in recording technology facilitated the rock musician's involvement in the sound-mixing process. Tape recorders and tapes became multitracked, with as many as 24 separate tracks available on a tape. Each instrument could be recorded separately and then replayed and edited in minute detail. Rock pieces now commonly consist of built-up layers of such studio performances, which are remixed and reduced to a final master tape. The rock musician could record a performance in the studio, store it on tape, and "mix" it later, thus taking over one of the functions previously left to the skill and judgment of the sound mixer. Formerly, single-track recording required a proper and final mix to be accomplished at the time of the actual studio performance by the musicians. The consequences of the new technology had a critical effect on the sound mixer's ability to control the recording process. One mixer notes: "That's why I'm in favor of the 'back to mono' thing. It'd give more power back to the engineer because he'd have to do all the mixing in one take."

However, the rock star's successful annexation of the sound mixer's craft could not occur until the balance of power in the *work organization* of studio collaboration had shifted in the rock musician's favor. For when these musicians first began to obtain recording contracts from the major record corporations, they found themselves confronted by the craft-union mode of collaboration and the "hands off the equipment" working regulations of the sound mixers. Marty Balin, a member of a highly successful San Francisco rock group, recounted some of his earlier experiences in the studio of a major corporation:

Because of certain union requirements, Balin hasn't been allowed to touch the board while the group was recording. "What bullshit that is. If I even touched the thing, they'd cancel the session. They slap your hands. Wham. 'Now, now, now, don't touch that Marty.' Like I'm some fucking moron kid."[11]

However, the equipment was precisely what the rock musician wanted to get his hands on.

In the mid-1960s the relationship between record corporations and popular artists underwent a revolution. Rock musicians developed the capacity to act as self-contained production units. Many formed groups in order to write, arrange, and perform their own music. After some preliminary experiences with working in recording studios, they often became less inclined to follow the editorial and administrative recommendations of company artists-and-repertoire men or independent entrepreneurs, especially when they realized that the use of middlemen substantially reduced their share of profits. One independent record producer explained:

"Groups want to spread their wings a little after they've been successful . . . If you're a success as an artist, it galls you to think there are other people who are taking 15 to 20 percent of what you do as an artist. And the thought is always in your head. 'Why do I need those extra people.' "

The revenues that rock musicians generated from the sale of millions of albums, publishing rights, and large-scale concert tours provided them with their own economic base in the music industry. Many artists used the newly acquired power to build their own recording studios and to establish their own record labels. From this emerged yet another mode of collaboration, even more antibureaucratic and anticraft union than the entrepreneurial mode: the art mode. A national recording manager's explanation of a major company's current policy indicates the rock musician's power in this mode of collaboration:

An established act will insist on going where he has been successful and we normally allow this. One of the reasons an artist goes to a particular studio is he likes to mix it himself or there is a mixer he has worked with and has confidence in. He doesn't want to change that system and you can hardly blame him.[12]

The distinguishing characteristic of art-mode collaborations is that middlemen representing the commercial interests of record companies or independent entrepreneurs are excluded from the studio production. The collaborators most directly involved in producing the popular music sound—the musicians, composers, and sound mixers—take responsibility for organizing the work to be done at the sessions and make the aesthetic decisions.

Often the rock star emerged as the ultimate arbiter in the process of determining what a good record should sound like. The standard for judging recordings is no longer a merely utilitarian one—that of capturing sound—

but rather a primarily expressive one—that of producing artistic sounds. One commentator notes: "Unlike on his *Something/Anything?* album Todd doesn't play all the instruments. 'I play the studio this time,' he says."[13] The rock musician views the studio equipment as practically another instrument.

As a result, the occupational ideology for sound mixing changed: work previously considered merely technical now became artistic. A look at the album cover credits of such rock stars as the Rolling Stones, John Lennon, the Beach Boys, and David Bowie demonstrates this fact. For example, the credits listed on one of David Bowie's albums—*Diamond Dogs*—read as follows:

> Written, arranged and produced by Bowie.
> Engineer Keith Harwood
> Tracks 1–5. Side one; 3, 4, 5. Side two mixed by Bowie and Visconti
> Tracks 6. Side one; 1, 2 Side two mixed By Bowie and Keith Harwood
> Strings on "1984" arranged by Tony Visconti.

The credits make it clear that Bowie is in control of all major creative tasks in the production of the recording. He goes to the trouble of detailing authorship of the sound mixing; he notes the assistance of two people, one of whom—Harwood—is a studio sound mixer; the other—Visconti—is a musical arranger. However, Bowie takes first billing for the mixes of all the selections. The rock star thus announces to his peers, critics, and audience that his sound mixing work is part of his art. The transformation of the craft to an art is complete.

FROM CRAFTSMAN TO ARTIST

The intrusion of rock stars into the craft world of sound mixers has also had its effects on the careers now available to them and the possible rewards they can expect from their work. As Becker has observed:

> When new people successfully create a new [art] world which defines other conventions as embodying artistic value, all the participants in the old world who cannot make a place in the new one lose out.[14]

The new convention in popular music, which makes sound mixing an extension of the musician-composer's art, has created the most problems for the craft-union sound mixers. They have found it difficult to accept the demands of rock stars who are often much younger than they are. One 48-year-old union mixer explained:

> "At a rock mixing session you might have twelve people telling you how to mix. . . . Often a group has one member who plays four or five instruments and wants control of the mix so he can get all of his parts in. Well, that won't sound good on a car radio. . . . But you can't push it on a session. That's why I like to stay in disc mastering these days: machines can't talk back. . . . The old school

engineers and producers used to work with talent. Now you get guys in who just play loud."

As rock musicians became aware of the resistance, resentment, and lack of appreciation for their music by craft-union mixers, they turned more and more to the entrepreneurial and art modes of collaboration, with the result that less work and fewer opportunities for advancement have been available to such mixers.

On the other hand, the desire on the part of rock stars to integrate studio techniques into their music created a demand for young sound mixers who were totally attuned to the conventions of rock music. In fact, one of the best credentials an aspiring mixer could have was being an ex-rock musician from a small-time band. This situation has led to the emergence of a hybrid type of studio collaborator—an artist-mixer. Again, Becker has noted that where the art and craft worlds overlap, craftsmen tend to speak of themselves as artists-craftsmen.[15] They seek recognition for their work beyond their in-group, although they must usually depend on the institutions of the ordinary craftsmen for their training and rewards. However, they hold an aesthetic ideology that goes beyond the utilitarian standards of the ordinary craftsmen and is in rapport with the aesthetics of the artists who work with similar craft materials.

In the field of recording, some critics have always insisted that sound mixing has an aesthetic dimension beyond merely capturing sound well. In 1956 one audiophile proclaimed: "I rate . . . the art of microphoning as the equal of any another interpretive art . . . the plain fact is that microphoning is an art unto itself with its own laws, principles, and its own special culture."[16] Other critics have suggested that a mixer's training should include musical as well as technical knowledge and should take place in special institutes or in music schools. But not until the late 1960s—when younger sound mixers realized that the chance for fast career advancement lay in allying themselves with the new generation of rock musicians rather than with the craft unions—did sound mixers begin aggressively asserting the aesthetic importance of their work. A young (early 30s) part-owner of an important studio in New York stated in a trade paper:

> The sound of today's record has become a much more important ingredient in the formula for a hit record than the hit of the 1940's. However, it is now more difficult for the arranger to exercise complete control of the final sound since now the engineer who may never have studied one note of music can improve on the arrangement, merely by adding one of the effects and that added effect could have more impact than the other two-thirds of the arrangement.[17]

In effect, some mixers began to develop and promote an artist-mixer ideology.

During this same period a new trade magazine appeared—*Recording En-*

gineer/Producer—which is, as its masthead states, "The magazine produced to relate Recording Art to Recording Science to Recording Equipment." In one of its early issues the editors announced the engineer of the year, "who danced with his fingers [on the recording console]."[18] The editors defended their analogy in an introduction:

> We think the analogy is not too strained when we compare the artistry of a great dancer to the artistry of a great recording engineer. Such an engineer is beyond the elementary repetition of "It worked then, and it'll work now. Why take chances?" just as the dancer is beyond carefully putting one foot in front of the other and merely walking. The techniques of the engineer and dancer are always growing, changing, expanding, in order to better express the music and feeling they deal with daily.

Significantly, the editors belittled the pragmatic, utilitarian standards of the ordinary craftsman and promoted an artistic aesthetic of experimentation and self-expression.

In this context it was not difficult for some mixers to put forth an artist-mixer ideology by claiming a total identity and equality with recording artists. They assert, "The recording engineer is another musician who has to know the score both musically and technically."[19] The corollary of this ideology of equality is that the sound mixer should share the rights and privileges of the recording artist's status: royalties on record sales, and professional and popular recognition as an artist. For the artist-craftsman, then, the development and promotion of an art ideology for his work can serve as a proposal to the art world to negotiate new terms for collaborating.

In practice, however, having status as artist-mixer recognized and rewarded has been problematic for sound mixers because of their marginality to the institutions of the rock musicians' art world. First, the reason a rock group values a mixer as an important aesthetic collaborator is often because of his special knowledge of "studio magic." The more resourceful and innovative the mixer is in applying studio technology to enhance or augment the recording, the more indispensable he is as an aesthetic collaborator. For example, mixers who are proficient in programming Moog synthesizers to be compatible with other rock instruments have recently been much in demand. Conversely, the more knowledgeable the recording artist becomes about studio techniques, or the more simplified and accessible the technology becomes, as in the case of newer models of Moog synthesizers, the less the sound mixer is able to claim a unique store of aesthetic resources, and the less necessary he becomes as an aesthetic collaborator.

Second, the artist-mixer is also vulnerable to charges that he is not really an artist because he does not fully take part in what is conceived of as the essential artistic act. One mixer attacked the artist-mixer ideology of his colleagues by arguing that "the engineer isn't playing the notes, he's on the other side of the glass [studio window], he's not in there with the group playing." Being "on the other side of the glass" is symbolic of the mixers' limited participation in the musicians' subculture wherein they develop their aesthetic ideals or "recording consciousness." Occupationally, the mixer is in a bind: sound mixers are typically affiliated with a particular studio while rock musicians are typically nomadic. Some aspiring artist-mixers have attempted to overcome the barriers to full participation in the rock musician's art world by plunging wholeheartedly into their life-style. This strategy of assimilation presents its own problems:

> "Then they want you to travel with them and do their sound on the road which isn't always fun. And you don't get much variety in sound problems. I know some of the younger engineers are doing this. But it easily goes to extremes. For example, there's a certain world-famous group . . . whose engineer wants so badly to be one of them that he's become a heroin addict too."

The demands of such a life-style limit the successful aspirants to the free, young, and hardy among sound mixers.

A third related problem that the aspiring artist-mixer must face when he throws his lot in with a particular group of artists is the mercurial nature of rock star careers. Like all those who assimilate, the sound mixer's destiny becomes tied to the host group's. Unfortunately, the cultural riptides that keep various recording artists' careers afloat often inexplicably run out, groups of collaborators founder, and the mixer is left stranded. As one mixer put it: "There's no job security. If the group goes, you go." Moreover, the taste for highly engineered music is neither universal nor constant among recording artists and audiences. Ultimately, the mixer who aspires to be an artist rather than a craftsman is subject to the same hit-or-miss career that plagues all those who attempt to create popular music. In general, the success with which an artist-craftsman moves from his craft world to an art world depends to a large degree on whether it is possible for him to abandon the established institutions and rewards of the craft world and successfully finesse the career contingencies of the art world.

During the early 1970s, several new institutions for rewarding mixers symbolically and materially evolved to accommodate the artist-mixer in his career. One important need that had to be fulfilled for the artist-mixer was that of making artists, critics, and audiences aware of his aesthetic contribution. Many of the rock groups who work in the art mode of collaboration in studio productions have recognized the new status of the artist-mixer by giving him artistlike credits on their record album covers. For example, the inner sleeve of the Rolling Stones' *It's Only Rock and Roll* album is devoted to their collaborators' captioned photographs, two of which picture sound mixers at their recording consoles. In addition, record company executives have made it a practice to award gold records to mixers as well as artists in recognition of their contribution to the aesthetic success of the recording as reflected in consumer sales figures.

The problem that has proved to be the most difficult to solve for the artist-mixer is that of receiving equitable compensation for his aesthetic contribution. Some recording artists have paid their mixers a bonus after a recording becomes a commercial success. Others have commissioned their mixers to design personal studios and public address systems for them. Mixers themselves are increasingly offering their services directly to successful recording artists as freelancers, at high fees, on a project-by-project basis. A few mixers have atained the ultimate artistic recognition that the music industry can give: a share in the royalties of record sales as co-producers with the recording artists. However, it is likely that artist-mixer careers will be institutionalized only if record companies and recording artists agree to provide royalties routinely to the sound mixer in addition to a recording session fee or salary.

Discussion of the artist-mixer's career problems indicates that for artist-craftsmen successfully to complete a transition from the craft world to the art world requires that the established art world agree to accept their ideology of artistic work, to recognize their work institutionally as art, and to make economic concessions to support it.

NOTES

[1] H. S. Becker, "Arts and Crafts," *American Journal of Sociology 83* (January 1978), pp. 864–70.

[2] "The Unsung Heroes," *Billboard* (28 October 1967), p. 72.

[3] Quotations accompanied by citations are from personal interview transcriptions.

[4] P. Lawrence, "Synthesthesia—Seen Any Good Records Lately?" *Recording Engineer / Producer* 5 (April 1974), p. 47.

[5] Three unions have organized sound mixers: the National Association of Broadcast Engineers and Technicians, the International Brotherhood of Electrical Workers, and the International Alliance of Theatrical Stage Employees and Motion Picture Machine Operators.

[6] R. Gelatt, *The Fabulous Phonograph* (New York: Appleton-Century, 1965), pp. 299–300.

[7] R. Williams *Out of His Head* (New York: Outerbridge & Lazard, 1972), p. 71.

[8] D. Laing, *The Sound of Our Time* (Chicago: Quadrangle, 1969), pp. 97–98.

[9] H. S. Bennett, "Other People's Music," Ph.D. dissertation, Northwestern University, 1972.

[10] I. I. Horowitz, "Rock, Recordings, and Rebellion," in C. Nanry (ed.), *American Music* (New Brunswick, N.J.: Transaction, 1972), p. 269.

[11] T. Cahill, "Marty Balin Sings Again," *Rolling Stone* (8 June 1972), p. 8.

[12] E. Tiegel, "Unions' Engineer Stipulation Irks Independent Producers," *Billboard* (1 April 1972), p. 14.

[13] "Half Notes," *Crawdaddy* (May 1973), p. 23.

[14] H. S. Becker, "Art as Collective Action," *American Sociological Review 38* (December 1974), p. 774.

[15] Becker, "Arts and Crafts," p. 866.

[16] E. T. Canby, "The Sound-man Artist," *Audio* (June 1956), pp. 44–45.

[17] "Ramone Stresses Gain Made by Sound in Producing Hit," *Billboard* (10 May 1969), p. 51.

[18] G. Koch, "Roy Halee, Engineer of the Year, 1971," *Recording Engineer/Producer 2* (April 1974), p. 11

[19] "Recording Studios in Profit Pinch," *Variety* (2 December 1970), p. 1.

H. Stith Bennett

THE REALITIES OF PRACTICE

1 9 8 0

○ ▲ ○ ▲ ○ ▲ ○

COMMITMENT TO A SCHEDULE

T he first consideration of the practice session is that it is a prear-ranged meeting, and there can be as many or as few sessions as the group cares to arrange. Observation of many groups shows that there is a great variation in frequency of practice schedules (from "never" to "every day"), and that the categorization of groups by their practice sched-uling yields an indicator of group career stages. It is, of course, not the number of practices, but the ideological framework which creates a partic-ular practice density that is indicative of the group's stage of development. When there is not enough material to play a three- or four-hour gig, the group is at an early stage, and the need for practice is great. If the "every day" schedule is actualized at this point, the shortest possible lag time ensues between the group's formation and the playing of its first gig. As the number of practices decreases from the practical limit (i.e., "every day," which means "almost every day"), the time it takes to construct a repertoire increases. Since the ability to accept an engagement depends on the existence of a repertoire, the practice schedule of a newly formed group determines its possibilities for succession to the steady-gig stage. It is, however, the fate of many groups to break up after initial formation because a workable practice schedule cannot be maintained. Here are some typical examples of nonmusical factors affecting the existence of group music.

J: There's one thing we're gonna have to do, and that's practice every day. If we don't do that there's no use in saying we've got a group together.

S: That was the reason my last group broke up. We coulda had a good band, too—Mike was a really steady bass player, and Jones was really into drums—but when nobody showed up for practice except every other Tuesday, all the energy just went down the drain.

J: Bob is working until five on weekdays, so we'll have to practice at night. . . .

B: If things work out with the group I'll quit that job. I just need enough money to pay off my amp and have something to live on.

S: Well, I know we can't play in here past about ten or something like that or else the neighbors will get pissed off and call the cops or something.

J: Let's do it between seven and nine then—no, six-thirty and nine, OK?

S: If we do that every day for two or three weeks we oughta be ready. [Group conversation after first session]

S: [Phone rings.] Hello.

M: Hello, this is Mike. I just wanted to call and tell you that I can't make it to practice tomorrow 'cause I'm sick.

S: You were sick yesterday and Monday.

M: Yeah, I know, but I just can't make it. Really, I'm sick.

S: Well, when are we going to get this thing together?

M: Look, I'll call you when I can practice again, OK? [Silence.] Hello?

S: Yeah?

M. Well, is that all right?

S: Whatever you say. It's up to you.

M: OK, well, I'll see you maybe the beginning of next week sometime, when I'm feeling better. I'll call you then, OK?

S: Goodbye, Mike.

M: Goodbye. [Telephone conversation between members of a dissolving group]

It is obvious that the practice schedule must coexist with a variety of nonmusical contingencies, and yet produce enough sessions to generate a performable repertoire. One of the perennial signs of a group in trouble is the absence of members from called practices, for when there is "something better to do" the special nature of the commitment to rock music is bastardized. Groups are founded on the commitment that *nothing comes before music*. When group members fail to show up for practice they are doing more than breaking commitments to the other individuals in the group. Their absence demonstrates that something means more than music—that, in short, they are not *musicians*. The ability of an individual to schedule everyday activities around the schedule of band practice is the ability of a group to exist.

"You know, if I had the most beautiful girl in the world, and she said, 'You're spending too much time with the band and not enough time with me; if you don't quit the band, I'll have to leave, because you love music more than you love me,' I'd say goodbye to her, even though I loved her and all, because nothing can get in the way of your music. Nothing. [Drummer]

Once this degree of commitment is obtained for the practice schedule the group moves along to the business of "getting down some songs."

SONG GETTING

What separates the rock musician's musical consciousness from that of rock audiences is the knowledge of how to *get* a song from a recording. This requires the resources of an instrument and a playback system. At first the process seems so simplistic that it might be unworthy of attention, yet its naive simplicity is its essential trait and is not to be overlooked.

HSB: How do you get your material?

G: Mostly from records.

HSB: Say some more. . . .

G: There really isn't much more to say, you just set [*sic*] down in front of the stereo with your guitar and play the record over and over until you learn it.

HSB: Do you think everybody does it that way?

G: I guess they'd have to . . . I can't think of how else you'd do it. Everybody I know does it that way.

HSB: What about buying sheet music?

G: I wouldn't know what to do with it—I can't read. Besides, I want to hear what the thing *sounds* like, and there ain't no way a sheet of paper sounds like Jimi Hendrix. [Guitar player]

What this account leaves out is a minute description of song-getting episodes, and therefore suppresses some of the most significant and problematic detail. Most musicians assume that this is "the way things are done" and lend it little importance, yet it is the event that is the key link in the transportation of musical ideas from the mass product to the individual mind, and bears further analysis.

In order to gain more detailed information I asked musicians to reminisce about their first song-getting attempts. Here is one of the richest responses.

HSB: Do you remember the first song you ever got off a record?

B: Yeah, it was "Sunshine of Your Love," you know, the Cream song.

HSB: How did that happen?

B: Well, it was mainly because I'd just gotten my guitar . . . just had it for a few weeks, and I would get somebody to show me a few chords and I'd practice them for a while and then I'd get frustrated. I mean I wanted to play something *specific* . . . a song.

HSB: And so. . . .

B: And so that riff kept going through my head: da-da-da-da-dum-dum-dum-da-da-dum, and I tried to play it but I kept losing it . . . forgetting how it went. So I'd get frustrated and put down the guitar, and then the damn riff would run thorugh my head again, or I'd hear it on the radio or some thing, and so

> I'd try to play it again, *but for the life of me I couldn't remember it while I was trying to play it.* [my italics]
>
> HSB: So what happened?
>
> B: You got to remember that this was four years ago and I'd never played any music in my life. I got so frustrated I just gave up . . . put the guitar in the corner and forgot about it. But it seemed like everywhere I went that song was on the radio or the stereo or something.
>
> HSB: Well, you obviously went back to it.
>
> B: Yeah, what happened was we got the album and so one day I got up all my nerve and tried to play along. Of course the guitar wasn't in tune with the record and I didn't understand about that, but somehow I managed to hit a note that sounded reaonably close and I kept putting the needle back in the grooves and trying to play along, and eventually I came up with something that resembled that riff. Some of the notes were wrong, but I had the rhythm down cold. I knew it wasn't much, really, but it was like I had won. [Guitar player]

Interaction with The Music is inescapable, and for the new instrument owner it provides the first "something specific" to play. It may not be obvious at first that a piece of The Music which has saturated a beginner's mind to the extent that it is completely memorized could be forgotten in the attempt to play it, yet this is the empirical evidence for which I have not found a negative case. This could be the point of departure for a deep discussion of the phenomenology of musical memory processes, a discussion that could be extended to include another piece of empirical evidence, which is that musicians report that they have the experience of hearing "music in the head," while some nonmusicians claim they have never had such an experience. I will save the phenomenology of music consciousness for another time, however, and simply point out that recorded songs are not *gotten* through the usual mode of audience exposure to playback events, but by the specifically defined event of copying a recording by playing along with it and using the technical ability to play parts of it over and over again.

The most important thing to notice about the initial interaction of recordings and musicians is its privacy. Although the self-taught student does not have the benefit of a more experienced musician as a guide, there is also freedom from the human expectation system of pedagogy. A beginner can therefore proceed at his or her own speed and, by manipulating the controllable electronic playback system, select certain temporal segments for focused attention. It is the conjunction of naive determination and the controllable repetition of recordings that makes an individual's song-getting skill possible. Similar learning techniques have long been employed in hard-sell radio and television advertising, and, of late, educational theorists have caught up with advertising practices by conceptualizing learning as repetition delivered by an electronic device (one notable example being *Sesame Street*).

One musically significant difference in song getting appeared in the case of a drummer.

HSB: Did you ever have any drum lessons?

J: Yeah, but I was playing in groups before that.

HSB: How could that be?

J: Well, I had my drum set—which was a Christmas present—in the basement along with my record player . . . I guess that was before stereo. And I would get a record and try to play along with it.

HSB: Did you ever play just certain parts of the record?

J: No, never. These were singles, see, and you'd put one on and then run over and sit down and try to play from the beginning. Sometimes when I was having a hard time I would just listen to a certain part, but I wouldn't try to play along—just listen.

HSB: And you did this alone?

J: Sure. I would have been too embarrassed at first to have anybody watch me, 'cause I was making a lot of mistakes. I didn't know what I was doing.

HSB: But you were just learning.

J: I'm still that way though. I don't like other people around when we practice— it makes me nervous . . . you know, I was just thinking . . . it's really pretty hard to play drums along with a record—even now.

HSB: Then you started the hard way?

J: Maybe . . . but it sure makes you listen. [Drummer]

The career of a local rock musician starts when the resource of the instrument is combined with the resource of The Music in a private copying episode. That it is possible to learn to play this way attests to the simplicity of The Music, but it also is indicative of the results of a private human-machine interaction where the human is in precise control of the stimulation that the machine gives.

The next career step is to expand the song-getting experience to the group situation. Here the individual's unique learning experiences are negotiated into a set of song-getting rules, and a group recording consciousness is invoked.

"The first big fight we ever had was about who had the song right. It was a four-chord change—regular old schlock rock . . . I don't even remember the name . . . well, anyway Pete had decided that the third chord was—let's say this is in G—a C, and I said it was an A minor. We'd play the song over and over and Pete, being the bass player, would play the C that the bass player on the record played, and I being the guitar player, would play the A minor which the guitar player of the record played. He was hearing the bass part and I was hearing the guitar part, and we both were right. It finally got to 'you stupid asshole, you can't play for shit anyway' . . . something like that . . . and I was so pissed off I just packed up my guitar and got about ten feet of rubber pulling out of the driveway. [Guitar player]

If an academic musical universe of discourse could hold in this situation, the concept of *relative minor* might be injected into the argument with some chance for resolution, since Am and C are closely related chords that can harmonize with or substitute for each other under certain circumstances.

What is determining these musicians' music, however, is not a body of knowledge—a *theory* of music—but the aural experience of the recording. The conflict about who was *right*—that is, whose interpretation of the recorded sound was to be considered legitimate—did not admit a consideration that varying interpretations can be derived from various ways of listening (aesthetics). Throughout it all the recording remained an unquestionable standard to be referred to "over and over" with expectations of revelation and resolution of doubt. Musicians may fail to reproduce recorded sounds, but the electronic god never fails.

It is such an important point to recognize this group song-getting sequence that I will give another detailed example. The song in this case is "C'mon," recorded by a group called Poco. It goes through a few more changes than the average rock song.

> R: [*At the turntable.*] OK, now I'll play the introduction . . . you got that?
> S: I'm not sure. How's this sound?
> R: No, no, it's "dah dah dit, dah, dah, dah."
> S: Play it again . . . [*He does.*] Damn that goes by quick.
> R: Well, that's close enough, how about running through the first verse.
> S: OK.
> R: Shit, what are those words there: "Dah, dah, dah . . . and it won't take long."
> S: I'm gonna sing this song?
> R: Yeah, of course, and it's just F and C.
> S: And then there's that little lick, which actually should be in harmony.
> R: Well, just play one note for now. But remember the C after the second one: "bow, dah, dah, dah" [etc.] [Getting "C'mon" from the record]

To get this song took at least two hours, and to be able to play it "all the way through without a mistake" took many rehearsals—perhaps fifty runthroughs over a three-day span. During that span the record was considered a few more times to clear up minor confusions about specific parts. After that the group agreed that they could play it "just like the record."

It seemed unlikely to me that *everybody* learned to play rock music simply by listening to recordings. I searched for negative evidence, which produced itself in the following way:

> HSB: Would you say that you got turned on to playing music through recordings?
> B: No. I mean records turn me on, for sure, but I started playing because I knew this guy that played, and I used to go over to his house and play, and then he had a band and I went to hear them practice and then I would even go with them to jobs. It was more like that.
> HSB: What kinds of things did you learn that way?
> B: I guess I learned all the songs he knew, which was all the songs the band knew. I used to know all his licks . . . the two of us would just sit around and play and when we would do something I wanted to learn I'd make him show me. [Rhythm guitar player]

Obviously one alternate account for learning to play rock music is the phenomenon of detailed face-to-face transmission, i.e., pedagogy. The empirical question then becomes: Where did the teacher learn what he knows? There is convincing historical evidence that the chain of connections between students and teachers of rock musicianship is not an infinite regression and that it ends in the process of white musicians copying recordings of black musicians' music. In the 1950s self-styled anthropologists of American black culture turned the uniqueness of black music into a product that was salable to white audiences, i.e., *rock and roll* music. The generalities of the process of American whites stealing American black cultural products (especially music) for their own economic gain are too well known to elaborate here. What is more important for the present is that the apparent negative evidence for my findings of transmission of rock musical knowledge through interaction with recordings, i.e., transmission by pedagogy, points to an entire historical process of impersonal interactional "pedagogy" through recordings. The point is that whether or not the initiate learns from a recording or from a teacher who has learned from a recording, the ability to get songs from records is the essential process for the transmission or rock music.

Here is another kind of alternate account:

HSB: How did you get into rock music?

K: I took classical piano lessons for twelve years . . . my dream was to be a concert pianist, and rock and roll was . . . well, you know, *commercial*, not really music. Then I got to college and these guys were starting a group and they heard me playing piano and they talked me into giving it a try. It was really hard for me at first because I had never tried to play without music in front of me, and so we went out and bought one of those books of sheet music from albums, and, of course, I could read that perfectly, and that broke the ice.

HSB: So you learned to play rock and roll from written music?

K: It's true in a way, but those transcriptions are so bad—they never match the record—so I stopped doing the sheet music trip really quick. It's so simple just to get things off the record, sheet music is just for people who can't hear. [Piano player]

The fact that rock sheet music exists as a salable item would seem to refute my song-getting argument. Much could be said about the market for those products. They are primarily aimed at the home market, but could conceivably be used by non-rock musicians who routinely perform from sheet music to "modernize" their repertoire. However, rock sheet music is itself derived from recordings in most cases, and although it is transcribed by experts into the conventions of traditional musical notation, the process differs little from the direct song-getting process that I have described. The generally poor repute in which rock sheet music is held among rock musicians is inherent in the limitations of the traditional notation system: rock musicians tend to play in ways for which conventional notation does not exist. This phenomenon has promoted and will continue to promote experimentation with written notation systems that can more adequately convey unconventional sounds, just as the art music world is now filled with experimental notation systems. In either case the primacy of sound over literature is surfacing.

Wherever I have sought out the basic process of learning to play rock music, the human–recording interaction—"getting the song from the record"—appears. In its typical cases there is a direct interaction between the initiate, with the instrument in hand, and the playback system: in the case of face-to-face transmission there is only a series of pedagogical links that separate the initiate from the song-getting event; and finally, in the case of transmission by written notation, experience with recordings is both logically and temporally prior to the writing down of the music, and is therefore a special case of song getting.

As a comparative case to the practice of getting songs from recordings, consider this account of the getting of a song in a Polynesian culture. The "musician"

> will go to the ocean side of the atoll at a propitious time accompanied by an assistant. He will enter the sea before dawn and swim beyond the ocean reef, a feat in itself involving no little danger. There, just beyond the line of breakers he will lie and swing up and down on the rollers as they pile themselves to crash on the reef, and chant his *tabunea* (or invocation) as follows: "O-ho, for I seize the leaf of the tree, the leaf of the tree the ocean—one, the Ocean-One. Come down to me, come to me, my inspiration verse. Come forth and be-drawn-forth from below, for I begin above, under the blowing wind of the southeast. It is finished, the tune, it is finished its-begetting." The words and music then come to him and he sings them out line by line so that his companion will hear and repeat them until the song is done. The companion will never forget or vary the song thus obtained. Anyone rash enough to attempt the above process without full skill and preparation will certainly end in trouble.[1]

Whether the god is oceanic or electronic, it is the unquestioned source of perfect music. Musical skill in both the Polynesian and rock examples is concerned with the process of *getting* music that already exists. The individual creative process of *making* music is not thought to exist in either case, and, instead, compositions somehow arrive intact and unquestioned.

Contrary to most academic definitions of their situation, contemporary popular musicians do, in fact, organize performances with the aid of a formal notation system. However, it is not a *written* system. What is established in every rock musician's mind is the set of sound possibilities that are responsible for the recorded sounds that reach one's ears. Electronic techniques provide the possibility for acoustic phenomena which break with the limitations of sound making that were in effect when the written notation system was developed. Therefore, an understanding of the acoustic control that is possible in the recording studio has promoted a unique consciousness of the makeup of sounds in general—what I call the *recording consciousness*. It is this consciousness that defines a group of people with expectations about the way things *sound* that are wholly different from the expectations of those who learned to listen without sound recordings in their environment, and demonstrably different from the expectations of those who learned to listen in an environment where reproduced sound was simply a poor imitation of an easily understandable acoustic event. A rock musician, through experience with recordings, conceptualizes acoustic phenomena in a historically unique way. Further, popular musicians know that audiences have also been exposed to the medium of recorded sound, and that their expectations about the way music sounds have similarly been given a context by the playback experience. The difference between the rock musician's acoustic consciousness and that of the audience is derived only from the manner in which interaction with recordings has occurred, i.e., that attempts have been made to play along with what has been heard on records. In this way the audience and the musician share an experience of sounds that have been produced through the various sound control possibilities that the recording medium has made possible, but only the musician can take on the task of delivering them in live performance. The special skills of rock musicians (or, for that matter, any contemporary popular musicians) involve the use of commercial recordings as formal notation systems.

THE WORK-UP

After a song is *gotten* it must be transformed into a performable entity. Although a song may be known in its individual parts, it cannot be said that the *group* knows the song until the process of *working up* (which is not so ironically also known as *getting down*) has been concluded. This process is the *practice* of the business of rock performance, and includes the dual aspects of repetition and alternation.

R: The only way you're ever gonna get a good group together is to go over and over your material until it's perfect.

HSB: How do you know when it's perfect?

R: You just do, that's all. Everybody plays his part without making a mistake, and if you can do that two or three times, you've got it down to where it just *feels* perfect.

HSB: How many times would you say you'd have to play a song before it's perfect?

R: Yesterday at practice we worked on the same song for more than an hour—closer to two hours. The lead was hard to do without mistakes and about halfway through we realized that the rhythm didn't sound quite right, so the drummer

had to unlearn one part and relearn another one. I'll bet we did it twenty times
straight.

HSB: Doesn't that get kind of boring?

R: It depends . . . if everybody's concentrating on getting the thing down it's not
boring. But it sure is work . . . no doubt about it. [Bass player]

At any one day's practice a song can be assessed as worked-up, yet at
succeeding practices it might not be played with its original perfection. To
be truly integrated into a group's immediately performable repertoire, the
work-up must stand the test of time, and today's forgetting of what was
familiar yesterday is a commonly understood part of the group's interactional form.

S: Let's do "Walk on the Water."

J: Which one is that?

S: Man, we only did it about fifteen times yesterday.

J: Yeah, I know but just play some of it and I'll remember.

S: [*Playing the song.*] Remember not to speed it up—OK?

J: OK. How are we gonna start it?

S: Same way as yesterday . . . one-two-three-four—

J: Hold on man, I don't even know where to come in . . . let's just practice the
introduction alone so I can get it straight in my head . . . [etc.] [Drummer]

Precise retention from day to day is neither expected nor expectable.
Fairly quick recognition (re-cognition) is expected, however, so that every
day that passes brings the group closer to the ability to perform its songs
at will, without preparatory huddling or reminders. The technique of alternating songs is evidence of a particular knowledge of the learning process:
that learning to play a song together is not a one-shot mechanism.

"We always have two or three songs to work on at practice. We do one until we
get tired of it and then start on another one. Of course, some songs go quicker
than others. When you're practicing steady with a group you know you can
always come back to it the next day, and that way there's no pressure and you
really learn the song." [Manager]

For a group to learn to play a song each member must learn to assimilate
a set of musical ideas (sounds) and then reproduce them at will. Yet at the
beginning stages of a group and at the stage of introducing new material to
an experienced group, the song materials are in such a state of disorgani-
zation that if there is to be willful reproduction of music, it will be of a
quality that is unacceptable in the performance reality. The secret of group
operation is, very simply, the shared knowledge that one has to be bad
before being good. The cooperative understanding at practice sessions must
operate with no negative sanctions for mistakes, and in fact must be con-
ducive to the correction and amendment of another's playing.

L: Man, I don't know what it is today, I just can't play for shit.

G: You just have to take it easy man, we'll get it down. You remember how long it took to get "Sympathy for the Devil" down, and now it's one of our best songs.

L: I just feel so tight, I need to loosen up. . . .

G: Just play whatever comes out and don't worry about it, we'll get it together, if you'd just play simple and not try to throw in that extra shit, it would sound a lot better.

The existence of a mistake, amendment, or correction is a recognition that, at least for a particular moment or day, the member in question could not play well. When it works, the practice reality is negotiated in such a way as to freely allow a member the ability to make mistakes and play poorly in front of his peers. The privacy of the practice session provides an offstage reality in which the privilege of actually editing the group's music is provided. To work up a song, then, is literally to repeat the various voices and segments of the song that were learned disparately from the recording until they flow together as a unitary performance experience. To the audience the practice reality, with its inevitable fumbles, is invisible. What is worked up in piecemeal over many days' time appears in the performance reality as an episodic whole, steadily unfolding and changing without apparent cues. To perform a song that is worked up is to compress the temporalities of many repetitions of the song (with other life activities) into a form that is spontaneously available to the collective memory of the group by voluntary fiat.

"If we played that song once we played it a thousand times. We practiced it one day, forgot it completely the next and relearned it the day after that. We played it in bars and at dances and concerts, and over the course of six months it just gets into your automatic system." [Flute player]

The practice of rock music is the worship of a sequential precision which is to be projected into the performance reality. The song has been gotten in parts—in the dual sense of the polyphonically separated instrumental lines and the sequential division of the song into copyable sections, such as "introduction," "first verse," "first dah-dah-dah," and so forth, which recapitulate the sequential playback of the song-getting process. Putting it all together collapses the analytic divisions of the recording into a coherent· experience. Having a song *down* is literally forgetting—removing from the group's awareness—the conceptual partitions that were constructed as an ordering or sequencing system so the song could be learned in the first place. The recording is a notation system precisely because its manipulation allows a representation of numerous segments and voices of the song outside of the temporality of the running-off of the recorded performance. Actually, the musician–recording interaction (song getting) is a partitioning of the music for analytic purposes. Once that partitioning has allowed the copying of individual parts, the whole is reconstructed in performance from that note-taking interaction. Local rock musicians are no different from any other kind of musician in the sense that they create performance realities from notes; it is just that those notes are remembrances of the partitions that the group placed in the playbacks of a recording while it was being *gotten*. As with any notation system, the notes provide an ordered boundary system that is elaborated in the play of the performance reality, but it should be remembered that transforming a song that is *gotten* into a song that is *worked up* involves removing the original partitions of the notation process and assimilating the song as an unbroken unity.

THE SET

The processes of song getting and working up have delineated the procedure of note taking and note breaking by which the group's aesthetic is constructed. The first part of the process is a unique way of listening to the recording (with the recording consciousness) to ferret out the aesthetic that was operating in the studio reality—finding answers to the question "How did they make those sounds?" The second part of the process is a unique way of reproducing the recording by using the recording consciousness as a notation system—finding answers to the question "How can *we* make those sounds?" From a sociological viewpoint these can be seen as two interactional forms: the musician–recording interaction and the musician–musician (i.e., group) interaction. A third interactional form must be seen in operation before an understanding of the practice of local rock is complete: the group–audience interaction.

I have shown that the economic category of gigs is the musician's avenue to audience access. Whether or not money exchanges hands at a gig, the musicians' services are exchanged with the audience, and it is in that sense that every event of audience access is an exchange event to the group. The stage at which the exchange idea and the idea of an aesthetic meet is in the process of *programming* the performance episode. The central concept of this practice is the *set*. A set is an anticipation of the exchange expectations of the audience; it is what the group knows about what the audience wants.

The physical evidence of the group's notion of a set is found in the phenomenon of the song list. A collection of song lists for different groups would provide the comparative cases necessary to see that although repertoires differ, the set form of local rock is the same. A typical song list provides an arrangement of titles and the key in which each song is played. I have seen some lists in which a small number of songs (say, five) comprises a set that is unified according to some programming standard (ballads or dance numbers, for example) so that after a set of five is played, any of the other sets may be chosen to fit the perceived "mood of the crowd." A more typical kind of song list is divided into sets that represent an entire playing episode from beginning to end. It is conventional to play forty-five minutes and break for fifteen minutes, so that each set is considered an *hour's worth of gig time*. This might represent ten or even fifteen songs per set, so that three such sets would mean that it is possible for the group to play a three-hour gig. The song content of such lists could provide a wealth of theoretical observations in and of themselves, but it is the *form* of the set that is of interest at the moment. It shows that the practice of local rock includes a projection of the group's future performance reality. The care and precision with which sets are constructed aligns the group's performance potential with particular markets for the group's services.

In this way the composition of a set is the product of group decisions that are made with particular types of gigs in mind. Consider this example of a local group with an established following that plays social gigs almost exclusively, with an occasional commercial or concert gig.

> HSB: How do you get a set together?
> B: By this time it's mostly a process of amendment of old sets that we're sick and tired of. Maybe there'll be one or two songs in a set that we keep and the rest we just throw out. Then somebody'll say, "Let's do this song," and if nobody violently objects, we'll do it.
> HSB: Does that mean a lot of Top 40 stuff?
> B: No. We don't play much of that . . . I mean if it catches somebody's ear then we'll do it, but not because it's popular with the audience or anything like that . . . we only play songs we want to do.
> HSB: How do you put those together?
> B: We've always had a thing about continuous sets—we try to play for at least an hour without stopping. Putting them in order is usually the old ratio of three or four fast songs to one slow song—that just sorta falls in place—and then you think of those weird ways of ending one song and having some kind of transitional riff to get into the next one. That's really the most fun—especially when you can pull off some mind-fucking key change. [Guitar player]

Here is a comparative example of set formation in a group that plays bar gigs exclusively.

> V: I don't know how it is out here, but to get gigs in North Dakota we were doing about half Top-40 stuff, about four or five country and western songs . . . and maybe we could slip in one or two good blues or rock songs a set. If you did too much of that the manager would come up and sorta let you know. . . . If you wanted to play steady gigs you had to pretty much be a Top-40 or country group.
> J: It's the same here, man. It's the same all over. [Conversation between traveling and local musicians]

When a group has established a local audience (i.e., a local market) in the economic setting of social gigs, set composition is primarily a function of perceived audience response—what *works* in the performance reality remains in the set, what doesn't work is replaced with something else, until an entire *good set* is derived by empirical test. Choice of material, however, is an option that the group retains. When a group is playing in the economic setting of a bar gig, the set composition is almost completely determined by The Music of the day as perceived by the bar owner or manager. Choice of material may be so completely specified by the management that specific songs are advertised to the potential audience. This control was exemplified to me through the newspaper advertisements of a Denver bar that promised "exciting, *live* entertainment" and then proceeded to list the week's "Top-10 songs" which would be performed.

To construct a three- or four-set repertoire is to transform an aggregation of musicians into a group that has audience access. To practice a set is not to practice the group's *music*, but to practice the programming of that music with a particular audience in mind. It is the subtlety of the set concept that it defines the rock event over long temporal slices, and therefore contextualizes "the next song" by what has gone before.

> "What really makes them a fantastic group is the way their sets build. If you think about it, there are a lot better groups musically, but when ——— gets an audience going, the next song just keeps taking you higher and higher and higher. Then they break into a sort of laid-back boogie blues which would be just an average song if it wasn't at the end of this amazing set of changes; but the energy carries over, and your mind just gets cleaned out." [Bass player referring to a local group]

For a group to organize its songs into sets is to allow the musician–audience interaction to become an element of its aesthetic, and in that sense to share an aesthetic—a way of listening—with an audience. When a musician is getting a song, the *studio aesthetic* is considered and assimilated. Then a *performance aesthetic* is invoked, which allows the group an acceptable rendering of the original even though they do not have studio sound controls at hand. Musicians quickly learn that audiences expect the recorded version of a song, and are likely not to appreciate the innovative musicianship required to turn the professionally produced and recorded product into a locally performable item. An original recording with ten studio musicians and overdubbed vocals is impossible for the local four-person group to play just like the record. Given this divergence between commercial recordings and live performance potential, groups often seek other avenues of connection to the audience. This is why the third aesthetic of the set is so important, for it is an aesthetic of programming that both the musician and the audience can share.

"It's like last night . . . we slipped in a few blues tunes because we felt like blowing really hard, you know. Of course, the audience was there to hear Top 40 and they just dug the shit out of that. When we took a break, a guy came up to me and said, 'That was a really good set.' Now, I know he wasn't listening to much of anything. He was drinking beer and hustling chicks, but that was the only way he could communicate with me, you know, the only way he could say OK." [Drummer]

If a group defines an hour as *a set of fifteen good songs*, the audience need only define that hour as *a good time*. In this way, the musician–audience interactional aesthetic of the set is program music; it is, for the audience, referential to experiences that the music accompanies. In fact, attention to popular music is programmed as a presentation of many selections in sequence. The radio station plays *one right after another*, or, if you are lucky, *four in a row* (without an advertisement); the album or the stereo at home plays *five or six in a row* and then the changer automatically programs another "set"; even the background music of shopping centers, offices, factories, elevators, and air terminals is organized in this fashion. If local rock is delivered in set form, then the audience need not listen to the live performance in the way the musician listens, and the exchange of the performance reality remains both undemanding for the audience and economically viable for the group.

THE COPY GROUP

After the group has learned to get, work up, and set The Music, an ironic economic reality presents itself: the services of the group are now marketable. This means that the career of becoming a rock musician becomes engaged with the various (and to some, devious) careers of rock entrrepreneurs. Those entrepreneurs might vary from college fraternity social chairmen to managers of bars to producers of rock concerts, but the similarity of all entrepreneurs is that they pose as experts who require a specific product. What keeps the local rock band viable is that it can supply that product to the local rock middleman. Although the demand for the group's services is represented by what I have called social and ceremonial gigs (and more rarely, concert gigs), the economic possibility of the local group having steady gigs is in the bar market. Bars are stable environmental configurations dedicated to sociability, and because there are those whose ideas of sociability include the presence of The Music, certain bars can, from the musicians' viewpoint, supply steady gigs. The meeting of demand and supply is, in this case, ironic, precisely because the spontaneous institution of a local rock band is originally unattached to the traditional institutions of sociability that it eventually learns to service. Bars and bands, although economically dependent on one another, are two distinct institutions whose participants' needs and desires cross only superficially. The bar manager is the musical go-between for his bar's clientele, and if he does his job well he chooses whatever musical experiences his clients desire with their talk and alcohol. It is the fact that the rock entrepreneur acts on a knowledge of "what the audience wants to hear," and that creates the economically and professionally stable social phenomenon of the *copy group*.

Top 40 group, *bar group*, and *copy group* have the same denotative meaning: bands that can be counted on to play The Music. The more subtle implications of a group which has as its main enterprise the human reproduction of sounds that have already been mechanically reproduced are sociologically devastating. The copy group is an enigmatic ideal type; it is as far as the local career of playing rock music tends to go, and it finds a market in those who do not want that way of playing to come to an end. The ability to copy music (the sounds of The Music) is the exhibition of a group's technical accomplishment—the finger exercises of popular music. In the same way that T. S. Kuhn speaks of scientists who do *normal science*, there are copy groups that play *normal rock*. Both the copy groups and the scientists are locked into a paradigmatic, interactional form that suppresses the next stage of a learning career. The reality of this "locked door" is in evidence when the twin heresies of eclecticism and originality are brought to the market for sale.

> "We went down to audition at this place and it was your average 3.2 joint with your average sleazy manager. We played a lot of stuff we'd written, some blues, and maybe an Allman Brothers tune or two. This guy kept asking for these particular tunes, you know, some stuff which I'd never heard of, which was probably that week's Top 40. Needless to say, we didn't get the gig." [Guitar player]

The method of operating as a copy group is to keep up with The Music by adding new songs to the repertoire as they are selected for release by the recording companies, heard on the radio, and popularized by advertisements. Taking on the permanent stance of copyists means that a copy group's performances attempt to recapitulate the aesthetic that was used in the production of particular commercial recording sessions. That this is likely to be humanly impossible means that the goal of a copy group is to approximate impossibility. The economically determined aesthetic of precision reproduction (precise, that is, in comparison to recordings) meets the group at every turn. If it is the economic reality that The Music must be played, then it is the musical goal of managing the *impression* of precise reproduction that is left as a local musician's ultimate specialty.

Once one's repertoire has been so precisely specified, the copy group musician knows at least one thing: the ears of both employers and audiences have been exposed to, and most likely saturated with, the songs they request.

"If you're playing steady gigs, you're playing the same songs over and over five or six nights a week. That will drive you crazy unless you can get into being as tight as hell. We've even gotten to the place where we can get off playing bubble-gum music. . . . The songs are for shit, but when you play one just like the record, you've got every part of the song straight in your mind. There's nothing sloppy about any of it, and it feels good just to be playing. . . . Besides, the audience eats it up." [Drummer]

Just like the record is impressionistic terminology. Left to their own devices a group of humans can rarely produce the sounds that a recording studio can produce, yet it can produce a sound that is *doctored* in such a way as to fool the ears of the typical bar audience. The intent of the members of a copy group is to see how close to identical-to-the-record they can sound. In the process of successive approximations to that impossible congruence a universe of sound-making skills is created.

"A lot of these overproduced Top 40 songs are overdubbed a zillion times. For one thing, it gives the vocal a kind of presence . . . You know what that sounds like. The way we get that is to get the drummer and the bass player to just sing along with the lead singer and just do exactly what he does. Those guys can't sing for shit, but if you mix their mikes down a little bit it sounds really close to an overdub. Or, a lot of times there'll be a string section or horn section part, and the organ player and I will work out the exact part they play and try to get the tone and the harmony the same too. You'd be surprised how close we can get." [Guitar player]

Whatever has been pounding the ears of the country for the past few weeks, or even the classic poundings of years gone by, is the reproductional challenge of the copy group. There is some doubt as to what the audience actually hears during a performance of this type. They sing along, dance, and expect every change in The Music, even as it is performed by different groups who necessarily have variable skills. It is as if the audience assembled at the American public house is not concerned with the performance of the here and now, but with some autonomically memorized set of sounds that is only sketched by the live musicians. As long as the copy group delivers its services, the collective memory of the audience seems to fill in the gaps between the sound of the group and the sound of the recording. When a copy group has fulfilled the expectations of its contractors it has played what it cannot play, and the audience has heard what it cannot hear.

NOTES

[1] This is taken from P. B. Loxton, "A Gilbertese Song," *Journal of Polynesian Society* 62 (1953).

HOW WOMEN BECOME MUSICIANS

1 9 8 8

○ ▲ ○ ▲ ○ ▲ ○

Two issues confront the novitiate band: (1) who will play which instrument and (2) what kind of music to play. The first issue is not one that typically confronts male bands. Male musicians are more likely to be able to play an instrument before joining a band, or at least they attend the first practice with some clear idea of what instrument they are going to play. Women are much less likely to be able to play already. Quite a number of women I interviewed had never played any rock instrument before, and the sheer shortage of female musicians means that often a woman who turns up intending to play one instrument is entreated to play a completely different one. The lack of female bass players and drummers is the main problem.

> SANDRA (who joined her band as a guitarist): We just couldn't find *any* good female bass players around. There were just none. We advertised and everything. We just couldn't find anyone who was good enough. So I said, "Oh, why don't I play bass and we'll look for a guitarist?" And they said "Yeah, OK." But then we looked for a rhythm guitarist and we didn't find one. Then we just decided to stay a three-piece. You've got to find the right sort of person to join.

> JOAN: Merle rang up and said, "What instrument would you like?" And they said "We wanted sax." And Merle hadn't played sax, ever. She got it and went along.

> ALICE: The first time we got together . . . I played guitar (not terribly well—I wasn't a great guitarist.) And we decided we were gonna have a band and we

were looking for a bass player. And we couldn't find a bass player. . . . We met and there was a bass and a bass amp. And I said, "Well, look, I'd quite like to have a go on the bass, you know, and if it's no good we'll carry on looking for a bass player." I really liked the idea of playing bass. We tried a song. I had a basic knowledge of the guitar, so it wasn't altogether too difficult.

Male musicians are usually drawn together to play a certain style of music. This is not necessarily true for female musicians. Again, the small size of the "pool" of players is a determining factor here. For a lot of the women I interviewed the desire to play in an all-women band was far more important than the style of the music itself—at the beginning, that is. Some novices had no preferred style, while others had to compromise to join a band at all. This can lead to problems later on.

> SUSAN: It would be nice to have more choice, other players to play with. It can be a problem, if you're really set on being a reggae player and you come from Leeds and there's only one girl-band, and they're not really into playing reggae. Then you're stuck . . . But I didn't know what I wanted to play until I joined the band. I only (recently) discovered that I'm really a sort of "funky" player . . . And I'd love to be in a heavy funk band.

For bands composed of already experienced musicians the pattern is different—the band starts out with an agreement on the style of music they are going to perform, their projected audience, and so on—but this is very rare among female bands because of the very small number of experienced rock performers.

> SUSAN: It's really difficult. Because if you haven't been through that whole thing of playing covers and Jimi Hendrix solos and Eric Clapton things . . . You have never experienced the whole thing of playing rock, and a bit of this and a bit of that—to have gone through it all and (then) put it aside, to know exactly what you want to play. So, for me, the three years that I've been playing have been an experiment, sorting out what direction I personally, and the band, want to go in. And I think it's really showed.
> I think it would be good for anybody that was thinking about being in a band to start at 12—get an electric guitar at 12 and do all those bedroom and garage things, go through all that so that you've got it all sorted out in your head. So you don't have to go through all that experimental period once you're in a band that's trying to be successful. You need to exhaust all that so that you've got a direction, once you're in a band.

This goes back to the fact that young girls do not see rock musician as a role to which they can aspire.

LEARNING TO PLAY ROCK INSTRUMENTS

For some band members the very rudiments of playing their instrument are learned within the band.

SUSAN: [Girls have not had] a whole history of having played guitar in garages and things. What girls have been confronted with . . . is being a girl-band in a male-orientated world. How can we do this? How can we go about this? We were all in the same boat together. None of us could play any better than anybody else. So we helped each other. We listened out, on my old record player, for the bass line and all those that could play guitar and bass tried to work it out, until we got it—in the end—and then the bass player played it. We listened to the horns and helped Merle work out the horns. So we helped each other. Right from the word "Go" there was this working-together atmosphere, each one having an equal say in the matter.

Other women have been classically trained and are therefore "musical" and may even define themselves as "musicians." But they still have to learn to play rock. An outsider might assume that a trained musician would easily be able to transfer her skills from one musical genre to another. This is not so. Being able to read and understand written music is no clear advantage in rock. Some even argue that it is a disadvantage.

ANDREA: That's the thing about being classically trained, you've got to throw it all away and start again!

I shall address this issue in some detail here because it applies to a lot of women in bands, especially keyboard players (more girls have piano lessons than boys).

From Classical to Rock

Classical music skills are not the same thing as rock skills, and my research clearly indicates that a lot of classically trained female musicians have trouble making the transition. This can be a source of great anxiety—a woman's identity as a musician is threatened; she experiences a crisis of technical confidence. Many years of classical training—and for some women I interviewed that included degree courses—means internalizing the norms and social structure of the classical world, so that, for example, the (male) composer is exalted while the individual (female) player has low status. It is difficult for women to rid themselves of the effects of this status hierarchy, which is part of the hidden curriculum of a course in classical music.

ROSALIND: You've got to get rid of all the ideas that you've got to play only the music that's written down, and you're sort of servicing the composer. You have to get rid of that. It did take a while to get the confidence to get away from the written music . . . That's the transition you have to make: from theoretical to "feel."

Having been trained to follow a written score, classical musicians find improvisation a major problem.

CAROL: I find it difficult freeing my brain to be able to initiate things. Because when you play classical music you just play what's written down by somebody else and all your energy and musicalness goes into expressing it in your own way. Whereas with rock music you're not just expressing something that someone else has written. You've got to think it up for yourself. And that's what I find difficult . . . Knowing what to play was my main problem; not having ever been in that situation where you're required to think something up for yourself, tied to the dots on the page . . . breaking away from that.

ALICE: It was quite difficult not having music to read, and to think of what to play without that. And I had to relearn it, in a way, to start from scratch. Even though I could play Beethoven sonatas the band for me was a complete learning experience.

As music is rarely written down in rock, players have to rely on their memories, another new experience for the classically trained.

ROSALIND: It was the first time that I had learnt things, learnt so much off by heart. And it was a real step into improvisation. I did tend to write things down at first. My first bass line I wrote down . . .

Playing pop means developing a different style from classical. On keyboards the hands are doing different and usually far less complex things. The keyboard player can feel redundant. As one woman put it, pop is more like creating a poster than an oil painting.

ALICE: The thing about playing in a band is, each individual doesn't have to do that much for it to sound good. And I didn't realize that at first. And I think, probably, I just put in too many fat chords, which isn't necessary. You can often play just a single line and it's really effective . . . It was very halting at first. I didn't know what to do with my left hand. I do feel I have evolved a style for playing pop music now, but I hadn't then and it was just trial and error, really.

This cutting down on classical skills is even more apparent with synthesizer playing. This woman played a monophonic synth and thus could not play chords:

CAROL: It just seemed rather a waste. It seemed that here's somebody who is able to be dextrous and yet not doing it, and being more of a technician. I mean, I like the sounds that I produce and it's nice to make them. It's just that, often, on stage I feel totally at a loose end. I think, "What the hell am I doing here? I'm not really doing anything. I'm only playing one note!"

Although Carol downgraded her contribution to the overall band sound and had problems deciding what to play, she still saw the opportunities which pop offered in a very positive light. If pop is like poster painting, "classical music is pretty well painting by numbers, because somebody is telling you what to do." Many classically taught musicians become critical in this way of their training, and it can be argued that getting into rock/pop is a form of rebellion against the norms of academic music.

> BEATRICE: The rules of harmony! I mean, the only rule you can possibly use is whether or not it sounds right! Even if you're writing music, surely you hear what you're writing down? But some people write music as a mathematical exercise.

Rock/pop also poses a new problem of audience.

> HELEN: Most of the stuff I've played before, I've had dots in front of me. And when you've got to concentrate on that, you can't think about your relations with the audience, because your relationship with the written music is more fundamental to the performance. Whereas, being in a rock band it's not. It's just you and the audience.

Finally, perhaps surprisingly, although used to analyzing classical music in great depth, "educated" musicians often do not think of being analytical about rock and pop.

> HELEN: It sounds really silly to me to say this, but . . . I haven't been really aware of listening to things closely at all, or analysing—which is a complete contradiction, having been involved in a music degree, done an analysis portfolio, listened to and pulled classical pieces apart, and yet had the attitude to pop music that I enjoyed it, but . . . I think I have listened to pop music very lazily.

Amplification

For many women, whether classically trained, from the folk tradition, or complete newcomers, joining a band is their first experience with amplification. There is a whole world here to come to grips with. First, there are anxieties about electricity which women, unused to this "masculine" domain, have to overcome. Many women spoke of their initial fear of feedback.

> SUSAN: I had to turn up for the audition . . . and I felt, 'Oh God!' 'cause I'd never played electric guitar—and with a plug! Into the wall! . . . I turned up and I was really scared."

Guitarists have to learn to overcome this fear of feedback, to see it as one of the distinctive resources of the electric guitar, to be tamed and exploited for effect. They have to learn the effect of amp settings; how speakers and speaker positions affect sound; the use of various kinds of pedals for sustain, compression, phasing, flanging, chorus effects, fuzz, delay, echo, geographical equalization, etc.; how to "slide" and "bend" notes to effect; how to play with their fretboard hand. Males pick up much of this arcane knowledge before they join a band; women come across it for the first time when they do.

> VERONICA: I think there is a tendency for us still to be scared of equipment: the "black-box-with-chrome-knobs" syndrome . . . I've obviously become very familiar with what I do but I still don't feel, physically I think, as at one with my equipment as I think most men do . . . It took me a year before I turned my volume up. Rosalind would see that my amp was turned up even if I turned it down, because I was still scared of it . . . of making a noise to that extent. I turned the knobs down on my guitar for a whole year. And then, suddenly, I thought, "Fuck it! I'm not going to do that anymore."[1]

For women who have been using books to learn from, being in a band enables them to learn the tricks of the trade which would otherwise be hidden from them—unlike men, very few women learn to play from records.

> JOAN: I've never really done the record scene—which I think you might find is common to a lot of women, for some reason. Men learn the whole set of Eric Clapton solos . . . And you get Billy Cobham drum solos off. And I listen to a record and I think, "Oh, that's good! That's great!" And then I sit down at a drumkit and nothing happens. And I never go on through that bit, thinking what he's doing and work out how he plays those two bars . . . And I think that's a female attitude.

Most female musicians know that analyzing records is a useful method of learning; it is just that, somehow, they do not do it. They lack confidence in their ability to be able, ultimately, to work it out and are therefore not willing to invest the very long hours it takes. It is only being in a band that gives women the necessary incentive. They can now learn from each other; they are not struggling alone. Boys learning usually know other boys who are also learning: they can compare work on records and figure sounds out in small groups. But girls tend not to be in rock music-making peer groups. If they do try to learn the electric guitar it is typically a solitary experience (unless they are going out with a musician boyfriend who is willing to help them). This goes back to "electric" music being perceived as male terrain. As they leave their teens, women buy fewer records than men and are far more likely to live without a record player. The point here is that while, for boys, joining a band is a stage in the gradual process of learning how to hear and play rock music, for young women, joining a band is when the learning starts.

Singers

Even singers may have new techniques to deal with, as they will have to sing through a mike, which is quite different from acoustic singing.

ALICE: I found that singing through a microphone is very different from singing not through a microphone and that I had to project my voice far more. And I don't think I sing very well through a microphone . . . It's just a completely different style, really. I feel I tend to shout a bit when I'm singing through a mike, 'cause I'm worried about it being heard. In fact, the more singing I've done the better I've got, obviously.

JILL: I'm only just learning how to use a microphone properly . . . I've got a sibilance which comes over on the microphone . . . For a lot of the time I was just diving on it, so I was shouting and then moving back again. So it was quite piercing. And also I was singing much higher than I ought to have been. Because all I'd ever experienced was watching people do it on *Top of the Pops* . . . and most of the time they are miming. And I was trying to do something that I didn't understand. And now I understand it I sing better. It sounded too piercing I think. I think sometimes it was so high it went off the mixing desk! . . . I think I sing from my head and from my neck. And I've been trying to sing from my stomach.

Because the voice is taken to be "natural," even in women's bands vocalists can feel insecure "just singing," as if they are not contributing (or learning) as much as the instrumentalists and are therefore more easily replaceable. Women singers thus often learn to play an instrument as well, even if it is just some form of percussion to be played occasionally, like the tambourine. (In feminist bands this can be a gesture too against the limited "chick singer" role prescribed for women in rock bands in the past.)

VERONICA: When we were just beginning to make music, I felt excluded from that because I was singing. Stephanie and I both started fiddling around with the bass guitar. But she got to it before I did. So I thought, "All right. I don't want to be left out of this. I'll try the rhythm guitar."

SARAH: I felt insecure in the band because, other than singing, I didn't have a good, solidly defined role . . . I've tried to fight for percussion to be an important, integral part . . . I've always played the tambourine but with the scraper, I picked it up because I wanted to stay up and play with everybody . . . there were eight of us. It meant that there was always somebody who had to sit out on some numbers . . . I didn't want to distance myself so much and feel like I'm just a singer, occasionally, with the band . . .

LEARNING TO PLAY TOGETHER

Apart from learning how to play their own instruments and to play in an amplified rock or pop style, band members must learn how to play with each other. There is a subtle and complex web of interlocking skills and norms involved in this. Band members must be able to listen to each other while the whole group is playing, which is one skill; they must be able to hear separate instruments—whether on a tape, record, or live—which is another. Some band members have always been able to pick out and listen to individual sounds while listening to a piece of music, others (more) learn this from being in the band, and all members improve this skill by practicing together. This is part of the general change that comes about when people first join a group: they become analytical about rock music. They do not let the noise just flood over them but break it up and figure out what is being played and how, instrument by instrument, section by section. The same record will be listened to very many times, and each time a different specific thing is being heard. Many of the women I interviewed mentioned this change in their listening habits.

> ANN: This has changed my whole way of listening to music. 'Cause I can no longer listen to it as a whole. I have to analyse it down to whatever everyone's doing.

> ALICE: I think Tanya showed me the first few things. We listened to some records. We listened to the bass part. And I've got a reasonably good ear and I could pick it out. And she helped me.

Norms regulate tempo, volume, and tone; how much and what to play; and when to play it. Some learners play too loud and/or too much and have to learn to give others "space." Such learning can be more or less competitive, which is one problem women musicians may have in male bands.

> HARRIETT: It was really awful—who was going to do the biggest and longest and loudest solo? The drummer was into playing Led Zeppelin. The guitarist was into playing something totally different. There was no communication. . . . [The drummer] was always playing very loud drums and not listening. That was the one thing they didn't do. They didn't listen to each other. There was no feeling of sharing in the music . . . like, you know, it goes backwards and forwards between people, this feeling. Whatever it is it never happened at all. It was just "Get in there and play as loud as you can."

For female (and indeed most male) musicians what matters most about group music is that the individuals show a sensitivity to what everyone else is playing. To borrow from George Herbert Mead, one could say that the novitiate band member must develop a "generalized other"—an overview of the whole "game" rather than an individualistic concern with her own role within it. The more that band members listen to each other, the better the group playing becomes. This point was mentioned often by my interviewees, many of whom did believe that it was easier to learn these skills at least initially in the context of an all-women group.

> ALICE: I think probably we encouraged each other far more, or allowed each other to progress at our own rates, far more than men would. And I think a lot of men are quite wanky about how they play.

On the other hand several women felt that some constructive (and necessary) criticism was missing in the carefully democratic atmosphere of women's bands:

> JILL: I kept thinking, "God, they must think this sounds awful and nobody's telling me!" It felt very much like I was working in a bit of a vacuum. Especially 'cause I'd done a lot of acting. You've got a producer [in acting]. You've got an outside eye, who'll say to you, "Right. In this scene you're looking at him . . ." And I found that really difficult in bands. That there's nobody to say, "That's wrong." And it's almost as if there are sort of sacred areas—you don't tell anybody that what they're playing on the guitar is crap. It's almost . . . people can do what they want, even if it's not particularly good.

> BEATRICE: We all tend to pussy foot too much. And we all tend to try not to hurt people's feelings.

In contrast:

> BELLE: Nobody gets upset about it. Like, if you say, "Oh, I don't like that bit. Could you . . . ?" You work it out one way or the other, so nobody gets upset about it. [And when conflict does threaten it is resolved thus:] It mainly happens at the end of rehearsing . . . You know what you're like after four hours playing. You're not fresh. So we just leave it till the next day. We say, "Oh let's not work on this because it's all loose . . . So let's leave it till next time and we'll start on that fresh." I think that's one of the reasons why we don't beat each other up!

For the band to gel and develop, some compromise between an easy tolerance and mutual criticism eventually has to be worked out. The overall good of the band is the main goal: the whole rather than the parts. But even when this is accepted problems remain: Who decides the good of the group? Is policy to be left to the people with the most obvious *musical* authority? The musicians I interviewed were all committed to notions of group equality. This may have been an aspect of the "postpunk" period: leaders were unfashionable. It was also a reflection of feminist politics: leaders were ideologically unsound. Either way, it raised a problem which is exacerbated in the next stage of a band's career: How is it to be "fronted"? Even in a group which sees itself as completely equal and democratic, someone has to introduce the numbers and generally talk to the audience.

> JILL: It's something we never thought of and when we were on stage, suddenly we were thinking, "Who's gonna say something, you know."

The question is double-edged: Who is capable and confident enough to perform this role? How can the resulting power be shared out?

Rehearsal

But before these issues have to be faced there are more mundane questions to answer. How many practices a week should there be? How long should they last? Should one smoke or drink during a practice? Should one engage in small talk and general conversation, and if so how much and when? Does one finish the practice in time to go to the pub? How important is punctuality? Decisions are made about all of these things and they become normatively "set" so that deviance incurs some degree of bad feeling or sanction.

All the bands in my research had norms of mutual help and tried to share out rehearsal tasks like loading and unloading the equipment and setting up. The breaking of norms occurred, of course, but it was recognized as such and was often referred to within the band. People who don't pull their weight create ill-feeling among the others. What's equally important, though, is that such discontent is expressed and resolved privately. It is thus very important that people other than band members are excluded from the practice space so that the band can concentrate on its tasks and come to see itself as a special kind of social unit. Privacy is necessary for reasons of both efficiency and morale, something which bands quickly learn for themselves if they have to deal with "outsiders" intruding on their space.

In particular boyfriends/husbands have to be kept out of rehearsals whether they are musicians or not. For women's bands, indeed, it is probably most important that male musicians are excluded—it is when women are trying to build up confidence on their instruments that male players are perceived (however fairly) as threatening and judgmental. It is clear from my research that if a women's band is to survive, the exclusion of male outsiders must be rigorously enforced in its early stages.

> KATHY: There was one girl . . . who was in our group whose boyfriend played guitar. And he was teaching her. And, at rehearsal, she'd say, "Oh, I can only stay for half an hour." And we used to get really fed up with her 'cause she didn't learn the songs. And her boyfriend was always with her, dragging her along. They used to sit there together all the time. And we got really fed up with her in the end. So my brother just said, "Let's play a twelve bar." 'Cause that's the first thing that everyone learns. He said, "You can play that, can't you?" And she was sitting next to her boyfriend and she goes, "Oh, I dunno Mick, can I play a twelve-bar?" So after that we decided to get rid of her and she hasn't done nothing since.

This example is from a mixed band. If it had been a women's band the boyfriend would probably not have been tolerated in the first place. It is important either way that women are seen to be learning to play for themselves and not depending endlessly on a man's direction.

Ancillary Skills

People who join electric bands not only learn how to play instruments together, they learn how to amplify them, set them up, and carry them in and out of vans together with all the rest of the equipment. Because people assume that strength is the prerequisite for such "humping," it is particularly important for women to discover that skill is just as necessary.

> ALICE: Equipment can be heavy but I don't think that's really a problem. Because women may not be as strong as men in terms of their physical force, but you don't need brute force to carry equipment, even heavy stuff. You need to know how to do it. You need to lift it carefully and the right way . . . There's been lots of times where we've had people come up to us at gigs—maybe it's a student union and there's three or four students delegated to help carry the PA out. And, like, you get two guys who pick up a bin and drop it half way down the steps, because they don't know what they're doing. And they're probably twice as strong as we are. And then Beatrice and Joan will come along and they can barely see over the top, and they'll pick it up and carry it onto the van. It's how to do it. Women carry plenty of heavy objects. Women carry babies around. Lifting things is like a knack. If you do it the right way you don't strain yourself.

Musicians must also learn how to repair equipment and do routine maintenance tasks. Mending jack plugs, for example, means soldering (typically the first time that women have ever done this), while drummers must learn how to change and repair their drumheads. In time the keyboard player learns how to change the guitarist's strings, the guitarist how to organize the keyboards. Everyone learns how to set up all the equipment—the practice PA if there is one, the drum set (which always takes a long time), the guitarists' amps, and so on. And when (as usual) some equipment fails to work, each band member must be willing to address the problem and demonstrate to the others that she has technical skills, that she is at least in control of her own equipment. Without these skills (not often thought of as "feminine," whether in formal schooling or informal peer culture), the band will never be able to gig.

Language

Becoming a member of a band means learning new languages. There is language which describes artifacts—technical terms, phrases, and abbreviations—and there is language which describes sound. Many women join bands quite ignorant of both.

> HILARY: Kelly had done this grade 17 piano [top level of standardized piano lessons] and knew all about musical theory. Merle knew what the names of the

notes were and also had some experience of arranging songs. And I didn't have a clue what they were on about most of the time.

HILARY: The bloke on the mixing desk said, "Do you want this through the foldback?" and we all looked at each other! We were saying, "What's he on about? What does he mean?" And we felt very stupid. And there's all sorts of things like that that you pick up. And so now I feel I've got more confident as a musician, to talk to musicians and play in another band.

A shared language is necessary simply to be able to communicate with other band members and, eventually, PA crews and the recording studio. As Wittgenstein said, the limits of one's language are the limits of one's world. Learning rock band language is learning about the world of rock bands, how that world operates, what one's place is within it.

A band member must obviously get to know what is meant by a "bar," "middle 8," "riff," "phrase," "bass line," and so on (a lot of miscommunication occurs at early practices because people mean such different things by these terms), and in time everybody is able to name each other's equipment parts and effects—"snare," "hi-hat," "toms." This is professional jargon and one can feel somewhat silly on first using a term like "gig" in nonmusician company. It sounds pretentious, it implies that you are a full-fledged rock player. Learning the language, in short, means taking on a new identity, making a new distinction between "insiders" and "outsiders." Such language also gives power, and I think that men typically use it in a less self-conscious way than women do—it is so clearly associated with the male power of the rock world. This has certainly been so in my own experience and has come out in my interviews with other women musicians, who are often reluctant to "talk shop" on makes of guitar or new amplifiers, and are hesitant about being too "technical" even among themselves or as they practice.

Getting Some Numbers Together

Bands often start by just jamming rather than working on any specific songs. "Jamming" may be defined as playing loosely and spontaneously, with no particular direction. Sometimes the first band song will emerge out of an initial jam. Other times someone will bring a semi-composed number to a practice and a band will jam around that until it gels. That is, jamming can be part of the composition process.

BONNY: Our most recent numbers have evolved more out of—there's the idea for a song and we've jammed around that idea and evolved things.

The danger here is that some bands never get beyond jamming. Unless bands get some numbers written and arranged it is unlikely that they will get to the stage of gigging:

BEATRICE: Before Maxine and Jane they were just jamming. They weren't into sitting down and working out the one song for hours and hours. I think that was the only difference between me and Kathy . . . and Maxine and Jane. 'Cause they were more into just playing free. And next time you can't remember *any* of it. I love doing that too. But I like writing songs as well—working hard on them. It does you a lot of good—sweat!

In order to perform in front of an audience a band must be prepared to conform to the norms of the gig. At most gigs this means that a set of carefully considered numbers be presented. "Just jamming" is only appropriate at exceptional gigs. But getting numbers worked out takes a lot of time and effort. It is more enjoyable, for beginners, just to play together as the mood takes them. But this immediate gratification has to be sacrificed if the band is to perform live. Some band members recalled their shock at this need for hard work. This was particularly true if they had never had any previous experience of arranging.

HILARY: It took a long time, because we weren't very musically capable, to work out what notes everybody ought to be playing . . . and how to arrange a song. We'd five numbers and it had taken about four or five months to work all that out. People like me and Maxine and Jane, who didn't know what was going on, used to get bored and pissed off because it took such a long time to do the arrangements, though I recognize that it was very important.

SONGWRITING

Most of the bands in my research wrote most, if not all, their own material. In some bands someone would go off alone, compose a number, and then present it to the group as a finished article—but this was a rare occurrence. The most typical case was someone (or sometimes two people) presenting the band with a number which was partly written. It might have, say, the lyrics, vocal line, and chords but no bass line, drum parts, or keyboards. Or else a number might be presented complete except for the lyrics and lyric line. All kinds of variation on this pattern existed, because the very nature of what is conventionally meant by a "song" or "number" had to be learned: a pop song is usually not much more than three minutes long; it has verses and choruses and often a "middle 8"; it needs some kind of "introduction" and some kind of ending; it has "lyrics" and not just a set of words. This knowledge is a prerequisite for composition.

A band is therefore both a context and an opportunity for writing. Many women who found themselves coming up with songs had never dreamed of doing so before (some have not done so since).

ANN: I never wrote a song until I joined the band. It was only joining the band that encouraged me to write anything. And I didn't know that I could before

I did it. I quite surprised myself. It was a good feeling to write songs that we played . . . I don't really write songs now, now that I'm not playing in a band. 'Cause it's stupid writing them 'cause I know they're not gonna get played. And so I don't. On occasion I might come up with the odd riff but that's as far as it goes.

JOY: For me, to sit down and write songs is not a natural state of affairs. It's not like [being] a poet, where you've got to write. I do it for a purpose. I don't do it for the sake of it. I think, "We've got a few gigs and we need some new material." I'll sit down and think, "Right, I'm going to write a song . . ." When we were doing it before I'd start to think, especially about lyrics . . . everything I read, every headline, "That would make a good song." But I've stopped that now. That was mainly 'cause I was looking for things. And now I'd have to sit at the piano and think about it.

If the band needs songs, then at least one woman has to step into the breach; it is often the exigency of a first gig which reveals songwriting talents for the first time. Resentment and conflict can emerge over this, even if at the start of a band's career, particularly before the first gig, they do not surface immediately. At this stage band members are still not confident enough to criticize each other. They are wary of upsetting each other's feelings and doubt that they are competent enough to criticize anyone else's material, especially if they have not themselves written anything yet. No group style or standard has yet emerged; the band is typically still experimenting and most things are tried out. Anyway, there is a shortage of material, so all songs offered are gratefully received:

HILARY: Anything that anyone had written was seized upon with great delight.

Later, however, as regular songwriters emerge from within the band, there can be too much material, and choices have to be made. The longer the band has been playing, the more likely this is to be the case. Conflict occurs between the goal of doing the best songs possible for the group and the value of self-expression for its individual members. Feelings easily get hurt—so much of the self is poured into songwriting that rejection of one's song may feel like rejection of one's person.

ANN: We had rows and rows and rows. And that was partly because we were so collective and everyone had to come to some kind of consensus, but also because it's a very intense kind of thing to be doing, playing music with other people. And then especially as we wrote our own stuff. I'm sure that had a lot to do with it. Because if you do cover versions, then you're not likely to argue so much about the arrangement and what different people are playing. Whereas, when people did their own songs it mattered much more what everyone did.

There is a norm in feminist bands that the original material they play must be written by women (it is usually written by the band themselves), and nonfeminist bands, too, are often unhappy about featuring new songs by "outsiders," particularly males.

> JOY: Jackie writes most of the material and I think the songs are pretty good. But none of us are actually sure how much is Jackie's and how much is Ian's. Because she says they do it together. But there's been a few practices that we've had where we've gone round to her house. And we've had to have Ian explain how it goes. And Jackie hasn't learnt it. So it's given the game away a bit. So it started to be apparent that Ian was sitting at home writing all these songs for our band because he wasn't in a band himself and it was his outlet. And so we started to weigh up—well, does that matter? Or not? I suppose I was more worried about it because I wanted to get some of my own songs out and I thought, "Well, they're not even Jackie's! They're Ian's." We were just doing it exactly as we were told. We were just becoming the vehicles for his writing. There wasn't anything of us there. It got too manufactured and anybody, whether they could play the keyboards or not, could just play these notes. There wasn't anything of me there. And I didn't like that. So I'd revolt against that, saying, "Oh, I'm not going to do that. I'm doing this."

Male rock and roll bands, even now, tend to start by doing covers and only later attempt to write their own material. Most women's bands mix originals and "standards" from the start.

> HARRIET: The main difference was that they [the men] hadn't got as much originality as the women I've played with. Or they wouldn't use it. They wanted to just do cover versions of things and be the same as other bands have been. And they just hadn't got the creative energy that women have got. They wouldn't use their own creativity or they were cut off from it . . . The guitarist in this band was technically really good. But he was just shit scared or couldn't find his own style. And he'd just copy things . . . They'd play the record and you were supposed to [copy it]. Having played with women before . . . I was really glad that I had done, because if that had been my first experience of trying to play it might have put me off for ever.

Women's "creativity" is more a matter of politics than inspiration. Some feminists in my research, for example, argued that women's bands should not do covers because the majority of existing songs have been written by men and it is about time women's voices were heard. The suggestion here is that women write different sorts of song than men, in terms of both lyric and sound. For these women songwriting is an ideological duty which is also fun!

But there are nonfeminist factors here, too. As already emphasized, many women join bands as complete novices. If such women play covers they run the risk of being compared, unfavorably, with the originals.

> SALLY: We did lots [of covers] to start with—badly, as well. Well, to start off with, you see, we didn't have any songs and we just fancied playing together as a band. So we thought, "Right, what songs do we like?" And we tried playing

those. "Hold on I'm Coming," "Keep on Running"—sixties kind of stuff . . . We just played it to the best of our abilities—which wasn't very much at that time.

This group quickly changed to writing its own material, and even when women's bands continue to perform standards they often adapt the lyrics to a new gender persona. Feminist bands, indeed, change the words as a matter of political subversion (though somtimes *not* changing the words can be equally subversive, as when a lesbian band sings a love song addressed to a woman).

> STEPHANIE: We did "I Saw Her Standing There . . ." A woman saying, "I saw *her* standing there" just gives a different twist to it. And we did "Da Doo Ron Ron" with "I met her on a Monday and her name was Jill." Changing the sex of it so that you had the whole lesbian undertones to it. I think that is fun. As well as finding those ones which were about how men were not to be trusted— which are there.

THE DEVELOPMENT OF A "MUSICIAN" IDENTITY

Most women starting out in groups do not define themselves as musicians. Those rock "beginners" in my sample who did tended to be the ones who had been classically trained, but that was certainly no guarantee of such self-definition—one woman I interviewed did not think of herself as a musician despite years of classical training, Grade 8 on the piano, and a few years' experience in a rock band!

> SALLY: At first, when people used to say, "What are you?" I wouldn't say a drummer. 'Cause even now I don't think of myself as a drummer. I just say, "Well, I sort of play drums." I can't say, "Oh I'm a drummer." 'Cause it used to sound really odd. I suppose I am, but . . .

This general lack of confidence makes women susceptible to criticism, especially from male musicians:

> SALLY: We're a bit sort of hesitant. We aren't confident enough. We're just hopeless. We sit there going, "Oh . . ." In everything else we're quite good at what we do—which is looking after kids. We're confident in that way.

Once a band member does start to see herself as a musician, or even just as a member of a band, this new identity functions beyond the temporary existence of the band at practices. It is carried around and affects the whole of the woman's life. For example, she will listen to music differently, discuss it differently, engage in technical talk with other musicians. Band members go to gigs together to watch other bands and pick up ideas, and so other people's gigs too come to be experienced differently—musicians tend to stand at the front and intently watch exactly what various members of the band are playing. Going out to live music ceases to be simply a social event, a chance to dance, talk, and meet people; it becomes part of band work, and in this setting the role of musician thus provides women with a shield against the strictures of the double standard. It is suddenly legitimate to go up and talk to the musicians during the break or after the gig. So long as her identity as musician is known or made known at the start of the conversation, she will not be put into the "groupie" category or be seen as on the lookout for sex.

> HILARY: When I was playing in that band I found it very much easier, then, to talk on more equal terms with blokes that I had known vaguely around the music scene in Coventry for a year or something—musicians. Once I was playing in a band—and word gets round, you know—and gradually they realise that you're actually playing in a band. And I was able to talk to them on a much more equal basis.

Not only is it thus easier to meet musicians and talk to them, it is also easier to be at a gig. You have a clear purpose and now look purposive. It gives you confidence. You feel more at ease in your surroundings. You've got a new place in the music world.

COMMITMENT

In doing my research I've interviewed women in bands which variously play the whole gamut of popular music: light pop, heavy rock, reggae, ska, jazz-rock, punk, new wave, mainstream, and feminist alternative. These women also span a wide range of experiences: from the local band which has played only a few gigs to the commercially successful band with records in the Top 10; from women who have been playing for only a month to women who have played for more than a decade. Whatever the differences, though, what has most clearly come out of my research is that all these women faced the same set of problems in becoming musicians in the first place. I have explored these problems in depth elsewhere,[2] but I do want to note one particularly important aspect of what it means to be a "woman in rock," and that has to do with commitment.

It is undoubtedly true that women find it hard to commit themselves to music in the way H. Stith Bennett shows that male musicians do (see preceding essay). Women do not typically have that *total* dedication. Bennett argues that the musician has got to be involved in his music to the exclusion of everything else. He has to be able to "get out of himself" at practices, so that he is unaware of the rest of his environment. We can assume then that the male musician who is a father will certainly not have the major responsibility for childcare. Male musicians do not take their babies along to band practices; indeed they would find the idea unthinkable. Yet some women do have to do this, and clearly, in this situation, their concentration cannot be exclusively riveted on the music; they cannot forget that they are mothers.

> JACKIE: When we first started I used to take Sam with me up to Joy's and he just used to play with the toys. [But] you couldn't get into it. You couldn't relax. My mind was always, "Oh, God! What's he doing? . . ." You've got to have children to understand that, I think. When they're around, you're just totally involved in them. I find I get them to bed and, if I'm going to a practice, it takes a while to readjust . . . to get into that other state of mind.

Having children affects the choice of practice place, what time of day or night practices can be held, how long they can last, how frequently they can take place.

> TANYA: We were going to Leyton, but since Linda's had her baby we need to have a place that has two rooms. In fact, this place is rather good. It doubles as a recording studio and has glass panels. So we can sit and peer at the baby through the panels.

> KATE: Sometimes we had to wrap up practices earlier because we didn't have a babysitter and the child wanted to go to bed. We had to stop. Or, she wanted to go and pick him up from school, or whatever.

Getting a babysitter can be a problem, and it is also costly. If a babysitter has to be hired for rehearsals, then it seems too much of a luxury to hire one in order to go to other people's gigs too. Women musicians who have children go out to gigs far less often than other musicians do—if they go out at all, that is.

> JOY: We undoubtedly get on differently because we're all women and it works differently. You see, we've got sympathy with each other, with our respective problems, you know, with fitting everything in. And if someone says, "Well, look, I can't do this because I've got to take this little child to the doctor," or, "He's ill and I can't . . . ," we'd all sympathise. Whereas, if you were in a male band and you said, "Oh, I'm sorry, I can't . . ." they'd say, "Oh, crikey, her and her kids!"

Musicians schedule their lives around music; mothers schedule their lives around their children. Only highly successful—and rich—women musicians can resolve this contradiction satisfactorily. Though men who are musicians are more likely to understand the importance of being in a band and to accept the complex arrangements this necessitates than other male workers (the women I interviewed who had young children were either single parents or married to musicians), it is also apparent that they see their own role in music as being much more important than that of their wives.

> ALICE: The baby comes with her . . . Her husband is a guitarist and he is the breadwinner and brings in the money to pay the mortgage. And she has the baby. So the baby comes to rehearsals . . . She's in this nuclear family setup and, of course, the way it's set up doesn't work around a woman being a sax player in a band. That's a big disadvantage in terms of work. So we all have to pull to help things work. Sometimes, I don't like it if I feel we're supporting this nuclear family setup but, on the other hand, why shouldn't we support *her* and be as helpful as we can be to *her* . . . He just goes off to his gig. I mean, can you imagine *him* turning up to *his* gig with a baby? I mean, what a joke, you know! . . . If Joan's husband turned up at a gig with a baby I should think they'd be shocked out of their brains! He wouldn't do it though.

Women are, then, expected to be most "committed" to their families, to their children and partners. A girl's search for a boyfriend is conventionally more important than a boy's search for a girlfriend. It takes up more time and effort, and boys thus give a far more wholehearted commitment to their hobbies than girls typically feel they can—this is one reason that girls' bands break up or, indeed, never properly get off the ground in the first place: boyfriends resent the amount of time band practices take up and put pressure on the girl to leave (and research makes clear that similar pressure is put on older women musicians by their partners). The problem is, again, exacerbated during the next career stage, gigging, when domestic arrangements of all sorts become problematic.

> ALICE: It was something so separate from the woman I was involved with, there was nothing she could relate to or be involved in. And it took up a lot of time and I was terribly excited about it, and it wasn't anything to do with her. People I know who are musicians who have relationships with people who aren't musicians find it very difficult.

But if women musicians aren't (can't be) committed as exclusively to their music as men, they do seem to have a greater commitment—an emotional commitment—to each other. In the bands I studied, friendship was a far more important aspect of musical life than it seems to be in accounts of male bands. There was less mutual detachment; less of a split between practice sessions and "normal" life; one could argue (as male musicians do) that there was less "professionalism." This was certainly true of bands just starting out.

> HARRIETT: I think the difference is that if somebody has had a row with somebody, or somebody isn't feeling too good, they don't come into the practice and pretend nothing's happened. It's real. Whatever's been going on in people's lives comes to the practice. And with guys it's not like that.

> SALLY: We're all moody. You get to a practice and somebody's in a bad mood or pissed off or something. And it always affects it. And in the four of us, with

kids and everything, somebody's bound to turn up at a practice each time feeling rotten. We used to try and go out for a drink and all sit there together and have a good natter and moan about kids and everything else. Some practices we'd play one number and spend the rest of the time talking. 'Cause it was an excuse for all of us to get out and go to the pub and have a drink and moan about this and that and the other. So, even if we didn't practice, it was nice just to get together as a group to chat. [Whereas when she played with men:] We didn't talk about bloody kids or anything. With them it was go there and you'd play. You don't piss around. You're paying for two hours and you make good use of it. So I wouldn't go along there and say, "Oh, I'm pissed off with X and Y keeps wetting the bed." I knew I was there for one reason only and that was 'cause they needed a drummer.

It is clear that practices were performing more than one function for Sally's band. They were social events, a chance to get together and talk. The band was not just a unit which produced music together; it was a friendship group. "Chats" seem to be important in all women's bands, especially in their early stages. There is usually a lot of getting together apart from practices, lots of phone calls and general contact, and the friendships built up within bands were often as important as the music itself. This aspect of "being in the band" seems often to outweigh the lack of money, the frustrations, the hard work, the scant chance of commercial success. For women—and this may be the paradoxical twist in the explanation of why they don't "make it" in rock as often as men—the immediate experience of playing together is a source of strength and pleasure and purpose far more important than individual commercial success.

KELLY: We're all in love with each other, in a way, but it's platonic. We do admire each other a lot and it feels like we're one person when we play . . . It's like a family. We are very close and it's given me all these extra people that I care about and they care about me. It's more than just working together. . . . It's adventurous, exciting. It's like a gang. You're mates. You're up there together.

BONNY: We have a good time when we play. We have a good time and a laugh when we rehearse. And we enjoy it. We're not striving for anything in particular . . . I've always enjoyed the gigs. Even bad gigs I've enjoyed on stage, because you get a good feeling going together. We know what's happening and we're all laughing at each other . . .

NOTES

1 All these problems have to be replayed when gigging starts. Women then have to confront not just the technology—in an even more amplified setting—but also the entrenched sexism of male technicians.
2 See Mavis Bayton, "Women in Music," Ph.D. dissertation (sociology), Warwick University, England, 1989.

SAMPLE AND HOLD

Pop Music in the Digital Age of Reproduction

1 9 8 8

○ ▲ ○ ▲ ○ ▲ ○

"Science fiction and nostalgia have become the same thing."
—T BONE BURNETT

POP EATS ITSELF

Surveying the state of pop music at the end of 1987, postmodernists and devotees of Walter Benjamin's cultural analysis could be forgiven for patting themselves on their theoretical backs and ruminating on the strange prescience of these two bodies of theory. Writing in *Critical Quarterly* two years ago, Peter Wollen established the link between Benjamin and the postmodernists thus:

> As Benjamin's "age of reproduction" is replaced by our "age of electronic reproduction," the trends which he discerned are further extended. Reproduction, pastiche and quotation, instead of being forms of textual parasitism, become constitutive of textuality.[1]

Within two years, the British pop act M/A/R/R/S was enjoying a huge international hit with the single "Pump Up the Volume"—a record that is made up largely of pieces of about thirty *other* records. At the same time, the dominant technology in pop's future is clearly going to be digital reproduction, as established in new processes of music production (such as sampling music computers), and in consumer software such as the compact disc (CD) and digital audio tape (DAT).

In addition to these technological developments, pop ideology is increasingly dominated by a sense that the future has now arrived, for good. Pop's sounds and visions appear to be caught in a stasis that is both aesthetic and political, and that is well summed up by the former leader of the Clash, Joe Strummer, in a recent *Melody Maker* interview: "All movements are bullshit." As traditional political movements have become marginalized in pop politics, so notions of pop's historical movement as "progress" have withered and died. "Progressive rock," that most diabolical symptom of pop's desire to evolve into Art, has ceased to progress; and the question "What comes after punk?" is heard less often. Instead, today's pop musicians are busy blurring historical and cultural boundaries, as the musics of "traditional" Hispanic (Los Lobos, Rubén Blades), Celtic (the Pogues), and African (*Graceland*, Hugh Masekela, Peter Gabriel) musics are made contemporary and enter the mainstream.

As Lawrence Grossberg has pointed out, our received notions of pop's margins and its center have ceased to apply.[2] So too have our ideas about generation. It isn't just that that pop's audience has grown older. That shift would merely return us to a prerock era of popular music. The essential change is that "older" music has become contemporary for audiences of *all* ages. In their year-end surveys of 1987, rock critics on both sides of the Atlantic pointed to the extraordinary number of reissues and old records on the charts. The link with the new technologies is unavoidable. On the one hand, CD reissues partly account for the latest wave of apparent nostalgia (including the resurrection of punk—CBS has released a CD package of greatest hits from the Clash). On the other hand, new digital technologies are being used to deconstruct old texts.

Digital developments appear to offer shattering evidence for the pertinence of Walter Benjamin's analysis, in the spheres of both production and consumption. In music production, the increasing use of digital recording and reproductive equipment gives enormous credence to Benjamin's celebration of the end of the '"aura." In the age of mass production, Benjamin stated that the audience is no longer concerned with an original textual moment. In the age of digital reproduction the notion of the "aura" is further demystified by the fact that *everyone* may purchase an "original." Digital recording techniques now ensure that the electronic encoding and decoding that takes place in capturing and then reproducing sound is such that there is no discernible difference between the sound recorded in the studio and the signal reproduced on the consumer's CD system. This is something new: the mass production of the aura.

More radical still is the technology of DAT, against which the music industry has mounted a huge and largely unsuccessful campaign.[3] Unlike

CD, DAT can record. It opens up the possibility that consumers will simply make their own perfect copies of CDs, via home taping, thus obtaining the aura gratis. One response, from the record industry in the United States, has been the introduction of Personics—a system that attempts to co-opt home taping by selling consumers customized cassette tapes, dubbed (legally, of course) in record stores. Consumers are thus able to reorder the program of music offered on records and tapes by the record company. Like the CD, Personics introduces new elements of consumer control. Furthermore, an increasing amount of contemporary pop music takes advantage of this technology to "sample" sounds, voices, and effects from other records and use them in new pieces of popular music.

These technological shifts go hand in hand (although sometimes just in parallel) with pop's changing attitude to its history. As old texts have become new again (through new media forms like music video and the increased use of pop as a film soundtrack, as well as CD reissues), pop has plundered its archives with truly postmodern relish, in an orgy of pastiche. The degree to which pop music in the 1980s has become self-referential is now so developed that some songs sound like copies of parodies. I recently attended a gig in Berkeley where the band supporting the Meat Puppets seemed to be pastiching the Cult—a British rock group who made their name in 1986 by resurrecting the hard rock sound of Led Zeppelin. (It should be noted that Led Zep T-shirts have now attained the status of symbols of "cool," rather than being icons of rock prehistory.) On his recent solo LP *Now and Zen*, former Led Zeppelin vocalist Robert Plant samples from his old recordings, having spent the last few years listening to new bands sample his old records.[4] Plant decided it was time to pastiche from his own pastiche.

If much of this lends ammunition to Benjamin's account of mass culture, then the postmodernists who've bothered to listen won't have failed to take account of the fact that one of Britain's leading new bands is called Pop Will Eat Itself. Aside from the fact that so much contemporary pop seems to be caught in a stasis of theft (as in "free sample") and reissues, many of its most celebrated new acts offer recycled versions of pop's past: from the sixties (Hüsker Dü, the Bangles) through heavy metal (the Cult, the Mission, Whitesnake), disco (Pet Shop Boys, the Communards), endless reruns of punk rock (Fuzzbox, Screaming Blue Messiahs). Other bands delight in the production of bizarre historical juxtapositions (Sonic Youth, the Replacements)—a trend exemplified in the 1980s fashion for new bands to compete to perform the most unlikely cover versions of 1970s songs in their live sets.

"It's like cruising the 50's again, dig?", says Mickey Mouse in the ads for Disneyland's latest attraction, Blast to the Past. "Shake, Rattle and Roll Back the Years" is the slogan. And the copy goes on: "During the Blast to The Past at Disneyland, everything then is now again, every day." What is significant about this advertisement is that the humans cavorting with Donald, Mickey, and company on the tail of a red and white convertible are all teenagers. No one who actually remembers the fifties is in sight—excepting the Disney characters, of course. The appeal, like Led Zeppelin's, is not nostalgic, it is postmodern; a sign that when the future arrives, pop teleology comes to a halt. Even its images of the future no longer connote progress. Just as Disney's "futuristic" monorail is now read as a quaint notion derived from a bad sci-fi novel, so its space age Tomorrowland rock groups (Laser, transtar), dressed in shiny silver suits and playing electronic instruments with all the latest gadgets, appear merely as an outdated idea of what we once thought the music of the future would be.

As I will try to show in this essay, the shiny "technology" that features so prominently in postmodern analysis can offer up some unexpected meanings. Without doubt the digital sampling music computer (the "sampler") is potentially the most postmodern musical instrument yet invented. I will argue that its use and meaning often remain wedded to earlier aesthetics.

SAMPLE AND HOLD

Digital sampling computers are relatively new machines that digitally encode any sounds, store them, and enable the manipulation and reproduction of those sounds within almost infinite parameters and no discernible loss of sound quality. (An important related technology is the digital delay line/pedal, which stores brief sequences of sound and replays them, often in rhythm with the music.) They do, however, have their roots in earlier analogue inventions.

The electronic synthesizer was of course used by pop and electronic musicicans to simulate the sounds of conventional instruments, from the harpsichords of *Switched On Bach* to the string sounds used on many pop albums—one version of the analogue synth is in fact known as a "string machine," for its ability to simulate (not very well) the sound of an orchestral string section. A technology that was closer to sampling is the Mellotron, an instrument that was used (rather excessively) in the 1970s by progressive rock groups like Genesis, the Moody Blues, and Yes. The Mellotron was a keyboard instrument that triggered analogue recordings of such sounds as human voices, strings, and flutes.

Sampling technologies made the Mellotron obsolete technically, just as it was going out of fashion aesthetically—late 1970s punk rock had little use for massed choirs and string sections! In 1979 the Fairlight Computer Musical Instrument came on the market, although its enormous cost restricted its use to all but the most successful musicians, producers, and studios. The Fairlight CMI was however followed, in classic music technology tradition, by a generation of machines that did the same thing more cheaply—the Emulator and the Synclavier, for instance; and then a further and even cheaper wave of samplers, such as the Greengate and Ensoniq Mirage. Eventually, in 1986, Casio brought out samplers which cost less than a hundred pounds.

What is typical about this development is the way the technology was used to mirror practices that derived from low-tech innovations, first taking them out of price range of most musicians, and then returning them, via the sale of the High Street Casio, to the "street"—or is it the spare room? For example: one common use of samplers is and was to mimic the stuttering effect of "scratching"—a technique initially developed by DJs using record turntables. Another instance is the use of samplers to dub in segments of speeches, effects, or music—a technique that art-punk bands of an earlier era achieved by splicing tape with a low-tech razor blade. I will try to show later in this essay that the new technologies have not removed the notion of "skill" involved in such (often extremely complex and delicate) procedures.

The question of skill is also raised, as I will demonstrate, by the fact that sampling computers are also music sequencers. Like some of their analogue predecessors, digital samplers can be programmed to play sounds and rhythms independently of a keyboard and/or human performer. This facilitated the development of a technology that is of paramount importance in recent pop history—the drum machine. Drum machines enable a musician to program rhythmic patterns without actually hitting any drums. Early analogue machines simulated drum sounds electronically, using elements such as "white noise" to approximate a snare drum sound. Sampling enabled manufacturers to create machines that digitally recreated a recording that exactly resembles a "real" drum recorded in a studio.

It is this combination of sampling and sequencing (as evidenced in drum machines and digital music computers) that has eroded the divisions not just between originals and copies, but between human- and machine-performed music. In each area, that of originality and of "feel," the new music technologies raise some fascinating questions for cultural theorists. They place authenticity and creativity in crisis, not just because of the issue of theft, but through the increasingly *automated* nature of their mechanisms.

THE REAL THING

The questions of theft and automation in modern pop production appear to challenge its essentially romantic aesthetic.[5] And yet strangely enough cultural studies discussions of these areas have so far said very little about the music itself. In what follows I will attempt to focus on that neglected level, through some comments on the new technologies and their impact on rhythm and timbre.

The most striking point in the analysis of both areas is the fact that music made by machines, or to *sound* like machines, has not taken pop's trajectory into electronic or art music, but has instead become the chief source of its *dance music*. Synthesizers, drum machines, and digital samplers are identified less with modern composers (like Brian Eno) than with dance genres like disco, hip-hop, Hi-NRG, and House. In other words, while cultural studies critics such as Simon Frith[6] debate the essentially critical and academic distinctions being made between technology on the one hand and "community" and "nature" on the other, pop musicians and audiences have grown increasingly accustomed to making an association between synthetic/automated music and the communal (dance floor) connection to nature (via the body). We have grown used to connecting *machines* and *funkiness*.

This observation doesn't discredit the arguments of Frith, since his position is essentially that cultural studies debates about authenticity carried over from literary theory don't travel well into the field of pop music. What I am suggesting here, however, is that Frith's analysis needs to be supplemented by a *musicological* critique. If anyone need be nervous about the arguments that follow it is surely the postmodernists, whose assertions about the role of technology in postmodern culture have rarely been tested via empirical analysis. It may be that all the high-tech wizardry of movies like *Blade Runner* and bands like Sigue Sigue Sputnik is merely yet more sci-fi iconography (hardly a postmodern phenomenon), while the more routine use of modern technology in pop music is thoroughly *naturalized*, through aural familiarity and via pop ideologies constructed beyond the level of the technical infrastructure (in art schools and in the music press, for instance).

The most significant result of the recent innovations in pop production lies in the progressive removal of any immanent criteria for distinguishing between human and automated performance. Associated with this there is of course a crisis of authorship. But where this crisis has generally been located at the level of copyright and ownership of intellectual property,[7] I want to focus on its musical manifestations. In order to get a sense of how far-reaching these changes are, consider this scenario, which is now common at the beginning of a pop recording session: before a note is committed to tape, a producer or engineer will use a sampling computer to digitally record each sound used by the group. At this point, it is sometimes possible for everyone but the producer to go home, leaving the computerized manipulation of these sounds to do the work of performance and recording. Indeed, the recent court case involving Frankie Goes to Hollywood, producer Trevor Horn, and his record company ZTT centered on this problem—what exactly did Frankie and their lead singer Holly Johnson actually *do?*

The question "Who played what?" isn't new, and allegations that the act didn't really play on their "own" records have been raised about many bands, from the Beatles to the Sex Pistols. What is new here is the increasing problem of distinguishing between originals and copies on the one hand, and between human and automated performance on the other.

There are four processes that lead to the blurring of distinctions between automated and human performance in today's pop. The first is the growing sophistication with which today's pop technologies can be programmed. If one listens to a recording that uses state-of-the-art computer technologies (such as Scritti Politti's *Cupid & Psyche 85*), it is clear that machines are being used to mimic many of the techniques normally developed over time by human "real-time" performers. These techniques include the elastic placement of the beat (slightly in front of or behind its "correct" mathematical position) to create "feel"; the use of subtle changes of volume or velocity to create "lifelike" dynamics; and deliberately making small changes in the tempo to emulate the way human performers speed up and slow down. Chris Lowe, who programs much of the Pet Shop Boys' music, has taken to boasting about his tambourines being "out of time," even though they are programmed, via a drum machine and/or computer. In other words, today's pop musicians are often technicians who have learned to program every bit as skillfully as earlier generations (up until punk) learned to play.

A second reason for the confusion is very simple. Much of today's technology allows musicians to play into the program, using drum pads, keyboards, or perhaps even the buttons on the machine itself. This information will often register at very fine degrees of subtlety, encompasses parameters such as velocity and extremely small shifts in tempo and placement of the beat, and might trigger digital samples of "real" sounds that are indistinguishable from the originals. The result can be that the machine program contains every bit as much information as any piece of "real" playing.

A third overlap arises out of one prevalent use of digital sampling technology in the modern recording studio. Drum or keyboard sounds stored on a digital music computer can be triggered by analogue recordings. In other words, a recording of a "real" drummer playing a drum set in a studio can be used to trigger *any* sounds that can be stored in the computer, including any other drum set sounds, any drum machine sounds, and an infinite number of percussive samples (including old standbys like breaking glass and the beating of sheet metal). Consequently, one modern recording process reverses the phenomenon described in the previous paragraph. Here, a "real" drummer, playing with human imperfections, can be made to sound like a machine, or a computer, through changes in timbre implemented via samples. Indeed, this technique has been consolidated into a piece of hardware called *The Human Clock*—a triggering device that enables a drummer to drive machines in synch, according to a varying human tempo.

Finally, there is the use of a studio "loop," in which a few bars of music (perhaps a drum pattern, guitar riff, or an entire rhythm section hitting a particular groove) are recorded in real time and then rerecorded and repeated as the rhythm track for an entire song. The effect is human feel within the loop, but consistency of groove throughout the song. (And if the loop is recorded digitally, there is no degradation of sound quality in the recording process.)

These confusions between human and automated rhythm are also evident at the level of timbre. Here the key distinction is between those sounds which seem natural and those which sound synthetic. It has become commonplace in both music production and consumption to observe that analogue sounds/recordings are "warmer" than digitally reproduced music. (The debate about CDs centers on this distinction; and J. Baird[8] discusses the analogue/digital debate in the field of production, where digital keyboards such as the Yamaha DX-7 became unfashionable almost as soon as they went into fashion, because of their allegedly "cold feel.")

The key shift here occurred in the 1980s, when a generation of pop musicians emerged who grew up listening to electronic synthesizers. What happened then was that the very technology (the synth) that was presumed in the 1970s to remove human intervention and bypass the emotive aspect of music (through its "coldness") became the source of one of the major aural signs that signifies "feel"! This is the sound of a bass analogue synth— often a Moog synthesizer (although the Prophet 5 is another popular analogue reference point). By the mid-1980s, the electro-pop band the Human League could talk about using analogue synths as a move *back* to their "authentic" musical roots.

This sense that analogue is warmer and more natural than digital also extends to its visual signification, which is appropriately enough also signified via the words we use to describe these patterns—*waves* as opposed to *numbers*. A year ago, when I bought a music program for the computer on which this essay was written, the salesperson showed me two different ways of visualizing musical information. A digital keyboard presented me with lists of numbers. But there was a software program that converted this information into an approximation of analogue-style wave-forms. Both were incomprehensible to me. But to the keyboard expert demonstrating the technology, it was "obvious" that the analogue waves were more "natural" than the digital numbers.

This confusion of synthetic and natural sounds (analogue electronic synths were supposed to be "cold" and "unnatural," according to rock's realist critics and fans at the time of their invention) is more strikingly evident in the story of the strange case of the "handclap." Use of the handclap in pop music has its origins in various American and African folk traditions. Indeed, the handclap is, along with the voice, music's most "authentic" sound; both are present in "traditional" musics of most cultures. Handclaps have also been used on record both as percussion and to signify audience involvement since the first popular music recordings. In the 1970s an electronically simulated handclap sound began to appear on many disco records. Its percussive appeal lies partly in the fact that it incorporates what drummers call a "flam"—that is, a spreading out of the impact of the beat that extends its duration beyond the point at which it is "supposed" to fall. (Record producers often amplify this effect by adding electronic delay in the recording process.) One of the most popular sources of this sound in the 1980s was the handclap on Roland's analogue TR-808 drum machine. (It can be heard prominently on Chic's 1970s recordings, and on Marvin Gaye's 1982 hit "Sexual Healing.") What is extraordinary about this is that by the time Roland came to work on its next generation of (digital) drum machines (such as the TR-707), the electronic handclap sounded so "natural" to pop musicians and audiences that they sampled their own electronic simulation from the TR-808 machine, rather than "real" handclaps. Similarly, many electro-pop bands and producers who use digital samplers began by storing and manipulating synthetic, analogue sounds on them—sounds that both musicians and audiences could recognize.

At first this looks like a perfectly postmodern instance. Our aural consciousness has become so invaded by the realm of synthetic signs that we now hear a mass-mediated electronically simulated "handclap" as the "real" thing. If however we abandon the idea that musical representation occurs via *mimesis* and consider its process of signification in relation to intrapersonal "states of mind," emotions, and so on, we might conclude that the electronic handclap *is* real. It *really* produces certain physiological effects when you dance to it.

My point is this: the "recognition" involved in knowing how to hear electronic music depends in part on understanding the associations attached to any given sound. One element of this is our recognition of rhythms and timbre. While digital technology might appear more "real" than analogue (since it can reproduce an actual snare drum sound instead of a synthetic simulation, a real bass guitar sound, not a synth-bass imitation), the opposite is often true: in pop's digital age, analogue sounds are the real thing, however automated or synthetic. And as electronic technology has become naturalized, audiences have become habituated to seeing pop performers as technicians, computer programmers, DJs, or studio engineers.

THE END OF AN AURA?

A landscape that revels in the fusion of originals and copies, and in which we cannot distinguish humans from machines, seems like unlikely territory for authors and auras. Yet despite the apparently postmodern nature of so much contemporary pop, the question of creativity and originality remains central. Once again, Frith focuses in his discussion on the demands of the industry.[9] I want instead to comment briefly on the role of authorship in pop's aesthetic, and then go on to look at the importance of the aura in contemporary digital pop.

The following comment, from Tim Simenon (creator of the sampled hit "Beat Dis"), perfectly illustrates my first point:

> "We got the records and found a common denominator beat—we chose roughly a range between 108 and 118, we laid down a beat at 114 b.p.m. and slowed down or speeded up the tracks I was going to use. But what differs about this kind of "street fusion" is that it isn't straight cut-up like a Double D & Steinski record, or Grandmaster Flash.
>
> "It's in that form, but the bassline is original, we've got a drum pattern around it, and that sound like a Shaft guitar isn't 'Shaft.' We sampled one note of wah-wah guitar and reconstructed it on the keyboards. You wouldn't be able to find that guitar pattern on any other record."[10]

Note how, in 1988, "creativity" has shifted so far from its 1970s progressive rock heyday (when musicians tried to invent new, unique musical forms, as well as original music) that Tim Simenon can lay claim to it merely by noting that he didn't *steal* something from another record.

This kind of practice and its ideology (that of the Age of Plunder) is grist to the mill of the postmodernists, for whom it provides evidence of our total absorption in "the realm of signs." Yet this is too simple. Simenon clearly *is* invoking the concept of creativity. And he isn't alone. Here is Martin Young of Colourbox and M/A/R/R/S:

> "Scratching is actually more creative than sampling. With sampling you are basically limited to a staccato effect whereas a good scratcher can really mess things up."[11]

But while the musicians/technicians themselves are well aware of the sophisticated work that goes into contemporary automation and plunder, there remains the problem of transmitting this information to the fans—indeed, this is precisely one purpose of interviews such as those I have just cited.

One recurring problem of pop history exposes postmodern interpretations of authenticity as inadequate: it is the persistent failure of all those acts who are marketed as a self-conscious hype. Sigue Sigue Sputnik is only the most spectacular failure in this category of pop about pop; even an apparently successful hype such as Frankie Goes to Hollywood ultimately failed to achieve long-term economic/artistic success, through career longevity. Neither of these bands could survive their image as postmod con men, because it deprived them of any position from which to market authorship. It implied that they were puppets—an image that *real* puppet groups (the Monkees, for instance) did their utmost to defuse. But the self-conscious hype is doomed precisely because its postmodern premises (audiences aren't interested in truth or creativity any longer) defy pop's romantic aesthetic.

Other acts, like ABC and the Pet Shop Boys, have overcome this difficulty by promoting themselves as the authors of their own *image*. The most audacious challenge to the "truth" of pop performance has been mounted by the Pet Shop Boys—a duo fronted, significantly, by a former journalist, Neil Tennant. Where most electro-pop acts who don't perform "live" persist in maintaining the pretense that they *can* play "live," either by announcing tours that never happen (a tactic they recently abandoned) or by touring with session musicians, Tennant recently upped the stakes of inauthenticity by boasting about their inability to actually play, or even sing, when they lip-synched at the American Music Awards:

> "It's kinda macho nowadays to prove you can *cut it* live. I quite like proving we *can't* cut it live. We're a pop group, not a rock and roll group."[12]

The Pet Shop Boys can defy some discourses of authenticity because they invoke others, such as the authorship of their own marketing images and a source of "truth" that lies in an explicit critique of "rock" music.

For other acts, authorship and authenticity reside in the ability to actually play. This competence needs to be demonstrated in live performance—one key element in pop's visual discourses. This factor is relevant every bit as much for those bands who rely on "postmodern" sampling technology:

> "We've had some things built which look like abstract objects standing on the back of our risers. We mike them with contact mikes, and treat the sounds as samples. In other words, we can produce all kinds of different sampled sounds by hitting these objects. Most people think we must be miming when we hit these things on stage, because they can't understand how all these sounds could be coming out of one piece of metal. In fact, we're not miming; we're triggering the sounds. I think we'd like to explore this a lot more next time we go out on the road, because it's an exciting way of producing lots of sounds through some physical effort. That creates some visual excitement. You actually see us working on stage, rather than just standing there."[13]

There are two points to pull out of this comment from the electro-pop band Depeche Mode. First, the notion of authenticity is still very much present in the need for pop musicians to demonstrate musical competence. Indeed, the new sequencing and samping technologies have cast such doubts upon our knowledge about just who is (or isn't) playing what that some bands have recently taken to placing comments such as "no sequencers" on album covers—the Human League (*Crash*) and Shriekback (*Big Night Music*) are two recent examples that recall the legend that the rock group Queen used to place on their 1970s albums—"no synthesizers"!

Playing analogue synthesizers is now a mark of authenticity, where it was once a sign of alienation—in pop iconography the image of musicians standing immobile behind synths signified coldness (Kraftwerk, for instance). Now it is the image of a technician hunched over a computer terminal that is problematic—but that, like the image of the synth player, can and will change.

Which brings me to my second point—that audiences need to *see* their pop musicians *doing* somthing. Depeche Mode are troubled by the perception that they are miming instead of playing (perhaps this is because it is true—much of their "live" show is replayed via tapes and/or sequencers), and yet they are happy to perpetuate it in the interests of visual spectacle.

This in its turn must prompt a question concerning why pop audiences continue to attend live events. The sound quality is often very poor, and the visual imagery is usually too distant to be of any great value. Indeed, most stadium concerts are now accompanied by simultaneous video replay onto large screens. Attending a live performance by a pop megastar these days is often roughly the experience of listening to prerecorded music (taped or sequenced) while watching a small, noisy TV set in a large, crowded field. I do not believe that the "community" that follows from being a participant in a social event begins to explain the appeal of the modern rock concert. What explains the pleasure of these occasions more fully is the *aura*.

As veteran U.S. rock promoter Bill Graham puts it:

> In actuality rock and roll has become so successful that the majority of fans don't go to see the artist but to be in the presence of the artist, to share the space with the artist.[14]

In other words, to consume the only truly original aura available in mass-produced pop—the physical presence of the star(s). If we abandon the abstractions of both cultural studies and postmodernist analysis of pop and consider the role of live performance in relation to musical meaning, it is clear that the role of the visual in live concerts serves three functions for audiences. First, it provides visual pleasure on an abstract level (the display of the body, the spectacle of special effects, etc.); second, it serves to authenticate musical competence;[15] and third, it offers us the consumption of a star presence, an aura. In this last area it is clear that the realm of signs gives way to something more fundamental—the desire for an audience with an original, even if it is shared with 50,000 others.

The importance of *presence* (crucially, a *musical* as well as an iconographic term) is also highlighted in a second area where the aura continues to dominate pop consumption. It constitutes a return to the consideration of digital technology set up at the beginning of this eassay.

It is clear that high fidelity is the very embodiment, in consumerism, of the fetishization of original performance. The digital reproduction offered by CDs takes this process to extremes, not just by promising greater sound quality than analogue systems, but by revealing to the listener at home "imperfections" in the original recording that went unnoticed at the time. CDs of the Beatles' early recordings apparently expose the sound of Ringo Starr's squeaky bass drum pedal. In addition, then, to the fetishization of the "original" recorded moment, CD appeals to a belief in a pure, unmediated reality (the location of the aura of music performance) which it supposedly reveals.

Thus while digital technologies like CD and DAT no doubt have the capacity to break the barrier between the original and the copy, they are in fact more likely to be used to enhance the power of the aura of the original moment of recording, via the consumerist practices of hi-fi.

THE POLITICS OF SAMPLING

I will finish by addressing the questions of realism and history in contemporary sampled pop. I want to suggest that there are really three strands of digital sampling in pop production, which roughly correspond to received cultural studies categories of realism (I would prefer the term "naturalism" myself, but the two seem to have become synonymous): modernism and postmodernism.

First, there is the "hidden" sampling involved in using a machine such as a Linn drum to reproduce "real" drum sounds, or in the process of using a Fairlight or Synclavier to steal a sound. This use of sampled sounds is motivated largely by economics rather than aesthetics—getting "good" sounds and the "right" performance from a machine is cheaper and easier than hiring musicians. In this kind of sampling the object is transparency, since the producer is using the technology to achieve a realist effect (the imitation of a "real" performance) without calling attention to the mediating role of production technology. And this use of sampling is indeed so pervasive that we no longer notice it. Most of the songs we hear on the radio today use computerized and sampling devices at some point.

A second kind of sampling is more explicit. Some producers have created records and remixes that celebrate playfulness, sometimes through a kind of baroque overindulgence. Trevor Horn (ABC, Frankie Goes to Hollywood, Malcolm McLaren), Arthur Baker (Afrika Bambaataa, Cyndi Lauper, New Order), Bill Lasswell, (Material, Sly & Robbie), Daniel Miller (Depeche Mode), and Rick Rubin (Beastie Boys, the Cult) come immediately to mind as producers who straddle a line between pop realism and the sometimes self-conscious exposure of their own craft.

The 1980s development of a mass market for extended 12-inch remixes of pop songs is central here. Samplers are often used on remixes, because they can store a few bars of music, as well as individual sounds. They can thus be used to manipulate, extend, and/or condense the *structure* of a song, as well as its texture, arrangement, and timbre. It is because this practice often seems to deconstruct the original text (the 7-inch single) that record producer Arthur Baker was once named Rock Critic of the Year.

This second layer of producers and musicians remain for me the most interesting group working with the new technologies, purely by virtue of the fact that their aesthetic radicalism takes place in what we once used to call the "mainstream"—the charts. Listen to Arthur Baker turn middle-of-the-road group Fleetwood Mac into modernist avant-gardists (on his remix of "Big Love") and what you hear is a steadfast refusal to settle for the pleasures of pop formula offered in the original. But the point here is that this aesthetic isn't postmodern at all—it is modernist, with a dance beat. It is Theodor Adorno mistreating Fleetwood Mac, not Walter Benjamin celebrating them. (Furthermore, the remix market is saturated with auteur theories focusing on the producer as author.)

Finally there are those DJs, musicians, and engineers, some of them associated with dance music and hip-hop, and others with punk and its aftermath, who have made an aesthetic out of sampling . . . and in some cases, a *politics* out of stealing. M/A/R/R/S, Cold Cut, Steinski, and Mantronix are in the former category. For this school of sampling, "stealing" segments from other records is a part of the meaning of the "new" text. The music press have dubbed this the Age of Plunder, and the *New Musical Express* in particular has tried to make a case for this aesthetic as the Next Big Thing. Punk collagists, my second subcategory, include Cabaret Voltaire, Big Audio Dynamite, and the Justified Ancients of Mu Mu.

The problem here, for theorists of the postmodern condition, is this: First, many of these producers appear to be working with fairly traditional notions of creativity and authorship—M/A/R/R/S, typically for pop, followed up their "postmodern" hit with a series of intra-band disputes designed to establish who was *really* the "creative" force behind their music. Second, and more devastating, is the argument that the Age of Plunder is in fact one in which pop *recuperates* its history, rather than denying it. This thread of interpretation is evident in the numerous instances in which digital montagists and scratchers claim to be educating the pop audience about its history, as Tim Simenon suggests: "Take James Brown, all of his records are being reissued. Kids of 18, 19 wouldn't have heard of him if it wasn't for hip-hop."[16] Arguments about authenticity, authorship, and the aura in contemporary pop are clearly very complex, and I don't claim to have even sampled the whole truth here. But it is clear, in my view, that the postmodern and Benjaminite positions cited by Wollen are much too simple, because they are (typically) too abstract. In the first place, it is clear that the pleasure of consuming pop auras has not disappeared in the age of its mass production. If the aura is now produced on a mass scale, this has not led to its demystification. Indeed, I have noted that attempts to expose the marketing of the star aura in pop (some of them initiated by entrepreneurs informed by political and social theories such as poststructuralism),[17] failed precisely because the discourses of authorship remain dominant, and because large sections of the pop audience refuse to consume self-consciously. Pop fans generally appear to want their stars clad in denim, leather, and spandex, not ironic quotation marks.

Postpunk pop's effort to make the past contemporary might just as easily be viewed as a new interest in its *history*, which is a further problem. Just as serious, it seems to me, are the continuing concerns with creativity informed via a romantic aesthetic, the dominance of "realist" and dance-oriented uses of sampling technology, and the naturalization of the "technology" that the postmoderns make so much of.

Pop might be eating itself, but the old ideologies and aesthetics are still on the menu. That, in my view, is indisputable. The fundamental questions for the postmodern theorists are these: First, do we need a postmodern theory of society/aesthetic in order to understand postmodern cultural forms? And, second, what is the status of the developing postmodern aesthetic? Is it, in Raymond Williams's terms, an emerging condition that will perhaps rise to aesthetic dominance? Or is it in fact an aspect of economic, historical, and technological developments in pop that need to be understood in the context of the continuing dominance of realism, modernism, . . . and romanticism?

In the essay I referred to in my opening comments, Peter Wollen confidently states: "Clearly, post-modernist forms . . . demand a post-modernist aesthetic." He goes on: "The old critical apparatus has tended, in practice, to lead either to an exaggerated cultural pessimism or to a polemical over-enthusiasm."[18] And yet the fact that so-called postmodern theory reproduces *exactly* that banal polarity (albeit sometimes as parody) suggests that this body of work has no privileged hold on postmodern cultural developments. In my view the reason for this is very simple: by conflating postmodernism as *theory* and as *condition*, the former finds itself with a vested interest in promoting the latter, if not morally and/or politically, then as a cultural form of far greater significance than the evidence often suggests. It is for this reason that we need to probe beyond the ritual incantation of pastiche.

NOTES

Acknowledgment: My thanks to Joe Gore for many suggestions and helpful comments on this essay.

[1] P. Wollen, "Ways of Thinking about Music Video (and Postmodernism)," *Critical Quarterly* 28, Nos. 1 & 2 (1986), p. 169.

[2] L. Grossberg, paper presented at the conference "Popular Music: Research Trends and Applications," San Jose State University, May 1987.

[3] As I write this in March 1988, the U.S. National Bureau of Standards has just ruled against record company proposals to include "copy code" (an electronic system for preventing home taping) on CDs.

[4] See J. Gore and A. Goodwin, "Your Time Is Gonna Come: Talking about Led Zeppelin," *ONETWOTHREEFOUR: A Rock and Roll Quarterly*, No. 4 (Winter 1987); and S. Pond, "The Song Remains the Same," *Rolling Stone* (24 March 1988).

[5] See J. Stratton, "Capitalism and Romantic Ideology in the Record Business," *Popular Music*, No. 3 (1983); and R. Pattison, *The Triumph of Vulgarity: Rock Music in the Mirror of Romanticism* (New York: Oxford University Press, 1987).

[6] S. Frith, "Art versus Technology: The Strange Case of Pop," *Media, Culture & Society 8*, No. 3 (July 1985).

[7] S. Frith, "Copyright and the Music Business," *Popular Music 7*, No. 1 (1987).

[8] J. Baird, "The Neo-analogue Revival Hits NAMM," *Musician No. 114* (April 1988).

[9] Frith, "Copyright."

[10] "Beat Generator," *New Musical Express* (27 February 1988).

[11] "Bytes and Pieces," *New Musical Express* (14 November 1987).

[12] "Random Notes," *Rolling Stone* (24 March 1988).

[13] "The Wilder Side of Depeche Mode," *Keyboard* (October 1986).

[14] Interview, *Calendar Magazine* (San Francisco) (1 March 1988).

[15] See J. Mowitt, "The Sound of Music in the Era of Electronic Reproducibility," in Richard Leppert and Susan McClary (eds.), *Music and Society* (Cambridge: Cambridge University Press, 1987).

[16] "Beat Generator," *New Musical Express.*

[17] I am thinking of the anarcho-situationist politics of Malcolm McLaren and Jamie Reid (the Sex Pistols, Bow Wow Wow), and the playful poststructuralism of Green Gartside (Scritti Politti) and Paul Morley (Frankie Goes to Hollywood, Art of Noise, Propaganda).

[18] Wollen, "Ways of Thinking," p. 169.

PART FIVE

Musicology
and Semiotics

○ ▲ ○ ▲ ○ ▲ ○ ▲ ○ ▲ ○ ▲ ○

The emergence of a fully developed musicology or semiotics of rock and pop remains a distant prospect; at present we have a collection of intriguing and highly suggestive fragments rather than a group of schools of thought with their own competing lines of investigation. The majority of musicologists are happy to ignore pop music because they believe it is so obviously of no great aesthetic importance (we, for our part, are delighted to be left to our own conceptual devices); and most semioticians are more confident about the study of visual and literary signs than the slippery world of music. Consequently, the textual study of the *music* itself (as opposed to its lyrics, iconography, or consumption) remains quite underdeveloped. Nonetheless, pop music studies may yet prove to be the first area of cultural studies in which traditionalists (musicologists) and contemporary theorists (semioticians) are able to speak to one another, simply because the field is largely occupied by enthusiasts whose concern for the empirical business of listening to pop usually outweighs slavish devotion to theory.

Susan McClary and Robert Walser discuss some of the problems of analyzing rock and pop in their contribution to this section, and in doing so illuminate both the textual and institutional difficulties that must be overcome in the essential project of developing musical analysis in pop music studies. The essays by Roland Barthes and Theodor Adorno address musics that don't strictly come under the rubric of "rock and pop" generally used in this collection; they are included because of their absolute centrality in contemporary debates. Barthes's essay considers the role of the voice in "classical music," and in doing so lays the ground for a reformulation of pop musicology. Adorno's account is a much-cited (and perhaps less often *studied*) essay concerned with jazz, written before the emergence of rock and roll. Its Frankfurtian pessimism has frequently been criticized—although one author has suggested that Adorno's conceptual framework can be rescued while reaching new conclusions.[1]

The remaining essays and extracts offer readings of some very different pop texts. Andrew Chester's distinction between "intensionality" and "extensionality" in music remains a key concept in the analysis of rock in relation to other musical forms.[2] Mark Booth examines a very different kind of pop soundtrack—the soda pop connection that forms an increasingly visible part of contemporary music culture. David Laing offers a model essay in the all-too-short history of detailed text analysis of rock auteurs in his discussion of the songs of Buddy Holly. And Barbara Bradby provides a linguistic analysis which draws on the formal techniques of semiotic analysis, in her reading of "girl-group" era songs.

NOTES

[1] Bernard Gendron, "Theodor Adorno Meets the Cadillacs," in Tania Modleski (ed.), *Studies in Entertainment: Critical Approaches to Mass Culture* (Bloomington: Indiana University Press, 1986).
[2] Iain Chambers, *Urban Rhythms: Pop Music and Popular Culture* (New York: St. Martin's, 1986).

● Susan McClary and Robert Walser ●

START MAKING SENSE!

Musicology Wrestles with Rock

1 9 8 8

○ ▲ ○ ▲ ○ ▲ ○

A comic strip: two members of the heavy metal band Billy and the Boingers—Opus (a penguin) and Hodge-Podge (a rabbit)—pore over a long-awaited review of their work in *Time*. It reads, "With their latest record, the newly relevant Boingers weave trance-like melodies that slip over the transom of social consciousness and insinuate themselves into your dreams." In the following frame, the two creatures stare disconcertedly at the magazine. Finally Opus (his brow furrowed with anxiety) asks, "Yeah, but do we kick butt?" "Read it again," replies Hodge-Podge. And with this, Berke Breathed, creator of the strip *Bloom County*, skewers much of what passes for rock criticism and academic writing about popular music—its vague pretentiousness and its chronic failure to address what really is at stake in the tunes.[1]

Bloom County / By Berke Breathed

WRITING ABOUT MUSIC

Though the point has often been made, it is still easy to forget that music is an especially resistant medium to write or speak about. While it does share with speech both sound and a mode of producing meaning that unfolds through time, most other aspects of music differ considerably from the patterns of verbal language. One of the principal differences, for instance, is that music relies on events and inflections occurring on many interdependent levels (melody, rhythm, harmony, timbre, texture, etc.) *simultaneously*. Each of these has something of a syntactical dimension—a grammar of expectations, normal continuity, etc.—and also a wide-open semiotic dimension that can make us think we hear sincere remorse or bad-ass sassiness, that can produce the image of "the authentic working-class hero" or "the virginal slut," that can engage associatively with anything from Louis XIV's Versailles to street gangs in the South Bronx. When all these levels are operating at the same time, whether reinforcing or contradicting one another or both, we are dealing with a tangle that pages and pages of words can only begin to unpack.

But this task is made even more difficult by the fact that the music of one's own culture often seems completely transparent. Music appears to create its effects directly, without any mediation whatsoever. Listeners are usually not aware of any interpretation on their part, of any cognitive processes that contribute to their understanding of a piece of music. The music plays, the body moves. No cultural code required, thank you very much. Moreover, it is precisely this illusion that one experiences one's own subjectivity or a collective subjectivity in music that is most prized. Music's ability to conceal its processes and to communicate nothing/everything "directly" is largely responsible for its peculiar power and prestige in society.

The sociologists who deal with music tend rightly to be suspicious of mystifications of this sort. They can feel the seductive pull of the music and witness its widespread impact on groups of listeners, but yet they cannot always explain how it is that this medium accomplishes its effects. Thus they turn to musicologists.

And the music at this point becomes opaque. What had packed its wallop seemingly without any assistance from the gray matter now becomes unrecognizably abstruse. For, in effect, the musicologist is being asked to reconstruct those levels of mediation that have always seemed so transparent. And these levels of mediation cannot easily be explained in words that mean anything to the listener. With literature or painting, critics can refer in ordinary language to characters, plots, colors, and shapes that resemble phenomena in the everyday world. To be sure, a viewer's affective response to a painting may be difficult for that viewer to grasp cognitively; but a critic can point to dimensions of the painting such as line, perspective, lighting effects, and so forth in order to help the viewer to understand the affective process. Similarly a literary critic can cause one to become conscious of underlying metaphors, the rhythmic patterning of sentence structures, or organizing narrative strategies to demystify (at least partially) the means by which moods seem to be created in texts without the reader necessarily understanding how. Even the visual effects of film and television (which, like music, rely on multileveled signification through time) can usually be explained to the nonspecialist through painstaking analysis of camera angles and editing decisions.

Something of that same procedure is possible in music criticism, except that the equivalents of colors, characters, or camera angles are explicable only up against abstractions in sound organization—abstractions that virtually all members of a society manage to absorb and internalize from an early age, but for which they have no conscious awareness and no vocabulary by means of which to verbalize their responses. Worse yet, it often turns out that listeners—even academic social science listeners—do not *really* want to have their organic musical experiences knocked apart into components and explicated.

For the sad fact is that what created a particular effect in a piece of music—an effect so powerful that it can make an arena full of nonmusicians jump to their feet and scream with ecstasy—can be the result of an E-natural rather than an E-flat or an anticipation of a mere thirty-second note's duration. The sociologist who has jumped up with excitement but who is cautious to understand such reflexes in material terms turns to the adjacent musicologist and asks: "How did that happen?" The musicologist calmly replies: "You were expecting an E-flat, and he sang an E-natural." And the sociologist explodes because she knows perfectly well that she was not expecting an E-flat, that in fact she would not know an E-flat from a hole in the wall, and that the musicologist is once again taking a perfectly transparent phenomenon and obfuscating—flaunting specialized and apparently useless information.

Some of this misunderstanding can be alleviated in live musical demonstration. That is, rather than whipping out the technical jargon, a musicologist can explain from behind a keyboard or guitar that you were expecting this (plays mock-up phrase) and instead you heard this (plays phrase as it actually occurred). Or the musicologist can demonstrate what direct metric attacks would sound like and then the huge difference it makes for the voice to set up a tension against the regular beats by means of minute hesitations or anticipations. Or an effect of sincerity can be located in the carefully calculated roughness of vocal production that accompanies a particular word. In all of these instances, the images themselves can be reconstructed *in sound*, along with alternatives that vary only enough to indicate how the effect is being materially produced.[2] In this context, no verbal mediation is required.

Without the possibility of live sound demonstration, however, musicologists seem to have two principal alternatives. They either write in an impressionistic manner that may capture something of the way the music feels and is received but that does not at all address the details that contributed to creating the effect; or they try to explain precisely how the effect was achieved, but in terms of graphs and vocabulary that are quite alien to the listener. A choice between poetic or technical mystification.

TRADITIONAL VERSUS POPULAR MUSICOLOGY

So far, everything we have said applies equally to all musicologists—those concerned wtih "serious" as well as popular music. But musicologists concerned with rock do encounter a number of extra problems. For one thing, they are working in a methodological vacuum. Not only does traditional musicology refuse to acknowledge popular culture, but it also disdains the very questions that scholars of rock want to pursue: How are particular effects achieved in music? How does music produce social meaning? How do music and society interrelate? Thus before (or at least at the same time as) discussing any piece or repertoire, the musicologist interested in popular music has to invent critical techniques, codes, and paradigms from scratch.

This usually comes as a surprise to people not familiar with the concerns of conventional musicology. If they do not pursue questions of this sort, then what in the world do musicologists do? The discipline of musicology traditionally is dedicated to the painstaking reconstruction, preservation, and transmission of a canon of great European masterworks. Academic scholars of music are usually divided into two principal groups: historians (who, incidentally, are the ones who go by the name "musicologists"), whose job it is to produce definitive editions of repertoires of the past and to track down all the factual information that surrounds the history of "serious" music; and theorists (who do not regard themselves as musicologists but who do much of the work that most resembles what musicologists of popular music do), whose job it is to construct models that account for the syntactical order of "serious" music. The radical division of labor between these groups is clearly defined: one group works with names, dates, and places, the other with musical structures. What makes this arrangement viable is that both groups simply assume *a priori* the quality of greatness in the music with which they are involved. They also assume that the music is autonomous, that it works in accordance with abstract patterns of organization that have nothing to do with the outside social world. Criticism and interpretations of any sort are very rare in academic music study: the positivism that regulates the historical branch and the formalism that informs theory consider such enterprises to be "subjective" and "speculative" rather than "true."[3]

Musicologists of popular music thus enter their field with several huge obstacles to overcome. First, they have chosen to work with music that is defined by their home discipline as the enemy. A good deal of musicology is still attached to the music-appreciation mission of instilling in the population a preference for European classical music over the "junk" of American popular music.[4] Thus in daring to take seriously the very music the discipline is designed in part to discredit, they risk being marginalized, alienated—regarded as betrayers to the missionary cause.

Second, they find themselves burdened with the hidden ideological claptrap of their musicological training. And unless the premises underlying that training are brought fully to consciousness, they continue to operate and to confuse the focus of new agendas. One of these is the assumption of "greatness" in classical music, which can hinder research in several ways. It prevents traditional musicologists from making socially grounded sense of art music (Who needs sense if you've got transcendental greatness?); it frequently leads to an apologetic tone in work on popular music (Well, this isn't *great*, you know, but people like it . . .); and it can lead to counterclaims of greatness—witness the numerous calls for "an aesthetic of rock," many based on precisely the same faulty, unexamined criteria of traditional musicology (rock is great music too—it has transcendental redemptive moments; it has abstract structures too complex for anyone to hear; it should be studied as though it too is autonomous from pressures of social production; etc.).[5] However, insofar as the traditional agenda of aesthetics is tied to appeals to universal consensus that eliminate the possibility of political struggle over discourse, aesthetic approaches per se are incompatible with studies that treat music as socially constituted.

Third, musicologists of popular music are required not only to deconstruct the premises of their discipline and all the theoretical tools they have inherited, but also to develop the tools they do need. On the one hand, the traditional obsession with pitch organization as the essence of music has to be understood both as ideologically saturated and as extraordinarily limiting (even in classical music): concentration on pitch gives the impression of total rational control of the music, but only so long as one dismisses as irrelevant those elements that are not so easily classified.[6] And it also gives the impression "objectively" that popular music (which is relatively simple harmonically) is vastly inferior to classical. The studies of popular music that try to locate meaning and value exclusively in pitch relationships are products of traditional musicological training, and they tend to make the music they deal with seem very poor stuff indeed. The blues suffer especially in the hands of unreconstructed musicologists, for the harmonic progression itself (simple and unvarying for the most part) cannot begin to explain what is significant about this reperoire.[7] The musical interest resides elsewhere, in the dimensions of music that musicology systematically overlooks.

On the other hand, developing methods for getting at those overlooked dimensions requires not only noticing them, but also constructing a vocabulary and theoretical models with which to refer to them and to differentiate among them. How does one talk about microtonal inflections when one has decided that therein lies a clue to Muddy Waters's genius? How does one account on paper for the strut—the strut one's body picks up and responds to immediately and without conscious thought—of Prince's "U Got the Look"? How does one deal with what Roland Barthes calls "the grain of the voice" in Janis Joplin's singing?[8] It is no wonder that musicologists have preferred sticking to pitch and meter (both of which are measurable and can be charted with some degree of certainty), for these other parameters resist—or have not thus far been subjected to—intellectual control. Yet inasmuch as popular music defies being explained in terms of harmonic structure and insists on these other parameters, the musicologist who wishes to make sense of this music must come to terms with these uncharted areas for which there is no shared critical apparatus or language— this at the same time as trying to account for a detail in a specific song.

Fourth, the objects of study in popular music are rarely notated. The tools for analyzing "serious" music assume a definitive written score which is regarded as the record of the "composer's intentions." Those distracting elements that "creep in" during performance can be ignored as irrelevant: the music is structure, pitches, rhythms. In popular music, one often is not dealing with a composer in the traditional sense at all; there often isn't even a score, except as such things may be constructed and sold after the fact as sheet music—usually a peripheral commodity transcribed by someone unconnected with the production of the music.

What popular music has instead of the score is, of course, recorded performance—the thing itself, completely fleshed out with all its gestures and nuances intact. What would seem to be an indisputable advantage over notated music converts to a disadvantage only because analytic methods are still tied to those aspects of music that can be fixed or accounted for in notation.[9] The musicologist is stuck with the predicament of whether or not to transcribe the piece into notation for the purposes of discussion. Ethnomusicologists have become sensitive to the ways in which transcription is not an innocent activity: to render an oral-tradition tune in staff notation shoves its pitches into Western diatonic patterns with important inflections showing up as irrational deviations; and to try to "capture" its rhythms in the square metric system of Western classical music usually either winnows out whatever was interesting about the piece in the first place or reveals the piece as a hopeless tangle of ties and switching meters. Yet not to transcribe is perhaps not to be able to demonstrate one's points in a written medium.

Finally, given that most musicologists of popular music recognize the centrality of the interrelationships between this music and society, they find it necessary to develop historiographic and sociological methods for dealing with those interrelationships. It has already been mentioned that traditional musicology dismisses questions of socio-musical interaction out of hand, that part of classical music's greatness is ascribed precisely to its autonomy from society.[10]

To be sure, there are methodological difficulties in making connections between *any* cultural artifact and social orgainzation: observe the flood of theoretical work in literary criticism dealing with these issues. But for music—which refers to the outside world less clearly than the other arts and which has long been treasured in Western culture precisely for its abstract, nonsignifying quality—the problems become staggering. For not only is there no obvious way of linking musical patterning to large-scale issues of social class or gender politics, but music does not even have the equivalent of a surface-level semantics from which to begin a discussion of meaning.

This has not always been the case: under the influence of Renaissance humanism, composers became concerned with developing techniques and codes for delineating various emotional types and thereby moving the passions of listeners.[11] Treatises from the seventeeth and eighteenth centuries were devoted to matters of how to represent (through choices of pitch, key, rhythm, tempo, articulation, and so forth) grief, joy, and myriad other affects—as are manuals for movie or TV composition. But then along came Romanticism and the desire to perceive the composer as an isolated genius who expresses his subjective self without mediation or social code. The old Baroque codes continued to operate, to be sure; but they were no longer acknowledged. There is still considerable resistance to semiotics in musicology, even when one is dealing with the music of the eighteenth century, for which contemporary treatises on musical semiotics survive. To admit to the social mediation of music is to undermine the illusion of the transcendence of social interests musicology so values in it.[12]

Thus to try to make the case that a particular configuration sounds mournful (something that may be obvious to virtually all listeners, especially those not perverted by musical training) is to have to invent a philosophical argument for meaning in music and to try to reconstruct forgotten codes out of centuries of music.[13] At first glance, for instance, much of Philip Tagg's work appears bogged down in what seem to be irrelevant issues (why semiotics) and irrelevant repertoires (what has a Bach passion got to do with ABBA's "Fernando"?).[14] If Tagg were in a context in which semiotics existed as a matter of course, he could simply refer. But, unfortunately, most of his steps are absolutely necessary—he has to rebuild the whole of Western musical semiotics before he can unpack the theme from *Kojak*.

And this only addresses the surface. Is it possible to locate dynamics of social change in this slippery medium? Here our principal model remains (paradoxically) Theodor W. Adorno.[15] On the one hand, Adorno developed methods for making sociological sense of classical music, even though those methods have continually been resisted by traditional musicologists who are committed to the belief in radical autonomy. On the other hand, he spent much of his energy trashing popular music. Yet it is the scholars of popular music who are most attracted to his methods—thus the common genre of article that attempts to strip Adorno's attacks on popular music of their content, to preserve the methods, and to use those methods toward the explication and legitimation of popular music.[16] For unfortunately it is still the case that the only music that seems to require such methods is that which is significant precisely because of its indisputable social impact. One of the extraordinary ironies of contemporary musicology is that the intellectual apparatus required of those studying "serious" music—as it is traditionally done anyway—is practically nonexistent ("just the facts, ma'am"); while that required of those studying popular music—where reception, social context, and political struggle are regularly regarded as central issues—is vast, frequently embracing not only Adorno but also Lyotard, Derrida, Barthes, Althusser, Kristeva, Gramsci, Attali, and many others.

So how does one go about making connections between music itself and social values? Adorno's methods rely on homology: on metaphorically linked similarities between dynamic processes in music and those most central to the society at the time. Jacques Attali works with models that take into account both the principles by means of which the music itself channels noise or violence and also networks of music production, distribution, and consumption.[17] Gramscian models address music as a discursive practice in which meanings are negotiated through appropriation and/or subversion of available codes of social signification.[18] And all of these approaches, because they are not useful to traditional musicology with its radical separation of music and society, must be developed from almost nothing whenever the musicologist of popular music wishes to make the slightest comment on possible relationships between a song and social context. At the very least, an elaborate theoretical covering of one's all-too-vulnerable disciplinary backside is required, often to the consternation of the general reader who wants to get straight at "the stuff"—at a very single confirmation of what large groups of listeners feel is at stake in a particular song or artist.

Despite the understandable impatience of general readers with the state of their work, musicologists of popular music have made enormous strides. It is not that they have been struggling to catch up to the standard of scholarship typical of traditional musicology; the reverse is rather more the case—because their area of study has required the exploration of a whole new set of issues and the development of a whole new set of methods, they are far beyond their conventional colleagues in sophistication.[19] Most Bach scholars would profit from studying how Elvis Presley is dealt with sociologically and musically.[20] For musicologists of popular music have begun to reconstruct the semiotic codes of Western music, have developed techniques for dealing with music as a discourse that both reflects and influences society, and have produced modes of dealing with aspects of music other than pitch organization. These achievements are impressive, and they ought to be recognized as such.

THE PITFALLS OF POP MUSICOLOGY

At the same time, problems do remain in some of the approaches applied to popular music. For example, many analyses of popular music rely too heavily on the lyrics. This should come as no surprise: the verbal dimension of a song is much more readily grasped and discussed in terms of meaning. Our techniques for dealing with texts are far better developed at this point, and they do not (or *need* not, anyway) involve the difficulty of mediating through a cumbersome professional jargon. The backbone of an analysis often is a discussion of the words—their versification, central images, and so on—and the music is dealt with only as it serves to inflect the ambiguities left unresolved within the text itself. Text remains prior to the music. The criticisms of rock by the PMRC (Parents' Music Resource Center) are all tied closely to verbal content. And the interpretation of Buddy Holly's "Peggy Sue" by Bradby and Torode concludes—after an exhaustive narrative tracing of minute verbal inflections, with nary a mention of the obsessive drumming that introduces and permeates the song—that "the rhythms of the song are the rhythms of *verbal images*."[21]

Yet it is not at the service of text that much popular music is constructed. Country music may strive to give the impression of personal communication from the singer to the individual listener: narrative structures are common and intelligibility is considered crucial. But it is certain that much rock is not received primarily in terms of text: indeed, the texts of some genres of popular music are not clearly discernible by its fans—those who are most devoted to the music—and the obscurity of the verbal dimension seems even to be part of the attraction.[22] Heavy metal fans, for instance, don't seem to be much concerned with verbal discourse; they go to concerts where lyrics are almost completely unintelligible, and they don't mouth the lyrics along with the songs even if they know them—they are much more likely to mime the guitar solos or make power gestures or yell. Narratives are relatively rare in metal; more commonly the texts evoke sequences of loosely related vivid images. Indeed, when an interviewer asked guitarist Eddie Van Halen, "Ever worry what your mother might think of some of [singer David Lee] Roth's lyrics?", his (probably slightly disingenuous) reply was, "I don't know what the lyrics are."[23] Whether in simplistic readings by the PMRC or in theoretically sophisticated readings of "Peggy Sue," excessive emphasis on text may lead to skewed perceptions.

The more musically oriented modes of analysis would seem to avoid that particular problem, though some of them fall into another trap—that of trying to control the music by means of a single totalizing method. Fortunately, pitch-obsessed analyses are rare in popular music criticism these days, for most musicologists studying popular music have recognized that approach's limitations. However, even some of the more socially grounded methods can prove guilty of attempting to determine too narrowly "the meaning" of a given piece. Semiotic studies, for instance, are invaluable so long as they are kept in some perspective: without them we have no way of explaining the associations, the conventional affective gestures upon which musicians and performers rely in communicating. But to remove a piece of music from its context and to dissect it solely on the basis of semiotic allegiances—and to abandon it thus dissected—is to compartmentalize it into atomic bits that no longer seem related to the entity that was able to seduce and move audiences. It is cut off from its power source.

What all these approaches have in common is a tendency to cover up or keep at arm's distance the dimensions of music that are most compelling and yet most threatening to rationality. As Opus the penguin asks after reading his review, "Yeah, but do we kick butt?" We would like to propose along with Opus that the inability or unwillingness to address this component of music—the bottom-line component, as it were, for most musicians and fans—is the greatest single failure of musicology.

Perhaps this is to be expected: it is, after all, the intellectually committed among us who become academics—those who are uncomfortable with inexplicable sensual responses and who wish to be able to control those responses rationally. Yet musicologists also are individuals who find themselves drawn to music so irresistibly that they dedicate their careers to trying to figure out what makes it tick. This combination of intense attraction and fear of the irrational or of the sensual creates a strange set of priorities: to seize the objects that are most profoundly disturbing and to try to explain away—through extensive verbalization and theorizing—that which caused the disturbance. If one can take a piece of music that provoked a reaction and then analyze it in a totalizing way (laying it out as text, labeling its chords, tracing its semiotic parts, reducing it to ideological agenda), then perhaps it won't bite.

In fact, musicologists sometimes approach music with the same attitude that gynecologists (quite rightly!) approach female sexuality: gingerly. In both situations, a concerted effort is made to forget that some members of society regard the objects of their scrutiny as pleasurable. The staff historian takes the vital information (date of birth, height, weight) of the patient. Up into the stirrups goes the song. And the theorist, donning "objectivity" as a methodological rubber glove to protect against contamination, confronts the dreaded thing itself. Graphs, pitch charts, semiotic dissections, guidelines of political correctness—the Pap smears of musicology—are marshalled to detect pathological deviation, to reduce the threat of individuality to normative order.[24] The song is buried under a barrage of theoretical insights, and—no, Opus—it doesn't kick butt any longer. That's the point.

But if kicking butt (or, as they would say in the Baroque, "moving the passions") is the mainspring of music for both its producers and consumers, then no wonder so many products of musicology seem so obfuscating. They aim precisely at displacing and obscuring the focus, at defusing the music's energy.

FEAR OF MUSIC

This is not to say that the foregoing techniques do not have their places, even necessary places. We are not advocating shutting off the mind and playing air guitar as a substitute for rigorous scholarship (though if more musicologists had an irresistible urge to play air guitar instead of lunging immediately for their distancing techniques, we all—readers and musicologists alike—might be the better for it). Rather, we are suggesting that considerably more attention has to be paid to those aspects of music that trigger adulation in fans, even if (*especially* if) those are just the aspects that strike terror in the scholar's rational mind.

Musicologists have been trained to perceive music through modes of "critical listening." Consequently, many of them tend to regard physically and emotionally oriented responses to music as naive and childish. Yet if rock has any political power (and those of us who lived through the sixties cannot doubt that it does), then that power most likely does not reside in the sophisticated abstractions that the theoretically trained alone are able to discern. Musicologists have to be able to use their analytical skills to explain how the effects listeners celebrate are constructed; they should not—in their attempts at establishing intellectual legitimacy—turn the object of study into something unrecognizable to the fan.

Part of the problem is one that chronically plagues the Left: a desire to find explicit political agendas and intellectual complexity in the art it wants to claim and a distrust of those dimensions of art that appeal to the senses, to physical pleasure. Yet pleasure frequently *is* the politics of music—

pleasure as interference, the pleasure of marginalized people that has evaded channelization. Rock is a discourse that has frequently been at its most effective politically when its producers and consumers are least aware of any political or intellectual dimensions:[25] those moments when subversive constructions of race or sexuality suddenly confront the mainstream with alternatives made appealing precisely because the music presents a new and irresistible mode of kicking butt.

A particularly explicit instance of such a moment is reported by Geoffrey Stokes in a discussion of mid-sixties "soul."[26] The historic occasion described is a session arranged by Jerry Wexler (Atlantic Records) between Wilson Pickett and the studio musicians of Stax Records:

> One of the most important of those ad-libs—one that helped define the soul sound for the next couple of years—was in effect danced by Wexler. They'd been doing a song for a while when suddenly, in the midst of the bridge, Wexler came bouncing out of the control booth and began to dance a version of the jerk. "Why don't you pick up on this thing here?" he asked.
>
> [Guitarist Steve] Cropper again: "He said this was the way the kids were dancing: they were putting the accent on two. Basically, we'd been one-beat-accenters with an afterbeat, it was like 'boom dah,' but here this was thing that went 'un-chaw,' just the reverse as far as the accent goes. The backbeat was somewhat delayed, and it just put it in that rhythm, and Al [drummer Jackson Jr.] and I have been using that as a natural thing now, ever since we did it. We play a downbeat and then two is almost on but a little bit behind, only with complete impact. It turned us on to a heck of a thing."

This account begins to locate the factor most responsible for soul's *musical* hook (though Stokes goes on to locate this analysis carefully within a complex political-musical framework). Along with this quirky shift of accent came, of course, a new set of images, flooding the mainstream, presenting challenges on many fronts: race, gender, class. What was once a bodily motion developed by urban black kids in the mid-sixties became something that continues to inform kinetic vocabularies worldwide. We all have learned how to "pick up on this thing here." It's engrained in our bodies.

To apologize for the rambunctious edge of music or to substitute for this dimension some intellectually respectable justification that avoids the rhythmic impulse, to attempt to reduce apparent noise to rational order is to stifle the music and willfully to ignore its source of political effectiveness. And this is true not only for work in popular culture but also for the study of important figures and style changes in classical music: the history of Western music is largely a series of struggles over which qualities of motion—of organizing or experiencing time, pleasure, and the body—are to prevail.[27]

To address these issues requires different strategies of speaking and writing than the more usual "objective" modes: a greater willingness to try to circumscribe an effect metaphorically, to bring one's own experience as a human being to bear in unpacking musical gestures, to try to parallel in words something of how the music *feels*.[28] Paraphrasing Pascal, the body has its reasons which reason knows nothing of—though it is, of course, the job of the musicologist to mediate between "the body's reasons" and musical discursive practices.

Simon Frith has on occasion been taken to task for having written that rock simulates sexual patterns.[29] That it does not do so in an unmediated fashion is clear enough: many layers of musical syntax, social encoding, and electronic technology lie between physical lovemaking on the one hand and a series of sounds played by a band on the other. Yet to dismiss this insight out of hand and to replace it with intricate hermeneutic readouts that nail down everything *except* the physical pulse is to try to render innocuous something that is important culturally precisely because it does what Frith (without knowing how to explain quite *how*) says it does.

To acknowledge the "groove" is not to reduce music to some essentialist notion of "the body" or to seek explanations in biological urges. The rhythmic impulses of rock music are as socially constructed as are the contrapuntal intricacies of the Baroque fugue. Yet to the extent that sexual appeal is central to the ways in which rock is produced, marketed, and consumed—and to the extent that members of society come to experience their bodies in the terms provided by rock—this dimension must be of central concern to the musicologist. For this is the dimension that both detractors and advocates of rock fight over—it's what's at stake, both in the music and in society at large.

Dealing with these issues responsibly involves legitimizing—or at least recognizing as vitally important—common responses to the music. It is the relative absence of such recognition that makes so much rock musicology seem so very alien. The critic or musicologist may and often should, in the final analysis, deplore the impulse behind the music's appeal or the pernicious nature of the message being swept along in its rhythmic wake: we are not simply saying, "let's boogie." But unless the sensual power of the music is dealt with seriously, the rest of the argument becomes irrelevant. It lacks credibility.

What is important in music is, indeed, elusive. But this need not force us back to some mystified plea of "ineffability." What musicologists can contribute to the discussion of the politics of popular music is some way of explaining how the powerful moments in music are accomplished, without discrediting the impression that they are exciting, disturbing, or pleasurable. The focus should be on constructing models that serve only as flexible backdrops, up against which the noise of the piece can reverberate. What do those norms signify? Whose are they? What is the piece's particular strategy of resistance or affirmation? What's the noise about?

To be sure, celebration of the beat is not the only aim of most writers on rock. The chords, melodic contours, and metric structures must be grasped analytically or else one has no way of addressing how in material terms the music manages to "kick butt." The reconstruction of semiotic codes is crucial, both for grounding musical procedures (including rhythmic) in terms of various discursive practices and for explaining how the music produces socially based meanings. Verbal texts, performance styles, and video imagery need to be analyzed carefully and in tandem with musical components. Modes of commercial production and distribution, the construction of band or star images, the history of a singer's career all have to be taken into account. And political issues (the positioning of the music with respect to class, race, gender) always must be dealt with seriously.

But none of these alone can be the whole story. And without some basic acknowledgment of the musical energy—the source of its power and ability to give pleasure or to threaten—they are not even satisfactory as part of the story. They are rightly viewed by readers as obfuscations. If musicologists are to start making sense, they must put aside, at least from time to time, the theories that serve so well as protective measures against the heat of the music, that keep the body firmly in check. If an article on popular music can't answer Opus's question, then maybe it needs to be rethought.

NOTES

Acknowledgment: We wish to thank Richard Leppert and George Lipsitz for reading and commenting on a draft of this paper.

[1] *Minneapolis Star and Tribune*, 8 May 1987, p. 17C.

[2] Philip Tagg's invaluable "interobjective comparison" involves precisely this kind of procedure, though it becomes quite cumbersome on paper. See his "Analysing Popular Music: Theory, Method and Practice," *Popular Music 2* (1982), pp. 47–62.

[3] For a recent account of academic music study and how it got to be that way, see Joseph Kerman, *Contemplating Music* (Cambridge, Mass.: Harvard University Press, 1985).

[4] The current bestseller by Allan Bloom, *The Closing of the American Mind* (New York: Simon & Schuster, 1987), argues that rock, feminism, and programs that study popular culture are major threats to civilization.

[5] Wilfrid Mellers, for instance, tends to apply criteria of musical complexity and the mystified image of the artist-as-genius from standard musicology to popular artists. See his treatment of Bob Dylan, *A Darker Shade of Pale* (London: Oxford University Press, 1984). Andrew Chester's "For a Rock Aesthetic," *New Left Review* 59 (1970), pp. 83–87, and "Second Thoughts on a Rock Aesthetic: The Band," *New Left Review* 62 (1970), pp. 75–82, are important early statements advocating that rock be dealt with in terms of aesthetics. For more recent thoughts on the subject, see Simon Frith, "Towards an Aesthetic of Popular Music," in Richard Leppert and Susan McClary (eds.), *Music and Society: The Politics of Composition, Performance and Reception* (Cambridge: Cambridge University Press, 1987), pp. 133–49.

[6] John Shepherd's work deals extensively both with the ideological implications of pitch studies and with neglected components of music such as timbre. See "Music and Male Hegemony," *Music and Society*, pp. 151–72. It is not at all clear that these other components are *inherently* more difficult to classify, but over the last millenium Western culture has

developed a theoretical apparatus that privileges pitch and meter, to the exclusion of most other parameters.

[7] Charles Keil explains well the difficulties of writing about the blues in *Urban Blues* (Chicago: University of Chicago Press, 1966), but then concentrates primarily on the sociological dimensions of the repertoire in his study. Andrew Chester's concepts of "extensionality" and "intensionality" continue to be extremely useful in studies of genres such as the blues. See his "Second Thoughts," pp. 78–80.

[8] Roland Barthes, "The Grain of the Voice," in *Image–Music–Text*, trans. Stephen Heath (New York: Hill & Wang, 1977), pp. 179–89.

[9] This overreliance on the notated score is detrimental to the study of "serious" music as well. The attention of the analyst is institutionally restricted to that which shows up as an event in the score, which means that sound imagery, qualities of motion, long-term rhythmic shapes, expressive inflections—in other words, most of the dimensions the listener responds to in music—are ignored. Likewise, classical performers typically are trained to play the notation as accurately as possible: a process that most often results in "braindead" performances. See Robert Walser, "Musical Imagery and Performances Practice in J. S. Bach's Arias with Trumpet," *International Trumpet Guild Journal 12*, No. 3 (February 1988).

[10] See, however, *Music and Society* for a series of essays that attempt to break through the ideology of autonomy and to put "serious" and popular music on the same methodological footing. See also Alan Durant, *Conditions of Music* (Albany: SUNY Press, 1984) for parallel treatments of both categories of music.

[11] See, for instance, Johann Mattheson, *Der vollkommene Capellmeister* (Hamburg, 1739), for an eighteenth-century treatment of signification.

[12] See Susan McClary, "The Blasphemy of Talking Politics during Bach Year," *Music and Society*, pp. 13–62, and "A Musical Dialectic from the Enlightenment: Mozart's Piano Concerto in G Major, K. 453, movement II," *Cultural Critique 4* (1986), pp. 129–69.

[13] Two standard studies on meaning in music are Leonard B. Meyer, *Emotion and Meaning in Music* (Chicago: University of Chicago Press, 1956), and Peter Kivy, *The Corded Shell: Reflections on Musical Expression* (Princeton: Princeton University Press, 1980).

[14] Tagg, "Analysing Popular Music."

[15] For Adorno essays dealing both with classical and popular music, see *Prisms*, trans. Samuel Weber and Shierry Weber (Cambridge, Mass.: MIT Press, 1981).

[16] Max Paddison, "The Critique Criticised: Adorno and Popular Music," *Popular Music 2* (1982), pp. 201–18, and Bernard Gendron, "Adorno Meets the Cadillacs," in Tania Modleski (ed.), *Studies in Entertainment: Critical Approaches to Mass Culture* (Bloomington: Indiana University Press, 1986), pp. 18–36.

[17] Jacques Attali, *Noise*, trans. Brian Massumi (Minneapolis: University of Minnesota Press, 1985).

[18] See, for instance, Richard Middleton, "Articulating Musical Meaning / Re-constructing Musical History / Locating the "Popular," *Popular Music 5* (1985), pp. 45–80; and George Lipsitz, "Cruising Around the Historical Bloc: Postmodernism and Popular Music in East Los Angeles," *Cultural Critique 5* (1986–87), pp. 157–78.

[19] Richard Middleton makes a similar point in his introduction to *Popular Music 2* (1982), pp. 1–8.

[20] See, for instance, Greil Marcus, "Presliad," in *Mystery Train: Images of America in Rock 'n' Roll Music* (New York: Dutton, 1982), and Middleton's discussion of Elvis's "boogification" in "Articulating Musical Meaning," pp. 15–18.

[21] Barbara Bradby and Brian Torode, "Pity Peggy Sue," *Popular Music 4* (1984), pp. 183–206.

[22] The same is true of opera reception. See Catherine Clément, *Opera, or the Undoing of Women*, trans. Betsy Wing (Minneapolis: University of Minnesota Press, 1988), for an especially interesting account of the will not to understand.

[23] From an interview reprinted in *Musician 100* (February 1987), p. 94.

[24] For a discussion of the silencing of music through music theory's imposition of order, see Susan McClary's afterword, "The Politics of Silence and Sound," in Attali's *Noise*, pp. 149–58.

[25] John Street demonstrates this point superbly in *Rebel Rock: The Politics of Popular Music* (Oxford: Basil Blackwell, 1986).

[26] Ed Ward, Geoffrey Stokes, and Ken Tucker, *Rock of Ages, The "Rolling Stone" History of*

Rock & Roll (New York: Rolling Stone Press/Summit Books, 1986), pp. 293–94. Thanks to Greg Sandow for bringing this passage to our attention.

[27] For an account of Bach's negotiations among available national discourses, distinguished by rival rhythmic impulses, see McClary, "The Blasphemy of Talking Politics"; and for a whirlwind history of tonality based on qualities of motion, see McClary, "The Rise and Fall of the Teleological Model in Western Music," in *The Paradigm Exchange* (Minneapolis Center for Humanistic Studies, 1987).

[28] For a philosophical discussion of the centrality of body-oriented metaphors in human knowledge and discourses, see George Lakoff and Mark Johnson, *Metaphors We Live By* (Chicago: University of Chicago Press, 1980); Lakoff, *Women, Fire, and Dangerous Things: What Categories Reveal about the Mind* (Chicago: University of Chicago Press, 1987); and Johnson, *The Body in the Mind* (Chicago: University of Chicago Press, 1987).

[29] Bradby and Torode, "Pity Peggy Sue," pp. 183, 204. We find evidence nowhere to indicate that Frith thinks that "these rhythms . . . express sexuality directly" (p. 204) and find the interpretation of the quotation from Frith on p. 183 to be a willful misreading.

THE GRAIN OF THE VOICE

1 9 7 7

○ ▲ ○ ▲ ○ ▲ ○

anguage, according to Benveniste, is the only semiotic system capable of *interpreting* another semiotic system (though undoubtedly there exist limit works in the course of which a system feigns self-interpretation—*The Art of the Fugue*). How, then, does language manage when it has to interpret music? Alas, it seems, very badly. If one looks at the normal practice of music criticism (or, which is often the same thing, of conversations "on" music), it can readily be seen that a work (or its performance) is only ever translated into the poorest of linguistic categories: the adjective. Music, by natural bent, is that which at once receives an adjective. The adjective is inevitable: this music is *this*, this execution is *that*. No doubt the moment we turn an art into a subject (for an article, for a conversation) there is nothing left but to give it predicates; in the case of music, however, such predication unfailingly takes the most facile and trivial form, that of the epithet. Naturally, this epithet, to which we are constantly led by weakness or fascination (little parlor game: talk about a piece of music without using a single adjective), has an economic function: the predicate is always the bulwark with which the subject's imaginary protects itself from the loss which threatens it. The man who provides himself or is provided with an adjective is now hurt, now pleased, but always *constituted*. There is an imaginary in music whose function is to reassure, to constitute the subject hearing it (would it be that music is dangerous—the old Platonic idea? that music is an access to *jouissance*, to loss, as numerous ethnographic and popular examples would tend to show?), and this imaginary immediately comes to language via the adjective. A historical dossier ought to be assembled here, for adjectival criticism (or predicative interpretation) has taken on over the centuries certain institutional aspects. The musical adjective becomes legal whenever an *ethos* of music is postulated, each time, that is, that music is attributed a regular—natural or magical—mode of signification. Thus with the ancient Greeks, for whom it was the musical *language* (and not the contingent work) in its denotative structure which was immediately adjectival, each mode being linked to a coded expression (rude, austere, proud, virile, solemn, majestic, warlike, educative, noble, sumptuous, doleful, modest, dissolute, voluptuous); thus with the Romantics, from Schumann to Debussy, who substitute for, or add to, the simple indication of tempo (*allegro, presto, andante*) poetic, emotive predicates which are increasingly refined and which are given in the national language so as to diminish the mark of the code and develop the "free" character of the predication (*sehr kräftig, sehr präcis, spirituel et discret*, etc.).

Are we condemned to the adjective? Are we reduced to the dilemma of either the predicable or the ineffable? To ascertain whether there are (verbal) means for talking about music without adjectives, it would be necessary to look at more or less the whole of music criticism, something which I believe has never been done and which, nevertheless, I have neither the intention nor the means of doing here. This much, however, can be said: it is not by struggling against the adjective (diverting the adjective you find on the tip of the tongue toward some substantive or verbal periphrasis) that one stands a chance of exorcising music commentary and liberating it from the fatality of predication; rather than trying to change directly the language on music, it would be better to change the musical object itself, as it presents itself to discourse, better to alter its level of perception or intellection, to displace the fringe of contact between music and language.

It is this displacement that I want to outline, not with regard to the whole of music but simply to a part of vocal music (*Lied or mélodie*): the very precise space (genre) of *the encounter between a language and a voice*. I shall straightaway give a name to this signifier at the level of which, I believe, the temptation of ethos can be liquidated (and thus the adjective banished): the *grain*, the grain of the voice when the latter is in a dual posture, a dual production—of language and of music.

What I shall attempt to say of the "grain" will, of course, be only the apparently abstract side, the impossible account of an individual thrill that I constantly experience in listening to singing. In order to disengage this "grain" from the acknowledged values of vocal music, I shall use a twofold opposition: theoretical, between the pheno-text and the geno-text (borrowing from Julia Kristeva), and paradigmatic, between two singers, one of whom I like very much (although he is no longer heard), the other very little (although one hears no one but him), Panzera and Fischer-Dieskau (here merely ciphers: I am not deifying the first nor attacking the second).

Listen to a Russian bass (a church bass—opera is a genre in which the voice has gone over in its entirety to dramatic expressivity, a voice with a grain which little signifies): something is there, manifest and stubborn (one hears only *that*), beyond (or before) the meaning of the words, their form (the litany), the melisma, and even the style of execution: something which is directly the cantor's body, brought to your ears in one and the same movement from deep down in the cavities, the muscles, the membranes, the cartilages, and from deep down in the Slavonic language, as though a single skin lined the inner flesh of the performer and the music he sings. The voice is not personal: it expresses nothing of the cantor, of his soul; it is not original (all Russian cantors have roughly the same voice), and at the same time it is individual: it has us hear a body which has no civil identity, no "personality," but which is nevertheless a separate body. Above all, this voice bears along *directly* the symbolic, over the intelligible, the expressive: here, thrown in front of us like a packet, is the Father, his phallic stature. The "grain" is that: the materiality of the body speaking its mother tongue; perhaps the letter, almost certainly *signifiance*.

Thus we can see in song (pending the extension of this distinction to the whole of music) the two texts described by Julia Kristeva. The *pheno-song* (if the transposition be allowed) covers all the phenomena, all the features which belong to the structure of the language being sung, the rules of the genre, the coded form of the melisma, the composer's idiolect, the style of the interpretation: in short, everything in the performance which is in the service of communication, representation, expression, everything which it is customary to talk about, which forms the tissue of cultural values (the matter of acknowledged tastes, of fashions, of critical commentaries), which takes its bearing directly on the ideological alibis of a period ("subjectivity," "expressivity," "dramaticism," "personality" of the artist). The *geno-song* is the volume of the singing and speaking voice, the space where significations germinate "from within language and in its very materiality"; it forms a signifying play having nothing to do with communication, representation (of feelings), expression; it is that apex (or that depth) of production where the melody really works at the language—not at what it says, but the vo-luptuousness of its sounds-signifiers, of its letters—where melody explores how the language works and identifies with that work. It is, in a very simple word but which must be taken seriously, the *diction* of the language.

From the point of view of the pheno-song, Fischer-Dieskau is assuredly an artist beyond reproach: everything in the (semantic and lyrical) structure is respected and yet nothing seduces, nothing sways us to *jouissance*. His art is inordinately expressive (the diction is dramatic, the pauses, the checkings and releasings of breath, occur like shudders of passion) and hence never exceeds culture: here it is the soul which accompanies the song, not the body. What is difficult is for the body to accompany the musical diction not with a movement of emotion but with a "gesture-support";[1] all the more so since the whole of musical pedagogy teaches not the culture of the "grain" of the voice but the emotive modes of its delivery—the myth of respiration. How many singing teachers have we not heard prophesying that the art of vocal music rested entirely on the mastery, the correct discipline of breathing! The breath is the *pneuma*, the soul swelling or breaking, and any exclusive art of breathing is likely to be a secretly mystical art (a mysticism leveled down to the measure of the long-playing record). The lung, a stupid organ (lights for cats!), swells but gets no erection; it is in the throat, place where the phonic metal hardens and is segmented, in the mask that *significance* explodes, bringing not the soul but *jouissance*. With Fischer-Dieskau, I seem only to hear the lungs, never the tongue, the glottis, the teeth, the mucous membranes, the nose. All of Panzera's art, on the contrary, was in the letters, not in the bellows (simple technical feature: you never heard him *breathe* but only divide up the phrase). An extreme rigor of thought regulated the prosody of the enunciation and the phonic economy of the French language; prejudices (generally stemming from oratorical and ecclesiastical diction) were overthrown. With regard to the consonants, too readily thought to constitute the very armature of our language (which is not, however, a Semitic one) and always prescribed as needing to be "articulated," detached, emphasized *in order to fulfill the clarity of meaning*, Panzera recommended that in many cases they be *patinated*, given the wear of a language that had been living, functioning, and working for ages past, that they be made simply the springboard for the admirable vowels. There lay the "truth" of language—not its functionality (clarity, expressivity, communication)—and the range of vowels received all the *signifiance* (which is meaning in its potential voluptuousness): the opposition of *é* and *è* (so necessary in conjugation), the purity—almost *electronic*, so much was its sound tightened, raised, exposed, held—of the most French of vowels, the *ü* (a vowel not derived by French from Latin). Similarly, Panzera carried his *r*'s beyond the norms of the singer—without denying those norms. His *r* was of course rolled, as in every classic art of singing, but the roll had nothing peasantlike or Canadian about it; it was an artificial roll, the paradoxical state of a letter-sound at once totally abstract (by its metallic brevity of vibration) and totally material (by its manifest deep-rootedness in the action of the throat). This phonetics—am I alone in perceiving it? am I hearing voices within the voice? but isn't it the truth of the voice to be hallucinated? isn't the entire space of the voice an infinite one? which was doubtless the meaning of Saussure's work on anagrams—does not exhaust *signifiance* (which is inexhaustible) but it does at least hold in check the attempts at *expressive reduction* operated by a whole culture against the poem and its melody.

It would not be too difficult to date that culture, to define it historically. Fischer-Dieskau now reigns more or less unchallenged over the recording of vocal music; he has recorded everything. If you like Schubert but not Fischer-Dieskau, then Schubert is today *forbidden* you—an example of that positive censorship (censorship by repletion) which characterizes mass culture though it is never criticized. His art—expressive, dramatic, *sentimentally clear*, borne by a voice lacking in any "grain," in signifying weight, fits well with the demands of an *average* culture. Such a culture, defined by the growth of the number of listeners and the disappearance of practitioners (no more amateurs), wants art, wants music, provided they be clear, that they "translate" an emotion and represent a signified (the "meaning" of a poem); an art that inoculates pleasure (by reducing it to a known, coded emotion) and reconciles the subject to what in music *can be said*: what is said about it, predicatively, by Institution, Criticism, Opinion. Panzera does not belong to this culture (he could not have done, having sung before the coming of the microgroove record; moreover I doubt whether, were he singing today, his art would be recognized or even simply *perceived*); his reign, very great between the wars, was that of an exclusively bourgeois art (an art, that is, in no way petit-bourgeois) nearing the end of its inner development and, by a familiar distortion, separated from History. It is perhaps, precisely and less paradoxically than it seems, because this art was *already* marginal, mandarin, that it was able to bear traces of *signifiance*, to escape the tyranny of meaning.

The "grain" of the voice is not—or is not merely—its timbre; the *signifiance* it opens cannot better be defined, indeed, than by the very friction between the music and something else, which something else is the particular language (and nowise the message). The song must speak, must *write*—for what is produced at the level of the geno-song is finally writing. This sung writing of language is, as I see it, what the French *mélodie* sometimes tried to accomplish. I am well aware that the German *Lied* was intimately bound up with the German language via the Romantic poem, that the poetical culture of Schumann was immense and that this same Schumann used to say of Schubert that had he lived into old age he would have set the whole of German literature to music, but I think nevertheless that the historical meaning of the *Lied* must be sought in the music (if only because of its popular origins). By contrast, the historical meaning of the *mélodie* is a certain culture of the French language. As we know, the Romantic poetry of France is more oratorical than textual; what the poetry could not accomplish on its own, however, the *mélodie* has occasionally accomplished with it, working at the language through the poem. Such a work (in the specificity here acknowledged it) is not to be seen in the general run of the *mélodies* produced which are too accommodating toward minor poets, the model of the petit-bourgeois romance, and salon usages, but in some few pieces it is indisputable—anthologically (a little by chance) in certain songs by Fauré and Duparc, massively in the later (prosodic) Fauré and the vocal work of Debussy (even if *Pelléas* is often sung badly—dramatically). What is engaged in these works is, much more than a musical style, a practical reflection (if one may put it like that) on the language; there is a progressive movement from the language to the poem, from the poem to the song, and from the song to its performance. Which means that the *mélodie* has little to do with the history of music and much with the theory of the text. Here again, the signifier must be redistributed.

Compare two sung deaths, both of them famous: that of Boris and that of Mélisande. Whatever Mussorgsky's intentions, the death of Boris is *expressive* or, if preferred, *hysterical*; it is overloaded with historical, affective contents. Performances of the death cannot be but dramatic: it is the triumph of the pheno-text, the smothering of *signifiance* under the soul as signified. Mélisande, on the contrary, only dies *prosodically*. Two extremes are joined, woven together: the perfect intelligibility of the denotation and the pure prosodic segmentation of the enunciation; between the two a salutary gap (filled out in Boris)—the *pathos*, that is to say, according to Aristotle (why not?), passion *such as men speak and imagine it*, the accepted idea of death, *endoxical* death. Mélisande dies *without any noise* (understanding the term in its cybernetic sense): nothing occurs to interfere with the signifier and there is thus no compulsion to redundance; simply, the production of a music-language with the function of preventing the singer from being expressive. As with the Russian bass, the symbolic (the death) is thrown immediately (without mediation) before us (this to forestall the stock idea which has it that what is not expressive can only be cold and intellectual; Mélisande's death is "moving," which means that it shifts something in the chain of the signifier).

The *mélodie* disappeared—sank to the bottom—for a good many reasons, or at least the disappearance took on a good many aspects. Doubtless it succumbed to its salon image, this being a little the ridiculous form of its class origin. Mass "good" music (records, radio) has left it behind, preferring either the more pathetic orchestra (success of Mahler) or less bourgeois instruments than the piano (harpsichord, trumpet). Above all, however, the death of the *mélodie* goes along with a much wider historical phenomenon to a large extent unconnected to the history of music or of musical taste: the French are abandoning their language, not, assuredly, as a normative set of noble values (clarity, elegance, correctness)—or at least this does not bother me very much for these are institutional values—but as a space of pleasure, of thrill, a site where language works *for nothing*, that is, in perversion (remember here the singularity—the solitude—of *Lois* by Philippe

Sollers, theater of the return of the prosodic and metrical work of the language).

The "grain" is the body in the voice as it sings, the hand as it writes, the limb as it performs. If I perceive the "grain" in a piece of music and accord this "grain" a theoretical value (the emergence of the text in the work), I inevitably set up a new scheme of evaluation which will certainly be individual—I am determined to listen to my relation with the body of the man or woman singing or playing and that relation is erotic—but in no way "subjective" (it is not the psychological "subject" in me who is listening; the climactic pleasure hoped for is not going to reinforce—to express—that subject but, on the contrary, to lose it). The evaluation will be made outside of any law, outplaying not only the law of culture but equally that of anticulture, developing beyond the subject all the value hidden behind "I like" or "I don't like." Singers especially will be ranged in what may be called, since it is a matter of my choosing without there being any reciprocal choice of me, two prostitutional categories. Thus I shall freely extol such and such a performer, little-known, minor, forgotten, dead perhaps, and turn away from such another, an acknowledged star (let us refrain from examples, no doubt of merely biographical significance); I shall extend my choice across all the genres of vocal music including popular music, where I shall have no difficulty in rediscovering the distinction between the pheno-song and the geno-song (some popular singers have a "grain" while others, however famous, do not). What is more, leaving aside the voice, the "grain"—or the lack of it—persists in instrumental music; if the latter no longer has language to lay open *signifiance* in all its volume, at least there is the performer's body which again forces me to evaluation. I shall not judge a performance according to the rules of interpretation, the constraints of style (anyway highly illusory), which almost all belong to the pheno-song (I shall not wax lyrical concerning the "rigor," the "brilliance," the "warmth," the "respect for what is written," etc.), but according to the image of the body (the figure) given me. I can hear with certainty—the certainty of the body, of thrill—that the harpsichord playing of Wanda Landowska comes from her inner body and not from the petty digital scramble of so many harpsichordists (so much so that it is a different instrument). As for piano music, I know at once which part of the body is playing—if it is the arm, too often, alas, muscled like a dancer's calves, the clutch of the fingertips (despite the sweeping flourishes of the wrists), or if on the contrary it is the only erotic part of a pianist's body, the pad of the fingers whose "grain" is so rarely heard (it is hardly necessary to recall that today, under the pressure of the mass long-playing record, there seems to be a flattening out of technique; which is paradoxical in that the various manners of playing are all flattened out *into perfection*: nothing is left but pheno-text).

This discussion has been limited to "classical music." It goes without saying, however, that the simple consideration of "grain" in music could lead to a different history of music from the one we know now (which is purely pheno-textual). Were we to succeed in refining a certain "aesthetics" of musical pleasure, then doubtless we would attach less importance to the formidable break in tonality accomplished by modernity.

NOTES

[1] "Which is why the best way to read me is to accompany the reading with certain appropriate bodily movements. Against non-spoken writing, against non-written speech. For the gesture-support." Philippe Sollers, *Lois*, (Paris, 1972), p. 108.

Theodor W. Adorno
(with the assistance of George Simpson)

ON POPULAR MUSIC

1 9 4 1

○ ▲ ○ ▲ ○ ▲ ○

THE MUSICAL MATERIAL

The Two Spheres of Music

Popular music, which produces the stimuli we are here investigating, is usually characterized by its difference from serious music. This difference is generally taken for granted and is looked upon as a difference of levels considered so well defined that most people regard the values within them as totally independent of one another. We deem it necessary, however, first of all to translate these so-called levels into more precise terms, musical as well as social, which not only delimit them unequivocally but throw light upon the whole setting of the two musical spheres as well.

One possible method of achieving this clarification would be a historical analysis of the division as it occurred in music production and of the roots of the two main spheres. Since, however, the present study is concerned with the actual function of popular music in its present status, it is more advisable to follow the line of characterization of the phenomenon itself as it is given today than to trace it back to its origins. This is the more justified as the division into the two spheres of music took place in Europe long before American popular music arose. American music from its inception accepted the division as something pre-given, and therefore the historical background of the division applies to it only indirectly. Hence we seek, first of all, an insight into the fundamental characteristics of popular music in the broadest sense.

A clear judgment concerning the relation of serious music to popular music can be arrived at only by strict attention to the fundamental characteristic of popular music: standardization.[1] The whole structure of popular music is standardized, even where the attempt is made to circumvent standardization. Standardization extends from the most general features to the most specific ones. Best known is the rule that the chorus consists of thirty-two bars and that the range is limited to one octave and one note. The general types of hits are also standardized: not only the dance types, the rigidity of whose pattern is understood, but also the "characters" such as mother songs, home songs, nonsense or "novelty" songs, pseudo-nursery rhymes, laments for a lost girl. Most important of all, the harmonic cornerstones of each hit—the beginning and the end of each part—must beat out the standard scheme. This scheme emphasizes the most primitive harmonic facts no matter what has harmonically intervened. Complications have no consequences. This inexorable device guarantees that regardless of what aberrations occur, the hit will lead back to the same familiar experience, and nothing fundamentally novel will be introduced.

The details themselves are standardized no less than the form, and a whole terminology exists for them such as break, blue chords, dirty notes. Their standardization, however, is somewhat different from that of the framework. It is not overt like the latter but hidden behind a veneer of individual "effects" whose prescriptions are handled as the experts' secret, however open this secret may be to musicians generally. This contrasting character of the standardization of the whole and part provides a rough, preliminary setting for the effect upon the listener.

The primary effect of this relation between the framework and the detail is that the listener becomes prone to evince stronger reactions to the part than to the whole. His grasp of the whole does not lie in the living experience of this one concrete piece of music he has followed. The whole is pre-given and pre-accepted, even before the actual experience of the music starts: therefore, it is not likely to influence, to any great extent, the reaction to the details, except to give them varying degrees of emphasis. Details which occupy musically strategic positions in the framework—the beginning of the chorus or its reentrance after the bridge—have a better chance for recognition and favorable reception than details not so situated, for instance, middle bars of the bridge. But this situational nexus never interferes with the scheme itself. To this limited situational extent the detail depends upon the whole. But no stress is ever placed upon the whole as a musical event, nor does the structure of the whole ever depend upon the details.

Serious music, for comparative purposes, may be thus characterized:

Every detail derives its musical sense from the concrete totality of the piece which, in turn, consists of the life relationship of the details and never of a mere enforcement of a musical scheme. For example, in the introduction of the first movement of Beethoven's Seventh Symphony the second theme (in C-major) gets its true meaning only from the context. Only through the whole does it acquire its particular lyrical and expressive quality—that is, a whole built up of its very contrast with the *cantus firmus*–like character of the first theme. Taken in isolation the second theme would be disrobed to insignificance. Another example may be found in the beginning of the recapitulation over the pedal point of the first movement of Beethoven's "Appassionata." By following the preceding outburst it achieves the utmost dramatic momentum. By omitting the exposition and development and starting with this repetition, all is lost.

Nothing corresponding to this can happen in popular music. It would not affect the musical sense if any detail were taken out of the context; the listener can supply the "framework" automatically, since it is a mere musical automatism itself. The beginning of the chorus is replaceable by the beginning of innumerable other choruses. The interrelationship among the elements or the relationship of the elements to the whole would be unaffected. In Beethoven, position is important only in a living relation between a concrete totality and its concrete parts. In popular music, position is absolute. Every detail is substitutable; it serves its function only as a cog in a machine.

The mere establishment of this difference is not yet sufficient. It is possible to object that the far-reaching standard schemes and types of popular music are bound up with dance, and therefore are also applicable to dance derivatives in serious music, for example, the minuetto and scherzo of the classical Viennese School. It may be maintained either that this part of serious music is also to be comprehended in terms of detail rather than of whole, or that if the whole still is perceivable in the dance types in serious music despite recurrence of the types, there is no reason why it should not be perceivable in modern popular music.

The following consideration provides an answer to both objections by showing the radical differences even where serious music employs dance types. According to current formalistic views the scherzo of Beethoven's Fifth Symphony can be regarded as a highly stylized minuetto. What Beethoven takes from the traditional minuetto scheme in this scherzo is the idea of outspoken contrast between a minor minuetto, a major trio, and repetition of the minor minuetto; and also certain other characteristics such as the emphatic three-fourths rhythm often accentuated on the first fourth and, by and large, dancelike symmetry in the sequence of bars and periods. But the specific form-idea of this movement as a concrete totality transvaluates the devices borrowed from the minuetto scheme. The whole movement is conceived as an introduction to the finale in order to create tremendous tension, not only by its threatening, foreboding expression but even more by the very way in which its formal development is handled.

The classical minuetto scheme required first the appearance of the main theme, then the introduction of a second part which may lead to more distant tonal regions—formalistically similar, to be sure, to the "bridge" of today's popular music—and finally the recurrence of the original part. All this occurs in Beethoven. He takes up the idea of thematic dualism within the scherzo part. But he forces what was, in the conventional minuetto, a mute and meaningless game rule to speak with meaning. He achieves complete consistency between the formal structure and its specific content, that is to say, the elaboration of its themes. The whole scherzo part of this scherzo (that is to say, what occurs before the entrance of the deep strings in C-major that marks the beginning of the trio), consists of the dualism of two themes, the creeping figure in the strings and the "objective," stonelike answer of the wind instruments. This dualism is not developed in a schematic way so that first the phrase of the strings is elaborated, then the answer of the winds, and then the string theme is mechanically repeated. After the first occurrence of the second theme in the horns, the two essential elements are alternately interconnected in the manner of a dialogue, and the end of the scherzo part is actually marked, not by the first but by the second theme, which has overwhelmed the first musical phrase.

Furthermore, the repetition of the scherzo after the trio is scored so differently that it sounds like a mere shadow of the scherzo and assumes that haunting character which vanishes only with the affirmative entry of the Finale theme. The whole device has been made dynamic. Not only the themes, but the musical form itself have been subjected to tension: the same tension which is already manifest within the twofold structure of the first theme that consists, as it were, of question and reply, and then even more manifest within the context between the two main themes. The whole scheme has become subject to the inherent demands of this particular movement.

To sum up the difference: in Beethoven and in good serious music in general—we are not concerned here with bad serious music which may be as rigid and mechanical as popular music—the detail virtually contains the whole and leads to the exposition of the whole, while, at the same time, it is produced out of the conception of the whole. In popular music the relationship is fortuitous. The detail has no bearing on a whole, which appears as an extraneous framework. Thus, the whole is never altered by the individual event and therefore remains, as it were, aloof, imperturbable, and unnoticed throughout the piece. At the same time, the detail is mutilated by a device which it can never influence and alter, so that the detail remains inconsequential. A musical detail which is not permitted to develop becomes a caricature of its own potentialities.

Standardization

The previous discussion shows that the difference between popular and serious music can be grasped in more precise terms than those referring to musical levels such as "lowbrow and highbrow," "simple and complex," "naive and sophisticated." For example, the difference between the spheres cannot be adequately expressed in terms of complexity and simplicity. All works of the earlier Viennese classicism are, without exception, rhythmically simpler than stock arrangements of jazz. Melodically, the wide intervals of a good many hits such as "Deep Purple" or "Sunrise Serenade" are more difficult to follow per se than most melodies of, for example, Haydn, which consist mainly of circumscriptions of tonic triads and second steps. Harmonically, the supply of chords of the so-called classics is invariably more limited than that of any current Tin Pan Alley composer who draws from Debussy, Ravel, and even later sources. Standardization and nonstandardization are the key contrasting terms for the difference.

Structural Standardization Aims at Standard Reactions. Listening to popular music is manipulated not only by its promoters but, as it were, by the inherent nature of this music itself, into a system of response mechanisms wholly antagonistic to the ideal of individuality in a free, liberal society. This has nothing to do with simplicity and complexity. In serious music, each musical element, even the simplest one, is "itself," and the more highly organized the work is, the less possibility there is of substitution among the details. In hit music, however, the structure underlying the piece is abstract, existing independent of the specific course of the music. This is basic to the illusion that certain complex harmonies are more easily understandable in popular music than the same harmonies in serious music. For the complicated in popular music never functions as "itself" but only as a disguise or embellishment behind which the scheme can always be perceived. In jazz the amateur listener is capable of replacing complicated rhythmical or harmonic formulas by the schematic ones which they represent and which they still suggest, however adventurous they appear. The ear deals with the difficulties of hit music by achieving slight substitutions derived from the knowledge of the patterns. The listener, when faced with the complicated, actually hears only the simple which it represents and perceives the complicated only as a parodistic distortion of the simple.

No such mechanical substitution by stereotyped patterns is possible in serious music. Here even the simplest event necessitates an effort to grasp it immediately instead of summarizing it vaguely according to institutionalized prescriptions capable of producing only institutionalized effects. Otherwise the music is not "understood." Popular music, however, is composed in such a way that the process of translation of the unique into the norm is already planned and, to a certain extent, achieved within the composition itself.

The composition hears for the listener. This is how popular music divests the listener of his spontaneity and promotes conditioned reflexes. Not only does it not require his effort to follow its concrete stream; it actually gives him models under which anything concrete still remaining may be subsumed. The schematic buildup dictates the way in which he must listen while, at the same time, it makes any effort in listening unnecessary. Popular music is "pre-digested" in a way strongly resembling the fad of "digests" of printed material. It is this structure of contemporary popular music which, in the last analysis, accounts for those changes of listening habits which we shall later discuss.

So far standardization of popular music has been considered in structural terms—that is, as an inherent quality without explicit reference to the process of production or to the underlying causes for standardization. Though all industrial mass production necessarily eventuates in standardization, the production of popular music can be called "industrial" only in its promotion and distribution, whereas the act of producing a song-hit still remains in a handicraft stage. The production of popular music is highly centralized in its economic organization, but still "individualistic" in its social mode of production. The division of labor among the composer, harmonizer, and arranger is not industrial but rather pretends industrialization, in order to look more up-to-date, whereas it has actually adapted industrial methods for the technique of its promotion. It would not increase the costs of production if the various composers of hit tunes did not follow certain standard patterns. Therefore, we must look for other reasons for structural standardization—very different reasons from those which account for the standardization of motor cars and breakfast foods.

Imitation offers a lead for coming to grips with the basic reasons for it. The musical standards of popular music were originally developed by a competitive process. As one particular song scored a great success, hundreds of others sprang up imitating the successful one. The most successful hits, types, and "ratios" between elements were imitated, and the process culminated in the crystallization of standards. Under centralized conditions such as exist today these standards have become "frozen."[2] That is, they have been taken over by cartelized agencies, the final results of a competitive process, and rigidly enforced upon material to be promoted. Noncompliance with the rules of the game became the basis for exclusion. The original patterns that are now standardized evolved in a more or less competitve way. Large-scale economic concentration institutionalized the standardization, and made it imperative. As a result, innovations by rugged individualists have been outlawed. The standard patterns have become invested with the immunity of bigness—"the King can do no wrong." This also accounts for revivals in popular music. They do not have the outworn character of standardized products manufactured after a given pattern. The breath of free competition is still alive within them. On the other hand, the famous old hits which are revived set the patterns which have become standardized. They are the golden age of the game rules.

This "freezing" of standards is socially enforced upon the agencies themselves. Popular music must simultaneously meet two demands. One is for stimuli that provoke the listener's attention. The other is for the material to fall within the category of what the musically untrained listener would call "natural" music: that is, the sum total of all the conventions and material formulas in music to which he is accustomed and which he regards as the inherent, simple language of music itself, no matter how late the development might be which produced this natural language. This natural language for the American listener stems from his earliest musical experiences, the nursery rhymes, the hymns he sings in Sunday school, the little tunes he whistles on his way home from school. All these are vastly more important in the formation of musical language than his ability to distinguish the beginning of Brahms's Third Symphony from that of his Second. Official musical culture is, to a large extent, a mere superstructure of this underlying musical language, namely, the major and minor tonalities and all the tonal relationships they imply. But these tonal relationships of the primitive musical language set barriers to whatever does not conform to them. Extravagances are tolerated only insofar as they can be recast into this so-called natural language.

In terms of consumer demand, the standardization of popular music is only the expression of this dual desideratum imposed upon it by the musical frame of mind of the public—that it be "stimulatory" by deviating in some way from the established "natural," and that it maintain the supremacy of the natural against such deviations. The attitude of the audiences toward the natural language is reinforced by standardized production, which institutionalizes desiderata which originally might have come from the public.

Pseudo-individualization

The paradox in the desiderata—stimulatory and natural—accounts for the dual character of standardization itself. Stylization of the ever identical framework is only one aspect of standardization. Concentration and control in our culture hide themselves in their very manifestation. Unhidden they would provoke resistance. Therefore the illusion and, to a certain extent, even the reality of individual achievement must be maintained. The maintenance of it is grounded in material reality itself, for while administrative control over life processes is concentrated, ownership is still diffuse.

In the sphere of luxury production, to which popular music belongs and in which no necessities of life are immediately involved, while, at the same time, the residues of individualism are most alive there in the form of ideological categories such as taste and free choice, it is imperative to hide standardization. The "backwardness" of musical mass production, the fact that it is still on a handicraft level and not literally an industrial one, conforms perfectly to that necessity which is essential from the viewpoint of cultural big business. If the individual handicraft elements of popular music were abolished altogether, a synthetic means of hiding standardization would have to be evolved. Its elements are even now in existence.

The necessary correlate of musical standardization is *pseudo-individualization*. By pseudo-individualization we mean endowing cultural mass production with the halo of free choice or open market on the basis of standardization itself. Standardization of song hits keeps the customers in line by doing their listening for them, as it were. Pseudo-individualization, for its part, keeps them in line by making them forget that what they listen to is already listened to for them, or "pre-digested."

The most drastic example of standardization of presumably individualized features is to be found in so-called improvisations. Even though jazz musicians still improvise in practice, their improvisations have become so "normalized" as to enable a whole terminology to be developed to express the standard devices of individualization: a terminology which in turn is ballyhooed by jazz publicity agents to foster the myth of pioneer artisanship and at the same time flatter the fans by apparently allowing them to peep behind the curtain and get the inside story. This pseudo-individualization is prescribed by the standardization of the framework. The latter is so rigid that the freedom it allows for any sort of improvisation is severely delimited. Improvisations—passages where spontaneous action of individuals is permitted ("Swing it boys")—are confined within the walls of the harmonic and metric scheme. In a great many cases, such as the "break" of pre-swing jazz, the musical function of the improvised detail is determined completely by the scheme: the break can be nothing other than a disguised cadence. Here, very few possibilities for actual improvisation remain, due to the necessity of merely melodically circumscribing the same underlying harmonic functions. Since these possibilities were very quickly exhausted, stereotyping of improvisatory details speedily occurred. Thus, standardization of the norm enhances in a purely technical way standardization of its own deviation—pseudo-individualization.

This subservience of improvisation to standardization explains two main socio-psychological qualities of popular music. One is the fact that the detail remains openly connected with the underlying scheme so that the listener always feels on safe ground. The choice in individual alterations is so small that the perpetual recurrence of the same variations is a reassuring signpost of the identical behind them. The other is the function of "substitution"—

the improvisatory features forbid their being grasped as musical events in themselves. They can be received only as embellishments. It is a well-known fact that in daring jazz arrangements worried notes, dirty notes, in other words, false notes, play a conspicuous role. They are apperceived as exciting stimuli only because they are corrected by the ear to the right note. This, however, is only an extreme instance of what happens less conspicuously in all individualization in popular music. Any harmonic boldness, any chord which does not fall strictly within the simplest harmonic scheme demands being apperceived as "false," that is, as a stimulus which carries with it the unambiguous prescription to substitute for it the right detail, or rather the naked scheme. Understanding popular music means obeying such commands for listening. Popular music commands its own listening habits.

There is another type of individualization claimed in terms of kinds of popular music and differences in name bands. The types of popular music are carefully differentiated in production. The listener is presumed to be able to choose between them. The most widely recognized differentiations are those between swing and sweet and such name bands as Benny Goodman and Guy Lombardo. The listener is quickly able to distinguish the types of music and even the performing band, this in spite of the fundamental identity of the material and the great similarity of the presentations apart from their emphasized distinguishing trademarks. This labeling technique, as regards type of music and band, is pseudo-individualization, but of a sociological kind outside the realm of strict musical technology. It provides trademarks of identification for differentiating between the actually undifferentiated.

Popular music becomes a multiple-choice questionnaire. There are two main types and their derivatives from which to choose. The listener is encouraged by the inexorable presence of these types psychologically to cross out what he dislikes and check what he likes. The limitation inherent in this choice and the clear-cut alternative it entails provoke like-dislike patterns of behavior. This mechanical dichotomy breaks down indifference; it is imperative to favor sweet or swing if one wishes to continue to listen to popular music.

THEORY ABOUT THE LISTENER

Popular Music and "Leisure Time"

In order to understand why this whole *type* of music (i.e., popular music in general) maintains its hold on the masses, some considerations of a general kind may be appropriate.

The frame of mind to which popular music originally appealed, on which it feeds, and which it perpetually reinforces, is simultaneously one of distraction and inattention. Listeners are distracted from the demands of reality by entertainment which does not demand attention either.

The notion of distraction can be properly understood only within its social setting and not in self-subsistent terms of individual psychology. Distraction is bound to the present mode of production, to the rationalized and mechanized process of labor to which, directly or indirectly, masses are subject. This mode of production, which engenders fears and anxiety about unemployment, loss of income, war, has its "nonproductive" correlate in entertainment; that is, relaxation which does not involve the effort of concentration at all. People want to have fun. A fully concentrated and conscious experience of art is possible only to those whose lives do not put such a strain on them that in their spare time they want relief from both boredom and effort simultaneously. The whole sphere of cheap commercial entertainment reflects this dual desire. It induces relaxation because it is patterned and pre-digested. Its being patterned and pre-digested serves within the psychological household of the masses to spare them the effort of that participation (even in listening or observation) without which there can be no receptivity to art. On the other hand, the stimuli they provide permit an escape from the boredom of mechanized labor.

The promoters of commercialized entertainment exonerate themselves by referring to the fact that they are giving the masses what they want. This is an ideology appropriate to commercial purposes: the less the mass discriminates, the greater the possibility of selling cultural commodities indiscriminately. Yet this ideology of vested interest cannot be dismissed so easily. It is not possible completely to deny that mass consciousness can be molded by the operative agencies only because the masses "want this stuff."

But why do they want this stuff? In our present society the masses themselves are kneaded by the same mode of production as the arti-craft material foisted upon them. The customers of musical entertainment are themselves objects or, indeed, products of the same mechanisms which determine the production of popular music. Their spare time serves only to reproduce their working capacity. It is a means instead of an end. The power of the process of production extends over the time intervals which on the surface appear to be "free." They want standardized goods and pseudo-individualization, because their leisure is an escape from work and at the same time is molded after those psychological attitudes to which their workaday world exclusively habituates them. Popular music is for the masses a perpetual busman's holiday. Thus, there is justification for speaking of a preestablished harmony today between production and consumption of popular music. The people clamor for what they are going to get anyhow.

To escape boredom and avoid effort are incompatible—hence the reproduction of the very attitude from which escape is sought. To be sure, the way in which they must work on the assembly line, in the factory, or at office machines denies people any novelty. They seek novelty, but the strain and boredom associated with actual work leads to avoidance of effort in that leisure time which offers the only chance for really new experience. As a substitute, they crave a stimulant. Popular music comes to offer it. Its stimulations are met with the inability to vest effort in the ever-identical. This means boredom again. It is a circle which makes escape impossible. The impossibility of escape causes the widespread attitude of inattention toward popular music. The moment of recognition is that of effortless sensation. The sudden attention attached to this moment burns itself out *instanter* and relegates the listener to a realm of inattention and distraction. On the one hand, the domain of production and plugging presupposes distraction and, on the other, produces it.

In this situation the industry faces an insoluble problem. It must arouse attention by means of ever-new products, but this attention spells their doom. If no attention is given to the song, it cannot be sold; if attention is paid to it, there is always the possibility that people will no longer accept it, because they know it too well. This partly accounts for the constantly renewed effort to sweep the market with new products, to hound them to their graves; then to repeat the infanticidal maneuver again and again.

On the other hand, distraction is not only a presupposition but also a product of popular music. The tunes themselves lull the listener to inattention. They tell him not to worry for he will not miss anything.[3]

The Social Cement

It is safe to assume that music listened to with a general inattention which is only interrupted by sudden flashes of recognition is not followed as a sequence of experiences that have a clear-cut meaning of their own, grasped in each instant and related to all the precedent and subsequent moments. One may go so far as to suggest that most listeners of popular music do not understand music as a language in itself. If they did it would be vastly difficult to explain how they could tolerate the incessant supply of largely undifferentiated material. What, then, does music mean to them? The answer is that the language that is music is transformed by objective processes into a language which they think is their own—into a language which serves as a receptacle for their institutionalized wants. The less music is a language *sui generis* to them, the more does it become established as such a receptacle. The autonomy of music is replaced by a mere socio-psychological function. Music today is largely a social cement. And the meaning listeners attribute to a material, the inherent logic of which is inaccessible to them, is above all a means by which they achieve some psychical adjustment to the mechanisms of present-day life. This "adjustment" materializes in two different ways, corresponding to two major socio-psychological types of mass behavior toward music in general and popular music in particular, the "rhythmically obedient" type and the "emotional" type.

Individuals of the rhythmically obedient type are mainly found among the youth—the so-called radio generation. They are most susceptible to a process of masochistic adjustment to authoritarian collectivism. The type is not restricted to any one political attitude. The adjustment to anthropophagous collectivism is found as often among left-wing political groups as among right-wing groups. Indeed, both overlap: repression and crowd-mindedness overtake the followers of both trends. The psychologies tend to meet despite the surface distinctions in political attitudes.

This comes to the fore in popular music which appears to be aloof from political partisanship. It may be noted that a moderate leftist theater production such as *Pins and Needles* uses ordinary jazz as its musical medium, and that a communist youth organization adapted the melody of "Alexander's Ragtime Band" to its own lyrics. Those who ask for a song of social significance ask for it through a medium which deprives it of social significance. The uses of inexorable popular musical media is repressive per se. Such inconsistencies indicate that political conviction and socio-psychological structure by no means coincide.

This obedient type is the rhythmical type, the word "rhythmical" being used in its everyday sense. Any musical experience of this type is based upon the underlying, unabating time unit of the music—its "beat." To play rhythmically means, to these people, to play in such a way that even if pseudo-individualizations—counter-accents and other "differentiations"—occur, the relation to the ground meter is preserved. To be musical means to them to be capable of following given rhythmical patterns without being disturbed by "individualizing" aberrations, and to fit even the syncopations into the basic time units. This is the way in which their response to music immediately expresses their desire to obey. However, as the standardized meter of dance music and of marching suggests the coordinated battalions of a mechanical collectivity, obedience to this rhythm by overcoming the responding individuals leads them to conceive of themselves as agglutinized with the untold millions of the meek who must be similarly overcome. Thus do the obedient inherit the earth.

Yet, if one looks at the serious compositions which correspond to this category of mass listening, one finds one very characteristic feature: that of disillusion. All these composers, among them Stravinsky and Hindemith, have expressed an "antiromantic" feeling. They aimed at musical adaptation to reality—a reality understood by them in terms of the "machine age." The renunciation of dreaming by these composers is an index that listeners are ready to replace dreaming by adjustment to raw reality, that they reap new pleasure from their acceptance of the unpleasant. They are disillusioned about any possibility of realizing their own dreams in the world in which they live, and consequently adapt themselves to this world. They take what is called a realistic attitude and attempt to harvest consolation by identifying themselves with the external social forces which they think constitute the "machine age." Yet the very disillusion upon which their coordination is based is there to mar their pleasure. The cult of the machine which is represented by unabating jazz beats involves a self-renunciation that cannot but take root in the form of a fluctuating uneasiness somewhere in the personality of the obedient. For the machine is an end in itself only under given social conditions—where men are appendages of the machines on which they work. The adaptation to machine music necessarily implies a renunciation of one's own human feelings and at the same time a fetishism of the machine such that its instrumental character becomes obscured thereby.

As to the other, the "emotional" type, there is some justification for linking it with a type of movie spectator. The kinship is with the poor shop girl who derives gratification by identification with Ginger Rogers, who, with her beautiful legs and unsullied character, marries the boss. Wish fulfillment is considered the guiding principle in the social psychology of moving pictures and similarly in the pleasure obtained from emotional, erotic music. This explanation, however, is only superficially appropriate.

Hollywood and Tin Pan Alley may be dream factories. But they do not merely supply categorical wish fulfillment for the girl behind the counter. She does not immediately identify herself with Ginger Rogers marrying. What does occur may be expressed as follows: when the audience at a sentimental film or sentimental music become aware of the overwhelming possibility of happiness, they dare to confess to themselves what the whole order of contemporary life ordinarily forbids them to admit, namely, that they actually have no part in happiness. What is supposed to be wish fulfillment is only the scant liberation that occurs with the realization that at last one need not deny oneself the happiness of knowing that one is unhappy and that one could be happy. The experience of the shop girl is related to that of the old woman who weeps at the wedding services of others, blissfully becoming aware of the wretchedness of her own life. Not even the most gullible individuals believe that eventually everyone will win the sweepstakes. The actual function of sentimental music lies rather in the temporary release given to the awareness that one has missed fulfillment.

The emotional listener listens to everything in terms of late romanticism and of the musical commodities derived from it which are already fashioned to fit the needs of emotional listening. They consume music in order to be allowed to weep. They are taken in by the musical expression of frustration rather than by that of happiness. The influence of the standard Slavic melancholy typified by Tchaikowsky and Dvořák is by far greater than that of the most "fulfilled" moments of Mozart or of the young Beethoven. The so-called releasing element of music is simply the opportunity to feel something. But the actual content of this emotion can only be frustration. Emotional music has become the image of the mother who says, "Come and weep, my child." It is catharsis for the masses, but catharsis which keeps them all the more firmly in line. One who weeps does not resist any more than one who marches. Music that permits its listeners the confession of their unhappiness reconciles them, by means of this "release," to their social dependence.

NOTES

[1] The basic importance of standardization has not altogether escaped the attention of current literature on popular music. "The chief difference between a popular song and a standard, or serious, song like 'Mandalay,' 'Sylvia,' or 'Trees,' is that the melody and the lyric of a popular number are constructed within a definite pattern or structural form, whereas the poem, or lyric, of a standard number has no structural confinements, and the music is free to interpret the meaning and feeling of the words without following a set pattern or form. Putting it another way, the popular song is 'custom built,' while the standard song allows the composer freer play of imagination and interpretation." Abner Silver and Robert Bruce, *How to Write and Sell a Song Hit* (New York, 1939), p.2. The authors fail, however, to realize the externally superimposed, commercial character of those patterns which aims at canalized reactions or, in the language of the regular announcement of one particular radio program, at "easy listening." They confuse the mechanical patterns with highly organized, strict art forms: "Certainly there are few more stringent verse forms in poetry than the sonnet, and yet the greatest poets of all time have woven undying beauty within its small and limited frame. A composer has just as much opportunity for exhibiting his talent and genius in popular songs as in more serious music" (pp. 2–3). Thus the standard pattern of popular music appears to them virtually on the same level as the law of a fugue. It is this contamination which makes the insight into the basic standardization of popular music sterile. It ought to be added that what Silver and Bruce call a "standard song" is just the opposite of what we mean by a standardized popular song.

[2] See Max Horkheimer, *Zeitschrift für Sozialforschung* 8 (1939), p. 115.

[3] The attitude of distraction is not a completely universal one. Particularly youngsters who invest popular music with their own feelings are not yet completely blunted to all its effects. The whole problem of age levels with regard to popular music, however, is beyond the scope of the present study. Demographic problems, too, must remain out of consideration.

Andrew Chester

SECOND THOUGHTS ON A ROCK AESTHETIC

The Band

1 9 7 0

○ ▲ ○ ▲ ○ ▲ ○

Western classical music is the apodigm of the *extensional* form of musical construction.[1] Theme and variations, counterpoint, tonality (as used in classical composition) arc all devices that build diachronically and synchronically outward from basic musical atoms. The complex is created by combination of the simple, which remains discrete and unchanged in the complex unity. Thus a basic premise of classical music is rigorous adherence to standard timbres, not only for the various orchestral instruments, but even for the most flexible of all instruments, the human voice. Room for interpretation of the written notation is in fact marginal. If those critics who maintain the greater complexity of classical music specified that they had in mind this *extensional* development, they would be quite correct. The rock idiom does know forms of extensional development; it cannot compete in this sphere with a music based on this principle of construction.

Rock however follows, like many non-European musics, the path of *intensional* development. In this mode of construction the basic musical units (played/sung notes) are not combined through space and time as simple elements into complex structures. The simple entity is that constituted by the parameters of melody, harmony and beat, while the complex is built up by modulation of the basic notes, and by inflection of the basic beat. (The language of this modulation and inflection derives partly from conventions internal to the music, partly from the conventions of spoken language and gesture, partly from physiological factors.) All existing genres and subtypes of the Afro-American tradition show various forms of combined intensional and extensional development. The history of jazz is largely a transition from one to the other, later punctuated by a reaction against "Europeanization" and a "return to the roots." The almost purely intensional form of the rural blues has only received critical attention in the past decade or so, and still largely remains a minority preserve. The 12-bar structure of the blues, which for the critic reared on extensional forms seems so confining, is viewed quite differently by the bluesman, for he builds "inward" from the 12-bar structure, and not "outward." Complexity is multidimensional and by no means strictly quantifiable, and the aesthetic capacity of a musical form cannot be measured by complexity alone, but the example of the country blues shows the complete adequacy of a purely intensional mode of construction to an immensely subtle and varied project of aesthetic expression.

If jazz aimed to transform intensional into extensional, musical structures, rock sought a reverse path. The founding moment of rock music was the creation of a white analogue of blues vocalism, which was achieved in its classical form with Elvis Presley's Sun recordings of 1954–55. Taking elements from both blues and country sources, the qualitative novelty of rock, first only effected at the vocal level, was a singing style that fit into the framework of country songs rather than 12-bar blues, and whose modulations and inflections were determined in the first instance by the cadences of Southern white speech and gesture. The primacy of the vocal that characterizes both blues and rock is almost inevitable in an intensionally constructed music which still uses instruments designed for extensional expression, and was noted in the fifties, not so much by the titans of Southern rock, Presley and Jerry Lee Lewis, for whom this development was almost intuitive, but by the more articulate of their disciples. Thus Eddie Cochran: "In rock 'n' roll the beat is only supplementary to the human voice. It's the voice, coupled with an extraordinary sense of emotion, which lends to rock 'n' roll a personality not sensed in other types of music."[2]

The conceptual pair of extensionality/intensionality is a step toward constructing a matrix for critical examination of the contemporary rock scene, and obtaining a purchase on the more strictly musical levels of the total product. Sixties rock derives essentially from the attempts of middle-class students in the early sixties to reproduce, at a more sophisticated level, the music that they had appropriated in the fifties, without at the time being able to work in it. After the demise of fifties rock, these musicians explored the roots and relatives of the rock genre, delving both into white country music (via "urban folk"/"protest"), but more fruitfully into the rural and urban blues. The idiom of the blues, which took some years to learn, was the key to the production of sixties rock, and opened up very substantial new fields of musical development. (British rhythm and blues in the sixties had a similar birth, though its development was mediated by its national setting.) But the limitation of sixties rock has been its inability to achieve a real integration of its adopted musical materials. In general, its intensional development is derivative from the blues, and its extensional development is parasitic on the European tradition. Paradoxically, though rock is recognized by both musicians and audience as a well-defined musical category, the interstices between rock and other genres seem far more habitable than the mainstream itself. Solutions adopted by major U.S. groups include acceptance of a derivative musical identity (blues groups such as Canned Heat), extensional elaboration of rock/blues formal elements (Grateful Dead); reliance on theme/lyric/stance and other nonmusical levels (Doors/ Country Joe); backsliding into country and western (Byrds) or jazz (Chicago; Blood, Sweat & Tears); fifties revivalism (Creedence Clearwater). Even Jefferson Airplane, perhaps the most impressive group of the sixties generation, whose music is least obviously parasitic on other forms, depend in the last instance on contrapuntal and harmonic structures that are firmly in the European/extensional tradition. Closely connected with the failure of sixties rock to achieve the new synthesis it explicitly aims at is the gross disparity between the caliber of its instrumentalists and its vocalists. Middle-class (male) white youths learned blues guitar well enough to be accepted as equals by black musicians; their singing rarely rises above mediocrity, a fact that demands psychoanalytic explanation.

The one major group that, for all its limitations, is firmly anchored in rock as an independent genre is the Band. They alone among important contemporary groups work at a purely intensional development which continues the enterprise begun with fifties rock. This is the reason they manage to produce work of musical value yet without significant lyrics or theme, without experimentalism, without recourse to a merger with other genres, and without any problems of presentation: the music alone speaks.

It is no coincidence that the Band's history has run an entirely different course to that of other sixties groups. Their origins are working class, and all except Levon Helm are Canadian. They were formed as far back as 1959, as backing group for the Arkansas-born Canadian rock king Ronnie Hawkins, and the "strange death of rock 'n' roll" passed them by. Later their work with Dylan in his most creative phase (1964–66) widened their horizons of composition and production, and after Dylan stopped touring they retired (like Dylan, but with very different consequences) to upstate New York to work for the first time at their own music. Their intense professionalism and the rigor of their collective instrumental work have never been endangered by the demand of being cultural symbols as well as musicians (the ruin of such promising groups as Country Joe or the Doors), and these qualities are absolute requirements of the ultra-sensitive capacity to turn thought instantly into sound that intensional construction demands.

An important determinant of the Band's particular style is that, unlike fifties rock (and mechanical attempts to revive this project, such as Creedence Clearwater), they do not rely on a unique vocalist. Given the role of the human voice in rock music, this absence determines both the vocal style affected by all four of the Band's singers, and its instrumental style. Lacking the vocal genius that the genre was originally designed for, the Band's vocals continuously strain against the upper limits of the male register (the region most responsive to changes of timbre), and even strain to emerge at all. Simultaneously, the backing instruments have a far more important role to play than in fifties rock. The simple country rhythms of guitar and acoustic bass (no drums) were sufficient against the virtuosity of a Presley. The Band has to rely predominantly on its rhythm section (a misnomer) for intensional development. Presley's vocal lines, designed to carry the whole musical message, could glide securely over a rhythmic backing that served only to underpin them. In the Band's music, the vocal constantly hesitates and hangs on a note while drums and bass build whole structures of arrival and non-arrival, anticipation and resolution, on the bridge passages between chord changes. The best example of this is the opening track on *Music from Big Pink*, the Dylan song "Tears of Rage," where these unconscious devices condense in a superb *musical* construct. Here the verbal message of the lyrics is clearly subordinate to the music, whereas the reverse is true even on Dylan's rendering of the song accompanied by the Band on the "basement tape." Dylan still works at delivering a verbal message. On *Music from Big Pink* the verbal message is a residue left after the lyrics have been bent to serve as a vocal line. What comes through more strongly than the precise events described are the connotations of the lyrics as a whole. The theme of filial ingratitude perfectly matches the Band's own performance, in which the music appears to have so painful a birth.

The Band's construction is astonishingly pure rock, whose aesthetic values are purely musical. It is not a synthesis that will propel the music on a radical forward course. This will not happen until or unless the problem of rock vocalism is solved. I am not suggesting that very different departures, such as cross-fertilization of rock with certain "serious" forms (e.g., Velvet Underground or Soft Machine) may not be a more secure way forward, and may not be from certain perspectives more aesthetically rewarding. There is no question here of a rank order—a conception quite alien to materialist criticism. Yet the extensional constructions of the "experimental" groups lead away from rock to realms where quite different critical canons must be applied.

To conclude, I would like to attempt some partial answers and correctives to the set of questions presented in my earlier article.[3]

Structural Coordinates and Sociocultural Base. The internal coordinates of a musical form are not mechanically determined by its social base.

The relationship is one of compatibility. Musical practice has a relative autonomy, and to each social group correspond certain acceptable genres. Analysis of this compatibility is an important and so far almost unexplored question which will require both historical materialist and psychoanalytic explanation. The role of *lyric* in rock music has been a major theme in the present discussion; as for *dance*, it is the intensional development of rhythmic inflection that made possible the qualitative break in dance styles that took place once rock music had been appropriated by its new audiences.

Dominance of the Vocal. What I attempted to grasp with this expression is in fact the dominance of intensional over extensional modes. In rock music, the overwhelming primacy of the vocal has been reduced with the development of electronic instruments and techniques, but rock remains a genre "dominated" by the vocal, which only tends to disappear in the "frontier" territories.

Music and Ideology. Artistic projects will continue to be distorted by ideological mystifications until dialectical materialism is generally accepted (and appropriated) as a world outlook. By "aesthetics is the politics of art" I meant to stress the importance of the ideological struggle against these mystifications, and of materialist analysis of artistic problems, by critics and the direct producers themselves as a requirement for the progress of all forms of art.

NOTES

[1] This statement is most strictly true of classical music in the narrower sense—i.e., as opposed to "romantic." But postclassical "serious" music only marginally departed from the extensional principle until the post-1945 era of electronic experimentation.
[2] Interview in *New Musical Express* (1958).
[3] Andrew Chester, "For a Rock Aesthetic," *New Left Review* 59.

JINGLE

Pepsi-Cola Hits the Spot

1 9 8 1

○ ▲ ○ ▲ ○ ▲ ○

To a twentieth-century American the street ballad carries overtones of other daily experiences besides those of sensational journalism. The song has much in common with the familiar boosting of consumer goods sung at us over radio and television: it is, in effect, a singing commercial. As a song exercise contrived for profit by one party for a second party, such a sold ballad has two collateral lines of descent in the modern marketplace. One is popular song, which sells directly whatever experience it offers in itself. The other is sung advertising, which is given away freely (insistently) to sell something else associated with the experience it provides.

The range of states of mind and heart sold now by the popular music industry takes in some species of boasting and marveling not too alien to that implied in the street ballad. Phallic boasting is obviously part of the first-person strut that first became noticeable in white popular music with Elvis Presley but that has an honorable longer history in black performance and recording. Songs about more or less mythic heroes also sell wonderment ("Big John," "Bad, Bad Leroy Brown," "Ballad of the Green Berets"). Some songs have won wide popularity by displaying prodigious events, like "The Wreck of the Edmund Fitzgerald." The consumer is usually given such a song free at first, over the radio, like the Londoner hearing his ballad first from the singing ballad-seller, and then pays for the recording so that he can replay at will whatever plays out in the song—the music, and also (in these cases) the chance to marvel.

In the most general terms, advertising song also relies on the consumer's readiness, even to the point of parting with money, to participate in attesting to marvels. The common content of all advertisements is that the given product or service is better than whatever presumes to compete with it. This pseudoinformation might be taken for merely conveyed information, as advertising must generally pretend that it is; but of course advertising is essentially rhetorical, concerned with transmitting the message in such a way as to induce acceptance of the message. The problem of the advertiser, then, is to seem only to be having his say to me, while really doing or saying something that will make his say into my say. I must be persuaded that his version of the world of bread or automobiles is the true version, so that I will attest to it in my behavior. If his message is that his particular product or service excels others, and his goal is to dispose me to adopt as my own view the view that it excels, it must be generally the case that he wishes me to enter into a marveling and even boasting attitude with respect to his product.

The principal mode in which this aim is pursued, of making his boast into my boast, is testimony. The testimonial commercial aims to be vicarious. When an athlete tells the television audience about the virtues of a car rental service, the advertiser has procured this admiring testimony to be delivered by a figure with whom much of the audience somehow or sometimes identifies: spectator sports are nothing if not vicarious. Movie and television stars are likewise nothing if not stand ins for ourselves, and their testimony is correspondingly valuable to advertisers. The most common endorser of all, the anonymous actress playing the housewife, is exactly the viewer's self as she wishes to be seen from the outside. When my stand-in tells the camera about rental cars, the significant transaction is not that he tells me but rather that I, by proxy, tell the world.

The utility of song in this promotional context stems from the inherent tendency in song experience for the listener to assume the perspective implied by the words. A successful singing commercial works like a successful testimonial commercial to put us in the place of attesting. What we have just noticed about spoken testimonial shows that song is not the only medium for this importation of sentiments into our consciousness. Most communication to us that feels satisfactory, that is not accompanied by a defensive discounting, achieves the status of what we accept, and in hearing or even reading it we participate in the communication. We admit it into consciousness and thereby admit it to have some validity.

The defensive discount is weaker as our capacity to identify with the source of the words is greater. Words in voice promote the identification more readily than words written. Printed advertising copy, with the exception of that pursuing certain special effects such as authoritativeness, runs naturally to the colloquial, to the speechlike—heavy, for example, with sentence fragments. With the beginning of radio in the 1920s and the flowering of television at midcentury, commercial persuaders were given immensely increased access to citizens' consciousness. A speaking voice for advertisers was of such value, and the addition of a speaking image to facilitate the self-projection of the consumer was such a grand bonus, that the commercial advertisers undertook and have sustained the sponsorship of the entire American broadcast culture.

The first commercial messages brought into homes by radio in the early twenties were formal and impersonal, but within that decade advertisers began to exploit the mechanism of identification natural to the medium. Performers made familiar by their radio programs were called on to deliver the messages; dramatization drew listeners into personal situations of appreciation for products; and in 1929 a barbershop quartet in Minneapolis sang the first broadcast jingle, for Wheaties. Ten years later, over network radio, jingle reached the level of national saturation that has since been available to it. The first massively promoted singing commercial was

> Pepsi-Cola hits the spot,
> Twelve full ounces, that's a lot,
> Twice as much for a nickel, too
> Pepsi-Cola is the drink for you!

It was played 296,426 times over 469 stations in 1941, and more than a million times by 1944, becoming in effect a new kind of golden disc hit, a recording sold a million times by broadcasting to advertisers. Its enormous success, reflected in its entry into playground folklore in a variety of parody forms, has been a signal ever since of what such jingles can achieve in making advertising copy intimate to the public.

The testimony on behalf of the product offered in such a jingle as this is different from spoken advertising testimony because of the nature of song. Jingle cannot have or even seem to have the discursive content of a talking commercial. Whatever one thinks of the information conveyed in a talking commercial script, some large part of what is brought over by such talk inheres in the discursive form itself, the impression being given that the product will sustain serious talk about it. Singing commercial sacrifices this appearance of rational discussability of the product. It also sacrifices a certain claim to responsibility, a sense that the words can be traced back to their source and that "you can take it from me." There is no apparent personal source of sung words. Spoken testimony comes from the pulpit or the witness chair, but sung witness is something that even the original, broadcasting performers seem merely to be joining in on.

The peculiar properties of song make both the strength and the limitations of jingle, compared with other tactics of advertising—for example, compared to the common practice of accompanying a spoken or visual message with instrumental mood music. Mood music can establish an association of the product with a feeling state; jingle can attach words to the state. Because the words are sung words, they will to some extent be experienced as the subject's own words, the more so the more effective the jingle.

The words are appropriated in this way when the commercial is heard, and consequently certain qualities attach to them when they are recalled. It is not exactly that they return as words one once uttered oneself. They are present in the mind as public words, verbal property not bearing the sign of ownership by someone else. Heard sung, they achieved the air of what we and the singer or singers joined in on, rather than of what so-and-so said. Recalled, they come in assembled jingling lines as common property objects, available to pass through inner or outer speech and so pass as one's own. The state of existence as unappropriated property is reflected in the availability of successful jingles for verbal play by children.

Such a state is close to the standing in the memory of proverb. Proverb is what every slogan aspires to become, but to describe the condition fairly easily arrived at by song as proverblike does not necessarily imply easy success for song in motivating sales. Jingle has not driven out other tricks of marketing, and like other tricks it is subject to debate over its effectiveness. The relationship of lines of words preserved in memory to any behavior at all is problematical.

If jingle words are like proverbs, it might seem that they would have better access to the will than is allowed them here: that they might be consulted in conscious choices. It may be suspected however that proverbs share the impotence of songs, rather than that songs partake of any supposed influence of proverbs. For one thing there are the pairs of contradictory proverbs, as of commercials, current in the same culture and advising opposite courses: "Look before you leap"; but "He who hesitates is lost." When both are available to consciousness, which will guide choice? Surely neither guides choice very often. What either can do is to confirm choice. Proverbs are solicited, like solicited advice, to confirm and support the choice of what one is otherwise inclined to do. Jingle words may very well appear in the mind on the occasion of a buying choice, as well as at other annoying times on the cue of verbal association, but they can seldom bring even pseudoinformation to bear on decision itself. At such a time they chorus reassurance about the choice just made.

The makers of advertisements have come to realize that jingles do little simple delivery of messages. One advertising executive was quoted in the *New York Times* as saying, "The days of merely rhyming a lot of product attributes are gone, or almost gone." A writer of jingles adds, "The point of jingles is the same as the point of popular music; finding a hook that is repeated and that the listener can't get away from." The idea of implanting hooked words in the mind, rather than true or false information, acknowledges the listener's tendency to take possession of suitably formed phrases and snatches of song and calculates that the hook can be attached to a string held by the merchant.

In popular songwriting the "hook" expression has long been used for the striking, catching turn of musical and verbal phrase that the writer hopes will attach itself to the listener, but there is an important difference in the two implied uses of this hook. The hook of popular song works to snag the listener into the song itself; purchase of the recorded song may naturally follow as a concrete taking possession of the song already held in the mind. The hooked sample attaches itself to us for its own sake. It is self-referring: the hook curves back on itself. Self-reference is often visible in the verbal form of such a hook, returning upon itself as paradox, or as repetitive regression, or as absurd phrase refusing to connect to expected context: consider, among the first-place successes of one year, 1973, where hook happens to coincide with title: "I Love You Love Me Love"; "Skweeze Me, Please Me"; "Can the Can"; "12th of Never"; "Rubber Bullets."

Advertising hook, on the other hand, aims not only to lodge in the mind but then also to pull buyers toward products. The crucial extra function is, as we have said, problematical; it must rely on semantic reference of the hooked words back along the attached line, and this reference is in conflict with the self-reference that lodges the hook. A well-made slogan or song hook is like a proverb in this as well. It will often show in its form the kind of recurved self-reference visible in many proverbs, like Benjamin Franklin's "Haste makes waste" or "Where there's marriage without love, there will be love without marriage": compare "When you're out of Schlitz, you're out of beer"; "When you say Budweiser, you've said it all"; "The one beer to have when you're having more than one"; "If you've got the time, we've got the beer."

The listener takes possession of such phrase-objects, and they take possession of him. The hook does draw us into the experience of jingle as song. No doubt that experience can associate good feelings with the sponsoring product, apart from or in addition to those of music alone; but direct payoff is doubtful. Being in the song is something the mind inclines toward, and the entry into commercial song can be more easily precipitated than exploited. Geoffrey Leech, in a study of British advertising, has observed that much advertising copy is dense with the kind of pattern noticed here in hooked jingles (where there is always, of course, the superimposed pattern of music, often similarily hooked), and that "such density of schemes and repetitions is not uncommon in traditional ballads and modern popular songs. But perhaps a more fitting analogy, bringing out the ritualistic aspect of advertising jingles, is with children's games and nursery rhymes."[1]

Professor Leech does not carry his suggestion further, but it seems helpfully suggestive in the present context. A chance to play these musical games is something that the buyer of recorded popular song pays for. The advertiser has reason to hope to tax this same delight in song games by using it against resistance to the buying of his product. The obstacle to his hope is that when we enter into jingles we may well not be listening to what the mind's voice is singing. Song is not always heard distinctly from the inside; following the curves of the jingle will not necessarily point us to the product. Even when we are annoyed with jingles, what they draw the mind into is play.

NOTES

[1] Geoffrey Leech, *English in Advertising* (London: Longman, 1966), p. 193.

"LISTEN TO ME"

1 9 7 1

○ ▲ ○ ▲ ○ ▲ ○

Buddy Holly's music developed considerably on the records made under his own name, mostly at Petty's studio in Clovis. The backing is usually by members of the Crickets, although the record labels only said "with instrumental accompaniment." These tracks are the twelve which appeared on the album *Buddy Holly in 1958*, with the addition of four later tracks—"Rave On," "Take Your Time," "Heartbeat," and "Well All Right"—and others not issued until after Holly's death, including "Love's Made a Fool of You" and two songs cut with the R&B saxophonist King Curtis: "Reminiscing" and "Come Back Baby."

The general impression given by these records is one of sparseness and simplicity, particularly in comparison with the baroque richness produced by the vocal backings on the Crickets' records. The principal elements are drums, guitar or piano, and voice, and often the drumming is pared down to a tom-tom or jelly. The songs are frequently loosely constructed, with each sung line countered by a meandering guitar line, on the call-and-response pattern of "Not Fade Away."

LYRICS AND SONG SHAPES

Most music in the rock 'n' roll tradition differs from other popular music and aligns itself with folk music in the relationship of the *song* to the *record*.

A Cole Porter song, for example, is more than just a recording by Ella Fitzgerald. It has an independent existence beyond that particular version, and it is easy to imagine Sinatra or Crosby making their own interpretations which would be equally acceptable. No single recording of a Cole Porter song exhausts its potential, whereas the Who's recording of "My Generation" or Jerry Lee Lewis's record of "High School Confidential" does precisely that. In each case it becomes impossible to disentangle the song from the recording of it. There is much less reason for anyone else to do another version of either song, unless they were prepared to make use of the Who's or Lewis's vocal and instrumental mannerisms. Cole Porter and Jerry Lee Lewis in this sense are polar opposites, and many rock performers will be found to be at neither extreme. It is worth examining this opposition because of the light it throws on the relationship between words and music in rock 'n' roll, and in particular in Buddy Holly's work.

It is useful here to draw a tentative comparison between popular music performers and film directors as seen by critics who analyze films in terms of the auteur principle. Both *auteur* and *metteur en scène* work from a written text, but, whereas the latter does no more than faithfully transfer that text to the screen, the auteur gives it certain emphases which change its meaning.

The musical equivalent of the *metteur en scène* is the performer who regards a song as an actor does a part—as something to be expressed, something to get across. The aim is to render the lyric faithfully. An obvious example of the genre is the "protest" singer, whose work subordinates music to message. The vocal style of the singer is determined almost entirely by the emotional connotations of the words. The approach of the rock auteur, however, is determined not by the unique features of the song but by his personal style, the ensemble of vocal effects that characterize the whole body of his work.

This dichotomy also holds among popular musicians who compose their own material. Those who, like Leonard Cohen, merely transpose their lyrics into song form cannot be considered rock auteurs because their musical style is entirely determined by the words on the page. But the meaning of Jerry Lee Lewis's "Whole Lotta Shakin' Goin' On" or of Buddy Holly's "Peggy Sue" on disc is infinitely richer than the words of the lyric on the page. In the work of these singers, the distinction between the composition and the performance, central to classical music, breaks down. The song "Peggy Sue" has no real existence outside Buddy Holly's record of it.

Within rock 'n' roll, examples of two kinds of auteur can be found. Carl Perkins is a singer of the first, weaker kind, a man who can impose a distinctive personal style on his material, but whose own songs are capable of having other singers' styles imprinted on them (e.g., Elvis Presley's record of "Blue Suede Shoes"). On the other hand Bo Diddley and Jerry Lee Lewis are two singers who inscribed their styles on the songs they recorded, thus

DIAGRAM A

"That'll Be the Day"

		M					M		

"Listen to Me"

			M				M		

"Peggy Sue"

"Heartbeat"

⌒M⌐   ⌒M⌐

| | vocal verses   instrumental passages   M "middle 8"
|---|

making it difficult for anyone else to perform those songs without imitating Diddley's "jungle beat" or Lewis's piano style with the famous swoop along the keyboard. Another major auteur of this kind is Buddy Holly, who found stylistic maturity at a time when it was becoming possible to play rock 'n' roll outside a rigid, conventional, 12-bar structure.

With his solo records, the shapes of Buddy Holly's songs start to match his vocal style in their originality. Short two- or three-line verse forms predominate. The effect of this in "Words of Love" or "Listen to Me" is to alter the balance between singing and instrumental work. Instead of having two large vocal sections separated by a shorter instrumental segment, these songs consist of a series of shorter singing and playing passages. Diagram A compares the Crickets' "That'll Be the Day" with three of the Holly solo records.

"Peggy Sue" has a two-bar instrumental embellishment at the end of each verse and no "middle 8." This omission partly accounts for the unrelieved excitement of the record, since the function of the "middle 8" in most songs is to provide a breathing space from a succession of verses, just as an instrumental break does.

The structure of "Listen to Me" is more orthodox, although the instrumental break, in which Holly repeats the title phrase over the guitar playing, is unusually long. In "Heartbeat," each line has its accompanying guitar response, except where the song returns from the "middle 8" back to the verse. It is based upon the call-and-response pattern, which probably reached the Holly fraternity ("Heartbeat" is written by Petty and Bob Montgomery) through the work of Bo Diddley. One of the Holly tapes issued after his death with a backing added by Petty is of "Bo Diddley."

The themes of these songs are similar to those of the Crickets. They are all love songs, and nearly all are sung directly to the girl. "Mailman Bring Me No More Blues"; "Love's Made a Fool of You" (which is a philosophical song addressed to men in general), and "Heartbeat," where the singer soliloquizes, are the main exceptions. In addition, there are "Ready Teddy," with a lyric in the "Rock Around the Clock" tradition—a general invitation to everybody to have a good time—and "Well All Right."

This last record is the nearest Holly and Petty ever came to making a rock 'n' roll protest lyric along the lines of Eddie Cochran's "Summertime Blues" or Chuck Berry's "Almost Grown," although there is none of the anger or irritation of those songs. The response to adult criticism of young people in "Well All Right" is: "Well all right / Let people say . . ." which is a shrug of the shoulders rather than a shake of the fist.

As with the Crickets' lyrics, the words of a large proportion of these solo songs are about a man trying to win a girl's love. This is the situation in "Little Baby," "Look at Me," "Words of Love," "Listen to Me," "I'm Gonna Love You Too" and "Peggy Sue." Two songs, "Wishing" and "Everyday," are slightly different, in that the singer passively hopes that a girl will "surely come my way" instead of being involved with someone already. Instead of using his own words to win a girl, he simply hopes that fate or chance will act for him. In "Wishing," he looks around for a wishing star to help him. "Everyday" straddles the gap between what might be called "confrontation" songs ("Listen to Me," etc.) and the large body of teenage daydream songs, typified by the Everly Brothers' "All I Have to Do Is Dream," in which the real girl has been eclipsed by the girl in the singer's imagination.

Few of the Holly solo songs possess regular four-line verses, like "That'll Be the Day." Only "Look at Me," "Take Your Time," "I'm Gonna Love You Too," and "You're the One" have verses of this kind. The other tracks have either two- or three-line verses, or a structure based on the 12-bar blues form, for example:

TWO-LINE: "Wishing," "Heartbeat," "Words of Love," "Love's Made a Fool of You"

THREE-LINE: "Everyday," "Listen to Me"

12-BAR BASED: "Mailman Bring Me No More Blues," "Ready Teddy," "Rave On," "Peggy Sue," "Baby I Don't Care," "Reminiscing"

("Well All Right" has eight-line verses, four lines of which form a chorus. "Um Oh Yeah" has verses which vary between two and three lines.)

Of the two-line verse songs, "Heartbeat" and "Love's Made a Fool of

DIAGRAM B

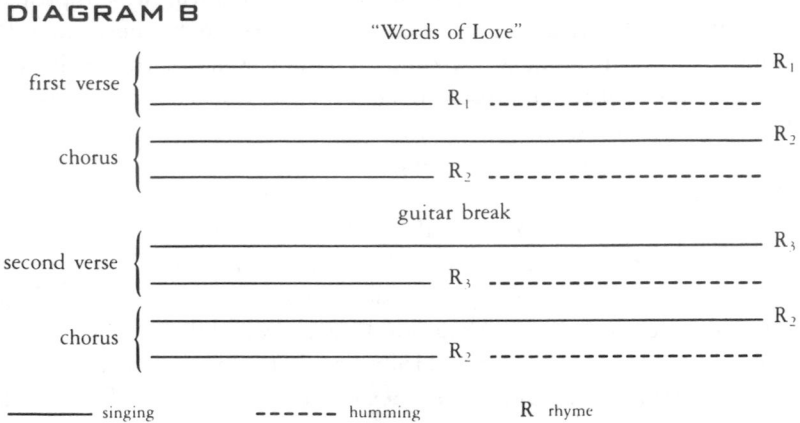

You" have complementary guitar lines following each vocal line. "Words of Love" has a chorus that is the same shape as the verse. Each vocal section (verse and chorus) is therefore four lines long. The second line in each pair is half the length of the first, and the other two bars are completed with humming. The shape of this intricate song is shown in Diagram B.

Although six songs have a structure based on the 12-bar blues, only one, "Mailman Bring Me No More Blues," has the classic blues form of three lines, with the second as a repetition of the first. "Ready Teddy," "Rave On," and "Peggy Sue" have another much-used blues form, in which the two lines spread over the last eight bars crop up in every verse, as a chorus. This structure is less obvious in "Peggy Sue" than in "Ready Teddy," where the chorus is clearly marked off from the rest of the verse. Two aspects of "Peggy Sue" combine to give it a spontaneous, unstructured appearance: quiet rhythm guitar work, which means that the chord changes are not emphasized, and constant repetition of the name "Peggy Sue" in both verse and chorus, blurring the division between the two.

The three-line verse shape of other songs also owes much to the blues, although its immediate ancestry was more likely the blues of C&W music than rhythm and blues. In both "Everyday" and "Listen to Me," the third line is almost the same in every verse and acts as a chorus, but the effect of this line is different from the type of chorus in "Ready Teddy." That chorus, introduced at regular intervals, acts as a bedrock for the song, as a firm construction underlying the lyric. In "Listen to Me" and "Everyday," however (as in "Peggy Sue"), the single line chorus seems to be reached each time by a less sure route, because the repeated phrases are not clearly set apart from the rest of the lyric; thus the listener hears them as a separate musical passage. The records give the impression of being one long, flowing unit, instead of songs composed of a series of structurally regular sections.

Another contributory factor to this flowing feeling is the use of rhymes: the units are very short, often only a phrase of three or four words. "Heartbeat" in particular has a complex rhyming scheme, with syllables echoing and bouncing off each other:

> Heartbeat why do you miss
> When my baby kisses me?
> Heartbeat why does a love kiss
> Stay in my memory?

It is worth listening to the whole sequence of rhymes, half rhymes, and echoes: do / you (line 1); why (lines 1, 3) / my (lines 2, 4) / stay (4) / ba- (2); -by / me (2) / -ry (4); does / love (3). Even the distant echo of a rhyme in the song's title contributes to the pattern.

These, then, are the features of the songs as they are before the records are made. What Buddy Holly and his backing musicians chose to make of them is the subject of the remainder of this chapter.

VOCALS

The powerful effect of Buddy Holly's singing does not come from what is normally thought of as vocal "power." In fact, his least interesting records are those in which he gives the song the full-blooded Little Richard or Elvis Presley treatment, like "Ready Teddy" or "Early in the Morning." Although he performs these songs adequately, the distinctive qualities of his singing seem to be submerged. These qualities need slower or more complicated songs than conventional rock 'n' roll tunes, to be fully effective.

Buddy Holly's singing voice was not strong, and this factor turned out to provide the basis for most of the vocal effects found on his records. Holly's voice was naturally higher-pitched than those of many rock 'n' roll singers, and lacked the body and resonance of Fats Domino or Elvis Presley. It was, in origin, like the voices of Buddy Knox, Carl Perkins, and the Everly Brothers, a typically country singing voice. Both Jimmie Rodgers and Hank Williams (the two greatest singers to fashion their own style in the C&W genre) possessed high-pitched voices, but with a wiry strength lacking in the more moping vocalizing of many of their successors.

Holly had a subtle strength allied to his relatively thin, high-pitched tone. The strength and subtlety came from a number of vocal effects or mannerisms, and a constant shifting from one to another of them, so that no phrase is sung in the same way as the preceding or the succeeding phrase. It is possible to isolate at least five distinct effects that appear frequently in the records Holly cut at Clovis as a solo artist, backed by members of the Crickets.

Contrast in pitch is the only one of his vocal mannerisms that Holly clearly borrowed from another artist, Elvis Presley. His version of "Baby I Don't Care," a song previously recorded by Presley, follows the original, where the title phrase is very low pitched. In other songs, alternate phrases are sung with contrasting pitch: in "Mailman Bring Me No More Blues," the final line of the last verse, which ordinarily would have a falling cadence, is sung with the second phrase much higher than the first: "One blue letter (LOW) / Is all I can use (HIGH)." In "Well All Right," the cadence at the end of the verse is the conventional falling one, but Holly overemphasizes the contrast between the high and low parts in a similar way.

In both these songs, one of the contrasting sections is made to sound "out of place" in the song. Holly sings the low part in the former song and the higher part in the latter, so that he seems to break out of the vocal range the song had set for itself: the listener is surprised by the change. This impression occurs in "Well All Right" because Holly's voice only sketches in the upward movement of the melody in the line "Well all right, well all right." The end of the word "right" is cut off sharply and the word itself is sung both times very softly. This contrasts with the next deeper line which is sung with greater power and assurance. In "Mailman Bring Me No More Blues" it is the Presley-like growl that is deliberately out of place. Contrasted high and low phrases in these records are not usually equally balanced. Holly's singing tends to place special emphasis on one of them, while the other is made to seem more integrated with the rest of the song.

More frequent than contrasts between phrases are contrasts in pitch within phrases. In "Peggy Sue," Holly's voice is continually darting up and down, so that the experience of the record is like that of a roller coaster or switchback ride. In the last two lines of the second verse quoted, the underlined words are those where low pitch is accentuated by Holly's singing, and those in capital letters are the emphasized high-pitched notes: "<u>Oh well</u> I <u>love</u> you gal / Yes I LOVE you PEGGY Sue . . ." (the last word is spread over several notes, on the last two of which the voice drops).

Variations in intonation are easily discerned in Holly's singing, but are more difficult to define. "Peggy Sue," Holly's most spectacular vocal performance, includes an important example in the verse preceding the guitar break. The tone of voice in which the first couple of lines are sung is new to the song; the voice is more nasal, and more "babyish," like the singing of the Crickets' "You've Got Love." It can be heard as a musical analogy to the private, intimate way of speaking two lovers might share; but it is only an analogy, not a representation of it. This new intonation within the record increases the tension and excitement.

In "Peggy Sue" the change in intonation is not related to the emotional mood or significance of the words, to reflect a particular feeling. It relates instead to the musical development of the record as a rock 'n' roll performance. Holly changes his vocal tone to take the music higher, to make it more exciting, as he would at a live performance.

The intimate intonation of Holly's voice on "Words of Love" has the same significance as the spoken phrases in the guitar passage of "Listen to Me." At one level, the latter represents Buddy Holly's dabbling in a convention found often in C&W ballads—the heart-felt recitation, but as well as addressing the girl in the lyric, "listen to me" is perhaps an injunction to the listener to notice the guitar.

Buddy Holly had a particularly individual *phrasing* technique. A large part of the art of ballad-singing lies in the singer's ability to hold a note with maximum emotional effect. Some sing in a traditional "true" manner, while others employ vibrato effects, designed to suggest choking or sobbing. Johnny Ray is the most obvious example of this last technique and he, more than anyone else, influenced young white rock 'n' roll singers of the fifties in singing ballads. Ray's style, in turn, derived from black singers, notably Roy Brown.

In the classic, early period of rock 'n' roll, the slow songs sung by Presley and others tended to be modeled on the kind of records cut by Ray and other "cry" singers. The rock ballad arrived later, at the end of the decade when rock 'n' roll seemed to become self-conscious about its lack of formal variety, with records like Ritchie Valens's "Donna."

Although Buddy Holly's best records were cut in this later period (1957–58), they stand outside the contemporary categories of beat and ballad, fast and slow, which nearly all the rest of the rock 'n' roll output of the time took for granted. His slower records are never bona fide ballads because of the way the singing on them is broken up by the guitar playing. Ballads depend on a steady buildup to a climax of joy or sadness, and consequently need at least four vocal lines uninterrupted by instrumental breaks. In comparison with the emotional explosions of most ballads, Holly's records are notably phlegmatic.

Holly puts one particular vocal technique—spreading one syllable over several beats of the music—to quite a different use from the straightforward ballad style. Holly does not actually hold the note, but substitutes several syllables for the single syllable of the lyric, in his famous "hiccup" manner. This means that his records lack the familiar effect of a long unbroken syllable held for a few beats and set off against that series of beats from the rhythm section. Instead of complementing the rhythm, Holly's staccato singing tends to imitate it and parallel it. On "Heartbeat," the syllable "be" (in the "middle 8" section just before the guitar break halfway through the record) is spread out over five beats: be-uh-ee-uh-ee. In singing it, Holly's voice spirals downward to rejoin the chorus line.

Few notes are held for more than one or two beats in Holly's records, so they avoid the overpowering emotion of the ballads of that period. Holly's listeners are not overwhelmed, as they are by a ballad, but continually have their attention redirected by the frequent changes of tone, pitch, and phrasing. Holly's music is, therefore, rarely sentimental.

Variations in vocal phrasing can be described in terms of their ornamental or dramatic function within a record. The vocal embellishment at the end of each verse of "Everyday" ("Love like yours will surely come my way *a-hey-a-hey-hey*") is predominantly ornamental. It arises out of the rhythmic and melodic patterns of the song. On the other hand, the sound Holly adds to the end of the title line of "Mailman Bring Me No More Blues" is dramatic, intended to suggest sobbing, and thus adds to the situation described by the lyrics rather than the purely musical character of the song.

These two instances constitute the two extremes of Holly's technique, and many of the vocal effects on his records combine elements of both the ornamental and the dramatic function, although the dramatic function is rarely dominant. On the last verses of "I'm Gonna Love You Too," his singing becomes more and more punctuated, with each word cut off and separated from the next. Sometimes an extra syllable is added (normally *-a*) to prevent two words running together. The extra syllable often coincides with Holly taking a breath and sometimes is sung falsetto. The technique has a dual role in the song: first, as Holly's response to the demands of performing the song, to bring it to a crescendo, and second, it is a more intense way of conveying the determination expressed in the words of the song. On this occasion, the dramatic and the ornamental are fused.

In "I'm Gonna Love You Too" Holly *sings wordlessly* for two verses, using only the sound "ah." The first begins the record, preceding the singing of the written words of the song, while the second forms a bridge between the guitar break and the next part of the lyric. The "wordless" verses thus act as an introduction to the lyric, and the syllable sung is the first syllable of the song's title: "ah'm a gonna love you too." Their effect is, in a way, like that of a stutter in ordinary speech.

The humming in "Words of Love" has some affinity with music as well as with words; it fills in the second half of a vocal line as a guitar phrase does in a conventional 12-bar blues. In the context of the lyric it also acts as the equivalent of the "um" sound people often use instead of "yes" to signify agreement. As a part of the lyric it gives added emphasis to the preceding words.

Buddy Holly was probably the first rock 'n' roll singer to *double-track* his voice so that he could harmonize with himself on record. The songs in which this occurs—"Listen to Me," "Words of Love"—provide interesting comparisons with the country-style close harmonies of Buddy and Bob on the recordings made three years earlier. In the verses of the two double-tracked records, Holly's two voices sing the same part, giving his sound a resonance that is not there on other tracks. In the middle 8 sections of these songs, however, he sings in a harmony close to the singing that he did with Bob Montgomery. But where Buddy and Bob had no distinctive sound to clearly differentiate themselves from other C&W singing teams, the later double-tracking is clearly recognizable as the mature Buddy Holly.

In addition to describing the vocal techniques that make up Buddy Holly's singing style, the aim of this section has been to suggest how that style relates to the meaning of the words Holly sings. It is clear that some records with poor lyrics turn out to be poor records, while others, with equally uninspired words, do not suffer the same fate. The difference lies in the relationship between *what* the singer is singing and the *way* he sings it in each kind of record. In the first kind, the singing style is dramatic, subordinated to the lyric: the singer is trying to get *something* across to the listener and if what he wants to express (the lyric or melody) is mediocre in itself, then the record fails, however well-executed the performance. But in records which succeed despite mediocre lyrics (and many rock 'n' roll records are of this kind), the performance achieves an autonomous character. Instead of trying to interpret the lyric, the singer uses it as a jumping-off point for his own stylistic inclinations. He uses it as an opportunity to play rock 'n' roll music, instead of regarding his role as one of portraying an emotion contained in the lyric.

The *auteur/metteur en scène* opposition already discussed is relevant here, and clearly Buddy Holly belongs in the second group of singers, although the picture is made more complex by the fact that he composed many of his own songs. Nevertheless, many of the vocal techniques he employs cannot be said to have emotional correlatives in real life. Their frame of reference is first and foremost the musical world of Holly's records. In other words, the appeal of Buddy Holly's music does not lie in what he says, in the situations his songs portray, but in the exceptional nature of his singing style and its instrumental accompaniment. In this context, it is relevant to recall that within the Holly-Petty partnership, Norman Petty wrote most of the lyrics and Holly concentrated on the music.

INSTRUMENTAL WORK

The tendency toward instrumental breaks tailored to fit closely into the rest of the song that had been apparent on the Crickets' records is taken further on the solo tracks. On the slower songs, the break is an almost exact recapitulation of the melody line ("Everyday") or a repetition of a riff that runs through the whole record ("Words of Love," "Listen to Me," "Heartbeat").

Norman Petty's influence on these records shows in the range of instruments that appear. Petty himself plays celeste on "Everyday"; piano on "Look at Me," "Rave On," and "Mailman Bring Me No More Blues"; and organ on "Take Your Time." King Curtis, one of the few black musicians Holly recorded with, plays tenor sax on "Reminiscing" and "Come Back Baby." The guitar playing is by Holly himself on "Peggy Sue," "Listen to Me," and the earlier records. On the tracks made after the split with the Crickets, Tommy Allsup takes the guitar breaks, notably on "Heartbeat."

The "dampened" style of guitar playing, which gives the instrument a dull instead of a ringing tone, is an important feature of several tracks. The clipped sound echoes Holly's own clipped, jerky style of singing. The two work together especially effectively on "Heartbeat," where the basic rhythms of singing and playing have a dramatic function, to suggest a pounding heart.

Buddy Holly is able to indulge his penchant for "down-home" rock 'n' roll playing on only three of these records. "Ready Teddy" has a rockabilly solo, with a pattern of chords and single notes familiar from "That'll Be the Day" and other earlier tracks. "Peggy Sue" and "Mailman Bring Me No More Blues" have breaks that erupt in barrages of chords, with a powerful "electric" tone—not merely an acoustic guitar solo amplified, but a unique metallic sound, where each chord echoes into the next. This playing is the main feature of what has been called the Tex-Mex style, and appears on "Words of Love," "Listen to Me," "Love's Made a Fool of You," and "Heartbeat," as well as several Crickets tracks. The intricate pattern of "open" chords that makes up the central motif of "Words of Love" and "Listen to Me" is the apparent Mexican aspect of Holly's work. As in the rocking style, the edges of the notes are blurred so that they begin to merge into one another. Holly's guitar tone is something almost without precedent in rock 'n' roll. It is closest to the sound of the young black musicians Berry and Diddley (whose style is in turn a deliberate mutation of the Chicago blues style), and to Ritchie Valens's playing on "La Bamba," a rock 'n' roll adaptation of a traditional Mexican dance tune. It clearly has nothing to do with the more expansive and emotionally diffuse guitar work of the white country tradition and the rockabilly style. Holly's Tex-Mex style is denser and more compressed, with a correspondingly greater expressive intensity.

The guitar break on "Love's Made a Fool of You," one of the lesser-known songs (which may be by Allsup), is a minor classic. It is a delicately played, thoughtful construction of single notes whose short phrases follow the line of the verse. It is like many blues guitar phrases, in that it seems to emulate the human voice.

As a descriptive term for Holly's playing, "Tex-Mex" is not very helpful because it does not take account of the major determinant of the style, which is the originality of the songs themselves. The discipline enforced on Holly—he could no longer cut loose with a raving rock 'n' roll break—

made his playing more economical and more integrated into the song. In addition, much of the fineness of tone came from the technical possibilities of the Fender guitar, a model Holly was one of the first to use among rock 'n' roll players.

RHYTHM SECTION

If the guitar playing moves beyond conventional rock 'n' roll on Holly's solo records, so does Jerry Allison's drumming. On several tracks, he uses only one percussive sound to tap out a single rhythmic pattern. "Everyday" sounds as though he is slapping a jelly. On "Heartbeat," he plays a single drum, and at the end of the track, a cowbell. The drumming on "Listen to Me" consists of a repeated pattern, which reinforces the guitar riff. Allison's outstanding performance is on "Peggy Sue," where the drumming makes itself felt by lightness and speed rather than by a powerful regular beat. The rhythm is beaten out on bass drum and tom-tom. Together with the rhythm guitar, whose continuous light strumming understates the chord changes, it makes possible the tremendous fluidity of the record.

The rhythm guitar playing on most of the tracks is by Niki Sullivan, or probably by Holly himself where Allsup plays lead. Holly's Stratocaster is the only guitar, taking both rhythm and lead parts, on "Peggy Sue." In "Well All Right" the traditional ringing, percussive acoustic sound of the rhythm guitar dominates the beat. The break is also taken by the rhythm guitar, repeating and stressing the chords that accompany the vocal. The bass playing, as before, is resolutely conventional, and never emerges from the general sound of the rhythm section.

On most rock 'n' roll records, the rhythm section has a simple but central role: to lay down a solid beat, usually accented on the off-beat, against which singer and instrumentalist can create their irregular lines of sound, but on many of Buddy Holly's Clovis tracks, the rhythm section sets up patterns that tend to work more closely with guitar and voice, becoming more than a mere background.

THE RECORDS

It is the greater flexibility of the rhythm section that enables "Peggy Sue" to take off where "Rave On" stays on the ground. The rhythm of "Rave On" is a well-delineated series of beats, while "Peggy Sue" is a constant stream of sound. "Rave On" has an easy foot-tapping rhythm that is also easy to dance to, but "Peggy Sue" has a rhythm not clearly divided up by accentuated beats. There is a repeated rhythmic pattern in the song, but the last note of it is marked by a slight dying away of the sound merging into the next repetition of the pattern.

The traditional distinction between rhythmic section, lead voice, and instrument begins to break down in "Peggy Sue," as the drums become more assertive. The notion of the stable lyric also seems to be under attack in the way that the title and certain other words and phrases appear and reappear constantly, as if Holly were improvising the words. A further contribution to the anarchic effect has already been mentioned: the chorus line is disguised because many of its words also appear in the verse lines.

Drums, guitar, and lyrics in "Peggy Sue" share a repetitive quality (in "Rave On" they share a regularity, which is very different). The one element of the record that is not repetitive is Buddy Holly's voice, which makes use of nearly all the techniques that have already been mentioned: continually shifting pitch, tone, and phrasing. It is a great vocal performance, as Holly responds to the relentless driving of the instrumental playing and manages to make the repeated words sound fresh every time he sings them. "Peggy Sue" is the record that extends Buddy Holly's vocal range fully, for on verse after verse, he finds new and more ingenious ways to sing a lyric of very limited poetic resources. The song almost assumes the character of a challenge, which, perhaps, is why it is such a compelling and exhilarating record to hear.

"Peggy Sue" gives the impression of spontaneous creation. In contrast, "Listen to Me" and "Words of Love" are carefully constructed tracks, where each vocal and instrumental element fits together like the pieces of a jigsaw puzzle. Each begins with a flowing guitar riff, continuing throughout the song ("Words of Love"), and recurring only in the spaces between the vocal ("Listen to Me"). The riffs are complemented by nimble drumming patterns that are relaxed versions of Allison's playing on "Peggy Sue."

The interplay between voice and guitar differs on these two records. "Listen to Me" has an alternation of voice and guitar riff, as shown in Diagram B. In "Words of Love" the voice emerges out of a continuous guitar background. The song is slower in tempo and Holly's singing is less animated. The effect of the steady guitar line is mesmeric, contributing to the calm quality of the track.

Vocally, "Listen to Me" contains far more of the restless side of Holly's singing. The first three lines of the verse are sung double-tracked in the familiar plangent, yearning, high-pitched way, the last line in a lower key. The greater variety in singing and playing is complemented by the loping character of the drumming, which is more active than the muted accompaniment to "Words of Love." Although the lyrics of both songs are very similar, the records have quite different emotional content. "Words of Love" projects a feeling of certainty and security, while in "Listen to Me" Holly seems far less sure that the girl will.

The most innovative single released by Buddy Holly before his death was the coupling of "Heartbeat" and "Well All Right." Although "Heartbeat" has a Latin rhythm far removed from the standard rock 'n' roll beat, the record is supple and lively. While the drums (with the ringing tone of the cowbell dominating the start and close of the record) and second guitar lay down the basic rhythm, the lead guitar fills in the breaks and plays behind the vocal so that it forms a bridge between the singer and the rhythm section. Allsup on lead guitar plays mostly dampened notes, which has the effect of emphasizing the rhythmic aspect of the notes, since they are "blunted" and without tonal variation. In contrast, the main guitar break on the record is played with the strings "open," a tone close to a steel guitar sound and that includes a number of bent notes. Here it is the actual sounds of the individual notes, rather than the rhythmic pattern they form, that is important.

There is no monolithic rhythm section behind Holly's singing on "Heartbeat," but a busy complex of guitars and drums. The rhythm guitar (played by Holly himself) has an important but unobtrusive role, providing a thin, constant texture of strumming between the more exotic patterns of lead guitar and percussion. Holly's vocal depends on timing and intonation for its effect: "Heartbeat why do you *miss* / When my baby kisses *me*." In the first line there is an almost imperceptible pause after "you," and "miss" is jerked out emphatically. "Me" is pronounced curiously, in the "babyish" tone of voice. Placed at the end of the line, it holds the listener's attention during the short, dampened guitar break.

"Heartbeat" is arguably Buddy Holly's most complete record, for within it many separate elements are perfectly synchronized. Each instrument plays its different role, but meshes in with the rest, and the main instrumental and vocal motifs—the staccato rhythm and jerky singing—echo the theme of the lyric: the heavy pounding of the excited lover's heart.

The dominant instrumental sound of "Well All Right," the acoustic rhythm guitar, is simple: the same chord pattern is maintained throughout the record. But it never becomes monotonous because of the subtle changes in emphasis, in light and shade, that are possible when an acoustic guitar is played harder or softer. The guitar sound moves into the foreground and recedes like waves on a shore. The drumming, in which the cymbals predominate, is related to the guitar, so that the light percussive tone melts into the equally light guitar sound.

The singing stands in the same relation to this rich instrumental sound as it does on "Words of Love." Instead of the music playing a minor role, to fill in the gaps between verses, the vocal seems to come out from behind the instrumental sound and to fade back into it as Holly's voice gets quieter and higher in the repetition of the title phrase.

CONCLUSION

Many of the Buddy Holly records cut in Clovis in 1957–58 diverge radically from existing rock 'n' roll song forms, both vertically (in the interaction of the instruments with each other and with the vocal) and horizontally (in the pattern of vocal and instrumental sections throughout the song). In particular, the contrast with the Crickets tracks that were made at the same time is striking.

Among the Crickets songs, the "one-track" ballads—"An Empty Cup" and "Last Night"—forced Holly's singing into a one-dimensional mold, where he had to concentrate throughout the song on achieving one specific effect. With "Words of Love" and the other slower solo songs, he had much more vocal play because they had broken away from the ballad genre.

Similarly, "Peggy Sue" stands outside the standard rock 'n' roll genre because the emphasis within it is on rhythm rather than beat. Chuck Berry sang in "Rock and Roll Music" that "It's got a backbeat, you can't lose it," but "Peggy Sue" lacks that accentuated backbeat, relying instead on a riff developed from Bo Diddley's style.

What distinguishes this music further from most white rock 'n' roll contemporary with it is the extent to which Holly's voice is integrated with the rest of the sound. To a considerable extent, the division between lead voice and accompaniment, in which the instrumental sound plays a subordinate role, is broken down. The fact that the musicians are now alongside him rather than in the middle distance gives Holly a stimulating musical context, with different contours on each track. On the earlier records and the Crickets tracks, Holly had been singing in an empty space, where the conventional rhythm section of the instrumental playing gave him merely rhythmic support, not musical inspiration.

The new instrumental arrangements provided the major impetus for Buddy Holly's vocal style on the solo records. Less important is the stimulus provided by the lyrics of the songs and their emotional themes. Sometimes, in fact, the characteristic emotional tone of Holly's voice goes against the apparent emotional message of the words: in "Peggy Sue" he sings: "If you knew Peggy Sue, then you'd know why I feel blue." It seems to be the cry of an unhappy man, but the record radiates energy and enthusiasm.

Holly's singing here and elsewhere epitomizes what Rick Nelson sings in one of his songs: "Rock and roll gets in your soul / It makes you feel so natural" ("Come On In"). Even where his singing had a dramatic function, where it interpreted the lyric, Holly was always a rock 'n' roll performer.

DO-TALK AND DON'T-TALK

The Division of the Subject
In Girl-Group Music

1 9 8 8

○ ▲ ○ ▲ ○ ▲ ○

SISTERS FROM BEHIND THE SPECTOR

E conomic analysis of the popular music industry has identified a cyclical movement whereby innovation is brought in by risk-taking small producers and is followed by a period of concentration in the giant record companies as they reproduce and capitalize on the new styles.[1] After a while the novelty wears off and a new generation protests against the decadence and commercialism of the old.

This equation of small with progressive and big with conservative can be easily overlaid with a gender analysis. For instance, Simon Frith and Angela McRobbie have pointed out that the creative bursts of rock 'n' roll, or of punk in late-seventies Britain, were both marked by an aggressive masculinity which they label "cock rock." By contrast, the late fifties saw the rise to popularity "of sweet black music and girl-groups like the Shirelles," so that "the decline of rock 'n' roll rested on a process of 'feminisation.' "[2] This undermining of the creativity of rock by commercialism functioned to normalize the socially challenging expressions of masculine sexuality in early rock 'n' roll.

On the other hand, "pop songs aimed at a female audience deny or repress sexuality." Girls' sexual feelings are interpreted through the dominant code of *romance*, which leads inexorably into the "harsh ideology of domesticity" and operates as "the dominant mode of control in popular music."[3] "Romance" isolates girls from each other in a battle to secure a boy against the treachery of female peers, and obscures housewives' material subjection as domestic laborers.[4] As such it presents no contradictions to the dominant ideology, and Frith and McRobbie state clearly: "For the contradiction involved in popular music's sexuality we have to look elsewhere, to the cock rock side of our ideal type distinction, to rock's ideological break with pop."[5]

While this theory exposes the exploitation of women both as performers and as consumers by the record industry, it does so at the expense of completely marginalizing women from the process of cultural conflict and change. In seeing the oppositional ideology of rock as one of "freedom from domesticity,"[6] Frith and McRobbie locate social and sexual contradiction not within either masculinity or femininity, but between them, in such a way that masculinity inevitably appears progressive and femininity conservative. While "cock rock" and capital play out an Oedipal drama, women's music appears only to reproduce mainstream cultural forms endlessly. In this essay, I shall argue against this version of rock history, in the awareness that I am challenging what is almost received opinion among rock and feminist critics.[7] Nevertheless, it does not appear to me to stand up to detailed examination, for it only follows the dominant ideology in assigning value to what is "masculine" and devaluing the "feminine."

In focusing specifically on the American "girl groups," who achieved a string of chart successes in the first part of the sixties, my aim is to show that this female-oriented music did bring important innovations to rock, and that the "feminization of rock 'n' roll" cannot simply be equated with its "decline." Of course, an alternative interpretation from that of Frith and McRobbie does see girl-group music as involving innovations, but, precisely in line with their theory of rock and sexuality, ascribes the innovations entirely to the creativity and risk taking of a few male producers. So, several of the best-known girl-group songs are reissued only as *Phil Spector's Greatest Hits*, and George Morton's "shadow" stalks the reissue of the Shangri-Las.

In fact, if one takes the girl groups as a genre, neither Spector's "wall of sound" nor Morton's minidramas are essential ingredients, but appear in retrospect as exaggerated variations on the theme. Nor is it enough to add in the professionalism of the songwriting teams or the intensity of much of the actual singing.[8] These explanations of the greatness of the best girl-group music inevitably posit the struggle of the *authentic individual* as triumphing over the stultifying tendencies of commercialism, whether it be Phil Spector's singlehanded pursuit of multitracking technique, the songwriters' dedication to their craft, or the authenticity of the streetcorner sound of the girls' voices. However, as the products of a complex division of labor, these recordings cannot be ascribed to any one "author." It seems wrong to single out ingredients which "shine through" the commercialism of the songs in this way. Each ingredient was part of that commercial success.

Instead, I wish to shift the focus and ask why these songs sold, as a question about the meanings created for an audience that is addressed in the songs themselves. If commercial success is defined as finding an audience that has money, we need to know not only why new groups in society may have money to spend (whether through employment or income redistribution), but also how that consumer group is "summoned up" and given an identity by the address of the song itself. From this point of view, the innovative character of a song or a genre derives not simply from the process of production objectified in the record as commodity, but also from the processes of circulation and consumption through which the meanings of the songs are appropriated and used by audiences.

In the case of the girl-group songs, a group of girls is usually constituted as an internal audience to the song in the form of chorus to the lead singer. This may not be the only audience addressed by the song, as it is one of them, we can take seriously the position of the female listener in relation to the song. This is to go against Laura Mulvey's influential theory that the female spectator in the cinema is necessarily "masculinized" by the address of the film, a theory that has been applied to rock music by Taylor and Laing.[9] Where, as in several girl-group hits, we can actually distinguish male and female "audiences" in the address of the song, it seems all the more urgent to theorize the position of the female listener as "different." This stance seems to be given weight by the claim that the main buyers of girl-group records were, in fact, young women.[10] In this way, the external audience for the song becomes part of the girl group that it addresses.

I shall argue that the "girl talk" represented in the songs can be analyzed to reveal a structure of *feminine discourse* which offers positions for the speaking female subject. In looking at the way in which this discourse is shaped within, but also *out of*, rock 'n' roll music, I shall be preoccupied with challenging the simple equation of masculinity with sexual "expression" and of femininity with sexual "repression" made by Frith and McRobbie. Although this equation has a surface plausibility in the conventional English-language usage of "masculine" and "feminine," it is one that feminists have sought to redefine. And if Freud did often see femininity as both repressed and repressive, the radical reformulation of his theory by Lacan sees *all* sexuality as involving both desire and its prohibition. For Lacan, the baby's "mirror" relationship with its mother is interrupted by the father's prohibition of incestuous desire. From then on language must come out of the gap created between self and (m)other; desire must speak in the hope of attaining that original one-ness. But at the same time, the child must speak from the knowledge that it does not possess the idealized "phallus" that appears to give the father possession of the mother and of the whole symbolic order of exchange. So, for Lacan, the subject always speaks from the place of the Other, from a position of lack, but desiring the wholeness that language seems to promise. The subject of language is always, then, divided against itself.[11]

By taking such a theory as starting point, it is hoped to avoid the functionalism of Frith and McRobbie's theory of rock and sexuality, which seems able only to posit an endless cycle of deviance and normalization. Instead of seeing cultural conflict as between masculine revolt and feminine repression, Lacan's theory predicts that there is division and conflict in all assumption of sexual identity. Feminists may well claim that since the fifties, women's role and women's sexual practices have changed more than men's, and been a site of more conflict. We must be careful, then, not to close off the possibility that "feminine" cultural products, such as girl-group music, may be part of that process of conflict and change.

On the face of it, while there were many ways in which conflict over sexuality was apparent in rock 'n' roll, the struggle of women for sexual autonomy was not one of them. Lesley Gore's "You Don't Own Me," a hit in 1965, is a magnificent but lone exception at the end of the girl-group period. Most commentary has seen rock 'n' roll as the revolt of "youth" for sexual autonomy, with race and class as intertwined themes in the "threat" perceived by the older generation; gender has been a dimension only in the form of masculinity seeking autonomy. It is therefore interesting that several recent commentators on the girl groups have heard the songs as expressive of a female standpoint. Greil Marcus, for instance, argues that among the qualities of the music were "a good deal of rage, and a lot more struggle—the struggle, one might think, of the singer—a young girl, black as likely as not—against the domination of her white, male producer."[12]

Simon Frith is perhaps pointing in the same direction when he remarks that on relistening to the Shangri-Las in the context of 1980s "alternative" women's music, he hears something of "female friendship" and calls for a reinterpretation of "girl-talk" songs.[13] Certainly it is striking that the name of the form "girl groups" prefigures the main organizational form of the women's movement, the "women's group," which was also a form for the development of "talk."

Perhaps the commentator who takes most seriously the idea that these songs express social conflict from a women's point of view is Aida Pavletich, who discusses the girl groups under the heading of "teen," which she describes as "a protest genre." She attributes the "belligerent toughness" of the performances to the streetcorner origins of many of the singers, as well as bringing out the generational conflict evident in many of the lyrics. But this is class and generation from a girl's point of view, which Pavletich captures in her image of the girl subject of the songs as a "hunter," out to get her guy against all odds of parents or the perennial Judy (the one that betrayed her).[14]

It is the way in which this position of active sexuality is elaborated in the songs that I wish to analyze in this essay. If active female sexuality had a history in the blues, the women blues artists sang mainly as mothers and experienced women. What was new in the girl groups was its articulation by schoolgirls.[15] But I shall argue that this girl talk is itself developed in contradictory opposition to the voice of the mother in the songs.

I wish to show, then, that the women's songs of the period *are* different from men's, and that they are not simply vacuous, commercial repetition of the bright ideas of the cock rockers. They are different in part because of the way in which the female subject in the performance is divided against herself. This division runs through to us as audience of the songs and does not allow us to argue that "the audience is always male."[16] But neither can we say that it is the "particular use of the female voice" that makes the music "dependent on a female response," as Frith has argued in relation to postpunk feminist bands. It is not that "the voice" itself directly expresses "a woman's point of view,"[17] but rather that the *different* voices always present in girl-group music *between* them produce a meaning for women.

BUDDY GROUPS AND THE EXCHANGE OF WOMEN

I shall in part be reading the girl-group songs against an analysis of male rock performances, which it may be useful to summarize here.[18] In this analysis, it was argued that the metaphor in the term "rock 'n' roll" encapsulates a central feature of the discourse of rock: the rock singer takes up the position of *mother* to the woman he addresses as "baby." The language of hushing a baby's crying is mapped onto the adult situation of a man's talk silencing a woman, while at the imaginary level, the rocking movements of the mother become those of a man's lovemaking. The successful rock 'n' roll song is a performance for other men, from which they can learn both the language and the body movements with which to overcome the imaginary crying of a woman.

These processes of identification constitute rock music as part of the secondary socialization process of adolescence. The original triangular relationship between a baby, the mother's voice, and the language of the father, through which the child underwent primary socialization and acquired a linguistic self-identity, is reworked as the son joins the father in adult male status. Rock music appropriates the love talk of the mother and redirects it (in a reversal of the power relations of mother over son) into the discourse of adult male–female relations.

The male rock performance, then, makes the woman into a silent object of exchange between men. Analysis of some Buddy Holly songs can demonstrate how this relationship of the singer to his male audience is set up. One way is through the use of pronouns as a form of address, as in the opening lines of "Peggy Sue": "If *you* knew Peggy Sue / Then *you*'d know why *I* feel blue." Here the "I" clearly addresses the audience as "you" about the woman. These lines form a structural preface to the song, and quite literally set the scene within subsequent verses, including the addressing of the woman as "you," will be enacted.

Alternatively, the relationship may be represented within the performance as an exchange between the singer and his male chorus. For instance, in "That'll Be the Day," the chorus represents the response of a male audience, picking up and repeating a limited form of the singer's words, always in harmony with him. The woman's incapacity to "say goodbye" is the message exchanged between singer and chorus. She has no independent voice; only her dependent "turtle-doving" is mimicked in the chorus's "oo-hoo." A similarly harmonious relationship with the chorus can be observed in "Oh Boy," where the singer's relationship with his fantasy woman is elided with his relationship with his male chorus/audience in the phrase "when you're with me, oh boy" in the first verse.

The ultimate in male solidarity is, of course, that rivalry over a woman cannot upset the bonds of brotherhood. In "I'm Gonna Love You Too" the pronoun address and the relationship with the chorus combine to represent this situation. At the beginning of the song, we understand the title phrase as meaning that the singer is going to reciprocate a woman's love. Then in verse 3, we are told that "another fella took you." When Holly goes on, "I'm gonna love you too," we are forced to understand, "I'm gonna love you as well as the other fella." In other words, the woman has been exchanged between him and the other fella without upsetting the buddy group. The wordless harmonies of the chorus beneath Holly's voice both represent this relationship and extend it into the whole group.

What is particularly important for our purposes here is that the male listener can identify with either singer or chorus without experiencing this as divisive. Whichever part he hums along with draws him into the buddy group. Preliminary analysis of other male group singing (doo-wop vocal groups of the fifties, the early Beatles) suggests that this analysis does have more general relevance for the male rock performance. When we turn to the girl groups, we find that no such easy identification is possible for the female listener. In a sense, the subject is much more openly divided against itself than in the smooth harmonies of "buddy" music. The following sections of this essay investigate this division, first by looking at pronouns in the songs, and then at the relationship between lead singer and chorus in the girl group. The conclusion returns to the general question of how "mother–baby" discourse is used in the female performance.

TALK ABOUT HIM NOW: PRONOUNS
AS FORMS OF ADDRESS

As a starting point for analyzing who the girl-group songs are addressed to, I looked at the pronoun structure of a sample of hit songs. The sample was based on the discography compiled by Greil Marcus,[19] from which I took only those songs that made the Top 10 on the U.S. *Billboard* charts. Of the 32 such songs that he lists, it was possible to find 24 on reissue. I have added four numbers,[20] giving 28 songs in all (see Table 1).

I transcribed the lyrics of these songs, distinguishing the "voices" of lead singer and chorus, and paying attention to repetition, interruption, and overlap of voices, as well as to the "fadeout," which is a feature common to all these songs. I then highlighted all personal pronouns in the songs and tabulated the number of times each occurred in each song. On this basis it was possible to distinguish three main groups: songs about "he/him," songs addressed to "you," and songs containing both "he" and "you." The latter group can be subdivided into those which address a female "you" and those in which the "you" is male, producing a number of variations on the triangular theme.

However, if we are concerned with the activity or passivity of the female subject in relation to the song performance, it becomes necessary to examine how pronouns act on each other. We need to know whether the female singer is singing of herself as object of the boy's desires and actions, or whether she herself is the desiring, acting subject. To this end, I looked for *sequences* of pronouns in the songs. Generally a "sequence" is just two pronouns related as subject and object (direct or indirect) of a verb. However, I have extended it beyond this purely grammatical notion to include some much looser relationships between pronouns, which still seem to be placing one in the position of subject to the other as object. For instance, I have counted "*I* sit at home alone and cry over *you*" as an "I–you" sequence, and "It's not the way *you* kiss that tears *me* apart" as a "you–me" relationship (both from the Shirelles' "Baby, It's You"). The results are summarized in Table 2.

From this table we can distinguish pronoun sequences which place the singer in an *active* relationship to the other (I–you, I–him) from those in which she is *passive* (you–me, he–me). I call this activity/passivity *discursive* since it is not inherent in the grammar but depends on our understanding of the positioning of the singer as subject in relation to the grammatical structures, as well as on an understanding of the song performance as gendered.

Added up over the whole sample, the numerical differences between these active and passive sequences was fairly small. Nor did counting the

TABLE 1

SAMPLE OF GIRL-GROUP SONGS REACHING U.S. TOP 10, 1960–1967

GROUP	SONG	U.S. CHART POSITION	YEAR
The Ad Libs	"The Boy from New York City"	8	1965
The Angels	"My Boyfriend's Back"	1	1963
The Chiffons	"He's So Fine"	1	1963
	"One Fine Day"	5	1963
	"Sweet Talkin' Guy"	10*	1966
The Cookies	"Don't Say Nothin' Bad (About My Baby)"	7	1963
The Crystals	"He's a Rebel"	1	1962
	"Da Doo Ron Ron"	3	1963
	"Then He Kissed Me"	6	1963
The Dixie Cups	"Chapel of Love"	1	1964
Lesley Gore	"It's My Party"	1	1963
The Jelly Beans	"I Wanna Love Him So Bad"	9	1964
Little Eva	"The Locomotion"	1	1963
Martha and the Vandellas	"Heat Wave"	4	1963
	"Jimmy Mack"	10	1967
The Marvellettes	"Please Mr. Postman"	1	1961
	"Don't Mess with Bill"	7	1966
Paris Sisters	"I Love How You Love Me"	5	1961
The Ronettes	"Be My Baby"	2	1963
The Shangri-Las	"Remember (Walkin' in the Sand)"	5	1964
	"Leader of the Pack"	1	1964
	"I Can Never Go Home Any More"	6	1965
The Shirelles	"Will You Love Me Tomorrow"	1	1960
	"Dedicated to the One I Love"	3	1961
	"Mama Said"	4	1961
	"Baby, It's You"	8	1962
	"Soldier Boy"	1	1962
	"Foolish Little Girl"	4	1963

* U.K. no. 4, 1972.

number of songs in which active sequences predominate over passive, and those in which passive predominate over active, yield any very significant results.

However, if we look at the way active and passive sequences are used in building up the meaning of particular songs, some rather striking results

TABLE 2
PRONOUN SEQUENCES IN GIRL-GROUP SONGS

	I–You	You–Me	I–Him	He–Me	You–Him	He–You	She–Me	Other
He songs								
"The Boy from New York City"			1	4				
"He's So Fine"			3	1				
"He's a Rebel"			2	4				1 They–Him
"Da Doo Ron Ron"			2	3				
"Then He Kissed Me"	1		4	15				
"I Wanna Love Him So Bad"		4	11	2				
"Heat Wave"			1					
"Leader of the Pack"	1		3	2	1	1		1 They–Me, 1 She–Him
You songs								
"One Fine Day"	1	9						
"Chapel of Love"	3							
"The Locomotion"	1	?						
"I Love How You Love Me"	13	17						
"Be My Baby"	8	3						1 We–Them
"Remember"	1							
"Will You Love Me Tomorrow"		6						
"Dedicated to the One I Love"	3	3						
"Mama Said"	2						1	
"Baby, It's You"	3	1						2 They–You
"Soldier Boy"	8	1						
He–Male you songs								
"My Boyfriend's Back"	2	1	2		1	4		
"Jimmy Mack"		1		1				
"Please Mr. Postman"		2		1				
He–Female you songs								
"Sweet Talkin' Guy"			1		1	2		
"Don't Say Nothin' Bad"	1	3	3	10				
"Don't Mess with Bill"	1		2	1				
"Foolish Little Girl"			8		7	4		3 Her–He
She song								
"I Can Never Go Home Any More"							4	2 You–Her
No sequences								
"It's My Party"								

TABLE 3
FANTASY AND REALITY IN RELATION TO PRONOUN SEQUENCES

SONG TYPE	FANTASY	REALITY
He songs	I–Him (active)	He–Me (passive)
You songs	You–Me (passive)	I–You (active)
He–You songs	You–Him (*you* active)	He–You (*you* passive)

emerge. Active and passive pronoun sequences do not occur randomly, but can be correlated rather precisely with a structural opposition in the meaning of the songs between *fantasy* and *reality*. A reading of these songs in terms of fixed gender positions (masculine = active, etc.) might still be possible if, say, all discursively active female positionings correlated with fantasy meanings. But this turns out not to be the case. For the *relationship between* the two pairs, activity–passivity and fantasy–reality, is consistently the opposite in the "he songs" from what it is in the "you songs."

To spell this out, in songs relating the first and third persons, the male "he" is the subject of narrative statements and the female "me" the object, whereas in fantasy expressions of desire, the female "I" is subject and the male "him" the object. In songs relating the first and second persons, the female "I" is the subject and the male "you" the object of narrative statements, whereas fantasy wishes are expressed as the male "you" acting on a female "me" as object. The third category, of "he–male you songs," combines elements from each of the other two patterns, so that the sequence "he–you" expresses reality, and "you–him" the female (or occasionally male) fantasy, again inverting the relationship between subject and object in narrative and fantasy. These relationships are summarized in Table 3.

These findings can be illustrated by looking at one example of each major type of song:

"Da Doo Ron Ron." This is a "he song" told as a simple story structured by the repeated he–me sequence, "And when *he* walked *me* home," which occurs in the refrain of each verse. This contrasts sharply with the I–him wish articulated by the lead singer in the final verse, "Some day soon *I'm* gonna make *him* mine" (picked up and reformulated by the chorus as "Yes, *I'll* make *him* mine"). This use of the I–him wish opens up a gap between the narrative and the desire of the singer, a gap which appears to be acted out when the voices of singer and chorus separate in the final coda which ensues.

"One Fine Day." This is a "you song," whose title aptly sets the stage for the you–me wishes that are repeated throughout the song, principally

the "One fine day / *You*'re gonna want *me* for your girl," which forms the refrain to verses 1, 2, and 4, and then, as the kernel of the song, is repeated over and over in the final coda/fadeout. Again, this is in sharp contrast with the single occurrence of I–you in the song in verse 3, where the lead singer introduces her *knowledge* of what the boy is really like:

> Though *I* know *you*'re the
> Kind of boy
> Who only wants to run around . . .

The music is also used to contrast this verse with the others. For the above lines, it modulates to the subdominant, the melody is different, and the chorus drops its persistent "shooby dooby" which "accompanies" the other verses. As this verse continues, the you–me fantasy is reintroduced, and the music moves back to the dominant of the original tonic, working up the chord of the dominant seventh over the last two lines, in prolonged anticipation of the return to the tonic at the beginning of the next verse:

> *I*'ll be waiting
> And some day darling
> *You*'ll come to *me*
> When *you* want to settle down . . .

As in the previous example, the *active* pronoun sequence introduces tension into the passivity of the rest of the song, but in this "you song" the "I" is active around the *reality* of "you," whereas in the "he song," "I" is actively shaping the *fantasy* of the future with "him."

"Sweet Talkin' Guy." This is a he–you song which relates "he" to a female "you." As can be seen from Table 3, the female "you" follows the pattern of the female "I" in the schema, being active in relation to fantasy and passive in relation to narrative action. The first verse of the song sets up this structure:

> Sweet talkin' guy
> Talkin' sweet kind of lies
> Don't *you* believe in *him*
> If *you* do, *he*'ll make *you* cry
> *He*'ll send *you* flowers
> And spend the time with another girl . . .

Here the expression of fantasy ("you believe in him") is complicated by the prohibition ("Don't"), which comes from the voice of an implicit "I." This "I" becomes explicit in the dramatic declaration which introduces the instrumental break:

> Why do *I* love *him* like *I* do?

Since all voices (i.e., of lead singer and chorus) join in on this phrase, it can be interpreted either as the exasperated reply of the "you" addressed in the first verse of the song or as a revealing confession by the voice giving advice to the "you." If it is both of these at once, as is suggested by the presence of both voices, the implication is of rivalry between two girls over the boy.

The first verse of the song had introduced the theme of rivalry in narrative form, by telling the story of "he," "you," and "another girl." The dramatic confession line brings this rivalry into the open as two identical, and therefore conflicting, fantasies around "him." The verses following this outbreak of emotion act out the rival fantasies in the "complicated" form in which fantasy was introduced in the first verse: each voice warns against the fantasy of "you" (the other voice) about "him." The sequence of pronouns and prohibition is here "him-no-you," in a sense the kernel of the song's meaning:

> Stay away from *him*
> No, no, no *you*'ll never win

In the fadeout, this sequence is sung by the different voices in a counterpoint of rhythms and melodies, with the lead singer adding in more elaborate lyrics to the faster rhythm and the chorus repeating the basic lyric to a moi drawn-out rhythm. The effect is of urgent pleading on the one hand. cor trasted with a more menacing threat on the other.

This song, then, contrasts the rival fantasies, you–him and I–him, with the he–you reality. In a sense, the fantasy of "him" becomes the object of ar xchange between "you" and "I." However, the song illustrates the fact that when "he/him" becomes a potential object of exchange between women in this way, the exchange is itself the object of negation and prohibition. All four hit songs in this "he–female you" category elaborate the language of "don't," two of them very prominently in a title line that is repeated throughout the song.

Together these three pairs of oppositions form a *structure* in which each side of the fantasy–reality opposition is itself a subject–object sequence where subject and object are of opposite genders in the song performance. Moreover, on opposite sides of the fantasy–reality divide, the two subjects are of opposed genders, as are the two objects.

It is, of course, possible to form pairs of sequences where both subjects (and both objects) are of the same gender. This is principally the case in the group of songs that contain both a "he" and a male "you." For example, the Angels' "My Boyfriend's Back" relates "he" to "you" and "you" to "him" directly, in a contest where "he" proves himself the real man and "you" consequently becomes feminized. The he–you sequences form the *reality* axis of the songs ("*he* knows that *you*'ve been lying"; "*he*'ll cut *you* down to size"), and form a contrast with the *picture* that "you" and "I" have of "him" ("when *you* see *him* coming"; "*I* can see *him* coming").

Space does not permit a full analysis of pronoun sequences in all the songs included in the sample. The next section, therefore, presents a summary of the results of this analysis, concentrating on the range of meanings achievable through the use of the contrasting sequences, and on the different possibilities inherent in the "he songs" and the "you songs."

YOU'VE GOT TO LET ME FOLLOW YOU: THE SIGNIFICANCE OF PRONOUN SEQUENCES

In the examples of a "he song" and a "you song" we have already looked at, the contrast between different pronoun sequences was perhaps exaggerated by the fact that in both cases, a single occurrence of a sequence in which "I" is active interrupts a long string of sequences in which "me" is passive. If we look at the wider sample of both types of song, we find that a commoner pattern is for the "I" sequence to occur first, being followed later by ones in which "me" is the object of "he" or "you," respectively. While the fantasy–reality opposition is not always so marked as in the songs we have looked at, the pronoun sequences on the fantasy side are particularly consistently deployed. More variation of meaning, though within very definite limits, was found to be available for those on the reality side.

In most of the cases where an I–him sequence is the first one to occur in the song, it expresses the desire of the singer for "him" as exaggerated, or ambitious in its intentions: for example, "*I* wanna love *him* so bad" (the Jelly Beans); "*I* love *him* so" (the Cookies); "That's no reason why *I* can't give *him* all my love" (the Crystals, "He's a Rebel"); "*I* loved *him* more than before" (the Marvellettes, "Don't Mess with Bill"); "*I* don't know how *I*'m gonna do it / But *I*'m gonna make *him* mine" (the Chiffons, "He's So Fine"); "Some day *I* hope to make *him* mine, oh mine" (the Ad Libs).

This expression of unlimited passion, or of socially ambitious marriage prospects, may be tempered with reality in quite a limited variety of ways, expressed through he–me sequences. First, the he–me sequences may serve as legitimation of an exaggerated expression of love. Such legitimation comes through the boy's reciprocation not of passion, but of good behavior and commitment: "*He*'s good/true to *me*" (the Cookies); "*He*'s always good to *me*" (the Crystals). The very sobriety of these statements of how "he" is to "me" lends authority to the girl's case.

Alternatively, the girl's expressions of desire may be tempered by doubt about the real situation, again expressed through he–me. So the Jelly Beans' "I Wanna Love Him So Bad" hits a snag with the line "If *he*'d only let *me*," which introduces an element of doubt into the song. The Marvellettes' "Don't Mess with Bill" turns doubt into ironic self-doubt with lines that describe a partial reality: "Though *I* tell myself *he* wants no one else / Cos *he* keeps coming back to *me*."

In the two songs where "I" is pursuing a boy whom she sees as of superior social status, he–me sequences come close to being an extension of the I–him wish. So in the last verse of the Chiffons' "He's So Fine," where "I" imagines the social situation as reversed, a he–me story is inserted within an I–him wish. The sequence of pronouns in this verse can be seen as I–(he–me)–him:

> If *I* were a queen
> And *he* asked *me* to leave my throne
> I'd do anything that *he* asked
> Anything to make *him* my own . . .

And in the Ad Libs' "Boy from New York City," a verse of he–me sequences are really extenstions of "I's" fantasy about "him," though expressed in narrative form: "Every time *he* says *he* loves *me*"; "Every time *he* wants to kiss *me*." But the last line of this verse, "*He* makes *me* feel so fine," again serves as legitimation of "I's" wish to make this rich boy hers, through the meaning of "fine" in American slang as of superior social class.

In all these cases where I–him is followed by he–me, it seems that the initial desire of "I" for "him" requries a he–me statement in order to legitimate it, in the sense of bringing the desire out of the realm of mere fantasy into some relationship with a reality of which "he" is subject. This structure is confirmed by a song where "he" has the authority to *negate* the legitimacy of "I's" desire for "him." The Shirelles' "Foolish Little Girl" takes the form of a dialogue between mother and daughter on the eve of an ex-boyfriend's wedding to someone else. The debate between them is crystallized in two sequences in the final fadeout, where the mother's voice sings: "Forget *him*, cos *he* don't belong to *you*," while the daughter continues to plead, "But *I* love *him*." The he–you sequence here establishes the *reality* of the situation between "he" and "you," a reality which "I" of course refuses to acknowledge as referring to "me." However, while "I" can continue in her fantasy world, she nowhere mangages to accord it reality with a he–me statement. The song does not resolve the debate in favor of either voice; instead it fades out with the two voices repeatedly affirming their difference.

Within this simple structure of an I–him wish legitimated by a he–me reciprocation/authorization, the "he songs" tell us a lot about the boy who is the object of desire. This description occurs in a series of statements of which "he" is the subject, the songs clustering around two types: the "fine" boy, who is the target of aspirations for upward mobility at marriage; and the "rebel," who is a vehicle for the defiance of parental aspirations, but represents commitment and understanding outside marriage.

When we turn to the "you" songs, we find that we learn virtually nothing about the "you" to whom the song is addressed but a lot about the "I"— her inner feelings, what she wants, and the strength of her convictions. It is perhaps this distinction that leads Alan Betrock to regard songs that use "he" as expressing "universal imagery," while songs that use "you" are more "specific." In discussing Phil Spector's relationship with the Ronettes (he married the lead singer), Betrock notes that the songs Spector produced with them always used "you" rather than the "he" of his previous successes with the Crystals, and remarks:

> Phil was expressing how he felt for the first time, sending these musical love letters out to Ronnie, and perhaps gaining pleasure by hearing Ronnie sing the words directly to him.[21]

This passage suggests a privileged position for the male audience of songs sung by women and addressed to a male "you." The female audience to such songs becomes more like a spectator to a performance between two others. We cannot perhaps, then, take for granted that this group of girl-group songs *does* appeal to girls, but will have to ask this question of the analysis.

As with the "he songs," it is the fantasy side of the contrast of pronoun sequences that turns out to be most consistently used in the "you songs." But, while in the "he songs" the fantasy sequence is an *active* one (I–him), in the case of the "you songs" it is the *passive* you–me (see Table 3). The consistent core of meaning of these you–me sequences is a wish for recip-rocation of love, always leaving room for doubt about whether this love of "you" for "me" will be forthcoming.

This you–me wish/doubt is well exemplified in the title line and repeated, unanswered question of the Shirelles' "Will *You* Love *Me* Tomorrow?"; in the first verse of the Ronettes' "Be My Baby" ("So won't you say *you* love *me?*"); and more tenuously in the refrain ("So won't *you* please . . . say to *me*, my darling"); in the Shirelles' "Soldier Boy" ("In this whole world / *You* can love but one girl / Let *me* be that one girl"); and in the same group's "Dedicated to the One I Love" ("Each night before *you* go to bed, my baby / Whisper a little prayer for *me*, my baby").

Generally, this rather uncertain you—me plea comes *after* one or more I–you sequences which have set up "reality" in one of two ways: I–you either expresses the absolute certainty and conviction of the love of "I" for "you," which then becomes "real" in relation to the wishes and doubts surrounding reciprocation; or it expresses the reality of separation of "I" from "you," a real distance which then contrasts with the fantasy that it can be bridged if "you" love "me."

The first alternative is exemplified in the first verse of the Ronettes' "Be My Baby" ("The night we met *I* knew *I* needed *you* so"), and in the Shirelles' "Soldier Boy" (the repeated "*I*'ll be true to you"). In both these songs what shines through is the absolute conviction of "I" about her feelings. The alternative of a reality of "separation" is set up at the beginning of the Shirelles' "Dedicated to the One I Love" ("When *I'm* far away from *you*, my baby"). An almost identical sequence occurs in the Paris Sisters' "I Love How You Love Me" ("And when *I'm* away from *you*"), although this is only a brief interlude of tension in an otherwise saccharine-sweet song. A separation due to the lack of reciprocation is represented in the Shirelles' "Baby It's You" ("*I* sit at home and cry over *you*"), where a sequence later in the song expresses the unshakeability of "I's" feelings ("*I* know *I'm* gonna love *you* any ol' way"), her resignation to the certainty of loving "you" even without a reciprocal commitment.

In all these I–you sequences, what we have is a complex statement by the girl *about herself*, a structure concisely exemplified in the two sequences quoted which use the format "I know I . . . you." This introspective detail on inner feelings may be part of what Betrock means by calling "you songs" more "specific." But at the same time, it suggests that his assumption that this specificity privileges the male audience is not correct. The male "you" to whom these songs are addressed is indeed nondescript and interchangeable (by contrast with the boys of the "he songs"). The introspection of the female "I," on the other hand, offers a ready means of identification for the female audience. We should also note that, because "you" is a genderless pronoun, a male audience can identify with the "I" of the song and still assume heterosexual address with the pronouns unchanged, a possibility which is excluded in the "he songs." It is therefore the "you songs" that on these criteria turn out to be more universal in their appeal, while the "he songs" are more specific in offering identification more exclusively to a subculture of girls.

In looking at the "he songs" we found ways in which "reality" virtually collapsed into "fantasy," notably in the use of the sequence I–(he–me)–him in the Chiffons' "He's So Fine." If we look at the way reality collapses into fantasy in the pronoun structure of the "you songs," some important differences in the possibilities of meaning in the two types of song emerge. The identity of the second person "you" as both subject and object of a verb makes it possible for the two "you" sequences to collapse into one: I–you–me. This sequence is found prominently in the Paris Sisters' "*I* Love How *You* Love *Me*," whose title line, and variations, are repeated throughout the song, and occurs less obviously in the central section of the Shirelles' "Dedicated to the One I Love" ("But *I* can be satisfied just knowing *you* love *me*").

What is special about this elision, in terms of the structure of meanings analyzed, is that it allows the activity of the "I" toward "you" or "him" to disappear into the passivity of the "you–me fantasy." No longer does "I" know "you" directly, as in "One Fine Day"; nor does "I" know "I," as in "Be My Baby," or in "Baby, It's You." Instead, in these I–you–me sequences, the "I" seems able only to know or want you–me.

We could see this I–you–me sequence as the pronominal structure of the Lacanian mirror phase. The "I" looking into the mirror of the, as yet, ungendered "you" sees reflected back the objectified "me," and misrecognizes that as self. That self's expressions of desire become caught in a circle of desire of "I" for "me." Instead of being the object of desire, "you" merely deflects desire back onto itself. This is indeed a "division of the subject" in which the subject must always misrecognize itself, and which seems peculiarly opposite for the position of the female subject in culture.

In fairness to the other songs, "I Love How You Love Me" is the only one in the sample that consistently performs this collapse into mirrorlike passivity. Apart from the fact that the song is not particularly "teen" either in its lyrics or the sound of its voices, there are other formal grounds for not considering it as a genuine girl-group number (see Table 4). It is therefore interesting that generally, the other "you songs" in the sample do not collapse the two pronoun sequences in this way, although they may make use of only one of them.

Unlike all the other personal pronouns, the third-person singular pronouns are inevitably gendered (he, she, etc.). Subject and object are also distinct, making it impossible for I–him to collapse into he–me. In Lacanian terms, this necessary gendering locates the subject within the symbolic order, where meaning is generated in the difference between reality and fantasy. With the gendered pronouns it is not possible to slip into the circularity of the mirror stage.

Against Lacan, however, these songs show that this is as much a feature of the pronoun "she" as it is of "he." This is all the more interesting as, in the two songs where "she" is related to "me," the "she" in question is the "I's" *mother*, Lacan's original "mirror." In the Shirelles' "Mama Said," a she–me sequence introduces reality into the fantasy of the daughter who has "almost lost her mind" over a boy. In a curiously ambiguous verse, the mother's *words* remind of the futility of desire without serious intentions on the part of the boy, at the same time as her *look* seems to perceive the reality of her daughter:

> And then *she* said someone might look at *me*
> Like *I'm* looking at *you*
> And then I might say
> *I* don't want *you* any ol' way . . .

Here the rather tenuous she–me sequence in the first line allows the daughter to translate this reality into her own I–you sequence in the last line ("I don't want you"). It does this via the ambiguity of "I'm looking at you," which both describes the present lust of "I" for "you" as well as invokes the gaze of her mother in the past.

The Shangri-Las' "I Can Never Go Home Any More" explicitly rejects the fantasy of "a boy" in favor of a same-sex love for "her," in this case the mother. The song establishes reality through a she–me sequence, again showing the mother's perspicacity toward her daughter ("*she* told *me* it was not really love") and counterposes a future fantasy for the female "you" of the audience ("Tell her *you* love *her*").

Returning to the more usual "he songs" and "you songs," we can conclude that the possibilities of meaning in songs about "him" are rather different from songs addressed to a male "you." In terms of the discursive activity/passivity outlined earlier, the structure of pronouns in the "you songs" appears to represent the *conventional* position allotted to women's desire. Here her fantasy is always the passive "desire to be desired": reality impinges as a constraint, whether that of separation/nonreciprocation or that of the need to prove her absolute faithfulness before she can plead for the return of her love.

The structure analyzed in the "he songs," by contrast, seems to allow for a much more interesting discursive activity, whereby the girl's active fantasizing shapes the very notion that she has of "him," and so the story of which she wishes him to be the active subject. Reality is brought in as confirmation of her fantasy, rather than as what she must do in order to dare to make herself the object of a male fantasy.

In relation to the thesis on girls and popular music that we started out with, the analysis so far has tried to show that the construction of romance from the girl's point of view is no simple matter of "waiting for her prince to come." Far from being always the passive object of a story in which the boy is protagonist, the girl in girl-group songs is passive only by contrast with her activity as a subject. The construction of herself as object of the boy's desire is a discursively complex activity which takes place within a series of well-defined relationships to her own construction of the boy as object of desire.

DON'T SAY AND DO LANG: THE CONTRADICTORY CHORUS

So far the analysis has performed a crucial oversimplification in treating the lyrics of a song as if emanating from a single voice. Although this may be part of the common experience of listening, it is, of course, to ignore the salient feature of these songs, which is that they are *group* music, in which different voices are articulated musically. What is more, it is immediately apparent on listening to the classic girl-group numbers that the singing of the group in the form of the chorus has much greater prominence than in most other genres of rock 'n' roll. In this section, we examine the meaning of this division of the subject into two voices in relation to what we have already found about the division of the subject into active and passive views of herself.

While it is not possible here to draw exhaustive comparisons between girl-group music and other group genres, the introduction to this essay did set up a comparison with Buddy Holly as a paradigm of the male rock 'n' roll singer's relationship with his backing group. It was argued that this relationship is one of consensus, achieved by the symbolic "exchange of women" between singer and chorus.[22]

If the traditional relationship of the chorus to lead singer is one of subservience, support, and sometimes of apprenticeship, this is often reversed in girl-group music. Even the term "lead singer" loses its meaning when the chorus both opens the song and sings consistently higher in pitch, as in many of the songs in the sample. Table 4 lists the presence of some of the features which make the chorus either formally equal to, or dominant over, the "lead" singer in the songs. The first two columns refer to the musical features already mentioned which often make the chorus the "lead" voice. The next two columns list the considerable number of songs in which the chorus does articulate pronoun sequences, and the songs where it articulates the pronoun "I."

The final two columns refer to features of the fadeout, so typical of the songs. Very often these codas represent the distillation of the meaning of the song, and the fact that they capture electronically the idea of an *endless repetition* is peculiarly apt for the representation of an unresolved conflict of desire, or of an indissoluble difference between voices. Two indicators of the nonsubservience of the chorus in these final fadeouts are given in these columns: the existence of a musical and verbal counterpoint between the two voices, which often involves the solo voice "wordwrapping" in between the lines of the chorus; and the maintenance by the chorus of a more verbal part than that of the solo singer, again reversing the normal relationship.

What this formal equality/dominance of the chorus means in practice of course differs according to the lyrics of the song and their arrangement between the voices. But there is a common thread of rivalry/restraint running through the chorus's relation to the lead singer in the song, which can now be illustrated.

Each verse of the Chiffons' "One Fine Day" (analyzed earlier as an example of a "you song") ends with the line "You're gonna want me for your girl." The chorus, which had been singing its vociferous "Shooby-dooby-dooby-dooby-doo-wah-wah" almost *against* the rest of the lead singer's words, withdraws on this line to a background "Ooh." The chorus is similarly silent in the contrasting middle verse where the lead singer states her knowledge that the boy "only likes to run around." When we reach the final coda

TABLE 4
FEATURES OF THE CHORUS IN GIRL-GROUP SONGS

	OPENS THE SONG	SINGS HIGHER IN PITCH	ARTICULATES PRONOUN SEQUENCES	ARTICULATES "I"	IN COUNTER-POINT WITH SOLO VOICE IN FADEOUT	HAS MORE VERBAL PART IN FADEOUT
HE SONGS						
"The Boy from New York City"	▲	▲			▲	▲
"He's So Fine"	▲	▲			▲	
"He's a Rebel"		▲	▲	▲	▲	▲
"Da Doo Ron Ron"			▲	▲	▲	
"Then He Kissed Me"		▲	▲			
"I Wanna Love Him So Bad"	▲	▲			▲	
"Heat Wave"					▲	▲
"Leader of the Pack"	▲		▲		▲	
YOU SONGS						
"One Fine Day"	▲	▲	▲		▲	▲
"Chapel of Love"			▲	▲		
"The Locomotion"		▲			▲	
"I Love How You Love Me"			▲			
"Be My Baby"					▲	▲
"Remember"		▲				
"Will You Love Me Tomorrow"			▲			
"Dedicated to the One I Love"			▲	▲	▲	
"Mama Said"	▲	▲			▲	
"Baby, It's You"	▲	▲				
"Soldier Boy"	▲		▲	▲		
HE–MALE YOU SONGS						
"My Boyfriend's Back"		▲	▲	▲	▲	
"Jimmy Mack"	▲	▲	▲		▲	
"Please Mr. Postman"	▲	▲		▲	▲	
HE–FEMALE YOU SONGS						
"Sweet Talkin' Guy"			▲	▲	▲	▲
"Don't Say Nothin' Bad"	▲	▲	▲	▲	▲	▲
"Don't Mess with Bill"					▲	
"Foolish Little Girl"		▲	▲		▲	
SHE SONG						
"I Can Never Go Home Any More"	▲	▲	▲	▲		
NO SEQUENCES						
"It's My Party"	▲	▲		▲		

and fadeout, the chorus picks up and repeats the final verse line. "You're gonna want me for your girl," and it does so in *counterpoint* with the lead singer. Because the chorus repeats the full you–me pronoun sequence, the effect is of two different voices clamoring for the attention of the "you." This of course makes a mockery of the intended sense of the line as sung by the lead singer, which envisages a time when the boy will want to stop running around with other girls and settle down with her.

The performance by several voices of a fantasy of being the boy's only girl places the chorus in the role of "mockingbird": the very repetition by a different voice subverts the intended meaning. This effect is achieved economically in the Shirelles' "Will You Love Me Tomorrow?" by just having the chorus join in the words each time the crucial question is asked. In this song "tonight" represents certainty for the girl ("Tonight you're mine completely"), while "tomorrow" stands for uncertainty, as in the title line and its repetition, "Will you still love me tomorrow?". The voices of the chorus represent this uncertainty musically. When the girl sings of the certainty of "tonight" her voice is heard solo. But when the doubt of the refrain question appears, so does the chorus, as if representing the future loves that will ask the boy the same question.

Similarly, the chorus's loud "Sha-la-lup-shup" accompanies the doubts expressed by the lead singer in verse 2: "Is this a lasting treasure?" In verse 3, the solo voice breaks away on a different melody and manages to sing alone again about "tonight" and certainty: "Tonight . . . you say that I'm the only one." But as doubt creeps in again, so does the chorus, in the dramatic climax to this verse:

Beats:	1	2	3	4	1	2	3	4	1	2	3	4	1	2	3	4	
	But	will	my	hea.......... rt	be		bro...... ken?										When the
	ni ...... ght		meets the mor		ning	su											n
	WHEN THE NIGHT MEETS THE MOR - NING SU																N

lowercase: lead singer
UPPERCASE: CHORUS

Here the two voices, heard first separately, then coming together, cleverly represent the idea of "night" meeting "morning" in the lyrics. The voice of the chorus, at first *following* that of the lead singer, catches up with her in the increasing urgency of the phrase and overwhelms her entirely in the crescendo of the "morning sun." The effect is of the moments just before sunrise and the sudden rush of light as the sun pushes over the horizon. The solo voice, and with it the certainty of "tonight," are swept away, the chorus bringing morning and uncertainty, and remaining with the lead singer for the rest of the song.

In these two songs ("One Fine Day" and "Will You Love Me Tomorrow"), it so happens that the relationship between singer and chorus exactly parallels that between pronoun sequences. In each case, the chorus joins in the you–me fantasy, the sequence used to formulate the uncertainty of reciprocation, and represents that uncertainty dramatically. Where the singer expresses "*I*'s" certainty about "you," as in "One Fine Day," she does so alone.

Like "Sweet Talkin' Guy," which was analyzed earlier, both these songs talk openly about unfaithfulness and possible noncommitment on the part of the boy. But what of songs where there is no such explicit fear of infidelity? It seems that even here the chorus plays a structural role similar to that in the songs analyzed. What should we make, for instance, of the counterpoint of two voices who each sing "Be my baby" in the refrain of the song of that name? The latent "maternity dispute" is brought out if we look at the way in which the accentuation falls on the different syllables. The chorus sings "be *my*, be my baby" on the first and third lines of the refrain, while it is not until her last entry (end of line 3) that the lead singer manages to emphasize the "*my*" in this way, in a passionate crescendo that can be heard as answering the "restraint" of the chorus:

With this song we meet "baby" language once more and can begin to address one of the questions with which we started out: If male rock singers have in some sense appropriated the language of the mother in singing to/

						So	won't	you
						OO		
(line 1) please							Be my	little
	BE	MY		BE MY			BA . . . . . BY	
(line 2) ba . . . . by							Say to	me my
	MY	ONE	AND	ON . . . . . LY			BA . . . . . BY	
(line 3) dar . . . . . ling					Be	my	baby	
	BE	MY		BE MY			BA . . . . . BY	
(line 4) no . . . . w,	o	o	o	o	o			
	MY	ONE	AND	ON . . . . . LY			BA . . . . . BY	

lowercase: lead singer
UPPERCASE: CHORUS

of girls as "my baby," and so forth, then how do female rock performances relate to this schema? The answer we can begin to suggest is that the representation of love in the girl-group performances is more complex than the one-sided activity of the male rock star toward his "baby." We have already seen that the girl singer by no means relapses into the role of passive "baby" in relation to a fantasized male, "maternal" activity. But neither, it turns out, can we say that any one female voice appropriates and internalizes mother talk. Instead there is a duality of voices that both present mother talk and re-present it in the voice of the daughter.

There are a few songs where this mother–daughter relationship to maternal discourse is acted out very explicitly (the Shirelles' "Foolish Little Girl," where mother and daughter are both represented as solo voices but the chorus backs and sometimes joins in with the mother's voice; and the Shangri-Las' "I Can Never Go Home Any More," where the chorus enacts the *singing* voice of the mother hushing the baby to sleep, by contrast with the *spoken* lyrics of the older and wiser daughter). But on the whole, a mother–daughter relationship between the voices of chorus and lead singer is only implicit in the songs, even when the word "baby" is used. Perhaps the most striking example of this underlying mother–daughter conflict is in the first verse of the Cookies' "Don't Say Nothin' Bad (About My Baby)," a verse that is repeated as four out of the six verses in the song:

1	2	3	4	1	2	3	4
	DON'T SAY	NOTHIN'. . .		BAD A. .BOUT MY		BA-BY	
							Oh
	DON'T SAY	NOTHIN'. . .		BAD A. .BOUT MY		BA-BY	
no						I	love him
	DON'T SAY	NOTHIN'. . .		BAD A. .BOUT MY		BA-BY	
so						Oh	don't you
	DON'T SAY	NOTHIN'. . .		BAD A. .BOUT MY		BA-BY	
know							He's
	HE'S	GOOD			GOOD TO ME		
good . . .		He's good	to	me . . .		'n'	that's all I
care about							

lowercase: lead singer
UPPERCASE: CHORUS

As "dialogue," this interchange is complicated, since although the second voice (the "lead" singer) appears to be replying to the first voice (the chorus), her words are not intended for the chorus to *hear*. Instead, the chorus appears to be talking to a third party (the "boy" and "everybody" of subsequent verses). The lead singer's voice, softer in volume and consistently lower in pitch than that of the chorus, is like the invisible fairy eavesdropping on the talk of the main characters in Shakespearean drama and subverting their meaning in witty replies, addressed to the audience but inaudible to the characters in the play. So, in this song, we in the audience hear the lead singer's "Oh no" as superficially complying with the injunction of the chorus, but quickly understand it to be a subversion of this compliance. For the chorus, to hear that her "baby" is "good" to someone else is exactly the "bad" news she does not wish to hear.

We may, of course, choose not to hear the song as a literal, interpersonal conflict in this way, but may take it as representing "inner" and "outer" voices of the same person. The reading then becomes even more complicated, as the lead's "Oh no" of line 1 must be addressed to herself, while the "Oh don't you know" of lines 2–3 must be addressed to an external "you." What is perhaps remarkable is the readiness with which we, as listeners, are prepared to perform such contortions in order to construct the two voices into a single "person" for ourselves.[23]

If the song is heard as conflict, then this is most readily understood as between two girls, whether these are different persons or part of the same person. But it is notable that only one voice (the chorus) uses the maternal language of "baby," and that only one voice (the solo singer) formulates the I–him fantasy of active desire. The chorus can, throughout, be heard as expressing a mother's worries, which reflect those of society ("everybody says he's lazy," etc.) and against which the solo voice must pit her fantasies and her knowledge of what "he" is like to "me."

It is on this he–me line at the end of each verse that the voices come most explicitly into conflict as rivals. The solo voice here does *lead*, with "he's good" prompting the chorus to imitate the phrase. The soloist's continuation, "he's good to me," then *interrupts* the chorus's completion of the same sequence. In addition, the emphasis on *"me"* by both voices as they hit the strong beat of the bar creates an unmistakable impression of voices in rivalry for the boy's, and audience's, recognition.

In all these songs the chorus acts in such a way as to restrain, or dampen, the exuberant fantasies and desires of the lead singer. Representing the mother, other girls, or just "everybody," the chorus is often the backdrop against which the lead singer must show her own strength and determination. But a chorus that mirrors the singer's words is often hard to outwit, as, while appearing to support, the chorus can often subvert the singer's meaning. We saw this in the divided voices of "Will You Love Me Tomorrow." Another example would be the way in which the chorus picks up and repeats the injunction of the lead singer, "Don't Mess with Bill" in the song of that name. If the chorus is heard as singing this *back* to the lead singer at the end of the song, then the lesson has been counterproductive. In "Don't Say Nothin'," the lead singer turns the tables on the chorus, subverting her meaning in a song which reverses almost all the "normal" relationships between the two voices.

By comparison with the analysis of the chorus in male group music which was briefly sketched earlier, the chorus in the girl-group songs is less submissive to, less supportive of, the lead singer. If the chorus is one way in which the voice of the mother is recalled, as the male or female adolescent struggles to articulate the first words of love in a world outside the family, then it is tempting to see these different relationships as paradigms for the way in which mothers relate to teenage boys and girls in everyday life. These relationships then map onto, and underlie, the relationship between boys and girls in same-sex groups. In this case, the girl-group model seems the more progressive in acknowledging, playing on, and working out differences between voices, while the boy group, or "buddy group," presents an apparent consensus which masks something more like a master–slave relationship.

CONCLUSION: FOR AND AGAINST ROMANCE

Popular in the early sixties, the girl-group songs were certainly one important source of the ideas, feelings, and words of *romance* for the generation of feminists that grew up to criticize the concept. As we saw in the introduction, these criticisms centered on the passive role that romance, particularly in its more commercial manifestations, was thought to allot to women, and led to the accusation that female-oriented popular music was sexually repressive. This cultural criticism paralleled feminist criticism of the equation of femininity with sexual passivity and repression in Freudian psychoanalysis. The criticism extended to the "compulsory heterosexuality" of romance, to the focusing of all of a woman's attention on the one aim of getting and keeping a man, again paralleling the psychoanalysts' theory of female desire.

The analysis of these songs, which are certainly all romantic and heterosexual in surface orientation, has shown that the elaboration of romance in practice is not so simple, or so negative for women, as these criticisms suggest. The in-depth analysis of the relationship between chorus and lead singer implies that none of these songs is simply "for" romance: the songs are always *both for and against* it. The analysis of the pronoun sequences has shown that to construct a meaningful relationship between fantasy and reality is, for the girl subject, to construct a relationship between her own activity and passivity, and one that can work in different ways. If sexuality is in some important way to do with *activity*, the argument of this paper shows that romance cannot be construed as its opposite: passivity and repression. Certainly as constructed in the girl-group songs, romance is a complex of active sexual desire tempered by real needs, such as that for reciprocation.

Although the songs are all initially about, or addressed to, boys, we have seen that the most interesting conclusions emerge around the relationship of the girl singers to their female audience, not to a male one. We have also found that the appeal of these songs to teenage girls is bound up with an appropriation of maternal discourse by the girls' voices in the songs. This discourse itself divides, to be used both as the conventional social restraint on the overenthusiastic love of a girl for a "bad" boy, and as the language through which the girl can herself express love for her "baby," "little boy," or just her "boy."

There were many questions raised in the sixties that continue to nag a generation that considers itself beyond them. One of them is the position of women in love relationships with either sex, once the traditional framework of marriage has been rejected. When schoolgirls today talk of their desire to "live" before getting married,[24] they echo the feminist slogan/question "Is there life after marriage?" The implied opposition of "life before" and "death after" marriage recalls the Lacanian placing of women in relationship to the distinction between the imaginary and the symbolic. If the symbolic order rests on the patriarchal *exchange of women* in language and marriage systems, the search for a prolongation of "life" for women may well lead us to explore the imaginary as a sphere of fantasy associated with the mother.

In the field of popular culture, romance has been the typically feminine manifestation of the imaginary. For women, it represents a sphere of *choice* which can be opposed to the ending of choice in marriage, where the woman is symbolically *chosen by* the man. For married women, listening to popular music may, like romance reading, be an escapism which at the same time expresses dissatisfaction with their lot. But for teenagers, the relationship between symbolic and imaginary is reversed: they live for real what for others is a fantasy world. If this notion of the teenager is an invention of the postwar imagination, it denotes a social space "in between" the patriarchal control of parents and the symbolic order of marriage. To explore the acquisition of identity by teenage girls is, in an important sense, to be looking at subjectivity "outside," or in a different relation to, the symbolic order.

The imaginary does not of course exist in isolation, but only in relation to the symbolic. The exploration of fantasy and romance in these songs has been fundamentally an exploration of discourse, or the way in which language allows subjects to position themselves in relation to it. Female subjectivity and feminine discourse do not turn out to constitute a "separate sphere" beyond the constraints of the operation of language as we know it. But music, and the musical arrangement of singing voices, takes us to the borderline between symbolic and imaginary. The divided voices of the girl groups take us outside language as the authorial "voice" of a text, just as the oscillating activity and passivity of the girl subjects continually cross the borders of reality into fantasy. And if the songs can still be analyzed as and through language, the conclusions show that there are more possibilities in language than the patriarchal dominance of symbolic over imaginary proposed as universal by Lacan. The divided, female subjects of the girl groups enact the possibility of a less monolithic, more egalitarian relationship between the two.

NOTES

[1] R. Peterson and D. Berger, "Cycles in Symbol Production: The Case of Popular Music," *American Sociological Review 40* (April 1975).

[2] S. Frith and A. McRobbie, "Rock and Sexuality," *Screen Education*, No. 29 (1979), p. 13. (Included in the present volume.)

[3] Ibid., pp. 11, 18.

[4] A. McRobbie, "*Jackie:* An Ideology of Adolescent Femininity," stencilled Occasional Paper No. 53, Centre for Contemporary Cultural Studies, University of Birmingham, 1978.

[5] Frith and McRobbie, "Rock and Sexuality," p. 12.

[6] Ibid.

[7] For a similar view of music aimed at a female audience on daytime radio see R. Coward, *Female Desire: Women's Sexuality Today* (London: Paladin, 1984). Coward sees DJs as channeling female desire into family and marital concerns through "dedications" (see the Shirelles' introduction to "Dedicated to the One I Love"). And for a restatement of her condemnation of girl groups see McRobbie, "Peggy Sue Got Marketed," *Times Higher Educational Supplement* (3 June 1988)—where *age* as well as gender is a reason for deploring the young singers appealing to a preteen female audience, and Bananarama can be dismissed for sounding "like a group of girls upstairs on the bus home from school."

[8] On singing: A. Betrock, *Girl Groups: The Story of a Sound* (New York: Delilah, 1982); on songwriting: G. Marcus, "The Girl Groups," in J. Miller (ed.), *The Rolling Stone Illustrated History of Rock and Roll* (New York: Rolling Stone Press/Random House, 1976), pp. 160–61 (1981); and A. Pavletich, *Sirens of Song: The Popular Female Vocalist in America* (New York: Da Capo, 1980).

[9] L. Mulvey, "Visual Pleasure and Narrative Cinema," *Screen 16*, No. 3 (1975), pp. 6–18; Mulvey, "Afterthoughts on 'Visual Pleasure and Narrative Cinema,' " *Framework*, Nos. 15–17 (1981), pp. 12–15; J. Taylor and D. Laing, "Disco-Pleasure-Discourse: on 'Rock and Sexuality,' " *Screen Education*, No. 31 (Summer 1979).

[10] Betrock, *Girl Groups*; Pavletich, *Sirens of Song*.

[11] J. Lacan, *Ecrits: A Selection*, trans. Alan Sheridan (London: Tavistock & Norton, 1977).

[12] Marcus, "Girl Groups," p. 160.

[13] S. Frith, "The Voices of Women," *New Statesman* (13 November 1981).

[14] Pavletich, *Sirens of Song*, pp. 78, 92, 94, 77–80, 88.

[15] Betrock, *Girl Groups*, provides ample documentation of the high school careers of the girl-group singers, many of whom were only 15 or 16 when they made their hits.

[16] Taylor and Laing, "Disco-Pleasure-Discourse."

[17] Frith, "Voices of Women."

[18] B. Brady and B. Torode, "Song-work: The Inclusion, Exclusion and Representation of Women," paper delivered to the annual conference of the British Sociology Association, Manchester, 1981; Brady and Torode, "Pity Peggy Sue," *Popular Music 4* (1984).

[19] Marcus, "Girl Groups."

[20] Marcus's discography ends at 1965. I have added three post-1965 songs that have become classical girl-group numbers (through reissuing). Two other issues arose in selecting the sample. One was the question of how many men can be included in the group and have it still count as a girl group. The Ad Libs sound and look like a girl with a male backup group, but they have been marketed as a girl group. In their hit song, the lyrical content of the chorus's interchange with the lead singer is so much more appropriate to the context of an all-girl group than a mixed-sex one ("tell us 'bout the boy from New York City") that it seems fair to count it as a girl-group performance.

   The other question is where to draw the line between Motown female groups and girl groups. Marcus draws the line at the Marvellettes, while Betrock goes the other way and includes the Supremes. Motown themselves produced an extraordinary reissue compilation of girl groups that includes numerous solo numbers and does not include the Marvellettes' "Please Mr. Postman," a song that was the company's second-ever hit and certainly their most "girl-group." My own criteria have been, first, whether lyrics are "teen" and from the girl's point of view and, second, whether the musical arrangement involves the kind of competitive relationship between singer and chorus that is analyzed in the second half of this paper. On these grounds, I have included Martha and the Vandellas' "Heat Wave," but it may well be that there are other early Motown girl-group hits that have not been reissued.

[21] Betrock, *Girl Groups*, p. 136.

[22] A more relevant comparison for girl-group music may be with doo-wop, the mainly black, mainly male vocal group music which flourished in the second half of the fifties. The relatively prominent role of the chorus, or of the whole group singing in harmony, as well as the predominance of *fadeouts* rather than formal endings, are features in common. But the way these formal features are developed in girl-group music gives rise to meanings that are different from anything found in doo-wop. The voices of chorus and lead singer, although occasionally found in musical counterpoint, do not, as far as I have been able to ascertain, develop conflicting meanings in doo-wop. The name "doo-wop" comes from the nonverbal syllables that form the bulk of the chorus's part in this music. The chorus does not on the whole sing words, but if it does, they are "learned" from those of the lead singer; it seldom sings pronouns, and virtually never sings pronoun sequences of the sort discussed here in girl-group songs. The chorus is *supportive* of the lead singer's expressions of desire in doo-wop: it does not articulate a voice with desires of its own that could conflict with those of the lead singer.

[23] In my experience of playing this song to audiences, this has been listeners' preferred "hearing." This raises the question of how listeners do construct a single melody out of two voices singing in counterpoint, an aspect that Stefani does not address in his interesting paper on melody as the "everyday" appropriation of music. G. Stefani, "Melody: a Popular Perspective," *Popular Music 6*, No. 1 (1987).

[24] S. Lees, *Losing Out: Sexuality and Adolescent Girls* (London: Hutchinson, 1986), pp. 95–96.

PART SIX

Music and Sexuality

○ ▲ ○ ▲ ○ ▲ ○ ▲ ○ ▲ ○ ▲ ○

One aspect of rock that has always been taken for granted by its proselytes and detractors alike is that it is a form of music that somehow *means* sex. The assertion of a "natural" relationship between sound and sensuality rests on a confusion of musicological, psychological, and racist assumptions about rhythm and the body, about adolescence and desire, about Afro-American musical "primitivism." These assumptions began to be unpicked by feminists concerned to expose the gender prejudice of 1960s theories of "liberation" through sex and drugs and rock 'n' roll. The counterargument that rock in fact works to organize sexuality along clearly differentiated gender lines was summarized in Simon Frith and Angela McRobbie's 1978 article, which is reprinted here. The distinctions it draws, between "teenybop" and "cock rock," for example, seem slightly crude in retrospect and, in the end, the article is more obviously about gender than sexuality. It remains an important and influential article, though, if only because the even cruder assumptions it criticizes continue to inform much rock practice.

Two such assumptions are featured recurringly in academic studies of rock. The first goes back to the suggestion (already implied by Riesman) that the pop/rock distinction is a matter of gender, with female (pop) consumers being described as essentially "passive," in contrast to the discriminating, engaged, male audience for rock. The essential male address of "real" rock is thus taken for granted and embodied in the standard history of rock as a succession of bold male heroes. Sue Wise's article on Elvis Presley challenges this sort of mythmaking directly. She not only raises questions about what is involved in the "passivity" of female pop fans, but also suggests that the domination of rock writing by men has led to a version of pop history that is both ideologically and empirically suspect.

Sheryl Garratt, in a chapter from her and Sue Steward's pioneering history of women in pop, *Signed, Sealed and Delivered*, develops Sue Wise's critique of the concept of passive female consumption in a celebration of the collective excitement of her days as a Bay City Rollers' fan. It is notable that both Wise and Garratt, in trying to make sense of women's use of music and its contribution to their own sense of female sexuality, draw directly on memories and feelings. Male rock writers (and academic rock writers, in particular) strive for a different sort of authority—more detached, more "rational," more rooted in the spurious notion of rock "knowledge" (a memory for names and dates) that has solidified over the years.

The second assumption that pervades writing on rock concerns sound and sexuality. The suggestion here is that there is a direct relationship between the body and a 4:4 beat, that the guitar-wielding, pelvis-thrusting *rhythm* of rock and roll is the norm of sexual expression. Richard Dyer challenges this from the perspective of disco culture. His questions concern the music itself: How do rhythmic and melodic structures work to "express" sexuality? By contrasting disco to rock in terms of both musical organization and social setting, he suggests that, in the end, to understand the sexual charge of sounds we have to know how they are placed in fantasy—a point to which we will return.

Finally, in his 1984 afterword to "Rock and Sexuality," Simon Frith shows how discussion of music and sexuality changed in the 1980s, under the influence of both new sorts of male and female pop stars like Boy George and Madonna, Green and Annie Lennox, and new sorts of ethical gurus, like Michel Foucault and Roland Barthes. The issue now was not how rock liberated, repressed, or channeled sexuality, but how the music contributed to its ever-fluid construction.

Simon Frith and Angela McRobbie

ROCK AND SEXUALITY

1 9 7 8

○ ▲ ○ ▲ ○ ▲ ○

Of all the mass media rock is the most explicitly concerned with sexual expression. This reflects its function as a youth cultural form: rock treats the problems of puberty, it draws on and articulates the psychological and physical tensions of adolescence, it accompanies the moment when boys and girls learn their repertoire of public sexual behavior. If rock's lyrics mostly follow the rules of romance, its musical elements, its sounds and rhythms, draw on other conventions of sexual representation, and rock is highly charged emotionally even when its direct concern is nonsexual. Rock is the ever-present background of dancing, dating, courting. "Rock 'n' roll" was originally a synonym for sex, and the music has been a cause of moral panic since Elvis Presley first swiveled his hips in public. It has equally been a cause for the advocates of sexual permissiveness—the sixties counterculturalists claimed rock as "liberating," the means by which the young would free themselves from adult hangups and repression. For a large section of postwar youth, rock music has been the aesthetic form most closely bound up with their first sexual experiences and difficulties, and to understand rock's relationship to sexuality isn't just an academic exercise—it is a necessary part of understanding how sexual feelings and attitudes are learned.

Unfortunately, knowing that rock is important is not the same thing as knowing how it is important. The best writers on the subject state the contradictions without resolving them. On the one hand, there is something about rock that is experienced as liberating—in Sheila Rowbotham's words, sixties youth music was "like a great release after all those super-consolation ballads."[1] On the other hand, rock has become synonymous with a male-defined sexuality: "Under my thumb," sang the Stones, the archetypical rock group, "stupid girl."

Some feminists have argued that rock is now essentially a male form of expression, that for women to make nonsexist music it is necessary to use sounds, structures, and styles that cannot be heard as rock. This raises important questions about form and content, about the effect of male domination on rock's formal qualities as a mode of sexual expression. These are more difficult questions than is sometimes implied. Lyrics are not a sufficient clue to rock's meanings, nor can we deduce rock's sexual message directly from the male control of its conditions of production. Popular music is a complex mode of expression. It involves a combination of sound, rhythm, lyrics, performance, and image, and the apparently straightforward contrast that can be drawn, for example, between Tammy Wynette's "Stand By Your Man" (reactionary) and Helen Reddy's "I Am Woman" (progressive) works only at the level of lyrics. It doesn't do justice to the overall meanings of these records: Tammy Wynette's country strength and confidence seem, musically, more valuable qualities than Helen Reddy's cute, show-biz self-consciousness. We will return to this comparison later.

There are few clues, then, in the existing literature as to *how* rock works sexually. Left accounts of popular music focus either on its political economy or on its use in youth subcultures. In the former approach, rock's ideological content is derived from its commodity form; rock is explained as just another product of the mass entertainment industry. But if we confine ourselves to this approach alone, we cannot distinguish between the sexual messages of, say, the Stranglers and Siouxsie and the Banshees. The contrast between the former's offensive attempts to reassert stereotypes of male domination and the latter's challenge to those stereotypes is lost if we treat them simply as equivalent bestselling products of multinational record companies. The problem of analyzing the particular ideological work of a particular piece of music is avoided with the assumption that all commodities have the same effect.

In the subcultural approach rock's ideological meaning is derived, by contrast, from the culture of its consumers. The immediate difficulty here is that existing accounts of youth subcultures describe them as, on the one hand, exclusively male and, on the other hand, apparently asexual. But even a good culturalist account of rock would be inadequate for our purposes. Rock is not simply a cultural space that its young users can win for their own purposes. Rock, as an ideological and cultural form, has a crucial role to play in the process by which its users constitute their sexuality. It is that process we need to understand.

Our difficulty lies in the ease with which the analysis of rock as an aesthetic form can slip past the comparatively straightforward sociologies of record production and consumption. An obvious indication of this problem is the complex reference to the term "rock" itself. As rock fans we know what we mean by rock empirically, but the descriptive criteria we use are, in fact, diverse and inconsistent. "Rock" is not just a matter of musical definition. It refers also to an audience (young, white), to a form of production (commercial), to an artistic ideology (rock has a creative integrity that "pop" lacks). The result of this confusion is constant argument as to whether an act or record is really rock—and this is not just a matter of subjective disagreement.

Records and artists have contradictory implications in themselves. The meaning of rock is not simply given by its musical form, but is struggled for. As a cultural product, a rock record has multiple layers of representation. The message of its lyrics may be undercut by its rhythmic or melodic conventions and, anyway, music's meanings don't reach their consumers directly. Rock is mediated by the way its performers are packaged, by the way it is situated as radio and dance music. Rock reaches its public via the "gatekeepers" of the entertainment industry, who try to determine how people listen to it. The ideology of rock is not just a matter of notes and words.

One of the themes of this paper is that rock operates both as a form of sexual expression and as a form of sexual control. Expression and control are simultaneous aspects of the way rock works; the problem is to explain how rock gives ideological shape to its sexual representations. We reject the notion, central to the ideology of rock as counterculture, that there is some sort of "natural" sexuality which rock expresses and the blue meanies repress. Our starting point is that the most important ideological work done by rock is the *construction* of sexuality. We will describe rock's representations of masculinity and feminity and consider the contradictions involved in these representations. Our concern is to relate the effects of rock to its form—as music, as commodity, as culture, as entertainment.

MASCULINITY AND ROCK

Any analysis of the sexuality of rock must begin with the brute social fact that in terms of control and production, rock is a male form. The music business is male-run; popular musicians, writers, creators, technicians, engineers, and producers are mostly men. Female creative roles are limited and mediated through male notions of female ability. Women musicians who make it are almost always singers; the women in the business who make it are usually in publicity; in both roles success goes with a male-made female image. In general, popular music's images, values, and sentiments are male products.

Not only do we find men occupying every important role in the rock industry and in effect being responsible for the creation and construction of suitable female images, we also witness in rock the presentation and marketing of masculine styles. And we are offered not one definitive image of masculine sexuality, but a variety of male sexual poses which are most often expressed in terms of stereotypes. One useful way of exploring these is to consider "cock rock," on the one hand, and "teenybop," on the other.

By "cock rock" we mean music making in which performance is an explicit, crude, and often aggressive expression of male sexuality—it's the style of rock presentation that links a rock and roller like Elvis Presley to rock stars like Mick Jagger, Roger Daltrey, and Robert Plant.

Cock rock performers are aggressive, dominating, and boastful, and they constantly seek to remind the audience of their prowess, their control. Their stance is obvious in live shows; male bodies on display, plunging shirts and tight trousers, a visual emphasis on chest hair and genitals—their record sales depend on years of such appearances. In America, the Midwest concert belt has become the necessary starting point for cock rock success; in Britain the national popularity of acts like Thin Lizzy is the result of countless tours of provincial dance halls. Cock rock shows are explicitly about male sexual performance (which may explain why so few girls go to them—the musicians are acting out a sexual iconography which in many ways is unfamiliar, frightening, and distasteful to girls who are educated into understanding sex as something nice, soft, loving, and private). In these performances mikes and guitars are phallic symbols; the music is loud, rhythmically insistent, built around techniques of arousal and climax; the lyrics are assertive and arrogant, though the exact words are less significant than the vocal styles involved, the shouting and screaming.

The cock rock image is the rampant destructive male traveler, smashing hotels and groupies alike. Musically, such rock takes off from the sexual frankness of rhythm and blues but adds a cruder male physicality (hardness, control, virtuosity). Cock rockers' musical skills become synonymous with their sexual skills (hence Jimi Hendrix's simultaneous status as stud and guitar hero). Cock rockers are not bound by the conventions of the song form, but use their instruments to show "what they've got," to give vent to their macho imagination. These are the men who take to the streets, take risks, live dangerously and, most of all, swagger untrammeled by responsibility, sexual and otherwise. And, what's more, they want to make this clear. Women, in their eyes, are either sexually aggressive and therefore doomed and unhappy, or else sexually repressed and therefore in need of male servicing. It's the woman, whether romanticized or not, who is seen as possessive, after a husband, antifreedom, the ultimate restriction.

Teenybop, in contrast, is consumed almost exclusively by girls. What they're buying is also a representation of male sexuality (usually in the form of teen idols), but the nature of the image and the version of sexuality on display is quite distinct from that of the cock rocker. The teenybop idol's image is based on self-pity, vulnerability, and need. The image is of the young boy next door: sad, thoughtful, pretty, and puppylike. Lyrically his songs are about being let down and stood up, about loneliness and frustration; musically his form is a blend of pop ballad and soft rock; it is less physical music than cock rock, drawing on older romantic conventions. In teenybop, male sexuality is transformed into a spiritual yearning carrying only hints of sexual interaction. What is needed is not so much someone to screw as a sensitive and sympathetic soulmate, someone to support and nourish the incompetent male adolescent as he grows up. If cock rock plays on conventional concepts of male sexuality as rampant, animalistic, superficial, and just for the moment, teenybop plays on notions of female sexuality as serious, diffuse, and implying total emotional commitment. In teenybop cults live performance is less significant than pinups, posters, and TV appearances; in teenybop music, women emerge as unreliable, fickle, more selfish than men. It is men who are soft, romantic, easily hurt, loyal, and anxious to find a true love who fulfills their definitions of what female sexuality should be about.

The resulting contrast between, say, Thin Lizzy fans and David Soul fans is obvious enough, but our argument is not intended to give a precise account of the rock market. There are overlaps and contradictions. Girls put cock rock pinups on their bedroom walls, and boys buy teenybop records. Likewise there are a whole range of stars who seek to occupy both categories at once—Rod Stewart can come across just as pathetic, puppylike, and maudlin as Donny Osmond, and John Travolta can be mean and nasty, one of the gang. But our comparison of cock rock and teeny bop does make clear the general point we want to make: masculinity in rock is not determined by one all-embracing definition. Rather, rock offers a framework within which male sexuality can find a range of acceptable, heterosexual expressions. These images of masculinity are predicated on sexual divisions in the appropriation of rock. Thus we have the male consumer's identification with the rock performer; his collective experience of rock shows which, in this respect, are reminiscent of football matches and other occasions of male camaraderie—the general atmosphere is sexually exclusive, its euphoria depends on the absence of women. The teenybop performer, by contrast, addresses his female consumer as his object, potentially satisfying his sexual needs and his romantic and emotional demands. The teenybop fan should feel that her idol is addressing himself solely to her; her experience should be as his partner.

Elvin Bishop's "Fooled Around," a hit single from 1975 captures lyrically the point we're making:

> I must have been through about a million girls
> I love 'em and leave 'em alone,
> I didn't care how much they cried, no sir,
> Their tears left me as cold as stone,
> But then I fooled around and fell in love . . .

In rock conventions, the collective notion of fooling around refers explicitly to male experience; falling in love refers to the expectations of girls.

From this perspective, the contrast between cock rock and teenybop is clearly something general in rock, applicable to other genres. Male identity with the performer is expressed not only in sexual terms but also as a looser appropriation of rock musicians' dominance and power, confidence and control. It is boys who become interested in rock as music, who become hi-fi experts, who hope to become musicians, technicians, or music businessmen. It is boys who form the core of the rock audience, who are intellectually interested in rock, who become rock critics and collectors (the readership of *Sounds*, *New Musical Express*, and *Melody Maker* and the audience for the *Old Grey Whistle Test* are two-thirds male; John Peel's radio show listeners are 90 percent male). It is boys who experience rock as a collective culture, a shared male world of fellow fans and fellow musicians.

The problems facing a woman seeking to enter the rock world as a participant are clear. A girl is supposed to be an individual listener, she is not encouraged to develop the skills and knowledge to become a performer. In sixth form and student culture, just as much as in teenybop music, girls are expected to be passive, as they listen quietly to rock poets, and brood to Leonard Cohen, Cat Stevens, or Jackson Browne. Women, whatever their musical tastes, have little opportunity and get little encouragement to be performers themselves. This is another aspect of rock's sexual ideology of collective male activity and individual female passivity.

MUSIC, FEMININITY, AND DOMESTIC IDEOLOGY

Male dominance in the rock business is evident in both the packaging and the musical careers of female rock stars. Even powerful and individual singers like Elkie Brooks can find success only by using the traditional show-biz vocabulary. Indeed, one of the most startling features of the history of British popular music has been the speed with which talented women singers, of all types, from Lulu through Dusty Springfield to Kate Bush, have been turned into family entertainers, become regulars on TV variety shows, fallen into slapstick routines, and taken their show-biz places as smiling, charming hostesses. Female musicians have rarely been able to make their own musical versions of the oppositional rebellious hard edges that male rock can embody.

Our argument is not that male stars don't experience the same pressures to be bland entertainers, but that female stars have little possibility of resisting such pressure. It may have been necessary for Cliff Richard and Tommy Steele to become all-round entertainers in the 1950s, but one of the consequences of the rise of rock in the 1960s was that mass success was no longer necessarily based on the respectable conventions of show biz; sexual outrage became an aspect of rock's mass appeal. But for men only. The rise of rock did not extend the opportunities for women; notions of a woman's musical place have hardly changed. The one new success route opened to women was the singer/songwriter/folkie lady—long-haired, pure-voiced, self-accompanied on acoustic guitar—but whatever the ability, integrity, and toughness of Joan Baez, Judy Collins, Sandy Denny, and the others, their musical appeal, the way they were sold, reinforced in rock the qualities traditionally linked with female singers—sensitivity, passivity, and sweetness. For women rockers to become hard aggressive performers it was necessary for them, as Jerry Garcia commented on Janis Joplin, to become "one of the boys." Some women did make it this way—Grace Slick, Maggie Bell, Christine McVie—but none of them did it without considerable pain, frustration, and, in the case of Janis Joplin, tragedy.

Perhaps the only way of resisting the pressures pushing women musicians into conventional stereotypes (and stereotyping is an inevitable result of commercialization) was to do as Joni Mitchell did and avoid prolonged contact with the mass media. Since her success in the sixties, Joni Mitchell has consistently refused to do TV appearances, rarely does concerts, turns down interviews with the music press, and exerts personal control over the making and production of her records. She, like Joan Armatrading, is rewarded with an "awkward" reputation; despite their artistic achievements, theirs is not the popular image of the woman musician. For that we have to look at a group like ABBA. The boy/girl group is a common entertainment device in both pop and disco music (Coco, the Dooleys, on the one hand, Boney M and Rose Royce on the other). ABBA provides the clearest example of the sexual divisions of labor such groups involve: the men make the music (they write and arrange, play the guitars and keyboards), and the women are glamorous (they dress up and sing what they're told—their instruments are their "natural" voices and bodies). *ABBA: The Movie* had a double plot; while a journalist pursued the men in the group, the camera lingered on Anna's bum—it was the movie's key visual image. In rock, women have little control of their music, their images, their performances; to succeed they have to fit into male grooves. The subordination of women in rock is little different from their subordination in other occupations; as unskilled rock workers women are a source of cheap labor, a pool of talent from which the successes are chosen more for their appropriate appearance than for their musical talents.

But the problems of women in rock reach much further than those of surviving the business; oppressive images of women are built into the very foundations of the pop/rock edifice: into its production, its consumption, and even into its musical structures. Pop music reaches its public via a variety of gatekeepers—radio producers, TV producers, and film producers. Disc jockeys at discos and dances, and writers in music papers and girls' magazines compete to interpret musical meanings. The Bay City Rollers, for example, were taken by girls' magazines to represent vocally and visually their own persuasive sexual ideology, were heard to articulate the comic strip vocabulary of true love.

Teenage magazines have used pop star images, male and female, to illustrate their romantic fantasies and practical hints since their origin in the fifties. *Jackie*, for example, the highest-selling girls' weekly magazine in Great Britain, interprets music for its readers exclusively in terms of romance.[2] The magazine depends for its appeal on pop, carrying two or three large pop pinups each week; but it never actually deals with music. It doesn't review records and never hints that girls could learn an instrument or form a band, that they should take music seriously as either a hobby or a career. Music is reduced to its stars, to idols' looks and likes. Head-and-shoulder shots loom out of the center and back pages, symbols of dreamily smiling male mastery. Nothing else in *Jackie* is allowed such uncluttered space— even the cover girl has to compete for readers' attention with the week's list of features and offers. Pop stars, in *Jackie*'s account of them, are not just pretty faces. Romance rests on more than good looks; the stars also have "personality." Each pinup uses facial expression and background location to tell readers something about the star's character—David Essex's pert cheekiness, David Cassidy's crumpled sweetness, Les McKeowan's reassuring homeliness. There is an obvious continuity in the visual appeal of teenybop idols, from Elvis Presley to John Travolta—an unformed sensuality, something sulky and unfinished in the mouth and jaw, eyes that are intense but detached; sexiness—but sexiness that isn't physically rooted, that suggests a dreamy fantasy fulfillment. These images tell us more about the ideology of female than male sexuality; the plot is revealed in the home settings of *Jackie*'s photographs. Teenage music is not, after all, a matter of sex and drugs and carelessness; these stars are just like us—they're rich and successful and love their families, they come from ordinary pasts and have ordinary ambitions: marriage, settling down.

Girls are encouraged from all directions to interpret their sexuality in terms of romance, to give priority to notions of love, feeling, commitment, the moment of bliss. In endorsing these values girls prepare themselves for their lives as wives and mothers, where the same notions take on different labels—sacrifice, service, and fidelity. In Sue Sharpe's words:

> Women mean love and the home while men stand for work and the external world . . . women provide the intimate personal relationships which are not sanctioned in the work organisation . . . women are synonymous with softness and tenderness, love and care, something you are glad to come home from work to.[3]

Music is an important medium for the communication of this ideological message, and its influence extends much further than our analysis of teenybop has so far made clear. The BBC's daytime music shows on Radio 1 and 2, for example, are aimed primarily at housewives; their emphasis is consequently on mainstream pop, romantic ballads, and a lightweight bouncy beat. On these shows there is little new wave music, few of the progressive, heavy, punk, or reggae sounds which creep into the playlists once the kids, the students, the male workers, are thought to be back from school and class and job. The BBC's musically interesting programs are broadcast at night and the weekend, when men can listen, and this programming policy is shared by commercial stations. The recurrent phrase in radio producers' meetings remains: "We can't really play *that* to housewives!"

Music has a function for women at work too, as Lindsay Cooper has pointed out.[4] Many employers provide piped music or Radio 1 for their female employees—indeed, piped music in a factory is a good indicator of a female workforce—and the service industries in which women work (offices, shops) also tend to have pop as a permanent backdrop. Music, like clean and pretty industrial design, is thought to soften the workplace, making it homey and personal, increasing female productivity and lessening female job dissatisfaction. Pop's romantic connotations are not only important for socializing teenagers, they also function to bring the sphere of the personal, the home, into the sphere of the impersonal, the factory. Music feminizes the workplace; it provides women workers with aesthetic symbols of their domestic identity; it helps them discount the significance of the boring and futile tasks on which they're actually engaged. If talk, gossip, passing round photos, and displaying engagement rings indirectly help women overcome the tedium of their work, then the pop music supplied by management is a direct attempt to foster a feminine culture, in order to deflect women from more threatening collective activities as workers. Women's music at work, as much as girls' music at home, symbolizes the world that is "naturally" theirs—the world of the emotions, of caring, feeling, loving, and sacrificing.

There's a feature on Simon Bates's morning Radio 1 show in which listeners send in the stories they attach to particular records. Records are used as aural flashbacks, and they almost always remind Bates's listening women of one of the following moments:

- ▶ when we first met
- ▶ a holiday romance I'll never forget
- ▶ when we broke up
- ▶ when I told him I was pregnant
- ▶ when we got together again
- ▶ when he first kissed me / proposed / asked me out

This request spot illustrates with remarkable clarity how closely music is linked with women's emotional lives and how important music is in giving sexual emotions their romantic gloss. The teenybop mode of musical appropriation has a general resonance for the ideology of femininity and domesticity.

A similar argument could be made with reference to cock rock and male sexuality, showing how the values and emotions that are taken to be "naturally" male are articulated in all male-aimed pop music. But music is, in important respects, less important for male than for female sexual ideology. "Maleness" gets much of its essential expression in work, both manual and intellectual; it isn't, as "femaleness" is for women, confined to the aesthetic emotional sphere. Boys can express their sexuality more directly than girls; they are allowed to display physical as well as spiritual desire, to get carried away. The excitement of cock rock is suggestive not of the home and privacy but rather of the boozy togetherness of the boys who are, in Thin Lizzy's classic song, "back in town."

Of course male sex is no more "naturally" wild and uncontrollable than feminine sexuality is passive, meek, and sensitive. Both are ideological constructs, but there is a crucial difference in the way the ideologies and the musics work. Cock rock allows for direct physical and psychological expressions of sexuality; pop in contrast is about romance, about female crushes and emotional affairs. Pop songs aimed at the female audience deny or repress sexuality. Their accounts of relationships echo the comic strips in girls' comics, the short stories in women's magazines. The standard plots in all these forms are the same: the "ordinary" boy who turns out to be the special man, the wolf who must be physically resisted to be spiritually tamed, and so on. Ideologies of love are multimedia products, and teenage girls have little choice but to interpret their sexual feelings in terms of romance—few alternative readings are available.

This remains true even though we recognize that pop music is not experienced as an ideological imposition. Music is used by young people for their own expressive purposes, and girls, for example, use pop as a weapon against parents, schools, and other authorities. At school they cover their books with pop pinups, carve their idols' names on their desks, slip out to listen to cassettes or radios in the toilets. In the youth club, music is a means of distancing girls from official club activities. They use it to detach themselves from their club leaders' attempts to make them participate in "constructive" pursuits. The girls sit round their record players and radios, at home and school and youth club, and become unapproachable in their involvement with their music.

Music also gives girls the chance to express a collective identity, to go out *en masse*, to take part in activities unacceptable in other spheres. Unlike their brothers, girls have little chance to travel about together; as groups of girls they don't go to football matches, relax in pubs, get publicly drunk. Teenage girls' lives are usually confined to the locality of their homes; they have less money than boys, less free time, less independence of parental control. A live pop concert is, then, a landmark among their leisure activities. The Bay City Rollers' shows, for instance, used to give girls a rare opportunity to dress up in a noisy uniform, to enjoy their own version of football hooligan aggression.

These moments of teenybop solidarity are a sharp and necessary contrast to the usual use of pop records in bedroom culture: as the music to which girls wash their hair, practice makeup, and daydream; and as the background music of domestic tasks (babysitting, housework) which girls unlike boys are already expected to do. But the ritual "resistance" involved in these uses of music is not ideological. Rather, girls' use of teenybop music for their own purposes confirms the musical ideology of femininity. The vision of freedom on which these girls are drawing is a vision of the freedom to be individual wives, mothers, lovers, of the freedom to be glamorous, desirable male sex objects. For the contradictions involved in popular music's sexuality we have to look elsewhere, to the cock rock side of our ideal type distinction, to rock's ideological break with pop, to its qualities as beat music, its functions for dance.

ROCK CONTRADICTIONS

The audience for rock isn't only boys. If the music tends to treat women as objects, it does, unlike teenybop romance, also acknowledge in its direct physicality that women have sexual urges of their own. In attacking or ignoring conventions of sexual decency, obligation, and security, cock rockers do, in some respects, challenge the ways in which those conventions are limiting—to women as well as men. Women can contrast rock expression to the respectable images they are offered elsewhere—hence the feminist importance of the few female rock stars, such as Janis Joplin, hence the moral panics about rock's corrupting effects. The rock ideology of freedom from domesticity has an obvious importance for girls, even if it embodies an alternative mode of sexual expression.

There are ambiguities in rock's insistent presentation of men as sex objects. These presentations are unusually direct—no other entertainers flaunt their sexuality at an audience as obviously as rock performers. "Is there anybody here with any Irish in them?" Phil Lynott of Thin Lizzy asks in passing on the *Live and Dangerous* LP, "Is there any of the girls who would like a little more Irish in them?"

Sexual groupies are a more common feature of stars' lives in rock than in other forms of entertainment, and cock rock often implies female sexual aggression, intimates that women can be ruthless in the pursuit of *their* sex objects. Numerous cock rock songs—the Stones' for example—express a deep fear of women, and in some cases, like that of the Stranglers, this fear seems pathological, which reflects the fact that the macho stance of cock rockers is as much a fantasy for men as teenybop romance is for women.

Rock may be source and setting for collective forms of male toughness, roughness and noisiness, but when it comes to the individual problems of handling a sexual relationship, the Robert Plant figure is a mythical and unsettling model (in the old dance hall days, jealous provincial boys used to wait outside the dressing room to beat up the visiting stars who had attracted their women). Cock rock presents an ideal world of sex without physical or emotional difficulties, in which all men are attractive and potent and have endless opportunities to prove it. However powerfully expressed, this remains an ideal, ideological world, and the alternative teenybop mode of masculine vulnerability is, consequently, a complementary source of clues as to how sexuality should be articulated. The imagery of the cheated, unhappy man is central to sophisticated adult-oriented rock, and if the immediate object of such performers is female sympathy, girls aren't their only listeners. Even the most macho rockers have in their repertoires some suitably soppy songs with which to celebrate true (lustless) love—listen to the Stones' "Angie" for an example. Rock, in other words, carries messages of male self-doubt and self-pity to accompany its hints of female confidence and aggression.

Some of the most interesting rock performers have deliberately used the resulting sexual ambiguities and ironies. We can find in rock the image of the pathetic stud or the salacious boy next door, or, as in Lesley Gore's "You Don't Own Me," the feminist teenybopper. We can point too at the ambivalent sexuality of David Bowie, Lou Reed, and Bryan Ferry, at the camp teenybop styles of Gary Glitter and Suzi Quatro, at the disconcertingly "macho" performances of a female group like the Runaways. These refer-ences to the uses made of rock conventions by individual performers lead us to the question of form: How are the conventions of sexuality we've been discussing embodied in rock?

This is a complex question, and all we can do here is point to some of the work that needs to be done before we can answer it adequately. First, then, we need to look at the *history* of rock. We need to investigate how rock 'n' roll originally affected youthful presentations of sexuality and how these presentations have changed in rock's subsequent development.

Most rock analysts look at the emergence of rock 'n' roll as the only event needing explanation; rock 'n' roll's subsequent corruption and "emasculation" (note the word) are understood as a straightforward effect of the rock business's attempt to control its market or as an aspect of American institutional racism—and so Pat Boone got to make money out of his insipid versions of black tracks. But, from our perspective, the process of "decline"—the successful creation of teenybop idols like Fabian, the sales shift from crude dance music to well-crafted romantic ballads, the late fifties popularity of sweet black music and girl groups like the Shirelles—must be analyzed in equal detail. The decline of rock 'n' roll rested on a process of "feminization."

The most interesting sexual aspect of the emergence of British beat in the mid-sixties was its blurring of the by then conventional teenage distinction between girls' music—soft ballads—and boys' music—hard line rock 'n' roll. There was still a contrast between, say, the Beatles and the Stones— the one a girls' band, the other a boys' band—but it was a contrast not easily maintained. The British sound in general, the Beatles in particular, fused a rough R&B beat with yearning vocal harmonies derived from black and white romantic pop; the resulting music articulated simultaneously the conventions of feminine and masculine sexuality, and the Beatles' own image was ambiguous, neither boys-together aggression nor boy-next-door pathos. This ambiguity was symbolized in Lennon and McCartney's unusual use of the third person: "I saw *her* standing there," "*She* loves *you*." In performance, the Beatles did not make an issue of their own sexual status; they did not, despite the screaming girls, treat the audience as their sexual object.

The mods from this period turned out to be the most interesting of Britain's postwar youth groups, offering girls a more visible, active, and collective role (particularly on the dance floor) than had previous or subsequent groups and allowing boys the vanity, the petulance, the soft sharpness that are usually regarded as sissy. Given this, the most important thing about late sixties rock was not its well-discussed, countercultural origins, but the way in which it was consolidated as the central form of mass youth music in its cock rock form, as a male form of expression. The "progressive" music of which everyone expected so much in 1967–68 became, in its popular form, the heavy metal macho style of Led Zeppelin, on the one hand, and the technically facile hi-fi formula of Yes, on the other. If the commercialization of rock 'n' roll in the 1950s was a process of "feminization," the commercialization of rock in the 1960s was a process of "masculinization."

In the seventies, rock's sexual moments have been more particular in their effects but no less difficult to account for. Where did glam and glitter rock come from? Why did youth music suddenly become a means for the expression of sexual ambiguity? Rock was used this way not only by obviously arty performers like Lou Reed and David Bowie, but also by mainstream teenybop packages like the Sweet and by mainstream rockers like Rod Stewart.

The most recent issue for debate has been punk's sexual meaning. Punk involved an attack on both romantic and permissive conventions. In their refusal to let their sexuality be constructed as a commodity some punks went as far as to deny their sexuality any significance at all. "My love lies limp," boasted Mark Perry of Alternative TV. "What is sex anyway?" asked Johnny Rotten, "Just thirty seconds of squelching noises." Punk was the first form of rock not to rest on love songs, and one of its effects has been to allow female voices to be heard that are not often allowed expression on record, stage, or radio—shrill, assertive, impure individual voices, the sounds of singers like Poly Styrene, Siouxsie, Fay Fife of the Rezillos, Pauline of Penetration; punk's female musicians have a strident insistency that is far removed from the appeal of most postwar glamour girls. The historical problem is to explain their commercial success, to account for the punks' interruption of the longstanding rock equation of sex and pleasure.

These questions can only be answered by placing rock in its cultural and ideological context as a form of entertainment, but a second major task for rock analysts is to study the sexual language of its musical roots—rhythm and blues, soul, country, folk, and so on. The difficulty is to work out the relationship of form and content. Compare, for example, Bob Dylan's and Bob Marley's use of supporting women singers. Dylan is a sophisticated rock star, the most significant voice of the music's cultural claims, including its claims to be sexually liberating. His most recent lyrics, at least, reflect a critical self-understanding that isn't obviously sexist. But musically and visually his backup trio are used only as a source of glamour, their traditional pop use. Marley is an orthodox Rastafarian, subscribes to a belief, an institution, a way of life in which women have as subordinate a place as in any other sexually repressive religion. And yet Marley's I-Threes sing and present themselves with grace and dignity, with independence and power. In general, it seems that soul and country musics, blatantly sexist in their organization and presentation, in the themes and concerns of their lyrics, allow their female performers an autonomous musical power that is rarely achieved by women in rock.

We have already mentioned the paradoxes in a comparison of Tammy

Wynette's "Stand By Your Man" and Helen Reddy's "I Am Woman." The lyrics of "Stand By Your Man" celebrate women's duty to men, implore women to enjoy subordinating themselves to men's needs—lyrically the song is a ballad of sexual submissiveness. But the female authority of Tammy Wynette's voice involves a knowledge of the world that is in clear contrast to the gooey idealism of Helen Reddy's sound. "Sometimes it's hard to be a woman," Tammy Wynette begins, and you can hear that it's hard and you can hear that Tammy Wynette knows why—her voice is a collective one. "I am woman," sings Helen Reddy, and what you hear is the voice of an idealized consumer, even if the commodity for consumption in this instance is a package version of women's liberation.

This comparison raises the difficult issue of musical realism. It has long been commonplace to contrast folk and pop music by reference to their treatments of "reality." Pop music is, in Hayakawa's famous formula, a matter of "idealization/frustration/demoralization"; a folk form like the blues, in contrast, deals with "the facts of life."[5] Hayakawa's argument rested on analysis of lyrics, but the same point is often made in musical terms—it is a rock-critical cliché, for example, to compare the "earthy" instrumentation of rhythm and blues with the "bland" string arrangements of Tin Pan Alley pop. A. L. Lloyd rests his assessment of the importance of folk music (contrasted with the "insubstantial world of the modern commercial hit") on its truth to the experience of its creators. If folk songs contain "the longing for a better life," their essence is still consolation, not escapism:

> Generally the folk song makers chose to express their longing by transposing the world on to an imaginative plane, not trying to escape from it, but colouring it with fantasy, turning bitter, even brutal facts of life into something beautiful, tragic, honourable, so that when singer and listeners return to reality at the end of the song, the environment is not changed but they are better fitted to grapple with it.[6]

Consolation derived not just from folk songs' lyrical and aesthetic effects, but also from the collective basis of their creation and performance: women's songs, for example, became a means of sharing the common experience of sexual dependence and betrayal. This argument can be applied to the realistic elements of a commercial country performance like Tammy Wynette's. But the problem remains: Is musical realism simply a matter of accurate description and consequent acceptance of "the way things are," or can it involve the analysis of appearances, a challenge to "given" social forms?

In analyzing the sexual effects of rock, a further distinction needs to be made between rock realism—the use of music to express the experience of "real" sexual situations—and rock naturalism—the use of music to express "natural" sexuality. An important aspect of rock ideology is the argument that sexuality is asocial, that music is a means of spontaneous physical expression which is beset on all sides by the social forces of sexual repression. Rhythm, for example, the defining element of rock as a musical genre, is taken to be naturally sexual.

What this means is unclear. What would be the sexual message of a cock rock dancing classic like "Honky Tonk Women" if its lyrics were removed? Rock's hard beat may not, in itself, speak in terms of male domination, power, or aggression, but the question is whether it says anything, in itself. Rock critics describe beat as "earthy" or "bouncy" or "sensual" or "crude," and so reach for the sorts of distinctions we need to make, but such descriptive terms reflect the fact that rhythmic meaning comes from a musical and ideological context.

We can best illustrate the complexities of musical sexuality with another comparison—between Kate Bush's "Feel It" and Millie Jackson's "He Wants to Hear the Words." Kate Bush is the English singer/songwriter who became famous with "Wuthering Heights." "Feel It" is a track on her debut album, *The Kick Inside*, and is, lyrically, a celebration of sexual pleasure:

> After the party, you took me back to your parlour
> A little nervous laughter, locking the door
> My stockings fall on the floor, desperate for more
> Nobody else can share this
> Here comes one and one makes one
> The glorious union, well, it could be love,
> Or it could be just lust but it will be fun
> It will be wonderful.

But, musically, the track draws on conventions that are associated not with physical enjoyment but with romantic self-pity. Kate Bush performs the song alone at her piano. She uses the voice of a little girl and sounds too young to have had any sexual experience—the effect is initially titillating; her experience is being described for *our* sexual interest. But both her vocal and her piano lines are disrupted, swooping, unsteady; the song does not have a regular melodic or rhythmic structure, even in the chorus, with its lyrical invocation of sexual urgency. Kate Bush sings the lyrics with an unsettling stress—the words that are emphasized are "nervous," "desperate," "nobody else." The effect of the performance is to make listeners voyeurs, but what we are led to consider is not a pair of lovers but an adolescent sexual fantasy. The music contradicts the enjoyment that the lyrics assert. Kate Bush's aesthetic intentions are denied by the musical conventions she uses.

Millie Jackson is a black American musician who has made a career out of the celebration of adult sexual pleasure. Her performances are put together around long risqué raps and her stance, in the words of *Spare Rib*, is somewhere between Wages for Housework and *Cosmopolitan*. "He Wants to Hear the Words" is a routine song on Millie Jackson's LP *Get It Outcha' System*. She sings the song to a new lover; "he" is the man she lives with:

> He wants to hear the words, needs to know that it's for real.
> He wants to hear me say that I love him in every way,
> Though he knows he's got a hold on me and I will stay.
> How can I tell him what I told you last night?

The song has a pretty tune, a gentle beat, and a delicate string arrangement. It has the conventional sound of an unhappy romantic ballad. But the passivity of this form is contradicted by the self-conscious irony of Millie Jackson's own performance. She gives the corny situation an interest that is not inherent in the song itself. She uses gospel conventions to express direct emotion, she uses her own customary mocking tone of voice to imply sexual need, and the effect is not to make the song's situation seem "real" (the usual way in which great soul singers are said to transcend banal musical material) but to reverse its meaning. Millie Jackson is so obviously in control of her torn-between-two-lovers life that it is the man she lives with who becomes the figure of pathos—so desperate for deception, so easy to deceive. Millie Jackson's contempt for her man's dependence on romance becomes, implicitly, a contempt for the song itself, and its own expression of romantic ideology. It is impossible to listen to her performance without hearing it as a "performance." Millie Jackson contradicts the sexual meaning of the song's musical form in her very use of it.

SEXUAL EXPRESSION / SEXUAL CONTROL

The recurrent theme of this essay has been that music is a means of sexual expression and as such is important as a mode of sexual control. Both in its presentation and in its use, rock has confirmed traditional definitions of what constitutes masculinity and femininity, and reinforces their expression in leisure pursuits. The dominant mode of control in popular music (the mode which is clearly embodied in teenybop culture) is the ideology of romance, which is itself the icing on the harsh ideology of domesticity. Romance is the central value of show biz and light entertainment, and in as far as pop musicians reach their public through radio, television, and the press, they express traditional show-biz notions of glamour, femininity, and so forth. These media are crucial for establishing the appeal of certain types of pop star (Tom Jones, Gilbert O'Sullivan, Elton John, etc.), and they are particularly significant in determining the career possibilities of female musicians, as discussed earlier in this essay.

It was against this bland show business background that rock was, and is, experienced as sexually startling. Rock, since its origins in rock 'n' roll, has given youth a more blatant means of sexual expression than is available elsewhere in the mass media and has therefore posed much more difficult problems of sexual control. Rock's rhythmic insistence can be heard as a sexual insistence, and girls have always been thought by mass moralists to be especially at risk; the music so obviously denies the concept of feminine respectability. In short, the ideology of youth developed in the 1960s by rock (among other media) had as its sexual component the assumption that a satisfying sexual relationship meant "spontaneity," "free expression," and the "equality of pleasure"; sex in many ways came to be thought of as *best* experienced outside the restrictive sphere of marriage, with all its notions of true love and eternal monogamy. The point is, however, that this was a male-defined principle and at worst simply meant a greater emphasis on male sexual freedom. Rock never was about unrestricted, unconfined sexuality. Its expression may not have been controlled through the domestic ideology basic to pop as entertainment, but it has had its own mode of control, a mode which is clearly embodied in cock rock and which can be related to the general ideology of permissiveness that emerged in the sixties: the "liberated" emphasis on everyone's right to sexual choice, opportunity, and gratification.

One of the most important activities to analyze if we're going to understand how sexual ideology works is dancing. The dance floor is the most public setting for music as sexual expression, and it is the place where pop and rock conventions overlap; for teenybop girls music is for dancing, and rock, too, for all its delusions of male grandeur, is still essentially a dance form. Girls have always flocked to dance halls, and their reasons haven't just been to find a husband; dance is the one leisure activity in which girls and young women play a dominant role. Dancing for them is creative and physically satisfying. But more than this, dancing is also a socially sanctioned sexual activity—at least it becomes so when the boys, confident with booze, leave the bar and the corners to look for a partner from the mass of dancing girls.

One function of dance as entertainment, from Salome to Pan's People, has been to arouse men with female display, but this is not a function of most contemporary youth dancing—it remains an aspect of girls' own pleasure, even in the cattle-market context of a provincial dance hall. The girls are still concerned with attracting the lurking boys, but through their clothes, makeup, and appearance—not through their dancing. This is equally true of boys' dances—their energy and agility are not being displayed to draw girls' attention; the most dedicated young dancers in Britain, the Northern soul fans, are completely self absorbed.

The concept of narcissism, like that of realism, raises more difficult questions than we can answer here, but we do need to make one concluding point: rock's sexual effect is not just on the construction of femininity and masculinity. Rock also contributes to the more diffuse process of the sexualization of leisure.

The capitalist mode of production rests on a double distinction: between work and pleasure, between work and home. The alienation of the worker from the means of production means that the satisfaction of her or his needs becomes focused on leisure, on the one hand, and family on the other. Under capitalism, sexual expression is constituted as an individual leisure need—compare precapitalist modes of production, in which sexual expression is an aspect of a collective relationship with nature. This has numerous consequences—the exchange of sex as a commodity, the exchange of commodities as sex—and means that we have to refer mass entertainment (films as well as music) to a theory of leisure as well as to a theory of ideology.

In writing this paper we have been conscious of our lack of an adequate theory of leisure. Underlying our analysis of rock and sexuality have been some nagging questions. What would nonsexist music sound like? Can rock be nonsexist? How can we counter rock's dominant sexual messages? These issues aren't purely ideological, matters of rock criticism. The sexual meaning of rock can't be read off independently of the sexual meaning of rock consumption, and the sexual meaning of rock consumption derives from the capitalist organization of production. In this essay we have described the ways in which rock constitutes sexuality for its listeners. Our last point is that sexuality is constituted in the very act of consumption.

NOTES

[1] Sheila Rowbotham, *Woman's Consciousness, Man's World* (London: Penguin, 1973) pp. 14–15.

[2] A 1967 issue of *Petticoat* magazine went so far as to urge girls to stop buying records and spend the money they saved on clothes, holidays, and makeup. "Borrow records from your boyfriend instead," the magazine suggested.

[3] Sue Sharpe, *Just Like a Girl* (London: Penguin, 1976).

[4] Lindsay Cooper, "Women, Music, Feminism," *Musics* (October 1977).

[5] S. I. Hayakawa, "Popular Songs vs. the Facts of Life," in B. Rosenberg and D. M. White (eds.), *Mass Culture* (New York: Free Press, 1957).

[6] A. L. Lloyd, *Folk Song in England* (London: Paladin, 1975), p. 170.

SEXING ELVIS

1 9 8 4

○ ▲ ○ ▲ ○ ▲ ○

"Whose are all those *ELVIS* records? Argh!" is a commonly heard question in my home, and always has been ever since it has been regularly frequented by feminists. I usually reply, sheepishly, "Well actually, er um, they're mine . . . but I never *listen* to them anymore!" "But how could *you* have ever *been* an Elvis fan?" is the predictable next question. "I was very young" I excuse myself, and this is usually enough to get me off the hook. Yet I know that if the truth was known—that I am still fond of Elvis's memory, that I love the records, that I still own a very large scrapbook of clippings, photos, and so on that I cannot bring myself to part with—then my feminist credibility would be open to question, my credentials reexamined, and my "right on–ness" wondered about in the light of this new information. And so it is not without some trepidation that I come out here for the first time publicly as—an *ELVIS FAN*.

Elvis Presley may not rank highly in most feminists' list of interesting and important subjects and, indeed, many have probably never given him a second thought. I hope it will be apparent from what follows that this essay is not "about" Elvis per se. Rather, I have taken my own involvement with Elvis as the topic for analysis, working from the starting point that to be a feminist *and* an Elvis fan is problematic, given the prevailing view of each that currently exists.

Tracing the strands of this involvement has raised ideas and problems for me which I take to be crucial for my own feminist understanding of the world. Among these are the relationship between subjective and objective accounts of reality and the existence of a powerful feminist orthodoxy which, paradoxically, accepts objective and "male" accounts of the world at the expense of personal and subjective experiences. And so although I examine this specifically in relation to competing constructions of "who" and "what" "Elvis" and "the Elvis phenomenon" was, the same kinds of things can (and should) be said about other features of many feminists' experience. These issues, clearly, are of interest to us all, including those of us who have never even heard of Elvis Presley.

And so, to begin at the beginning, I pose the same question—how is it possible for me to be, at one and the same time, a feminist *and* an Elvis fan?

ELVIS THE BUTCH GOD

That Elvis is portrayed as a macho folk hero is easily apparent from any number of written accounts:

> The teddy boys were waiting for Elvis Presley. Everyone under twenty all over the world was waiting. He was the super salesman of mass distribution-hip . . . he was a public butch god with the insolence of a Genet murderer. . . . Most of all he was unvarnished sex taken and set way out in the open. . . . The Presley riots were the first spontaneous gatherings of the community of the new sensibilities.[1]

This quotation beautifully encapsulates the main elements, posited over and over again, which supposedly explain Elvis's impact on popular culture. First, it suggests that Elvis's impact had worldwide cultural significance. Second, it assumes that his appeal was to young people, inciting them in rebellion against the "old order" of adults, thus creating or expressing a "generation gap." And, third, it also assumes that the central component of this extraordinary impact was his expression of rampant male sexuality.

The cultural significance of the emergence of Elvis in the 1950s is never doubted by those who write about him:

> Before Elvis, rock had been a gesture of vague rebellion. Once he'd happened, it immediately became solid, self-contained, and then it spawned its own style in clothes and language and sex, a total independence in almost everything—all the things that are now taken for granted. This was the major breakthrough and Elvis triggered it. In this way, without even trying, he became one of the people who have radically affected the way that people think and live.[2]

In such accounts the 1950s are depicted as a time of stagnation, with a postwar younger generation disillusioned by the war and looking for a symbol of rejection of the past and hope for the future. That change, that revolution, which youth throughout the world was waiting for was, they suggest, epitomized in the expression of Elvis's sexuality. Consider this:

> Always, he came back to sex. In the earlier generations, singers might carry great sex appeal but they'd have to cloak it under the trappings of romanticism, they'd never spell anything out. By contrast, Elvis was blatant. When those axis hips got moving, there was no more pretence about moonlight and hand-holding; it was hard physical fact.[3]

There are any number of accounts like this, which purport to describe the atmosphere of the 1950s and the consequent impact of Elvis on a world which was "waiting" for a modern, *positive*, exciting challenge to the old order. That this "challenge" should turn out to be an uncontrolled and rampant male sexuality is invariably accepted as unproblematic by the male writers who wax lyrical about Elvis's hips and "revolutionary" impact:

> Presley's breakthrough was that he was the first male white singer to propose that fucking was a desirable activity in itself and that, given sufficient sex appeal, it was possible for a man to lay girls without any of the traditional gestures or promises. . . . He was the master of the sexual simile, treating his guitar as both phallus and girl, punctuating his lyrics with the animal grunts and groans of the male approaching an orgasm. He made it quite clear that he felt he was doing any woman he accepted a favour. He dressed to emphasize both his masculinity and basic narcissism, and rumour had it that into his skin-tight jeans was sewn a lead bar to suggest a weapon of heroic proportions.[4]

"The revolution" seems to be war under the name of sex, with the phallus (of course a heroic one!) as the main weapon—so guess who is the enemy?

Elvis's appeal is traditionally depicted as an appeal to young girls who, overwhelmed by his animal magnetism, were able to lose their sexual inhibitions and, albeit in the safety of a concert hall, "respond" to being turned on by the male sexual hero, a response in which they displayed mass (sexual) hysteria. But some of the preceding quotations suggest very clearly the rarely mentioned and never analyzed impact that Elvis had on boys. It was the teddy *boys* who were "waiting" for Elvis, it was young *men* who identified with him and his supposed ability to "lay girls" with ease and without consequence. It is no coincidence that the male archivists of popular culture were only interested in Elvis while he represented their sexual fantasies. Although he had a career of over twenty years, male writers dwell upon only the first couple of these, when they can identify with the super butch sexual hero that they themselves have promoted and lauded. And when their folk hero loses his "potency" as they see Elvis as doing, they look to explanations outside of his control in order to explain his "downfall," just as they do for other "failed" rock stars:

> What is interesting is that his appeal in the first place was to young males. . . .
> Each successive pop music explosion has come roaring out of the clubs in which

it was born like an angry young bull. . . . Commercial exploitation advances towards it holding out a bucketful of recording contracts, television appearances and world-wide fame. Then, once the muzzle is safely buried in the golden mash, the cunning butcher nips deftly along the flanks and castrates the animal. . . . The trick is to shift the emphasis so that the pop idol, originally representing a masculine rebel, is transformed into a masturbation fantasy-object for adolescent girls.[5]

Perhaps this is where I come in.

ELVIS THE TEDDY BEAR

I've always been an Elvis fan. My mother loves to embarrass me by telling how I used to jig around in my pram when his records came on the radio (perhaps a mum's poetic license, as I was born in 1953 and at least a toddler before Elvis arrived on the scene). This story demonstrates how, within my family, I was identified as an Elvis fan and this was seen as an important part of my life.

I must have been about eleven or twelve when Elvis became for me a full-time preoccupation and hobby. By this age I was able to actively seek out all things Elvis. I saved spending money to buy his records, see his films, buy fan magazines, and stick posters on my bedroom walls. My closest childhood friend was also an Elvis fan and we would spend hours discussing him, listening to records, and swapping pictures and stories. But mostly my interest in Elvis took the form of a solitary hobby, a private thing between "him" and me. If I spent large amounts of my time in my (shared) bedroom alone fixing pictures in my scrapbook, this was OK because I was absorbed in my "hobby." So it was also a way of spending a considerable time alone in an overcrowded household which was accepted as legitimate by my family.

I remained actively interested in Elvis throughout my teens, up until the age of twenty or twenty-one, when I "got feminism." The "getting of feminism" was, for me, a fairly lengthy process. Not for me any shattering bolt of lightning, but instead a slow and gradual reshaping of my view of the world brought about by things I read, talked about, and heard over a couple of years, as this was sifted through my own unique biographical history, experience, and consciousness. During this period I, of course, began to reconstrue present and past events in a new light.

The overwhelming feature of this period in my life is that of rejection. So many things were reconstrued and rejected at this time, when I had a sort of clearing out of twenty years of accumulated sexist junk. And of course feminism touched every inch and every aspect of my existence, from relationships to the way that I looked, to my goals and ambitions in life, to the things that were dear to my heart. And so at the same time that I came out as a lesbian, threw out the frocks and makeup, changed my career and stopped feeling obliged to be interested in men, I also rejected Elvis.

This rejection of Elvis along with the rest is interesting to me in retrospect. I had never analyzed my fondness for or interest in him as I grew up. He was just there as an important part of my life—he had always been important to me and I had never questioned how or why (or the exact nature of the "him" I was interested in). Similarly, when the time came to leave him behind I did it without question or analysis. All I knew was that he did not fit into my new-found beliefs and was frowned upon by my newly acquired peers.

I don't remember reading or hearing any specific feminist analysis which said that "Elvis can seriously damage your health." Occasional feminist references to rock music in general invariably pointed the finger at the Rolling Stones and Elvis as epitomizing the male-dominated, woman-hating bias of rock music. But the main pressure came from incredulous friends, who were always quick to point out the ideological impurity of Elvis—they never explained why, beyond somehow embodying in person the message of the "feminist finger," and I never asked. I guess we all thought we knew what the problem was without having to spell it out—Elvis was the very worst kind of male superhero—no further explanation was necessary. Somehow (quite how I don't know) Elvis was a central part of the patriarchal plot, for "Elvis" consisted of a social phenomenon and personal image which downgraded women by elevating the male macho hero to unprecedented heights. And of course being a "fan" of any description was also highly suspect, unless the "star" was a certified right-on woman like Dory Previn or Joan Armatrading, for "being a fan" was to collude in one's own oppression.

This took place during what I call my "zealot" period, when I rejected many things from my past because they did not fit neatly into my new way of life. My feminist consciousness acted as an all-purpose purgative; having expurgated myself of all unwholesome things past I had achieved the desired effect: I felt pure, newly born, I fit in with feminst friends, my life was an integrated whole.

Integrity is vital to sanity, as any woman knows only too well. But as the years went by echoes of my past (in the voice of Elvis?) have from time to time surfaced, demanding to be analyzed and explained. Such a thing occurred in 1977 when Elvis died. I was surprised at how much his death touched me. I hadn't thought about him for years; as far as I was concerned he was a relic of a past "false consciousness." And yet his death was terribly significant to me and it made me very sad. Of course it said something about my own mortality, about the fact that I was growing older. Elvis had always been around and suddenly his not being around anymore was a reminder of time moving along and death coming closer to us all. But it was also more than that.

I felt I had lost something that was very special and dear to me, something that had played an important part in my life. As a now mature feminist something simply didn't fit—I had to try and understand why I was sad. Why was I grieving for a "butch god" when he represented everything that I loathed and fought against? Was it just nostalgia, a yearning for my youth, or was it more than this?

In order to answer these questions for myself I turned to the proliferation of books and articles that appeared to cash in on his disintegration and then death. And, yes, there it was in black and white—Elvis the butch god, Elvis the phallus, Elvis the macho folk hero. And then I turned to my own mementos of Elvis; I listened to the records and I dragged out the scrapbooks (significantly, I had never been able to completely discard these and they had been relegated to dusty shelves and cupboards).

As I listened to records and delved into clippings, cuttings, and photos they evoked memories and feelings from my youth. And the memories that were evoked had nothing to do with sex, nothing even to do with romance. The overwhelming feelings and memories were of warmth and affection for a very dear friend.

As an adolescent I had been a very lonely person, never feeling that I fit in anywhere, never "connecting" with another human being. In later years I understood this in terms of my early awareness of being gay, but at the time it was just confusing. Elvis filled a yawning gap in my life in many different ways. He was an interesting hobby when life was boring and meaningless. He was a way of being acceptably "different" because it simply wasn't fashionable to be an Elvis fan when I was one. Most of all he was another human being to whom I could relate and be identified with. When I felt lonely and totally alone in the world, there was always Elvis. He was a private, special friend who was always there, no matter what, and I didn't have to share him with anybody. He was someone to care about, to be interested in, and to defend against criticism. In my own private Elvis world I could forget that I was miserable and lonely by listening to his records and going to see his films. Some people who feel so alone in an alien world turn to religion or to drink or to football teams to give their lives purpose. I turned to Elvis; and he was always there and he never let me down.

This experience of Elvis is one I find difficult to explain, but I know it is one which was shared by many other people. Flipping through the pages of *Elvis Monthly*'s and remembering conversations with other fans reminds me time and again that very many female *and* male fans experienced Elvis in this way. For us Elvis the macho superhero might just as well have been another and totally different person, for he certainly wasn't *our* Elvis.

WILL THE REAL ELVIS PRESLEY . . .

The two accounts of Elvis, as butch god and as teddy bear, are so dissimilar that one could be forgiven for thinking that they describe two different people. But of course they are describing the same person from two quite different perspectives, and *neither* can be said to be the "true" or "real" picture of what Elvis "meant" in terms of popular culture. Some people will have experienced Elvis as I did; to some he will have been a butch god;[6] and to others he will have meant very little or nothing at all. Yet archivists do not present such a relativist view. On the contrary, the overwhelming feature of their accounts is their similarity, their complete accord that Elvis was first and last about rampant male sexuality. But once we accept that some people did not experience him in this way (as I didn't), it becomes interesting to ponder the question of how such a one-sided view came into being, why it gained the currency that it did, and why it has remained largely unquestioned for so long.

I have already suggested that most writers about Elvis, then and now, are men; and it remains true that women have written very little about him. The first component in this artful construction of Elvis is therefore the simple and familiar one to feminists: that of men interpreting and encoding knowledge, in their own interests and after their own image, and then calling this an objective account of the world as it truly is.

The second feature of this construction is the careful selection of particular bits of Elvis's career to support their theories. Elvis had a show business career spanning over twenty years, and yet these writers invariably focus on only the first couple of years as the most significant and important part of it. This period is seen as representing the elemental Elvis, the sexual hero who is subsequently "castrated" by the American army/commercial exploitation/his manager/his mother (take your pick), leaving just a eunuch/teddy bear/pap for adolescent teenage consumption. It's this that they mean when they talk about Elvis's appeal having first been to men and why they feel so betrayed by all the rest—the "real" Elvis, their Elvis, got taken away from them.

Elvis's rise to fame was inextricably linked with the moral panic surrounding the behavior of women and girls at his live performances. They screamed and cried and lost control in large numbers (and must have presented a quite stupendous spectacle in their own right, just as with the female response to the Beatles later). The media found it disturbing on one level, but they also loved it and fueled and fostered it. Since this kind of mass crowd expression of power from women and girls was supposedly both unprecedented and unthinkable, explanations for it were sought. What better way to explain the frightening spectacle of hordes of uncontrollable females than by "discovering" that they were only responding to being sexually stimulated and manipulated by a man—literally *man*-ipulated.

How suitable! How unthreatening! And how ego-stroking for the men who looked on approvingly. By turning Elvis from what in effect he was— an *object* of his fans—into a *subject*, the girls' behavior was de-threatened and controlled. It was but a small "logical" step from here to say that if Elvis could do this then what he represented must be the phallus—after all, it must have been something rather wonderful to produce this reaction in girls, and what is more wonderful than the phallus? Lead bar in his trousers or no, when these male writers saw him on stage they saw a "weapon" of "heroic" proportions, for how else could he have this effect on women? Paradoxically, there was nothing new about this at all, for Elvis was merely invested with all the properties and preoccupations that had previously been reserved as a stereotype for black men. So not only did this view of Elvis explain away threatening women, it also transformed folk devil into folk hero in a way that was extremely ego-enhancing to white men.

The main point about all of the foregoing is that it is about *men*. It was men who claimed Elvis as their butch god, men who bathed in his reflected glory, men who felt betrayed when the girls stopped screaming, men who depicted this phallic hero as having worldwide cultural significance. What women thought then and now is largely unknown because, quite simply, no one bothered to ask or even thought that our views were worth anything. After all, what is the point in talking to someone, let alone taking what they say seriously, who merely *reacts* to male cues?

This version of Elvis is so widespread and accepted that it is difficult to question it without firsthand knowledge of what "really" happened. For all practical purposes it is the only extended version of "Elvis" that exists. And it demonstrates how people who are involved in the production of "knowledge" find exactly what they set out to look for—by looking in selective places, asking only some questions and ignoring, or failing to see, information that is uncomfortable or doesn't fit. And this is something which we, as feminists, must recognize: that is, we must never take anything on trust, we must ask our own questions, seek out our own knowledge, and always look gift horses, in the form of other people's knowledge, firmly in the mouth.

Perhaps feminists have adopted the butch god version of Elvis because there just hasn't been another version available to those who didn't go through the kinds of experiences that I did. Yet it still seems paradoxical to me that *feminists*, myself included, have taken over these *male* ideas about rock music without ever bothering to ask how women experienced this phenomenon. Feminism was supposed to be about questioning all male constructions of reality and knowledge, about reworking male common-sense understandings of the world. In the case of Elvis, male writers have taken their subjective sexual fantasies and turned them into "objective fact." And feminists have gone along with this—the media hype has succeeded, the image swallowed, the feminist reworking left undone.

There is still much feminist reworking and challenging to be done, and I have used my personal experience of a public phenomenon as an example of a totally taken-for-granted view of reality which is open to a different interpretation. It is in the examination of personal experience that the disjuncture between subjective and objective realities is most clearly seen. Feminist reclaiming and renaming of the world is still important and necessary, and when it does take place it invariably reveals deep complexity and multiple reality, and raises many interesting questions. Of course it's only the beginning of doing this around "Elvis" that appears here, but I hope that making an analytic version of my experience available to other people has shown that even beginnings can be interesting!

NOTES

[1] Jeff Nuttall, *Bomb Culture* (London: Paladin, 1969), pp. 29–30.
[2] Nik Cohn, *A WopBopaLooBop A LopBamBoom* (London: Paladin, 1969), p. 23.
[3] Ibid., p. 25.
[4] George Melly, *Revolt into Style* (Harmondsworth: Penguin, 1970), pp. 36–37.
[5] Ibid., pp. 39–40.
[6] For another woman's "Elvis," see, for example, Vivienne Welburn, "Elvis: The Way It Was," *Forum 15*, No. 7 (1982), pp. 46–51.

TEENAGE DREAMS

1 9 8 4

○ ▲ ○ ▲ ○ ▲ ○

> *It's a teenage dream to be seventeen*
> *And to find you're all wrapped up in love.*
> "GIVE A LITTLE LOVE," BAY CITY ROLLERS

One of my clearest memories is of a bus ride from my housing estate in Birmingham into the city center. An atmosphere like a cup final coach, but with all of us on the same side and with one even more radical difference—there were no boys. At every stop, more and more girls got on, laughing, shouting, singing the songs we all knew off by heart. We compared the outfits and banners we had spent hours making, swapped jokes and stories, and talked happily to complete strangers because we all had an interest in common: we were about to see the Bay City Rollers.

That was 5 May 1975. I know the exact date because the ticket stub was carefully preserved in my scrapbooks, along with every one of that year's press cuttings to refer to the Rollers. And they were mentioned a lot. Tartan was the year's most fashionable accessory; you could buy Bay City socks, knickers, watches, shoes, lampshades, and countless other fetish objects to fantasize over. For a while at least, the Rollers were big business. Yet nine years later, I see that they didn't even play on their early records; the songs that reached the Top 10 on advance orders alone were weak and sloppily made, with words so wet they almost dripped off the vinyl. Considering that we were supposedly driven into a frenzy the second they walked on stage, they weren't even that pretty.

So what *was* the appeal? Johnny Ray, Sinatra, Billy Fury, Cliff Richard, the Beatles, Bolan, the Osmonds, Duran Duran, Nik Kershaw . . . the names have changed, the process of capitalizing on the phenomenon may have become more efficient and calculated, but from my mother to my younger cousin, most women go through "that phase." Most of us scream ourselves silly at a concert at least once, although many refuse to admit it later, because like a lot of female experience, our teen infatuations have been trivialized, dismissed, and so silenced. Wetting your knickers over a pop group just isn't a hip thing to have done, much better to pretend you spent your formative years listening to Northern soul or Billie Holiday.

Even the artists making money out of girls' fantasies are usually embarrassed and at pains to point out that they have *male* fans, too; to get out of the teeny trap and aim their music at a more "mature" or serious audience seems to be their general ambition. Once they've attained those heights, they're quick to sneer at the girls who helped make them in the first place. Of course, the serious, thinking rock audience they want is mainly male. In spite of a number of women journalists (and some men do make the effort), the music press is mainly written by men for other men. "Primarily for men" is a message that permeates the ads and the way they use women's bodies to shift product, and that informs the casual sexism of articles on women artists (the references to "dogs" and "boilers" in *Sounds*, for example). As part of the same bias, "teenybop" music is either ignored or made into a joke. Often with justice, of course: the Rollers may have been atrocious, but later bands have plumbed depths that my little Scots boys couldn't have dreamed of.

But no matter how bad the music, what the press or any of the self-appointed analysts of "popular culture" fail to reflect is that the whole pop structure rests on the backs of these "silly, screaming girls." They bought the records in millions and made a massive contribution to the early success of Elvis, the Beatles, the Stones, Marc Bolan, Michael Jackson, and many of the others who have since been accepted by the grownups and become monuments, reference points in the rock hierarchy. Before you sneer again, boys, remember that it's often their money that allows you your pretensions.

But the real question is, of course, why? Why do adolescent girls go loopy over gawky, sometimes talentless young men? The answer lies partly in the whole situation of adolescent women in our society. We live in a world where sex has become a commodity—used to sell everything from chocolate to cars, sold in films and magazines, and shown everywhere to be a wonderful, desirable ideal that is central to our lives. The pages of *Jackie*, *My Guy*, and countless other magazines have a clear message: look good, shape up, and flaunt it. Yet hand in glove with this dictum there goes another: *nice girls don't do it*—or at least not until they're 16 / married / going steady (and even then, they don't take the initiative). Sex is the sweetest con-trick of our time, a candy-coated sweetie with a guilt-filled center. At adolescence, we start to realize that this magic/punishment may actually apply to us, too.

A confusing and often traumatic time for everyone. For girls, however, these new expectations, the new rules and roles they have to conform to, are even more perplexing. Growing aware of our bodies and needs is alarming, because while male sexuality is exaggerated by society—portrayed as insatiable and uncontrollable—ours has been virtually obliterated. It is men who *need* sex; women supply it (though it is our responsibility to keep them at bay until the time is right). With double standards, feelings we aren't supposed to *have*—let alone enjoy—and a body or ambitions that may not fit the acceptable stereotypes, it can be a pretty tough time. Falling in love with posters can be a way of excluding real males and of hanging on to that ideal of "true love" for just a little longer. It is a safe focus for all that newly discovered sexual energy, and a scream can often be its only release. It is the sound of young women, not "hysterical schoolgirls" as one reporter would have it—a scream of defiance, celebration, and excitement.

"When their fans are old enough to start looking for *real* boyfriends," sneered a *Birmingham Evening Mail* review of that May 1975 show, "the Rollers will soon be forgotten." But it's not that simple: some of us were lesbians, some of us *did* have boyfriends. In any case, girls mature earlier than boys, so it was more a question of us waiting for *them* grow up than the other way round.

Carol Bedford, who wrote *Waiting for the Beatles* about her experiences as an avid Beatles follower, firmly dismissed the idea that their obsession was due to any fear of sex. In an interview in the *News of the World's* Sunday magazine (5 April 1984), she says:

> We weren't neurotic and we weren't all virgins. I knew what sex was, I'd lived with a man—so it can't be true. And I didn't get afraid or hysterical when George [Harrison, her favorite] did touch me. I didn't want to go further because if he did have a "stable," I didn't want to be one of a crowd. Of course, it must have been an escape from reality into an idealized relationship. But that's wonderful and I wish I had an escape now. I knew what was important then—seeing George. Today, I couldn't answer that. I keep in touch with the other Scruffs [the name adopted by the gang of women who sat outside the band's offices all day]. We remember it as a giggling and happy time. Life is much harder now.

Part of the appeal is desire for comradeship. With the Rollers at least, many became involved not because they particularly liked the music, but because they didn't want to miss out. We were a gang of girls having fun together, able to identify each other by tartan scarves and badges. Women are in the minority on demonstrations, in union meetings, or in the crowd at football matches: at the concerts, many were experiencing mass power for the first and last time. Looking back now, I hardly remember the gigs themselves, the songs, or even what the Rollers looked like. What I *do* remember are the bus rides, running home from school together to get to someone's house in time to watch *Shang-a-Lang* on TV, dancing in lines at the school disco, and sitting in each others' bedrooms discussing our fantasies and compiling our scrapbooks. Our real obsession was with ourselves; in the end, the actual men behind the posters had very little to do with it at all.

But why those particular men? It is interesting to note that although many of their lyrics tell how girls continually lust over their irresistible bodies, Rainbow, Whitesnake, or even the more enlightened, younger heavy metal bands just don't get women screaming at them. The people most attracted to the ideal of the hard, hairy, virile hunk of male are, in fact, other men, who form the majority of the audience at any heavy metal gig. Women seem far more excited by slim, unthreatening, baby-faced types who act vulnerable and who resemble them. Androgyny is what they want: men they can dress like and identify with, as well as drool over. With so few women performers to use as models, perhaps girlish boys are the next best thing. There's no way you could imitate Whitesnake's David Coverdale; a Rollers loo-brush haircut or a Brian Jones pageboy, on the other hand, was easy. Furthermore you, too, could wear the same clothes as those slim-hipped, pretty young boys. It is easy to forget that even the Rolling Stones—now Real Men without question—were once condemned for their effeminacy and implied to be gay.

A touch of homosexuality seems to *enhance* a male star's popularity with women, in fact—especially if it is carefully denied elsewhere. When Marc Bolan's former manager, Simon Napier-Bell, took on Wham! after seeing them on *Top of the Pops*, he knew that their exclusive, buddy-boy act would go down as well with a young female audience as it had with the clientele of Bolts, a North London gay club. Many stars are openly bisexual, knowing that it adds to their infamy and appeal. Even Frankie Goes to Hollywood—whose first record was banned from the BBC due to its gay overtones—found they had attracted a teen audience. This success caused them to consider toning down their act, they said in the gay magazine *Square Peg:*

> I think we are paddling backwards, because we've realized that there's a lot of money to be made out of 13-year-old girls, which is sad. But we've been told by people in office buildings that we're treading on thin ice now, to be careful—not that we're going to be that careful. I'm not singing for 13-year-olds, I'm still singing for men.

Roxy Music, Bowie, Bolan, the Sweet, Adam Ant, and Boy George have all used camp presentation to advantage; one of the Bay City Rollers had formerly posed for gay porn magazines (which, of course, says more about his financial state than his sexuality). Even cuddly Barry Manilow, the aural equivalent of Mills and Boon, began his career playing the gay clubs with Bette Midler. This isn't to say that all of the people mentioned here *are* gay—but the notion that they *may* be somehow enhances their appeal to women. Perhaps it makes them safer. Or perhaps this hint of deviancy titillates. Maybe even women feel that they would be the one to mother the boy, to love him and set him back on the right path.

The idea of the hero as an outsider is very important. After all, young women are having problems adapting to that same alienating society themselves. This "bad boy" image has been a powerful theme for pop heroes. It links together groups like the Stones and early Wham!—who are otherwise very far apart. These boys are the ones your parents definitely wouldn't like—nor, for that matter, would your straight and prissy classmates. They, like you, don't fit in. But they're rebels not rejects, and by liking them, you too become a rebel.

A lifetime of suppression means that few girls dream of themselves becoming exceptional—instead, they fantasize about having boyfriends who do it for them, projecting their desires yet again onto men. With songs such as "He's a Rebel," "Home of the Brave," and, of course, "Leader of the Pack," the Crystals and the Shangri-Las built careers around the contradictions that male stars often pander to. Rebels by proxy, girls envied for their associations with wild men, they were still ultimately safe, took mom's advice, and snuggled sadly back into the family fold.

Most groups choose a safer path, and are at pains to present a reassuringly wholesome image for parents and the media. Girls' magazines are usually happy to help, as in this conversation overheard in a record company office:

REPORTER: What do you eat for breakfast?
SINGER: Fried eggs, bacon, beans, and tea.
REPORTER: Isn't that a bit lumpen?
SINGER: How about champagne and kippers, then?
REPORTER: A little too exotic, I think.
SINGER: OK. Coffee, toast, and marmalade?
REPORTER: Great. What's your favorite drink?

And a thousand 12-year-olds cut it out and put it in their scrapbooks, knowing they'll be able to cook him what he wants when he comes to stay.

Even with the sickeningly wholesome Osmonds or the Rollers, however, the feeling of going against normal society, of rebellion, persisted. One of the most important points about most teeny groups is that almost everyone else hates them. With the Rollers, everyone but the fans continually made fun of us, insisting that the band was stupid and couldn't play. They were right, of course, but that wasn't the point. It was us against the world—and, for a while at least, we were winning.

For the girls' magazines, the band meant big circulation. When guitarist Alan Longmuir tried to escape from the band pleading old age (probably yet another publicity stunt), many even printed petition forms. Presumably in exchange for the endless color posters and the fawning coverage they gave the band, *Mirabelle* and *Fab 208* were allowed to print weekly "letters" from the boys. I hardly missed a copy. The few brave souls who did dare to criticize were usually forced to retract due to the sheer volume of abuse; next to each of these apologies, I lovingly drew a little skull-and-crossbones victory sign. We were invincible, a tartan army defying critics, DJs, newspapers, and everyone else who spoke against "our boys."

In the end, media attention was so focused on the fans and the mass hysteria that the music itself was forgotten altogether. The Rollers were accused of engineering their first U.S. TV appearance so that fans surged forward and knocked two of them unconscious minutes into their act. The estimated 50 million viewers of the satellite broadcast didn't get to *hear* much, but they saw what manager Tam Paton wanted them to see: Rollermania. It means that when they made their first visit to the United States a week later, there were already tartan hordes waiting at the airport, ready to join the fun. It takes an efficient publicity machine to escalate one single teeny band into a mass phenomenon, and Tam Paton was a slick manipulator of the media and pop. As he trumpeted in a *Daily Mirror* piece:

> I used to pick Rollers on personality rather than on skill. I felt you could take someone who had an image and teach him to play. You can have the most fantastic musician in the world, but what's the point if you have to spend a fortune in plastic surgery to get him right as far as image is concerned?

The ultimate in this selection process is perhaps the New York / Puerto Rican Group, Menudo, whose members have to be under 16, and good looking. They are unceremoniously sacked on their sixteenth birthday, and replaced.

It is looks that attract the magazines that tell young women how to look and what to buy. "Personality" is what these magazines promote: they will interview stars about food, pets, or (clean) funny stories about life on the road. They are not interested in music: how or what the artists play—lyrics aside—is usually irrelevant; even the inevitable color posters rarely show the band actually performing. What girls are sold is a catchy hook, and an image and lyrics they can identify with. Fantasy fodder. This is the male as sex object, posed, airbrushed, and marketed just like any female model. He, however, is usually imperfect and ordinary enough for the fans to believe that, one day, he could be theirs.

That myth, the illusion of accessibility, is essential—and artists aiming for this market are careful never to mention a girlfriend or even the type of woman they prefer in any but the vaguest terms. Once again, the Rollers had the routine down to perfection: "It's not looks that count, it's personality," said Les McKeowan, giving hope to plain girls everywhere, while forgetting to mention his friendships with women like Britt Ekland.

A fan's mind is a curious thing, though. It picks and chooses from the information available, giving credence only where it wants to, and even managing to retain and believe quite contradictory facts simultaneously. Fantasy, unlike reality, isn't binding, which is the big advantage pop heroes have over real men. You can turn Boy George into your gentle, cuddly, funny, dream romance and still enjoy your father turning purple with anger over his effeminacy.

In every interview there's an endless litany of "no permanent girl at the moment . . . someday I'll find the right girl . . . believe in romance . . . we love all our fans." You know it's you he's really waiting for. But you also know he's unavailable. And there's the crunch. Normally, even the most obsessive fan knows that her chances are so slight as to be negligible. Jona MacDonald first saw Chris Hughes on *Top of the Pops* in 1979, drumming with Adam and the Ants. She went on to follow him with an energy, persistence, and ingenuity that begs admiration in spite of its being so pointless and oppressive. In 1983, she sat on the steps of the Abbey Road Studios morning and night for a total of 110 days (she counted), while he produced Wang Chung's first album, *Points on a Curve*. Years before, Beatles fan Jill Pitchard sat waiting outside those same studios for so long that she was eventually made the receptionist: she is still there, and when EMI opened the room in which the Beatles recorded to the public, Jona was offered a job alongside Jill, ushering in awestruck fans.

So what's the appeal of famous men?

> "I don't look on him as being famous now that he's not in the Ants any more. I just think he's really good looking. I'd like to be a friend of his. Well, I'd like to go out with him, that's my ambition. But then there's somebody else, isn't there? I know deep down I'll never get anywhere with him. I just wish it wasn't true, I'm going out with someone now, but I still keep in contact with Chris. And if I go off him, I won't forget him: I've still got my scrapbooks and everything."

And so have I. Four volumes of carefully pasted cuttings and pictures. It is this retentiveness that makes teenage girls such a lucrative market. And how exploitable is this urge to collect not only the records, but the posters, tour programs, fan club specials, books, magazines, and any other product companies wish to foist on them! Birthdays, names, measurements, likes, and dislikes are all learned by heart, and fans can often relate more statistical information about an artist than he could himself, offhand. Yet the picture they build up is the one they want to believe, with faults rationalized or glossed over, and virtues often invented. It is easy to create an idealized fantasy man with none of the flaws of real men, and to transfer those attributes on to an inaccessible, but real, star. For most, it's just a way of brightening up dull, ordinary lives: the cynical comments written in my scrapbooks show that even at my most infatuated, I knew half of what was written was lies. For a minority, though, the dream can become an obsession. It happens gradually, as Carol Bedford explained:

> "You realize that you could ask for an autograph, and then you start to think, 'Wouldn't it be nice if he knew my name?' I've tried to understand why that is important. Perhaps it's an inferiority complex . . . you got special status for length of service. When he singled you out, all those hours of waiting didn't seem to exist."

Carol's waiting ended after a record company Christmas party in 1971, when George Harrison asked her to stop wasting her life in such a way:

> "It was a very moving conversation because it showed he cared. It was also a low point because I realized I would have to quit. If that was the only thing I could give to him, then I would. It took two months to build up courage to even ask myself if I could survive without seeing him: could I go through a week without the most important thing in the world to me—watching George Harrison walk out of the building?"

Carol had come to England from Dallas to follow her band. "Polythene" Pat Dawson, on the other hand, was a fan in Liverpool before the Beatles became famous. She recounted her memories to Mike Evans in *Let It Rock* (July 1975):

> "There was a hierarchy of people who'd been watching them for a long time, and they were quite matey with us—they used to pull birds from this group but when the newer fans arrived, they were already beginning to get 'distanced.' The older fans tended to like them for their music, and as fellas in the personal sense, whereas the newer ones liked them because they were the Beatles. This was long before they made records or anything, but they were already a big cult in Liverpool. It wasn't like seeing people who were stars. You still saw them as a bunch of lads you might get off with."

As they became better known, many of the early fans refused to buy the records, not wanting their boys to leave them. Pat clearly recalls her sadness at their success:

> "The night Bob Wooler [the Cavern DJ] announced as they were going on stage that 'Please Please Me' had reached number one, it was awful, because the reaction was the opposite to what they expected. Everyone was stunned. That was the end of it as far as we were concerned."

Men become obsessed, too, of course. But the difference between, say, the man who changes his name to Elvis and the woman who spends all her savings following Spandau Ballet to the United States is that, for her, a close, socially acceptable relationship—marriage—is at least a possibility, no matter how remote. It is also difficult for a woman to actually fantasize about *being* her hero in the same way as a man could. With so few role models to follow, to fantasize about being on stage as a *female* performer may be almost a contradiction in terms. Instead, most of us dream of being a pop star's girlfriend: fame and recognition by proxy. Girls are taught to wait for men to give us what we want, rather than to get it ourselves. In the world of the Mills and Boon, romance, passion, wealth, status, and excitement are conferred on the passive heroine by the men who come into her life. That idea is a persistent one. My favorite daydream in boring classes at school was of a famous star suddenly walking into the room to take me away, leaving my classmates sighing in regret that they hadn't realized I was so wonderful. I felt that my lover could actually transform me, and many of my friends have confessed to similar Cinderella fantasies.

While women are judged—and taught to value themselves—by the status of their men, they will continue to follow personable young groups. Perhaps, even, the most obsessive are also the most ambitious. Most of the fans I have met waiting outside studios and concert halls have been bright, energetic, articulate young women—hardly the stereotypical "groupie" described in the songs, videos, and fantasies of the Real Men of rock 'n' roll.

The term "groupie" is a dangerous one, for it is often used as a putdown for *any* woman involved in the industry. In February 1969, the newly formed *Rolling Stone* magazine devoted a whole issue to "Groupies: The Girls of Rock," explaining to the reader that "some of the girls of rock, girls who are very much part of the scene—everybody knows them—never were groupies in the strict sense, but are somehow cut from the same fabric. Like Trixie, the girl bass-player, and Dusty, the girl recording engineer." Pauline Black told of similar false assumptions being made by men when she was the singer in the Selecter, on the 2-Tone national tour:

> "Guys, when they're on the road, have a different attitude to when they're at home, and invariably I'd find myself with a whole load of young girls outside my door saying, 'Oh, so-and-so's thrown me out of his room because I won't do whatever.' Really young, naive girls who were just into the whole thing and had come back to the hotel expecting to have a bit of a drink and a good time without thinking of the consequences of hanging around hotels with loads of guys."

If a woman wishes to be involved in any way, it is often assumed that she is only there ultimately because she is attracted to the man. It is worth bearing this in mind whenever the term "groupie" is used. And then there's the question of how "groupies" see themselves. Pat Hartley, an American woman involved in the New York–Andy Warhol music scene, when interviewed by *Spare Rib* (1974), saw it as a form of autonomous female activity:

"The whole groupie thing turned itself around. It used to be that the guys could pick and choose. Well, after the first three years it was us choosing, the guys had no choice. In the end, when the groups came to town, the girls would decide whether . . . I mean, after having Stevie Winwood, was it worth it to have anyone less? And for the groups, in a way it was part and parcel of selling the albums. It was 1964 that the Beatles first came to the States, and around that year the groupies started. It was a different kind of thing then: the place was littered with 14-year-old girls, and there were people like me, Jenny Dean, Devon and others who were going into it from an intelligent point of view. We'd just find out who was in town and what hotel they were in. It's not that difficult, if one decided to put a little effort behind it. It's a society of a kind, the way it functions, it has its own strange rules. A lot of it is women dressing for women; a lot of it had to do with the competition between the chicks. We paired off in twos and there were always couples who were like married couples. Very few chicks would go in one at a time. Going in twos was sort of an adventure and it was fun. It was a weird thing. When it started, it started like a teenage sex vibe . . . all those women standing outside the Plaza Hotel screaming our knickers down for these incredible pop groups, and at the time, it really was the girls after the boys."

The freedom to be used by the consumer of your choice. But what happens when the stars themselves are women? Girls scream at girls, too. When the Ronettes or the Shangri-Las played to a live audience, the front rows were full of young women screaming, reaching, and hand-dancing in their seats. The girl-group era told women that they could be stars, that they could dress up and look strong and sexy, get up there with the boys. "I knew I was going to sing," says Ronnie Spector firmly on the video of Alan Betrock's "Girl Groups." "I knew, I had no qualms, nothing. I was going to sing, and I was going to sing rock 'n' roll." For Ronnie it was 13-year-old Frankie Lymon, a boy with a girl's high voice, who showed the way. For the girls watching her, Ronnie herself was opening up new possibilities. The girl groups told young women that their dreams were possible, and even as their songs reinforced the most reactionary ideas of love and marriage ("He Hit Me, and It Felt Like a Kiss"), they were showing that it *was* possible to be something more than somebody's girlfriend: a singer and a star.

In the August 1982 issue of *Ms* magazine, Marcia Gillespie talks of the significance for black girls of one of the few groups to survive the Beatles and the British invasion that followed:

The Supremes were important—symbols of the idea that integration could happen, that we could make it and still have the dream. That black girls could be glamorous and beautiful and celebrated for it—at home and abroad. . . . The idea that black managers and recording companies could take three girls from the ghetto, take rhythm and blues, and move it and them from the back of the bus and to a limousine was daring and visionary for its time.

Women have continued to idolize women, to pin them up and objectify them in just the way any boy would. In the late 1970s, the most popular pinup in girls' bedrooms was not John Travolta or Johnny Rotten, but Debbie Harry. It's often hard to tell if they just want to *be* them, or if they are in love with them. In adolescence, the line is thin between admiration and lust (*boys* screamed at both Bolan and Bowie)—although, with a little help, most of us grow out of it and become as anti-gay as the society which raised us. Helen Terry describes her relationship with her Culture Club fans:

> I get loads of letters, and the other day I met two girls with "I Love Helen Terry" scratched on their arm. That's really beyond me—all these girls screaming, "I really love you!" It's so unreal. I think half of it is that they'd like to be me, they'd like to be close to George, to be able to sing, maybe. The other half is that, basically, I'm very safe: I'm like everyone's best mate, I talk to anyone. I'm fairly low-key.

On the whole, the word "fans," when applied to women, is derogatory. It is always assumed that they are attracted to a person for the "wrong" reasons, that they are uncritical and stupid. As an audience, they are usually treated with contempt by both bands and record companies. The "real" audience is assumed to be male, and advertisements, record sleeves, and even stage presentation are nearly always aimed at men. Yet a substantial majority of women own a stereo, and music is a constant background to our lives—on the radio at home, piped into supermarkets and factories, in the disco, records played while we do our chores. And in the brief time when the majority of girls *are* actively involved as fans, the fun and the thrills are unlike anything most men will ever experience. For us, in 1975, the real excitement had little to do with the Bay City Rollers: it was about ourselves.

IN DEFENSE OF DISCO

1 9 7 9

○ ▲ ○ ▲ ○ ▲ ○

All my life I've liked the wrong music. I never liked Elvis and rock 'n' roll; I always preferred Rosemary Clooney. And since I became a socialist, I've often felt virtually terrorized by the prestige of rock and folk on the Left. How could I admit to two Petula Clark LPs in the face of miners' songs from the North East and the Rolling Stones? I recovered my nerve partially when I came to see show-biz music as a key part of gay culture, which, whatever its limitations, was a culture to defend. And I thought I'd really made it when I turned on to Tamla Motown, sweet soul sounds, disco. Chartbusters already, and I like them! Yet the prestige of folk and rock, and now punk and (rather patronizingly, I think) reggae, still holds sway. It's not just that people whose politics I broadly share don't *like* disco, they manage to imply that it is politically beyond the pale to like it. It's against this attitude that I want to defend disco (which otherwise, of course, hardly needs any defense).

I'm going to talk mainly about disco *music*, but there are two preliminary points I'd like to make. The first is that disco is more than just a form of music, although certainly the music is at the heart of it. Disco is also kinds of dancing, club, fashion, film—in a word, a certain *sensiblility*, manifest in music, clubs, and so forth, historically and culturally specific, economically, technologically, ideologically, and aesthetically determined—and worth thinking about. Second, as a sensibility in music it seems to me to encompass more than what we would perhaps strictly call disco music, and include a lot of soul, Tamla, and even the later work of mainstream and jazz artists like Peggy Lee and Johnny Mathis.

My defense is in two parts: first, a discussion of the arguments against disco in terms of its being "capitalist" music, and second, an attempt to think through the—ambivalently, ambiguously, contradictorily—positive qualities of disco.

DISCO AND CAPITAL

Much of the hostility to disco stems from the equation of it with capitalism. Both in how it is produced and in what it expresses, disco is held to be irredeemably capitalistic.

Now it is unambiguously the case that disco is produced by capitalist industry, and since capitalism is an irrational and inhuman mode of production, the disco industry is as bad as all the rest. Of course. However, this argument has assumptions behind it that are more problematic. These are of two kinds. One assumption concerns *music as a mode of production*, and has to do with the belief that it is possible in a capitalist society to produce things (e.g., music, such as rock and folk) that are outside of the capitalist mode of production. Yet quite apart from the general point that such a position seeks to elevate activity outside of existing structures rather than struggles against them, the two kinds of music most often set against disco as a mode of production are not really convincing.

One is folk music—in the U.K., people might point to Gaelic songs and industrial ballads—the kind of music often used, or reworked, in left fringe theater. These, it is argued, are not, like disco (and pop music in general), produced *for* the people, but *by* them. They are "authentic" people's music. So they are—or rather, were. The problem is that we don't live in a society of small, technologically simple communities such as produce such art. Preserving such music at best gives us a historical perspective on peasant and working-class struggle, at worst leads to a nostalgia for a simple, harmonious community existence that never even existed. More bluntly, songs in Gaelic or dealing with nineteenth-century factory conditions, beautiful as they are, don't mean much to most English-speaking people today.

The other kind of music most often posed against disco, and "pap pop" at the level of how it is produced, is rock (including Dylan-type folk and everything from early rock 'n' roll to progressive concept albums). The argument here is that rock is easily produced by nonprofessionals—all that is needed are a few instruments and somewhere to play—whereas disco music requires the whole panoply of recording studio technology, which makes it impossible for nonprofessionals (the kid on the streets) to produce. The factual accuracy of this observation needs supplementing with some other observations. Quite apart from the very rapid—but then bemoaned by some purists—move of rock into elaborate recording studios, even when it is simple and produceable by nonprofessionals, the fact is that rock is still quite expensive, and remains in practice largely the preserve of the middle class, who can afford electic guitars, music lessons, and the like. (You have only to look at the biographies of those now professional rock musicians who started out in a simple nonprofessional way—the preponderance of public school and university-educated young men in the field is rivaled only by their preponderance in the Labour Party cabinet.) More importantly, this kind of production is wrongly thought of as being generated from the grassroots when, except perhaps at certain key historical moments, nonprofessional music making, in rock as elsewhere, bases itself, inevitably, on professional music. Any notion that rock emanates from "the people" is soon confounded by the recognition that what "the people" are doing is trying to be as much like professionals as possible.

The second kind of argument based on the fact that disco is produced by capitalism concerns *music as an ideological expression*. Here it is assumed that capitalism as a mode of production necessarily and simply produces "capitalist" ideology. The theory of the relation between the mode of production and the ideologies of a particular society is too complicated and unresolved to be gone into here, but we can begin by remembering that capitalism is about profit. In the language of classical economics, capitalism produces commodities, and its interest in commodities is their exchange value (how much profit they can realize) rather than their use value (their social or human worth). This becomes particularly problematic for capitalism when dealing with an expressive commodity—such as disco—since a major problem for capitalism is that there is no necessary or guaranteed connection between exchange value and use value. In other words, capitalism as productive relations can just as well make a profit from something that is ideologically opposed to bourgeois society as something that supports it. As long as a commodity makes a profit, what does it matter? Indeed, it is because of this dangerous, anarchic tendency of capitalism that ideological institutions—the church, the state, education, the family—are necessary. It is their job to make sure that what capitalism produces is in capitalism's longer-term interests. However, since they often don't know that that is their job, they don't always perform it. Cultural production within capitalist society is, then, founded on two profound contradictions—the first between production for profit and production for use; the second, within those institutions whose job it is to regulate the first contradiction. What all this boils down to, in terms of disco, is that the fact that disco is produced by capitalism does not mean that it is automatically, necessarily, simply supportive of capitalism. Capitalism constructs the disco experience, but it does not necessarily know what it is doing, apart from making money.

I am not now about to launch into a defense of disco music as some great subversive art form. What the arguments above lead me to is, first, a basic point of departure in the recognition that cultural production under capitalism is necessarily contradictory, and, second, that it may well be the case that capitalist cultural products are most likely to be contradictory at just those points—such as disco—where they are most commercial and professional, where the urge to profit is at its strongest. Third, this mode of cultural production has produced a commodity, disco, that has been taken up by gays in ways that may well not have been intended by its producers. The anarchy of capitalism throws up commodities that an oppressed group can take up and use to cobble together its own culture. In this respect, disco is very much like another profoundly ambiguous aspect of male gay culture, camp. It is a "contrary" use of what the dominant culture provides, it is important in forming a gay identity, and it has subversive potential as well as reactionary implications.

THE CHARACTERISTICS OF DISCO

Let me turn now to what I consider to be the three important characteristics of disco—eroticism, romanticism, and materialism. I'm going to talk about them in terms of what it seems to me they mean within the context of gay culture. These three characteristics are not in themselves good or bad (any more than disco music as a whole is), and they need specifying more precisely. What is interesting is how they take us to qualities that are not only key ambiguities within gay male culture, but have also traditionally proved stumbling blocks to socialists.

Eroticism

It can be argued that all popular music is erotic. What we need to define is the specific way of thinking and feeling erotically in disco. I'd like to call it "whole body" eroticism, and to define it by comparing it with the eroticism of the two kinds of music to which disco is closest—popular song (i.e., the Gershwin, Cole Porter, Burt Bacharach type of song) and rock.

Popular song's eroticism is "disembodied": it succeeds in expressing a sense of the erotic which yet denies eroticism's physicality. This can be shown by the nature of tunes in popular songs and the way they are handled.

Popular song's tunes are rounded off, closed, self-contained. They achieve this by adopting a strict musical structure (AABA) in which the opening melodic phrases are returned to and, most importantly, the tonic note of the song is also the last note of the tune. (The tonic note is the note that forms the basis for the key in which the song is written; it is therefore the harmonic "anchor" of the tune, and closing on it gives precisely a feeling of "anchoring," coming to a settled stop.) Thus although popular songs often depart from their melodic and harmonic beginnings—especially in the middle section (B)—they also always return to them. This gives them—even at their most passionate, as in Cole Porter's "Night and Day"—a sense of security and containment. The tune is not allowed to invade the whole of one's body. Compare the typical disco tune, which is often little more than an endlessly repeated phrase which drives beyond itself, is not "closed off." Even when disco music uses a popular song standard, it often turns it into a simple phrase. Gloria Gaynor's version of Porter's "I've Got You Under My Skin," for instance, is in large part a chanted repetition of "I've got you."

Popular song's lyrics place its tunes within a conceptualization of love and passion as emanating from "inside," the heart or the soul. Thus the yearning cadences of popular song express an erotic yearning of the inner person, not the body. Once again, disco refuses this. Not only are the lyrics often more directly physical and the delivery more raunchy (e.g., Grace Jones's "I Need a Man"), but, most importantly, disco is insistently rhythmic in a way that popular song is not.

Rhythm, in Western music, is traditionally felt as being more physical than other musical elements such as melody, harmony, and instrumentation. This is why Western music is traditionally so dull rhythmically—nothing expresses our Puritan heritage more vividly. It is to other cultures that we have had to turn—above all to Afro-American culture—to learn about rhythm. The history of popular songs since the late nineteeth century is largely the history of the white incorporation (or ripping off) of black music—ragtime, the Charleston, the tango, swing, rock 'n' roll, rock. Now what is interesting about this incorporation or ripping off is what it meant and means. Typically, black music was thought of by the white culture as being both more primitive and more "authentically" erotic. Infusions of black music were always seen as (and often condemned as) sexual and physical. The use of insistent black rhythms in disco music, recognizable by the closeness of the style to soul and reinforced by such characteristic features of black music as the repeated chanted phrase and the use of various African percussion instruments, means that it inescapably signifies (in this white context) physicality.

However, rock is as influenced by black music as disco is. This then leads me to the second area of comparison between the eroticism of disco and rock. The difference between them lies in what each "hears" in black music. Rock's eroticism is thrusting, grinding—it is not whole-body, but phallic. Hence it takes from black music the insistent beat and makes it even more driving; rock's repeated phrases trap you in their relentless push, rather than releasing you in an open-ended succession of repetitions as disco does.

Most revealing perhaps is rock's instrumentation. Black music has more percussion instruments than white, and it knows how to use them to create all sorts of effects—light, soft, lively, as well as heavy, hard, and grinding. Rock, however, hears only the latter and develops the percussive qualities of essentially nonpercussive instruments to increase this, hence the twanging electric guitar and the nasal vocal delivery. One can see how, when rock 'n' roll first came in, this must have been a tremendous liberation from popular song's disembodied eroticism—here was a really physical music, and not just mealy-mouthed physical, but quite clear what it was about— cock. But rock confines sexuality to cock (and this is why, no matter how progressive the lyrics and even when performed by women, rock remains indelibly phallo-centric music). Disco music, on the other hand, hears the physicality in black music and its range. It achieves this by a number of features, including the sheer amount going on rhythmically in even quite simple disco music (for rhythmic clarity with complexity, listen to the full-length version of the Temptations' "Papa Was a Rolling Stone"); the willingness to play with rhythm, delaying it, jumping it, countering it rather than simply driving on and on (e.g., Patti Labelle, Isaac Hayes); the range of percussion instruments used and their different effect (e.g., the spiky violins in Quincy Jones and Herbie Hancock's "Tell Me a Bedtime Story"; the gentle pulsations of George Benson). This never stops being erotic, but it restores eroticism to the whole of the body and for both sexes, not just confining it to the penis. It leads to the expressive, sinuous movement of disco dancing, not just that mixture of awkwardness and thrust so dismally characteristic of dancing to rock.

Gay men do not intrinsically have any prerogative over whole-body eroticism. We are often even more cock-oriented than non-gays of either sex, and it depresses me that such phallic forms of disco as Village People should be so gay identified. Nonetheless, partly because many of us have traditionally not thought of ourselves as being "real men" and partly because gay ghetto culture is also a space where alternative definitions, including those of sexuality, can be developed, it seems to me that the importance of disco in scene culture indicates an openness to a sexuality that is not defined in terms of cock. Although one cannot easily move from musical values to personal ones, or from personal ones to politically effective ones, it is at any rate suggestive that gay culture should promote a form of music that denies the centrality of the phallus while at the same time refusing the nonphysicality which such a denial has hitherto implied.

Romanticism

Not all disco music is romantic. The lyrics of many disco hits are either straightforwardly sexual—not to say sexist—or else broadly social (e.g.,

Detroit Spinners' "Ghetto Child," Stevie Wonder's "Living in the City"), and the hard drive of Village People or Labelle is positively antiromantic. Yet there is nonetheless a strong strain of romanticism in disco. This can be seen in the lyrics, which often differ little from popular song standards, and indeed often are standards (e.g., "What a Difference a Day Made" by Esther Phillips, "La Vie en Rose" by Grace Jones). More impressively, it is the instrumentation and arrangements of disco music that are so romantic.

The use of massed violins takes us straight back, via Hollywood, to Tchaikovsky, to surging, outpouring emotions. A brilliant example is Gloria Gaynor's "I've Got You Under My Skin," where in the middle section the violins take a hint from one of Porter's melodic phrases and develop it away from this tune in an ecstatic, soaring movement. This "escape" from the confines of popular song into ecstasy is very characteristic of disco music, and nowhere more consistently than in such Diana Ross classics as "Reach Out" and "Ain't No Mountain High Enough." This latter, with its lyrics of total surrender to love, its heavenly choir, and sweeping violins, is perhaps one of the most extravagant reaches of disco's romanticism. But Ross is also a key figure in the gay appropriation of disco.

What Ross's records do—and I'm thinking basically of her work up to *Greatest Hits* volume 1 and the *Touch Me in the Morning* albums—is express the intensity of fleeting emotional contacts. They are all-out expressions of adoration which yet have built on to them the recognition of the (inevitably) temporary quality of the experience. This can be a straightforward lament for having been let down by a man, but more often it is both a celebration of a relationship and the almost willing recognition of its passing and the exquisite pain of its passing—"Remember me / As a sunny day / That you once had / Along the way"; "If I've got to be strong / Don't you know I need to have tonight when you're gone / When you go I'll lie here / And think about / the last time that you / Touch me in the morning." This last number, with Ross's "unreally" sweet, porcelain fragile voice and the string backing, concentrates that sense of celebrating the intensity of the passing relationship that haunts so much of her work. No wonder Ross is (was?) so important in gay male scene culture, for she both reflects what that culture takes to be an inevitable reality (that relationships don't last) and at the same time celebrates it, validates it.

Not all disco music works in this vein, yet in both some of the more sweetly melancholy orchestrations (even in lively numbers, like "You Should Be Dancing" from *Saturday Night Fever*) and some of the lyrics and general tone (e.g., Donna Summer's *Four Seasons of Love* album), there is a carryover of this emotional timbre. At a minimum, then, disco's romanticism provides an embodiment and validation of an aspect of gay culture.

But romanticism is a particularly paradoxical quality of art to come to terms with. Its passion and intensity embody or create an experience that negates the dreariness of the mundane and everyday. It gives us a glimpse of what it means to live at the height of our emotional and experiential capacities—not dragged down by the banality of organized routine life. Given that everyday banality, work, domesticity, ordinary sexism, and racism are rooted in the structures of class and gender of this society, the flight from that banality can be seen as a flight from capitalism and patriarchy as lived experiences.

What makes this more complicated is the actual situation within which disco occurs. Disco is part of the wider to and fro between work and leisure, alienation and escape, boredom and enjoyment that we are so accustomed to (and which *Saturday Night Fever* plugs into so effectively). Now this to and fro is partly the mechanism by which we keep going, at work, at home— the respite of leisure gives us the energy to work, and anyway we are still largely brought up to think of leisure as a "reward" for work. This circle locks us into it. But what happens in that space of leisure can be profoundly significant; it is there that we may learn about an alternative to work and to society as it is. Romanticism is one of the major modes of leisure in which this sense of an alternative is kept alive. Romanticism asserts that the limits of work and domesticity are not the limits of experience.

I don't say that romanticism, with its passion and intensity, is a political ideal we could strive for—I doubt it is humanly possible to live permanently at that pitch. What I do believe is that the movement between banality and something "other" than banality is an essential dialectic of society, a constant keeping open of a gap between what is and what could or should be. Herbert Marcuse in the currently unfashionable *One-Dimensional Man* argues that our society tries to close that gap, to assert that what is all that there could be, is what should be. For all its commercialism and containment within the to and fro between work and leisure, I think disco romanticism is one of the things that can keep the gap open, that can allow the *experience of contradiction* to continue. Since I also believe that political struggle is rooted in experience (though utterly doomed if left at it), I find this dimension of disco potentially positive. (A further romantic/utopian aspect of disco is realized in the noncommercial discos organized by gay and women's groups. Here a moment of community can be achieved, often in circle dances or simply in the sense of knowing people as people, not anonymous bodies. Fashion is less important, and sociability correspondingly more so. This can be achieved in smaller clubs, perhaps especially outside the center of London, which, when not just grotty monuments to self-oppression, can function as supportive expressions of something like a gay community.)

Materialism

Disco is characteristic of advanced capitalist societies simply in terms of the scale of money squandered on it. It is a riot of consumerism, dazzling in its technology (echo chambers, double and more tracking, electric instruments), overwhelming in its scale (banks of violins, massed choirs, the limitless range of percussion instruments), lavishly gaudy in the mirrors and tat of discotheques, the glitter and denim flash of its costumes. Its tacky sumptuousness is well evoked in *Thank God It's Friday*. Gone are the restraint of popular song, the sparseness of rock and reggae, the simplicity of folk. How can a socialist, or someone trying to be a feminist, defend it?

In certain respects, it is doubtless not defensible. Yet socialism and feminism are both forms of materialism—why is disco, a celebration of materialism if ever there was one, not therefore the appropriate art form of materialist politics?

Partly, obviously, because materialism in politics is not to be confused with mere matter. Materialism seeks to understand how things are in terms of how they have been produced and constructed in history, and how they can be better produced and constructed. This certainly does not mean immersing oneself in the material world—indeed, it includes deliberately stepping back from the material world to see what makes it the way it is and how to change it. But materialism is also based on the profound conviction that politics is about the material world, and indeed that human life and the material world are all there is; there is no God, there are no magic forces. One of the dangers of materialist politics is that it is in constant danger of spiritualizing itself, partly because of the historical legacy of the religious forms that brought materialism into existence, partly because materialists have to work so hard not to take matter at face value that they often end up not treating it as matter at all. Disco's celebration of materialism is only a celebration of the world we are necessarily and always immersed in. Disco's materialism, in technological modernity, is resolutely historical and cultural—it can never be, as most art claims for itself, an "emanation" outside of history and of human production.

Disco's combination of romanticism and materialism effectively tells us— lets us experience—that we live in a world of materials, that we can enjoy them but that the experience of materialism is not necessarily what the everyday world assures us it is. Its eroticism allows us to rediscover our bodies as part of this experience of materialism and the possibility of change.

If this sounds over the top, let one thing be clear—disco can't change the world or make the revolution. No art can do that, and it is pointless to expect it to. But partly by opening up experience, partly by changing definitions, art and disco can be used. To which one might risk adding the refrain, if it feels good, *use* it.

AFTERTHOUGHTS

1 9 8 5

○ ▲ ○ ▲ ○ ▲ ○

There was, it seems, a moment last summer (my source is a baffled Australian tourist) when the only pop stars left in Madame Tussaud's were David Bowie and Boy George (Michael Jackson was added later). "Gender bending" had got its final accolade; Britain's peculiar contribution to Western pop music was preserved, appropriately, in wax.

The Australians weren't the only people baffled. For more than a decade now American youth magazines like *Creem* have been filled with anxious readers' defenses of rock 'n' roll masculinity, and as a traveling rock critic last year I was repeatedly asked to explain Culture Club. I couldn't usually give much of an answer, just reply that the sexiest performer I'd seen was, in fact, a boy in Depeche Mode, a dyed blonde in mini-skirt and skimpy top. His shoulder straps kept slipping, leaving me, a "heterosexual" man, breathlessly hoping throughout the show to get a glimpse of his breasts.

In general, 1984 was a playful pop year. It began with Annie Lennox's appearance on the U.S. Grammy Awards Show, not with her usual close-cropped unisex look but in full drag, as a convincing Elvis Presley. It ended with the British record biz awards. Holly Johnson opened the envelope for Prince: "Oh yes, I've had telephone sex with him!" A huge bodyguard rose up (I thought he was going to thump Holly) and cleared a path for the little master, who walked daintily behind. Prince sings about incest, oral sex, pornography, obsessional lust, and masturbation.

Otherwise it was Frankie Goes to Hollywood's year. They made records about sexuality: Welcome to the Pleasure Dome! Their triumph was "Relax," a huge-selling single that was banned by the BBC for "sexual offensiveness," but the importance of the Frankie story wasn't its outrage but its coziness. Their very success made them part of the Radio 1 pop family—by the end of the year, Mike Read, the DJ who'd initiated the ban on "Relax," was the voice-over on Frankie's TV commercials. They had become family entertainment. What did it mean?

In 1978 Angela McRobbie and I wrote an article titled "Rock and Sexuality" for *Screen Education* (which is included in the present volume). It was not a very profound piece but it was, surprisingly, a "pioneering" attempt to treat rock's sexual messages analytically. It was reprinted in an Open University reader and is, to our embarrassment, still regularly cited. To our embarrassment because the piece was a jumble of good and bad arguments. We confused issues of sex and issues of gender; we never decided whether sexuality was a social fact or a social discourse.

Our aim was to counter the common assumption that rock 'n' roll somehow liberated sexual expression; we wanted to pick open terms like "raunchy," to challenge rock naturalism. Rock, we suggested, works with conventions of masculinity and feminity that situate both performers and audiences along clear gender lines—males as active participants, females as passive consumers. Musically, the distinction is marked by the contrast between "cock rock" and "teenybop."

In terms of who controls and consumes music, our points still seem valid. For all the current celebrations of the postpunk, postmodernist condition, teenage courtship rituals have changed remarkably little since the 1950s, and pop still plays much the same part in the organization of adolescent gender roles. We described a pattern of power in the music industry, men in charge, that hasn't altered since. Punk did have an effect on images of sex and romance, but it did little to improve women's career opportunities in or out of show biz. The most important female stars—Madonna, Cyndi Lauper, Tina Turner, Sade—are still important because of their complex (and contradictory) relationships to femininity. Male and female sexuality alike are still referred to male desires; if homosexual, bisexual, and asexual men can now use their confusions (and zest) as a source of pop success, lesbianism remains a secret.

And this is where the problems of our original piece start: our account of how music carries sexual meaning now seems awfully dated. We rejected rock naturalism but we retained the suggestion that sexuality has some sort of autonomous form which is expressed or controlled by cultural practice.

We were writing, ironically enough, just as the fashion in pop cultural analysis became do-it-yourself structuralism, and critics were quick to point out our "essentialist" view of sex. We were reminded that "cultural pro-

duction occurs always in relation to ideology and not to the 'real world' ";
we were instructed that rock is not about something other than itself—
sexuality—but is a "signifying practice" through which a particular "discourse of sexuality" is constituted. The task of criticism, in short, is not to
show how performers articulate a predefined ideology, but to trace the way
sexuality is constructed by the performing conventions themselves, by the
responses they compel listeners to make.

Take Frankie's "Relax." Everyone knew this was a "sexy" record, sexy
in a way most records aren't, but nobody could quite say why, as the BBC
found, to its discomfort, when it tried to explain the "Relax" ban. Sound
as such isn't offensive—BBC bannings always refer to lyrics. But the key
word in "Relax" was the innocent "come," and, in the end, the head of
Radio 1 had to refer his decision to what the group said about the record
in interviews, how they put pictures to it on the video. The record was
offensive for what it *represented*.

The irony of this is that a "deconstructive" reading of "Relax" reveals a
commonplace account of desire (which is why Frankie so quickly found
their place in the British pop establishment). "Relax" is a naughty record,
a singalong party pooper from the tradition that brought us Gary Glitter's
"Do You Wanna Touch Me" and Dave Dee, Dozy, Beaky, Mick, and Tich's
"Bend It." The original "Relax" video (which, seen on *The Tube* by Trevor
Horn, led to Frankie's ZTT contract) had a limited budget, crude camera
angles, and a tacky SM imagery that was much more unsettling than ZTT's
big-budget, snickering lust.

The ZTT "Relax" was a knowing record not just as a production number
but also as a marketing exercise—Frankie were the first pop group to be
sold by a huckster, Paul Morley, inspired by French critics Barthes and
Foucault. And Morley was, in turn, the child of a particular pop age. In the
1960s, when value judgments about music rested on notions of authenticity,
musicians were respected for their sexual honesty. Built into the original
rock aesthetic was the idea that sexual feelings/preferences/desires/anxieties
were either expressed (a good thing) or concealed (a bad thing). Sexuality
was either spoken out—lustily, painfully—or made false by pop's treacly,
romantic norms. The John Lennon story is the most complex example of
this opposition of romance and reality: having rejected pop's romantic lies,
Lennon could only authenticate his love of Yoko Ono by public accounts
of their sex life. And it's instructive too to remember that the Rolling Stones,
who now sound ridiculously camp, were once honored for their truthfulness
in revealing hidden, unrespectable desires.

Since David Bowie and early 1970s glam rock, the aesthetics of British
popular music have changed. Pop stars became valuable for their plasticity
and so their sexuality too became a matter of artifice and play, self-invention

and self-deceit. As rock entered its modernist, formalist stage, punk and disco became they key codes. The Bowie / Alice Cooper / Donna Summer / Malcolm McLaren / Blondie lessons in star-making were learned by everyone. These days, indeed, heavy metal bands, cock rockers writ large, are the most elaborately made-up groups of all.

Put together glam/punk/disco dressing up with the history of British youth posing (and, as Jon Savage has pointed out, every style, from teds to new romantics, took inspiration from the gay underworld), and you get a sociological explanation for Boy George. The general implications for rock and sexuality are, though, less clear. Sociologists themselves seem still wedded to the misconception that boys' concern for fashion somehow "feminizes" them (and it's hard not to assume that skinheads are more "masculine" than their more fancily dressed peers, even in this age of football terrace "casuals"). Rock critics, equally, still draw an instinctive line between the "natural" sexuality of rock tradition and the "artificial" sexuality of the gender benders. This has become obvious in 1985's New Authenticity movement (and the rise of Bruce Springsteen as a popular icon). Part of the appeal of the new generation of guitar/pub/roots bands (and the musicians are almost all male) is their restatement of old rock 'n' roll truths of sex and gender—rutting, romantic men, mysterious, deceptive women.

Such nostalgia can't undo the changes the 1970s made. The best evidence I know for this is Fred and Judy Vermorel's remarkable book, *Starlust*, "the secret fantasies of fans." These obsessive, devotional voices supply the missing strand in accounts of rock and sexuality: the consumer view.

The most misleading of our original arguments was the distinction we made between male activity and female passivity when, in fact, consumption is as important to the sexual significance of pop as production. Teenybop culture, for example, is as much made by the girls who buy the records and magazines as by the boys who play the music and pose for the pinups, and once we start asking how pop produces pleasure, then notions of passivity/activity cease to make much sense. There's pleasure in being fucked as well as in fucking, and how these pleasures relate to gender is the question at issue. What's obvious in the Vermorels' book is that fan fantasies (however masochistic) are a form of vengeance—in dreams we control the stars who in our fandom seem to control us. What's equally apparent is that these private games with public faces are for many fans, male and female, a way of making sense of their own sexuality.

Pop stars' sexual games have changed the rock and sexuality questions. What is interesting now is not how the objects of desire are made and sold—as pinups, heroines, stars—but how sexual subjectivity works, how we use popular music and imagery to understand what it means to have desires, to be desirable. The most important effect of gender bending was to focus the problem of sexuality onto males. In pop, the question became, unusually, what do men want? And as masculinity became a packaging problem, then so did masculine desire—whether this was resolved by Boy George's espousal of chastity, by the careful shot of Marilyn's hairy chest during his drag appearance on *Top of the Pops*, or by the record company instructions to the director of Bronski Beat's first video: he had to make a promo clip that would be, simultaneously, obviously gay in Britain, obviously straight in the United States. In its attempt to make normal such "abnormal" men, the pop process simply drew attention to the fragility of sexuality itself.

Part of the fun of pop lies in this tension between reality and fakery, between experience and expression. *Smash Hits* became Britain's most successful music magazine precisely because of the delight it takes in the collision of pop star myth and mundaneness. Its editors know that pop's sexual come-on lies in the way stars tantalize us with the suggestion that we can get to know them as they *really* are (all those interviews). All fans dream of casual intimacy with their idols (I thus count Dylan, Jagger, and John Lennon among my friends), and even the most torrid sexual fantasy rests on the assumption that to fuck a star is to get to know them most intimately—their sexuality and reality are equated (an equation we make in everyday life too).

In the Vermorels' book the key term is "possession." Fans want to possess their idols just as they feel possessed by them. In material terms this comes out as manic consumer fetishism: every sight and sound of the star is collected, stored, inspected (and the replay button on the VCR adds a new dimension to what can be lovingly yours, again and again and again). In fantasy terms possession is, by its nature, erotic.

Pop effects are usually explained in terms of identity—the key words in most pop songs are "I" and "you," and in "Rock and Sexuality" we suggested that, for the most part, boys identify with the performing "I," girls with the addressed "you." But once we start looking at pop genres in detail, the play of identity and address becomes rather more complicated. Whether in the teenybop education of desire, sixth-form miserabilism (from Leonard Cohen to the Smiths), the Springsteenian community or torch singing, the best records (the ones that give most pleasure) are the ones that allow an ambiguity of response, letting us be both subject and object of the singers' needs (regardless of our or their gender).

And what's crucial to this, of course, is the grain of the voice, the articulation of sexuality, the body, through its timbre, texture, and pulse. Great voices, the ones that make us fans, are distinctive sounds that seem to hold in perfect balance words, rhythm, and personality. (One of the effects of video promotion has been a displacement of the pop voice—Simon LeBon simply isn't as evocative a singer as, say, Cliff Richard. On video, music can be mediated through the body directly; sexual representations are taken from established film codes like pornography and advertisement.)

Most pop songs are love songs but the critical problem is not, as I once thought, to contrast love as show-biz cliché (or romantic ideology) to real life, but to find out first what love is meant to mean. Obsession? Pain? Beautiful feelings? Power? Love songs give private desires a public language, which is why we can use them (and our uses are not necessarily gender divided).

The Vermorels show how much resentment there is in fans' feelings for their stars. Pop stars demand our attention and use their power (the weight of their public presence) to keep it. And the more their songs mean to us as private messages the more we can be unsettled by their public display. The voyeurism involved in pop concerts works both ways; it's not just the *stars'* emotions on show. The power struggle between stars and fans is what gives concerts their sexual charge.

In *Adam Bede*, George Eliot writes of her teenage heroine: "Hetty had never read a novel: how then could she find a shape for her expectations?" Nowadays our expectations are shaped by other media than novels, by film and television fictions, by pop stars and pop songs. Popular culture has always meant putting together "a people" rather than simply reflecting or expressing them, and the popularity of popular singers depends on their emotional force, their ability to build a mass following out of intensely personal desires. There's a way of reading pop history, then, that is profoundly depressing. Who, except for a Barry Manilow fan, could be heartened by his effect on his followers? But what's involved here is not just the appropriation of people's fantasy lives by some very silly love songs (and some very hackneyed porn imagery). The *Starlust* fantasies also express a kind of sexual utopianism, a dream world in which care and passion, abandon and affection can coexist.

What amazes me about pop history is how little the fantasies it has put into play have impinged on everyday life, how few demands they've made of it. The sixties, for all their bad press now, remain important, therefore, as an expression of hedonistic greed—which is why Frankie Goes to Hollywood videos returned, in the end, to hippie imagery, why Paul Morley remains caught on the cusp of provincial bohemianism and metropolitan poise. For him, as for many of us, Patti Smith was the key to the link between modernism and postmodernism, punk and beat, sexual liberation and sexual play. As children now of Barthes and Bowie rather than Marx and Coca-Cola, we may understand the discourse of sexuality better than we did in the 1960s, but the coordination of theory and practice seems as difficult as ever.

PART SEVEN

Reading the Stars

○ ▲ ○ ▲ ○ ▲ ○ ▲ ○ ▲ ○ ▲ ○

In the end, the most important commodities produced by the music industry—as important for the circulation of desire as for the realization of profits—may not be songs or records but stars. Songs work on us and records sell to us because of our identity with or response to them—an identity and response almost invariably mediated through a performer, a person who stands for what we possess, how we are possessed. Record company marketing strategies have long depended on the creation of performers and groups who can thus guarantee sales, and in his essay here, David Buxton describes and criticizes this process from a Marxist perspective. He draws on the traditional Frankfurt School critique of mass culture (see, for example, Adorno's essay in this volume) and more recent French theories of signification.[1] What makes his piece particularly interesting is his suggestion that rock was, in fact, crucial to the making of a consumer society.

The remaining pieces in this section are contrasting readings of specific stars, and we have chosen them partly to supply an instant overview of the most significant positions in rock criticism. Tom Carson's celebration of the Ramones treats them straightforwardly as *representatives* of and for their audience, while Holly Kruse's tribute to Kate Bush is a lyrical reading, a search for the "true" meaning of Bush's songs in her biography. Kruse's approach is an example of the literary critique of rock which first emerged in the late 1960s, following English Department appropriations of Bob Dylan—from this "auteurist" perspective the music business is simply a vehicle that makes available artists whose significance must be rooted in their own imagination. But Kruse also captures the way in which a particular sort of star creates a particular sort of listener (just as Tom Carson's knowing irony is produced by the Ramones' own artfulness). For Kruse, the sheer pleasure of *interpreting* Kate Bush's lyrics is a direct sign of one sort of fan-star identification.

Simon Reynolds represents the 1980s generation of British rock critics and writes about "new pop" in a cooler, more cynical way. He takes the society of the spectacle for granted: he is interested in the star effect on pop's critical discourse itself. His gleeful name-dropping and his playful sense of the provisional nature of all rock meaning stand in sharp contrast to the more earnest American rock critical traditions represented by Carson's street sociology, on the one hand, and Kruse's literary analysis, on the other.

Finally, Greil Marcus pulls together the various strands of European cultural theory and American populist rhetoric in two linked meditations on stars and their meanings in people's lives. He makes clear what is implicit in all good rock criticism: the interpretation of a particular sound always takes place at a particular political moment, in a particular political mood.

NOTES

[1] See, for example, Jean Baudrillard, *For a Critique of the Political Economy of the Sign* (St. Louis: Telos Press, 1972).

ROCK MUSIC, THE STAR SYSTEM, AND THE RISE OF CONSUMERISM

1 9 8 3

○ ▲ ○ ▲ ○ ▲ ○

Rock music permeates all areas of social life, from supermarkets to homes. The intensity of its reception ranges from the fanatical devotion of youth subcultures to cheery accompaniment for household chores. The following deals primarily with analysis of the stars in rock music and rock's relation to consumerism. It does not pretend to be exhaustive of its subject—other obviously important factors like sexuality are artificially left aside. Marxism has tended to attack rock music (and earlier, swing music) because of its commodity basis, and has upheld folk music as ideologically superior. The American Communist Party consciously used folk music as part of its political strategy in the 1930s and 1940s.[1] Thus, following the Bolsheviks' example, classical and contemporary popular music (the swing and jazz music favored by the new American urban population) were declared to be "tools of the ruling class." The canons of socialist realism, that proletarian art should be "national in form and revolutionary in content," led to the search for a national folk music. The folk music of rural Southern hamlets selected for this task, however, was a foreign, esoteric form to urban dwellers outside the South who made up an ever-increasing proportion of the American population after 1920. The impact of this musical strategy never went beyond its Southern, rural roots. Radical folk singers took shelter in their extreme isolation, waiting for the revolutionary leap that never occurred.[2]

This folk-purist approach resurfaced in the late 1950s and early 1960s, this time linked with a wider, non-Communist Left, and enjoyed wide commercial success. Whereas the American Communist Party consistently worked outside the commodity market, using direct participatory singing on picket lines and at meetings (albeit, at a time when records and radio had established their dominance), the new folk singers were successful recording artists. While the older radical singers of the 1930s had kept to a strict ethic of anonymity, the folk revival was marked by the heightened individuality of its stars. The feeling that "every artist's first responsibility is to himself" was shared by Tom Paxton, Bob Dylan, and Phil Ochs, among others. These stars expressed themselves mostly through recordings, saturating the market with issues and rhetorical protest statements. The later folk purists were mistaken in the belief that with the use of nonelectric technology, they were somehow less compromised with monopoly capitalism and its advanced technology: folk music was a commodity on the mass market, and no less "commercial" than the rock and roll they criticized.[3]

This argument had become displaced by the mid-sixties, as influential critics like Jon Landau argued that rock music was, in fact, a genuine folk music, with shared values between audience and performer. The mass consumption of rock, supposedly a folk form with radical, "alternative" values, was seen as evidence of political change among American youth.[4] Ideologues like Tom Hayden and Eldridge Cleaver agreed that the "liberation" of white youth could be rooted in rock: this was only a short step from the idea that "cultural revolution" or "freeing one's mind" (through psychedelic means or otherwise) was an alternative to, or the very manifestation of, political revolution.

Robert Christgau has argued that "rock and roll, as we all know, was instrumental in opening up the generation gap and fertilizing the largely sexual energy that has flowered into the youth lifestyle, and this lifestyle, as we all know, is going to revolutionize the world."[5] Yet rock music, in spite of its apparent desire to be a vehicle for rebellion, had somehow become a valuable corporate interest. A Columbia record advertisement in 1967 claimed: "The Man can't bust *our* music . . . Know who your friends are. And look and see and touch and be together. Then listen. *We* do" (my emphasis). An advertisement for *Rolling Stone* in 1967 appealed for subscribers: "you know rock and roll is more than just music; it is the energy center of the new culture and youth revolution."[6] How had this extraordinary situation come about, in which the radical Left and multinational record companies both proclaimed the central importance of rock as a radical cultural force?

There was nothing pre-given in the emergence and dominance of the record commodity form in popular music. Although the anonymous, participatory, and localist folk tradition had largely diminished in both England and the United States by the turn of the century due to the breakdown of rural commodities under the influence of rapid industrialization, popular music still largely existed outside of the commodity market or as a marginal part of it. Tavern singing, amateur performance, and minstrelism predominated. The most common commodity form of popular music in this period was sheet music, which reinforced amateur performance. The rapid growth of the record into a mass commodity cannot be postulated as the satisfaction of some preexisting "need." Even after the emergence of the record as a musical commodity, no *a priori* reason why this form should have predominated can be given, especially to the extent it became an almost mandatory aspect of youth culture by the late 1960s, largely replacing the significance of live performance. The record could conceivably have remained a marginal commodity for music lovers and collectors. Economic explanations also presuppose an ahistorical concept of need and do not tell us why consumers spend their extra money on records in particular. The emergence of the record as a *mass* commodity was dependent on the corresponding creation of a new social use value for popular music in its record form. However, the specific social "usefulness" of the record must be explained.

According to Baudrillard, use value as conceived by Marx is essentially naturalist: the commodity has use value because it "satisfies human wants of some sort or another." The fetishization of the commodity then is a socially mediated form, exchange value. Baudrillard, however, argues that use value is a fetishized social relation as well. Use value today should not be understood as something "natural" or even as being broadly determined by historical and social factors, but as a fluctuating, variable factor within the commodity itself, which depends on transformations or shifts in the abstract code of signs that regulate social use value in general. This code goes beyond mere "functional" use value,[7] all the more so in products lacking any precise functional use like the record; in this case the ability of the commodity to absorb signifiers is potentially infinite. This absorption can be called the commodity's *enhanced use value.*

This process of absorption, achieved by capitalism through advertising, seeks to generalize the commodity to increasingly mass status by loading it with symbolic value. The synonymity of denim jeans with relaxed, energetic, anti-puritan youth is an example of enhanced use value. The product transcends its immediate functional use to become a key symbol of a whole "life-style," and an anthropomorphized sexuality of the commodity has been a major strategy in this enhancement. This argument implies that the accession of the record to mass status has been a consequence of the symbolic strategies invested in it, rather than any inherent quality of the music recorded on it.

Unlike sheet music, the record is intimately associated with a star system. Once blues music (which can be considered a folk music) was recorded in the 1920s, it developed a tradition of "great singers." Initially, the invention of the microphone as an aid to recording favored a relaxed style of singing, which heightened the nuances of "personality" in each singer, rather than the rigorous technical perfection of the operatic tradition. Moreover, the freezing of social relations as a characteristic of recordings, their congealment into commodity form, circulates the human voice without physical limits, thus fulfilling one of the essential preconditions for the star system: that the star be known without reciprocation by a mass of individuals, whose only common point lies in being represented by the same star. The development of radio technology, which also served to distribute recordings on a mass scale, corresponded with the decline of regional cultures. And whereas in the past, one became a famous personality through the performance of extraordinary deeds, the recording artist became known to hundreds of thousands simply through "being" on record. The emphasis changed from what one "did" to what one was "like."

If we conclude that the record brought with it, for a number of contingent reasons, a star system, what then was the "usefulness" of this star system which enabled the record to accede to mass status? In his historical etymology of the word "consumer," Raymond Williams argues that its original meaning of devouring, waste, and using up was highly unfavorable. Early uses of "consumer" carried over this general sense of destruction or waste. "In a context where value is derived from the land or the direct appropriation of nature, consumption is suicide. It is to use up that which must be maintained and replenished in order to survive."[8]

For the nonurban or the newly urbanized, the wage system represented an intrinsic violation of a basic assumption. The initial reaction was a compulsion to *save*, to appropriate money as if it were land. However, the American economy in the 1920s needed to expand and create new consumer demands—to educate the "masses" in the culture of consumption. The mass production of commodities in ever-increasing abundance demanded a mass market to absorb them. Previously, the worker was seen as a beast of burden, whose leisure time was of little interest, provided it remained within certain moral boundaries. Few employers understood that mass production required the organization of consumption and leisure as well. As Boston magnate Edward Filene stated in 1919: "Mass production demands the education of the masses; the masses must learn to behave like human beings in a mass production world. They must achieve, not mere literacy, but culture."[9]

However, this "enlightened" attitude was not sufficiently predominant to prevent the Great Depression, which was essentially a crisis in the circulation of capital, or "inefficient consumption." It was not until the stability of the mid-1950s that consumerist themes became consecrated in social practice, although they had already been well established. As early as 1892, Simon Patten, an apostle of industrial consumerism, affirmed that the mechanical reproduction of *images* would be decisive for a new economic order.[10]

Monopoly capitalism needed to increase its consumers; markets had to grow horizontally (nationally), vertically (into the working classes), and ideologically (enhanced use values). Of course, this was not an automatic process. While capitalism could discipline people in work, it could not *make* them consume. For the ideologues of the new consumerism, leisure time could no longer be wasted.

As Ewen has shown, advertising theorists were directly influenced by the work of behaviorists, who placed the emphasis on the social construction of personal identity. The transition to a consumer economy required a careful supervision of consumer demands. In other words, the consumer had to be produced along with the product. Advertisers preferred "blank-slate" characters, uncontaminated by a puritan reluctance to consume—the "young" were the logical contenders for this honor.

Advertisers presented a world in which values were no longer communicated in the localized private sphere but rather in the marketplace where the commodity held the promise of "mass" community. Consumerism was the basic social relation; the "liberation" of the self from the traditional family or regional solidarity was the highest form of existence. Having wrenched the self from the security of the traditional, advertisers shattered the body into a series of potential physical and social disasters that only commodity consumption could avert. In the commodity lay the possibility of a united self, the fulfillment of "liberation."

The breakdown of traditional social relations due to urbanization and mass production left personal identity in a void, which consumerism filled as *the* basic social relation. An individual bombarded with a mosaiclike set of commodities (especially those that move beyond comfort-oriented or obviously functional uses), through which an individual identity is established, was likely to make decisions conforming to a certain life-style. These life-styles found conceptual models, in various degrees of specificity, in the person of celebrities. Complete or, more often, partial acceptance simplified the numerous consumer decisions confronting the individual.

The rock star as a life-style model was the outcome of a long process that corresponded to the rise in the 1960s of a large, affluent middle class in the West. Pop singers of the 1930s, who also were associated with a middle-class public, had conveyed a relaxed image which implied that spending on leisure activities was acceptable social behavior. Bing Crosby was an archetype of what later would be described as a role model: a casual, athletic, conformist family man, who stated that "every man who likes me sees in me the image of himself." Participation in advertising furthered the development of the star's life-style model. Kate Smith advertised cigars, while several bandleaders promoted cheese, beer, and household items. The star's personality was embodied in the product sold. Thus, a fan could describe the cigars promoted by Kate Smith as being "really mellow and full of contentment." The presentation of the life-style of the stars as the ideal of sophisticated modern living grew as part of the American dream manufactured during the 1930s.

Some stars were active in defining their role. In 1932, Joan Crawford published a manifesto entitled "Spend!" In response to widespread complaints that film stars were grossly overpaid, Crawford replied that it was the stars' *duty* to maintain the life-style the public associated with their highly visible position. She argued that she must surround herself with the height of luxury so that fans would be satisfied, and further exhorted them to imitate her; "I, Joan Crawford believe in the dollar. Everything I earn, I spend."[11]

This quasi-direct role of the star in organizing consumption was later to be lost as consumption norms became interiorized and advertising more sophisticated.[12] However, Crawford's manifesto does remind us of the extent to which the star played a normative role in promoting consumption. It was only with rock music in the 1960s (and by this time, rock stars had replaced film stars as the dominant star figures)[13] that the essential themes of the 1920s, namely consumption as "liberation" (and no longer as a "duty") and the key role of youth in accelerating the consumption cycle (and thus the circulation of capital) were finally realized. This "liberation" from the puritan restraints on consumption (and sexuality) was realized when youth were sufficiently well off to assume their role as consumers.

In *Discipline and Punish*, Michel Foucault details the development, elaboration, and refinement of a new series of disciplinary techniques that emerged in the army, schools, and workshops. The human body was the object of these measures. Movements and gestures were studied in order to be broken down into simple, machinelike movements. The most obvious impact of this "training of docile bodies" was in work discipline. As the industrialization process increasingly reduced the worker to a mere appendage of a machine, the body was trained to be a machine as well. In this context, physical comfort and relaxation were subversive to work discipline, which extended beyond the factory gate. From an early age, schoolchildren were trained to sit erect; failure to do so was punished.

Public moralists have always sought to rein in the "loose morals" inevitably connected with popular music and dancing[14] which involved body movements that violated work discipline. The undisciplined consumer body was defined in part by the functional relation between music and dance in rock music, a relation enhanced by rhythmic borrowings from the blues and jazz; the sexual freedom widely accepted to be inherent in the music and dance of American blacks provided an apparently liberating element: eroticism. Rock music could be said to have given back to middle-class whites their bodies.[15]

At the same time that rock music assisted in loosening cultural norms against consumption in favor of material fulfillment, there emerged a discriminating consumer "awareness." Typical of this new trend were the mods, a cultural movement in Britain in the 1960s that expressed itself primarily through music and fashion. Mods distinguished themselves through commodities, using goods "as weapons of exclusion, to avoid contamination from other, alien worlds of teenage taste. . . . Mods exploited the expressive potential within commodity choice to its logical exclusion . . . they 'chose' to make themselves into Mods, attempting to impose systematic control over the narrow domain which was theirs and within which they saw their real selves. . . . When the Italian scooter was first chosen . . . it was lifted into a larger unity of taste. . . . Value was conferred upon the scooter by the simple act of selection."[16] The same idea of active, "life-style" consumption is shared by Charles Reich, an ideologue of the American counterculture. According to Reich, "A new generation can come along and can say we're going to take all these things, the stereo, the motorcycles, the things in the supermarkets and the music above all, and we'll command them. Now they'll be tools of revolution instead of tools of repression because we'll use them as we wish. [Now] in both films, and in music, people are making their own culture right in the heart of the repressive machine. . . . That's the miracle of it."[17]

What this analysis presupposes is the internalization of *taste* or *style*: in buying even functional products one must choose among a series of styles, only a few of which *fit* one's personality. However, the development of an individual style reintroduces discipline in respect to consumption norms at another level. Style (and by extension sexuality) becomes publicly visible through externalization. Failure to consume "in style" becomes the basis of social rejection.

Just as the labor process was rationalized by advanced industrialism, consumption had to be made efficient for the stabilization of cyclical economic developments. "Consumer discipline" necessitated not only the confinement of psychological release to the leisure sphere, but also—on a higher level—the cultivation of individual style.

Consumer discipline, however, could not be repressive because (1) the freedom to choose was the basis of "market democracy" and (2) in bourgeois ideology, there has always been a fundamental antinomy between work and leisure. The historical identification of the star system and rock music with "liberation" can be understood better as constituting a reverse image of Bentham's Panopticon.[18] Whereas in the Panopticon, one hidden surveillant in a central tower could survey many individuals while remaining invisible to them, the star, unable to see outward and exposed in intimate detail, is the object of the relentless gaze of an anonymous mass society. The seduction exercised in obtaining this gaze becomes synonymous with "liberation."

Rock stars, as agents of consumer discipline, help to define the norms and limits of the existing sociohistorical consumer, and thus individual possibilities.[19] They anchor a chaotic aesthetico-ideological discourse and represent it in a "humanized" form by investing the human body itself. Thus the record managed to achieve an enhanced social usefulness far exceeding the mere "need" for recorded music. It has become one of the key elements in the constitution of the modern self, increasingly defined in terms of lifestyle. It is not without reason that the more farsighted record executives of the 1960s were enthusiastic over the identification of rock with the "youth revolution."

This is not to suggest that genuinely countercultural values were not an important part of rock music during the 1960s. It is undeniable that rock music served a key role in the struggle over cultural norms. However, it is important not to see rock music as a perpetual conflict between two pure entities, counterculture and corporate capitalism, in which the latter always unfortunately appropriates the former to its own ends. There is no easy demarcation line between radical and capitalist strategies; after all, participants in the countercultural movement were as enthusiastic about McLuhan's "wired-up global village" as were media executives.

Apart from contradictory ties to the political New Left, the counterculture was marked by two discourses: McLuhanism and psychedelia. McLuhan's arguments can be briefly summarized: because electronic media are extensions of people, they have come to determine social being (and not the inverse). The "radical" conclusion of this argument was that one must work through the media for social change. Rock music (along with advertising) was the area in which McLuhan's ideas made the most headway, valorizing a previously despised cultural form into the vanguard of technico-cultural revolution. Countercultural McLuhanites thus argued that the music of Dylan, the Rolling Stones, or the Beatles had done more to change people's consciousness than radical theory or practice. McLuhan and Buckminster Fuller were declared to be "more revolutionary than Marx."[20]

Just as McLuhan served as a bridgehead between "rebellious youth" and economic restructuring, rock music was the fruit of a historically unique alliance between organic cultural forms continually reanimated by a popular base and advanced technology. In the 1960s, the extent to which McLuhanism converged with rock music can be seen in the way it integrated one of the latter's central canons, the "sexual revolution." As McLuhan argued: "the electric media, by stimulating all senses simultaneously, also give a new and richer sensual dimension to everyday sexuality that makes Henry Miller . . . old-fashioned and obsolete."[21]

The other major element of the counterculture, the belief in the spiritually therapeutic value of psychedelic drugs, was not unrelated to McLuhanism. Psychedelia played an important role in the aestheticization of social life in the 1960s which accompanied the media explosion and arguably led to a greater sensibility to color and design, both essential for a more discriminating consumer consciousness. LSD, which in Richard Neville's words "transforms the mundane into the sensational," was to have a profound influence on pop culture, media style, and advertising. Rock music was a key terrain for psychedelia, not only because of the traditional involvement of musicians with drugs, but also because rock music's McLuhanist outlook for social change conferred on psychedelic drugs a complementary role of transforming consciousness.

With the relative success of the alternative life-style wing of the counterculture over its more political counterpart and the heavy media promotion of the "Woodstock Nation," a large aesthetically responsive middle-class youth audience that transcended regional tastes became visible. Furthermore, the association of countercultural ideas with instrumentally dominated "progressive rock" provided a ready frame of reference for the music to penetrate non-English-speaking Europe. From the period after 1970 emerged new rock music genres, marketing types, and "supergroups," a prelude to the sclerosis from which rock music has not yet recovered.

Attempts to link rock with political action, despite their naiveté, were forgotten. Rock music became synonymous with radicalism *tout court*. This is not to suggest that rock music was "reactionary," but that its potential for critical judgment seems to have been suspended. Castigated from the outset as being symptomatic of moral disintegration, vulgarity, and the lowering of cultural standards, rock music has grown into an established aspect of modern personality—it seemingly is beyond criticism. Rock music is strikingly devoid of critical concepts, apart from the elitist arguments of Adorno and the occasional references to corporate domination. It remains immersed in the hubris of individualism, and sexism, and has become an important agent for the Americanization of western culture. By ignoring the possibilities of an alternative organization of culture in favor of symbolic radicalism, rock music helped play an important role in the production of the necessary creative imaginary for capitalist reorganization.

The star is a recent phenomenon. Music hall singers of the nineteenth century cannot be considered stars in the modern sense of the word. They were rather personalities whose celebrity was rooted in local traditions. The fame of popular singers in the Caruso mold, however, depended on their talent being widely recognized in order to transcend local audiences. Their "image," if one can use this word, was "functional"—it conformed to the standards of their profession. Attempts by entertainers to identify with their audiences were initially criticized as "unprofessional."[22]

The large-larynxed concert-style voice effected by earlier popular singers like Al Jolson proved, however, unsuitable for the microphone and radio. The role of the microphone in establishing a singer's personality can be seen in the sex appeal attributed to Rudy Vallee on the basis of his broadcast voice alone. The primary personality attribute of the popular music star was "sincerity."[23] Second-level stars also tried to embody this characteristic but with less authenticity and aura. As Robert Merton suggests in his study of Kate Smith, this sincerity of the star is a denial "of a discrepancy between appearance and reality in the sphere of human relationship."[24] The star seemed to be a guarantee of community in a world where it is lost.

The emphasis on personality continued through the rock music period, in spite of a sharp musical rupture. Personalities, however, were now young, and aimed at a youthful audience.[25] They referred to other personalities not always musical, and were manufactured accordingly: Elvis Presley was described as a "guitar-playing Marlon Brando," while Terry Dene and Cliff Richard in Britain were modeled as Elvis Presley lookalikes. Adam Faith was modeled on James Dean. In short, stars were manufactured on the basis of already-proven personalities, preferably as physical lookalikes of established idols.

Whereas previously the style of singers and their music was supposed to flow naturally from their personality, style was now constructed to suit the music, and was arbitrarily related to the singer's "personality." This opened the way for the total integration of the singer into fashion and design. With the wave of British groups from 1964 onward, little attempt was made to promote individual personalities: rather, a distinctive group style was presented that borrowed heavily from fashion. Styles were reproduced instead of personalities. This is not to suggest that the age of the great personalities was over (the Beatles successfully traversed both formats), but rather that a "group style" replaced stars at the second level of the pop hierarchy.

As the work of design engineers became oriented toward the creation of artificial differences between products, rock groups too began to be distinguished on the basis of superficial stylistic features. No form of visual overkill was excluded to make the "product" *interesting*. The very success of styles originating in pop music in formulating a design aesthetic in the wider sense (mod, psychedelia, glitter rock, and even punk rock to some extent) suggests that rock music plays a role in product design, creating enhanced use values in abstract form which can subsequently be transferred to other products. The rock star mediates between this abstract enhanced use value and the consumer in anthropomorphic form, thus creating new use values which engender specialized consumers. Rock stars, like commodities, move within a totally designed environment.

Rock musicians, in response to what they saw as the increasing commercialization of music during the 1960s, sought to distinguish themselves from this trend by emphasizing the internal convictions of the *artist* as opposed to the external trappings of style. In opposing stylistic manipulation, musicians returned to "sincerity," a previous criterion of the star, manifested by a commitment to counterculture values and the themes of nineteenth-century romanticism, from the communication of higher spiritual values like "love" (Shelley, Donovan, Jefferson Airplane) to the exaltation of decadence (Baudelaire, Velvet Underground, the Doors).

The later, more violent critique of established rock stars by the punk rock movement (which questioned the social relations involved in the production of music as well) also, in its own way, resurrected the criterion of sincerity to mythical rock values. Its polemic condemned the failure to conform to the norms of rock musical stardom: shared values between audience and performer, and youth.

The "homological" relation between pop subcultures and a life-style manifested in symbolically laden objects does not necessarily mean that all pop subcultures are capable of transferring enhanced use value on a mass scale. Nevertheless cultural movements are always *potentially* capable of being repackaged for mass marketing and aesthetically generalized. This process of generalization has more to do with the specific aesthetico-ideological conjuncture than any inherent, self-defined quality of "rebellion" or the lack of it. To the extent that rock music in the late 1960s embodied "alternative values" for a mass of middle-class youth, it raised the enhanced use value of the record to new heights.[26]

There is evidence that the star is a declining force today. This decline is a complex process that cannot be reduced to one or several causes. A large part of the reason, however, is the decline in record sales. This decline cannot be explained away as an effect of the general economic crisis, for all leisure commodities have not been similarly affected. The record has lost much of its aura as a commodity; its social use value has fallen. This is especially evident with the rise of disco music, in which music was reduced to its most functional use as dance music.[27] There are other reasons as well; rock music as an art form is undoubtedly in crisis. Musically limited from the beginning, it has vainly sought to extend itself through eclectic borrowings from other traditions. The musical stagnation of the 1970s is reflected in the number of re-releases and endless revivals of rock music's own past.

Another factor in the decline of the star has been the emergence of computer technology in music, which bypasses the relation between musicians and traditional instruments, on which a large part of the star mythology was based. Music making has become an affair of technicians and record producers. Kraftwerk, an electronic group, has pushed this development to its logical conclusion by employing robots as onstage replacements.

Record production for a smaller market will probably follow the same path as film production after the latter lost most of its audience to television.[28] In most cases, a record must break internationally to become profitable. Under these circumstances, stars become homogenized and abstract, deprived of any organic content. Moreover the criticism of a "moral-decay" and "sixties permissiveness" as causes of America's economic decline also implicates the hedonism that is essential to rock star mythology.

As argued earlier, the star system presupposes the breakdown of traditional forms of organic culture and the creation of a mass audience. This lack of organic community has enormous consequences for the way in which we think of popular music. If the quality of individual life depends on the coherence and depth of social relations, then the existence of stars and the individual–mass society dialectic on which they draw implies not only an impoverished sphere of social relations, but also an impoverished sense of the individual; it is not insignificant that mass culture aims at "average" individuals who make up a *silent* majority.

In spite of its reputation for radicalism, albeit almost entirely limited to the symbolic level, rock music remains one of the last bastions of laissez-faire capitalism. Whereas in most domains, the advanced capitalist countries have, to a greater or lesser extent, instituted a public sphere to protect society against the excesses of the market, such a sphere is singularly lacking in popular music, thus making it an abnormally conservative domain. The notion of a public sphere, involving complex relations between state and civil society, is not, of course, unproblematic: nothing could be worse than state control of licensed pop groups as in the Soviet bloc.

Such a public sphere would encourage the flourishing of forms of popular music that do not obey the logic of a market increasingly content to pack stadiums with bland supergroups. It is also important that rock music and the issues surrounding it (sexism, youth culture, computerization) be subject to much more *critical* discussion than has been hitherto the case. What is desperately needed are forms of cultural intervention that allow pleasure, satisfaction, and aesthetic experience outside the dominant modes of commodity consumption. The present stagnation in capitalist cultural industries, due largely to a "petrification of the social" (Baudrillard), demands imaginative alternatives.

NOTES

[1] The political idealization of folk was of Bolshevik and Stalinist origin (Stalin reputedly liked folk music). In the revolution, folk songs and fairy tales were used to win over an illiterate peasantry, and in the 1920s rural culture was deemed "proletarian." In 1929 the Proletarian's Musicians' Association of Moscow is reported to have characterized folk music "as the true expression of the working class."

[2] For more detail, see Serge Denisoff, *Great Day Coming* (Chicago: University of Illinois Press, 1971).

[3] A similar confusion appears in the critique of disco by rock "purists" as "mass-produced," as if rock retained artisan status. This attitude often rests on a naive humanism of the artists and their "work." As Landau put it: "To me, the criterion of art in rock is the capacity of the musician to create a personal, almost private universe and to express it fully." Landau, *It's Too Late to Stop Now* (Straight Arrow Books, p. 15). The initial folk versus pop opposition surfaced within rock in the sixties in the demarcation of what was characterized as "progressive" or "art" rock, from "mass art" (commercial pop).

[4] As Christopher Lasch points out, as politics becomes more and more unmistakably an occupation of elites, ordinary citizens feel they can make their influence felt by designing an "alternative lifestyle." C. F. Lasch, "Happy Endings," *New York Review of Books*, 12 March 1981.

[5] Christgau, *Any Old Way You Choose It: Rock and Other Pop Music*, 1967–73 (Penguin), p. 95.

[6] The previous quotes are from Michael Lydon, "Rock for Sale," In J. Eisen (ed.), *Age of Rock 2* (New York: Vintage Books, 1970).

[7] This is not to suggest, of course, that there is any isolable, "zero-degree" of functionality. The difference between Marx and Baudrillard may be more historical than conceptual. In the *Grundrisse*, Marx does remark that the capitalist "searches for means to spur workers on to consumption, to give his wares new charms, to inspire them with new needs through constant chatter, etc." Karl Marx, *Grundrisse: Introduction to the Critique of Political Economy*, trans. Nicolaus (New York, 1973), p. 287.

[8] Stuart Ewen and Elizabeth Ewen, "Americanisation and Consumption," *Telos* 37 (Fall 1978), p. 45.

[9] Stuart Ewen, *Captains of Consciousness* (New York: McGraw-Hill, 1976), pp. 54–55.

[10] Patten was also to announce the end of the work ethic in *The New Basis for Civilization* (1905). This new civilization was to be based on "self-expression" rather than "self-denial."

[11] Kenneth Anger, *Hollywood Babylon* (New York: Straight Arrow, 1975).

[12] This can be seen in the evolution of record album covers, which followed general patterns in advertising. At first (1950–mid-1960s), a full-frontal image of the star dominated covers; later, a more subtle, complex image was to be given by codes or design motifs which constituted the star's image in his or her *absence*. This coincides with the decline of personality sponsorship in advertising and the rise of signs of connotation, often totally arbitrary to the function of the product. This evolution indicates the integration of rock music into the world of fashion and design. See the *Album Cover Album*, ed. Roger Dean and Hipgnosis, 1977.

[13] Rock music assumed the liberation ethic of consumerism to the full, as unlike the stars of another new medium, television, they were not directly overseen by sponsors aiming at a mass market. "The stars of TV are very circumspect, because the people who sponsor them won't put up with any nonsense. So you have . . . people who are not particularly colorful, not particularly maverick." Walter Scott's Personality Parade in 1958, quote by A. Cockburn in *Celebrity*, ed. James Monaco (New York, 1978). The difference between film and rock stars is more difficult to theorize because of a long tradition of frequent crossovers between the cinema and popular music. Rock stars replaced cinema stars in the 1960s, especially among the young; this was to a large extent a consequence of the decline of film. American filmmaker Paul Morrissey, known for his work with Andy Warhol, commented: "You had this vacuum in the 1960s, there were no young stars put out by Hollywood. . . . So the kids wanted heroes, and in the vacuum, they turned to the dreariest source material—musicians . . . but at least they were young." Interview in *Rolling Stone*, 1971 April 15. In their preconsumer affluence period, and before the "embourgeoisement" of film in the 1930s (E. Morin), film stars were "interesting personalities" who, surrounded by luxury, brought glamour into the lives of fans. Apart from obvious exceptions, the reverse is probably more true of rock stars: dull professionals are made glamorous by the excitement and imagination of fans. However, the distinction between the worlds of rock and television remains significant—to a large extent, television personalities have taken over the circumspect, normative, family-oriented role of pre–rock and roll popular singers.

[14] Before the 1920s, dancing was equated with the suffragette movement by conservative moralists who saw dancehalls, and the debauchery popularly associated with them, as a radical alternative to the "hearth and home." Jazz was seen as a threat to business life. The *Ladies Home Journal* traced the moral downfall of 1,000 black girls in Chicago between 1920 and 1922 to jazz.

[15] However, the acceptance of the "black body" requires mimicry by white musicians. Elvis Presley imitated black singers and achieved mass popularity, while none of the singers he copied achieved a similar status.

[16] Dick Hebdige, "Object as Image," *Block* 5 (1981).

[17] Interview with Charles Reich, *Rolling Stone*, 4 February 1971.

[18] For a more detailed discussion of the Panopticon see Michel Foucault, *Discipline and Punishment: The Birth of the Prison*, trans. Sheridan (New York: Pantheon, 1979) pp. 195–228; and Norberto Bobbio, "Democracy and Invisible Government," *Telos 52* (Summer 1982), pp. 50–51.

[19] It should be emphasized that rock music stars are overwhelmingly male and that the few women in rock music are generally constrained by stereotypes of female sexuality. This does not mean, of course, that women are uninfluenced by rock music life-styles. However, the current new wave music features an increasing number of women as musicians and "stars," a development that requires the analysis of women in rock music concerning their influence on life-style making. This lies beyond the scope of this study.

[20] In retrospect, this "revolution" accompanied a profound restructuring in which computers, electronics, and the media began to replace the old industrial base of capitalism. McLuhanism was the natural ideology of the new technocratic strata, which still bathe in McLuhan's glamour.

[21] An interview in *Playboy*, March 1969.

[22] Commenting on the behavior of popular singer Eddie Jobson, who went so far as to take off his collar and tie, and stroll among the audience, critic Patterson James wrote in the December 1921 issue of *Billboard* that a more sophisticated audience "will decline to be put on a footing of personal social intimacy, and will demand that he work at his business of entertaining, not by using them, but by using the stage and his own wits for material."

[23] The rise of the singer as personality threatened bandleaders, who saw popular singers as rivals to their own "professional" fame. While a singer in Paul Whiteman's band, Bing Crosby had to pretend he was a musician by fiddling with a rubber-stringed violin or guitar between verses. After World War II, singers replaced bandleaders as "stars."

[24] Robert Merton, *Mass Persuasion* (New York: Harper, 1946).

[25] "The main point about pre–rock and roll culture is that society conducted itself as if it were homogeneous. . . . It was, in brief, theoretically possible for everyone to dig the common culture. . . . [This] worked very effectively until kids demanded music the family couldn't take." Howard Junker, "Ah, the Unsung Glories of Pre-rock," *Rolling Stone*, 2 December 1970.

[26] Conversely, that record sales do not necessarily follow economic trends can be seen in the relatively low sales growth during musically "unexciting" years. See R. Peterson and D. Berger, "Cycles in Symbol Production; the Case of Popular Music," *American Sociological Review 40* (1975), pp. 158–73.

[27] Disco music was problematic for record companies because it was "noncreative," i.e., it did not easily transmit other cultural spinoffs. See "Industry in Crisis," *Melody Maker*, 30 June 1979.

[28] See Armand Mattelart, *Multinational Corporations and the Control of Culture* (1979), ch. 6.

ROCKET TO RUSSIA

1 9 7 9

○ ▲ ○ ▲ ○ ▲ ○

In midsummer of 1977, Sire Records released "Sheena Is a Punk Rocker," a new single by the Ramones. That summer was the high-water mark of the punk era—an era that had begun the year before, when the first wave of New York underground club bands started getting record contracts, and would end, for all practical purposes, with the breakup of the Sex Pistols in January of 1978. After that, though punk survived, it was no longer a revolution. But that hadn't happened yet. At CBGB's and Max's Kansas City, the atmosphere was heady with confidence. Everyone was ready to believe that by the end of the year punk rock would have taken the Top 40 by storm, and brought the mainstream of the culture to submission in one quick and easy battle; it was the old fantasy of the American bohemian underground, of finally being accepted by the rest of the country—a dream much older than rock 'n' roll itself. There was a sense that people all around you were doing fine things, in a way they might never have the chance to again. To be in New York that summer was to have some sense of what it might have been like to live in San Francisco in 1966 or 1967, or in London when the Beatles and the Stones first hit.

"Sheena" caught the mood. From the shout of "Go!" that kicked off its raucous guitar attack, the chords bumping into each other in an endlessly ascending spiral, to the ethereal, soaring fadeout two minutes and forty-five seconds later, it was an unremitting frenzy of all-out exhilaration: it blew away the posturing nihilism of "Blank Generation," the only previous punk-rock anthem, in an explosion of pure, cataclysmic joy. Sheena, the girl who didn't want to go to a disco and went out looking for something better, was punk's first great convert, and there was a whole world of tension teetering in the infinitesimal pause after "Sheena is . . ." before the band broke loose into the yammering liberation of the chorus; the pride of "Well New York City really has it all" told the other half of the story. It was as casual as a throwaway—a good dance tune, no more—but it was also one of those rare songs that not only define the tempo and aura of a certain time and place but suggest, almost compel, a whole way of life.

At that time, the Ramones had released two albums—*Ramones* and *Leave Home*—and occupied a position of almost unparalleled authority in the punk community. More than any other band, they had defined the music in its purest terms: a return to the basics that was both deliberately primitive and revisionist at the same time, a musical and lyrical bluntness of approach that concealed a wealth of complex, disengaging ironies underneath. It was zero-based rock 'n' roll, and the conquest was so streamlined that the smallest shifts in nuance, when they came, had enormous implicit resonance.

At the same time, the band set the attitude: a comic resentment toward the rest of the world, a defiant pleasure in trashiness, and the tawdry excesses of urban lowlife. Punks, in the original sense of the word, were the sort of people who were such hopeless losers that they couldn't even be convincing as outlaws; far from romanticizing that status, the Ramones glorified their own inadequacy. Their leather jackets and strung-out, streetwise pose weren't so much an imitation of Brando in *The Wild One* as a very self-conscious parody—they knew how phony it was for them to take on those tough-guy trappings, and that incongruousness was exactly what made the pose so funny and true. And yet they were genuinely sexy, too; in spite of everything, they were cool. American myths are never so immediately recognizable, and irresistible, as when they're turned into a joke.

The Ramones lived out that double-edged vision in all sorts of ways. They were raised on the pop-culture religion; they believed in the Top 40 as the melting pot of the teenage American dream, where clichés and junkiness and triviality take on the epic sweep of a myth and the depth of a common unconscious. But they themselves were minority artists, working far outside the mainstream, and that, paradoxically, gave them the freedom to live out everyone's private fantasy that the Top 40 really told the truth, instead of being the shoddy compromise it always actually was; they were also sophisticated modern ironists, working with all the alienation and distance that implied. *Rocket to Russia* isn't imitation Top 40; it's a fan's vision of what the Top 40 ought to be.

What that meant, among other things, was that they could play as fast, loud, and mean as they wanted to; they could deliver on the anarchic promise hidden beneath the pieties of AM radio. And because they had no use at all for the empty fluency and virtuoso craftsmanship of most seventies rock

(" 'tasty licks,' and all that Traffic twaddle," as Lester Bangs once put it, being a little unfair and dead right at the same time), they could get their effects with an economy and verve. On stage, they rammed their way through their sets at the speed of a subway express slamming from station to station; Johnny and Dee Dee leaped to the rim of the stage, thrusting out their axes with the comic ferocity of Popeye tripping out on spinach, while Tommy acted smooth and unruffled and Joey just wrapped himself around the mike stand, hanging on for dear life. On *Rocket to Russia*, there's never any grandstanding, none of the careful preparation you hear in most modern rock 'n' roll: there just isn't time for any of that. Even the occasional flourishes—the perfect simplicity of the four tom-tom beats that break into the last chorus of "Rockaway Beach," the faint echo on the shouts of "lo-ba-to-*may*!" that open "Teenage Lobotomy"—have a utilitarian speed. The musicians just grab for what they need, set it down, and rush on, and it all goes by in a blur.

Ramones was a tour de force of deadpan comedy; there was a furious, galvanizing wit in its reduction of rock 'n' roll to the dumb, howling noise everyone always loved it for before they loved it for anything else, and in its reduction of modern urban horror to the glazed-eyed banality of a punk's "What, me worry?" shrug. It had the kick of a shared secret dragged out into the open—of a high-school dirty joke that you suddenly realize every other tenth grader in the country knows, too. Shortly after it was released, I remember running into a redneck acquaintance of mine from Virginia, a sort of teenage derelict-in-training whom I hadn't seen in years; he wanted at once for me to tell him everything I knew of the Ramones, and later on in the evening I remember him chanting the lyrics to "Beat on the Brat" with an expression of blissful contentment on his face. It was about the only thing we had in common, but it was enough.

The sequel, *Leave Home*, necessarily didn't have quite the immediate excitement of *Ramones*, but in many ways it had more depth, lurking beneath the bombed-out surface. If there were plenty of parodic songs with titles like "You're Gonna Kill That Girl," there was also "I Remember You," with that lovely moment when the excitement in Joey's voice turns the single word "you" into pure poetry; and the wistful "What's Your Game." Most important, perhaps, in retrospect, was "Oh Oh I Love Her So," a near-perfect evocation of teenage romance in the neon-lit urban landscape which the Ramones had already claimed as their own turf: "I met her at the Burger King," Joey began, "we fell in love by the soda machine. . . ." All very funny, but genuinely evocative, too. Having completely negated the whole superstructure of received ideas which had been the bane of rock 'n' roll for years, the band could now begin to approach the old clichés and stereotypes as their own discovery, and make them come alive again in this new, ironic framework.

Even so, "Sheena" was a breakthrough. Formally, the playful Beach Boys harmonies and the bouncy freedom of the riff went far beyond anything the band had done before; the lyrics, though full of teasing allusiveness, were utterly without the disengagement of irony—they drew you inside in a spirit of open celebration. Once again, the Ramones were reworking a hackneyed genre—the rock 'n' roll song about rock 'n' roll—and making it their own. On *Ramones*, there had been a cut called "Judy Is a Punk," which was no more than another comic-horrible put-down; it's the addition of the word "rocker" that makes all the difference, and the message of "Sheena"— like that of Lou Reed's classic "Rock & Roll" itself—is that her life was saved by rock 'n' roll. For all their tongue-in-cheek humor, the Ramones, like Reed, meant it literally; in fact, it was the only kind of redemption they would admit to.

Rocket to Russia followed in late autumn. Though "Sheena" was easily the best song on it, there were still many surprises; the rest of the album took its cue from "Sheena," and took off in all sorts of new directions to affirm what "Sheena" was all about. More than anything else, it was the band's new assertiveness, their brazen pride in their own identity, that opened up the album. From the punning title—"rocket" for "rock it"—to the invocation of "Ramona" and the wonderful double entendre of "Rock, rock, Rockaway Beach," the Ramones never let you forget that this was rock 'n' roll, and they had just as much of a stake in it as anyone else.

The music was manic, driving, exquisitely controlled; the songs were as barbed and funny as ever, but they also had surprising warmth. "Teenage Lobotomy" was another portrait of a modern urban zombie, but now it had turned into a gleeful, openly self-delighted boast; "I Can't Give You Anything" sounded more like a promise than a threat; the free-floating, merry-go-round rhythms of "Locket Love" belied the bitterness of its lyric. The ballad "Here Today, Gone Tomorrow," put the disassociated bleakness of the Ramones' sound to tellingly emotional use in a painfully, comically direct account of the burned-out end of a love affair.

Everywhere on the album, the Ramones pushed their punk ironies to the limit, and then turned around and trampled those boundaries with an infectious, all-embracing zest. Conceptually, perhaps, a song like "Rockaway Beach" is an East Coast takeoff on a California surf epic—since Rockaway Beach, in Queens, is one of the few beaches in America you take a subway to get to—but it breaks the parodic mold to become a genuine celebration of the place; there's a palpable delight in the very absurdity of this artificial teenage paradise stuck in the middle of the urban concrete. Very little in seventies rock is genuinely urban; in fact, most of it doesn't have much sense of place at all—synthetic substitutes, like the Eagles' *Desperado*, seem to come at you out of a vacuum. The triumph of the Ramones is that they *were* urban, and modern as Martians in their black leather jackets, and were able to find pleasure and even joy in that transient, junky, corrupt milieu.

One of the chief delights of rock 'n' roll is that it's trash music for a trash culture; when Chuck Berry wrote down his version of the American dream, it wasn't any chaste pastoral grandeur he chose to mythologize, but juke-boxes and hamburgers and neon. What makes the music liberating is that it's resolutely not respectable. This is obvious enough, but it's something rock 'n' roll is trying to forget—as jazz, for instance, successfully forgot: I'm sure that there are all kinds of people out there who would give a *moue* of distaste if you told them the stuff started out as whorehouse music.

When rock turned classy and "mature" in the late sixties, the move was inextricably tied up with the utopianism of the counterculture; the possibility of revolution was the only thing that gave *Sergeant Pepper* and the flood of pretensions in its wake credibility. When the countercultural dream died, it turned all that visionary artiness into pure sludge—icing with the cake shot out from under it. The first five years of the seventies were a long tunneling out from the wreckage of the sixties, and they were among the worst years in rock 'n' roll history, as smugly reactionary as the void between the apostasy of Elvis and the arrival of the Beatles; like the generation it created, the music had lost its focus. What gave a postpunk resurgence like *Some Girls* its marvelous kick was that after years of playing the seventies game, and being depressingly polite about it, the Stones were turning around and pissing on respectability, pissing on the gas station walls again—while Mick wrote obscene put-downs of his own ex-wife in the men's room, no less!—and sounded as if they were having a great time doing it, too. They had remembered trash.

The Ramones, however, never needed to be reminded. The Edenic, antimaterialist sentimentality of an event like Woodstock would have been utterly alien to them, as alien as the glossy emptiness that followed it; they were living out Nabokov's dictum that nothing is more exhilarating than philistine vulgarity. They took Berry's message even further than he had, because they capitalized on the random violence and brutality that went hand-in-hand with the raw, funky charge of big-city life; it's that sense of danger—instant and enormous—that gives their music its panicky, brutal-ized edge. And yet the violence was so extreme, and so anonymous, that it became just another pop cartoon. If that was a depressing truth, the Ramones were cocky enough, and heretical enough, to say that it was ridiculous, too; and even to say that it was not without its appeal. Their reveling in the trashy vitality of such an overwrought atmosphere was a life-affirming manifesto.

So their songs were two-minute artillery barrages of pounding rhythm without a shred of melodic soothing, and both on stage and on record they played the role of mutant Dead End kids, brain-damaged cripples, teenage fascists. Some of that was pure shock tactics; some of it was a deliberate subversion of the whole sixties peace-and-love, acid-trance sensibility, which by the time they came around had turned into the Quaalude sensibility, and which they loathed because it was false. But mostly it was just a caricatured, hence accurate, reflection of their own experience. ("The young . . . are Germans, one and all, from fifteen to twenty-one," Leslie Fiedler once wrote, in a line that rings a lot truer than almost anything the youth-consciousness pundits ever said; "We're the members of the master race," the Dictators told the teenagers of America, not too long before the Ramones came out with "Blitzkrieg Bop" and "Today Your Love, Tomorrow the World.") The Ramones turned themselves into campy pseudo-Nazi grotesques because identity justified their reality, and their rebellion, as much as Jerry Garcia's acid-fuzzed religiosity justified his.

Their best anthem before *Rocket to Russia* was a song called "Pinhead," from *Leave Home*, which was both a joke ("I don't want to be a pinhead no more / I just met a nurse that I could go for") and a call to arms: they used to finish their stage shows with its closing chant of "Gabba Gabba Hey!" with Joey holding those words aloft on a placard. "Pinhead," of course, derived from Tod Browning's 1932 underground classic *Freaks*. When it was first released, the movie—a story about the assorted cripples, geeks, and pinheads of a circus sideshow, who wreak their revenge on the normality symbolized by the icily beautiful blonde trapeze artist who betrays one of them—was presented as straight horror. When it was revived in the seventies, however, the new teenage underground had no trouble identifying with the freaks' attack on the straight world. Self-proclaimed freaks themselves, they dug the misshapen outcasts on the screen as their own mythic self-image.

The Ramones brought that identification into the open, and if they instinctively treated it as black comedy, they also glorified it. By the time *Rocket to Russia* came out, those images had become familiar, and the jokes had become a great deal more than jokes: they had taken on the faceless universality of the girls in the Beatles' early rockers or the Beach Boys' California surf. "Cretin Hop," the lurching dance song that opens *Rocket to Russia*, has a crazed grandeur that goes all the way back, in its arrogant, incandescent silliness, to "Rock Around the Clock" or Little Richard's earliest assaults on human sanity. It's no accident, either, that "Teenage Lobotomy," on side 2, segues immediately into the classic, sensual grace of "Do You Wanna Dance": the grotesque and the celebratory are one.

But for the Ramones there had never, really, been that much of a distinction to be made; they had inherited a sense of life as pure camp from the early sixties, from Twiggy and Warhol and movies like *Beach Blanket Bingo*. The bands that influenced them most weren't the established greats of the era, either—just to cite the most obvious example, Dylan might just as well never have been born for all the Ramones cared—but such semicool, semilaughable second-echelon groups as Herman's Hermits (not only Joey's put-on Cockney accent, but a lot of his phrasing, too, derives directly from Peter Noone), the Troggs, the 1910 Fruitgum Company, the Ventures, and Paul Revere and the Raiders (what was the black leather and jeans uniform, after all, but a seventies equivalent for those neat little colonial outfits?). It was music that was close to bubblegum, and in the seventies the Ramones remained, subversively, close to bubblegum: from the cute conceit of their assumed names down to their logo—a caricature of the Great Seal with a baseball bat in the American eagle's claw and the message "Look Out Below" clutched in its beak—their whole iconography came out of the cheerful travesties of sixties pop. They were like a teenybopper magazine's Dream Date gone film noir.

Rocket to Russia had all the fun of bubblegum, but it was emphatically not innocent: precisely what makes a song like "Sheena" so satisfying is that its exuberance is knowing and earned, not ingenuous. The peculiar astringency of the Ramones' style—Joey's insistence on keeping the "I" in his vocals separate from himself, and in a song like "Why Is It Always This Way" separating that "I" from everything it observes—is the result of their not being a sixties bubblegum band, but seventies revisionists fully aware of everything that's happened in between. The Rolling Stones depended instinctively on that kind of relativism from the start, which is why a cut like "Out of Time" sounds as up-to-date as ever, while the Beach Boys and a lot of the early Beatles, for all the undeniable greatness of the music, now sound, not false, maybe, but incomplete: you have to forget a little of what you know to enter into that world completely. The sixties harmonies on *Rocket to Russia* are intentionally distant echoes—they're like a half-forgotten memory floating in the background of the songs.

However, implicitly from the start, and overtly by the time *Rocket to Russia* came out, the Ramones weren't content to point up that ironic distance; if they were the children of sixties pop absurdism, they never really succumbed to the pop nihilism that was its psychological nerve. For all its images of alienation and disjunction, *Rocket to Russia* is comically exultant, a conquest; the affirmation has an overwhelming power because it's wrestled out of such debased and ugly circumstances.

The attractiveness of the comic loser, the man at the end of his rope whose private victory is his own defiant pride in not letting go, is the closest thing we have to the idea of the holy fool. You can hear him in Lou Reed shrugging off the sex-and-suicide despair of *Berlin* with the hilariously tight-lipped moral, "Just goes to show how wrong you can be"; or in Gary Gilmore saying irritably to a *Playboy* interviewer, "Accidents can happen to psychopaths just as easily as anybody else, man." In most places, a line like "Hang on a little bit longer / Hang on, you're a goner" from *Rocket to Russia*'s "Locket of Love" would be a baffling paradox. In America, it makes perfect sense, because failure is the national joke; failure is freedom. When, in "I

Wanna Be Well," Joey follows the line "Daddy's broke" with the gee-whiz bemusement of "Holy smoke," and answers "My future's bleak" with the mocking question, "Ain't it neat?", he sounds outrageously pleased with himself.

The low appeal of turning failure into comic pride, of twisting the whole hierarchy of success and defeat around to make it say the opposite of what it seems to mean—of the subversive gesture—is most of the fun of *Rocket to Russia,* and most of its art as well. "Why Is It Always This Way" is about a suicide, but it's set to an almost frolicsome, upbeat rhythm, with a bouncy "hey, hey, hey" in the chorus; "Here Today, Gone Tomorrow" is as lovely and open a song as any the Ramones have done, but it's still played off against the up-yours kiss-off of its title; and these flippancies, far from blunting the impact of the songs, are exactly what gives them their vitality and kick. It's not graffiti transformed into art so much as it's art redeemed by the spirit of graffiti.

The Ramones are such a pure expression of American pop culture— devious, dumb, brilliant, and exhilarating—that it's an almost irresistible temptation to intellectualize about them. You can have analytical fun trying to figure out the interplay of irony and authenticity in "Teenage Lobotomy," say, or noticing the way the word "time" is used in three consecutive lines, with three different meanings, in "Here Today, Gone Tomorrow." That may not be completely irrelevant, but it somehow misses the point. The real revelations come elsewhere. They come when Johnny, for instance, plays a guitar solo on "Here Today, Gone Tomorrow" that lifts the song right off the ground, not just because the idea of Johnny playing a solo is so beautifully unexpected but because it suddenly seems so exactly right and necessary. Or when you hear the ecstatic longing in Joey's singing on "Do You Wanna Dance," struggling to stay afloat above a churning storm of heavy-metal riffing. Or in the sudden sweetness of "Ramona," a song that captures the essence of what the Ramones mean to their audience, and vice versa, in four wonderfully easy and seductive lines:

> *You're getting better and better*
> *It's getting easier than ever*
> *Hey you kids in the crowd*
> *You know you like it when the music's loud . . .*

Or in a dozen other moments one could name, when the guitar; the pumping, insistent bass; the graceful punctuation of Tommy's drumming; and Joey's back-street, punky-tough voice twisting itself around a lyric all come together with a throat-catching immediacy that has nothing to do with analysis and everything to do with the galvanizing, primal joy of rock 'n' roll itself. You could say that it's all a joke, done just for fun; but in America, simply having a good time is an elusive, tricky ideal, and even jokes have a moral significance. The achievement of *Rocket to Russia* is that it makes its own brand of fun stand for something a lot deeper and more liberating than all the heavy profundity of most of the profound and heavy albums you could name. It's the kind of deadly serious kidding that rock 'n' roll, and America, couldn't live without.

IN PRAISE OF KATE BUSH

1 9 8 8

○ ▲ ○ ▲ ○ ▲ ○

In the American musical mainstream, the most innovative performers are usually the least commercially successful. This may be less true in Great Britain, where avant-garde artists such as Laurie Anderson have reached the number one position on the pop singles chart, but even that was considered a novelty, and it remains surprising that the most commercially successful female recording artist in Britain is Kate Bush. Kate Bush's music integrates intellectually challenging subject matter into complex and often experimental instrumental arrangements. Her 1985 album *Hounds of Love*, for example, which was a Top 10 record in the United Kingdom, contained songs dealing with out-of-body experiences, the later life of Wilhelm Reich, and witch trials; and Bush frames her visions in arrangements that combine ancient folk instruments with the latest in synthesizer technology. How has such an apparently "uncommercial" artist been able to succeed within the constraints of the music industry? This question is the focus of the first half of my essay. In the second half I examine the ways in which Bush's music—specifically that found on *Hounds of Love*—employs intricate musical and narrative structures to convey her vision of a human essence that transcends temporal boundaries.

THE MAKING OF AN
UNLIKELY POP STAR

Kate Bush's entry into the music business was in itself unconventional. She began writing songs while still in her early teens, and by the time she was in her mid-teens, she and her family had produced a demo tape that contained fifty of her compositions. Though every record label to which the tape was circulated turned it down, it was not long after that friends of the Bush family brought Kate's music to the attention of Pink Floyd's guitarist David Gilmour. Gilmour was impressed by Bush's songwriting skill and vocal range and in 1974 financed a three-song demo for Bush, made with Pink Floyd's producer Andrew Powell. The tape was sent to EMI, Pink Floyd's record company, where it was heard by Terry Slater, the executive who signed the Sex Pistols to a major label contract. Slater was quite impressed with the demo and signed Kate Bush, even though she was only sixteen years old. In recognition of her relative youth, EMI made an unusual move and gave Bush some money "to grow up with," and Bush spent three years continuing her dance studies, honing her vocal skills, and developing a more mature songwriting style.[1] In 1977 she recorded her first album, *The Kick Inside*, and the first single, "Wuthering Heights," reached the number one spot on the British pop chart just one month after its release in early 1978.

Whatever the curiosity value of "Wuthering Heights," the young singer proved to be no one-shot wonder. Though Kate Bush's next album, 1979's *Lionheart*, was a critical disappointment, it did produce a Top 20 single in the U.K., and there have been a couple of British hits on all her subsequent LPs: 1980's *Never For Ever* on which she debuted as co-producer, 1982's self-produced *The Dreaming*, and *Hounds of Love*, recorded in the studio she had now built in her home. EMI is obviously well satisfied with Bush's success, but it seems unlikely that the company could have predicted Bush's profitability at the time of her signing. Even her earliest recorded material dealt with unusual subjects, such as life after death, poisoning, metaphysical understanding, and supernatural phenomena; and Bush's vocal phrasing has always been unconventional. Undoubtedly, then, Bush's contract with EMI was the result of several conspiring factors. Though the relative importance of each element can only be guessed, EMI's market position and the nature of the recording industry in the 1970s provide clues into the conglomerate's motives for signing Kate Bush.

That it was David Gilmour who brought Kate Bush to the attention of EMI certainly helped Bush's career get off the ground. At the time of Bush's signing in 1974 Pink Floyd was a very important act to the company. The progressive band released its eternally selling *Dark Side of the Moon* on

EMI's Harvest label in 1973, and Pink Floyd was a respected and successful veteran of the art rock scene. Other members of Pink Floyd were seeking out fresh talent at the time, and EMI management would have surely thought it in the company's best interests to cater to the band members' whims.

The importance of Pink Floyd to EMI was symptomatic of a larger development in the British music industry in the early seventies. A number of progressive artists were selling substantial quantities of records in both Great Britain and the United States. The acid rock of the late sixties had evolved into the art rock of the seventies, with bands like Pink Floyd, Emerson, Lake and Palmer, Jethro Tull, Traffic, and Genesis becoming industry mainstays. These artists experimented with synthesizers and other emerging technologies in order to create new sound experiences. Once the commercial viability of these musicians had been proved, record companies were eager to jump on the progressive bandwagon. One study of the musical tastes of British teenagers done in 1972 found that almost half of the middle-class teens surveyed favored "progressive" music over mainstream pop.[2] Undoubtedly the middle-class teen market was one that record companies desired to tap. EMI had already shown its commitment to progressive rock by launching the Harvest label in 1968, and by the early seventies it was clear to industry executives that adventurous musicians could actually make money for a company. Thus, in 1974 EMI would have been more likely to believe that an experimental performance artist like Kate Bush could sell records than it might have been later in the decade.

Another factor that cannot be overlooked is EMI's dominant position in the British record industry during the early seventies. Since 1950 the record industry in the United Kingdom had been dominated by two giants, EMI and British Decca, and EMI's position was strengthened substantially in the early sixties when the label signed the Beatles. Although increasing competition from American labels hurt the industry leader as the decade drew to a close, EMI remained in control of an array of interests that gave it both horizontal and vertical control over numerous aspects of the recording and distribution process in Britain—even in the middle of the 1970s, EMI was still manufacturing one-fourth and distributing one-third of all records sold in the U.K.[3]

Financial success gave EMI the economic means to invest in the development of new talent. Moreover, it is in the long-term interest of a large company to recruit new talent continually, because "nobody wants to depend on a small number of acts."[4] Labels lose artists to other companies, life-style alterations, and death, as EMI was painfully aware with the breakup of the Beatles. Record companies depend on a constant influx of new talent to ensure that the organization will survive, and, in the words of one observer, "the larger the company, the greater its need for new 'product.' "[5]

The mid-seventies were definitely a key time for labels to be on the lookout for new talent. The British record industry was reaching a stagnation point and EMI was particularly conscious that it failed to sign the major British successes in the United States like the Who and Led Zeppelin. Artist and repertoire (A&R) people were searching for anything that might prove to be "a 'Next Big Thing,' the new Beatles phenomenon," that would invigorate the industry.[6] After all, one reason behind the continuous search for talent is the recognition by industry executives that they are working in a "taste" business. The commercial success of a particular artist or musical genre is often difficult to predict; therefore, the record industry must produce a variety of musical sounds. If, for example, Kate Bush or a Kate Bush clone became the Next Big Thing, a label would not want to miss out financially on the trend. Record companies, particularly record companies resourceful enough to carry numerous failed gambles, see that it is wise to invest in a wide range of talent just in case something outside of the musical status quo captures the public's attention. EMI may have been gambling when it signed Kate Bush, but it was a gamble that paid. When "Wuthering Heights" reached the top of the British chart, only EMI had a Kate Bush, and the idiosyncratic nature of Bush's music made the construction of a Kate Bush clone an accomplishment almost beyond the powers of imagination.

In addition, one should not forget that EMI signed Kate Bush at a time when visually oriented rock performers were growing in popularity. Kate Bush's early career was aided by her training in dance and mime and her striking good looks. The visual presentation has always been an important component of Bush's music: her single "Wuthering Heights" was released with a video at a time when such promotional clips were rather rare. By the time the video explosion reached Britain in the early eighties, old hands like David Bowie, Bryan Ferry, Peter Gabriel, and Kate Bush found themselves in advantageous positions from which to exploit the medium. Bush's lengthy experience in the realm of music video has allowed her to direct clips for "Hounds of Love," "The Big Sky," and "Experiment IV."

There is a last point to be made here: although by the mid-1970s U.S. tastes and sales strategies dominated the rock scene, and EMI suffered competitively as a result, it was still the dominant record company in non-English-speaking markets—in Europe, Japan, and South America—and the company seems to have been aware of Kate Bush's potential in these markets from the start. Although she is, formally, a "singer-songwriter," she did not really compete with early-seventies U.S. stars like Joni Mitchell or Carole King. She was a solo performer who gained popularity with quiet, though offbeat, songs like "Wuthering Heights" and "The Man with the Child in His Eyes." Unlike Mitchell at this time she did not foreground the acoustic guitar in her music but instead composed on the piano, and on some early songs, especially "James and the Cold Gun" and "Hammer Horror," she relied heavily on the electric guitar. And unlike King, Bush was not content to restrict her vocals or her subject matter to a conventional pop range. It was, rather, the "exoticness" of her sound and image that made her, from EMI's point of view, a possible star in, say, Japan.

The musical climate of the 1970s, EMI's position in the British and international music industry, the involvement of David Gilmour as a "gate-keeper," Kate Bush's undeniable talent, and a number of other factors thus interacted at a specific point in time to make the addition of Kate Bush to EMI's stable of musical talent seem a wise maneuver. And once Bush proved a profitable artist, the company probably thought it best not to tamper with a successful formula and allowed Bush a great deal of artistic freedom.

However, though Kate Bush has been a bestselling artist in the U.K. for almost a decade, she is virtually unknown in the United States. It was only with *Hounds of Love* in 1985 that Bush received any significant recognition in the United States. Though none of her previous albums had been able to crack the Top 100, *Hounds of Love* reached the thirtieth position on the *Billboard* album chart, largely on the strength of the single "Running Up That Hill," which peaked at thirty-one in November of 1985. But Bush has yet to attain the kind of success in the United States that she enjoys in her native England and in Europe; and though "Running Up That Hill" brought Kate Bush new fans in American dance clubs, she seems destined to remain a strangely British and European phenomenon. If her popularity in non-English-speaking European, Asian, and South American countries suggests that factors other than the unusual subject matter of her songs have allowed her to succeed, these factors have not been sufficient to ensure her success in the U.S. market.

Putting that to one side, for a moment, perhaps one reason that Kate Bush's popularity in England has not been duplicated in the United States is because she is a very English singer. Throughout most of the history of rock music in Britain, performers have used accents imported from America.[7] This began to change in the early seventies when singers like David Bowie and Bryan Ferry employed English accents, and Bush herself acknowledges the importance of these male artists in the formation of her own vocal style.

> "I think most of the stuff I have liked has been English. With the majority of other people—well, they were listening to Elvis and people like that and most of their heroes were American. The artists I liked, such as Roxy Music and David Bowie, were all singing in English accents and, in fact, were among the few in England who were actually doing so at that time. I mean, Elton John, Robert Palmer, and Robert Plant sound American when they sing."[8]

Moreover, Bush's Englishness is not confined merely to her accent. Her image is largely constructed around her British heritage. As Terry Slater of EMI states:

"Kate is a real English girl, she's from the roots of Great Britain. It's not a gimmick or produced. She's the first really *English* girl singer for a long time."[9]

Bush has contributed to this perception by celebrating her native land in songs like 1979's "Oh England My Lionheart." The essential English quality of Bush's music and image has certainly had a profound effect on her popularity in the United Kingdom and perhaps on her inability to achieve widespread recognition in the United States; in particular it made her hard to classify as a "rock" performer (and until recently she was not well regarded in the British rock press). Still, even as a "pop" singer Kate Bush was fortunate to appear at a moment in Britain when a great deal of space for a singer like her had just opened up. In *One Chord Wonders*, Dave Laing notes one of the victories won by female singers in the punk era of the mid-seventies was the opportunity to experiment with a wider range of vocal sounds. Certainly Bush, who gained popularity in postpunk England with a repertoire of unearthly shrieks and guttural whispers, took advantage of this space to convey a disturbing breadth of emotion. Yet Bush's music was also a reaction against the one-dimensional angst and unorchestrated discord of punk, using melody and often frail vocals to create a surreal world of affect. Once again, Bush was extremely hard to "place" in terms of the usual music market labels.

Which brings us back to her image. Described by Laing as "poetically enigmatic," Kate Bush transcends mere voyeuristic objectification.[10] In her videos and live performances, Bush presents a series of dramatic personas that distance the viewer, even as the lyrics appear to invite him or her into the most recessed enclaves of her soul. The Kate Bush the viewer sees is merely a projection. Bush herself affirms this: "When I perform, I'm definitely someone else. She's a lot stronger and I wouldn't be as daring as her."[11] On stage, she becomes Catherine of "Wuthering Heights," the outlaw of "James and the Cold Gun," the child-woman of "Feel It." Bush's enigmatic image has been important to her success in non-English-speaking countries where the idea of a poetic chanteuse has great appeal, as well as in the faddish, often image-oriented British Isles. And those listeners who were initially hooked by the novelty of "Wuthering Heights" soon discovered that there was a profound intelligence behind the image, an intelligence that allowed Bush to pass from the realm of show-biz spectacle into the world of respected musicians.

The relatively small size and integrated promotion of the British and other European pop music markets makes them more susceptible to the influence of fads and images than their American counterpart, and this fact undoubtedly accounts in part for Kate Bush's inability to achieve anything more than a cult following in the United States before the mid-eighties. Rather than focusing on her sexuality and striking physical appearance,

American fans and critics have tended to praise Bush for her musical skill and artistic vision; and the complex nature of these elements has generally limited Bush's American following to a handful of devotees. With "Running Up That Hill," however, Kate Bush gained fans in American dance clubs, while the album *Hounds of Love* received considerable airplay on album-oriented rock radio. Thus, Bush was at once occupying the seemingly contradictory roles of progressive rock heroine and dance-funk queen, neither of which converged in any significant way with the American pop mainstream. Furthermore, few Americans were aware of the image so popular in England, Europe, South America, and Australia. Although MTV gave substantial airplay to one of the two videos for "Running Up That Hill," visual exposure to Kate Bush has been quite limited in the United States. Her only tour, in 1979, was confined to England, and her controversial performance on *Saturday Night Live* in that year did not create a lasting impression in this country.

Though Kate Bush herself has not been a significant commercial presence in the United States, her influence has been felt. Perhaps more than any other female artist, Kate Bush legitimized the use of the rather eccentric vocal ranges and phrasing that one can now find in the music of artists like Cyndi Lauper. Bush has also been one of the pioneering users of the Fairlight synthesizer, especially on *Never For Ever* and *The Dreaming*. By moving beyond pre-set and artificial synthesizer sounds, Bush discovered new ways to sample a variety of natural resonances in order to deepen the structure of her music. Only now are mainstream artists catching up with experimenters like Bush in their uses of synthesizer technologies.

In spite of her importance in these two areas, Kate Bush has probably had the greatest impact in her role as a performance artist. To Bush, the visual presentation of the music and the music itself cannot be divorced; thus, it is not surprising that she was the first female pop star to combine her music with classical and modern dance training. Bush's idea that the combination of music and movement allows the artist to express a more complex range of emotion has been translated, though in simplified form, into the work of American music video superstars like Madonna and Janet Jackson. What was once novelty has now become the norm.

To summarize, then, in terms of both her music and her market position, Kate Bush does not fit easily under any label, whether general ones like "rock" and "pop" or more specialized categories such as "singer-songwriter" or "video star." Rather, she has expanded the notion of auteur that began to be applied to rock songwriters and performers in the late 1960s to cover the expressive control of performance, movement, image, and even studio ambiance. What is she using her remarkably individual pop authority to say?

HOUNDS OF LOVE: A WINDOW TO HUMANITY'S ONCE AND FUTURE ESSENCE

One aspect of Kate Bush's performance that can never be successfully borrowed by other artists is the unique vision she creates. Her songs are intensely personal, whether they tell a story about a specific character (as in "Don't Push Your Foot on the Heartbrake" from *Lionheart* or "Babooshka" from *Never For Ever*) or reveal Bush's own fears and desires (as in "Feel It" and "Sat in Your Lap"). The personal nature of Kate Bush's music has been reinforced in recent years by her near total control of the production process. She has always written all of her own material and plays a variety of instruments on her albums, including piano, Fairlight synthesizer, Yamaha CS80 keyboard, violin, and cello. For the most part, Bush has kept a loyal corps of backing musicians who have stayed with her throughout her public career. One of these musicians is her brother Paddy, who plays mandolin, strings, percussion sticks, bullroarer, didjeridu, fugare, and balalaika on his sister's records, as well as providing backing vocals.

As Kate Bush gained control of her career, her music matured. Her first two albums, *The Kick Inside* and *Lionheart*, produced by Andrew Powell, emphasized piano and orchestral arrangements and featured Bush's ethereal soprano vocals. With 1980's *Never For Ever*, the album she coproduced with Jon Kelly, Kate Bush expanded her vocal and conceptual range. Character songs, so representative of her early work, remained a mainstay, but "Babooshka" and "The Wedding List" were clearly the products of an adult mentality. The newfound Fairlight allowed Bush to create atmospheric pieces like "Egypt." Psychoanalysis and spiritual questions appeared in songs on the album, and "Army Dreamers" represented Bush's first attempt to integrate Irish folk melodies and modern instruments. As Bush's transitional album, *Never For Ever* paved the way for *The Dreaming* (1982) and *Hounds of Love* (1985).

The Dreaming is an unorthodox journey through a songwriter's soul. "Sat in Your Lap" starts off the album with pounding tribal drums and a variety of nontraditional vocals, all underscoring Bush's crisis of faith: "Some say that knowledge is something that you never have / Some say that knowledge is something sat in your lap." Her impatience with the process of spiritual understanding is articulated in the demand "Give me the karma, mama," a demand restated later on the side in "Suspended in Gaffa" when she asks, "Can I have it all now?" In "Suspended in Gaffa" Bush blends ancient instruments like bouzoukis and mandolins with guitars and synthesizers, implying a kind of coexistence between the past and present, a theme that recurs throughout her recent music. The album's title song, "The Dreaming," also invokes this motif. Not only does Bush use an Australian aboriginal instrument, the didjeridu, in the song; the very title of the composition is taken from the aborigines' concept of the eternal dreamtime. The dreamtime is an aboriginal cult's mythology, a mythology that is eternal because it is continually reenacted in rituals celebrating the creation. It is like dreaming because through the rituals the past, present, and future coexist as aspects of a single reality.[12] "Night of the Swallow" continues this temporal confusion by working an Irish jig into the chorus.

Supernatural concerns about issues like life after death remain prominent on *The Dreaming*, but Kate Bush also turns the magnifying glass inward to examine her own psyche. In "Leave It Open" Bush recognizes the evil that exists in humanity, "harm in us but power to arm," and vows to control her own baser urges. The album ends with the angst-ridden "Get Out of My House," in which Bush uses the house analogy to describe the innermost enclaves of her being: "This house is full of madness / This house is full of mistakes." The certainty of conviction displayed in this final song closes the 1982 album on a positive note, but there is an overall feeling of disjointedness on *The Dreaming* that is left to be resolved on *Hounds of Love*.

Many techniques employed on *The Dreaming* reappear on *Hounds of Love*. Tribal drum rhythms that drove songs like "Sat in Your Lap" and "The Dreaming" play a larger role on *Hounds*, and the mixture of traditional and contemporary instruments is also included in a more highly developed form. However, the discontinuities between the two albums are as important as the similarities. The piano, for example, is no longer the central instrument on *Hounds*; it has been replaced by the Fairlight, which possesses the capability of integrating a variety of sounds into a melodic whole. This shift reflects the difference in the two albums' contents. While the idiosyncratic piano proved the ideal accompaniment for *The Dreaming*'s introspection, *Hounds* requires an instrument that mirrors its focus on interpersonal relationships and the interrelatedness of life.

The first side of *Hounds* is titled "Hounds of Love," and the first two tracks, "Running Up That Hill" and "Hounds of Love," center on Bush's problems in male-female relationships. In "Running Up That Hill" Bush addresses the misunderstandings and unintentional pain lovers cause. She sees the solution to the problem in an exchange of perspectives, singing "If I only could / I'd make a deal with God / And I'd get him to swap our places." Bush realizes that she is part of the problem, for she is "unaware I'm tearing you asunder" and wonders, "Is there so much hate for the ones we love?" The most important function of "Running Up That Hill" is its role in setting up the rest of side 1. This first song tells the listener that the narrator, presumably Kate Bush, has difficulty in her relationships, and the rest of the side attempts to trace the origins of the problem.

Like "Running Up That Hill," the second song, "Hounds of Love," concerns awkwardness in intimate relationships. Both tunes are sung by

Bush in an accessible pop style and are structured around reasonably conventional instrumentation. "Hounds of Love" replaces the rat-a-tat snare rhythm of "Running Up That Hill" with a more emphatic, complex beat and uses a cello to create a steady melodic flow—another avoidance of the fragmentation found on *The Dreaming*.

The lyrics of "Hounds of Love" suggest that a regression in Bush's emotional development is taking place. The song's first lines ("When I was a child / Running in the night / Afraid of what might be / Hiding in the dark / Hiding in the street / And of what was following me / Now hounds of love are hunting") indicate that the roots of her difficulties lie far in the past. Though Bush realizes her peril is much less than that of a fox run to ground by hounds, she cannot bring herself to abandon social conventions for love. Were Bush's lover to take her "shoes off and throw them in the lake," she would be "two steps on the water" in pursuit of them. The water imagery foreshadows the motif that provides the basis for the second side, "The Ninth Wave." Here, as later, the water is a primordial ooze in which the individual enters a presocial state. On side 1 Bush is not yet ready to enter that realm, though she knows that avoiding her primal emotions is foolish, at once complaining "I don't know what's good for me" and realizing "I need love."

The third track, "The Big Sky," finds Kate Bush in an even more childlike state than the previous song. Bush lies on the ground and stares at the clouds, imagining them to be Ireland and Noah's Ark. Appropriately, Bush uses a girlish voice to describe her activity. Though she begins the song in an earthbound state, she is soon "leaving with the Big Sky" where "we pause for the jet." "The Big Sky" is not the only song on *Hounds* in which Bush explores the atmosphere's upper reaches. On side 2, "Hello Earth" places her spirit in suspension above the world. Yet while Bush's astral projection on side 2 is intensely personal, here it affects others, for "The Big Sky" is directed at someone about whom Bush petulantly complains, "You never understood me / You never really tried." For her part, Bush finds watching clouds more interesting than working on a relationship: "You want my reply? / What was the question?" The communication failure seems intrinsically linked to the problems articulated in "Running Up That Hill" and "Hounds of Love," but even more than in those songs Bush's interpersonal difficulties are linked to nature and childish emotions. Once again, the implication is that the dilemma's origins are in the early stages of Bush's development.

The feeling intensifies with "Mother Stands for Comfort," in which Bush creates an eerie mood with hushed vocals, unearthly Fairlight accompaniment, disembodied background drones, and the sound of breaking glass. One gets the feeling that the relationship with Mother is not warm, but almost supernatural. Mother has powers of omniscience—"She knows that

I've been doing something wrong"—but she is biased in the application of her powers, since "she won't say anything."

"Mother Stands for Comfort" contains two major Bushian themes: the evil within mankind and the need to turn to "Mother." Bush, or her character, knows there is harm in her and doubts her ability to contain it: "It breaks the cage and fear escapes and takes possession / Just like a crowd rioting inside / Make me do this, make me do that." Her doubt extends to her ability to evaluate the morality of her actions, asking "Am I the cat that takes the bird?" To Mother, however, the answer is clear; her child is "the hunted, not the hunter." Mother stands for comfort because for her there is no ambiguity; she must protect her child. Moreover, there is comfort in realizing this is a universal maternal quality. In the song's title the words "Mother Stands" imply that Mother is a symbol, standing for something else. Also, the word "Mother" is always capitalized in the lyrics printed on the album's inner sleeve, hinting that this is a mythic mother. Throughout side 2 Bush has looked back in time and into nature to determine the basis of her confusion, and now she has returned to the womb. She puns "Mother will stay Mum," but the lyrics and arrangement do not make Mother sound entirely comforting, for she is inextricably linked with the dark side of human nature.

On the other hand, in "Cloudbusting," the side's final cut, a father is warmly remembered. The song is based on *A Book of Dreams* by Freudian theorist Wilhelm Reich's son Peter. In his later years, Wilhelm Reich grew obsessed with the notion that the Earth is governed by a delicate balance of energies, and he developed a device called an "accumulator" to realign the natural forces at Organon, his Maine home. One of the accumulator's purported abilities was the capacity to make rain. Young Peter was deeply involved in his father's projects, and in his book he recalls the events that led to his father's arrest and imprisonment for fraudulent practices.[13]

The close emotional bond shared by father and son is conveyed by Kate Bush through the warm strings that continue throughout "Cloudbusting." When examined on its own, "Cloudbusting" is an interesting narrative, but when viewed in the context of the rest of *Hounds* the song seems full of omens and allusions. Anyone familiar with Peter Reich's book who listens to *Hounds* will be struck by the similarity in structure between side 2, "The Ninth Wave," and *A Book of Dreams*. In the book Peter is hospitalized and wavers between consciousness and dreaming. While awake he lives in the present, but when he is unconscious he is a child. As in the eternal dreamtime, the past and present are blurred, all part of one reality. Kate, and Peter Reich, is able to keep the dead father alive: "But everytime it rains / You're here in my head / Like the sun coming out / I just know that something good is going to happen."

In several ways, "Cloudbusting" previews "The Ninth Wave," the mini-concept album that occupies side 2 of *Hounds*. "The Ninth Wave" finds Kate Bush adrift in the water, battling to stay awake and avoid drowning. Through the night Bush slips in and out of consciousness, much as Peter Reich does in his book. As with the eternal dreamtime, the past and future exist as elements of the present, in this case through hallucinations and dreams. It is undoubtedly significant that side 1 ends with Bush making rain in "Cloudbusting," an act in which the waters are at her mercy. In contrast, Bush is at the whim of the drowning pool on side 2, as if her rain making got out of hand.

"The Ninth Wave" is also previewed by the back of the album jacket, where a photograph of a wet, seaweed-strewn Kate Bush appears. Beneath the picture the following explanation is given:

> Wave after wave, each mightier than the last
> 'Til last, a ninth one, gathering half the deep
> And full of voices, slowly rose and plunged
> Roaring, and all the wave was in flame . . .
> —*Tennyson, "The Coming of Arthur"*

At this point it is not surprising to learn that Tennyson's poem possesses a muddled chronology, beginning with the meeting of Arthur and Guinevere and ending with a fantastical account of Arthur's birth. The four lines on the jacket refer to the night of Uther's death, but the quotation ends before the reader can learn that the infant Arthur, swathed in flame, is borne on the ninth wave. As Merlin declares that the child washed to his feet is Uther's heir, the wave encircles the two with flame. When the wave recedes, calm ensues.[14]

The temporal confusion in Tennyson's tale is in keeping with Kate Bush's narrative and musical devices, and the invocation of Arthur weaves a mythic web around the second side of *Hounds*. The cycle of birth, death, and messianic rebirth central to Arthurian legend is also vital to "The Ninth Wave." Like Arthur, Kate Bush experiences a death and rebirth, though hers is in the water. According to Carl Jung, water symbolizes the subconscious mind into which one must descend before aspiring to the heights of enlightenment. In dreams, the conscious mind fights the pull of water, just as Bush does. Like the subjects of Jung's analysis who thought "spirit" comes from above, Bush is disturbed to be in the midst of the water, "the fluid of the instinct-driven body, blood and the flowing of blood, the odor of the beast, carnality heavy with passion."[15] For Bush, the water is another vehicle for an introspective ordeal.

"And Dream of Sheep," a lullaby played on the piano, sets up the scenario in which Kate Bush, as the narrator, tries to stay awake in the water and awaits rescue. "Little light will guide them to me," she sings, wishing that she could doze, desiring her radio as a link to civilization in the primal pool.

The struggle for consciousness proves futile as the sheep take her "deeper and deeper." Her error is immediately signaled by the ominous strings and deep vocals of "Under Ice." The water of Bush's dreamworld has turned to ice over which she skates, but "There's something moving under / Under the ice / Moving under ice—through water / Trying to get out of the cold water." Kate pleads, "Something—someone, help them!" until she reaches the awful realization, "It's me!"

The claustrophobic dream jolts Bush back to consciousness, though the process is difficult. Employing a variation of a technique used in "All the Love" on *The Dreaming*, a variety of voices urge Bush to awaken, and many make reference to Bush's situation. Some mention the "little light," others recite lines from songs elsewhere on the side, such as "We are water in the holy land of water" from "Jig of Life." This lead-in to "Waking the Witch" contains the first appearance of garbled vocals that sound like Kate Bush's cries for help as she bobs in and out of the water, gasping "—help me baby help me—talk to me talk to me—."

Once again, Kate slips into hallucination. This time she has confessed to a priest, but the priest uses the confession against her in a witchcraft trial. The jury of "good people" affirms that the defendant is "Guilty! Guilty! Guilty!" and though the clergyman pities the girl—"poor witch"—he condemns her. By announcing "I am responsible for your actions," the priest removes from the girl's hands power over her own karmic destiny. Thus, in some way the "witch's" predicament parallels that of the drowning victim whose fate lies with potential rescuers. The priest's reassurance, "You won't burn / You won't bleed," simply serves to affirm that the witch will die by drowning. "Help this blackbird / There's a stone around my leg," Bush cries. "Wake the witch," the clergyman's final command, is answered by the sound of a helicopter and a man shouting "Get out of the waves! Get out of the water!"—a command later uttered by Bush in "Hello Earth." The priest's voice is a demonic growl, contrasting strongly with the song's angelic refrains and enhancing the perception that symbols of good often conceal fundamental evil. Loss of control is underscored by the frenetic, electric guitar-driven melody.

Disillusionment gives way to resignation in the quiet, droning "Watching You Without Me." No longer does Kate see herself in the world of the living, but instead imagines that her disembodied soul has returned home to watch a loved one. "You watch the clock / Move the slow hand / I should have been home / Hours ago—but I'm not here," she observes; yet this is the time of a distant world, a different reality. Bush, as the narrator, has entered the realm of spirit where ethereal voices sing, "We receive thee," and her links to the physical plane are dissolving: "You can't hear me." She seems ready to accept the spirits' invitation—"You won't hear me leaving"—when she is rudely jerked back to physical existence by the earthy Irish instruments of "Jig of Life."

The traditional jig begins with the line "Hello old Lady / I know your face well," conjuring images of the mythic Mother on the album's first side. Kate is told by the old Lady that "Now is the place where the crossroads meet"; she must choose between life on the Other side and continued existence on Earth. The old Lady urges her to struggle for her worldly existence, the aspect of Kate's being that is the old Lady, the Earth Mother. A decision to enter the spiritual realm is not without consequences for others: "This moment in time / It doesn't belong to you / It belongs to me / And your little boy and your little girl." The recitation by John Carder Bush, Kate's brother, at the end of the song serves to reinforce the old Lady's message, advising Kate that her past, present, and future are inextricably linked; though "now does ride in on the curl of the wave," she must also remember "all that's to come runs in at the first on the strand." Kate Bush's ordeal has brought her to the crossroads, the place where past, present, and future converge, where she must choose between physical and spiritual existence. In the song's arrangement, the feeling of the presentness of the past is intensified by the inclusion of a number of traditional Irish folk instruments.

As "Hello Earth" fades in, the ancient mood of "Jig of Life" is disrupted by space radio chatter. The song finds Bush in the aerial position she occupied at the end of "The Big Sky," and from her elevated station she can make our planet seem insignificant: "Hello Earth / With just one hand held up high / I can blot you out / Out of sight." But she cannot affect events on Earth, she can merely watch. "Watching the storms / Start to form / Over America / Can't do anything / Just watch them swing with the wind / Out to sea." Though Kate wants to warn seagoers of the potential danger, the danger that placed her existence in peril, she is helpless—she gave in to her desire to ascend the heights before experiencing the primal depths, forfeiting her earthly power.

However, Kate Bush's journey through the collective unconscious has shown her that it is not too late to reclaim her physical existence. Though she seems resentful of the forces that interfered with her plans to cease her struggle for life, Bush also sees that she was wrong to give up so easily and accepts her baptismal trial:

> I was there at the birth
> Out of the cloud burst
> The head of the Tempest,
> Murderer, Murderer of calm!
> Why did I go?
> Why did I go?

At the end of "Hello Earth" Bush descends to the physical plane, asking in German if there is a light and whispering "tiefe, tiefe," which in German is synonymous with "deep" in the sense of "profound." Thus, Bush's perception of being taken "deeper and deeper" in "And Dream of Sheep" has been borne out in a spiritual way as well as physically.

"Hello Earth" is the most dramatic track on *Hounds of Love*. Bush uses piano, bass, folk instruments, guitar, sound effects, and her voice to create a melodramatic mood and cinematic scope. The most remarkable feature of the song, however, is the integration of a Gregorian-type chant into the melody. The liturgical chant acts much like traditional folk instruments on other tracks; it brings an element of the past into present reality. Yet unlike didjeridus and pipes, such chants suggest a Christian culture and tend to imbue lines like "I was there at the birth" with Christian connotations.

Its lyrics, soaring melody, and placement on the album make "Hello Earth" a climactic moment. The song represents Bush's epiphany. "The Morning Fog," a joyous celebration of Kate's spiritual rebirth, follows "Hello Earth" to close the album. After surviving the night, Bush welcomes the light of morning as it burns off the fog, and she greets the Earth: "D'you know what? / I love you better now." Her declaration that "I am falling / Like a stone" seems to imply that Kate is being pulled underwater for a final time, but the gaiety with which she sings the line suggests she is falling from the spirit world back to the material realm. In fact, Bush tells us that the descent is "Like a storm / Being born again." The enlightened appreciation she has gained for humanity and the Earth will be demonstrated when she is back among the living: "I'll kiss the ground / I'll tell my mother / I'll tell my father / I'll tell my loved one / I'll tell my brothers / How much I love them." Lest anyone doubt that "The Ninth Wave" is a description of Kate Bush's own struggle for spiritual understanding, it is interesting to note that these lines from "The Morning Fog" accurately describe the Bush family unit.

Kate Bush leaves it up to the listener to decide whether the drowning person of "The Ninth Wave" is rescued. "The Morning Fog" is such an upbeat song that one might be tempted to argue that help must be in sight. Yet when "The Ninth Wave" is taken as a whole, physical salvation is much less important than the spiritual enlightenment Bush has already received. Rather than turning from the primal drives and the evil that lie at the core of humanity, Bush realizes that she must face and accept this part of her soul. Within each individual the past, present, and future coexist, and no element in the balance can be neglected. Humans strive to cultivate their civilized exteriors, but without a recognition of the natural forces that spring from their primitive essences there can be no true understanding.

NOTES

[1] Fred Vermorel, *The Secret History of Kate Bush* (London: Omnibus Press, 1983), pp. 86–87.

[2] Graham Murdock and Guy Phelps, "Responding to Popular Music: Criteria of Classification and Choice among English Teenagers," *Popular Music and Society 1*, No. 3 (1972), p. 150.

[3] Simon Frith, *Sound Effects* (New York: Pantheon Books, 1981), pp. 140–43.

[4] "Records: The Gorillas Are Coming," reprinted from *Forbes* (10 July 1978) in Michael Emery and Ted Curtis Smythe (eds.), *Readings in Mass Communications* (Dubuque, Iowa: Brown, 1980), p. 326.

[5] Jon Stratton, "Reconciling Contradictions: The Role of the Artist and Repertoire Person in the British Music Industry," *Popular Music and Society 8*, No. 2 (1982), p. 91.

[6] Dave Laing, *One Chord Wonders* (Milton Keynes: Open University Press, 1985), p. 7.

[7] Ibid., p. 26.

[8] Peter Swales, "Kate Bush: A British Cult Heroine-Turned-Superstar Passes Through the Realm of the Subconscious," *Musician* (January 1986).

[9] Vermorel, *Kate Bush*, p. 92.

[10] Laing, *One Chord Wonders*, p. 89.

[11] Vermorel, *Kate Bush*, p. 83.

[12] A. P. Elkin, *The Australian Aborigines* (New York: Doubleday, 1964), p. 210.

[13] Peter Reich, *A Book of Dreams* (New York: Harper & Row, 1973).

[14] Alfred Lord Tennyson, *Idylls of the King and Other Arthurian Poems* (London: Nonesuch Press, 1968), p. 20.

[15] Carl Gustav Jung, *The Basic Writings of C. G. Jung*, ed. Violet Laszlo (New York: Modern Library, 1959), pp. 302–3.

NEW POP AND ITS AFTERMATH

1985

○ ▲ ○ ▲ ○ ▲ ○

I am a punk. I always have been, and always will be.
MARTIN FRY, *Melody Maker*, 1985

This claim—from the leader of ABC, the group who (briefly) made gold lamé suits and string sections hip—takes us to the heart of new pop. Back to 1979 and its consensus—where punk had "failed" was in straying from the "original point"—individualism, discovery, *change*—and becoming new orthodoxy, a tradition. This positive, constructive redefinition of punk ignored and erased crucial elements in punk's heterogeneity (rage, aggression, nihilism, chaos, outrage), rationalizing it to little more than the idea of "progression." Punk had been apocalyptic; there wasn't meant to be a day after. But here one was, in the future—what to do but "flee to the edges," finish the "incomplete revolution"—make modern(ist), eighties music (using new inputs like jazz, European avant-garde, dub, disco); demystify and decentralize the means of production (independent labels). The years 1978–79 saw the creation of a "space for growth."

Serious rock's dream is that people can be changed, minds opened. So the great nightmare is when *pop* becomes *industry*, when efficient marketing ensures music is channeled *only* toward the people who are already receptive—rather than working for an overall education of desire. The year 1979 was haunted by the fear of this death of communication—complaints about compartmentalization, demands for access (to radio), and diversity. Within a year it was the alternative scene itself that was blamed for reinforcing "barriers"; progression slurred as "progressive rock"; what was once a space seen now just as confinement, (a) retreat; a former purity now a niggling purism/puritanism. Behind the shift lay the fear of the moment when *stimulation becomes comfort*—there was a torrent of rhetoric against "the new hippies," cozy cults. Fretting beneath the imagery of mud, stagnation, skulking in the shadows, was the dilemma of entryism—what to do with your good intentions—stay pure but marginal, or try to reach the masses and risk compromise (the hard Left faces the same dilemma). Two rival definitions of musical "power"—either purity of vision or extent of influence. Eventually a number of groups/labels/writers launched an attack on the "sterile" conceptuality and "purgative innovation" of groups like Pop Group and Scritti Politti, arguing that there was no *real* provocation without crossover, just relations of mutual comfort, impotent elitism. "The good groups should be in the charts." So came the dream of a *new* pop—for the "brown rice indies' " defeatism, there would be ambition, a pragmatic response to the demands of accessibility (technology, color, image). If punk was about *change*, then this "all change!" was *truer* to the "spirit of punk." The "movement" had to keep *moving*.

New pop involved a conscious and brave attempt to bridge the separation between "progressive" pop and mass/chart pop—a divide which has existed since 1967 and is also, broadly, one between boys and girls, middle-class and working-class leisure: "serious" music (from acid rock to punk to post-punk) is *head* culture—implicitly antidance, bodily passive, oriented toward contemplation, treatment of records as statements (artistic or social), based around LPs and lyrics. Mainstream pop is *body* culture—oriented to dance and sex, based around singles and stars, radio and clubs. New pop aimed to unite *head* and *body*, serious ideas and surface plesaures, theory and *love*. Faced with the specter of punk turning *into* what had been its original target—progressive rock—the only way out was *pop*: the investment in the word "pop," against "rock," was a renewal of faith in the possibility of breaking the boys/girls divide. Pop intellectuals like DAF, Stimulin, and ACR *thought* their way back to (an idea of) the body, dance, sex—the idea "free your ass and your mind will follow," dance as a valuable loosening up, even antifascist (in reality dance is just as much a discipline, an exploitation of the body as a resource—*the* major resource of working-class kids—that slots into a range of uses—sport, violence, "handling yourself," sexual flaunting). There was an attempt to confuse gender distinctions within the individual as well as the pop marketplace—an interest in androgyny, ambiguity, and male glamour; attempts to exlode the fixed male critical hierarchies, the disdain for "mass-produced" pop, to attend seriously to the pleasures of dance, the formulaic and the transient, artifice, the uses of stardom.

All this came directly out of punk. New pop kept from punk an emphasis on economy (the single), awareness of the business (the importance of *control*), DIY—but this time the goals were higher, the charts, aided by technology (synths, drum machines). Once again, it was intended as the fulfillment of punk's failed *musical* revolution. New pop turned away from the tradition of American rock 'n' roll that punk was squarely entrenched within—to Europe (electronics, avant-garde noise) and black pop (David Byrne had said: "Black dance production techniques are a more radical breakthrough than punk") to forge a futurist(ic) music. Others returned to classicism and ornament in sound (against 1979's minimalism, the modernist fear of the conventional structure) but leavened with postmodern mixing of styles, ironic and exposed intertextuality. Sources were the sixties, torch songs, cabaret, jazz. But there was also hunger to recover punk's lost shock of the new—we can see the same trajectory in a number of punk careers: Martin Fry and his tuxedo, Vic Godard and swing, Morley and McCullough praising Dollar, Tight Fit, Haircut 100, Adam Ant, Julie Burchill burying rock for Oklahoma, Radio 4, Diana Dors, Jackie Collins. This time the target of iconoclasm was rock's own petrified doxa—but the very vehemence of these debunkings was pure punk, the litany "Rock Is Dead" the ultimate rock act.

Color, dance, fun, style were sanctioned—they were both strategically necessary, being the terms of entry into pop—and pleasurable, allowed under the new creed of guilt-free hedonism. What went wrong was when new values became new dogma, new barriers—such as snobbery against uncommercial but valid musical initiatives (dealing with art concerns, musical innovation, dark things). So Birthday Party were abused, while Level 42 was hailed as part of the new brightness ("a pop ECM" indeed!) and Adrian Thrills said of Talk Talk: "They are preparing the first pop masterstroke of 1982." The undoing of new pop was that it allowed for literal and liberal interpretation. Ambition became virtue in itself—Wham!'s "Make It Big" at any cost. The Thompson Twins talked of *aiming* to make "disposable music." New pop ideology was vague—Adam Ant talked of giving people hope and pride, through entertainment, ABC of choice and change and value—almost just a vision of better, more exciting and efficient consumer capitalism. Worse still was the elaboration of an idea of health— a typical testimony being Green's account of his pop rebirth as recovery from illness (his squat life/indie angst had given him heart trouble)—new pop as healthy narcissism, healthy optimism, healthy appetites. All this was recuperable to a conventional *Cosmo* idea of the good life—hedonism as intense consumerism, suntan, and smiles—or the whole *Face* life-style mentality. Fun was scoured of derangement and dissipation; new pop subsumed into show biz; and from new pop hatred of immobility—(Oi's "wallowing" in its exploitation)—it was a short step to upward mobility. New pop's other problem was that its makers were driven more by an idea of pop than musical instincts, resulting in sublimated pop criticism, meta-pop. The music groaned under the weight of manifestos about pop's lack—Positive Noise's "Give Me Passion," Dexy's "Burn It Down" and "Let's Make This Precious," Adam Ant—or self-consciously considered the institution of the pop song or the lover's discourse—Scritti Politti, ABC.

New pop made the pop hell we now inhabit. As well as the planned obsolescence of teenybop, it spawned a new category of *adult-oriented pop*, stardom tempered by sobriety. These "artists" make attempts to do good work with pop, to extend lyrical language, to mix depth and pop appeal— leading to graceless, ungainly writing (Howard Jones, Tears for Fears, China Crisis, Kershaw.) There are dismal echoes of new pop themes—Paul Young's "Sex" for the Stimulin slogan "Sex and Sweat Is Best," Eurythmics' references to "the language of love" learned from Scritti's deconstruction, aimless eclecticism, postmodernism (a knowing, hollow use of clichés, e.g., Eurythmics' "There Must Be an Angel"). These people have reduced new pop to *reformism*.

New pop is also responsible for the smug introversion of our alternative scene, as ever defining itself *only* as pop's other. New pop's idea of health and cleanliness provoked a revolt toward sickness and dirt—initially useful, a different way to recover punk's lost outrage than new pop's anti-rockism, toward ever more unmanageable forms of the forbidden. But this quickly became ritual—the Membranes / Yeah Yeah / Riley school of thrash takes noise as a value in itself, the Foetus / Sonic Youth / P. Orridge / Bargeld axis assume it is enough simply to *depict* a censored "reality" of vile urges and general ghastliness, in order to subvert pop normality. And of course new pop Europeanism has given way to the return of America (country 'n' southern, tough but tender masculinity, bar bands, all that *alcohol*). And the fucking Pogues . . .

New pop was about making the best of what was *inevitable*—synths, video, new production, glamour's return—an optimistic response to the potential of technology. What's survived of that determination? In very different ways, ZTT, Weller/Respond, Scritti Politti, New Order, and Malcolm McLaren have a commitment to getting across, spreading new values. Morley and McLaren go together, and not necessarily how Burchill would have it. Both realized that the idea of a rock community, rock as folk, was dead—superseded by the media—and that it was there you had to operate, using the techniques of hype and contrivance. Both turned to the rootless, modern sound of Trevor Horn. Both were sick of the hip fraternity, our imperturbability, and vested hope in teenagers' receptivity to new ideas. Both have an idea of the entrepreneur as adventurer, both hate what McLaren called the "grocer mentality" of the independents, seeing that the independent scene's problem is its *too* successful demystification—turning pop into just work, business. McLaren and ZTT are aware that pop involves myth, staged confrontations, sensation, charades if you like. What they both lack is *music*. ZTT have no group that can bear the weight of their ideas. None of their groups has presence or musical body; the ideas and music are bitty, overeclectic, unrealized. It isn't enough just to refer to dreams, obsession, visions, and crime, to quote J. G. Ballard on "madness"—the music itself must embody the themes, enforce the magic. The pop song must be a "spell." ZTT should be more circuitous, less upfront about their designs. Ultimately the music is just too *overlit* to disturb or arouse—pop for public spaces, cutting a swathe through club or chart, but not music to take to your bed(room). As with ABC the aims are unclear—not to be as "mediocre" as the rest of the biz, "choice and value," a more effective music industry. Still ZTT are trying—even if this means both endeavor *and* exasperation.

Like ZTT, Paul Weller's Respond label is a meta-pop commentary on pop's lack—"Shout It to the Top," "Speak Like a Child." Weller's an important part of the new pop picture—with the Jam, the most successful punk band, he faced the same dilemma about progression, and ever since he copied "The Look of Love" and used string sections on "The Bitterest Pill," he's gone along with the new pop tenets—Rock Is Dead (he's turned to sixties and seventies soul), Europeanism (Respond's Parisian chic), eclecticism (the shambles of "Cafe Bleu"), optimism and cleanliness. But Weller is still activated by the idea of the sixties—the dream of a youth community, classless pop, based on the real coincidence of mass and hip taste between 1963 and 1967 (where ABC were inspired by Bowie, Ferry, and Bolan, who took their art-school / underground ideas and tried to reach a mass audience). Weller's pop is marred by an un-pop decency, by its *use* as a vehicle for messages of sanity and responsibility. He isn't really very young at heart.

Scritti Politti try to work within anonymous dance music, but Green's subversive intent runs foul of marketing—the subtle feminism of "The Word Girl" undermined by a video that made use of beautiful models; the packaging of the records inviting misinterpretation—intended as ironic contrast to the indie Scritti covers (photographs of filthy bedrooms, *photocopies* of litter), the pictures of luxury commodities are easy to take literally, just as the Scritti sound fits too well in our affluent-sounding chart. Green's pop is too airbrushed and deodorized to transfix or pierce (me). The Smiths and New Order surpass pop at being pop. They have a color and brightness, but it's natural rather than cosmetic—like flowers or stars. (There is little more remarkable in eighties music than New Order's alchemy of the base matter of Hi-NRG). They keep alive that strand in new pop of male fragility—but are perhaps too delicate for pop competition 1985 (the Smiths won't, *can't*, do video). The Smiths and New Order—like Joy Division, Echo, and Birthday Party earlier—indicate that if the spirit of the blues (an

attitude, not a form—gloom as exhilaration) persists, it is in white music—
not in modern black pop and its white copyists.

New pop came directly out of punk, and was about faith—faith in the
*break*age of barriers (the class, sex, and race barriers that are the reality of
"youth culture"), the *break*through into personal consciousness. Whatever
their failings, the new pop activists understood that the point and the liberation of pop was when it was of such heavenly extravagance as to be a
reproach to the tired world; today people want pop that reflects only the
most straight(forward) probable of desires. When I spoke of a new bohemianism in Monitor 3, I didn't mean dirt and scruffiness—for we have our
indie refuge already—but a pop that was entryist, that had new pop strategies
and optimism of the will, but that wore, in the charts, a mark of its difference
and exile. A pop of unearthly presence, poetry, blasphemous reverence in
the face of the facetious and practical, a pop that demands the impossible
of life. (I'm thinking of the likes of Siouxsie and the Associates—who
burrowed up within glamour, cabaret, disco, a *new psychedelia*, pop that
covered questions of loss of identity and collapse of language). Will we ever
see its like again? Maybe the dream of *breakthrough* is the final pop illusion,
but . . . we can't stay at home any longer.

CORRUPTING THE ABSOLUTE

1 9 8 5

○ ▲ ○ ▲ ○ ▲ ○

CORRUPTING THE ABSOLUTE

Sue got off work and drifted down the midway in a wet heat, past the American-flag petunia gardens. Screamers rammed circles in the Whirl-A-Gig cars, pasted in stand-up Roll-A-Turn cages by their own gravity. They whistled and moved in droves behind raw hot dogs. At night she lay in the top bunk naked with the lights off. Fan on full aimed at her crotch while janitors lounged in front of the garages watching the rows of windows. Rod Stewart, scratchy and loud, combed his hair in a thousand ways and came out looking just the same.

That paragraph is the last of three in a Jayne Anne Phillips story called "What It Takes to Keep a Young Girl Alive"; the title is a play on a line from Rod Stewart's "Every Picture Tells a Story," the tune drifting through Sue's window. I sometimes wonder how good a song has to be to make its way into fiction like that—into lives like that. I wonder what the song does there. This isn't the old "soundtrack of our lives" routine: you know, when Sue gets older and "Every Picture Tells a Story" comes on the radio as an oldie she'll remember working at the amusement park. Something is happening in Phillips's story, to her character and to the song. It isn't clear what; maybe the contact itself is all that can be dramatized.

Beneath the drama, though, there's an ugly, blank feeling, as if, lying on her bed in the heat, a girl with a dead-end job has found herself humiliated by Rod Stewart's wild-oats ramble from Paris to Bangkok—or as if the facts of her life have humiliated the romanticism of the song. Or has the girl ignored the tale Stewart tells and stolen a moment from it, a moment that comforts because it tells her she's not the only one who can't change her life? Or is the empathy inside out—Fuck you, Rod Stewart, who gives a shit how your hair looks? Maybe none of that matters here; maybe the point is simply that Stewart was right. If a song is good enough, one story leads to another, which is what else there is after birth, copulation, and death.

As it happens, "Every Picture Tells a Story" is Stewart's greatest performance. That means either Phillips has good taste in pop song references or that the capacity of the song to enter a situation, transform it, and be transformed by it confirms its quality. Or it means neither. The thirty-year winnowing-out of rock history by oldies programming has more or less proved that quality talks and bullshit walks—Jimmy Gilmer's "Sugar Shack," the top single of 1963 and, according to a private survey, one of the three most loathsome records ever made, has disappeared—but bad records too enter people's lives, perhaps just as easily as good ones. What do they do there? Just because a bad record has been removed from the air by the common critical work of mass taste doesn't mean the bad record disappears from the life of whoever absorbed it in the first place.

Now, by a good record I mean one that carries surprise, pleasure, shock, ambiguity, contingency, or a hundred other things, each with a faraway sense of the absolute: the sense that either for the entire performance (as in the Rolling Stones' "Gimmie Shelter"), or more often for a stray moment, someone (the singer, the guitarist, the saxophonist) wants what he or she wants, hates what he or she hates, fears what he or she fears, more than anything in the world. The wonder of "Every Picture Tells a Story" is that such absolute moments occur all over the place: in the acoustic guitar licks after each verse, in the drum roll at the end of the first, in Maggie Bell's answer to Stewart's "Shanghai Lil never used the pill" with an out-of-nowhere "SHE CLAIMED THAT IT JUST AIN'T NATURAL!", in a dozen of Stewart's lines, in the unmatched openness of the rhythm—which somehow shuts up tight for the long coda, exactly as if a bunch of studio hacks had been brought in to finish off the number because, after shaking the world off its axis, the original musicians were kind of worn out. By a good record I mean one that, entering a person's life, can enable that person to live more intensely—as, whatever else it does, "Every Picture Tells a Story" does for Jayne Anne Phillips's Sue.

By a bad record I mean one that subverts any possibility of an apprehension of the absolute, a record that disables the person whose life it enters into living less intensely. Words like "corrupt," "faked," or "dishonest" suggest themselves, but there are plenty of corrupt, faked, or dishonest records with moments just as deep and powerful as any in "Every Picture Tells a Story"—not just honorable "let's get rich" records like Freddy Cannon's "Palisades Park," but "this is a load of shit but let's get rich, maybe we can change our names and not have to tell our mothers" records like the Diamonds' white-boy ripoff of "Little Darlin'," which was originally made by the noble black rhythm and blues group the Gladiolas, whose version wasn't as good. As Kim Gordon of the New York band Sonic Youth once wrote, in "rock 'n' roll, many things happen and anything can happen." (Who knows what happened to the Diamonds? I saw them more than fifteen years ago in a Reno casino, singing evergreens, pretending—even though by then their mothers were probably dead—that they weren't even the same group that had recorded "Little Darlin'," which was still on the air.) By a bad record I mean a record that is so cramped and careful in spirit that it wants most of all to be liked—to be accepted, to be acceptable.

I'm thinking of Julian Lennon, his hit album *Valotte*, his hit single "Too Late for Goodbyes," and a letter in *Rolling Stone* where a mother wrote in with her my-kid-said-the-darndest-thing: "Mom, you had John Lennon, now we have Julian." Good luck, kid, I thought: What kind of wishes will be sparked in you, what kind of life can you make, out of these pathetic little Family Favorites tunes about nothing? It hurt to read that letter, not because Julian Lennon is corrupt, fake, or dishonest, but because he is probably worthy, sincere, and true.

Julian Lennon is so promotable it makes you wonder if he really is John Lennon's son. Yes, his voice sounds just like John's—it's uncanny, and that's the hook. He looks like John. But just as John's bright sneer is beyond Julian's smooth, sad-eyed face, the endless emotional complexities in the dumbest lyrics John ever sang are beyond Julian's Xerox voice. Even on the earliest Beatle records, when John Lennon sang badly, which is to say emptily, you could hear failure; on *Rock 'n' Roll*, released in 1975, his last album before the 1980 *Double Fantasy* LP (his last), when Lennon sang badly you could hear self-loathing and doubt. When Julian sings badly, emptily, which is all he does, you hear success. It's the success not of carrying off some intimation of the absolute, but of carrying a phrase to its completion.

What happens when a song like Julian Lennon's "Too Late for Goodbyes" enters a life as easily, as mysteriously, as unconsciously, as "Every Picture Tells a Story"? What happens when such a song frames and defines the possibilities of life? When Julian Lennon's songs enter a life, I can only imagine that they reduce it. His songs reduce it because, in the immediate context, they say that the person's parents had something richer, they lived in a better time. They made or rejected better choices, their successes or failures can be more fully dramatized, they had the real thing, which is no longer on the market. But it is in the context of time passing that the real process of a bad song in a real life begins its work. A bad song is absorbed whole, in the moment, unconsciously. The person whose life it enters barely knows it's there: it's just part of the day. But as time goes on, and the song fails to live up to life, it begins to break down. It reveals itself as a corrupt, faked, dishonest tumor in the pysche. Never saying its name, it frames the bits and pieces the person who absorbed it was willing to settle for—and that's all there is.

Of course, almost everyone settles. No one wins. The absolute was denied in the Garden of Eden, and the defining characteristic of human beings remains their ability to want more than they can have. That contradiction produces rage, desire, hate, and love, and real art brings all those things to life. Art that quiets or buries those cultural instincts can't survive the human faculty—it falls apart. But as it does, it humiliates whoever carries it. If Jayne Anne Phillips's Sue was humiliated by Rod Stewart's "Every Picture Tells a Story," that humiliation made her realize what she had given up, and it made her want it even more.

ONE STAR PER CUSTOMER

Rock 'n' roll, as anyone will tell you these days, is now simply "mainstream music"—pervasive and aggressively empty, the sound of the current sound, referring to nothing but its own success, its own meaningless triumph. For the first time, rock 'n' roll really is everywhere: Madonna's wedding or Springsteen's tour are hard newsbreaks. Old hits spout ad-agency lyrics every time you hit the dial or change the channel; with Michael Jackson's purchase of Beatle copyrights, Beatle music may soon be run through a commercial revival that will definitely erase whatever mnemonic power the songs still retain. Imagine:

> *She's leaving home, she's leaving home . . .*
> Is she? Has she?
> Call NATIONAL CHILDWATCH, INC.
> We can help—and you can
> *Get by with a little help from your friends*

And that's just the public service version—a Jackson tax credit.

All this is obvious. Less so is the way the shapeless mainstreaming of pop music has produced a perfect, balancing compensation: the process by which the pop milieu, now merely the milieu of everyday diversion, is continually reorganized around a single replaceable figure.

Since 1984's Jacksons tour, performer after performer has been brought-forth-to-come-forth as a unitary, momentarily complete symbol of individual fulfillment and public conquest. As Jackson was replaced by Prince, Prince was replaced by Madonna, who has been replaced by Springsteen. At the given moment, their faces appear on every magazine cover (Bruce on the cover of *Star* in the supermarket: "HOW MARRIAGE HAS CHANGED HIM." Inside: "IT HASN'T"). Every single and LP, every tour, sets "records," generates "unprecedented" amounts of money. The Guinness people can't keep up with the ever-lengthening number of hours logged by fans camping in line for tickets. It's no matter that much of this is pure hype; what counts is the result, and the result is a sort of consumer-fan panic, a *Konsumterror* (the phrase was Ulrike Meinhof's) that suspends one's very identity in the fear of missing out on what's happening, or what is said to be happening. It's a social version of the TV quiz show where contestants are asked to guess not the true answer to a question, but the answer that polls have shown most people believe is true—or is it the answer most people believe most people believe is true?

Whatever signs and meanings a performer might bring to this process are nothing compared to the process itself. Meanings are dissolved, or attached to the dominant sign systems of the moment ("BRUCE—THE RAMBO OF ROCK," reads a bumper sticker), or trumpeted as spurious, glamorized oppositions to fake versions of the dominant sign systems ("DO YOU WANT YOUR DAUGHTER TO GROW UP LIKE MADONNA?"), making real opposition incomprehensible. And as their meanings are dissolved, so are the performers. They're used up, exiled into the wilderness where dwell those who, once, were. Jackson was not just replaced by Prince; exposed at the height of his fame and power as a celibate zombie, he was discredited by a self-made fucker. But then Prince was revealed as a megalomaniac, and so he was discredited by a down-to-earth slut, who was discredited by a man who stands for the values that made this country great, who was discredited by—

It's true that this voraciously entropic process has a constant need for weirdos, for people who in prerock times would have been inconceivable as public icons. "Anarchy had moved in," Nik Cohn writes of the mid-fifties in *AwopBopaLooBopAlopBamBoom* (1972). "For thirty years you couldn't possibly make it unless you were white, sleek, nicely spoken and phoney to your toenails—suddenly now you could be black, purple, moronic, delinquent, diseased, or almost anything on earth, and you could still clean up." Thirty years later, though, that touch of anarchy has turned out to be a legitimating principle of control. This is the rock 'n' roll contribution to mainstream hegemony.

Think of the sense of freedom and resistance Cyndi Lauper must have wanted to communicate. The sensual social pluralism of her "Girls Just

Want to Have Fun" video, its affirmation of the pleasure of self-invention, became a reifying star turn in her following "Time after Time" piece, where her boyfriend didn't like her new haircut. What happened to all those people on the "Girls Just Want to Have Fun" screen, whose discovery of their own autonomy created a dance in the street? They were shoved back into the same anonymous crowd that may soon receive Cyndi Lauper, and from that crowd they will watch whoever comes next, and wonder where she came from, who he is. They will stand in line for a record-breaking number of hours, pay a record-breaking number of dollars to find the answer, or anyway what most people are said to think the answer is.

Just as present-day politics are a reaction against the utopianism and doubt of the sixties, present-day rock 'n' roll is a reaction against the punk negation of the late seventies. As Dave Marsh has written, "the aim was to eradicate the hierarchy that ran rock—ultimately, to eradicate hierarchy, period." But in modern societies revolt is almost always a minority tendency, and unless the moment is seized, the silent majorities always take the game away. An astonishing ten million people were on strike in France in May 1968; Charles de Gaulle came within hours of abandoning the nation to its fate, but finally he stood fast, and the next month he won a landslide vote of confidence. Punk attacked a smoothly functioning but increasingly bland celebrity culture and gave it the frisson it had lacked. Less than a decade later, the celebrity culture that punk attacked looks primitive next to our own—and the centering of that culture on a single, replaceable figure is not even its real center.

Just as, in the pop milieu, there is at any given time only one real star in the United States, today there is only one real person: Ronald Reagan. Behind all the replaceable center figures of pop is an irreplaceable center: product of grand historical forces, function of his time and place and all that, but also a unique individual with his own goals, his own fears, his own way of using his institutional power to take social power as a supercelebrity. An autonomous individual, Reagan seals the autonomy of all others, and also seals the limits of that autonomy, since all autonomy must finally be returned to him, and to what he chooses to represent. He is omnipresent, as naturalistically at home dancing the night away on the cover of *Vanity Fair* as he is, through the magic of electronics, chatting with the winners of the Super Bowl, making their victory his.

Making their victory his—in its primitive form, that's how the process seems to work. In its fully realized form—the 1985 Super Bowl, say, where Reagan actually appeared in the locker room as a video hologram—it is apparent that the supercelebrity does not take, but gives. In 1985 it was made to seem as if the 49ers had not won until Reagan had joined the event—in other words, until he made it real.

This is altogether a pop process. Yes, Ronald Reagan has never said a public word about Prince or Madonna, only had Michael Jackson to the White House and appropriated Bruce Springsteen for a campaign speech. But by those acts and thousands like them, he validated the process by which stars are validated. He became bigger; so, for the moment, did they. The difference is that he is not in it for the moment.

PART EIGHT

Last Words:
The Fans Speak

○ ▲ ○ ▲ ○ ▲ ○ ▲ ○ ▲ ○ ▲ ○

Fred and Judy Vermorel's book *Starlust* was the first publication of its kind—a study that offered a theory of the music industry through the words of the fans themselves. These extracts from that book serve as the best conclusion to this reader that we can imagine: a reminder that pop meanings are ultimately made by the consumers (albeit under social conditions that are not of their own choosing) . . . whatever the intentions of industries, musicians, and critics.

STARLUST

1 9 8 5

○ ▲ ○ ▲ ○ ▲ ○

WHAT LOVE SHOULD BE

Joanne

When I make love with my husband I imagine it's Barry Manilow. All the time.

And after, when my husband and I have made love and I realize it's not him, I cry to myself.

It's usually dark when the tears flow and somehow I manage to conceal them.

It happens to an awful lot of people, too. I didn't realize how many until I got involved with Barry fans. A lot of them are married and around my age and they feel the same way and they do the same thing. It's comforting to know I'm not the only one.

But it's still not easy sometimes. It can be very, very upsetting. 'Cos sometimes, besides everything else, I've got this terrible guilty feeling.

But I can't help the way I feel. There's no one can change the way I feel. Not me, or anybody. You can't just press a button and hope it will change.

I always say you can't make yourself love somebody and you can't stop loving somebody. It's just something that happens and you've got no control over it. You don't particularly want it to happen but it does. There's nothing anyone can do about it.

It can cause a lot of problems sometimes.

And I do feel guilty sometimes, very guilty. But mostly I go along with it because it's easier to.

I suppose it's the same kind of thing people get out of religion. I can't really explain it more than that. But they obviously get something from God to help them through their lives. And Barry is—maybe I shouldn't say it but it's the way I feel—he's the same sort of thing. He helps me through my life.

Helen

Most husbands can't cope with it.

I know one particular girl, for instance, whose husband ripped her posters down. And he also taped over her concert videotapes.

I mean, our concert videotapes are our pride and joy—we don't let them go at all—and for someone to record over them is sacrilege.

He also tried to stop her going to the convention.

Her best friend was also very much into Barry so when the husbands were out during the day the girls were always together. He resented that as well. He resented everything to do with Barry.

He actually used to come along to the local gang meetings and sit there all night. Never say anything. Just watch his wife all night. It spoiled it for her because she couldn't relax and have a good time like the rest of us.

One of the girls who went to the Chicago convention last year got some really special photographs. And I found Millie in a side room, away from everybody, sitting and sobbing her heart out over these photographs. She had to go and lock herself away. She didn't dare react or show any kind of emotion in front of her husband. That must be a really big strain on her.

I've known other husbands just as jealous.

Another girl I know, a very dedicated Barry follower, can't talk about Barry in her husband's presence at all. He gets very, very jealous and aggressive and will go off in fits of sulks and not speak to her, or he throws a tantrum or something. Just because she's talking about Barry or watching Barry on the video.

Julie (16)

I'm an only child, and earlier this year my father died. He knew how mad about Nick [Heyward] I was and even when he was dying he asked about Nick. He meant the world to me, and I never knew something could change your life so much. I still haven't got over it but I only have to look at my posters or play Nick's records to feel a little better. My mum says I'm in a world of my own, as I'm involved so much with Nick.

TOUCHING ANOTHER WORLD

The Cassidy Family

The Cassidy family (Marc Bolan fans) live in a small Welsh village. Present are Lorna (54), her son, Ewan (30); her daughters, Sheila (34) and Anne (20); two nieces, Jan (18) and Maggie (20); Pat, the daughter-in-law (29); and Lorna's three grandchildren, Deborah (4), Clare (9) and David (11).

LORNA: Really it was Ewan got us all hooked. He used to play his records so loud the kids used to stand on the corner of the street and listen to him.

SHEILA: It wasn't a question of hooked—you could hear nothing but him in the Terrace!

ANNE: As far as me and Maggie were concerned, we were seven at the time and he used to take us into his room and shut the door and sit us there on the window sill. And we were stuck there for the rest of the day. In the end we just started singing the songs.

PAT: Brainwashing.

ANNE: Yeah, it was. We just got hooked on him, didn't we?

LORNA: At first it was just a noise and I thought: Ewan do you have to keep on playing that?

And he said: "Come in here, Mum. Sit down and listen. Just listen." And I did and I got hooked.

And after that I just kept playing him. I still do. I mean, if I don't play a track of his some time during the day it's not right. It's like withdrawal symptoms from cigarettes—I can feel there's something wrong: I haven't played Bolan today. Isn't that true, Anne?

ANNE: Yes, it is.

LORNA: This is the thing nobody can explain. Only another Bolanite can understand.

I mean, Ewan—he's not poetic in any way—I don't think I've ever known him write a piece of poetry, but he wrote—what was it he wrote?

ANNE: *In the deep dark corners of my mind*
I still see you bop and grind . . .

LORNA: *Marc, they tell me you've gone to a far better place.*
Where you can dance in a wide open space.

ANNE: *Dancing with your red shoes on*
Dancing all night long.

LORNA: And he put all his love he had for him in that little poem.

LORNA: People say to us: "How come you *love* Marc?" Because even boys, I mean butch boys now I'm talking about, not gays, they really love him. They don't just like him, they really love him. And girls can't understand it. I know

Bolan fans who've lost girlfriends because they can't figure it out, you know. And you can't explain. It's just *different*. It's a totally different affection.

Marc ignites people. He really does.

There's a magic about him. I don't know what it is.

[There is a special room in the house set aside for Marc.]

Q: How did Marc's room come about?

LORNA: Well, Ewan had him everywhere. He had him on the ceiling, on the walls, you name it.

SHEILA: It was purple, the room, wasn't it?

LORNA: Psychedelic. And Marc was everywhere.

EWAN: Purple and green.

PAT: Errrr!

LORNA: And when he got married Pat said it all had to come off. Because . . .

SHEILA: *[whispers]* Pat doesn't like him.

PAT: I don't *dislike* him . . .

SHEILA: Actually the reason it was redecorated was because Ewan was moving out to get married and Dad thought: Well, this is the end of Marc now, so he thought he'd decorate it.

ANNE: We left it like that until '77. And then when the crash happened in '77 it all went back up again.

LORNA: Now kids who can't put stuff up because their parents won't have it send it to me and I put it in Marc's room so at least it's up somewhere.

It's known as Marc's room. It's never the spare bedroom—it's known as Marc's room.

And it's funny, all the girls who sleep in that room have a most beautiful night's sleep.

PAT: Boys don't though, do they?

LORNA: No. They toss and turn.

LORNA: When we heard about the crash, I think it was on the five o'clock news and it came on and I said, "Oh my God, no." It just felt as if the world had come to an end.

It was crazy. Here I was a grandma with all the kids, all the family, plenty of other people around that I love, but it just felt as though the world had crashed, you know? It was just disastrous.

And then Ewan came through the door looking white as a sheet and then Anne came home from school and threw herself in my arms.

The day of the funeral I stood there and I cried nearly all day. Father said: "Oh come on, we'll go out and buy some wallpaper."

SHEILA: That's father's answer to everything.

LORNA: We went to buy the wallpaper and then he bought me a rose tree, same as Marc's at Golders Green.

But it wasn't only then, I mean it's *now*. I can be up in Marc's room playing a record and I just look around me and I say: "Oh, God." And I just start crying.

And you think to yourself: Well, this is crazy. *[To Anne]* And it still happens to you, doesn't it?

ANNE: You can't explain it. Unless you're a Bolan fan you can't explain what the love is. It's not any love you can explain.

LORNA: It's not sexual.

ANNE: It's not like a family love. If family died and was buried in Golders Green and we went to see their grave it still wouldn't be the same feeling as going to see Marc.

LORNA: But it's not a feeling that drags you down. I mean, you have a cry but then you're up again, aren't you? There's an elation. Oh, I can't explain it. It's impossible to explain.

Q: How many times have you been to Golders Green?

ALL: Every year.

LORNA: Every year since he died. And we go every year to the tree, the tree his car crashed into. We go to the tree to be there for the dreaded five to five. That's when it happened. His fans come from everywhere: Japan, Germany, France, Canada, Israel, Switzerland . . .

ANNE: They walk, don't they?

LORNA: The ones from Japan actually walked and hitchhiked all the way from Japan just to be there. I mean, they couldn't speak a word of English but they didn't have to.

We stay there all night, just playing his music and what have you. Then when five to five comes we go to the tree . . . we just sit and talk. It's a happy occasion. There's very few tears. You can't be sad when you're with Marc's fans because they're such a happy band to be with.

Henry (16)

I don't own anything of Cheryl's but I wish I did. I know this may sound perverted, but I'd like a pair of her pants to hang on my wall! Mind you I wouldn't mind any other article of clothing or such.

The smaller items of my Bucks Fizz collection I put in drawers. The records go into cases and the larger items go under my bed. Occasionally I like to look at the things but usually I leave them until night and then "check" to see none of the souvenirs have been jolted out of their position.

I really enjoy my collection because it feels like I have a piece of them in my possession.

Hollies Fan

As we walked through the door I saw Allan Clarke. He was sitting round a table with his wife and some friends, together with their children. I couldn't believe it, I nearly shouted out loud—here was this great star sitting drinking tea in an ordinary café, and being ignored by everyone. We sat down nearby. I felt ill, I thought I was going to be sick my stomach churned so much. I wanted desperately to talk to him but didn't know how to. In the end my wife could stand it no longer and we got up together and went over. I said: "Mr. Clarke, sorry to bother you but may I have your autograph?" He looked up and said: "Of course." I told him I had all his albums and he seemed surprised. He wrote: "Thanks, Allan Clarke" on the back of my wife's checkbook (the only paper we had) and shook both our hands. Then we thanked him and sat down, and he carried on as if nothing had happened!

SPANKING BOY GEORGE

Lilian

I always imagine pop stars in physical pain.

At the moment it's Boy George.

I think that's a very good choice because you can get all the stuff you need in the paper whereas before, with Blondie, it was difficult to get much to feed it with . . .

I don't think I'd have this kind of fantasy about someone I admired or agreed with. Like Robert Wyatt for instance, or the Raincoats.

But with pop groups, you don't really take them seriously—or I don't—because the music is so sort of throwaway.

I also think it's to do with how pop stars are presented. Because there's this unrealistic situation of them being famous.

And I've thought: How would I feel if people had fantasies and thought all these things about me? I mean what would it do to someone's brain? It would be awful. I couldn't stand it if *one* person was like that about me, never mind hundreds or more.

But then I suppose they are there for people to fantasize about.

Like that Mark Chapman killing John Lennon—it was the same sort of thing in a way. He idolized him and actually thought he was him, and he went through all these sorts of feelings.

In fact, I find the idea of murder quite exciting because it's a new feeling and because it's so dramatic. I can't really understand it or explain it.

They're really time-consuming, my fantasies, because once I get involved with them I'm just obsessed with that person for ages.

It's sort of like falling in love with someone—you spend so much time on them and get so absorbed by them.

And I think: I must be wasting a lot of time. But then you think: Well, everyone does this because everyone needs fantasies. And anyway I'm not wasting that much time.

I think perhaps that really my fantasies are a way of controlling my own life. Because I always feel people are trying to take control of my life all the time.

I feel sort of helpless in a way.

I often feel like when people have nightmares and they're walking down the street and they're really inappropriately dressed or walking down the street in the nude and everyone else is fully clothed, and it's that feeling of helplessness—that you can't stop people invading you.

It's as though people are taking bits of you and pulling bits off you and twisting them round and making them how they want you to be. Like a hole being cut in the top of your head and someone putting their hand inside and taking everyone out.

They're taking your soul out.

I HAVE TO SHOUT

Nichola

Usually I take one of my magazines to school with me with a picture of Nick Rhodes and I leave it out during the lesson so that he's there and he's looking at you.

Because in these pictures it's like he's looking at you. And that's how I imagine it usually—that he's there and he's looking at me and he can see me and hear me through the magazine.

When I stare at one picture for a long time, especially where he's sitting on his own and staring at you, and then I look away quickly, I can see from the corner of my eye that his lips are moving and he's smiling and everything.

He's come alive and he's watching me, and he can see and he can move. So I imagine he's here with me all the time and he's watching me all the time.

So if I do something I'm careful, because Nick Rhodes is watching me.

Like when people say he's ugly I'm careful not to get angry and swear at them. I'm careful to speak nice. Because if Nick Rhodes was in this position he'd speak nicely. He wouldn't shout and everything. So I think: Oh, he's watching me so I've got to be good.

That's not all the time because I'm not always good!

Usually what I think about is that they're human beings and they've got to be doing something this very moment and I wonder what it is.

'Cos I know Duran Duran exists. I know Nick Rhodes exists and I like him and I'm spending money buying things for him and everything.

But he doesn't know I exist.

BEAMED THROUGH THE AIR

Bernard

From an early age I was interested in science fiction and spacy things like paranormal beings. And Bowie was a personification of that kind of thing.

So it was quite scary to see someone on stage who did look like an alien. He didn't look like a boy and he didn't look like a girl. But he did look very threatening and androgynous. For someone as young as I was, that was quite a frightening experience.

I think Bowie's got a strange face and a very fascinating face, and I don't think there could be another David Bowie—to have everything perfect in the way he has.

I remember I got really confused and at one point I really did think he was something alien. Seeing photographs of him I thought: he can't be real.

And when I saw him in '73 at the Hammersmith Odeon—my sister took me—in all that Ziggy get-up, he was such an awe-inspiring figure.

That impression was left with me.

The clamor for tickets for the '83 concerts was so immense because you are sharing two hours of your life with him—two hours in the life of someone you know won't be there one day. It's quite a marvelous experience to be able to at least say: "I shared two hours with him."

Maybe, you know, with 10,000 other people, but it's still a very solid thing in the eyes of the world.

For the Hammersmith show me and some of the other fans got together an arrangement of flowers in the shape of a red shoe. And we put a card on it with everyone's names who had donated. So that, you know, they were then a name to Bowie—which is nice.

It's nice for people to know Bowie's read their name.

At one point during the song "Breaking Glass" he points to a member of the audience who then has a pointing match with him. And that was me at one of the gigs—we were pointing at each other.

And at another moment he whirled round again with his finger out-stretched and I was there too. At the time it seemed quite incredible because it seemed telepathic. And you think: Well, was it just coincidence or . . . ?

People were actually quite amazed that it was going on. They were turning to me and saying: "I think he recognized you."

But that wasn't the best one. The strongest feel of any kind of link I've had with Bowie is actually knowing that whatever I do in terms of writing the fanzine, that he is reading it and that he does actually own your work— which I think is the most amazing thing that could ever happen to any artist who does feel strongly about Bowie.

It is a bit odd really, having devoted so much time to him and never having actually met him. But then again it's quite nice in a way. I don't have any regrets about not meeting him. I think I will meet him one day, but it would be nice if there was an arrangement where I could actually sit down and talk to him at length.

I think that would mean much more as a first memory than just rushing up to him and saying: "I'm Bernard from ——— fanzine."

[*Bernard is 22 and edits a successful Bowie fanzine from which he earns a living.*]

Julie

A lot of what I read about him was fantasy reading made up for the immediate public to entertain the suckers. But then you do believe what you read. We people do believe the written word—it's all we have to go on. And kids of 16 or 18 they really take it all in because they really do worship these people.

And that's how I think it's dangerous. Because kids lose their own identity—which is so important.

The star expresses something up there that's very real to you and so you mistake that thing for yourself. And you get caught up in his life.

But you're another person with another story to tell.

You mistakenly think you can live his life and you get caught up in his success and think it's perfectly possible to achieve all those things.

They represent the success story up there and they're giving it out to the public, doling it out by the ton. Then they give out trite comments to the press and expect pe ple to take it on the chin.

And you do, because you're so absolutely gullible.

It's almost pathetic that kind of idol thing.

But then he was extraordinary and he deserved all that idolatry, even though he's probably laughing now.

So I don't regret any of the money I spent or any of the things I used to do, the obsessions I had.

I think it was part and parcel of what I am now. I'd like to talk to him about it some time, I really would.

He was so stylish and so completely different from any other pop star of that time that he was lost in his own isolation. Because having created that complete balloon around him he mustn't let it burst. The pressure must have been enormous to keep all that fantasy going.

But he achieved it by sheer tactics, you know: Try this, let's see how the kids react to that. And then completely washing his hands of the whole business. Not actually accepting the responsibility for what he's done by becoming a besuited man with a blond hairdo and a lot of money and the ability to make his own films.

I just wonder if he doesn't think that everyone's a sucker. He's riding on the crest of a wave and he's a legend.

But I sometimes wonder who kicked it all off, whether it was some massive publicity stunt or whether it was actually David Bowie who had the initiative.

Because I'm sure he's extraordinary, but I don't think that he's so extraordinary that he didn't have a lot of help from the right people to create all that and to bring out those records.

I think he should be made aware of how he's influenced people's dress, their manners, their behavior.

Because I now have the kind of wisdom to know how pop stars can damage people by their life-styles and by the kind of money they throw around and the kind of images they present on television.

People can get so taken away with it that they're actually in danger of believing that they are that person.

Well, I never believed I was David Bowie—I mean, I couldn't have been further from it, being rather fat and frumpy and very much a virgin—but I actually believed that I could have a relationship with him.

This was *his* influence and it was rather damaging. And I think he's so detached now from what he's done to people that he doesn't realize in all his wealth how he's influenced them.

Because he's actually walked away from them and has lived a life of cream because we've allowed him to.

It's a terrible thing he did really.

He's got a lot to answer for.

[*Julie is 25. She's an actress and worked with David Bowie on* The Hunger.]

THE ART OF DAYDREAMING

Sophie

I suppose daydreaming is an art. It's just something you work on and get better and better at. You don't lose it if you try to keep hold of it. It's a wonderful thing to have. I think I'd crack up if I couldn't do it.

Acknowledgments

Theodor W. Adorno, "On Popular Music": from *Studies in Philosophy and Social Science* 9 (1941); reprinted by permission of Suhrkamp Verlag, Frankfurt am Main.

Roland Barthes, "The Grain of the Voice": extracted from *Image-Music-Text*, translated by Stephen Heath. Translation copyright © 1977 by Stephen Heath. Reprinted by permission of Hill and Wang, a division of Farrar, Straus, and Giroux, Inc.

H. Stith Bennett, "The Realities of Practice": reprinted from *On Becoming a Rock Musician* (Amherst: University of Massachusetts Press, 1980). Copyright 1980 by University of Massachusetts Press. Reprinted by permission of Sage Publications, Inc.

Mark W. Booth, "Jingle: Pepsi-Cola Hits the Spot": extracted from *The Experience of Songs* (New Haven: Yale University Press, 1981). Copyright Yale University Press 1981.

David Buxton, "Rock Music, the Star System, and the Rise of Consumerism": reprinted from *Telos* 57 (1983).

Tom Carson, "Rocket to Russia": reprinted from *Stranded: Rock and Roll for a Desert Island*, Greil Marcus, ed. (New York: Knopf, 1979).

Andrew Chester, "Second Thoughts on a Rock Aesthetic: The Band": first appeared in *New Left Review* 67 (1970).

Gary Clarke, "Defending Ski-Jumpers: A Critique of Theories of Youth Subcultures": originally published as a mimeo paper by the University of Birmingham Centre for Contemporary Cultural Studies, 1981. Copyright by Gary Clarke and the CCCS.

Richard Dyer, "In Defense of Disco": reprinted from *Gay Left* 8 (1979), and reproduced with the permission of the author.

Simon Frith, "Afterthoughts": reprinted from *New Statesman*, August 23, 1985.

Simon Frith and Angela McRobbie, "Rock and Sexuality": reprinted from *Screen Education* 29 (1978) and reproduced with the permission of the Society for Education in Film and Television, London.

Sheryl Garratt, "Teenage Dreams": reprinted from *Signed, Sealed and Delivered*, by Sheryl Garratt and Sue Steward (London: Pluto Press, 1984), and reprinted with the permission of Drake Marketing Services.

Andrew Goodwin, "Sample and Hold: Pop Music in the Digital Age of Reproduction": reprinted from *Critical Quarterly* 30 (3) 1988. Copyright 1988 by Andrew Goodwin.

Lawrence Grossberg, "Is There Rock After Punk?": reprinted from *Critical Studies in Mass Communication* 3 (1) 1986, with the permission of the author.

Stuart Hall and Paddy Whannel, "The Young Audience": extracted from *The Popular Arts* (London: Hutchinson, 1964).

Dick Hebdige, "Style as Homology and Signifying Practice": extracted from *Subculture: The Meaning of Style* (London: Methuen, 1979).

Antoine Hennion, "The Production of Success: An Antimusicology of the Pop Song": reprinted from *Popular Music* 3 (Cambridge University Press, 1983); reprinted with the permission of Cambridge University Press.

Paul M. Hirsch, "Processing Fads and Fashions: An Organization-Set Analysis of Cultural Industry Systems": reprinted from *American Journal of Sociology* 77 (University of Chicago Press, 1972), with the permission of the author.

Donald Horton, "The Dialogue of Courtship in Popular Song": reprinted from *American Journal of Sociology* 62 (University of Chicago Press, 1956–57).

Edward R. Kealy,"From Craft to Art: The Case of Sound Mixers and Popular Music": reprinted from *Sociology of Work and Occupations* 6 (1979).

Dave Laing, "Listen to Me": extracted from *Buddy Holly* (London: Vista, 1971).

Angela McRobbie, "Settling Accounts with Subcultures: A Feminist Critique": reprinted from *Screen Education* 34 (1980) and reproduced with the permission of the Society for Education in Film and Television, London.

Greil Marcus, "Corrupting the Absoute" © *Artforum* (April 1985); "One Star Per Customer" © *Artforum* (November 1985).

Richard A. Peterson and David G. Berger, "Cycles in Symbol Production: The Case of Popular Music": reprinted from *American Sociological Review* 40, 1975.

Simon Reynolds, "New Pop and Its Aftermath": originally appeared in *Monitor* 4 (1985).

David Riesman, "Listening to Popular Music": reprinted from *American Quarterly* 2 (Summer 1950) and reproduced with permission of the author and the American Studies Association. Copyright 1950, American Studies Association.

Fred and Judy Vermorel, "Starlust": extracted from their book *Starlust: The Secret Fantasies of Fans* (London: W. H. Allen, 1985). Copyright Fred and Judy Vermorel 1985.

Roger Wallis and Krister Malm, "Patterns of Change": extracted from *Big Sounds from Small Peoples* (London: Constable, 1984).

Paul Willis, "The Golden Age": extracted from *Profane Culture* (London: Routledge and Kegan Paul, 1978).

Sue Wise, "Sexing Elvis": reprinted with permission from *Women's Studies International Forum* 7 (1984). Copyright 1984 Pergamon Journals, Ltd.

The *Bloom County* cartoon on p. 277 is © 1987 Washington Post Writers Group. Reprinted with permission.